THE
PLACE
NAMES
OF
MARYLAND

HAMILL KENNY, Ph.D.
*(Author of West Virginia Place Names,
Their Origin and Meaning, 1945;
Origin and Meaning of the Indian
Place Names of Maryland, 1961.)*

1. Garrett
2. Allegany
3. Washington
4. Frederick
5. Carroll
6. Baltimore
7. Harford
8. Baltimore City
9. Howard
10. Montgomery
11. Prince George's
12. Anne Arundel
13. Calvert
14. St. Mary's
15. Charles
16. Worcester
17. Somerset
18. Wicomico
19. Caroline
20. Dorchester
21. Talbot
22. Queen Anne's
23. Kent
24. Cecil

THE
PLACE
NAMES
OF
MARYLAND
*Their Origin
and
Meaning*

HAMILL KENNY

MARYLAND HISTORICAL SOCIETY

BALTIMORE

© 1984
MARYLAND HISTORICAL SOCIETY
201 West Monument Street
Baltimore, Maryland 21201

Founded 1844

Second printing 1999

Library of Congress Catalog Card Number 84-060803

ISBN 0-938420-28-3

To ORA, my infinite inspiration

CONTENTS

PREFACE

This book discovers and sets forth the origin and meaning of the various words and phrases used in Maryland to name the state's most representative villages, towns, cities, mountains and watercourses. Such words and phrases are called placenames, which means simply that they are the names of places. In Maryland the placenames are both Algonquian and English. Examples of them are ALLEGANY, CHESAPEAKE, CUMBERLAND, RISING SUN, SILVER SPRING. The skeptical reader who wonders what there is to uncover and explain in the name of a place will readily perceive that a placename, besides being the symbol of one locality or another, always has a hidden historical meaning involving pioneer founders and families, storekeepers, postmasters and politicians, churches and churchmen, geographical and maritime phenomena, fauna and flora, and a treasure trove of folklore, speech ways, and local history. A placename, redolent of home and hearth, is a glorious word.

This is my third full placename study. The first was on West Virginia placenames (1945), and the second was on the origin and meaning of Maryland's Indian placenames (1961). I have undertaken this third book because I feel that Maryland—one of the more historical central Atlantic states to be heretofore neglected by placename authors—needs a more compendious placename treatment than my Indian book allowed. The Indian placenames, all included here, have had the benefit of the Algonquian knowledge given me by the late Catholic University professor, James A. Geary. As for the non-Indian names, I am fortunate to have had, throughout, counsel and information from the late William B. Marye, Maryland's leading local historian.

As years pass by and the origins of placenames fade into history, it becomes increasingly rare (so it seems to me) to encounter citizens who know how their home towns were named. Indeed, perhaps owing to the mobility and pressures of the present day, the institution of the home town is somewhat in limbo; and many people, with no occasion any longer to think about local origins, seem to regard their village abodes as hardly more than dormitories. Nevertheless, I have had scores of successful placename conversations with Maryland mountaineers, watermen, homeowners, housewives, storekeepers, farmers and postmasters—many of whom corresponded with me and all of whom were polite and cooperative. To each of these good informants I take this opportunity to say, "Thank you, heartily!"

In addition to conversation, fieldwork and correspondence, my sources of information were state histories, county histories, magazines, newspaper articles, gazetteers, directories and maps. In this regard, perhaps I owe most to the *Maryland Historical Magazine* and to the detailed accounts of the original *Maryland, A guide to the Old Line State* (N.Y., 1940).[n] I have had to use many libraries. The most important and helpful of them were the State Law Library (Annapolis [Mrs. Shirley Rittenhouse]), the Anne Arundel County Public Library (Annapolis), the Enoch Pratt Free Library (Baltimore), the Library of Congress, and the Maryland Room of the McKeldin Library (College Park). I feel especially grateful to Mrs. Harold Hayes, of the McKeldin Maryland Room, for her help in the early stages of my research. Finally, for his patience and careful advice, I express my sincere thanks to Mr. William Sager, Publications Director of the Maryland Historical Society.

I leave this study with a warm feeling for the state of Maryland. Its placenames are a gallery of memorable pioneers and founders. Its streams and mountains are celebrated by undying words from the Algonquian and English languages. Maryland is not a land of vast monumental antiquities. Indeed, its best monuments are perhaps its placenames.

Note: See also Edward C. Papenfuse (et al.), *A New Guide to the Old Line State . . .* (Baltimore and London, 1976).

ABBREVIATIONS AND RECURRING REFERENCES

I. General (including County Abbreviations).
II. Newspapers and Magazines.
III. Chronological list of Directories, Gazetteers, Catalogues, Guides.

I. *GENERAL ABBREVIATIONS* (Incl. County Abbreviations)

B. & O. R.R.	Baltimore & Ohio Railroad
b.	born
C. & D. Canal	Chesapeake & Delaware Canal
ca.	*circa* "about"
C. & O.	Chesapeake & Ohio Canal
cf.	*confer* "compare"
DAE	Dictionary of American English, 1938–44
d.	died
Dir.	Directory
E. Sh.	Eastern Shore
et al.	*et alii* "and others"
fl.	*floruit* "flourished"
GMd 1941	Gazetteer of Maryland, 1941
LC	Library of Congress
n.	note
OED (NED)	Oxford English Dictionary
PA	Proto (Primitive) - Algonquian
PG	U. S. Postal Guide
PHC	Postal History Catalogue 1960
P. M.	postmaster
p. o.	post office
P. O. D.	Post Office Department
q. v.	*quod vide* "which see"
Reaney	R. H. Reaney, A Dictionary of British Surnames, London, 1968
sic	"thus, so"
TDr.	Telephone Directory
v.	*vide* "see"
W. Md. (R.R.)	Western Maryland (R.R.)
*	Formerly, lost, obsolete; hypothetical, if Indian
vol., vols.	volume (s)
Wentworth	H. Wentworth, Am. Dialect Dictionary, N.Y., 1944

KEY TO COUNTY ABBREVIATIONS

A	Allegany
AA	Anne Arundel
B	Baltimore
BC	Baltimore City
C	Calvert
Co	Caroline
Cl	Carroll
Ce	Cecil
Ch	Charles
D	Dorchester
F	Frederick
G	Garrett
H	Harford
Ho	Howard
K	Kent
M	Montgomery
PG	Prince George's
QA	Queen Anne's
SM	St. Mary's
S	Somerset
T	Talbot
W	Washington
Wi	Wicomico
Wo	Worcester

II. *NEWSPAPERS, MAGAZINES*

Am. Sp.	*American Speech* [Quarterly of Linguistic Usage]. 1926 -.
BASD	Bull. of the Archaeological Soc. of Delaware. Wilmington, 1939–1949.
Capital	The Evening *Capital* [Annapolis, Md.].
Extra	Sunday magazine of the [Baltimore] *News American.*
GS	The Glades *Star* [Centennial Eds.] 4, 1972. Oakland, Md.
MHM	The *Maryland Historical Magazine.* 1906 -. Md. Hist. Soc., Baltimore.
Names	Journal of the Am. Name Society. 1953 -.
Star	The Washington *Star.*
Sun	The Baltimore *Sun* [and Sunday magazine].

III. *CHRONOLOGICAL LIST of CATALOGUES, DIRECTORIES,*
    and GAZETTEERS

PHC	Postal History Markings. R. T. Powers, ed. Markings 1766–1855. . . . 1960.
Heads 1790	Heads of Families. First Census U. S. 1790, Maryland.
Morse 1794	J. Morse, *The American Geography* . . . London, 1794.
Kuethe 1795	J. L. Kuethe, "A List of Maryland Mills, Taverns, Forges and Furnaces of 1795," *MHM*, 31 (1936), 155–169.
Kuethe Map	_____, "A New Map of the Province of Maryland . . .," *MHM*, 32 (1937), 28–30.
List 1803	*List of the Post-Offices in the United States . . .* Washington, 1803.
Scott 1807	J. Scott, *A Geographical Description of Maryland*, Philadelphia, 1807.
Table 1811	*Table of Post-Offices . . . United States.* Washington, 1811.
Table 1819	*Table of Post-Offices . . . United States.* Washington, 1819.
Table 1825	*Table of Post-Offices . . . United States.* Washington, 1825.
List 1828	*List of the Post-Offices in the United States.* Washington, 1828.
Register 1833	*Register of . . . Officers and Agents . . . United States . . . 1833.* Philadelphia, 1834.
Fisher 1852	R. S. Fisher, *Gazetteer of Maryland*, Baltimore, 1852.
Lewis 1878	J. Lewis & Co., *The Maryland Directory*, Baltimore, 1878
Webb 1880	*Webb's Cumberland Directory*, 1880–81. New York, 1880.
Lewis 1882	J. F. Lewis, *The Baltimore Directory*, Baltimore, 1882.
Dir. 1893	Directory of . . . Cumberland . . . Barton /et al./. Bell Pb. Co. Baltimore, 1893.
Oakland 1900	*Oakland,. . . Guide to Walks, Drives, Excursions*, Oakland . . . 1900 /LC/.
GMd 1904	Gannett's *Gazetteer of Maryland*, Washington, 1904.
Guide 1940	*Maryland, A Guide to the Old Line State*, New York, 1940.

GMd 1941   Md. State Planning Commission's *Gazetteer of Maryland*, Baltimore, 1941.

Manual 1947   *Manual of Coordinates for Places in Maryland*, Md. State Planning Commission . . . 1947.

Pilot 1947   *United States Coast Pilot: Atlantic Coast*, Section C . . . 5th ed., Washington, 1947.

Arrow 1948   *Polk's Official Arrow Street Guide of Baltimore*, Washington, 1948.

WMd 1952   Western Maryland Co. *Passenger Time Tables*, Baltimore /1952/.

Mont 1960–61   *Montgomery County Handbook*, Mont. Co. Ch. of Commerce, 1960.

Manual 1962   *Maryland Manual of Coordinates 1962*, Md. State Planning Department /Baltimore/.

Arrow DC 1963   *Arrow Street Guide . . . Washington*. Polk & Co., Boston, 1963.

Pr. Geo. 1962–63   *Your Guide to Prince George's County 1962–63* . . . Pr. George's Chamber of Commerce.

Binnacle 1966   The *Binnacle*. Yachtsman's Guide to the Chesapeake Bay Country, 2 (1966).

Calvert 1969   W. A. Dando and T. D. Rabenhorst, *Atlas of Calvert County* . . . Univ. of Md., Dept. of Geography, 1969.

Manual 1969   *Maryland Manual of Coordinates*, 1969 /3rd ed./, Md. Department of State Planning. . .

New Guide 1976   *Maryland, A New Guide to the Old Line State* . . . Baltimore, 1976.

INTRODUCTION

I.
Previous Writings

A serious study of Maryland's placenames was begun in the 1930's by J. Louis Kuethe, of Johns Hopkins University. In addition to sending forth questionnaires, he published such articles as "Runs, Creeks, and Branches in Maryland" (*Am. Sp.*, X, 1935), "A List of Maryland's Mills, Taverns, Forges, and Furnaces of 1795" (*MHM*, 31, 1936), and "Maryland Place Names Have Strange Origins" (*Sun*, Sept. 8, 1940). What was perhaps his last article was "Words from Maryland," which appeared in *American Speech* in December 1940. At about that time Kuethe abandoned his project.

However, past and presently, various articles on Maryland placenames have appeared in the Baltimore *Sun*, The Baltimore *News American*, the *Maryland Historical Magazine* (*MHM*), *American Speech*, and *Names*, the magazine of the American Name Society. Of these, *MHM*, in its earlier volumes, has been Maryland's best placename medium. In 1907 it published C. W. Bump's explanation of *Patapsco*; in 1945 it published Ethel Roby Hayden's "Port Tobacco, Lost Town of Maryland"; and in 1954 it published the present author's "Baltimore: New Light on an Old Name." But *MHM*'s greatest service to Maryland placename study has been the publication, during a period of forty years (1918–1959), of some twenty-three articles on the state's placenames and local history by William B. Marye. The abundance and exactitude of these contributions make him the dean of Maryland placename studies.

In more recent years the magazine *Names* has published Kenneth Robb's "Names of Grants in Colonial Maryland" (17:1969) and my own "Place-Names from Surnames: Maryland" (18:1970). The publication in 1961 of my *Origin and Meaning of the Indian Place Names of Maryland* (Waverly Press) gave the state the first full length account of an important group of its names of places. The present book repeats the Indian names and, going a step farther, undertakes an account of representative Maryland placenames in general.

II.
Quantity and Selection

Throughout the present century the number of cities, towns, and villages in Maryland has evidently been growing. To judge from standard gazetteers and manuals, the state had 3901 places in 1904, 7922 places in 1941, and 12,000 places in 1947. The 1947 list, when subjected to recent map study, seems to have lost 4000 old places, and to have gained 3000 new places. At present, Maryland may therefore be said to have about 11,000 placenames. Included in this number are about 315 Algonquian Indian names. Included also are those of the state's 770 runs, creeks, and branches that have names. It is not thinkable that the state has any properly defined villages that are unnamed. However, there are "lost" villages, such as *MONOCACY, and submerged villages, such as *SELBY-SPORT.

When I began to collect, describe, and explain the names of Maryland's numerous and fluctuating places, I was at once faced with the problem of what names to include and what names to leave out. With the best of intentions, I found that, for reasons of time and space, I would have to shorten the number of my entries. With the best of intentions, I found that there are many names (MELITOTA? OREGON? MONKEY LODGE HILL?) that defy accurate explanation. Obviously, all important placenames should be included; but importance is often a matter of opinion. BALTIMORE, CHESAPEAKE, and POTOMAC are highly important; Maryland's eleven MUDDY CREEKs and four SMITHVILLEs are of little importance. However, a Smithville could be the birthplace of a future president; and a muddy creek could be the habitat of the much-prized snail darter.

In the light of these disturbing contradictions, I have concluded that wide representation should be my goal. Not every name, but every *kind* of name, should be dealt with. To bring this about I have followed three principles: (1) to include all the state's genuine Indian placenames, because of their linguistic, historical, and cultural value; (2) to include a large number of town and village names, because of their human interest; and (3) to include a moderate number of geographical placenames, especially those that are significant because of historical incident or natural wonder. The names here assembled on the basis of the three foregoing groups thoroughly represent Maryland's infinite placename variety. And each of their explanations has a well-founded source.

III.
The Kinds of Names

I have divided the state's placenames into eight categories. They follow, and constitute Part III of the Introduction.

1. *Surnames, given names, names from foreign places.* About 54% of Maryland's names of places are from British family names (CHISHOLM, KAYWOOD, LANHAM), and they often preserve old words and meanings no longer elsewhere recorded. Of course English is not the only language found; witness WOYTYCH, CAYOTS, and YONKERS. A feature of the village names that come from surnames is their frequent double

meaning. MOUSETOWN (W), for instance, is probably not for *mouse* but from the German family name *Maus, Mause*. *Sam(m), Sams*, can be either a surname or a given name. What, then, can one securely say, without investigation, about SAMS COVE (AA) and SAMS CREEK (2; Cl and F)?

Villages from given names are also subject to misinterpretations because of a possible double meaning. HELLEN (HELLEN CREEK, HELLEN GUT, C) is not from a girl's name but from Nathaniel Hel(l)en. There is little doubt that *Elva* (in ELVATON, AA) is a given name; but LAURAVILLE (BC) could be from *laurel*.[n] RUTHBURG, by the way, is from the family name *Ruth*. The state's placenames from foreign villages, hills, and streams are usually British (SALISBURY, *LONDONTOWN, DUNDALK, WYE RIVER). They can easily be confused with names derived from surnames. CAMBRIDGE and OXFORD evidently come from England's two university towns. But MANCHESTER (Co) and WINCHESTER (4) could be from the family names *Manchester* and *Winchester*. Maryland's commemorative names of places are by no means all British. Examples from other countries are LITTLE ORLEANS, NEW WARSAW, NEW GLATZ.

Note: As it turns out, so I have lately learned, *Laura* is the name of the daughter of John Henry Keene, who established a post office here.

2. *Manors, estates, and the houses thereon.* The first country habitations to be given names were the manors created by the Lords Baltimore. The Baltimores had the royal right to "alienate, sell or rent" the land in their new lordship. And there ensued in Maryland what may be called a manorial period lasting from the days of Cecilius and Leonard Calvert to the enthronement in England of William and Mary (1669). During that time sixty-two "true manors" came into being, twenty-six of which survive today in the form of standard names of places. Examples are CHARLES GIFT, PORTLAND STATION, WORTON.

Maryland ceased to be a proprietary colony in 1692. All "manors" that arose after that date are "pseudo-manors." Some present-day placenames, usually dating from the eighteenth century and incorrectly looked upon as "true manors," are DOUGHOREGAN (with "Doughoregan Manor" adjacent), CARROLTON MANOR, COLMAR MANOR, and FRANKLIN MANOR.

Maryland today has a multitude of places whose names originally belonged to tracts and manor houses of manorial pretension. One thinks of GLENELG (from "Glenelg Manor"), LA PLATA (from "La Plata," the Chapman Farm), RIVERDALE (from "Riversdale," a Calvert mansion), and CHEVY CHASE (from the estate, "Chevy Chase"). Homes of a "manorial" style are still being renovated and built in suburban Maryland.

3. *Names relating to religion.* In 1941 there existed eighty-seven places named for saints. Some of these names are merely geographical (ST. CATHERINE ISLAND, ST. CLEMENT BAY, ST. LEONARD CREEK). NERI (from St. Philip Neri, the "Apostle of Rome") is found twice (A, AA). Villages from saints' names are usually scantily populated. In 1961 only six of them were post offices (ST. GEORGES ISLAND, ST. INIGOES, SAINT JAMES, SAINT LEONARD, SAINT MARYS CITY, SAINT MICHAELS). The saints' names ending in -s, -'s indicate possession. One asks (e.g.) "ST. CLEMENTS what?" in SAINT MARYS the answer to this question is "City." For ST. MICHAELS the answer is "Church" (1667).

Next in quantity to saints' names are names from biblical mountains. In 1947 there were sixty-five. The mountains most commemorated are Zion (24) and Olivet (Mount of Olives/10/). There are five names from Calvary, and four from Tabor. I suppose that ZINE MINES (F) is from Zion; MT. ZORA (Manual 1947; Ce) should be *Zoar.*

Biblical names and family names are easily confused. HEBRON could be from the family name (Hebron, Heborn, Hepburn); BEULAH could be from a given name. SOLOMONS ISLAND is not from King Solomon, but from Captain Isaac Solomon, of Philadelphia, who set up a fishery here in 1867. ISRAEL CREEK (2; F and W) raises questions. Genealogists speak of "The line of John Israell, Gentleman" (d. 1723) and state that Robert Israel (d. 1795) married Priscilla Baker (or Beall), of Frederick. Wyand mentions the naturalization, in September 1751, of a certain Angel *Israollo.* "Midshipman Israel," of Washington County, is mentioned by Williams as "a promising son." He was blown up in Tripoli Harbor on September 4, 1804.

Besides names from saints and the Bible, the state has a micellany of placenames that are related to religion. One finds PROVIDENCE and ROSARYVILLE; there are GRACEHAM, HAVRE DE GRACE, and GODS GRACE CHURCH (on GOD'S GRACE POINT). The spiritual enthusiasm of MT. GLORY CHURCH is noteworthy. Less animated names are PROTESTANT POINT, BRICK MEETING HOUSE, and such church names as CHURCH, CHURCHTON, and CHURCHVILLE. The possibility of confusing surnames with seemingly religious names is ever present. CHRIST ROCK and some of the church names could well be from the family names, *Christ* and *Church.* EDEN(S) reminds us that *Eden Street* (BC) and DENTON (Eden + ton?) probably commemorate Sir Robert Eden, Maryland's last colonial governor (1769–1776).

4. *Names from royalty, nobility, and Jacobean history.* Seven counties were named for the Calverts and their families (BALTIMORE, CALVERT, CAROLINE, CECIL, CHARLES, HARFORD, and TALBOT). ANNE ARUNDEL COUNTY takes its name from the wife of

Cecil Calvert, second Lord Baltimore. In addition there are BALTI-MORE (city), BENEDICT, CALVERT, LEONARDTOWN, MT. CALVERT (etc.). Was FREDERICK (city) named for Frederick Calvert, sixth Lord Baltimore, or for his friend, Frederick, Prince of Wales? From noble men and women have come, of course, MARYLAND (Queen Henrietta Maria), ANNAPOLIS (Queen Anne), QUEEN ANNE'S COUNTY, and QUEENSTOWN.

It has been debated whether PRINCESS ANNE (S) owes its name to Queen Anne or to a lesser Anne, the daughter of King George II. To Prince Frederick, oldest son of King George I, is attributed PRINCE FREDERICK (C). Two *Annes* have been involved in the name ANNAPOLIS. The capital's first name, *ANN ARUNDEL TOWNE, comes from Anne Arundel, the wife of Cecil Calvert, second Lord Baltimore. In 1695 it became ANNAPOLIS, from Queen Anna Stuart. Anne Arundel's father was Baron Thomas Arundell. WARDOUR BLUFF (AA) and Wardour, a section of Annapolis, apparently bear the name of his Wiltshire castle. The family-name, *Arundel*, appears in ARUNDEL, ARUNDEL GARDEN, and ARUNDEL-ON-THE-BAY.

Kings are remembered in several of the state's placenames. A defunct *KINGSTON (KINGSTOWN), on Chester River, was named in 1732 "... presumably in honor of the reigning monarch." GEORGETOWN is for King George III; FREDERICKTOWN, opposite Georgetown, is for Frederick, George III's brother. Names from dukes are CUMBERLAND, from the Duke of Cumberland (1721-1765), the son of George II, and UPPER MARLBORO and LOWER MARLBORO from the Duke of Marlborough (1650-1722). These military dukes were never in the American colonies: but Lafayette was here,[n] and the ill-fated General Edward Braddock.[n] Marquis de Lafayette is remembered in *Fayette Street*, *Lafayette Avenue*, and *Lafayette Square* (BC). Braddock's name occurs in BRADDOCK, BRADDOCK HEIGHTS, BRADDOCK ROAD, and BRADDOCK RUN. Braddock's quartermaster, Sir John St. Clair, is remembered in SIR JOHNS RUN, a West Virginia stream in Bath District, Morgon County.

5. *American history, local and national.* GARRISON (B) and SOLDIERS DELIGHT (B) seem to have arisen in connection with early Indian marauders in Baltimore County. BRANDYWINE (PG) commemorates the Revolutionary Battle of the Brandywine (1777). The Civil War gave rise to McCLELLANS LOOKOUT, PAROLE (AA), and FORT MEADE, the latter place having been named for General George Meade, victor at Gettysburg (1863). *SURRATTSVILLE was changed to CLINTON (1878) because of Mrs. Surratt's suspected connection with Abraham Lincoln's murder.[n] CLINTON probably celebrates DeWitt Clinton, Governor of New York (d. 1828). An interesting name, relating to the Civil

War era, is BUREAU, which arose from a unit of the Freedman's Bureau, 1865.[n]

Note: Mention should here be made of FREE TOWN, an active black community near PASADENA, Anne Arundel Co., and *UPPER FREE TOWN, Somerset County. The former originated in about 1800; the latter came into being from *Upper Hill after the Civil War. These names are sufficiently accounted for by the facts that blacks were numerous in the Chesapeake Bay region from the days of the Calverts and in 1860 Maryland had more free Negroes than any other state. See: Benjamin Quarles, *MHM*, 71:1, Introd.

Notes: Marquis de Lafayette (1757-1834) made American sojourns in 1777, 1780, 1784, 1824-25. Braddock (b. 1697) was killed at Fort Duquesne in 1755. Mrs. Surratt and three others were hanged.

Maryland has a handful of names from local industrialists, philanthropists, and politicians. John W. Garrett, Baltimore and Ohio Railroad president, is commemorated by GARRETT COUNTY and GARRETT PARK. George Peabody and Johns Hopkins, philanthropists, are celebrated by *Peabody Heights* (BC) and *Hopkins Plaza* (BC). As for state politicians, one thinks of Colonel John Eager Howard ". . . of Revolutionary fame." He was Governor of Maryland from 1788 until 1791; later he was a United States Senator and a candidate for vice-president. From the Howard family come HOWARD COUNTY, HOWARD HEIGHTS, HOWARD PARK, HOWARDSVILLE, and *Howard Street* (BC). Governor Oden Bowie was prominent in administration and politics; Senator Arthur Pue Gorman aspired to the presidency, and controlled Maryland politics from 1869 until 1895. For Gorman, GORMAN (G) was named; from Bowie have come BOWIE and ODENTON.

National politics may account for KINDY HOOK (Ch). The analogous KINDERHOOK, N.Y., was the birthplace of President Martin Van-Buren, who was nominated in Baltimore in 1835. Other presidents are directly represented. Examples are WASHINGTON COUNTY, WASHINGTON GROVE, JEFFERSON, and LINCOLN. Indeed, George *Washington* accounts for twenty-four names of places in Maryland. Another national figure, Benjamin Franklin, has his name in twenty-three Maryland places, such as FRANKLIN, FRANKLINTOWN, FRANKLINVILLE, etc. However, since *Franklin* is an abundant surname, it is not likely that all of Maryland's Franklin names are from *Benjamin* Franklin.

6. *Agriculture, manufactures, shipping.* Maryland's first industrial machine was probably the water-mill. At the earliest moment possible the settlers of St. Mary's set up, "adjoyning to the Towne," a water-mill "for the grinding of corne." Mills quickly became numerous. In 1795 there were 180 mills; in 1941, 146 years later, there were 186. Nondescript mill names are MILL CREEK, MILL POINT, MILL SWAMP. More descrip-

tive are WINDMILL ISLAND CREEK, SAW MILL COVE, SAWPIT RUN, etc. Some mills with family names, such as HOOD'S MILLS, McKINSTRY'S MILL, and BACHMAN MILLS, have become villages. MILLINGTON (K), though it had mills, probably takes its name from the family name *Millington*.

Planting of corn and the commercial production of tobacco gave rise to a number of early placenames. The gazetteers give names like CORN-FIELD, CORNFIELD CREEK, CORNFIELD HARBOR, CORN-FIELD POINT, CORN HAMMOCK ISLAND. Cornbread, called *pone*, gave rise to PONE ISLAND and HALF PONE POINT. The tobacco industry is marked by TOBACCO RUN, TOBACCO STICK, PORT TO-BACCO, and ROLLING ROAD.

To pass from milling and agriculture to a broader placename description of Maryland industry past and present, one notices, first of all, names relating to pioneer life. Examples are SALTWORKS CREEK, SLAUGH-TERHOUSE RUN, SMOKEHOUSE COVE. Mechanics were important; one finds MECHANIC VALLEY (Ce), MECHANICS TOWN, ME-CHANICSVILLE (4). General mining was a pioneer activity; and in the case of iron and coal it was an early, if short-lived, giant. One finds SALT-PETER CREEK, CHROME HILL, BOXIRON CREEK (from bog iron); one finds, all pertaining to iron mining, HEMATITE (Co), IRON ORE RIDGE (Al), BLOOMERY, and OLD FORGE BRIDGE. The coal industry eventually outgrew the iron industry. Typical placenames from coal mining are SHAFT, KLONDIKE, PEKIN, MOSCOW. In the early days of the colony, *mill* usually meant a *flour* mill. But in 1852, especially in central Maryland and the Baltimore area, a mill was often a textile factory or a paper mill. At about that time, in addition to a number of cotton mills, there were 187 paper manufacturers and thirty-nine paper and "band-box" makers. Existing placenames from these sources are PAPER MILLS (BC), LAUREL (from *Laurel Factory), and SAVAGE (*SAV-AGE FACTORY). Mid-nineteenth century maps show that Maryland had a "Toy Fac" (toy factory), a "Carp. Fac" (carpet factory), a "Cot Fac (cotton factory), a "Fulling M" (fulling mill). But no placenames have survived to commemorate them.

The term *transportation* conveniently comprises the rest of Maryland's industrial placenames, which I divide into names from shipping and fisheries, names from canals, and names from railroading. To begin with shipping, one finds that in 1852 the state had 673 shipbuilders, 108 "ship smiths," 83 ship Joiners, and ten ship manufacturers. Current placenames relating to this industry are SHIPYARD CREEK(K) and HARTGES BOATYARD (AA). In a wider sense, shipping is further represented by THE ANCHORAGE (T) and ANNAPOLIS ROADS. Also quite pertinent are placenames containing *haven, harbor, port* and *wharf*, such as CASTLE HAVEN, HARBOR COVE, PORT DEPOSIT, and CONTEES

WHARF. Names for the kinds of ships built in Maryland are rare; I think of CANOE NECK CREEK, SHIP CREEK, and SLOOP CREEK.[n]

Note: With credit to Elaine G. Breslaw, let me point out that Thomas Todd, a shipwright, established a boatyard in Annapolis in 1651 and gave his name to both a creek (TODD'S CREEK, now SPA CREEK) and a street (*Shipwright Street*).

Related to ships and shipping, the disappearing ferry and Maryland's two aged canals have left their mark in the state's placename annals. In 1947 there were twenty designations containing the word *ferry*. Examples are FERRY BAY, FERRY BRANCH, and FERRY FARMS. There is even FERRY SLIP (QA). The two major canals—the defunct Chesapeake and Ohio (from 1828) and the active Chesapeake and Delaware (from 1804)—have given BIGPOOL (W) and PIVOT (Ce), respectively. CHESAPEAKE CITY commemorates the C. and D. Canal. Maryland has no placenames from the Chesapeake and Ohio Canal's historic Paw Paw Tunnel, which stands near the Paw Paw Bends of the Potomac River, Allegany County. However, on the opposite side of the river is the village of PAW PAW, Morgan County, West Virginia.

The idea of a railroad from Baltimore to the Ohio River was conceived in February 1827; and in 1830 Peter Cooper's first steam engine made a round trip from Baltimore to Ellicott's Mills. Names that arose from the Baltimore and Ohio Railroad are RELAY, PLANE NO. 4, JESSUP (from *Jessups Cut), HIGH GRADE JUNCTION, and VIADUCT JUNCTION. The Western Maryland Railroad (chartered in 1856) gave rise to TWENTY—FIRST BRIDGE and *TANK (near Patapsco). With the railroads came placenames ending in *switch, summit, junction, siding*, and *station*. Examples are BASKET SWITCH, WATERSVILLE JUNCTION, BEELER SUMMIT, FIERY SIDING, and RED HILL STATION. In Anne Arundel County, BESTGATE, IGLEHART, and WOYTYCH were all once railway stations; and some station names added the term, *switch* (*PATUXENT SWITCH STA. P.O.; *DORSEY SWITCH STA., etc.). *SPARKS SWITCH STA. has become SPARKS (B); *PUMPHREY STA. has become PUMPHREY (AA).

7. *Fauna and Flora (beasts, birds, fish, plants, trees, fruits).* Names of this kind bring up two arresting points. The first point is that family names and Christian names are readily mistaken for animal and plant names; the second point is that placenames, while they often record the early presence of an animal or plant, give no clue to whether or not an animal or plant is today extinct. At first sight COW SPRING (F) appears to denote the animal. But this explanation becomes less certain when one finds out that Frederick *Cow* and Dewalt *Cow* both lived in Washington County in 1790. Since there were also people in 1790 by the name of *Hog(g)*, *Wolf(e)*, and *Bear (Baer)*, the same doubt arises as to HOG COVE,

WOLFSVILLE, and some of the *bear* names, such as BEAR CREEK (W). One must be cautious, also, about names like BULL BRANCH (B), BULL MOUNTAIN (Ce), and BULLOCK CREEK, since *Bull* and *Bullock* are both family names. The reader can believe with certainty that BULL FROG (Ce) and BULL MINNOW POINT are from frogs and minnows; he can also safely attribute BEE TREE DITCH to the *bee*. And yet there is need of continual awareness: APE HOLE CREEK is probably from the family name *Abe, Ape*; TICK NECK is probably from "Conrod" Tick, a German of Anne Arundel County, naturalized in 1762.

As for the extinction of the larger mammals, one can say with certainty that—despite BUFFALO RUN, ELK RIVER, PANTHER BRANCH, and WOLF TRAP CREEK—the buffalo, the elk, the panther, and the wolf are no longer found in our woods. Curiously, the black bear (the subject of perhaps twenty-seven placenames [e.g., BEAR HOLLOW, A]) is still present. In the summer of 1981, according to news stories in the Piedmont (W.Va.) *Herald*, a black bear was seen on two occasions in the George's Creek region of Allegany County. It had probably wandered into the state from Pennsylvania.

Local naturalists say that the wildcat was driven out of Maryland in the 1880's, but that there are still bobcats. Perhaps it was the panther that was driven out. Maryland has no placenames for the bobcat. But there are WILDCAT BRANCH (3), WILD CAT CREEK, and WILDCAT POINT. Moreover, there is the debatable CAT ROCK (F). The Maryland rattlesnake is assuredly rare, except perhaps in Western Maryland. Placenames for it and other reptiles are illustrated by SNAKE DEN BRANCH (M), RATTLESNAKE ISLAND (Wo), and TERRAPIN SAND COVE. SNAKE LANE (H) suggests a hair-raising encounter from out of the past.

Colonial historians give a stirring account of the primeval animals of Maryland and Virginia. The 1635 *Relation* lists "Bufeloes, Elkes, Lions, Beares, Wolves, Foxes, Otters"; Alsop, 1666, adds "the Cat of the Mountain, the Rackoon, the Possum, the Squirril, and the Musk-Rat." William Penn mentions the panther; and Captain Smith enumerates small creatures, such as hares, martins, "Powlecats, weassels, and minkes." One cannot be sure of names with *martin*, such as MARTIN COVE; and *hare* has been replaced by *rabbit*, as in RABBIT HOLLOW (G). But most of the other smaller creatures mentioned are still found. Representing them are MINK TUMP ISLAND, MUSKRATTOWN, POLECAT HOLLOW, POSSUM POINT, RACCOON CREEK, and SQUIRREL HILL. *Skunk*, derived from Algonquian, occurs in SKUNK HOLLOW.

Note: The otter (evidenced by ten old placenames, such as OTTER POND) is not extinct.

All of the foregoing creatures are wild. Maryland's placenames from tame or domesticated animals remind us that the first colonists of Virginia and Maryland were not only men and women but also domesticated farm and house animals hitherto unknown and unseen in the pagan Delmarvan fields and forests of the New World. The *Relation* (1635) mentions "Cattell, Hogges, Poultry ... bought thither from England, Virginia and other places"; Alsop (1666) describes "Cows, Sheep and Horses" as "Beasts that were carried over at the first seating of the country." The horse was the most important of these newcomers, and, after the horse, the cow and the pig. Placename examples are HORSEBRIDGE CREEK, HORSE HAMMOCK ISLAND, HORSEPEN BRANCH, COW CREEK, HOG ROOTING POND, HOGS SKULL, and PIGSKIN RIDGE. Virginia writings of 1624 allude to "Dogges, Catts, ratts." The Indian had a domesticated dog, but it is likely that Maryland's five *dog* names are from the imported breeds (DOG CREEK, DOG RIDGE, DOGTOWN /2/, DOG and BITCH ISLAND).

Birds and fish make up the rest of Maryland's fauna. Mockingbirds must have been abundant. In 1697 King William III had 200 Maryland mockingbirds sent across the Atlantic for his royal aviary. The state has MOCKINGBIRD CREEK, and MOCKINGBIRD POND. Miscellaneous placenames from the plenteous birds of yesterday are CRANE ISLAND, GOOSE POINT, HAWK COVE, HERON ISLAND, DUCK ISLAND, SWAN CREEK, BRANT HOLE, and WIDGEON (a village).

FOWLING CREEK (Co) names the sport that has decimated the peregrine falcon and emptied the skies of the geese and ducks that once filled Maryland's heavens "like a cloud." The question of extinction again arises. The wild passenger pigeon, so abundant in 1687 in Quebec that holy water was used to exorcise it, began to disappear in about 1875 and has been completely extinct since 1914. Maybe PIGEON HILL (Ce) and PIGEON CREEK (S) refer to the passenger pigeon. But it is virtually certain that PIGEON HOUSE (AA) and PIGEONHOUSE CREEK (S) are from the domesticated bird. It is gladdening to know that, despite rumors and misgivings, the eagle and the wild turkey, unlike the passenger pigeon, are *not* extinct. Relatives of the eagle are represented here by such names as BUZZARD FLATS, HAWK COVE, FALCON POINT, and MERLIN GUT. From the eagle itself are EAGLE MOUNTAIN, EAGLE NEST POINT, and EAGLE ROCK. How safe from extinction is the Baltimore Oriole? It was described in 1947 as a "natural resident in all sections of the state." However, it has given only one placename, ORIOLE, a Somerset County village.

It remains to consider Maryland's stream, bay, and ocean animals, whose mention here at the end somewhat belies their great importance. In 1635 the state abounded in "Whales, Sturgeons, Grampuses, Porpoises, Mullets, Trouts, Soules, Place, Mackarell, Perch, Crabs, Oysters, Cockles, and Mussles." There were also rock fish, shad, and menhaden. As late as 1800, porpoises and sharks occasionally swam up the St. Mary's River in search of food; but with the passage of time these larger denizens have become rare. This is true also of the smaller shad, sturgeon, and rock fish. Illustrative placenames are HERRING BAY, TROUT RUN, POR-POISE CREEK, WHALE POINT (K), PERCH GUT, COCKLES POINT, MUSCLE HOLE STREAM, and SHAD POINT. STINGAREE ISLAND (BEND, CREEK) calls to mind Captain Smith's *STINGERAY ILE, of 1608. EEL HOPE POINT is comparable to MARSHY HOPE CREEK, old English *hop* ("valley, enclosure") being the common element of each name. WHALE POINT is perhaps misleading; Warner notices that *whale* in Eastern Shore watermen's dialect sometimes denotes a large soft crab. Maryland's celebrated crabs are responsible for CRAB ALLEY (BAY, CREEK, NECK), CRAB CREEK, CRAB POINT, and CRAB POINT COVE. Almost equally celebrated are the clam and the oyster. Relevant placenames are BIVALVE, CLAM ISLAND, and diverse *oyster* names such as OYSTER BAY, OYSTER COVE (3), OYS-TER CREEK (3), and OYSTERSHELL POINT (a village).

Turning from the state's fauna to its flora, one may well pause, first of all, to observe a group of plant and tree placenames containing words of Algonquian and Caribbean origin. In such a group certainly belongs the native American tree, the hickory, whose name is from Virginia Algonquian. It occurs fourteen times in Maryland nomenclature and furnishes the colonial example, *POHICK, and such later examples as HICKORY BAR POINT, HICKORY GUT, and HICKORY THICKET. Also of Algonquian origin are *chinquapin, persimmon,* and *tuckahoe,* found in CHINKAPIN RUN (B), PERSIMMON CREEK (SM), PERSIMMON TREE ROAD (M) and TUCKAHOE CREEK. Several more difficult Algonquian names turn out, upon analysis, to be descriptions of Maryland flora. *ASKIMINIKONSON (Wo), for example, suggests *strawberries* and probably means "Stony place where they pick early berries"; *MONOPONSON, the Indian name of Kent Island, suggests *tubers,* and probably means "It is an island where tubers are dug." Several additional Algonquian placenames, such as AQUASCO, CUTMAPTICO, QUAN-TICO, and TRANSQUAKING, refer to vegetation and trees.[n] However, I no longer believe that PAGAN POINT (SM) is from Algonquian for *pecan;* the family name *Pagan* seems to me to be a more likely source. I call

---

Note: An unusual example is TIPPITY WICHITY, an island at the head of St. Mary's River, near Great Mills. The word is apparently Virginia Algonquian and refers to the Tipitiwitchet, once the popular name for Venus's fly trap (*Dionaea muscipula,* a remarkable insect-eating plant from North Carolina). See: *Handbook,* II, 759.

Caribbean the Indian words from Spanish America that one finds in PAW PAW HOLLOW (SM) and TOBACCO RUN (H). *Sassafras,* as in SASSA-FRAS RIVER and SASSAFRAS HAMMOCK, has a strain of American Indian; *hammock* is from the language of the Arawakan Indians.

Alsop (1666) writes about Maryland's "plenteous soyle," and mentions oak, walnut, cedar, pine, chestnut, elm, ash, poplar, vines, plums, straw-berries, persimmon and violets. In 1972 the state's "Wye Oak" (T) was described as being "still the state and national champion." The Wye Oak itself has not given rise to any placenames; but there are OAK CREEK and forty-four other *oak* names. From trees in general have come ASPEN RUN, BEECH SWAMP, CEDAR BRANCH, CHESTNUT GROVE, LOCUST GROVE, PLUMTREE RUN, POPLAR GROVE, and MAPLE RUN. From the standpoint of placenames, the pine tree, as in PINE HILLS, is the state's most abundant tree, with ninety-four placename ex-amples. Four other trees arranged in order of their placename abundance are the cedar, the oak, the poplar, and the locust.

Many of Maryland's berries, flowers, fruits, and vegetables are com-memorated in the placename manner. Berries in general are probably rep-resented by BERRY LANE and BERRY RUN; however, there could be confusion with the family name, *Berry.* There can be no doubt about the genuineness of *cranberry* and *mulberry;* examples are CRANBERRY BRANCH and MULBERRY FIELD CREEK. The rose is a favorite placename flower, as in ROSECROFT, ROSEDALE, ROSEMONT; but in some cases it may be from the family name or the given name. VIOLETSVILLE could be from the given name *Violet;* however, ARBU-TUS, naming John Burrough's favorite spring flower, a sort of wild straw-berry, probably refers to the plant. Examples of grain and vegetable names are CORNSTACK (S), and PEA RIDGE. Most names with *bean,* such as BEANTOWN, are from the family name. Maryland's water-courses have weeds and vegetation, such as sea lettuce, cordgrass, wid-geon grass, and eel grass. Unless it be SALT GRASS POINT, these aquatic plants have left no placenames.[n] It should be so arranged, of course, that this note (see next page [note on *sedge grass...*) follow the *Tippity Wichity.*

Note: I find an exception in *sedge* grass, used in the former name (*SEDGE-FIELD) of SHADY SIDE (AA).

8. *Geography; topographical terms.* Except for bays and ocean, and the glades and mountains of Western Maryland, denoted by such names as SIDELING HILL, KEYSERS RIDGE, and GREEN GLADE RUN, the state conforms to this early geographical description by Alsop: "... gen-erally plaine and even, and yet hath some pritty small hills and risings; It's full of Rivers and Creekes and hath store of Springs and small Brookes."

Kuethe found six brooks, "Chiefly in the central section." An example is MEADOW BROOK, which also illustrates the extensive occurrence of *meadow* (15). Placename examples of the features mentioned by Alsop are NORTHEAST RIVER, LICKING CREEK, FLY HILL, FORT HILL, CLEAR SPRING (village), and MARDELA SPRINGS.

It is apparent from the foregoing that Maryland's geography is hardly spectacular. Its topographical terms are mainly those that are in common use in the British Isles, such as *bay, cove, forest, hill, island, lake, marsh, mountain, point.* However, one does not find *down, fen, firth, mull,* and *moor.* When certain English terms (such as *falls, glade, narrows*) have meanings different from their usual sense, they are called "Americanisms." Some Americanisms in Maryland are CRAB ALLEY CREEK, GWYNNS FALLS, GLADE RUN, OLD GROUND RUN, NARROWS PARK (A), and THOROFARE COVE. The term *mountain* usually denotes a high elevations. When, in Anne Arundel County, one finds it naming several low hills on Gibson Island, and an adjacent low point, MOUNTAIN POINT, one recognizes what is probably both Americanism and folk whimsy.

IV.
Vocabulary (Americanisms)

Now, using placename examples, let us consider more thoroughly the vocabulary of the Americanisms that gradually came into use in colonial Virginia and Maryland. There are three kinds: (1) words taken into English from the Algonquian Indians of the Atlantic coast; (2) words taken into English from Spanish and Portuguese adaptations of native words picked up in the West Indies; and (3) Americanized words and phrases from British English.

1. *Algonquian borrowings.* Placename examples of most of these have been given earlier under Fauna and Flora. *Moccasin* is Narragansett Algonquian and, in MOCCASIN POND (Wo), may refer to a lily. CO-HOUCK POINT (SM) may contain Algonquian *cohoke;* PUCKUM BRANCH (D) may contain Algonquian *pokoone.* HALF PONE POINT (SM) appears to be from Powhatan *appoans* "bread." Maryland has no surviving placenames from *pocosin* (Algonquian *poquosin* "marsh, swamp"). However, "Pocosin" occurs several times in the Baltimore County Rent Rolls of 1700.

2. *Words from the West Indies through Spanish and Portuguese.* PAW PAW COVE and TOBACCO RUN are mentioned under Fauna and Flora. Other instances are HAMMOCK ISLAND and SAVANNA LAKE. Additional clearcut words in this category are hard to find. *Canoe* (as in CANOE NECK CREEK) is an example. *Guinea* (as in GUINEA MARSH, D), however, is probably from West Africa.

3. *Americanized words and phrases from British English.* The English
stream names, *branch, creek,* and *gut,* took on new meanings in America.
Creek, meaning an inlet, or a small stream, in England, often means a
lengthy watercourse here. Maryland's TEN MILE CREEK is an example. As for *branch* and *gut,* one supposes that they are used in an American way in COONFOOT BRANCH and GUT MARSH (H). *Fork* is probably an Americanism; Maryland has FORK NECK, FORKED CREEK,
NORTH FORK BRANCH, etc. In some instances the settlers, to describe the new streams, salvaged British dialect terms, such as *drain,
frosh,* and *gully.* Examples are LLOYD DRAIN, ALLEN(S) FRESH,
and ROCK GULLY CREEK. On the Eastern Shore, tidewater Americanisms abound; one thinks of CRAB ALLEY and THOROUGHFARE
CREEK.

The natural peculiarities of terrestrial features such as mountains and
valleys are more conspicuous than the natural features of streams. And
the Americanisms they gave rise to are more evident. *Field* and *town* are
Americanisms, especially when modified by *old,* as in Maryland's OLD
FIELD and OLDTOWN. *Bottom,* a word found in British dialects, is used
in an American way in FOGGY BOTTOMS GUT (Ch), SANDY BOTTOM
and *DELAWARE BOTTOM. Another term from British dialect is *hole,*
meaning a small valley. In Maryland one finds it in APE HOLE CREEK,
MUDDY HOLE MARSH, and MUSCLE HOLE STREAM.

When one turns from Americanisms, and scans the state's placename
vocabulary in a search for the archaic and the unusual, it appears convenient to set up four divisions: (1) topography; (2) buildings; (3) industries,
activities; and (4) artifacts.

1. *Topography.* The state has unusual *barrens, glades,* and *narrows.* The
barrens, which are naturally sterile areas where there are only stunted
trees, have given rise to BARREN POINT and BARREN ISLAND
THOROFARE. Unfortunately, the phonetically similar family name
Baron brings to such names the possibility of confusion. The state's
glades, found in Garrett County and consisting of natural meadows with a
wet, marshy soil, are marked by GLADE RUN, GREEN GLADE RUN,
and ASHER GLADE. *Narrow(s)* is used for both land and water. In THE
NARROWS and NARROWS PARK, it means a narrow mountain pass; in
KENT NARROWS and WYE NARROWS, it designates the narrowest
part of a neck of land or island. Some of Western Maryland's mountains
sidle or slope sideways. The term *sideling* is used, as in SIDELING HILL
(and MOUNTAIN).

2. *Buildings.* Homes and houses are represented by LOG CABIN
BRANCH, BLOCK HOUSE POINT, FODDER HOUSE COVE, MEET-
ING HOUSE BRANCH, SALTHOUSE COVE, SWEATHOUSE
BRANCH, TANHOUSE CREEK, TENTHOUSE CREEK, and WARE-
HOUSE CREEK. Mills are named by BRICK MILL LANDING, POW-

DER MILLS, ROLLER MILL (K), and TUBMILL BRANCH. Two unusual bridge names are BLOCK BRIDGE and PUNCHEON BRIDGE. Pens and pits are represented by COWPEN RUN, HOGPEN CREEK, HORSE PEN BRANCH and SAWPIT RUN. Kilns and dams were abundant; the manuals list twenty-eight names from the *beaver dam*. Examples of kiln names are LIMEKILN HOLLOW, MAPLEKILN RUN, TANKILN RUN, and TARKILL (TARKILN) RUN. Miscellaneous structures are suggested by PITCHERDAM CREEK, FISHING BATTERY (LIGHT), and SCAFFOLD CREEK.

Some of the foregoing names need an explanation. The sweathouse was a lodge where baths were taken, especially by Indians. The rolling mill rolled and flattened metals and grain; in a tubmill water fell on tub-wheels placed in a vault. The maple kiln boiled maple sap to make sugar; the tar kiln was used to extract tar from wood and coal. In a sawpit one of the sawyers stood in a pit. *Battery* in names like FISHING BATTERY LIGHT means a battery or embankment of stone.

3. *Industries and activities*. One finds common terms used in an outmoded sense. Examples are BRICKYARD ROAD, STEELYARD CREEK, TANYARD COVE, SALTWORKS CREEK, and WATERWORKS CREEK. Swimming is denoted by DIPPINGPOND RUN and JUMPERS HOLE CREEK.[n] Collecting the eggs of wild birds was called "egging"; Maryland has LITTLE EGGING BEACH. "Striking," which was the strictly forbidden activity of catching a fish by striking it, is commemorated by STRIKING MARSH.

Note: This creek name bristles with frustrating explanations. John Mellin (*Capital*, April 2, 1983) cites an Arnold (AA) woman who was told that Jumpers Hole Road was the site of frog-leaping contests in the early 1900's. However, it appears that as early as 1802 a Maryland legislative document mentions Jumpers Hole Road in connection with a ferry across the headwaters of the Severn. My own opinion is that "Jumpers Hole" was simply a swimming hole where one could dive.

4. *Artifacts*. Some of the many colonial artifacts mentioned in Maryland's placenames are BUTTER POT POINT, FRYING PAN CREEK, KITTLE (kettle?) HILL, ROSINBARRELL SLAUGH, STIRRUP RUN, GRINDSTONE RUN, and WHETSTONE RUN. The butter pot was a low, stone jar, holding about a gallon; resin was kept in barrells. As for Indian artifacts, INDIAN SPRINGS (F) marks a likely locality; PIPE CREEK (Cl) is more specific.

V.

Matters Linguistic

A. *Pronunciation and dialect*. One ascertains the pronunciation of a placename by hearing it spoken or by reading a description of how it is spoken. Accordingly, we *hear* SAWLZ-berry for Salisbury and REE-vuh for Riva; and for Fairmount (S) and Wingate (D) we *read* "Fire-mint" (v. Warner) and "Wing-git." Journalists enjoy joking about the pronunciation of *Baltimore*. The Baltimore dialect has been called "Balmorese." Its dialectal pronunciation has been written as BOLL-ih-mer, Bollimer, Bollmer.

In general the state's placenames are not hard to pronounce. However, some of the Indian names would certainly baffle a stranger. Examples are Chicone (she-COHN), Conococheague (KAHN-uh-co-CHEEG), Lonaconing (Loan-uh-COHN-ing), Manokin (muh-NO-kun), Mattaponi (Matta-po-NYE), Monie (mo-NYE), Shawan (shuh-WAHN), Wicomico (wye-KAHM-i-co), Youghiogheny (yahk-ee-ah-GAINEY) In the realm of non-Indian names, Bowie (BOO-ee) and Taneytown (TAHNI-town) are deceptive, as are also Principio (prin-SIP-io) and Benevola (benny-VOHL-uh). La Plata is properly (lah-PLAY-tuh). In Dorchester County Crapo is (CRAY-po) and Warner writes "crow-sher-on" for Crocheron; however, I have heard (*KROH*-shun).

In both pronunciation and spelling, placenames reveal local dialects. Thus the old spelling *Spaw for Spa Creek, Annapolis, indicates that the *ah* sound of today was once an *aw* sound. That this sound lingers as a trace of dialect is shown by the fact that Calvert County is still sometimes pronounced (CALL-vert). Books about Eastern Shore speech indicate that *oyster* there is often pronounced "arster" and *turtle*, "turkle." One would therefore expect the local pronunciation of OYSTER COVE and TURTLE EGG ISLAND to be "Arster" COVE and "Turkle" EGG ISLAND. In Western Maryland, where the folk reputedly say "holler" for *hollow*, BEAR HOLLOW and RABBIT HOLLOW are no doubt often pronounced BEAR "Holler" and RABBIT "Holler." The folk pronunciation "crick" for *creek*, though rarely found spelled in this way, is common in Appalachia; Carey has found "Crab Crick" in an Eastern Shore folk poem.

G. *The omission of s ('s)*. In Western Maryland one hears "corp" for *corpse*, "licen" for *license*, and "mile" for *miles*. In nearby West Virginia one hears "year" for *years*, "child" for *child's*. In Maryland placenames the omission of *s* is frequent. RIVERDALE, for instance, omits the *s* of "Riversdale," the mansion its name is from; KEYSER RIDGE omits the *'s* of *Keyser's Ridge, thereby obscuring the original meaning. In 1933 the U.S. Geographic Board made the bad decision that WILL'S CREEK should be WILL CREEK. Happily, the Maryland gazetteers and manuals still spell this name with an *'s*. Since *Will(s)* can be a family name, not to do so would cloud the tradition and possibility that "Will" was a Shawnee Indian.

For the sake of accuracy *s* and *'s* should not be omitted in placenames that are plural or possessive. Laxity in this regard makes it questionable whether or not RHODE RIVER means "Rhode's River." In the case of family names, such as *Gannon* and *Lappan*, that do not end in *s*, one supposes the GANNONS and LAPPANS indicate something possessed. Investigation shows that GANNONS comes from "Gannon's Store" and that, as early as 1843, LAPPANS was "Lappon's Cross Roads." In the case of ambiguous family names the presence or absence of *'s* in a place-name is crucial. With no *'s* in LONG CORNER, one is left in a quandary as to whether this is a *long* corner or Mr. Long's corner. In the case of TRAVERS (TRAVERSE) COVE, either spelling could be correct; but "Traver's" would be wrong because the family name (Travers) correctly ends in *s*. Some speakers tend to add *s* rather than omit it; for SILVER SPRING one still hears the erroneous "Silver Springs."

C. *Maryland and Delmarvan R.* In Western Maryland one hears "arn" for *iron*, "sir-up" for *syrup*, "Carlin" for *Carolyn*, and "born" for *barn*. In central Maryland one sometimes hears "curl" for *Carroll*; and the "ur" of *Baltimore* ("Ball-uh-mur") is often derided. In the Delmarvan dialect of the Eastern Shore, *Delaware* is pronounced DELLA-wur, and *America* is uh-MURR-ica. One even hears THUR-uh-pee for *therapy!*

Maryland's most striking placename examples of this speech characteristic are the result of an *a, e, i,* or *o* being followed and affected by an *r*. Thus the German family name *Gartner* has given GORTNER, *Morgan* sometimes appears as "Margan" (MARGANTOWN, QA), and *Sherman* becomes "Sharman," as in SHARMAN (W). There is no doubt that Terrapin (TERRAPIN SAND COVE) appears also as "Turpin" (TURPIN SAND COVE) on account of an *r* influence. This influence also explains why *ROASTING-EAR POINT appears as ROASTING GAR. "Carnishes," which sometimes occurs for CORNISH POINT (SM), illustrates the r-effect; it is more than a mere "corruption."

R can be transposed or interchanged; it can intrude. Examples of an interchanged *r* are MT. ZORA, an incorrect variant of Mt. Zoar, COBRUMS WHARF, which should be "Coburns" (adjacent to COBURNS), and "Harve De Grace," incorrect for HAVRE DE GRACE. Examples of intrusive *r* are CHEVERLY, from *Cheveley*, DRUNKARD LICK RUN, from *Dunkard*, and OUTWARD LICK TRUMP from *Tump*. A final speech peculiarity is the occasional appearance of an *r* after *oi (oy)*. This occurs in Western Maryland, where one hears "orl" for *oil*. In central Maryland WOYTYCH (AA) is pronounced WUR-tik; on the Eastern Shore, OYSTER COVE (D) may be "Arster."

D. *Folk etymology.* A folk etymology is an early attempt on the part of the folk to make sense of a difficult word or name by ignorantly altering its pronunciation and spelling. Thus the family name *Throck(g)morton* has been altered by the folk to give FROG MORTAR CREEK; and the family name *Honeycutt* has been altered to give "Honeygo," as in HONEYGO RUN. The name of a settler, *Luke Raven*, has been altered to give LOCH RAVEN. By the same process, the family name, *Delahyde*, has been transformed to "Dolly Hyde," as in DOLLYHYDE CREEK.

Since Maryland's early settlers knew little or no Algonquian, they necessarily applied folk fancy to the new Indian sounds they heard and altered them on the analogy of familiar English words. The *-woman* of MATTAWOMAN, the *Chop* and *tank* of CHOPTANK, the *Rock* and *walk* of ROCKAWALKING are all the invention of the folk; the real Indian words had sounds that were similar. PORT TOBACCO is what the folk made out of the original Algonquian **Potopaco*; VIENNA is what they made out of **Unna-*, a shortened form of *Unnacocassinon*, the name of a Nanticoke chieftain. Folk etymology is both the bane and the delight of the placename student. Chericoke (Virginia) and ROMANCOKE (QA) are good placenames, but they entirely obscure the early Algonquian words they are from.

Finally, folk etymology is a branch of folklore and often involves folk phrases and folk stories. Warner relates that BESTPITCH, though it comes literally from the family name, *Bestpitch*, is explained locally by the phrase "Best Bridge." And Carey relates that HEBRON, evidently biblical, is explained by the folk as a mispronunciation of "Heaven." Yarns woven to explain a word or name are called etiological stories. An example is the explanation of DAMES QUARTER as having arisen from the angry exclamation "Damn quarter!" by a fisherman who had lost a quarter. GUNPOWDER FALLS, *POMPEY SMASH, and TRED AVON RIVER are but a few of the many Maryland placenames that have folk explanations. With few exceptions, folk etymologies, though entertaining, are incorrect.

E. *Combinations.* Maryland's placename compounds are mainly of two sorts. The first sort consists of syllabic combinations of *Maryland* and the names of her bordering states; the second sort consists of syllabic combinations of family names, in whole and in part. Examples of the first sort (containing *Mar-*, *Mary*, *Del-*, *Pen-*, and *Syl-* /Pa./) are DELMAR, MARDELA SPRINGS, MARYDELL, PEN MAR, and SYLMAR. Examples of the second sort are LORDOLPH (the surname *Lord* + the last syllable of Ran*dolph*?), MORGANZA (*Morgan* + *-za*), MORGNEC (*Morgan* + neck), COKESBURY (*Coke* + *Asbury*), and TOLCHESTER (*Tol*son + *Chester* River). In KEYMAR, *Mary*land is combined with the surname *Key*; in KLEJ GRANGE one finds the first letters of the given names *K*ate, *L*ouise, *E*mma, and *J*osephine. Since *-polis* (Greek "city") and *-wood* are standard suffixes, compounds such as ANNAPOLIS, PHILOPOLIS (Greek *filos* "loving"), and EUDOWOOD (Greek *eudios* "clear, fair") are not surprising.

Maryland has its share of bewildering and insoluble placenames that, to speak colloquially, are simply "Greek." One of them, indeed, *is* Greek. I refer to MELITOTA (K), which appears to be from Greek *melitoutta* "honied (cake)." Some of the state's Indian placenames completely defy explanation. Happily, an interesting but difficult one, TIPPITY WICHITY ISLAND (SM), turns out to be the Algonquian word *Tipitiwitchet*, the popular name of Venus's-flytrap (v. *Handbook*, ii, 759). But a score of tantalizing names defy explanation and belong in the guessing grounds. Instances are MA LEG ISLAND (C), ROHN PITCH (Wi), a stream, and SKYWATER ROAD (AA).[n] Admariothria (a coinage on the analogy of the word *idolatry*, means "Homage to Mary" and was the former name of George Tompson's colonial manor in Piscataway Hundred. But this place is not listed in the gazetteers and manuals.

Note: I was inclined to treat PADDY PIDDLE COVE (Ce) jocularly. But I now wonder whether, somehow, it is related to the *Piddle* or *Puddle* River (a small stream), Dorsetshire, England.

SKYWATER ROAD (AA) is easily explained when one considers that it is on Gibson Island, a region of handsome homes, sky and water. Cf. BYWATER ROAD, Gibson Island.

VI.
Ethnology and Migration

1. *The Algonquian Indians.* They were in Virginia and Maryland before the Roanoke voyages, before Captain John Smith, and before the Calverts. The majority of the placenames on the early Virginia maps are Algonquian. In Maryland, such placenames, though they usually originated from the streams, often, in a secondary way, designated the native tribes. A study of these names today shows that they corroborate the history of the northern wandering of the Piscataway (Conoy), Shawnee and Tuscarora, and enlighten the migration of such tribes as the Delaware, the Seneca, and the Nanticoke.

As for specific examples, let us begin with the Piscataway or Conoy Indians, whom the Maryland settlers found on Piscataway Creek, and who, after a sojourn in the region of the District of Columbia (1673?) and again on nearby Heaters Island (earlier *CONOY ISLAND), trekked north into Pennsylvania and settled near Conestoga (ca. 1704). The placenames that mark this passage are PISCATAWAY CREEK, *CONOY ISLAND, *INDIAN TOWN LANDING (Md.), *CANAVEST (Md.), *Conoy Creek* (Pa.), and even *Kanawha* (W.Va.), if the theory can be maintained that the names *Conoy* and *Kanawha* are related and that the Conoy once lived on the Kanawha's banks.

Another well-known Maryland tribe, the Nanticoke, also migrated to Pennsylvania, beginning in 1792. They removed from their Maryland domain, NANTICOKE RIVER, carrying with them the bones of their ancestors. One may plot their line of march by WETIPQUIN CREEK at the Maryland end and Towanda Creek at the Pennsylvania end. *Wetipquin* means "Place of interring skulls," and *Towanda* means "Where we bury the dead." These Indians are remembered in Pennsylvania by *Nanticoke*, a town in Luzerne County.

Finally, some notice should be taken of the wanderings across Maryland of the Shawnees, the Delawares, the Tuscaroras, Senecas, and Mingos. In 1677 and for the next thirty years the Shawnee Indians crisscrossed western and northern Maryland on their way from the Savannah River, South Carolina, to Pequea Creek, Pennsylvania. The placenames that record these expeditions inlcude *Shawanese Oldtown, *Old Field(s), OLD-TOWN, TOWN CREEK, SHAWAN, and *SHAWAN CABIN BRANCH. The Tuscarora Indians, making a trek similar to that of the Shawnees, spent ninety years, after an Iroquoian treaty in 1712–1715, emigrating from North Carolina to Tuscarora Valley, Pennsylvania. During that time they often had temporary encampments in Maryland. Placenames commemorating their presence are Frederick County's two TUSCARORA CREEKs. Meanwhile, the Delaware and Seneca Indians often crossed Maryland on the Old Indian Road, a path between the Susquehanna and the Potomac. One finds in this connection DELAWARE RUN, Worthington Valley; and it is significant that the South Branch of the Patapsco River was once called *Delaware Falls.

MINGO BRANCH (B) and the two Baltimore and Cecil County SENECA CREEKs indicate the early presence of the Iroquoian "Minqua or Sinigo Indians" in the backwoods of that area. Names locating the Seneca are in Cecil County (SENECA POINT), Baltimore County, and Montgomery County (SENECA, SENECA BRIDGE, SENECA CREEK). Thus, marked by placenames, one finds a Seneca Indian path.

2. *The English.* In 1631 William Claiborne, Secretary of the Virginia Colony, established a trading post of about "one hundred souls" on Kent Island. Evidently they were the first white immigrants and settlers in what is today Maryland. There followed the settlers of 1634. Such placenames as CHARLES COUNTY, CALVERT COUNTY, PRINCE GEORGES COUNTY, LEONARDTOWN, BRETON BAY, BENEDICT, and ALLENS FRESH will evoke from many future generations the exclamation "English!"

3. *The Celts.* By this heading I mean the Irish, Scotch and Welsh. They came here with the English; later they came in ethnic groups. The Irish have given an abundance of placenames; but the various Baltimore names (BALTIMORE, City and COUNTY, BALTIMORE CORNER, etc.), although Irish, are from the Calverts and hardly indicate migration. However, Colonel George Talbot, the second Lord Baltimore's cousin, when he brought 100 Irish people to "Susquehanna Manor" in 1680, indulged in a penchant for Irish placenames. Such extinct places as *NEW IRELAND, *NEW LEINSTER, and *MUNSTER arose; and Talbot renamed the NORTHEAST RIVER, the *SHANNON. Of these places only DUBLIN is left. Today, sprinkled throughout the state, one finds references to the Irish in BELFAST, COVE OF CORK (AA), IRELAND, IRELAND CREEK, IRISH CREEK, and IRISHTOWN.

Similar to the foregoing signs of the Irish are such plain Maryland references to the Scotch as ABERDEEN (H), SCOTCH HILL (A), SCOTCH-MAN CREEK (G), SCOTLAND (W, SM), SCOTLAND CREEK (D), and SCOTCHMAN POINT (Ce). As SCOTCH HILL (A) suggests, the George's Creek coal fields of Allegany County were early haunts of the Scotch. Not only are there CALEDONIA HILL and MIDLOTHIAN, but also, from Scotch and Scotch-Irish family names, GRAHAMTOWN (A), JACKSON RUN (A), JENKINS HILL (G), LAUDER (A), SHAW (A), SLOANE (mine and village), and perhaps MORRISON and REYNOLDS. WILSON (G) and McCOOLE (A) are from Scotch-Irish surnames. *Garrett* (as in GARRETT COUNTY) and *Mc Henry* (as in Mc HENRY, G) are Scotch-Irish family names; but the founders, John W. Garrett and James McHenry, were from the Baltimore area.

The Scotch-Irish have been defined as ". . . the descendants of the Scotch and English who settled in the north of Ireland, with an infusion of Irish blood in some few instances." There was an influx of the Scotch-Irish to the Eastern Shore in about 1692; and so abundant were they in Somerset County that an early writer describes that region as ". . . a place pestred with Scotch & Irish." It often requires special research into genealogy and local history to determine exactly whether a particular name betokens the Scotch-Irish. It is likely that McKINSTRY'S MILL (C1) and RANDALLSTOWN (B) are Scotch-Irish. One would expect to encounter a multitude of Scotch-Irish placenames in Somerset County. Several examples are BARKLEY BRANCH, LAWSONIA, and SCOTT POINT.

It remains to describe the Celtic placenames left on our maps by the Welsh. There were Welshmen among the Western Maryland miners in 1860; *LLANGOLLEN (now BLOOMINGTON, G) attests to this. There were Welshmen in Baltimore, as marked by GWYNNS FALLS. And there were Welshmen in central Maryland and on the Eastern Shore, in particular Edward and Philemon Lloyd, as marked by the rivers SEVERN, TRED AVON, and WYE. From Philemon Lloyd's name has come LLOYD CREEK; from the storied Welsh patronymic, *Jones*, come our four JONESTOWNs and our one JONESVILLE. Other Welsh placenames in Maryland are MORGANVILLE, REESE, and LINTHICUM. Names like CARDIFF and LANDAFF probably commemorate small groups.

4. *The French and Germans.* The French are somewhat scantily represented by Maryland placenames.[n] FRENCHTOWN (Ce) may have derived its name from a group of Acadians who settled here in 1755; the old "Frenchtown" quarter of Baltimore is similarly explained. Another Baltimore quarter, "San Domingo," denotes the arrival here, in 1793, of some 2000 whites, mulattoes, and blacks, following an insurrection in Haiti. These French speaking refugees considerably influenced Baltimore culture, but the only French name they left is *Ducatel Street*, for Edme Du

Catel, originally from Auxerres, France. To the Eastern Shore, after the revocation of the Edict of Nantes (1685) came a small number of Huguenots. Perhaps CRAPO and CROCHERON reflect this movement. The French family name *De Courci*, is seen in CORSICA RIVER, COURSEY POINT, and DE COURSEY CREEK. These names are from Maryland's Colonel Henry Coursey, whose ancestors had been in England since the eleventh century.

Note: Gregory A. Wood (*The French Presence in Maryland 1524-1800*, Baltimore, 1978) makes it plain, however, that, judging by placenames, there were more French colonists in the state than one would suppose. John Jarbo(e), of Dijon, France (b. 1619), is remembered by *JARBOESVILLE (today LEXINGTON PARK, SM), HARDESTY (PG), CHANEYVILLE (C), PARDIE BRANCH (Wo), SOLLARS (C), PARRAN (C), and PARROTT POINT (T) are all probably from French settlers. Among notable Huguenots one finds Marin Duval and Antoine LeCompte. Apparently they gave their names to DUVALL BRIDGE (AA), DUVALL CREEK (AA), LECOMPTE CREEK (D), and LECOMPTE BAY (D). It appears from Wood that at the time of the Acadian experience Baltimore had *Frenchman's Alley* and, on S. Charles Street, *French Town*. Baltimore's Bentalou Street is from Paul Bentalou (1754-1826), a French hero of the American Revolution. He was on a committee to help the Santo Domingans.

LAPPANS CROSS ROAD, LIPINS CORNER and SILLERY (sometimes "Silvery") BAY are all French.[n] And it should not go unmentioned that HAVRE DE GRACE, with a completely French spelling, memorializes what tradition says was an exclamation favored by the Marquis de Lafayette when he crossed the Susquehanna River in 1784 on a visit to George Washington.

As it turns out, Maryland's German immigrants are last in this account; but the abundance of German placenames in Maryland shows that they were by no means least. Indeed, one of Maryland's first naturalized citizens, Augustine Herrman (Md. denizen, 1661), a distinguished representative of the Dutch of New Amsterdam, was a German. His presence in Maryland is commemorated by BOHEMIA RIVER, from his place of birth, by PORT HERMAN, and by ST. AUGUSTINE, from his given name.

Note: "Silvery" is a folk etymology. However, I have not been able to determine whether SILLERY BAY (AA) has any connection with a Maryland family by this name.

It was from Pennsylvania that the bulk of the Maryland Germans eventually came; they were in Frederick County in 1732, Alleghany County in about 1780, and Garrett County in about 1788. The Frederick County immigrants settled in the "Green Glades" and populated the safer backwoods communities, "Aurora" and "Redhouse." Excepting *GERMAN

SETTLEMENT (1827), today Aurora, W.Va., there is nothing about these remote placenames to indicate their former migratory significance. However, now one finds in Garrett County NEW GERMANY, village and state park.

It sometimes seems as though the more one looks in Western Maryland the more German placenames one sees. In Frederick and Washington Counties one finds HAGERSTOWN, FUNKSTOWN, LEITERSBURG, MYERSVILLE, *NEW BREMEN (1784), CREAGERSTOWN, and *HARBAUGHS (HARBAUGH VALLEY). In Allegany County one finds ECKHART, BOETCHERVILLE (near Cumberland), KREIG-BAUM (Conrad Creighbaum), and KIEFER. And in Garrett County one finds BITTINGER, GORTNER, FINZEL, KITZMILLER (compare *Kutzmueller*), SINES, STEYER, STRECKER, and WEBER. However, though these western counties have a special history of German settlement, it is possible to find striking German placenames in almost every corner of the state.

To continue, in Montgomery County, for instance, one finds, north of Gaithersburg, GERMANTOWN, OLD GERMANTOWN, CLOPPER, and PRATHERTOWN. Somewhat southeast, in Prince George's County, are BADEN, NEW GLATZ, and SILESIA. BADEN, both placename and family name, represents the Grand Duchy of Baden, Germany; NEW GLATZ is from the countship of Glatz, Silesia; and SILESIA betokens the duchy of "German Silesia."

Finally, to complete this account of the placename signposts of Maryland's racial groups, attention must be paid to the small but valuable nomenclature of the state's Negroes, Jews, Italians, and Poles. They follow up the rear, so to speak, because, despite their importance, the placenames that commemorate them are few and hard to locate. Of all such names, places that may be called "Black communities" are the most numerous. Usually they are small villages, often suburbs, in central and Southern Maryland, and on the Eastern Shore. Examples are ARUNDEL-on-the-BAY (AA), COPPERVILLE (T), HIGHLAND BEACH (AA), LAKELAND (PG), SUGAR HILL (PG), and TOBYTOWN (M).

Maryland's Jewish people have at least one explicit placename to commemorate them. I refer to the almost forgotten village of *JEWSBURG (C1), today known as MARSTON. I learn (1981) from the Wilt brothers, of Marston, that the name arose in the nineteenth century, when *JEWSBURG had several Jewish families and a country store. As for placename references to Italians and Poles, there is some certainty, and there is also some doubt and dissension. Certain it is that in the days (ca. 1895–1930) when Polish crop pickers came into Anne Arundel County every summer from Baltimore there was a section in Baltimore called "Little Poland"; and certain it is that to this day there exists a neighborhood in Baltimore named "Little Italy." But it is not certain that the celebrated signer, William Paca (1740–1799), whence *Paca Street*, Baltimore, was an Italian, as some Italians claim; nor is it certain that POLISH MOUNTAIN (A) is from an early Polish family or enclave. Stiverson and Jacobsen[1] satisfactorily demonstrate that William Paca, despite his Italian-sounding surname, was probably an Englishman. And a worthy Allegany County local historian,[2] decrying a racial origin, believes that the *Polish* of POLISH MOUNTAIN (Colton 1852, map) originated from the *polished* look of the sunny mountain leaves on some past occasion. I am inclined to reject the "polished leaf" theory. Not only is it phonetically difficult to explain how *polished* (pa-) lost its *-ed* and became *Polish* (poe-) but there is the additional objection that ordinarily English usage does not favor the adjective *polished* in such phrases as "polished leaves" or "polished mountain." The racial origin is further favored by the fact that in Joan Hume's *Index to the Wills of Allegany County 1784–1960* (Baltimore, 1970) approximately twenty-five Polish families are listed, some of their surnames being Blonskey, Jesinovsky, Rensky, Jablinsky, and Kabovsky. Webb's *Cumberland Directory 1880–81* lists Blonsky, Lashansky, and Shausky.

---

[1]See Gregory A. Stiverson and Phebe R. Jacobsen, *William Paca a Biography* (Baltimore: Md. Hist. Soc., 1976). The surname of Robert Paca, the immigrant, had such contemporary spellings as *Peaker*, Pecker, *Peaca*, *Peca*, and *Paka*. Comparable English surnames are *Pace*, *Packe*, and *Pake*. In his discussion of PACKINGTON, Leicestershire, England, Ekwall (*Concise Oxford Dict. of English Place-Names*, 1960) mentions a hypothetical *Pac(c)a's* town (people, wood) and remarks that Old Norse *Pakki* occurs as a by-name.

[2]See POLISH MOUNTAIN in the accompanying alphabetical text.

Conclusion

Now that there are nuclear weapons that could bring it to pass, the withdrawal and disappearance of the American Indians in Virginia and Maryland might one day be followed by the withdrawal and disappearance of our present black and white citizenry. Since the days of the Calverts Maryland has become sprinkled with a myriad of populated places, each of which has a name. No one quite knows what will be the future of these names. Will alien invaders, overriding the countryside, change them to another language? Or—perhaps a sadder fate—will our smaller towns become deserted, like Goldsmith's Auburn, with the Indian water and mountain designations lasting longer than the rest? In any case, we presently have here a pantheon of lesser gods, a gallery of the worthy persons who have achieved a sort of immortality by having places named for them. Let us, in the accompanying pages, see who they were and give them their due.

ALPHABETICAL TEXT

A

ABERDEEN. A village near Havre de Grace, Harford County. Two earlier names were *Halls Cross Roads and *Mechanicsville. According to postmaster William N. Michael, the station was named *Aberdeen* when the Pennsylvania, Wilmington, and Baltimore Railroad came through here in 1892. C. Milton Wright, in *Our Harford Heritage, A History of Harford County*, attributes the name to a Mr. Winston, of Aberdeen, Scotland. Mr. Winston settled alongside the railroad and was the first postmaster. Incorporation was in 1892.

ABINGDON. A village near Van Bibber, Harford County. William Paca (1740–99), Maryland governor and a signer of the Declaration of Independence, founded Abingdon in 1779. The name is probably from the market town and municipal borough of Abingdon, Berkshire, England. W. B. Marye, Maryland local historian, recalls that the Paca Place was called Paca's Park and the original survey was called Collett's Neck. (See: Gannett, 1905.)

Note: Abingdon, a town in Illinois, was so called because a native of Abingdon, Maryland, was one of its founders.

ACCIDENT. A village near Kaese Mill, Garrett County. A tract of land here was called "Accident" as early as 1774. A village arose in about 1800, and the post office was established in 1838. The accident that probably gave rise to the name happened in 1774 when two separate surveying parties accidentally claimed and surveyed the same tract of land. At the time of these surveys Lord Baltimore had just opened for settlement his lands "westward of Fort Cumberland." During the next three months twenty land speculators, with their agents and surveyors, rushed into the mountains with land warrants in their pockets. (See: GS 30, June 1948; Weeks, pp. 19–20).

ACCOKEEK. A village near Sharpsville, Prince George's County. Evidently it takes its name from *Acquakick*, a small stream it is near. *Accokeek* is Indian, and probably contains two Algonquian elements, "up to" and "hill, rising ground." Its most likely meaning is "At the edge or limit of the hill or rising ground."

Note: The basic elements of the PA archetype are *ahkwi* "up to" and *ă'kiwi* "hill, rising ground."

ADAMS. A village on St. George Island, St. Mary's County. In 1790 there were only six heads of families by the name of *Ad(d)ams* in St. Mary's County. In 1963 the combined telephone list of *Adamses* in Charles and St. Mary's Counties contained about 66. Austin L. Adams, of St. George Island, is perhaps a modern descendant of the founding family.

ADAMSTOWN. On the Baltimore and Ohio Railroad, near Doubs, Frederick County. It has been known by the three earlier names, *Adamsville, Adamstown Junction,* and *Davis' Warehouse.* The name was changed from Davis' Warehouse to Adamstown in 1840, when Adam Kohlenburg became station agent.

ADELPHI. See RIGGS MILL. Pronunciation: uh-DELL-fye.

ADY. A village near Scarboro, Harford County. The name is evidently from the Ady family. In 1790 William Ady was the only Ady in Harford County. In 1878 S. M. Ady lived near Coopstown, Harford County. The name has persisted to the present day. In 1963 one finds I. B. Ady living on Sharon Road about five miles from Ady. (See: Lewis 1878).

AIKIN (AIKEN). A village near Perryville, Cecil County. It appears that Glasgow, Maryland, was once named Aikens or Aikenstown, for a man called Aiken who kept a hotel here. In 1790 Robert Aiken was in North Susquehanna Hundred, Cecil County. Samuel Aikin, Jr., was living in Aiken in 1963. (Source: Johnson, p. 334). See *GLASGOW.

AIREY. A village near Linkwood, Dorchester County. It has been described as "Aireys ... a little village and railroad station on the Cambridge and Seaford Railroad." The forefather of the local Airey family was Thomas Airey of Kendall, Yorkshire. He came to Maryland in 1726, and in 1728 became Priest of Great Choptank Parish. Henry Airey lived here in 1781. Compare MOUNT AIRY. (See: Jones, pp. 94–95; 276–77).

ALDINO. A village near Level, Harford County. Sandra Williams (Avondale Store, Aldino) has 19th century deeds to her parents' property that describe the locality as "Woods Meadow Enlarged," on the Old Mudtown Road. The village has had the two earlier names of Mudtown and Avondale. The present name, according to Miss Williams, was suggested by the Post Office Department. The pronunciation is Ell-DINE-Uh.

*ALL/A/NS MILL. See NEWTON.

ALLEGHENY. In Western Maryland, the name of mountains, coal mines, a county (ALLEGANY), and two villages, ALLEGANY and ALLEGANY GROVE. All these names come, directly or indirectly, from "The Allagany Ridge of Mountains." *Allegheny* is a Delaware Algonquian word whose last two syllables are from the Algonquian element meaning

---

Note: The principal PA stem is, specifically, *-aha(n)* "alternate motion, lapping." It appears as *-hanna* in Loyal*hanna,* Susque*hanna,* Toby*hanna,* Occa*hannock,* Rappa*hannock,* and even Youghio*gheny.* For "good" one may consider B & A (Delaware) *welhik.*

"alternate motion, lapping." The opening syllables (Alle-) may mean "good." Hence the meaning of *Allegheny* is probably "Good river."

ALLEN. A village in Trappe District, Wicomico County. Allen has had the two earlier names, *Trap* and *Upper Trappe*. Joseph W. T. Smith, Circuit Court Clerk, Wicomico County, informs me: "My great uncle, Mr. Joseph S. C. Allen, was postmaster and merchant there and the . . . village changed its name from Upper Trappe to Allen after his family." See LOWER TRAPPE, and TRAPP(E).

ALLENS FRESH. One of the freshes of Wicomico River, near Faulkner, Charles County. Spelled *Allenfresh*, it was also a post office. The name probably arose in 1674, when John Allen built a courthouse and prison about four miles from Port Tobacco River. There was also Allen's Mill ("now called Fresh"). (See: BK, p. 17, p. 25 and p. 101).

Note: "Fresh" is an Americanized British dialect term meaning (v. OED; McJimsey, III) "A stream of fresh water running into tidewater; also that part of a tidal river next above the salt water."

ALLOWAY. A village near Ashton, Montgomery County. The name is from "Alloway," a farm in Drayton, west of Stabler, Montgomery County. A relative of the owner suggested the name, apparently because it had a pleasant sound and reminded him of Scotland, where Alloway is a suburb of Ayr. (See: Farquhar, p. 93).

ALLOWAY CREEK. It flows into Maryland from Pennsylvania and enters the Monocacy River at Palmer, Carroll County. Early spellings are *Willoloway* and *Willoway*. *Alloway* is a shortened form of *Willoway*. The original *Willoloway* is Indian and the counterpart of Delaware Algonquian *wulalowe* "beautiful tail." The reference is probably to the black fox, and a plausible meaning is "Fox Creek."

Note: The pith of the word is probably PA *weli-*, *uli-* "good, fine, pleasant, beautiful." Cf. *Allegheny*.

ALLVIEW. A new community near Laurel, Howard County. It was being built in about 1963. The name is descriptive and suggests an elevation (See: *Star*, Dec. 14, 1963).

ALTAMONT. A village near Wilson, Garrett County. This place marks the summit (2632 ft.) of the Baltimore and Ohio Railroad's "Seventeen-mile Grade." The Latin meaning is "high mountain." Terra Alta, W. Va., fifteen miles west on the same railroad, marks another summit and means "high ground."

AMERICAN CORNERS. A village near Concord, Caroline County. The town is at a ' 'right-angled crossroads." There is little doubt that the *American* of this name is a folk modification based on the family name, *Merrikin*. Mr. Wilbert Merriken, of the Caroline County Historical Society, bears this name, and the 1963 telephone directory lists seven *Merri-*

kens in the vicinity of Denton and Federalsburg. The spelling of this family name is properly MerriKIN, from *Mary* plus *-kin* ("small").

AMMENDALE. A village near Beltsville, Prince George's County. It was probably named for General Jacob Ammen, a Beltsville farmer and miller. This family name is rather old in Maryland; Richard *Ammon* is mentioned in 1699, in a list of Baltimore County taxables. (See: Lewis 1878).

AMOSS. A village near Fallston, Harford County. The name is related to *Amos's Island, Susquehanna River, now submerged owing to the Conowingo Dam. In Harford County in 1790 there were fourteen persons with the surname *Amos*, and one with *Amoss*. The name has persisted. The 1963 Harford County telephone directory has twenty-two *Amos* and eleven *Amoss*. William H. Amoss is listed for Fallston, near present-day Amoss.

AMOS MILL. A 200-year-old mill on Amos Road, near Norrisville, Harford County. Its earlier name was *Wiley Mill, or *First Wiley Mill, from Matthew Wiley (d. 1840). Isaac Amos bought the mill and property eight-six years ago. In 1964 it was owned by John W. Amos. See FALLSTON.

ANACOSTIA. A section of southeast Washington, D.C., on the Anacostia River. Anacostia has been known by two other names, *Twining and *(Old) Uniontown. *Twining was on the site of the old Anacostin Indian Fort; the name *Uniontown was withdrawn owing to postal confusion. See *Twining: see *Uniontown.

ANACOSTIA RIVER. A branch of the Potomac River flowing from Prince George's County through the District of Columbia. In early Maryland patents, the Potomac River between Oxon Run and Rock Creek was called the *Annacostin River. The name *Anacostia* is from the Nacostines, an Algonguian tribe. Wallace Tooker thought that it means "At the trading town"; but a translation based on Algonquian *-ehtan* ("stream, current") is equally acceptable. The Latin ending *-ia* was probably added by the Jesuits.

ANDERSONTOWN. Near Hobbs, Caroline County. The name is ascribed to "a certain" James Anderson who, many years ago, owned considerable land here and did much business. (See: Cochrane, p. 245).

ANDREWS. A village near Crapo, Dorchester County. Mary Andrew lived in Dorchester County in 1790. A telephone list for Dorchester County in 1963 contains 28 *Andrews*. Ruby Hughes, postmistress at Crapo, states that "Andrews P.O." was closed in 1967, and that its mail is now handled at Crapo. Passano's *Index* of Maryland source records mentions John Andrews, a Maryland settler in 1654.

ANDREWS AIR FORCE BASE. Near Camp Springs, Prince George's County. In about 1942 this field was known as Camp Springs Army Airfield. In March 1945 it was renamed in honor of Lieutenant

General Frank M. Andrews, who (when he was commander of U. S. forces in Europe) was killed in an Icelandic plane crash. See CAMP SPRINGS.

ANGOLA-by-the-BAY. A resort near Rehobeth, Somerset County. Compare "City of Angola," *Book of Mormon*.

Note: It is a possibility that this Somerset County name is a relic of "Angola," which the younger John Johnson named in 1677, "perhaps out of a sense of family heritage." "Angola" was a forty-four acre lot and represented part of the estate of the Johnson clan, descendants of Anthony and Mary Johnson, Africans who came to Virginia in 1619, and to the E. Sh. (Somerset Co.) in about 1660. (See: Ross M. Kimmel, "Free Blacks in Seventeenth-Century Maryland," *MHM* 71:1, 1976.)

ANNAPOLIS. Capital city of Maryland, it is on the Severn River, Anne Arundel County. Its earlier most important names were *Providence, Town Land* at *Proctor's*, and *Anne Arundel Town*. These three names originated as follows: *Providence*, from the Puritans (1649); *Proctor's* for Michael Proctor, early settler; and *Anne Arundel Town*, for Anne Arundel, wife of Cecil Calvert, second Lord Baltimore. At the time of the first Annapolitan Assembly (28 February 1695) the name was still *Anne Arundel Town*. Thereafter, with the encouragement of Gov. Francis Nicholson, it became *Annapolis* (1695). The name is from Anna Stuart (1655–1714), later (1702) Queen Anne of England.

ANNAPOLIS JUNCTION. Near Savage, Howard County. Its name was *JUNCTION in 1842. Steven Latchford, Mt. Rainier, Md., writes that for many years "a railroad line with small engines and small passenger cars" ran between Annapolis Junction (on the Baltimore and Ohio Railroad) and Annapolis, "a distance of twenty miles." This was the Annapolis, Washington, and Baltimore Railroad.

Note: Mr. Latchford's father was an early B. & O. station agent at Annapolis Junction. Mr. Latchford contends that the first American telegraph message was sent from Annapolis Junction to Baltimore. Compare *Telegraph Road*, a secondary route to Friendship Airport.

ANNAPOLIS ROADS. At the mouth of Severn River, beyond Annapolis harbor, Chesapeake Bay. This is a vicinity more open than a harbor, where ships may ride at anchor. Compare Hampton ROADS, Virginia.

ANNE ARUNDEL COUNTY. It lies south of Baltimore County, on the western shore of Chesapeake Bay. It was created by a legislative act in 1650 and takes its name from Lady Anne Arundel, wife of Cecilius Calvert, second Lord Baltimore.

*ANN-ARUNDEL TOWN. This is the place that became *Annapolis* when the Legislature, in 1694–1695, met for the second time in Anne Arundel County. (Source: Riley, p. 124). See *ANNAPOLIS*.

ANNEMESSEX. Pronounced Anna-MESS-ick. The name designates two Somerset County rivers and a bay (*Anamessex Bay*). The word is Indian, and its opening syllables probably constitute the general Algonquian element, *anām* "beneath." One authority thinks that the last syllable means "log, board." However, for technical reasons, I prefer to define the last syllable as "rush, fly." The resulting meaning would be "It rushes beneath (the bank)."

ANNESLIE. A town near Towson, Baltimore county, today a suburb of Baltimore City. Houses were first built here in the 1920's. The name is for the estate "Anneslie," which Frederick Harrison, Jr., named for Anne R. Wilson, when they were married in 1837. (See: *Extra*, March 19, 1972).

ANTIETAM. A village near Sharpsburg, Washington County. It is on Antietam Creek near its junction with the Potomac River. The village takes its name from the creek. See: ANTIETAM CREEK.

ANTIETAM BATTLEFIELD. near Sharpsburg, Washington County. A Civil War battle, sometimes called the "Battle of Sharpsburg," took place here on September 18, 1862. *Sunken Lane*, thereafter, was called *Bloody Lane*. See SHARPSBURG.

ANTIETAM CREEK. A tributary of the Potomac River in Washington County. It had such strange spellings as *Odieta* (1721), *Antieatum*, and even *Andirton* (1730). The name is Indian and may contain the general Algonquian word *-ehtan* for "flow, current." An 1868 authority gives the meaning as "swift water." (See: Jones, *Indian Bulletin II*, 1868).

APE HOLE CREEK. A small branch of the Pocomoke River, Somerset County. It is *Apes Hole Creek* on Martenet's map of 1866. The original spelling was probably **Abes Hole Creek*. The *s* of Abes could cause a phonetic change from *b* to *p* (thus giving Ape). In colonial times *hole* meant a purlieu or vicinity. *Abe* can be from a family name, or from either *Ab*salom or *Ab*raham. Compare Abb's Valley, Virginia, from *Absalon* Looney.

Note: There are five families named *Abe* in the Baltimore telephone book (1977).

APPLEGARTH. A village on Middle Hooper Island, Dorchester County. George, Thomas, and William Applegarth were living in Talbot County (near Dorchester County) in 1790. During the War of 1812 Captain Nathaniel Applegarth was a volunteer in the Dorchester County Militia Company. (See: Jones, p. 259).

AQUASCO. A village near Eagle Harbor, Prince George's County. The name of this place has an unbroken descent from Capt. John Smith's **Acquackack*. The word is Indian and appears to contain the two general Algonquian elements, "edge, extremity" and "weed." It probably means "The edge or extremity to which the vegetation extends."

Note: The Algonquian words are PA **axkwi* "edge, extremity" and PA **ackwi* "weed."

ARABY. A village near Frederick, at Frederick Junction, Frederick County. It was a post office in 1866. "Araby" takes its name from a large tract of land patented as "Araby" to James Marshall, a native of Scotland. Marshall built his manor house in 1780.

Note: Maryland has had at least three other similar names: (1) "Arabia Petrea," Deer Creek, Harford County, surveyed in 1721; (2) "Araby," an 18th century house near La Plata; and (3) "Deserts of Arabia," an Anne Arundel County tract in about 1800. A local historian has suggested that "Arabia Petrea" was selected because of the barrenness of the surrounding land. (See: Footner, p. 301; W. B. Marye).

ARBUTUS. A village near Halethorpe, Baltimore County. Arbutus, first called *Crowdentown, takes its name from the abundance of arbutus on the local hills. It appears that in earlier times "arbutus parties" were sometimes held to pick this trailing spring flower.

ARCADIA. A village near Upperco P.O., Baltimore County. It was still a Western Maryland Railroad station in 1969. The name may be from an estate or tract called "Arcadia," whose farmhouse can still be seen on "the new U.S. Route 40" near St. John's Lane.

ARLINGTON. A Baltimore city suburb and railroad station (ARLINGTON JUNCTION). The name is said to have been given owing to a mistake on the part of one Douglas, a local shop keeper. Mr. Douglas at a town meeting voted to name this Maryland place *Arlington*, because he believed that Arlington, *Virginia*, had been the home of George Washington. "The mistake made a hit and everyone said, 'Let's call the town Arlington.' " The new name (earlier *Hookstown*) was inscribed on the door of the railroad station. (See: Davidson, p. 273). See HOOKSTOWN.

ARMIGER. There appear to be two villages by this name in Anne Arundel County, one near Jacobsville, the other near Winchester. In 1878 Jacob and Joseph Armiger were living near here. The family name Armiger means "armour-bearer, squire."

Note: Sometimes probably pronounced ArmiNger.

ARNOLD. A village about four miles northwest of Annapolis, Anne Arundel County. In 1866 it was *Arnolds Store P.O.* Postmaster Franklin B. Spriggs states that Arnold takes its name from an old resident, Tom Arnold, who had the first store. In 1878, when the place was called *Arnold's Store*, E. F. Arnold was postmaster and general merchandiser.

ARUNDEL. A village near Baltimore (Arundel Garden); a village near Bay Ridge, Anne Arundel County, (Arundel-on-the-Bay). In 1969, there were twelve Arundels, including *Arundel Manor, Arundel-on-the-Bay*, and *Arundel Garden*—all in Anne Arundel County. The ultimate source of these names is Anne Arundel, wife of Cecil Calvert, 2nd Lord Baltimore. See ANNAPOLIS.

ASHLAND. A village near Cockeysville, Baltimore County. In 1878 Ashland was the seat of the Ashland Iron Company, Iron Manufacturers.

The name is from the Ashland Iron Furnace. This is the furnace mentioned in the 1941 Maryland Gazetteer as *Ashland Furnace* near Marble Hill, Baltimore County.

Note: Ashland is a rare family name. The likelihood is that ASHLAND was named owing to ash trees.

ASHTON. A village near Sandy Spring, Montgomery County. In May 1889, a post office was established here, and Alban G. Thomas, a Quaker merchant, became postmaster. The name is a combination of *Ash-* and *-ton*, from "Ashland" and "Clifton," two neighboring estates in the Thomas family. (See: Farquhar, *Annals* II, p. 159).

ASPEN. A village near Rockville, Montgomery County. In Montgomery County there are also *Aspen Hill*, *Aspen Hill Park*, and *Aspen Knolls*. In Carroll County there are two streams known as *Aspen Run*. The Maryland Barrens would have been congenial to aspens. These are old original names. See BARRENS, The.

ASSACORKIN ISLAND. In Chincoteague Bay, Worcester County. The original spelling was AssaQUAKIN. The ending *-corkin* is an invention by the folk. The name is Indian and appears to contain either Algonquian *ācaw-* "across," or Algonquian *asāw-* "brown, yellow." The *-quak-* may mean "earth." The full translation is either "Where there is land across or beyond," or "Where there is brown or yellow earth."

ASSATEAGUE. An island, bay, and sound bounded by Chincoteague, Sinepuxent, and Assawoman Bays, Worcester County. The name is Indian and, like ChincoTEAGUE, probably contains the Algonquian element *-tuk* "river." The opening part of the name is either *ācaw-* "across" or *asāw-* "brown, yellow." The full meaning is either "River beyond or across," or "Brown or yellow river." See CHINCOTEAGUE.

ASSAWOMAN. Northern extension of Isle of Wight Bay, Worcester County. An early spelling is *Assawommon*. The name is Indian, and the two opening syllables (*assa-*) seem to be from either Algonquian *ācaw-* "across," or Algonquian *asāw-* "brown, yellow." For technical reasons the rest of the word cannot be satisfactorily solved, and the full meaning of *assawoman* remains unknown.

Note: The *-woma(e)n* of these names is a folk spelling on the analogy of English *woman*. Perhaps the *-wom-* of ASSAWOMAN is a cognate of Natick *amäëu* (*amáei*) "He goes away." See MATTAWOMAN.

ASYLUM. A vicinity, Baltimore County. This is probably the locality of the Spring Grove State Hospital.

ATHAL. A village in Athel Neck, near Mardela Springs, Wicomico County. Athaloo Landing (Nanticoke River) is nearby. The name is probably from *Athel* Neck, the name of a tract. The ultimate origin of these names is *Atholl*, Perthshire, Scotland.

ATHALOO LANDING. On the Nanticoke River, Wicomico County. *Athaloo* is from the name *Athal*. It no doubt means *Athal* Landing. The -*oo* could be caused by an extra vowel between the two *l*'s.

ATHOLTON. Near Simpsonville, Howard County. Nearby *Atholton Manor* is the site of "Athol," built by Rev. James McGill, who was born in Scotland in 1701. Atholl, Perthshire, was perhaps his birthplace. See ATHAL.

ATTAWA. This name, appearing as "ATTAWA Sept. 1, 1938" among inscriptions found at Friendship Methodist Church, Friendship, Anne Arundel County, is described as follows on p. 37 of *Tombstone Inscriptions of Southern Anne Arundel County* (Upper Marlboro, 1971): "the above is found directly at the foot of a large, old tree, and there was some question as to whether the inscription might not have significance for the tree, and perhaps not be a tombstone. This exotic looking word (Attawa) is probably a variant of the simple English surname *Attaway* "Dweller by the roadside" from OE *weg* "way, road." Cf. the surname *Ottaway* (Wall Street *Journal*, 1980).

AVALON. Tilghman Island, near Tilghman, Talbot County. It is built on a man-made island of oyster shells and has been called "the little island town of Avalon." The suggestion has been made that Avalon was named "after the Calverts' ill-fated Newfoundland settlement." However, there seem to be no historical connections. And it is highly likely that *Avalon* was chosen simply because it is a symbolic name for "island paradise."

Note: George Calvert's Newfoundland tract, Avalon, was chartered in 1623. Somewhat interesting in Maryland are the historic *Avalon Iron Works*, Patapsco River, and an early Baltimore County area, the "Avalon Purchase."

AVENUE. A village near Oakley, St. Mary's County. This place is located on old St. Clements Manor, whose manorial lord in 1637 was Dr. Thomas Gerard. Local historians decry *Avenue* and think the name should be *Gerard*. As for *Avenue*, Edwin Beitzell, of Abell Md., explains: "... people going out to the Avenue would speak of 'going out to the Chapel' and then that changed to 'going out on the avenue,' which meant going out to the church or one of two store-bar rooms located on that stretch of road, which later became Route 242." There is also AVENUE BRANCH (SM).

AVILTON. A village near Piney Grove, Garrett County. Earlier names were *McKenzie Settlement* and *Pea Ridge*. Between 1874 and 1885 the name was *St. Anns*, for St. Ann's Catholic church. The present name arose with the coming of a post office in 1885. Garrett County courthouse documents indicate that "Auvil" was a military lot in 1839. Later Garrett County documents record a transfer of land relating to *Avilton* and Herman *Auvil*. Evidently Avilton takes its name from the family name *Auvil*. Compare *Auvilton*, Tucker County, West Virginia, which was named from another branch of the *Auvil* family.

AVONDALE. A village on the Western Maryland Railroad, near Westminster, Carroll County. Martenet's 1866 map describes it as *Avondale Station*, near "Iron Ore Banks." The name is probably from "Avondale," a historic Georgian brick manor house near Westminster. The house "Avondale" was known as "Furnace Hill" when it was built in 1740. Now filled with water, the pits used to smelt iron ore are still here. See "Avondale" tracts.

AVONDALE CREEK. A branch of Little Pipe Creek, Carroll County. Its name is from the village of Avondale, where it begins its course.

"AVONDALE" TRACTS. In Maryland there are: "Avondale," Fell's Point; "Avondale, or Turner's Point," Talbot County; and "Avondale," the Snowden Plantation, Prince George's County. Names with *Avon* have poetic associations and come ultimately from the British river name *Avon*. "Avondale, or Turner's Point" probably has its name from the Tred *Avon* River.

B

BACHMANS MILLS. A village on Big Pipe Creek, near Deep Run, Carroll County. There is also Bachman Valley. In about 1780 Bower's Mill became *Bachman's Mills*. In 1834 there was a post office. On two occasions members of the Bachman family have been postmaster—in 1834, David Bachman, and in 1882 A. C. Bachman.

BACK WYE RIVER. Queen Anne's County. What is today Back Wye appears to have have been known in 1660 as *Morgan's Creek*, from Evan Morgan. The Front Wye and the main stream are probably the St. Michael's River.

BACON HILL. A village near Northeast, Cecil County. Bacon Hill is a folk development from the earlier name *Beacon Hill*. It has been explained that *Beacon Hill* was the site of one of the beacon fires George Talbot and his rangers used to forestall raids by the few Indians who still lingered in the region north of New Ireland.

George Talbot was Charles Calvert's Irish kinsman and frontier lieutenant.

BADEN. A village, near Cedarville, Prince George's County. The name is from the Baden family. In 1964 many persons by that name still lived here. Compare Lt. Nehemiah Baden, first commandant of "The Maryland Line Confederate Soldier's Home of Pikesville."

Note: Heads 1790 lists, for Prince George's County, John Baden, John Baden, Jr., and Robert Baden.

BAKERSVILLE. Near Tilghmanton, Washington County. Elias Baker was the postmaster in 1833, and the name is for him. In 1903 Allen

Denton Eakle bought the "old" Elias Baker property, Bakersville, and took up residence there. See EAKLES MILLS.

BALD FRIAR. A village and hill on the east side of the Susquehanna River, near Pilot, Cecil County. This is the site of the ancient and historic "Bald Friar Ferry." The name has been explained by the story that the ferry was run by a baldheaded man named Fry. However, in 1696 there was a tract here called "ye Bald ffryar"; and in 1723 Governor Charles Calvert spoke of "Maidens Mount," commonly known as "bald Fryar." The origin from "Mr. Fry" is probably wrong. It is more likely that the name comes from some ancient natural feature of Bald Friar hill (elev. 380). (See: Johnston, p. 345; Marye, 4).

BALDWIN. A village near Jenkins, Baltimore County. Under *Baldwin* in 1878 Lewis lists Thomas Baldwin, general merchandise, and A. S. Baldwin and Charles A. Baldwin, physicians.

BALLS. A village near Hagerstown, Washington County. Turner Alfred Ball (1821–1887), son of Turner Ball, Montgomery County, bought a 120-acre farm in Funkstown District, Washington County, in 1867. BALLS is two miles from Funkstown.

*BALTEMORE M(anor), *BALTIMORE TOWN. Historic tracts once situated near present-day Elkton, Cecil County. These places were founded as early as 1670. One authority believes that *BALTIMORE TOWN was the *first* Baltimore Town and flourished between 1659 and 1674. (See: Hill, MCC, pp. 116–17, Leakin, *MHM*, 1906).

*BALTEMORE TOWN. A lost village once existing near a ferry on Bush River, Harford County. This place was known in 1683, and has been called "Old Baltimore." There was a court house here, and it was the first seat of Baltimore County. Armistead Leakin visited "Old Baltimore" in August 1875 and found two log houses, a spot covered with alder bushes, the abutting stones of a decayed wharf, and a burial ground.

Note: It appears that a third *Baltimore was laid out in Dorchester County in 1693.

BALTIMORE. A city on the Patapsco River, Chesapeake Bay, Baltimore County. Commissioners appointed by the Legislature laid the city out in 1729 on the lands of Thomas Carroll. In 1745 it was consolidated with *Jones-Town (Old Town)*. The origin of the Maryland Baltimore was the Calvert family, especially Cecil, whose father, George Calvert, had become Lord Baltimore, of the Barony of Baltimore, in Ireland, in 1625. It has been debated whether the name of George Calvert's Irish title and barony comes from Baltimore, a seaport in County Cork, or from an obscure unmapped *Baltimore* on the River Rinn, in County Longford. Lord Baltimore's barony was in County Longford, and in recent years "Baltimore Fields" and "Baltimore Lane" were discovered there on the River Rinn. However, it was an established custom for Irish lords to take their titles from local seaports. All in all, the evidence seems to favor the origin from Baltimore, County Cork. This is also the opinion of the Irish Placenames Commission. The Gaelic elements of the name *Baltimore* are *bailte* and *mora*. The meaning is "big houses, homesteads, estates." (See my "Baltimore: New Light on an Old Name," *MHM*, 49: 2, 1954; *Sun*, Jan. 13, 1957; "Baltimore's Name Conjectures," *Extra*, July 16, 1972).

BALTIMORE COUNTY.   It lies below Pennsylvania and between Carroll and Harford Counties. It was formed in 1659 and takes its name "From the Proprietary's Irish Barony" of Baltimore, in County Longford. *Baltimore Town, on Bush River, was probably the county's first seat. See *BALTIMORE TOWN. See also CECIL COUNTY, HARFORD COUNTY.

BARBADOES POND.   A village near Andrews, Blackwater River, Dorchester County. In 1706 Governor John Seymour commented on the advantage to Maryland of the vicinity and commerce of the Spanish West Indies. The present name probably comes from the West Indian trade. Compare "Barbadoes Hall" and SPANIARD NECK, Queen Anne's County. (See: Emory, pp. 32–33).

BARBER.   A village near Trappe, Talbot County. The name may be for Ambrose Barber, at one time a member of the Maryland House of Delegates. He was born in 1852, a Friend, and came to Easton from New Jersey to practice homeopathic medicine.

BARNESVILLE.   Near Dickerson, Montgomery County. It was a post office in 1818. The *Barnes* of this name was probably related to the Barnes family of Anne Arundel and Howard Counties. Records indicate that the founder of the family came to Maryland in 1678. His son, Adam Barnes (d.1769) married a Dorsey and became an extensive landowner in Howard County.

BARRACKS.   GMd. 1941 locates this place in Carroll Co. The name is probably from the family name *Berwick* (*Berrick, Barwick, Barrick*). In 1850 in Woodsboro District, Frederick County, there were John, George, Solomon, Henry, Ezra, and Jacob *Barrick*.

BARRELLVILLE.   Near Mount Savage, Allegany County. This was the post office *Barrallville* in 1852. Here the *-ville* appears to be added to either the family name *Barrell* or the family name *Burrell*. Since families by the name of *Burrell* live in this area, the origin from *Burrell* seems more likely. The spelling *Barrell* suggests a popular etymology.

BARREN CREEK.   A creek and village near Mardela Springs, Wicomico County. The creek was known in 1747. The village abbreviates its name from *Barren Creek Springs*, a post office in 1824. Some early records give "*Baron* Creek Springs." The name of the creek is probably from the family name *Baron* (*Barren, Barron*). Neville *Baron* was living in Pocomoke City in 1964.

BARRY. Frederick County. Barry was a post office in 1832. Passano has ten genealogical items on various families by this name. In 1790 there were six Barrys in Maryland, half of them in Anne Arundel County.

BARTON. A village near Westernport, Allegany County. Coal here was "opened up" in 1854 and the village was settled in the spring of that year. In 1866 there were "Barton Mines." There was also a Barton Coal Company. Andrew Bruce Shaw founded Barton, on land owned by Major William Shaw, his father. The name is from Barton, England, Major Shaw's birthplace.

Note: It is an interesting sidelight on early Western Maryland immigration to notice that this place, with its typical British name, has a recently restored cemetery of more than a hundred Irish graves. Many Irish people migrated to the George's Creek area during the 1800's. *Condon* and *Rafferty* are among the family names. (See: "St. Gabriel's Cemetery at Barton Restored," Piedmont (W. Va.) *Herald*, 25 May 1982).

BASKET SWITCH. Near Newark, Worcester County. It was known by this name as early as 1901, and its location on a branch and siding of the defunct Pennsylvania Railroad accounts for *Switch*. According to E. Randolph Bradford, neighboring farmer, baskets were once made here from the local gum trees. Such trees yield slats or laths for baskets, chicken crates, and the like. In 1947 Chester Thomas, of Ocean City, had a basket factory here; but it is evident that the local basket industry began much earlier. (See: Reppert, *Sun*, Sept. 17, 1961).

BATTLE, BATTLE CREEK. A village and stream near Adelina, Calvert County. It was spelled *Battaille* Creek in the will of Thomas Tasker (1699/1700). Robert Brooke gave this name to the creek in memory of his first wife, Mary Baker, whose family was from Battle, Sussex County, England. The English village takes its name from Battle Abbey, the monastery that was founded in memory of the Battle of Hastings.

BATTLE CREEK CYPRESS SWAMP. It is at the head of Battle Creek, Calvert County, and takes its name from that stream. This region is the most northern of all East Coast swamps to contain a tract of bald cypress trees.

BATTLE SWAMP. This is the same place as Woodlawn, Cecil County. Kuethe lists Battle Swamp Tavern for 1795. In 1866 it was *Battle Swamp* or *Woodland P.O.* There is only the tiniest sign of a swamp here, but in 1722, near Battle Swamp, there was, according to Johnston, a fine spring of water known as the Indian Spring. The origin of the name is unknown (See: Miller, p. 133). See WOODLAWN.

BEALLSVILLE. Near Poolesville, Montgomery County. Grove, remarking that the Beall family was very prominent, and that Samuel Beall was sheriff in 1760, attributes "Beallsville in Montgomery County," and

"Bealls Rock near Frederick Junction," to Elisha Beall, a lieutenant in the Revolutionary Army. (See: Grove, p. 381).

BEALLSVILLE.   Catoctin Creek, near Harmony, Frederick County. This was the post office of *Beallville* in 1834. The name is probably from Colonel Samuel Beall, the grandson of Alexander Beall, who came to Maryland in 1666. Colonel Beall married the granddaughter of the fabulous Ninian Beall. Later he became sheriff of Frederick County, a member of the Committee of Correspondence, and a Justice of the Frederick County Court. (See: TW, I, p. 45).

Note: Thomas Beall, the son of Colonel Samuel Beall, laid out *Washington Town* on the site of Cumberland two years before the Assembly "erected" Cumberland under its present name (1787).

BEANTOWN.   Near Waldorf, Charles County. Beantown was a post office in 1844. The name is from the family name *Bean* (Beane, Bain, Bayne). In 1669 Edith, the daughter of "Walter Bean or Bayne," married a Charles County minister. In 1683 John Bayne was a commissioner to buy town lands for the advancement of trade. The 1790 census lists Benjamin Bean, Charles County. (See: BK, p. 32; pp. 35–37).

Note: Mrs. James Ryon states that in 1870, when the Pope's Creek Railroad was built, Beantown P.O. was moved to the railroad and called *Waldorf*. (See: Schmidt, *Sun*, 7 October, 1962). See WALDORF.

BEARDS CREEK.   A branch of the South River, at Riverview, Anne Arundel County (GMd 1941). This name, and Beards Point, are from various members of the Davidsonville *Beard* family, whose progenitor, Richard Beard, received Anne Arundel County's first land grant, in 1650. See Jacqueline Duke, "A Love Affair," Evening *Capital*, Dec. 17, 1981.

BEAVER CREEK.   A village and stream near Wagners Cross Roads, Washington County. *Witners* became Beaver Creek post office in 1836. The village takes its name from the stream it is on. It was an early 19th century milling center.

BEAVER DAM.   A village near Beaver Dam Ditch and Ingleside, Queen Anne's County. *Beaver's Dam* was a post office in 1811. In 1866 it was charted as *Long Marsh P.O.* or *Beaver Dam*. Today it has become *Ingleside*. See INGLESIDE.

BEAVERDAM.   A village southeast of Pocomoke City, Worcester County. There was a stream called *Beaver Dams Branch* in Worcester County in 1759. In 1960 there were no beavers here; however, there were still muskrats.

Note: In 1941 Maryland had one Beaver Branch, three Beaver Creeks, and fifteen stream and village names containing *beaverdam*.

BECKLEYSVILLE.   Near Albantown, Baltimore County. In 1878, Daniel Beckley, paper manufacturer, was the postmaster here.

BEELER SUMMIT. A summit (650 ft.) on the Baltimore and Ohio Railroad, near Rohrersville, Washington County. The name is from the Beeler family. On a farm near Rohrersville George W. Beler was born in 1835. His father was Samuel Beeler (1811–1884).

BEL AIR. The county seat of Harford County, near Fallston. It was spelled *Bellair* in 1794. The name is from the French and means "fine air." "Bel Air" names are abundant. Compare Bellaire, Ohio, which takes its name from Bel Air, Maryland.

BEL ALTON. A Charles County village two miles n.w. of Faulkner. The Guide (1st ed., 1941) states that Bel Alton "grew up in the 1890's" after the Pope's Creek Railroad was built. *Bel,* here probably means "beautiful, fair, fine, pretty." *Alton* could be from another American town (e.g., Alton, Illinois), or from an English town (e.g., Alton, Derbyshire, where *Alton* probably comes from O. E. *Aldatūn* "Oldtown"). Cf. BEL AIR.

Note: The place is important on account of its locality. Near here Maryland's earliest Jesuits circumvented the land laws and built churches to "Christianize" the Indians. Cf. Chapel Point.

BELCAMP. A village near Abington, Harford County. Known as early as 1900, it probably means "good camp" or "good field." However, there is the possibility that *Bel-* is from the family name *Bell.* Cf. *BALTIMORE CAMP, an omnibus connection to Owings Mills when the Western Maryland railroad was completed to Owings Mills on Aug. 5, 1859. See: Harold Williams, *The Western Maryland Railway Story,* Baltimore, 1952, p. 26.

BELMONT. A village on Johnnycake Road, near Woodlawn, Baltimore County. The name was known as early as 1906. The elevation here is 440 ft., and the name may refer to a beautiful hill. It is also possible that it is from a nearby mansion. Compare "Belmont," Howard County, the historic home built by Caleb Dorsey in 1738 with bricks brought here from England.

Note: "Belmont," as the name of a house, probably came here from England. There are twenty-two *Belmonts* in Bartholomew's Gazetteer of the British Isles.

BELTSVILLE. Near Muirkirk, Prince George's County. In 1811 the name was *Vansville, with G-G. Van Horn postmaster. In 1835 the Vansville post office was moved three quarters of a mile south, and the name was changed to *Beltsville.* The name *Beltsville* comes from Truman Belt, the original landowner, from which the Baltimore and Ohio Railroad at this point acquired the right of way. The railroad gave the name in his honor in 1835. See CHEVY CHASE.

BENEDICT. A village opposite Hallowing Point, Patuxent River, Charles County. In 1695 it was *Benedict-Leonard Town;* in 1747 it was *Benedict-Town.* It was "erected" in Charles County in 1683 and commemorates Benedict Leonard Calvert, the fourth Lord Baltimore (1675–1715).

BENEVOLA.   A village near Boonsboro, Washington County. It was a post office in 1850. Benevola Chapel, of the United Brethren in Christ, was organized here in 1858. The name is probably from the word *benevolent* and suggests a friendly community. Pronunciation: benny-*VOE*-la.

BENFIELD.   A village north of Severn Crossroads, Anne Arundel County. "Benfield Road" is well-known in the Annapolis region. The name is from the family name *Benfield*. Samuel Benfield was in Montgomery County in 1790. In 1978 Virgil O. Benfield lived in Herald Harbor, Anne Arundel County.

BENGIES.   A village and point, Middle River Neck, Baltimore County. Hopkins maps *Benjies Pt.* in 1878. Bengies, four miles from the point, is a station on the defunct Pennsylvania Railroad. The name of the point is from Robert Benger, who laid out "Benger's Horse Pasture" in 1679. Bengies takes its name from the point. (See: Marye 4, pp. 340–41).

BENTLEY SPRINGS.   A village near Walker, Baltimore County. Lewis in 1878 describes the springs here as "highly medicinal." At that time the place was owned by C. W. Bentley, of Baltimore.

BENVILLE.   Near Middletown, Charles County. Compare *Bensville*, Charles County, which was a post office in 1817. Compare also Bensville, near Pomfret.

BENVILLE.   On Smith Creek, Potomac River, St. Mary's County. Wynne and Benville Wharf were mentioned together in 1912. But the U.S. Geographic Board has since preferred *Benville*. The name is probably from the given name *Ben*, but the family name *Benfield* is a possibility.

*BENTZTOWN.   A lost village in Frederick County. But once it was well-known owing to Folger McKinsey, "The Bentztown Bard." There is a Bentz Street in Frederick; in about 1825 there was a Bentz family near Boonsboro. Lewis in 1878 listed, for Frederick City, "Bentz & Son, Manufacturers of and Dealers in Harness, Saddles, etc."

BEREAN.   A village near Mt. Carmel, Baltimore County. The name occurs as early as 1902. The primary origin of the name is Berea (Beroea). Macedonia, where Paul and Silas went. "Berean" refers to a citizen of Berea. In Maryland it may be taken as an adjective meant to describe a utopian place of "Primitive Christianity." (Consultant: Prof. R. B. Drake, Berea College, Berea, Ky.).

*BERLIN.   A lost village near Brunswick, Frederick County. In 1811 it was a post office. The name suggests German settlers. In 1905 there were thirty-seven U.S. post offices with the name *Berlin*. See BRUNSWICK.

BERLIN.   A town near Ocean City, Worcester County. It was a post office in 1820. The name is probably a combination of the English name *Burleigh (Burley)* and *Inn*. Early records refer to "Burleigh Cottage" and "Burleigh Manor." The town was built on land patented as "Burleigh" by

_____

Note: Pronounced *BURR*-lin.

William Stevens in 1677. One supposes there was also a "*Burleigh Inn*." Compare nearby GERMANTOWN, though I see no connection.

BERRY. A village near Bolton, Charles County. According to Arthur L. Keith, all the Berrys of Charles County, before 1800, probably descended from Samuel Barry, who first appears in the county records in 1690. (See: *MHM*, 23, March 1928).

BERRY. A village near Rigley, Prince George's County. Stein mentions the Berry family founded by James Berry, Puritan leader. He came to Maryland from Virginia in 1649, and settled in Prince George's County, where James and William Berry acquired large landed estates.

BERWYN, BERWYN HEIGHTS. Near College Park, Prince George's County. The two places are adjacent; each has the same elevation (85 ft.). Simon writes: "Berwyn came into existence about 1883. In 1885 Berwyn Road, then known as Central Avenue, was built." The name is probably from the Berwyn Mountains and River, Denbighshire, Wales.

BESTGATE. A village near Annapolis, Anne Arundel County. On the Washington, Baltimore, and Annapolis Railroad in 1905. The story is told that there was once an illegal harness racing track here, and that this was the "best gate." It is much more likely that the name is from a Dr. Best, whose farm gate opened upon a road paralleling the railway. (Informants: Howard Willet; Margaret Worthington).

Note: John A. Mellin's "Vignettes" (*Capital*, April 2, 1983) points out that G. M. Hopkins' 1878 map of the Second District (A. Ar. Co.) locates "Beth Gap Station" at General's Highway and Bestgate Road. Mr. Mellin cites C. E. Parker, Sr., whose family owned property here for many generations, as saying that the region was originally cultivated by a man named Beth. ". . . and when he sold it to a man named Best the latter placed a gate at one end of the old road leading through it." Perhaps this was the "Dr." Best referred to above.
Query: Is Beth/Best a coincidence?

BESTPITCH. A village on the Transquaking River, near Bucktown, Dorchester County. In 1884 there was *Best Pitch Ferry*. The name is from the family name *Bestpitch*. In 1778 Levin Bestpitch was a first Lieutenant in the Upper Battalion of the Dorchester County Militia, and John Bestpitch was an Ensign in the Lower Battalion. Reppert attributes the village name to "a man named Bestpitch, who had a farm in the vicinity early in the last century."

BETHEDEN, BETHEDEN CHURCH. A village near Klej Grange, Worcester County. The name is a combination of *Beth* (Hebrew "house") and *Eden*. Pronunciation: Beth-E-dun. See EDEN.

BETHEL. A village near Patapsco, Carroll County. It is Hebrew for "House of God." Compare *Bethel near Jarrettsville, described as being, in early days, in the wilderness of Upper Node^n Forest, Baltimore County. Other Maryland *Bethels* have the same meaning.

Note: I suggest that *Node* here means "area, region." Query: Land of Nod?

BETHESDA.   Washington, D.C. suburb, near Chevy Chase, Montgomery County. It was a post office in 1852. The name is from the Bethesda Presbyterian Church, around which the village grew. Fifty years before the American Revolution Bethesda Presbyterian Church had been "Captain John Presbyterian Church." The Hebrew meaning of the name may be "House of Mercy" (biblical). Or it may come from *Bethsaida,* a pool or public bath near Jerusalem. See CABIN JOHN.

BETHLEHEM.   A village near Preston, Caroline County. It was a post office in 1866. A 1969 road sign here called attention to "Ye Little Town of Bethlehem in Maryland." The name may have been given by Methodist Bishop Francis Asbury. It is hard to determine whether this is the Maryland *Bethlehem* that was first called *Brannock's Crossroads."* (See: *Sun,* Dec. 25, 1960, p. 11).

*BEVANSVILLE.   A lost village in Allegany County. In 1834 the postmaster here was Henry Bevans. (See: Register 1834).

BEVANSVILLE.   Near Grantsville, Garrett County. Passano makes genealogical references to *Beavan, Beavens, Bevan,* and *Bevends.* There is only one *Bevan* in Garrett County phone book, 1972.

BEW (BEAU) PLAINS.   In Prince George's County. Compare "Blue Plains sewage treatment plant along the Potomac River in Anacostia" (1976). Oxon Cove is nearby. In 1714–15 there was a Prince George's County plantation called "Bew (or Beau) Plains." Has this *bew,* by popular etymology, become *Blue*? (See: Keith, *MHM,* 22, June 1927, p. 146). See BLUE PLAINS.

Note: In *Beaufort,* N.C., *beau* is pronounced *bew.*

BIG POOL.   A village and B. and O. railroad station near Ernstville, Washington County. Williams (I, 212) states that the big pool here came into existence with the building of the C. & O. Canal: ". . . opposite Fort Frederick the canal passed through a piece of low swampy land, which immediately filling up to the canal level, formed the 'Big Pool.' " Once it was 700 feet wide and abounded in fish and water fowl.

BILLINGSLEY.   A village near White Plains, Charles County. "Billingsleys Tavern" existed in Charles County, near Prince George's, in 1795. The name is from the Billingsley family, whose founder, Francis Billingsley, a Virginia Puritan, came to Anne Arundel County in 1652. Later generations of the Billingsleys moved to Prince George's County. (See: Stein).

BIRDSVILLE.   Near Davidsonville, Anne Arundel County. In 1866 this was *Birdsville,* or *South River P.O.* According to Reppert, Birdsville was settled in colonial times by a man named Bird, who crossed the bay in a dugout and brought with him an Indian wife. They built a cabin near the Rhodes River. In 1878 Jacob Bird, Joseph Bird, Mary Bird, and Frank and Jacob Byrd, lived here. (See: *Sun,* 16 Dec. 1962).

BISHOP. Near Showell, Worcester County. This is a station on the Penn Central Railroad, two miles from Bishopville. See BISHOPVILLE.

*BISHOP'S TAVERN. Baltimore County. The postmaster in 1834 was Elias Bishop. (See: Register).

BISHOPVILLE. Near St. Martin's River, Worcester County. Bishopville "originated" as *Milltown*. The present name is from the Bishop family. In 1790 there were nine entries for *Bishop* in Worcester County. The current Somerset-Worcester phone book lists eleven.

BITTINGER. A village near Bevansville, Garrett County. The Guide (p. 343) describes Bittinger as a mountain village named for "Henry Bittinger or Bedinger," who bought military lots here in 1814. He was the "ancestor of the numerous Bittinger family of this county." (See: Weeks, p. 20).

BIVALVE. A village near Tyaskin, Wicomico County. Bivalve was *Waltersville in 1877. In 1887, when a post office was established, it was renamed *Bivalve* at the suggestion of its postmaster, J. E. Willing. The Bivalve Oyster Packing Company had a shucking house here. *Bivalve* refers to the two valves or hinged shells of the oyster. Compare Bivalve, N. J., an oyster-shipping port.

Note: *Waltersville* represents the heirs of G. D. Walter, who lived here in 1877.

*BLACKFOOT TOWN. This was on Pepper's Creek, Somerset County. On parochial records the land here was described as being near Black*ford*. Evidently Black*foot* is a corruption of Blackford, or vice-versa. Compare Black*foot* Creek, Dorchester County.

*BLACKHORSE. Near Shawsville, Harford County. *Blackhorse* was a post office in 1834; in 1846 it was changed to *Shawsville*. A road marker here tells about George Washington and the "Black Horse Tavern." The name is said to refer to the team of black horses owned by the first innkeeper. (See: Anson, *Sun*, March 25, 1962).

Note: The inn was also called "Sutton's."

BLACKISTON (BLAKISTONE) ISLAND. Potomac River, St. Mary's County. The settlers of 1634 gave this island the name *St. Clements*. Later it was renamed *Blackistone* for Nehemiah Blackstone, who received it as a dowry from Thomas Gerrard, his bride's father. See CLEMENTS.

BLACKROCK. A village one mile north of Blackrock Run, near Mount Carmel, Baltimore County. *Black Rock* was a post office in 1846. The name is related to a nearby feature called "The Black Rock." See BLACKROCK RUN.

BLACKROCK RUN. A stream near Butler, Baltimore County. A natural feature, "The Black Rock," is nearby. Scott's *Geographical Descrip-*

44   THE PLACENAMES OF MARYLAND

tion mentions the Maryland "black stone, which contains a certain portion of iron."

BLADENSBURG.   Near Hyattsville, Prince George's County. It was a post office in 1789. The Eastern Branch of the Potomac River, which the village is on, became filled with silt in the beginning of the 19th century. *Garrison's Landing* had been an early name. The original settlement, however, was *Beall Town*, from John Beall (1688–1742), who owned the land. Bladensburg was laid out in 1742 and takes its name from Thomas Bladen, Governor of Maryland from 1742 to 1747.

BLOODY POINT, also BLOODY CREEK.   Kent Island, Chesapeake Bay, Queen Anne's County. Emory mentions two traditions: (1) that the colonists massacred a group of Indians here; (2) that in this region a French pirate was hanged to death in chains. In early times Kent Island was known as the "bloody ground" of Maryland. (See: Scharf, I, p. 138).

BLOOMINGDALE.   A village near Queenstown, Queen Anne's County. An earlier name was *Mount Mill*, which took its name from "Mount Mill," a fine colonial homestead of 1792. Dr. Edward Harris, of Baltimore, bought "Mount Mill" in 1817. During the lifetime of his sisters the name was changed to "Bloomingdale," which suggests a dale of flowers.

*BLOOMING ROSE SETTLEMENT.   Near Friendsville, Garrett County. Settlement in this historic community was as early as 1832. The name, given by Jonathan Boucher, an Anglican clergyman, paraphrases the biblical sentence (Isaiah, ch. 35) ". . . the desert shall rejoice, and blossom as the rose." (See: Weeks, p. 50).

BLOOMINGTON.   Near Luke, Garrett County. The first settlement was in 1849, and the first name was *L(l)angollen*, probably from the Llangollen Mining Company. The present name, perhaps given by the first Baltimore and Ohio Railroad workmen, is a reference to the many spring wild flowers.

Note: "Borderside," a historic mansion (1865; Wm. A. Brydon) was once situated here. In a sense, it borders both the Potomac and Savage Rivers, and the Allegheny-Garrett County boundary. Lately it was razed to make way for a Credit Union. In the vicinity of the razed mansion (*"Borderside") the archeologist will find a rock formation bearing the tracks of a prehistoric animal.

BLUE PLAINS.   District of Columbia sewage treatment and disposal area, near Forest Heights and Oxon Hill, Prince George's County. Wilstach mentions "Blue Plains" as a historic estate between Oxon Creek and the Anacostia River. See: BEW (BEAU) PLAINS.

*BOETCHERVILLE.   Near Cumberland, Allegheny County. Apparently this village no longer exists. However, the 1968 Allegany County phone book has two instances of the family name *Boethcher*.

BOHEMIA RIVER.   A branch of Elk River, Cecil County. This name, Bohemia Mills, and "Bohemia Manor" all commemorate Augustine Herrman, who was born in Prague, Bohemia, in 1621. Herrman, one of Maryland's first naturalized immigrants, received his letters of denization in 1660, and moved from New Amsterdam to "Bohemia Manor," Maryland, with his family in 1662. His lands in Maryland were in payment for his famous map of Virginia and Maryland in 1670.

BOND. A village and railroad station, near Bloomington, Garrett County. Stein states that the Bond family, probably of English origin, has several branches in Maryland. The 1972 Garrett County phone book gives R. W. Bond, of McHenry, and Richard D. Bond of Hoyes.

"BOOMTOWN," a strip of shops and saloons catering to Fort Meade soldiers; near Odenton, Prince George's County. This vicinity flourished in the early 1940's. It was almost abandoned by merchants in the postwar period. In the early 1950's it "boomed" again to serve a new generation of servicemen. (See: *Capital*, Dec. 16, 1968).

BOONSBORO. A village near Keedysville, Washington County. George and William Boone settled here in 1774. Tradition relates them to Daniel Boone. In 1801 this was the post office of *Boonesburg*; lots were laid out in 1829.

BORDEN SHAFT. A George's Creek village, near Frostburg, Allegany County. This was the site of *Borden Mines*, and the place had a coal mine *shaft*. Passano makes two genealogical references to a *Borden* family. See SHAFT.

BORING. A village and post office near Fowblesburg, Baltimore County (GMd 1941, Manual 1947). An item in *Capital* (July 12, 1982) indicates that Boring was named in 1905 for David Boring, the first postmaster. There are fifteen Borings in the Baltimore City TDr. The family name *Boring* is probably a variant of the British surname *Bowring*.

Note: On July 14, 1982, the *Wall Street Journal* published a similar story about Boring, a town and post office in Boring District, Oregon. The Oregon town was named in 1874 for homesteader, William H. Boring. Jokes and puns come easily when dealing with the two names.

BOSTETTER. A village near Hagerstown, Washington County. Andrew Bostetter, founder of the family in this region, came to Maryland from Germany "at an early day." John Bostetter, grandson of Andrew Bostetter, died at Bostetter in 1879.

BOWENS. A village near Barstow, Calvert County; notice also BOWENSVILLE. Stein points out that David Bowen, the "original ancestor of the Bowen family," was probably a Puritan. He owned "Bowen" or "Bowen's Neck," and made his will in 1670.

BOWIE. A town near High Bridge, Prince George's County. The name is from Oden *Bowie* (1826-1894) who, from 1867 to 1872, was the thirty-seventh governor of Maryland. He was a native of Prince George's County, and had earlier been a state delegate and a state senator. Governor Bowie's father was William Ducket (see *DUCKETTSVILLE). And his mother was Eliza Oden Bowie (see ODENTON). Bowie is a British surname. Pronounced BOO-E.

BOXIRON.   A village near Girdletree, Worcester County, also BOX-IRON CREEK. The name is from *bog's iron*, a product formed in the bogs of the Eastern Shore from stagnant water containing oxide of iron. There were once extensive bog iron factories here. The product was shipped as pig-iron to England.

BOZMAN.   A village near St. Michaels, Talbot County. The name is from the Bozman family known in Maryland as early as 1663. The Guide describes John Leeds Bozman (1757–1823) as "the first of a long list of state historians."

BRADDOCK.   A village near Frederick, Frederick County. This place was called *Old Braddock* to distinguish it from Braddock Heights. It was once a stagecoach stop on the "National Road," General Braddock's fateful route in 1755. See BRADDOCK HEIGHTS.

BRADDOCK HEIGHTS.   A village southeast of Middletown, Frederick County, and several miles west of Braddock. The elevation is 950 ft. "Braddock's Spring" here was used in 1755 by the troops of General Edward Braddock, and near the spring is a bronze marker relating that this was the National Trail, over which General Braddock and the young George Washington travelled in the disastrous summer of their defeat near Fort Duquesne (1755).

BRADFORD SIDING.   A railroad siding in Harford County. The earliest Bradfords, among them William Bradford, Sr., settled near the head of Bush River in the 18th century. Augustus W. Bradford, born at Bel Air in 1806, was governor of Maryland between 1861–65.

BRADY.   Allegany County village, near Cresaptown. In 1852 this was probably the post office, *Brady's Mill*. In 1878 John C. Brady was a cattle dealer here. An early list of settlers in "the county lying west of Fort Cumberland" mentions Benjamin Brady. (See: TW, I, pp. 3–5).

BRADY'S RUN.   A Baltimore city placename recorded as *Porcosen Run* or *Brady's Run*. See POCOSIN.

BRANCHVILLE.   Near Lakeland, Prince George's County. The stream, Paint Branch, is near Branchville at the point where Branchville Road begins. The name is from the branch.

BRANDYWINE.   A village near T. B., Prince George's County. It was a post office in 1835. The name probably commemorates the Battle of Brandywine, fought during the War of American Independence on Sept. 11, 1777, at the forks of Brandywine Creek, southwest of Philadelphia. Eight American places are named for this battle.

BRANNOCK BAY.   A branch of Trippe Bay, Dorchester County. According to Dr. Guy Steel, of Cambridge, the name is from "a very large family of Brannocks who lived in Dorchester County since its early settlement." In Dorchester County records, one finds mention of Edmund Brannock, 1684, and John Brannock, 1690.

BREATHEDS STATION. Baltimore and Ohio Railroad. See below.

BREATHEDSVILLE. Near Lappans, Washington County. Williams mentions John W. Breathed, Curator of St. James College, "the first agent of the Baltimore and Ohio Railroad at Breathed's Station, which got its name from him."

BRENTLAND village. Near Welcome, Charles County. See below.

BRENTWOOD. A suburban community, near Mt. Rainier, Prince George's County. There are two adjacent districts here; one is *North Brentwood*, with black people, and the other is *Brentwood*, with white people. These places were settled simultaneously by Washington commuters after World War I. The region was often described as "the newly developed highlands on the banks of the Anacostia River." The name is from the Maryland *Brent* family. Giles and Fulke Brent were in Maryland in 1638. Compare BRENTLAND, Charles County, and BRENTWOOD, Baltimore County.

BREW MAHR MILL. A village near Muddy Creek Falls, Garrett County. George T. Brew had a shingle mill on Muddy Creek in 1899 or 1900. The present name suggests joint ownership and probably comprises the family names, *Brew* and *Mahr*. *Mahr* is probably from *Maher* and illustrates a typical local pronunciation. (See: Schlosnagle, pp. 272-73).

*BRICK MEETING HOUSE, east of Rising Sun, Cecil County. In about 1802 it was called *Nottingham. According to Miller, General Lafayette left Elkton in 1781 and travelled "by way of Brick Meeting House, now called Calvert." See CALVERT.

BRIDGETOWN. Near the headwaters of Tuckahoe River, Caroline County. The post office, "Nine Bridges," was changed to "Bridgetown" in 1841. At one time there were nine small bridges here. Later they were reduced to one single, large, concrete bridge. Compare *Bridge Town*, now GREENSBORO, where there was a bridge over the Choptank River. See GREENSBORO.

Note: Scott in 1807 mentions a "strong bridge," over the Chester River, leading to *Sandtown.

BRINKLOW. A village near Sandy Spring, Montgomery County. In the late 1880's Hallie Lea, local homeowner and storekeeper, named this village *Brinklow* after "a place in England just because she thought it a pretty name and one not used anywhere in the United States." (Source: Mrs. J. C. Williams, Columbia, Md., 1975).

Note: The English place could be Brinklow, Warwickshire.

BRISTOL. A village near Drury, Anne Arundel County. The post office *Pig Point* was changed to *Bristol* in 1840. Compare *BRISTOLL,

Hunger River, Dorchester County, which was established by the Legislature in 1686. Both names commemorate Bristol, Gloucestershire, England.

Note: When Bristol was called *Pig Point* it was on the Patuxent River.

BROCKATONORTON BAY. This body of water is off Chincoteague Bay at the mouth of Boxiron Creek, Worcester County. It is pronounced bog-uh-NARTIN. In 1670 it was spelled *Bauchitinaughton*, an Algonquian name evidently changed by the folk to *Pocketty Norton and later, to Brockatonorton—where the family names *Brock* and *Norton* were imagined. It is reasonable to consider *Brockatonorton* an Anglicized form of Virginia Algonquian *Bocootawwonauke*. In Powhatan, *boketawh* means "fire." An acceptable translation of *Bocootawwonauke* is "Fire people or nation."

Note: Perhaps the nearness of Boxiron Creek is more than a coincidence.

BROOKEVILLE. Near Sandy Spring, Montgomery County. It appears that Brookeville, founded in 1780, and Laytonsville, were additions to "Brooke Grove" (1728) surveyed by James Brooke in 1762. Postmaster William J. Boswell, Brookeville, has stated: "Named by founding fathers for their three Brooke wives (or was it to flatter father-in-law)." (Postal information: 1967).

BROOKLYN. Anne Arundel suburb of Baltimore, separated from it by the Patapsco River. Brooklyn owes its origin to the Patapsco Company, which the Maryland legislature incorporated in 1853. R. W. Templeman, a company employee, probably gave the name in 1857. Early residents saw a geographical similarity between this Brooklyn and Brooklyn, N.Y., in that each place was separated from a larger adjoining city by a river. (See: Riley, pp. 111–112).

BROOKVIEW. Near Ennalls, Dorchester County. The village overlooks a swampy region of Marshyhope Creek. It was *CROTCHERS FERRY in 1866. (Source: James G. Marine, Brookview, 1966).

BROWNING MILL. Northwest of Swallow Falls, Garrett County. Compare *Browning Bear Hill, Browning Dam*, and *Browning Mill*. The name is for the Browning family and has historical significance because it indirectly commemorates Garrett County's prodigious huntsman and pioneer, Meshach Browning (b. 1781). The title of Browning's vigorous and celebrated book is *Forty-four Years of the Life of a Hunter Being Reminiscences of . . . A Maryland Hunter Roughly written Down by Himself.* Philadelphia: Lippincott, 1928.

BROWNSVILLE. Near Gapland, Washington County. It was a post office in 1833. Tobias Brown, son of Rudolph Brown, was one of the first settlers of Washington County. He owned a tract of land extending from Gapland to Brownsville. Andrew Jackson appointed Rudolph Brown's grandson, John, to be postmaster at Brownsville. In 1878 C. Brown was postmaster. (Source: Williams, II, p. 932).

BRUCEVILLE. Near Keymar, Carroll County. Hoye states that Bruceville was laid out by Colonel Norman Bruce of St. Mary's County. He came to Maryland from Edinburgh, Scotland, in about 1758.

Note: Another name for Bruceville is York Road.

*BRUCEVILLE STATION. At Keymar, Carroll County. Grove remarks: "Now Keymar junction where the Northern Central connects with the Western Maryland Railroad, about ten miles from the Mt. St. Mary's College." See KEYMAR.

BRUNSWICK. A railroad town near Knoxville, Frederick County. A tract called "Merry Peep o' Day" was laid out here in 1787 as *Berlin*. In 1890 the name was changed to avoid confusion with Berlin, Worcester County. In 1890 the Baltimore and Ohio Railroad had built extensive repair shops here. Both names (*Berlin* and BRUNSWICK) suggest German settlement.

BRYANTOWN. Near Hughesville, Charles County. In 1790 there were six *Bryans* living here; and one was a mulatto. See PATUXENT CITY.

BUCKEYSTOWN. Near Adamstown, Frederick County. George and Michael Buckey established the Buckey Tannery here in 1775. In 1834 it was sold to Daniel Baker, and the site of the old tannery was occupied by the brick and tile plant of the Baker Brothers. (See: Grove, p. 110).

Note: My thanks to Mrs. Nancy Bodmer, of Buckey's Antiques (Buckeystown, 1980), who writes me that the Buckey family, Huguenots, were originally from a place about forty miles north of Paris. They fled from France "apparently settling in Minfield [sic] which is in the Alsace region." Ms. Bodmer adds that earlier spellings of the family name were *Buquet, Bucka, Bucke, Bocke, Bookay, Bocky*, and *Bouquet*.

BUCKTOWN. Near Aireys, Dorchester County. Since *Back*garden Creek and *Back*garden Pond, near Bucktown, probably are a folk mistake for *buck* or *deer garden*, it seems likely that Bucktown has its name from an early abundance of *buck* or deer. However, there is a possibility that the name contains the family name *Buck*.

Note: *Garden* is frequently used to designate animal haunts, as in Bear *Garden*, Elk *Garden*, etc.

*BUFFALO MARSH. Six miles from Bittinger, Garrett County. The first white settlers found the carcass of a large buffalo in this marsh. (See: Schlosnagle, p. 771). See Mc HENRY.

BUFFALO RUN. A stream and village, in Garrett County. A tract was surveyed here in 1772. The run was given this name because an early settler killed a buffalo on the north bend near the mouth of the stream. (See: *Glades Star*, No. 11).

BUREAU. A village near Williston, Caroline County. As part of a federal program for the care of emancipated slaves, the U.S. Government built a Freedmen's Bureau building here in 1865. The program was discontinued in 1870; the building burned down in 1938. The vicinity of the brick foundation is still called "the Bureau." The story is told that the lumber for the bureau was meant for Denton, and was delivered to this out-of-the-way place by mistake. (See: Guide; Cochrane). See FREE TOWN.

BURKITTSVILLE. Northwest of Petersville, Frederick County. In 1824 the post office here was *Harleys Store*. The change to *Burkittsville* was in 1828. The founder of the Burkitt family was Christopher Burkhart, who was in the Leitersville District in 1755. The village was laid out in 1829 and takes its name from Henry Burkitt. (See: Guide; Bell, p. 166).

BURNT STORE. A village near Grosstown, Charles County. It is on Martenet's Map of 1866. An inquisitive historian, trying to find this place, met a Negro farmer, who drew up with a team of mules and pointed to a tangle of high underbrush. Said the Negro: "Used to be a store here but it burned down."

BURRISVILLE. On Coon Box Road, north of Centerville, Queen Anne's County. The pronunciation is BURRZ-ville. The name is from the Burriss family, represented in Queen Anne's County, in 1790, by Hannah Burriss. Phone lists for 1965 give ten instances of *Burriss*, and one of *Burruss*, for Kent and Queen Anne's Counties.

BURRSVILLE. Near Anthony, Caroline County. It was a post office in 1830. *Union Corner* and *Punch Hall* were at first called *Burrsville*. Cochrane states: "The name of Burrsville was probably selected for the post office, without reference to any suggestions in the neighborhood." In any case Burrsville reflects the abundant family, and family name, Burroughes (Burrus, Burris, Borrows). In 1963 in Caroline County there were phones for one *Burris*, one *Burroughs*, and five *Burrows*. See *PUNCH HALL; see *UNION CORNER.

BURTONSVILLE. Near Spencerville, Montgomery County. R. A. Burton, blacksmith and wheelwright, was the postmaster here in 1878. Farmers in the vicinity at that time were Isaac, George H., and George D. Burton.

BUSH. A village near Abingdon, Harford County. This was the post office, *Harford*, in 1789. *Harford Town was the first seat of Harford County. *Harford Town bears the name of Henry Harford, illegitimate son of the last Lord Baltimore. The site is at the head of Bush River, which accounts for the present name. See *HARFORD TOWN.

BUSH RIVER. Harford County branch of Chesapeake Bay. In 1658 Bush River was unnamed; later one finds it in the Maryland *Archives*, between 1667 and 1687. Perhaps this is the stream which Captain John Smith, in 1608, called *Willoughby's River*. In early days "barrens" alternated with saplings and bushes along the streams of the upper Chesapeake, and it appears very likely that *Bush* River means simply "bushy river." Compare Bushkill, Pennsylvania, which means "bushy creek."

BUSHWOOD (WHARF). Wicomico River, at Blackistone, St. Mary's County. See BLACKISTONE.

BYNUMS RUN; also BYNUM, a village. Northwest branch of Bush River. James Bynum, an early settler, was murdered by the Indians at a bend in this branch.

C

CABIN CREEK. A village near East New Market, Dorchester County. A tributary of the Choptank River, Dorchester County; also a village. Compare CABIN BRANCH, Anne Arundel County, about which Riley relates: "Here the last Indian to remain in this section is said to have had his wigwam."

CABIN JOHN. A village near Glen Echo, Montgomery County. In 1819 this was the post office, *Captain John's Mills*. "Cabin" in CABIN JOHN is evidently a folk corruption of "Captain." There is also a CABIN JOHN CREEK, Elk River, Cecil County.

CACAWAY. An island and point, Langford Bay, Kent County. This Algonquian name was spelled *Cackaway* in 1688. The opening syllable, *Cac-*, may be from the Algonquian element for "wild goose" (Delaware *kaak*) or from the Algonquian element for "porcupine" (Ojibwa *kag-*). The end of the word, *-away*, is perhaps Algonquian "fur, plumage." Of the two possibile translations, "Goose feathers" and "Porcupine quills," I prefer the latter for technical reasons.

CAIUCTUCUC. The early Algonquian name of Wills Creek and vicinity, Alleghany County. In 1787 it appears as *Caicuctuc* or *Wills Creek*. The opening syllable may represent Algonquian "wild goose" (Delaware *kaak*). The middle part of the name may be a form of Algonquian *-e?tekw* "stream." With the ending *-uc* taken as the Algonquian *-ahk* "it is," one reaches the meaning, "Where goose creek is."

CALIFORNIA. A village near Jarboesville, St. Mary's County. It is on Martenet's map, 1866. The original name was *BENITIA. The present name arose more than a hundred years ago, when lumber was shipped here from California to build an estate called "California Farmstead." (See: Dobbin, "California in Maryland," *Sun*, 23 Sept. 1962).

CALVERT. A village near the West Branch of Little Northeast Creek, Cecil County. Calvert was known as *BRICK MEETING HOUSE until 1880–81, and it was also once called *EAST NOTTING-

HAM. The first meeting house—perhaps the earliest church in Cecil County—was built on land granted in 1701 by William Penn. Both Cecil County and CALVERT were named for *Cecil*ius *Calvert*. Compare CE-CIL, near Zion, Cecil County. Calvert is on one of the thirty-seven Nottingham Lots (each named Nottingham) built by William Penn on George Talbot's Susquehanna Manor grant.

CALVERT COUNTY. It lies below Anne Arundel County, between the Patuxent River and Chesapeake Bay. Permanent settlement took place in 1650 when Robert Brooke arrived as "Commander" of a new county. It was founded in 1654, and the name is for Cecil Calvert, second Lord Baltimore.

*CALVERT TOWN. On Battle Creek, Calvert County. Here was the original seat of the Calvert County government. Robert Brooke named it *Battle Town*. But it soon became known as *Calvert Town*. After 1725 the courthouse was moved to Prince Frederick. See BATTLE, BATTLE CREEK.

CAMBRIDGE. A city on the Choptank River, Dorchester County. The Maryland Assembly in 1684 established this town on Daniel Jones's plantation, alongside the Choptank River. In 1686 it was named *Cambridge*, from the English university town; in 1745 it was incorporated. *CAMBRIDGE CREEK, now Dorchester Avenue, was at first its eastern limit.

CAMP DAVID. Catoctin Mountain presidential retreat, near Thurmont, Frederick County, Alt. 1880. This area, a 6000-acre tract, was improved in 1939 by CCC and WPA workers and called *Hi-Catoctin*. Franklin Roosevelt dubbed it "Shangri-la." Dwight Eisenhower renamed it *Camp David* for his grandson (later Richard Nixon's son-in-law). The place had rustic cabins; hence *camp*.

*CAMP PAROLE. Near Annapolis, Anne Arundel County. This place developed from a camp (estab. 1862) for paroled federal prisoners. See PAROLE.

CAMP SPRINGS. A village near Silver Hill, Prince George's County. Camp Springs was originally a rural area, with fresh springs where people came to picnic and camp.

CANTON. Baltimore suburb, junction and dock. What was once *Hampstead Hill* (Baltimore) is now CANTON, named for the first commercial voyage from China to Baltimore. Footner gives the date as 1785. The ship was the *Pallas*, commanded by Captain John O'Donnell.

CAPITOL HEIGHTS. Prince George's County village adjacent to Southern Ave., S.E. Washington, D.C. Elevation 100 feet. Nearby are Fairmount Heights, District Heights, and Forest Heights. The name indicates a somewhat elevated region (heights) near Washington, the national capital. There is no view of the Capitol building.

CAPITOLA. A village near Whitehaven, Wicomico County. Mrs. Eloise Darby, of this place, explains that the name originated from certain phrases relating to a Captain White, who lived here. For instance: "*Cap'n* [White] *tol' ya,*" etc.

CARDEROCK. Near Great Falls, Montgomery County. Also Carderock Springs. The name is evidently from "Carter Rock," in the Great Falls. In this case the *t* of *Carter* has become *d* because of the following *r*.

CARDIFF. A village near Whiteford, Harford County. Cardiff is a "heavily" Welsh community on the Pennsylvania border. In 1733 slate-quarrying began here and attracted waves of Welsh miners. Welsh used to be spoken in every home. The other half of the settlement is Delta, Pa. Together with Whiteford, Md., the three villages make one community. The name is from Cardiff, on the Bristol Channel, Wales. (See: Reppert, *Sun*, May 20, 1962).

CAROLINE COUNTY. East of Talbot and Queens Anne's Counties and adjacent to Delaware. This county was created in 1774 and takes its name from Caroline Eden, the wife of Sir Robert Eden, English Governor of Maryland. She was the sister of Frederick Calvert, the last Lord Baltimore. Since it parallels Eden Street, it is likely that Caroline Street, Baltimore, was also named for this lady.

CARPENTER POINT. Chesapeake Bay, near Charlestown, Cecil County. William Carpenter or Carpender settled at Carpenter's Point in 1658. He was Cecil County's first permanent settler.

CARROLL COUNTY. It borders Pennsylvania and lies between Baltimore and Frederick Counties. The county was formed in 1836 and takes its name from Charles Carroll of Carrollton, who had large land grants in this vicinity.

CARROLLS MILL. A village near Mayfield, Howard County. My notes indicate that the post office here was *Doughoregan,* from the name of the estate of Charles Carroll, I. A 1793 deed mentions the main road "... from Baltimore Town to Dr. Charles Carroll's Mill and Iron Works lying on Gwins Falls." This was "Charles Carroll, Chyrurgeon.'" See DOUGHOREGAN.

*CARROLLSBURG. Early community on the present site of Washington, D.C. There was also Carrollsburg Square, S.W. It existed along with *FUNKSBURG (from Henry Funk?) and *HAMBURG. Daniel Carroll established *Carrollsburg. *Carroll Street, S.E., also for Daniel Carroll, has been obliterated to make way for the new Madison addition to the Library of Congress. (See: Williams, II, 992-93).

Note: Daniel Carroll's estate, Duddington Manor, 1663, lay along the north side of the Anacostia River and comprised the site of the present U.S. capitol.

*CARROLLSBURG. Emmitsburg in 1786 was described as "a wood," and the land on which St. Joseph's Catholic Church, Emmitsburg, was built in 1793 belonged at first to "Mr. Carroll of Annapolis." It was *Carrollsburg*. See EMMITSBURG.

CARROLLTON. A village near Reese, Carroll County. At first Carrollton was not a village but the manorial estate, "Carrollton Manor." "Carrollton" was surveyed for Charles, Daniel, and Eleanor Carroll in 1723. In the beginning, it consisted of 10,000 acres. When the famous Charles Carroll inherited it, it had grown to 40,000 acres. The celebrated phrase, "Charles Carroll of Carrollton," means "Charles Carroll of Carrollton" *Manor*.

CARRS CORNER. Annapolis, Anne Arundel County. The general store of Virgil and Everd Carr, at this familiar corner, closed in 1970. Benjamin Carr, the founder of the local "Carr Clann," came to America from Scotland in the 1730's. Compare *Carrs Hills, Lothian.

CARSINS, CARSINS RUN. A village and stream, Harford County. This is only a different spelling of the family name *Carson*. In 1878 the place was *Carsin's Run P.O.* At that time a farmer, William Carsins, lived here.

CARTHAGENA CREEK. Two neighboring streams in St. Mary's County. The name is from Cartagena, Colombia, which Admiral Edward Vernon, after taking Porto Bello, unsuccessfully besieged in 1741. History mentions the £5,000 Supply Act of 1740 for the Carthagena Expedition. See MOUNT VERNON; see PORTO BELLO.

CARTERSVILLE. Community. Anne Arundel County. In 1651 Captain Edward Carter had 600 acres near Herring Creek Bay, Anne Arundel. In 1790 Joseph Carter resided in the county. The 1971 Annapolis phone book lists 119 Carters. Compare Carters Cross Roads, Carroll County.

CARVILLE STATION. Near Centreville, Queen Anne's County. The place has been spelled *Carville's Corner* and *Carville's Station*. The name is from the family name *Carville*. John Carvill was Kent County Commissioner in 1706; Edmund Carville was Kent Island parishioner in 1805. The surname may be related to *Tancarville* or *Courville*, Normandy, France.

Note: In 1874 Thomas R. Carville was an incorporator of the Bank of Centreville.

CASSATT. A village on the Pocomoke River, Somerset County. It is in the 1941 Gazetteer; it is absent in Manual 1947. I learn that the

---

Note: I include this name for whatever connection it may have with the ancestry of Mary Cassatt, the American painter.

branches of this family differentiate themselves on the basis of whether the name is written with one "t" or two "t"s. Cf. K. A. Cassat, Pasadena, Maryland.

CASSELMAN RIVER. A branch of the Youghiogheny River, near Grantsville, Garrett County. The name is attributed to Jacob Casselman, a pioneer settler on the Pennsylvania part of the river. The first traders called this stream "Old Town Creek". In 1813 it was known as the "Little Youghiogheny." At first there was probably an Indian village or "Old Town" here.

CASTLE HAVEN. A village near Lloyds, Dorchester County. There is a natural harbor or haven. In 1659, on a patent of 800 acres, Anthony Le Compte, a Huguenot refugee, built a castle-like house here named "Antonine." The present house was built in 1730. LE COMPTE CREEK and LE COMPTE BAY are adjacent.

CATOCTIN. A tributary of the Potomac River, Frederick County; also, mountains stretching from north to south in that county. The last part of this Indian name contains -*atin*, -*adina*, etc., a general Algonquian word for "mountain." The first part is probably a form of Algonquian -*ketagi* (Fox) "spotted, speckled." The meaning is "Speckled Mountain." Statuary Hall, U.S. Capitol, has columns of speckled rock from the Catoctin mountains.

CATONSVILLE. A village near Ellicott City, Baltimore County. Catonsville was first called *JOHNNYCAKE for an inn here that was noted for its cornbread. The present name is for Richard Caton who in 1787 married the daughter of Charles Carroll of Carrollton. The estate Charles Carroll gave the couple comprised the present site of Catonsville.

*CAUSE, BIG, LITTLE. Anne Arundel County. *Big Cause, Little Cause* were tributaries of the Severn River near Fort Madison in 1878. I suppose that "Cause," as used here, means *causeway*.

CAVETOWN. Near Smithsburg, Washington County; elevation 750 ft. The oldest known cave in Maryland once existed here. There was room for 1000 people; it had a lake big enough for a small boat. In 1912 quarriers made the cave unsafe. It had disappeared by 1920. (See: Dorsey, *Sun*, 6 January 1963).

CAYOTS. A village in Chesapeake District, near the Bohemia River, Cecil County. It was Cayots Corner in 1877. The name is for "a Frenchman who lived here for a time . . ." This is probably a form of the French family name, *Cayouette*. (See: Miller, p. 43).

CEARFOSS. A village near Maugansville, Washington County. It is on Martenet's map of 1866. Living here in 1878 were Simon *Cearfoss*, shoemaker, and Daniel *Cearfoss*, farmer and stock dealer.

CECIL COUNTY. It is separated from Harford County by the Susquehanna River, and lies south of Pennsylvania and west of Delaware.

The county was created by proclamation in 1674, and takes its name from Cecil Calvert, the second Lord Baltimore. Thirteen years earlier Augustin(e) Herrman had proposed a *Cecil County* and a *Ceciltown*. The town was never built, but the site it was to occupy is remembered today in *Town Point*.

CECILTON. A village near Fredericktown, Cecil County. Earlier names were *SAVIN(G)TON and *CECILS CROSS ROADS. The name is for Cecil Calvert, second Lord Baltimore. In 1730 and in 1731 attempts to establish a *Cecilton had failed.

*CECILTOWN RIVER. Erstwhile name of the Elk River, mentioned in the records of the Council, in 1662, in connection with one of Augustine Herrman's surveys.

CENTERVILLE. Maryland has Centervilles in Frederick, Charles, Prince George's, Somerset, and Washington Counties. Howard County has a *Centre*. Places so named were evidently in the center of a particular region or county. Compare *Centralia, at Annapolis Junction in 1864, whose name arose from its central location in regard to Washington and Baltimore. For CENTERVILLE, Washington County, see KEEDYS-VILLE. (See: Riley, p. 114).

CENTERVILLE LANDING. Corsica River, near Centreville, Queen Anne's County. The Guide describes this landing as a place "... from which freight is carried on a branch of the Pennsylvania Railroad ..."

CENTREVILLE. Town and county seat, Queen Anne's County. *Chester Mills, an earlier name, was changed to *Centreville* in 1797. The town, situated in the center of Centreville District, is a development from "Old Chester Church" and "Old Chester Mill," and was laid out in 1792.

Note: According to Emory, the spelling *Centreville* is French and was intended to honor the French for their help during the American Revolution. However, *Centre* is a valid British spelling for *Center*; and *-ville* is the usual ending of English village names.

CERESVILLE. A village near Walkersville, Frederick County. *Ceresville Mill was built in about 1745 by Cornelius Shriver. Perhaps the name is from Ceres, Greek goddess of agriculture. Compare Ceres, Fifeshire, eastern Scotland.

*CHAKAKITQUE (SAHAKITKO). An erstwhile stream and trading post at the junction of Big and Little Elk Creeks, near Elkton, Cecil County. Prof. C. A. Weslager, of Hockessin, Delaware, believes that "the basic word is certainly a Maryland Indian place-name." On that assumption, I shall proceed to study it.

I can find no occurrences in Maryland or Virginian placenames of the final syllables *-kitco, -kitque* ... However, the general Primitive Algonquian stem *ke?tci* "big. great" is suggested by the *Cha-* (*Saha-*) of *CHA-

KAKITQUE. It appears in Virginia and Maryland in *Chaptico, Che*sapeake, *Ch*optank, etc. In New England (see Huden) *Chi*comico Creek is translated "big house."

However, with the second syllable (*-ka-* [*-ha-*]) unaccounted for, and no Algonquian clue whatever to account for the *-kitko, -kitque,* one turns to Iroquoian. The results are negative, though; for nowhere in Iroquoian can I find jot or tittle of *Chaka-* [*Saha-*].

The location of the place indicates that its name may end with a locative. Beauchamp's various Iroquoian etymologies show that *-que* is the French form of normal Iroquoian (locative) *-ga*; and Powell (see Beauchamp) makes it evident that *-ke* (French form *-que, -gwe*) is the Iroquoian local preposition for *at* or *on*. Sarato*ga*, Ticondero*ga* (etc.) are examples. Cuoq bears out Beauchamp, noting that Iroquoian *-ke* means "sur," and that *-ka* means "where, from where, par ou." An example is *Onontoharake* "sur la montagne."

Supposing that *-ko* (*-que*) stands for the Iroquoian locative (*-ga* [Cuoq-*ke*]), I feel that *CHAKAkitque (SAHAKITKO) is an Iroquoian placename in the locative sense. Maybe it means "at, on, near" a waterfall. But I can find no Iroquoian analogy to the opening syllable(s).

CHAMP. A community near Oriole, Somerset County. *ST. PETER'S PENINSULA was the earlier name of this place. The present name is for I. Frank Beau*champ*, once an optometrist here. When he petitioned for a post office bearing his own name, the postal authorities, preferring a shorter word, made the compromise of *-champ*.

CHANCE. A village near Dames Quarter, Somerset County. The story is told that Capt. James Whitelock, after the postal authorities turned down the name "Rock Creek" for this place, petitioned that it be called "Chance," because the chances were that they would not get a post office at all. They got it, and the name was *Chance*. This story should not obscure the fact that many early land grants, such as "Chance" (Calvert County 1712), "Come by Chance," and "Accident" had the same or a similar name.

CHANEY, CHANEYVILLE. Below Dunkirk, Calvert County. The Chaneys responsible for Chaneyville were the descendants of Richard Cheyney or Chaney, who came from Kent County, England, and settled in Anne Arundel County in 1658. The first Chaney to settle in Calvert County was Thomas Chaney, grandson of Richard Chaney, the immigrant.

CHAPEL POINT. A village and point, Port Tobacco River, Charles County. From earliest colonial days the land here was known as St. Thomas Manor, and the first manor house and chapel were built in 1662. It and later chapels burned down. The present St. Ignatius Catholic Church is perhaps the nation's oldest active parish.

Note: Reverend Robert Thoman believes that Chapel Point was once *Kittama-quindi Point, where Father Andrew White and other Jesuits built a log and skin chapel which was used by the Indians. Earlier authorities, however, locate *Kitta-maquindi at the junction of Tinkers and Piscataway Creeks, Prince George's County.

CHAPTICO. A creek, bay, and village, Wicomico River, St. Mary's County. In 1651 it was spelled *Choptico*. The principal elements of this Indian name are Algonquian "big" (Ojibwa *kitci*, Fox *kehtci*, etc.) and Algonquian "wave, current" (*tekwi*). The meaning would be "It is a big (or deep) stream." Pronunciation: CHAP-tee-coe.

CHARLES COUNTY. It is below Prince George's County and is largely bounded by the Potomac River. A proclamation by Gov. Josias Fendall created this county from St. Mary's County on May 10, 1658. It was named, to use Cecil Calvert's words, "in honor of our only son and heir apparent, Charles Calvert Esquire."

CHARLESTOWN. Near Northeast, Northeast River, Cecil County. The citizens of Cecil County felt the need for a town, and the act to incorporate *Charlestown* was passed in 1742. The name appears to commemorate the fifth Lord Baltimore.

*CHARLESTOWN. Former seat of Prince George's County. On a tract of land surveyed here in 1652 for Philip Calvert a town, *Charlestown, developed. It was the seat of Prince George's County in 1695. In 1732 Upper Marlboro became the county seat. At *Charlestown a house, "Mount Calvert," is all that today remains. See MOUNT CALVERT; see UPPER MARLBORO.

Note: The name probably commemorates Charles Calvert, third Lord Baltimore.

CHARLOTTE HALL. A village near Mechanicsville, St. Mary's County. Charlotte Hall was established in 1698. It was a health resort, and was usually called "Ye Cool Springs of St. Maries." The school, Charlotte Hall, was ordered to be built in 1774. It was named for Queen Charlotte of England (m. George III in 1761).

CHARLTON. A village near Clear Spring, Washington County. The name commemorates Captain John Charlton and his plan to colonize in Maryland's interest what is today York County, Pa. In 1736 fifty German settlers in this area renounced Maryland's authority, and Governor Ogle issued a warrant to evict them and make a resurvey. The land was then to be occupied by fifty-two Marylanders, including Edward, John and Thomas Charlton. Nothing came of these plans; and soon afterwards Captain Charlton seems to have become a resident of Leitersburg District, Washington County. (See: Bell, p. 158).

CHASE. A village near Cowentown, Baltimore County. This place was first *Chase's Station* (present Pennsylvania Railroad). The name arose seventy-five years ago when Charles Chase, a New England lawyer, came south to this place for his health. He was related to Samuel Chase, a "Signer."

CHASE CREEK. Severn River, near Arnold, Anne Arundel County. Samuel Chase, "Signer" and Associate Supreme Court Justice, lived in Annapolis until 1786.

Note: Samuel Chase (1741–1811).

CHATTOLANEE. A village in the Green Spring Valley, Baltimore County. *Chattolanee* is the name of the "green spring" of *Green Spring Valley*. The name is Muskhogean and means "yellow rock"; but the reference here is to a mineral spring. In 1892 Baltimoreans were drinking Chattolanee mineral water.

CHAUTAUQUA. Montgomery County village, near the Washington, D.C., Amusement Park *Glen Echo. *CHAUTAUQUA* is an Iroquoian Indian word, from Lake Chautauqua, N.Y. Between 1874–1888 it was used nationally to designate summer programs of lectures and musicals. This region of Montgomery County has about fifteen imported Indian street names. An example is *Saranac Road*.

Note: *Chautauqua* (Iroquoian) has been given a half dozen meanings. One of them is "Where the fish was [sic] taken out."

CHESACO PARK. Back River, near Rosedale, Baltimore County. Numerous local businesses, such as Chesaco Sand Co., have taken this name; and there is a Chesaco Avenue, Baltimore. The first two syllables, of course, are from *Chesapeake*.

CHESAPEAKE BAY. It divides the eastern and western shores of Maryland, and extends from the Susquehanna River in the north to the Potomac River and the Atlantic Ocean in Virginia. In 1585 it was spelled *Chesepiooc*. All authorities agree that the first syllable of this Indian name means "big, great," from Algonquian *kehtci* (*kitci*, etc.). The second syllable may be regarded as Algonquian *äs*, meaning "*shellfish*, oyster, clam." The end of the word is evidently *-āpyäki* "expanse of water." The name means "Great shell-fish bay."

CHESAPEAKE BEACH. A village and resort below West Beach, Chesapeake Bay, Calvert County. Chesapeake Beach, conceived as a bayside resort, was named and incorporated in 1894 by an Act of the Maryland Assembly. The actual town appeared in 1900 when the Chesapeake Beach Railway Co. completed its tracks and built an amusement area, a power plant, and a water system. Trains began to run in July 1900. (Source: J. M. Rector, late president of the Washington Railway Co.).

CHESAPEAKE CITY. On both sides of Back Creek, Elk River, Cecil County. The town is at the Maryland end of the Chesapeake and Delaware Canal, and it arose in 1804 when the canal began. It was incorporated in

1815. Mayor Harry H. Griffin writes me: "This town was named after the Chesapeake Bay ..." See PIVOT.

CHESTER. A village near Stevensville, Queen Anne's County. There is a reference to the "parish church at Chester" for Dec. 19, 1718. It appears likely that the name arose owing to the nearness of the Chester River, though both names reflect *Chester*, Cheshire, England.

CHESTERFIELD. A village near Mt. Tabor Church, Anne Arundel County. The name is probably from an early tract named "Chesterfield." The original source is probably Chesterfield, Derbyshire, England.

*CHESTER MILL. This is now CENTERVILLE, Queen Anne's County. A deed of 1780 mentions "... the grist mill situated on the land called Chesterfield and known as Chester Mill ..." However, there are court records that mention it as early as 1713. In 1789 the name Centreville was substituted for *Chester Mill to avoid confusion with nearby similar placenames.

CHESTER RIVER. Eastern Shore tributary of Chesapeake Bay; dividing line between Kent and Queen Anne's Counties (*Chester R*, Herrman 1670). The Chester was known as such "as early as 1667," when William Hemsley described himself as being of Coursey Creek, Chester River. The name is from the Roman walled city of Chester, Cheshire, England. (See: Emory, p. 17).

CHESTERTOWN. On the Chester River, near Radcliff Creek, Kent County. *New Town became a port of entry for Cecil, Kent, and Queen Anne's Counties in 1708. An act of 1730 mentions "Chester-Town or New-Town," and lays out "a-new" a "TOWN" to be called "CHESTER-TOWN." The present name is from the Chester River.

CHESTERVILLE. Ten miles east of Chestertown and two and a-half miles north of Chester River. It is mentioned by Lewis in 1878. The nearness of the Chester River probably accounts for the name.

CHESTNUT. Maryland has chestnut *groves*, *hills*, *knobs*, and *ridges* in Garrett, Calvert, Frederick, Harford, Baltimore, and Montgomery Counties. Stein, speaking of Chestnut Hill, Calvert County, remarks that "In former days before the blight, chestnut trees abounded in the forests."

CHEVERLY. A town near Bladensburg, Prince George's County. Robert Marshall named Cheverly in 1918 after Cheverly Gardens, an adjoining tract near Landover Station. Mrs. Marshall thus explained the name: "(It) was named after a rich man's estate in England. It has no other significance except English sentiment." Recent researches reveal that Cheverly, with an "intrusive *r*," is from Cheveley, a village, parish, and manor, Warwickshire, England. The English name is Anglo-Saxon, containing *ceaf* "chaff" and LEAH "field, meadow." It means "twig field." (See: Papers of Raymond W. Bellamy, Cheverly; Hirzl, *Star*, Nov. 2, 1976).

CHEVY CHASE. Montgomery County suburb of Washington, D.C. The name appears to have come from "Chevy Chase," a tract patented to Colonel Joseph Belt in 1751, and advertised for sale as "Chevy Chase" in 1760. The Chevy Chase Land Co., formed in 1890, made the first "energetic development" of the area; the first sixteen houses were built before 1909.

Note: Compare "Chevy Chase," a tract in Gunpowder Hundred, surveyed in 1695 for John Thomas Chase. The name seems to be a pun on Mr. *Chase's* family name.

CHEW. A village near Upper Marlboro, Prince George's County. The original Col. John Chew came to Virginia in 1622. In general, the Chews came from Somersetshire, England, ". . . where the manorial mansion of Chew Court may still be seen at Chew Magna, in Chewton Township, fifteen miles from the Severn River." (See: Bowie, p. 514; Mc Grath, p. 152).

CHEWSVILLE. Near Cavetown, Washington County. The village occupies part of a tract granted to Samuel Chew, Jr., in 1736, and it appears that "Chews Farm" and "Chews Manor" were granted to Samuel Chew, Jr., in 1763. It was a post office in 1839. (See: Williams, I, p. 22).

CHICAMACOMICO RIVER. A tributary of the Transquaking River, Dorchester County. The latter part of this Indian name is probably Algonquian *-ahkamikwi* "dwelling place." The first part of the name may be Alonquian *Kehtci-kami-* "big water." The meaning would be "Dwelling place by the big water."

Note: *kehtci-kami-* is Longfellow's GICHEGUMEE or "shining big sea water."

CHICAMUXEN. A creek and village, Potomac River, Charles County. It was spelled *Chingomuxon* in 1650. The opening part of this Indian name may be either Algonquian *chi* (from *kehtci*) "big" or Algonquian *tcink* "elevated raised." If one chooses the latter element (*tcink*), the rest of the name could be *amehki* "ground, surface." The meaning would be "(There) lies high ground."

Note: The alternative translation (taking *-cam-* as "expanse of water" and *-uxem* as "stone") gives the meaning "Stone at the big bay."

CHICONE CREEK. A tributary of the Nanticoke River at Vienna, Dorchester County. Pronunciation: she-CONE. Early spellings indicate that the final letters of this Indian name were originally *-awan, -awone*. Powhatan *coan* "snow" befits this ending. If then one regards the opening syllable *chi-* as Algonquian *kehtci* "big," the meaning of *Chicone* becomes "Big snow."

Note: To quote from my 1961 book on these subjects, "I propose, then, that *Chicone* be regarded as *kehtci-akoni* (Fox-*akoni*, Powhatan *coan*, B & A *guhn*) 'Big snow.' Cf. Algonkin (Cuoq) *cagakon 'soft snow.'* "

62   THE PLACENAMES OF MARYLAND

CHILDS. A village near Singerly, Little Elk Creek, Cecil County. This was *Childs* Station, on the Baltimore and Ohio Railroad. The name is for George W. Childs, editor of the Philadelphia Public *Ledger*. It appears that he owned the Marley paper mill near here. (See: Guide; see Miller, p. 75).

CHILLUM. Washington, D.C., suburb near Takoma Park, Prince George's County. "Chillum Castle Manor," once situated here, had its name from "Chillum Manor," properly *Chilham* Manor, the ancestral home of the Digges family, Chilham, Kent County, England. Chilham, Kent, is the site of Chilham Castle. And in Chilham Church there is a monument to Sir Dudley Digges. William Digges came to Maryland in 1650.

CHINCOTEAGUE BAY. In Stockton and Snow Hill Districts, Worcester County. Pronunciation: sheenco- TEEG. In 1608 it was spelled *Cinquoteck*. This Indian name evidently contains Algonquian *chingua-* "large" and *-tegw* "wave, flow." The consequent meaning is "Large stream or inlet."

CHINKAPIN RUN. A tributary of Herring Run, Baltimore County. In 1685 it was spelled *Chincopin*. The opening syllables of this Indian word are no doubt from Delaware Algonquian *chinqua* "large, great." The last part of the word may mean either "nut" or "tuber." The more likely meaning is "Big nut."

CHINGVILLE. A village near Clifton Mills, St. Mary's County. A St. Mary's County deed for 1882 mentions John F. Ching.

CHISHOLM RUN, CHISHOLM'S MILL. Youghiogheny River, near Oakland, Garrett County. On June 23, 1849, James Chisholm bought from Norman Bruce the land here, the old mill, and the water rights. (See: Weeks, p. 92).

CHLORA POINT. Choptank River, near Oxford, Talbot County. Ingraham spells it *Cloras Point* and states that "Clora Dorsey" was the name of a home there. He ascribes the name of the point to the owner of the "Hier- Dyer-Lloyd" tract, and declares (ridiculously?) that the tract in early days was owned by a Spaniard named *Clora* Adora.

*CHONK RIVER. This obscure stream is described by W. B. Marye as "... the Chonk River up near the Little Monocacy." I have no knowledge whatever of its origin and meaning. Since the Little Monocacy is a branch of the Potomac River, one of whose early names was *Cohongoronto* (*Cohongaroota*), "River of the wild geese," I suggest that *Chonk* is somehow related to Delaware and Powhatan *Kaak, Kahunge* "goose." See "William B. Marye's 'Dig' at Bryn Mawr" (B. M. Key, ed.), *MHM*, 75: 1 (March 1980).

CHOPAWAMSIC ISLAND. It lies in the Potomac River at the mouth of the Virginia stream, Chopawamsic Creek. Across the river is Charles County, Maryland. One assumes that the island takes its name from the creek. This Indian name is an Algonquian sentence, and apparently contains: *kehtci* "big"; *api* "extent, expanse (river)"; *oom* "go"; and *-eke* "they." The meaning would be "They go down to the river."

CHOPTANK. A large tributary of the Chesapeake Bay, Talbot and Dorchester Counties. Also a village. This Indian name is probably a composition of Algonquian *kehtci-* "big," *-api-* "back again," and *-ehtan* "current, flow." The final *-k* may be taken as a verb ending. The consequent meaning would be "It flows back strongly," a reference to tidal changes.

CHROME HILLS. A village near Coopstown, Harford County. The elevation is 480 feet. An 1878 map of Harford County mentions "Chrome Ore & Magnesia." At that time the lands here were described as being composed "of mineral, mostly cleared." Compare "Chrome Pits" in Cecil County. Isaac Tyson, of Baltimore, began mining chrome in 1830. See RISING SUN.

CHURCH CREEK. Found as both stream and village in Anne Arundel, Cecil, Dorchester, Kent, and other counties. Church Creek, Anne Arundel County, borders "Priest's Farm," where there is a graveyard and where there was once a Catholic church. The Kent County Church Creek is called "a reminder" of the site of the first lasting landing of white colonists on the Eastern Shore. See *NEW YARMOUTH.

CHURCH HILL. A village near Price, Southeast Creek, Queen Anne's County. This place became a post office in 1802. In 1878 there were M. E., M. E. South, and P. E. churches here. The church responsible for the name was on Southeast Creek near Collins' Mill.

CHURCHTON. A village near Deal, Anne Arundel County (GMd 1904, 1941; Manual 1947). Ms. Martha C. Dawson, former postmistress here, tells me (1983) that the post office was established in 1885. The name is explained by there being several churches in the area.

CHURCHVILLE. Near a branch of Tobacco Run, Harford County. As for postal history, in 1828 Churchville was known also as *Herberts Cross Roads. One of the "elders" of Churchville had come here in 1740. In 1878 there were two churches, Holy Trinity and Presbyterian. "Priest Neale's Mass House" was in this region. Also nearby is the village of CALVARY.

CLAGGETTS. A community in Washington County. Compare *Claggetts Mill, Washington County, 1795. See CLAGETTSVILLE.

CLAGETTSVILLE. A village near Damascus, Montgomery County. The name is for the Clagett family, whose founder, Captain Thomas Clagett, the settler of "Clagett's Delight," 1682, came to Calvert County in 1670. He was from Claygate, England, where his family name originated.

CLAIBORNE. A village on Eastern Bay, Kent Island, Talbot County. The Baltimore and Eastern Shore Railroad established Claiborne in 1886 as a ferry point on its line. In 1940 this was the eastern end of the Romancoke-Claiborne ferry. The name commemorates Captain William Claiborne, whose trading post on Kent Island in 1631 was the first place of settlement within what is today Maryland.

CLARKE. A village near Severn, Anne Arundel County. Compare "Clarkenwell," surveyed on May 23, 1664, for John Clark of Herring Creek Hundred, Anne Arundel. There was also Thomas Clark, an Englishman, who came to the Province with Daniel Dulany and studied law under him in Annapolis. His marriage (1727) is recorded in the registry of St. Anne's Church, Annapolis.

CLARKSBURG. A village near Neelsville, Montgomery County. There is a tradition that Clarksburg is on the site of an Indian trading post. It became a post office in 1800. The land here, granted originally to Henry Griffith in 1761, was known as the "cow pasture." John G. Clark built the house. (See: PHC; Boyd).

CLARKSVILLE. A village near Highland, Howard County. Local history mentions "the late" William Clark, "an extensive farmer of the limestone section of Clarksville." His father was David Clark, one of three brothers who came from the north of Ireland after the American Revolution. (See: Warfield, p. 410).

CLARYSVILLE. Near Eckhart Mines, Allegany County. An advertisement of the "Clarysville Inn and Motel" (1968) indicates that the inn here was built in 1807, and that the Clary family was the original owner. For many years the manager was Jerrard Clary.

Note: Compare the (surname?) spelling *M(a)c Clarysville*.

CLEAR SPRING. A village near Indian Spring, Washington County. It was a post office in 1823. In the vicinity are Big Spring, Indian Spring, and Green Spring Furnace. Clear Spring was founded in 1821 by Martin Meyers. The name is from a spring ("behind the hotel") so large that at one time it turned a mill wheel.

CLEMENTS. A village at the head of St. Clement Bay, St. Mary's County. Lord Baltimore granted St. Clement's Manor to Thomas Jerrard, who came to Maryland in 1637. *Clements* is short for *St. Clement's*. This illustrates how, in the brief Puritan regime that began in 1643, *saint* was omitted from names.

Note: The ultimate origin of these names is apparently St. Clement's Bay, Jersey, one of the Channel Islands.

CLINTON. A village near Camp Springs, Prince George's County. In 1854 the post office here was *Surratts*. *Surratts* is still the election district, and the place is still known locally as *Surrattsville*. Because of Mrs. Mary Surratt's suspected connection with the murder of Abraham Lincoln, the name was changed from *Surratts* to *Robeystown* three weeks after the tragedy. It became *Clinton* in 1878. The old name is from Surratts Tavern and John Harrison Surratt; *Clinton* may be from Governor De Witt Clinton, New York.

CLOPPER. A village near Gaithersburg, Montgomery County. Its name is from Francis Cassatt Clopper, who bought a plantation here in 1811. Clopper, born in Baltimore in 1786, was related to Mary Cassatt, the American painter. Compare CASSATT, a village near Costen, Somerset County.

COHILL. A village near Roundtop, Washington County. Edmund Pendleton Cohill, born 1855, was a Washington County school board member, the president of the Tonoloway Orchard Company, and an organizer of the Hancock Bridge Company. His name belies the fact that his father was from Germany.

COKESBURY. There are two villages, one near Craigtown, Cecil County, and the other near Wellington, Somerset County. In each instance the name has come from *Cokes-bury*, a compound of the surnames of Bishop Thomas *Coke* and Bishop Francis *Asbury*, Methodist theologians.

COLBOURN, COULBOURN CREEK. Village and stream, near Marion, Annemessex River, Somerset County. William Coulbourne, of Somersetshire, England, settled in Annemessex between Oct. 1663 and January 1663/4. In March 1664 he became a Lieutenant of a Foot Company, and in February 1670 he was a member of the Commission of Peace for Somerset County. He died in 1689. Compare COLBOURNE, Worcester County.

COLEMAN. A village near Stillpond, Kent County. A likely namesake was the early Harford settler, Rev. John Coleman, Protestant Episcopal minister and Revolutionary soldier, usually known as "Parson Coleman." He was a native of Dinwiddie County, Virginia (d. 1816).

COLESVILLE. Near Glenmont, Montgomery County. It was a post office in 1816. There are also Colesville Farm Estates, Colesville Gardens, and Colesville Park. The name is from the English family name *Cole* (*Coale*), meaning "coal black, swarthy." Cf. the ubiquitous *Colesville Road*.

COLLEGE GREEN. A village near Farmington, Cecil County. *Farmington* became *Principio* in 1840, and in 1849, Principio became *College Green*. In 1853 it was changed back to Principio. The name is from the estate, "College Green," which Rev. John Beard, perhaps an Irishman, bequeathed to his sons in about 1771. See PRINCIPIO.

COLLEGE PARK. A town near Riverdale, Prince George's County. In 1866 it was mapped as "Md Agr Coll/ *Agricultural College*." It had been chartered in 1856 as a private corporation. Here at first there was only "College Station," an unscheduled railroad stop. Later a Washington real estate developer drained the land and subdivided it. In 1890 the name was changed to College Park. The college street names so abundant here came later and were probably suggested by the presence of the college. (See: Callcott).

*COLLEGE ST. JAMES. Bygone village, near Breathedsville, Washington County. It was a post office in 1847. In 1906 it was "St. James Sta. or St. James School P.O." Callcott includes "St. James (Episcopalian) 1843" among nine Maryland church-supported colleges that were established before 1860.

COLORA. A village near Rising Sun, Cecil County. The name, given in 1845, comes from "Colora," the home of Lloyd Balderston, who came here in 1842 or 1843. The name of the home is a combination of Latin *aura* ("breez/y/") and Latin *culmen* (*columen*), "ridge." "Breezy Ridge" is its meaning.

COLUMBIA. A bygone village and a recently planned city, the one a development of the other, near Simpsonville, Howard County. The old Columbia lay on what was known as the Columbia Pike, and probably took its name from the Pike. The new Columbia, planned in 1964, is on the site of the old Columbia, after which it was named.

Note: One supposes that *Columbia* Pike owes its name to the proximity of the District of Columbia.

COMEGY BIGHT. Cove and creek. Chester River, near Pomona, Kent County. Cunz attributes "Comegy's Bight" to Cornelius Commegys, a Hollander who settled on the Eastern Shore in about 1680. He was sometimes called Commegys from Vienna, but he was really a Dutchman from Vianen, South Holland. Comegys and his family were naturalized by Act of Assembly in 1672.

Note: A *bight* is a small bay or cove. McJimsey gives an instance of where it is spelled *bite*.

COMUS. A village near Barnesville, Montgomery County. The name is an abbreviation of the family name *McComa(u)s*. Louis E. McComas, in 1898, was a U.S. Senator from Maryland.

CONOCOCHEAGUE. A creek flowing into the Potomac River at Williamsport, Washington County; also a village. Pronunciation: KAHN-ohko-CHEEG. This Indian name had such early spellings as *Conigochego*, *Conegocheek*. The opening part of the name appears to be general Algonquian for "long, lengthy" (Delaware *guneu*). The rest of the word is perhaps Algonquian *-chin(g)we* "dull sound." The meaning would be "A dull sound is heard afar off," possibly a reference to boulders striking each other during a flood.

CONOWINGO. A tributary of the Susquehanna River, Cecil County; also a dam and postal village. Unlike most of Maryland's Indian names,

Conowingo is probably Iroquoian. The last part of the word (-*wingo*) shows a popular etymology. "At the waterfall" would be a plausible meaning.

*CONOY ISLAND. In the Potomac River, near Point of Rocks, Frederick County. Today this is HEATERS ISLAND; in about 1711 it was *Conoy Island and had the two villages, *Indian Town Landing and *Canavest. The name is from the Piscataway or *Conooi* Indians, who resided here for a while when they abandoned their lands in Charles County. *Conoy* may be from the Algonquian element *guneu, kenwi,* "long, lengthy, far off." Cf. Kanawha. See PISCATAWAY.

CONTEE. Village near Laurel, Prince George's County. Lewis 1878 lists Contee's Station and notes that the postmaster was C. S. Contee. The first Contee in Maryland was Colonel John Contee, of the Colonial Militia (1707), and a member of the Council of State.

CONTEES LANDING WHARF. Rhodes River, near Birdsville, Anne Arundel County. *Hopkins 1878* has a store where Contees Wharf is today. Nearby are the homes of Chas. Contee and Rich. Contee. The Contees, French Huguenots, claim descent from the French family *Conde*. Alexander Contee, the forefather, emigrated from Barnstable, Devonshire, England, between 1693 and 1713.

COOK(S). Point, village, cove, etc. Choptank River, near Hudson, Dorchester County. Andrew Cooke, "Gentleman," of London, England, came to Maryland in about 1661. In 1662 he bought "Maulden" or "Cook's Point" in Dorchester County. This "Andrew the First" probably gave the two names. His son was Ebenezer Cooke, poetical author of "The Sot-Weed Factor" (1708).

COOKSVILLE. Near Lisbon, Howard County. In 1824 Larkin S. Cook was the postmaster. In 1825 when General Lafayette, revisiting the United States, had breakfast at Joshua Roberts' tavern, Cooksville, "Mr. Thomas Cook lived just opposite."

COPPERVILLE. On Big Pipe Creek near Oregon School, Carroll County. The name appears to be related to a copper mine discovered in about 1804 near Libertytown. (See: Scott 1807, p. 29).

COPPERVILLE. Near Unionville, Talbot County. Oral history indicates that Copperville, an all-black town in the vicinity of Leed's Creek and Tunis Mills, was founded after the Civil War by Uncle John Copper, a favorite slave who had house privileges at the Wye Plantation, learned how to read, and made clever military plans. The land was sold to blacks, never rented. (See: Jones, "An Echo of Slave Days," *Sun* (Mag.) Nov. 19, 1978).

CORDOVA. Village on the Pennsylvania Railroad near Queen Anne, Talbot County. Cordova is on Martenet's map of 1866. The story is told that once during railroad times a *cord* of wood was left *over* here. However, that is a folk explanation, and it is far more likely that the name is from Cordoba, Spain. In 1905 there were thirteen *Cordobas* in the United States. Compare LISBON.

CORNERSVILLE. Near Hills Point, Dorchester County. In 1878 Samuel *Corner* was the postmaster here.

CORNISHTOWN. Dorchester County. Compare Cornish Pt., St. Mary's County. Probably from the family name, *Cornish*, "from Cornwall." In 1790 Anney and Sam Cornish were in Dorchester County.

COROMANDEL. Allegany County. Compare "Coromandel," the later name of "Flint Hill," Montgomery County. The name commemorates the Coromandel Coast, on the eastern seabord of India.

CORRIGANVILLE. Near Cumberland, Allegany County. Historians mention "the village of Kreigbaum (now named Corriganville)." Matthew Corrigan came to Kreigbaum in 1869. When he became the first postmaster, *Kreigbaum* was changed to *Corriganville*. See *KREIGBAUM.

CORSICA CREEK, RIVER. Between Corsica Neck and Spaniards Neck, Queen Anne's County. By legislative enactment, *Corsica Creek* was changed to Corsica River in 1886. Colonel Henry Coursey *(De Coursey)*, erstwhile Clerk of Calvert County, moved in 1660 to a tract of land on the Chester River, Queen Anne's County, as large as the space he could cover on a map with his thumb. This was "Coursys Lords Gift" or the "Thumb Grant," given to the De Coursey family in 1658 by the second Lord Baltimore. Evidently CORSICA, *COURSEYS, COURSEY POINT, DE COURCY ISLAND, etc., are all variations of the family name *De Coursey*.

Note: The De Courc(s)ey family in America originated in Calvert County. Maryland *Archives* in 1671 mention the "branches of Coursaca Creeke" near the Patuxent River. See *COURSEY'S CREEK.

COSTEN. A village near Davis Corner, Somerset County. The name is from the *Costin, Costine* family. Henry Costin (Costing) was probably in Somerset County in 1665–1668. Phone lists of 1964 give at least seven families of *Coston* in the vicinity of Pocomoke City, Snow Hill, and Girdletree.

COTTAGE CITY. Washington suburb. Near Bladensburg, Prince George's County. Simon states that Cottage City began to develop appreciably in about 1920 "when a builder began the construction of the one-story cottages that suggested the name of the community."

COTTINGHAM. A village near Corbin, Pocomoke River, Worcester County. Also known as *Cottingham Ferry*. Probably from the family name *Cottingham*, which had nine representatives in Worcester County in 1790. However, there is the possibility that the name commemorates the village of Cottingham, Northamptonshire, England.

COULBORNE. Village. Somerset County. Compare Colbourne, Wicomico County.

*COURSEY'S CREEK. Queen Anne's County. In 1658 John and William Coursey, younger sons of the Courcy family, gave their name to the present Queenstown Creek—mentioned in land records as *Coursey's Creek—and also to the neck of land between that creek and the Wye (then known as *St. Michael's). See QUEENSTOWN CREEK.

COWENTON. Village near Whitemarsh, Baltimore County. This was earlier *Whitemarsh, from Whitemarsh Run. In 1904 it was *Cowenton Sta.* The name is from the Cowen family. John K. Cowen (1844-1901) was an early president of the B. & O. Railroad.

COWENTOWN. Near Appleton, Cecil County. It was a post office in 1823-24. An earlier name was *Turkeytown. In 1790 there were five *Cowan*, 4 *Cowen*, and two *Cowin* in Maryland. The majority (six) were in Harford County.

*COWPENS. A village in Baltimore County; also "Cow Pen Creek." The village may be from "Cowpens," an estate east of Towson to which John Eager Howard gave this name to commemorate the Battle of Cowpens, in which he fought. Compare HORSEPEN BRANCH (Montgomery County; Prince George's County).

COX'S STATION. Charles County. It is on the Pennsylvania Railroad. In 1878 Samuel Cox was the postmaster, and Samuel Cox, Jr., attorney at law, lived here.

*COXTOWN. Calvert County. Henry Coix gained land in Calvert County in the 1660's; his brother Thomas settled on the Patuxent River at "Cox's Choice." When Lower Marlboro was laid out in 1683, it was first named *Cox Town* because it stood on Henry Cox's land. The name was changed to Marlboro after the victory of the Duke of Marlboro at Blenheim in 1704. See LOWER MARLBORO.

*CRABTOWN. Another name for Annapolis, Anne Arundel County. Stevens remarks that "Irreverent midshipmen spoke of the Ancient City as 'Crabtown,' an allusion to one of the important, if malodorous, sources of income."

CRAMPTON GAP. South Mountain, near Burkittsville, Frederick and Washington Counties. John E. Crampton was the postmaster here in 1834. In 1836 the postal name was changed to *Rohrersville*. Thomas Crampton, born at sea in 1735, came to Pleasant Valley, near Crampton's Gap, before 1759. The Gap is in South Mountain near Gapland. El. 930. See ROHRERSVILLE.

CRANBERRY. A village on Cranberry Creek, near Cranberry Station, Carroll County. More than a hundred years ago, when there were only a few scattered farmhouses, the newly built Western Maryland Railroad made the place "an official way point." Wild cranberries were abundant then; and the name given was *Cranberry*. Today both the station and the cranberries are gone. (See: Reppert, *Sun*, Jan. 29, 1961). Compare CRANBERRY RUN, Harford County.

CRAPO. A village near Lakes Cove, Honga River, Dorchester County. In 1866, *Woodland Town was on the present site of CRAPO, which Jones calls a "modern name." The spelling is a version of French *crapaud* "toad." A name meaning "frog" was no doubt intended. Compare Frog Point, Dorchester County, Frogeye, Somerset County, and Frogtown, Howard County. Pronunciation: CRAY-po.

CREAGERSTOWN. Four miles from Thurmont, near the Monocacy River, Frederick County. Creagerstown, known as *Crugerstown until 1819, is about one mile from the site of *Monocacy, a ghost town that flourished for more than a quarter of a century. Between 1760 and 1770 John Creager built "a new village," Creagerstown. *Monocacy began to die; Creagerstown, on one of the first crossroads, became an important stagecoach point.

Note: The postal spelling (*Cruger...*) suggests that the founder's name may have been *Cruger* (German *Krüger*).

CRELLIN. A village near Hutton, Garrett County. Crellin is mentioned in an 1860 resurvey record. For more than thirty years it was known as *Sunshine*. In the 1890's the associates of Rolland P. Crellin, a Pennsylvania capitalist, built a new sawmill here. The post office became *Crellin* in 1892. (See: *Glades Star*; see: Schloss nagle).

CREMONA. A creek and village in Mechanicsville District, St. Mary's County. In the mid-seventeenth century the creek was known as *Mud Creek. And the site of the present community was West Ashcom, granted after 1653 to John Ashcom, who came to Calvert county in 1649 from Berkshire, England. Professor Norton Dodge, who owned "Cremona" in 1972, states that it was built after the War of 1812 and finished in 1819. Dr. Thomas, the builder, fancied violins, and admired Virgil, who was educated in Cremona, Italy.

CRESAPTOWN. Near Cumberland, Allegany County. Postal history indicates that it was *Cresapburg from 1800 until 1823. And it is probably the place that was once known as *Cresap Station, near Rawlings. Here Daniel Cresap, father of Edward Cresap, of Cumberland, built a brick house. (See: FBC, p. 20).

Note: This name commemorates the family of the celebrated Colonel Thomas Cresap, whose fort and home were at *SKIPTON (now OLDTOWN), near Cumberland. His son, Daniel, gave his name to DAN'S MOUNTAIN. See OLDTOWN; see *SKIPTON.

*CRESWELL'S FERRY. Cecil County. Port Deposit, before it was incorporated in 1824, was known as *CRESWELL'S FERRY. Most of the town was built on an estate formerly owned by Col. John Creswell. The estate is still in the possession of the Creswell family. Robert Creswell was enrolled in the Virginia Company in 1620. Compare CRESWELL, near Abingdon, Harford County.

CRISFIELD. A town on Little Annemessex River, Somerset County. The tract was surveyed in 1663. The town's welcoming brochure (1966) states that Crisfield was first known as *ANNEMESSEX, and later as *SOMERS COVE. The present name is for John W. Crisfield, founder of the Eastern Shore rail system. He is said to have fallen off a gangplank into the river here during celebrations in 1866. (See: Warner, p. 277).

Note: *SOMERS COVE is from Benjamin Summer (Somer).

CROCHERON. A village on Tedious Creek, Fishing Bay, Dorchester County. Eugene Crocheron was a county commissioner after the "Constitution of 1850." In 1902 he was the postmaster. Pronunciation: CROACH-n.

CROFTON. A residential community near Bowie, Anne Arundel County (Manual 1969). Ms. Barbara Swann, Administrative Assistant at Crofton, tells me that Hamilton Crawford (now of Louisiana) completed the construction of this village in late 1964. Ms. Swann is uncertain; but it is supposed by some that *Crofton* consists of the *Crawf-* of Mr. Crawford's surname combined with *-ton*. However, since the cultural motif of the local design is plainly English, with such English street names as Shaftsbury, Swinburne, and Eton, I am inclined to attribute the origin to one of the following English Croftons: Crofton, Cumberland; C—Kent; and C—Lincolnshire.

CROMWELL. The name of places in Anne Arundel County, Frederick County, and Baltimore County. "The original settler" was Richard Cromwell, a Puritan, who was among those who were appointed to determine the boundaries of Anne Arundel and Baltimore Counties in April 1698.

Compare *Cromwell's Point, Talbot County, where the planter, Gershon Cromwell, who came to Maryland in 1653, owned a tract called "Cromwell."

CROOM, CROOM STATION. Near Upper Marlboro, Prince George's County. The will of Christopher Rousby, 1684, mentions: "... Land yt belong to me att ye head of Potuxon Riv[r] called Crome." The present Croom was named for an estate patented to Thomas Clagett, Calvert County coroner in 1789. These names memorialize Croom, County Limerick, Ireland.

Note: The station was on the Popes Creek Branch of the Baltimore and Potomac Railroad.

CROSIADORE CREEK. Near Trappe, Dickinson Bay, Talbot County. "Crosiadore" was the home of the Dickinson family from 1634 to 1959. The name, from French *Crosier d'Or*, is thought to be from the Dickinson family coat of arms; they had been on Medieval crusades. John Dickinson, Governor of Pennsylvania and founder of Dickinson College, was born here in 1732. See CHLORA Pt.

Note: A crosier was a staff resembling a shepherd's crook.

CROSS KEYS. Places by this name are found in Prince George's County and in Baltimore City. Compare "Keys Tavern," established by John White in 1717 near the Brick Meeting House, Cecil County. The name *Cross Keys*, emblematic of St. Peter and his successors, was probably brought here from England, where it was an old and common name for taverns. It is possible, however, that one or more of these names may commemorate the Civil War battle at Cross Keys, Virginia, (8 June 1862).

CROSSMORE'S SLOUGH. A tidal inlet of the Great Falls of the Gunpowder River. This is perhaps the only example of the term *slough* ("swamp") among Maryland placenames. In colonial times it was *LITTLE CREEK; until 1917 the land on both sides of the creek belonged to the Crossmore family.

Note: I seem to have overlooked RAINBARREL SLOUGH (Wo), DUNNOCK SLOUGH (D), and The SLOUGH (S), etc.

CROSS ROADS. A village near Grayton, Charles County. Compare *The Cross Roads, Crossroad District, Wicomico County, and *Cross Roads, otherwise Gravelly Hill, Harford County. There are obscure *Cross Roads* in Montgomery and Howard Counties. *Cross Roads, Washington County, appears to be more properly, *Wagners Cross Roads*, q. v.

*CROW HILL. This settlement lies between Black's Station and Chesterville, Kent County. Named many years ago, because—"from time immemorial"—crows assemble here every evening to spend the winter nights in the scattered trees. (See: Usilton, pp. 235–36).

CROWBERRY CREEK. Near Bethlehem Choptank River, Caroline County. The name indicates the presence of the crowberry, a shrub bearing black, edible, berry-like fruit. It is found in the British Isles. The name is from a German word and has no connection with *crow*.

CROWDENTOWN. Near Arbutus, Baltimore City. This name appears to commemorate the tiny village of Crowden, Yorkshire, England.

CROWNSVILLE. Near Waterbury, Anne Arundel County. It was *Crownsville* post office in 1851. In 1866 the spelling was *Cronsville*. The origin is either the lost Irish family name *Cron*, or the English family name, *Crown (Crowne)*. In 1976 the Annapolis phone book had one *Crown*, one *Crowne*. Compare Cron Island, Rhode River, Anne Arundel County.

CRUMPTON. Near Pondtown, Chester River, Queen Anne's County. In about 1708 the name was *McALLISTER'S FERRY. The present name is for William Crump, who "took up a large tract of land." (See: Hanson; see Usilton).

Note: Emory cites the Centreville *Record* (23 Sept. 1875) for the statement that Crumpton was founded in 1858 by James C. Shepperd and Maurice Welsh of Salem, N.J., who bought the entire Crumpton tract and laid out fifty or seventy-five acres in streets and building lots.

CUCKOLD CREEK. Village and stream, Potomac River, near Tompkinsville, Charles County. Compare CUCKOLD CREEK, St. Mary's County, and CUCKOLD POINT, Baltimore County. Among the tract names of Frederick County are "Cuckolds Horns," 1749, and "Cuckolds Point," 1751. In a Hall of Records deed for 1722, one finds mention of land called Cuckholds Pointe laid out for William Cockey "living in Anne Arundel County . . . on a river called Magotty . . ." George Alsop, colonial poet, wrote to his father: "Herds of deer are as numerous . . . as Cuckolds can be in London, only their horns are not so well drest and tipt with silver as theirs are." Perhaps some of Maryland's cuckold names are a humorous reference to deer.

CUMBERLAND. City on the Potomac River, near Wills Mountain, Allegany County. The fort that was begun here on July 4, 1754, was at first called "Fort Mount Pleasant." When the militia continued the work, Col. James Inness renamed it *Fort Cumberland* to honor George II's son, William Augustus, Duke of Cumberland (1721-1765). He fought at Dettingen in 1743 and at Culloden in 1746.

Note: Two years before the Assembly "erected the town under its present name" (1787) Thomas Beall had laid out "Washington Town" here. See *KING OPESSA'S TOWN; see OLDTOWN.

CUMBERSTON(E). A village near Owensville, Anne Arundel County. In the Hall of Records, Annapolis, there are these four patents for John Cumber and his son: Cumberston, 1659; Cumberston Grange, 1663; Cumber Ridge, 1664; and Cumberton, 1677. Kelly identifies John Cumber as "Captain," and states that the present name was given in 1798 when the tract on which the house stands, a part of "Cumberstone," was resurveyed. Cumber's name is also found in CUMBER CREEK.

CUNNINGHAM CROSS ROADS. It is adjacent to Crossroads, Cearfoss, Washington County. Martenet in 1866 mapped it as *Cunningham X Roads/Cearfoss*. The name is for the Cunningham family. Samuel Shields Cunningham was a merchant in Williamsport from 1825-1831. He was cashier of the Washington County National Bank until 1880. He died at Williamsport.

CUNNINGHAM FALLS, CUNNINGHAM FALLS STATE PARK. See HUNTING CREEK.

CURTIS BAY, CURTIS CREEK. The bay is in Baltimore City; the creek lies to the south in Anne Arundel County. It was mapped in 1755 as *Curtis's Creek*. Compare CURTIS POINT, near Shadyside, West River, Anne Arundel County. In 1790 there were eight *Curtis* for Baltimore County, none for Anne Arundel. The precise Curtis responsible for the name is elusive. See FURNACE CREEK.

CUSHWA(S) MILL. A village near Hicksville, Washington County. The Cushwa family was Alsatian and English, and its paternal ancestors reached Pennsylvania at the close of the 17th century. John Cushwa was at Dry Run (near Clearspring) in 1760. Capt. David Cushwa, active in the War of 1812, gained a large landed estate, "Cushwa's Establishment." His sons became business men in Hagerstown and Williamsport.

CUTMAPTICO CREEK. A tributary of the Wicomico River, Wicomico County. Pronunciation: Cut-MAP-tee-coe. An early spelling was *Cutty Mocktico*. This Indian name probably consists of three Algonquian elements, *kehtci* "big," *mehittuk* "tree," and the complex ending *ā-wi* (which became *ō*). The meaning would be "Big tree (creek)."

CYLBURN. Baltimore city suburb. On Cold Spring Lane. "Cylburn Mansion or Park" was originally known as the Cotton Estate. The tract was willed to the city to be made into a public park. In 1942 it began to be used as a children's home. In 1957—less than two miles away—the (municipal) Cylburn Home, keeping the original name, came into being. Mr. F. C. Stevens attributes the name to a manor or estate in Scotland. Pronunciation: SILL-burn.

D

DAHLGREN CHURCH. Village. Near Bolivar (Zittlestown), Frederick County. From the rare family name Dahlgren (Dahlgreen). Compare Dahlgren Hall (U.S. Naval Academy), for Admiral John A. Dahlgren.

DAMASCUS. Village. Near Purdum, Montgomery County. Elevation 875 ft. The land here is undulating, and the original land grant was "Pleasant Plains of Damascus." The name is from Damascus, Syria, and has religious significance. (Boyd, 126; Guy Jewell, Damascus).

DAMES QUARTER (town); DAMES QUARTER CREEK. Monie Bay, Somerset County. In 1670 it was spelled *Damnd Quarter*; in 1794 it appears as *DAMES QUARTER*. Although it has been suggested that the name arose from a whimsical land grant name, and even that it may have designated a region of beaver *dams*, the usual explanation, supported by the nearness of Deal (earlier *Devils*) Island, takes it as a reference to the land or quarter of the *damned*. There is a humorous but unacceptable explanation based on the report that colonial settlers, sailing past Deals Island, espied Indians running, hopping, and squatting. Later they encountered similar Indians on the Wicomico, and one settler cried: "Look! There's some more of those *damned squatters!*" See: DEAL ISLAND; see: QUARTER.

Note: The possibility that the family name *Dame(s)* is involved in this mystery should not go unnoticed,. *Archives* mentions John Dames, for 1780, and Captain Frederick Deames, for 1781. (See Reppert, *Sun*, May 1961).

DANIEL. Village, near Winfield, Carroll County. Daniel was mapped in 1909. Compare *Daniels, Howard County, a mill town scheduled for destruction in 1968, probably named for the Daniel family, although the given name, Daniel, is a possibility.

Note: *DANIELS (Howard Co.) was earlier known as **ALBERTON.

DANS MOUNTAIN (el. 2898), DANS ROCK (el. 2892). Near Midland, Allegany County. Both names are from Daniel Cresap, the son of the doughty pioneer, Colonel Thomas Cresap. The story is that here one day, while hunting with an Indian named George, Daniel Cresap killed a mother bear and climbed a tree to capture the cubs. A branch broke, and he and the cubs fell to the rock. As for the mountain, it appears that Daniel Cresap was later killed there in a gun fight with an Indian. Schaeffer narrates that the Indian, George, who accompanied Daniel, had been taken by Colonel Cresap to raise. Was he the elusive *George* of George's Creek? See CRESAPTOWN; see GEORGES CREEK; see NEGRO MOUNTAIN; see SAVAGE MOUNTAIN.

DARBY'S. Montgomery County. No doubt from Darby's *Mill* or *Store*. Heads (1790) has eight *Darby*, one *Darbey*. The Suburban Maryland Phone book for 1974–75 lists forty *Darby* (*Darbie*) in the Montgomery and Prince George's area. Compare "Darby," a 1764 tract of land given to the Indians by an Act of Assembly.

DAR. Near Freeland, Baltimore County. Dar was named for Billy Dar in about 1900. The family name, usually spelled with two *r*'s, was represented in 1790 by two entries. In the Baltimore phone book for 1969 there are twenty-two entries.

Note: My informant was the postmaster at Freeland, Nov. 29, 1974.

DARES, DARES BEACH. Chesapeake Bay, Calvert County. James Dare, a 1662 immigrant, came to Calvert County in 1670. His son, Nathaniel, obtained "Hooper's Cliffs," "Dares Addition," and other tracts.

DARLINGTON. Near Dublin, Harford County. *Darlington*, was a post office in 1819. It was changed to *Woodlawn* in 1821, and in 1853 it became *Battle Swamp*. Ruth B. Smith, postmistress at Darlington, states that a member of the Society of Friends proposed the name. It had earlier been *RED DOOR. *Darlington* is an infrequent surname in Maryland; I am inclined to attribute the Harford County name to Darlington, Durham, England.

DARNALL. Near Bristol, Anne Arundel County. In 1878 there was no such village in Anne Arundel County. However, there were the residences of F. & P. Darnall and P. Darnall Jr. Earlier, John Darnall (d. 1684) had lived at "Portland Manor," Anne Arundel County. His older brother, Col. Henry Darnall, was called ". . . of the Woodyard." "Woodyard" was a tract in Prince George's County.

DARNESTOWN. Northeast of Seneca, Montgomery County. *Darnes* was the first name. Between 1821 and 1823 it was changed to Darnestown.

William Darne, of Mountain View, at the foot of Sugar Loaf Mountain, later moved to Darnestown. He represented Montgomery County several times in the state legislature, and was a director of the C. & O. Canal.

*DASHIELL'S CREEK. On the Wicomico River, Eastern Shore. The name is from James Dashiell (1634-97), who came to the "Wicomico Section" (later Somerset County) from Virginia in 1663-64. He lived on the south side of the Wicomico River, at the mouth of Dashiell's Creek. (See: Torrence, p. 440).

Note: Wood includes James Dashiell in a list of most notable Huguenots.

DAVIDSONVILLE. Near Birdsville, Anne Arundel County. Thomas Davidson was the postmaster here in 1834. The progenitor was James Davidson, who came to Pennsylvania from England in 1775 and later served in the Maryland line under General Smallwood during the American Revolution. In the War of 1812 he was one of the "Old Defenders" at the Battle of North Point. He died at Davidsonville in 1841. (See: Warfield, p. 329).

Note: Recorded history began at Davidsonville in 1665 when Lord Baltimore granted "the Indian Range" to Robert Franklin, merchant, and Richard Beard, shipwright. Thus are explained BEARD'S CREEK and BEARD'S POINT ROAD, two places in the Davidsonville vicinity.

DAVIS, Village; also DAVIS BRANCH. Near Woodstock, Howard County. The Davis family was among the founders of Anne Arundel and Howard Counties. The family is extensive in Maryland. See Passano, pp. 88–89.

DAVIS CORNER. Near Costen, Somerset County. Lord Baltimore granted lands in Somerset County to two Davis brothers. In a list of loyal subjects in Somerset County in 1689 appear Samuel and John Davis.

*DAVISES TOWN. Anne Arundel County. An Anne Arundel patent of 1701 mentions "Davidstone," owned by Thomas Davis.

Note: "Davidstone" appears to be a jumble of *Davis* and *town*.

DAWSON. Village. Potomac River near Black Oak (Bottom) and Rawlings, Allegany County. Register 1833 gives Thomas W. Dawson as postmaster. In a list of settlers "located in lands in the country lying west of Fort Cumberland," one finds Samuel, William, Edward and Thomas Dawson.

Note: A "Captain Dawson" was awarded military lots "westward of Fort Cumberland" for service during the Revolutionary War. The grant was probably "Yough Lake Manor."

DAWSONVILLE. Four miles from Poolesville, Montgomery County. Dawsonville was a post office in 1825. *Seneca Mills* was an earlier name. In 1878 Americus, Frank, James, and Randolph Dawson, all farmers, were living here.

DAY; DAYSVILLE. (2). Day is near Woodbine, Carroll County. One Daysville is in Carroll County; the other Daysville is near Libertytown, Frederick County. The Carroll County Daysville owes its name to the Day family, represented here in 1862 by Aquila, Lloyd, and Milton Day.

DAYS POINT. Gunpowder River, Gunpowder Neck, Harford County. The name is for Edward Augustus Day (1833–1917), of "Taylors Mount." In the last half of 1800, when *Day's Island was formed during a storm, he drove a carriage and horses through the new thoroughfare. (See: Marye, 10, p. 41, p. 46).

Note: There was evidently a senior Edward Day. Marye notices that *Day's Fishery was owned by Edward Day, of "Taylor's Mount," in Nov. 1770.

*DE LA BROOKE MANOR. One authority locates it on "the middle Patuxent River"; another authority describes it as being near Oraville, "On the old Three Notch state road." The name is for Robert Brooke, of White Church, Hampshire, England. Brooke was an Oxford graduate, who in 1652 became acting governor of Maryland.

DEADMAN RUN. Western Run, near Dover, Baltimore County. The area has not been submerged. Compare *Dead Man's Hollow, Loch Raven, Baltimore County, which *has* been submerged. Notice, also, Dead Run, Baltimore County. See HOLLOW.

DEAL ISLAND. Island; village. Manokin River, Tangier Sound, Somerset County. The name is spelled *Devil's Island* in *Archives* 1783; in 1866 it is *Deil's I., Deils Island P.O.* Evidently the original *Devil's* Island became Scotch *Deil's*; today it is *Deal.* The spelling *Deal,* is probably a Post Office Department change. The area is so largely a marsh that, originally, it was perhaps thought of as being fit only for the devil. The the Scotch Irish, *Deil* may have sounded better than *Devil.* See DAMES QUARTER; see *DEVIL'S ISLAND.

Note: *Deil* is the Scotch word for "devil." Cf. Deil's Dyke, Scotland.

DEALE. Near Churchton, Anne Arundel County. On an Anne Arundel Atlas Map of 1878 on finds "J. Deale Heirs." The name appears to be from James Deale, who bought three tracts of land here in 1736. Local history mentions a public road leading from Cedar Point ". . . on the land of James Deale." Mrs. Marshall Nelker writes of Martin Deale and "Dr. James *Deale* of James" (b. 1809). (See: Nelker, *Capital,* 13 March 1969; Bisbee, *Capital,* 24 September 1979).

DE COURCY ISLAND. Wye Narrows, Wye River, Queen Anne's County. *Coursys Lords Gift* is on Herrman's Map of 1670. The name is for Henry Coursey, the recipient of "My Lord's Gift" for his loyalty to Lord Baltimore. He was one of the ancestors of the Coursey and Decourcy families of Queen Anne's County. See CORSICA RIVER; see COURSEY Pt.

DEEP CREEK. Maryland has ten *Deep Creeks.* Among the ten, it appears that Lerch Creek, Anne Arundel County, was formerly *Deep

Creek. And Deep Creek, the source of Deep Creek Lake, Garrett County, is called *Green Glades Creek* "on old maps."

DEEP CREEK LAKE. Near Oakland, Garrett County. It is "partly in McHenry, Thayerville, and Swallow Falls." The lake is the result of a hydroelectric plant and dam, built between 1923 and 1925. The impounded waters of Deep Creek, having submerged the area, flow through a tunnel in Marsh Mountain and propel two turbines. El. 2427.

DEER PARK. Village. Near Oakland, Garrett County. Deer Park was on the "Deer Park" survey of 1774. An early name was *Davis Mills*, for Henry G. Davis, who spent his summers here and had saw mills on nearby Deep Creek. The present name arose because of the early abundance of deer. Compare Elk Garden (W.Va), ten miles away.

DELAWARE RUN. A stream in the Worthington Valley, Baltimore County. In 1678 the Delaware Indians claimed the upper parts of Baltimore and Cecil Counties. It is likely that they used the Indian road that once ran towards the Potomac from the Susquehanna across Harford County and the Great Falls of the Gunpowder. This would account for DELAWARE RUN, for *Delaware Falls*, the former name of the Patapsco's South Branch, and for *Delaware Bottom* and *Delaware Hundred*.

DELMAR. A town on the Delaware-Maryland border, north of Salisbury, Wicomico County. In 1859, when the town was founded and the Delaware Railroad reached here, the locality was still a pine forest. The name is a compound of the opening syllables of *Del*aware and *Mar*yland.

DENNINGS. Near Taylorsville, Carroll County. This village was a post office in 1818. As the Register indicates, Charles Denning was an early postmaster.

DENTON. Town. Choptank River, Caroline County. Though the name was *Eden-Town* in about 1773, this place was locally known as *Pig Point* until the building of a courthouse in 1791. The present name, with the omission of *e* and the addition of *-ton*, is for Sir Robert Eden, the last royal governor of Maryland, 1769–1774. Authorities agree that the opening *e* was "diplomatically dropped" when Eden left for England soon after the American Revolution.

Note: A Caroline County deed of 1709 mentions Thomas Todd's brother, "late of Denton," Durhamshire, England. Perhaps other early Colonists were from Durhamshire. This may have influenced the change from *E*denton to *Denton*.

DENTS. See DENTSVILLE.

DENTSVILLE. East of Zekiah Swamp, Charles County. The name commemorates the early Dent family of Southern Maryland. John Dent (1645?–1712), who came to Maryland from Yorkshire, England, died in St. Mary's County. He was Captain of Chaptico Hundred; his great grandson, Reverend Hatch Dent, was a worthy officer in the American Revolution.

In 1960 "Dents Palace," near Bryantown, Charles County, was described as the ancestral home of the Dents.

Note: There is a Dent Memorial at Charlotte Hall, St. Mary's County.

DETMOLD. Village. George's Creek, near Lonaconing, Allegany County. From C. E. Detmold, who in 1846 leased an iron furnace from the George's Creek Coal and Iron Company, which had began to dig iron ore, limestone, and coal in this region as early as 1837. Detmold abandoned his furnace in 1856 and took control of what became known as the Detmold Farm. It was he who opened up the "Big Vein," later bought by the Central Coal Company, whose superintendent was Alexander Shaw. See *CENTRAL (from Central Coal Company); see SHAW.

DETOUR. Near Keymar, Carroll County. *Double Pipe Creek was the post office here in 1825. The name was changed to DETOUR because the earlier name was too long for Western Maryland Railroad timetables. And Detour was chosen perhaps because the creek and the new railroad detoured around the high places nearby, perhaps because (so the story goes) Bishop Daniel P. Sayler suggested it after seeing so many detour signs in his travels on the roads of the Middle West. The earlier name, *Double Pipe Creek, is from the stream that is formed here by the junction of Little Pipe Creek and the Big Pipe Creek. It should be considered that at this point Little Pipe Creek makes a sharp curve or detour.

*DEVIL'S DANCING GROUND, or *DEVIL'S WOODYARD. On Bush River Neck, Abby Island Creek, Harford County. Marye remarks that this old unrecorded name marks a bare spot where (traditionally) nothing will grow.

*DEVILS ISLAND. See DEAL ISLAND.

DEVIL'S ISLAND. Marye speaks of an island in Assawoman Bay called Devil's Island. See DEAL ISLAND.

DICKERSON. Baltimore and Ohio Railroad village near Barnesville, Montgomery County. W. H. Dickerson was the postmaster and general storekeeper here in 1878. N. C. Dickerson was among the farmers in the neighborhood.

Note: A member of the Dickerson family was one of the thirty-two joiners of "Chiswell's Exile Band," a group of young Montgomery County men who, at the opening of the Civil War, deserted Maryland and crossed the Potomac River to fight for the South. Another family represented was Veirs. (See: E. L. Meyer, "Faded Legacy of Montgomery County Exiles," Washington Post, 4 Sept. 1981).

DICKEYVILLE. Baltimore City suburb along the banks of Gwynns Falls. *Wetheredsville was the post office name in 1848. The village had come into existence in the 1790's as the site of a mill which the Quaker Wethered family took over in 1829 to manufacture wool. During the Civil War this mill supplied both armies; the Union Army confiscated it in 1863. Dickeyville became the name when William J. Dickey bought the land, the house, and three mills in 1871. He paid $82,000; in 1934 the entire town was sold for $42,000. See WETHEREDVILLE.

DISTRICT HEIGHTS. District of Columbia suburb near Forestville, Prince George's County. The elevation is 280 ft. Similar names in the vicinity are Bradbury Heights, Capitol Heights, Forest Heights...

DODON. Village near Birdsville, Anne Arundel County. Probably from "Dodon," a tract of land surveyed in July 1669 for Fran Stockett "... in the woods to the northward of Ann Arrundell Mann^r ..." Perhaps "Dodon" is from Dodona, an old Greek shrine sacred to Zeus.

DOLLYHYDE CREEK. A branch of Linganore Creek, near Libertytown, Frederick County. In 1839 this was the locality of the Dolly Hyde copper mine, no doubt named from the creek. Dollyhyde is a folk spelling of the Anglo-Norman family name Delahide, Delahoyde, in which -hide means "a measure of land." In Ireland this family (e.g., Roger de la Hide) settled in Dublin, Meath, and Kildare.

DORSEY. Village near Harmans, Anne Arundel County. *Dorsey's Switch Sta. existed in 1878, and at that time E. Dorsey, A. Dorsey, and Lloyd Edgar Dorsey were local residents. The stream Dorsey Branch is nearby. The first of these Maryland Dorseys was Major Edward Dorsey, who bought land on the Severn River in 1650. The early Dorseys have been called the "Dorseys of Hockley," a reference to "Hockley-in-the-Hole," near Annapolis, originally owned by Edward Dorsey and patented in 1669 to his sons, Edward, Joshua, and John. A tract of Dorsey land, called "Dorsey," was situated on *Dorsey Creek, now College Creek, Annapolis. See HOCKLEY.

*DOUBLE PIPE CREEK. A post office in 1834. See DETOUR.

DOUBS. Also DOUB and DOUB'S SWITCH. Near Adamstown, Frederick County. According to Grove "a Mr. Doub" owned a mill here, and the railroad put a switch alongside the mill for use in the shipment of flour. It was called Doub's Switch. "... About 1885 the Baltimore and Ohio Railroad established a station here and called it Doub."

*DOUGHOREGAN MANOR. Historic house and estate in Howard County five miles west of Ellicott City. It was spelled Doohoregan in 1773. Pronunciation: doe-REE-gan. The house, with a Doric portico and a Roman Catholic chapel, was built about 1727. It dominates the 10,000-acre tract granted by Lord Baltimore to his land agent, Charles Carroll, the Settler (arrival 1688). Ellen Hart Smith (Charles Carroll of Carrollton, Cambridge [Mass.], 1942) states that the original Carroll named his manors for the family estates back in Ireland—Ely O'Carroll, Litterlouna, etc. Doughoregan is said to mean "House of Kings." Manor Road is adjacent.

DOUGHOREGAN P.O. See CARROLLS MILL.

DOVER. There are two, one near Butler, Baltimore County, possibly also known as MANTUA, and the other in Talbot County. The names are probably from Dover, Kent, England. Manuals still list Dover, Talbot

County, though it is really a "vanished" Choptank River port where a courthouse planned in 1778 was never built. *BARKER'S LANDING was the early name of Dover, Talbot; today there remain "Dover Bridge," on the Choptank, and *Dover Street*, Easton.

DOWELL. A village on St. John Creek, near Appeal, Calvert County. The name refers to the Dowells, who moved from Anne Arundel County to Calvert County in the eighteenth century. In 1733 John Dowell was on the Tax List as a resident of Lyon's Creek Hundred, Calvert County. And for the same year John and Philip Dowell are listed as owning parts of "Lingan's Purchase," near Lower Marlboro.

DOWNES. Near Ridgely, Caroline County. This surname village is more than eight miles north of DOWNES LANDING (Choptank River). It appears that what is now Downes Wharf once bore the name *Indian Landing.

*DOWN'S CROSSROADS. See GALENA.

DOWNSVILLE. Near Spielman, Washington County. It was a post office near Downey Branch in 1855. The village, founded in 1852, takes its name from Grafton Downs' grandfather, Charles Downs, who died in 1857. He was district constable and a life-long Democrat.

DRAYTON. Near Spencerville, Montgomery County. It was a post office in 1852. The family name is rare: there were no *Draytons* in Maryland in 1790; there are only two in the Maryland-D.C. phone book of 1967–68. Indeed, it appears likely that the name is from an estate or manor house and commemorates *Drayton*, Buckinghamshire, or *Drayton*, Staffordshire, England.

DRY SENECA CREEK. A small branch of Seneca Creek, Montgomery County. See SENECA.

DUBLIN. Near Darlington, Harford County. It was a post office as early as 1814. The town was situated on "Arabia Petria," a tract surveyed in 1821 for Charles Carroll of Annapolis. Here in the eighteenth century a Scotch-Irish settlement stretched from Cecil County into what was then Baltimore County. The region was called "New Ireland," and abounded in Irish tract names, such as "Clarke's Demury in Antrim." An 1845 deed mentions "the Great Road to Dublin." (See: *Sun*/mag./April 29, 1962).

DUHAMEL CORNERS. Near Sudlersville, Queen Anne's County. A Duhamel genealogy mentions ". . . Dr Peter Duhamel, our earliest known ancestor in Maryland." Duhamel settled on the Eastern Shore in 1725 and was probably in Queen Anne's County in 1727. He lived at Duhamel Corners, was married in about 1730, and died before 1755.

Note: It is not certain whether Pierre or Peter Duhamel, of Duhamel Corners, and Pierre Duhamel, son of Huguenot Isaac Duhamel, were one and the same person. The latter had studied medicine in France and returned to America as a surgeon on Lafayette's staff.

DUKES.   A village near Adelina, Calvert County. There is a tradition that James Duke, the ancestor of the Duke family of Calvert County was the son of Richard Duke who came to America in 1634 and settled at St. Mary's. Though he became a member of the Council, he later returned to England, leaving his offspring behind. The final *s* of the name suggests possession, perhaps of a tavern or country store.

*DULANEY VALLEY.   A submerged village in Baltimore County. It was inundated during the construction of Loch Raven Dam. In general, the name is from the Dulaney Valley, "anciently" known as the *Valley of Jehosophat. In particular, the name is from Daniel Dulany (1685-1753), "one of the great lawyers of colonial Maryland." Dulany was born in Queen's County, Ireland, and came to America in 1703. He bought the Valley property from the Smith family. In 1745 he laid out *Frederick Town (now FREDERICK).

DUMBARTON.   Near Pikesville, Baltimore County. Compare "Dumbarton," Col. Ninian Bealls's estate in what is today Georgetown, D.C.; also "Dumbarton," near Rockland, Baltimore County, a stone house built in 1853. The name in this country commemorates Dumbarton, seaport and county town of Dumbartonshire, Scotland. Above the Scottish city lies the Rock of Dumbarton (*dun Breatuin*, "fort or hill of the Britons"). See BEALLSVILLE.

DUNDALK.   Baltimore City suburb, near St. Helena. The name arose when Henry McShane, seeking a name for the railroad siding at his bell foundry, chose *Dundalk*, in memory of his birthplace on Dundalk Bay, off the Irish coast. Several other places in the Baltimore Dundalk area have names from Dundalk, Ireland. An example is *St. Helena*, which comes from the name of a park in the center of Dundalk, Ireland. (See: Greenbury series).

DUNKIRK.   Near Chaneyville, Calvert County. The name is from "Dunkirk," one of the landed estates of lawyer William Groome (about 1661). He was counsellor for most of the English merchants who did business with Calvert County planters. See "Smithville."

DURBUROW MILL.   Village Near Little Antietam Creek, Leitersburg, Washington County. The alternate name, ". . . Winter Mill," is from Daniel Winter, the father-in-law of Isaac H. Durboraw (1796-1873). The latter was born in Franklin County, Pennsylvania, and came to the Leitersburg vicinity to take charge of "the Longmeadows or Martin's School." Later he became a farmer and also owned and operated the "Winter or Durboraw mill."

E

EAGLE HARBOR.   Near Aquasco, Prince George's County. Greene states that Eagle Harbor was incorporated in 1929, ". . . with provisions for a complete town organization." The area is about two miles west of the

Patuxent River, where there were probably eagles. However, there is the possibility of an origin from the family name *Eagle*.

EAKLES MILL(S). Village. Antietam Creek, near Keedysville, Washington County. Lewis in 1878 gives Martin Eakle as postmaster, and describes Martin Eakle and H. M. R. Eakle as local millers.

EARLEIGH HEIGHTS. A village near Pasadena, Anne Arundel County (elevation 70 ft). It was a post office in 1904. The name is from the variable family name, *Early (Earley, Erleigh, Erley)*. Compare *Earley*, Berkshire County, England.

EASTON. On the Tred Avon River, Talbot County. A post office in 1789. Easton was at first the hamlet, *Pitts Bridge. In 1778 it was *Talbot Town, the county seat; in 1789 it became *Easton*. Although Easton has been spoken of as being "easterly of St. Michaels," and even as being the "East Capital of Maryland," the best authorities attribute the name to Easton, Somersetshire, England, the county in which one finds the Welsh river *Avon*. See TRED AVON.

EASTPORT. The southeastern part of Annapolis, Anne Arundel County. During the War of 1812, Fort Horn, from Congressman Van Horn, stood here; and the community's first name was *Horn Point. In 1887 the name *Severn City* came and went; and in 1888, when a post office was sought, *Horn Point* permanently became EASTPORT. The name is from Eastport, Maine, the hometown of Charles Murphy, who in 1893 retired from the U.S. Navy and bought and developed Annapolis real estate.

ECKHART (ECKHART MINES). Village. Near Frostburg, Allegany County. In 1852 this was *Eckart's Mines*, on the Eckart Rail Road. *Eckhart District* was laid out in 1889. The name is from the Eckhart family, John, George, and Adam Eckhart, who had Military Lots in Western Maryland in 1788. In 1968 Charles F. *Eckhart* lived here.

EDEN. Village. Northeast of Loretto, Somerset County. This name, like Eden Street, Baltimore, probably commemorates Governor Robert *Eden*, who arrived in the province in 1769 and departed "under a flag of truce" in June, 1776. When Somerset and Worcester Schools were united in 1770 they were named *Eden School* in Governor Eden's honor. See DENTON.

EDESVILLE. Near Rock Hall, Kent County. This was *Edesville P.O.* in 1866. Forks in the road here probably account for the earlier name, *Forktown. The name is from the family name *Ede(s)*. In 1790 there were 3 *Eads*, 1 *Eades*, and 1 *Edes*. This rare surname is probably a pet form of *Edith*.

EDGEWOOD. Village. Near Van Bibber, Harford County. It was *Edgwood Sta.* in 1866. The U.S. Army Arsenal is a half mile south. Perhaps the village was thought of as being at the *edge* of the 10,000-acre "domain" of the late General Cadwallader.

EDMONSTON. Village. Near Bladensburg, Prince George's County. Compare the prominent Edmonston family. One of Ninian Beall's daughters married an Edmonston; Archibald Edmonston, a distinguished Prince George's juryman in 1697, was one of Beall's kinsmen. The present place involves the old historic *Edmonston Road,* whose name is from a prominent Baltimore resident.

EDNOR.   Village. Near Ashton, Montgomery County. The name is for *Edna,* the eight-year-old niece of Dr. Francis Thomas, who had a home and store here and became the first postmaster. To explain the *-r* at the end of the name, it has been suggested that the postal officers misread the handwriting, or that there was already a post office in Maryland called *Edna.* However, a final superfluous *-r* is often heard in some American dialects. Ednor post office closed in 1959.

EDWIN.   Community? Near Manokin, Somerset County. In July 1966 a farmer here explained to me that EDWIN is "Just a name on the map."

EKLO.   Village. Near Dar, Baltimore County. It was named in 1892 and appears again in 1979–80.

ELDERSBURG.   Near Sykesville, Carroll County. Welch's Tavern was an early landmark; John Elder, an owner of much land here, laid out the town before 1800.

Note: See Sr. Louise Donnelly (of Springfield, Va.), "The Maryland Elder Family and Kin," N & N, *MHM,* May–June, 1976.

ELDORADO.   Near Marshyhope Creek and Brookview, Dorchester County. The present name is from the name of ". . . the former Becky Taylor farm, owned in 1955 by Mr. and Mrs. Willis Brinsfield, Sr." Pronunciation: El-do-RAY-do.

ELIOAK.   Village. Near Columbia, Howard County. Carrolls Mills, Doughoregan P.O., and Doughoregan Manor are nearby. But it is perhaps more important that the Dorsey family was in this vicinity before 1700. The name is probably from a manorial estate. There was a tract, "The Isle of Ely," there was a tract "Ely O'Carroll"; and Owen Dorsey had built a large brick house at Elioak. The *Eli-* of the name is from Ely, Cambridgeshire, England. The *-oak* may be descriptive or it may stand for the *O'C* of a Celtic surname (perhaps *O'Carroll*). See DOUGHOREGAN.

*ELIZABETH-TOWN.   See HAGERSTOWN.

ELK MILLS.   A village on Big Elk Creek, Cecil County. In about 1775 this was Elk Forge, with two forges and eighteen slaves. Later it was the site of the Elk Mills Cotton Factory. The *Elk* of the name refers to Big Elk Creek.

ELK NECK.   A village on the Neck between Northeast and Elk Rivers, Cecil County. It was a post office in 1853. Compare "Elk Neck," Harford County, which was laid out in 1663 for John Collett.

ELK RIDGE.   This name describes a ridge that begins at the Potomac River, Washington County, and runs northwest for about nine miles. The name indicates the former abundance of elks.

ELKRIDGE. A village on the Patapsco River, near Relay, Howard County. It was a post office in 1815. This was the locality of *Elkridge Landing P.O.* in 1866. The name is from a spiny, thickly-wooded ridge that runs twenty miles north from the Annapolis region and turns sharply east to the valley of the Patapsco.

*ELKRIDGE LANDING. Baltimore County. A colonial shipping point. See above.

ELK RIVER. A branch of the Chesapeake Bay, Cecil County. It is mentioned as early as 1652. The colonial spelling was Elke.... Evidently there was once an abundance of elks. See: ELKTON.

ELKTON. Town. At the head of the Elk River, Cecil County. The land tract here was patented in 1681 as "Friendship," and the first name of the village was *Head of Elk. It became Elkton by an Act of the Legislature in 1787, though for several years *Elktown* persisted.

The original name, *Head of Elk, has counterparts, such as "Head of Chester," *Head of Sassafras, and *Head of Severn. In each case *head* refers to the geographical head of the stream mentioned. Thus *Head of Elk* refers to the head of the Elk *River* and not to the erroneous idea of an elk's head shaped (in appearance) by the junction of Big Elk Creek and Little Elk Creek to form the Elk River.

Maryland's *elk* names show that the state once had great herds of elks in its woods. In 1832 a few elks remained in Pennsylvania. In 1852 a small herd of elks was hunted in Elk County, Pa.

ELLENGOWAN. This is the less well-known name of TEXAS, a village twelve miles north of Baltimore. Before 1850 the post office was *Taylor Hall.* In 1866 it was *Texas* or *Ellengowan P.O.* The name appears to be a compound of *Ellen* and the Irish family name *Gowan (Gowen, Gowans).* Pronunciation: *Ellen-GOW-an.* See TEXAS.

ELLERSLIE. A village five miles north of Cumberland, Allegany County. The post office here was established in 1868. The name is from Elderslie, Renfrewshire, Scotland, the birthplace of the wife of Judge Buchanan, a resident here. Elderslie, Scotland, was also the birthplace of Sir William Wallace, Scotch national hero. Compare Ellerslie, Georgia, named in 1828 for Elderslie, Scotland. The American spelling, without *d*, indicates the true folk pronunciation. The Scotch name was *Ellirsly* in 1499.

ELLICOTT CITY. On the Patapsco River, Howard County, three miles west of Catonsville. Earlier names in 1797 were *Ellicotts Mills, *Ellicotts Lower Mills. The present name is from John, Joseph, and Andrew Ellicott, who bought water rights here in 1774 and transported their milling machinery from Philadelphia to Elkridge Landing. Andrew Ellicott, Sr., a Quaker, founded the family. He had emigrated in 1730 from Devonshire, England, to Bucks County, Pa.

ELSIO. Village. Baltimore County. Perhaps it is from a given name (Elsa? Elsie?); perhaps it is from a surname (Elza, Elzey). The Baltimore phone book for 1969 lists 3 *Elsey*, 7 *Elza*, 6 *Elzey*. Truitt mentions Luther Elzey, a Laurel /Md./ horticulturist.

EMMERTSVILLE. Near Tilghmantown and Fairplay, Washington County. In 1866, near this site, were *Fair Play* and *Downsville P.O.* Ezra D. Emmert, the son of Daniel Emmert, was born in West Virginia and went to Fairplay when he was a boy. Ezra Emmert's son, William Edgar, was born at Fairplay in 1866. He became a Downsville farmer. The name of the village is probably from this family.

EMMITSBURG. A town on Toms Creek, Frederick County. It was a post office in 1800. In 1795 *Emmits Mill was near here. And it appears that *Silver Fancy* and *Poplar Fields* were early names. Helman attributes the present name to Samuel Emmit, an Irish emigrant who patented land here in May 1757 and laid out the town in August 1785.

Note: On a back road in the Catoctin National Park there is a milestone inscribed "10 mi to AMMITS TOWN." The reference is to *Emmitsburg* and indicates not only that one early pronunciation of *Emmit-* was *Ammit-*, but also that the place was once known locally as a *-town*...

EMORY GROVE. A village near Reisterstown, Baltimore County. This was the site of the Emory Grove Camp Ground, a Methodist institution, where the celebrated Billy Sunday once preached. The first Camp Meeting was at nearby Glyndon in August 1868. The name commemorates Bishop John Emory, of the Methodist Episcopal Church.

Note: Compare *Emory Grove*, a low-income black community in about 1967, near Gaithersburg, Montgomery County.

ENGLE MILLS. Village near Accident, Garrett County. In 1878 Samuel Engle was a miller here.

ENGLISH CONSUL. Village near Lansdowne, Baltimore County. In 1948 Baltimore City had an *English Consul Avenue*. The name is from the British Consul, Will Dawson, who came to Baltimore in 1816.

ENNALLS. Near Hurlock, Dorchester County. There are also Ennall's Mission, Ennalls Spring(s), Ennalls Station, Ennalls Wharf. These names are for Bartholomew Ennalls, of York County, Virginia, who transported ten people from Virginia to Maryland, and had tracts of land surveyed for him and his son, Thomas, in 1672. In January 1668 Ennalls had bought land on Transquaking Creek. In 1676 he became Commissioner or County Justice in Dorchester. He died in March 1688.

ERNSTVILLE. Near Big Pool, Washington County. John G. Ernst (b. Germany, ca. 1803) and John Ernst (b. Wurtemberg, Germany, 1820) had farms at Clearspring, about five miles from Ernstville, before the Civil War. John G. Ernst settled near Smithburg and made shoes; his son, Joseph Ernst, became Commissioner of Washington County in 1899. John Ernst of Wurtemberg died in Clearspring District in 1864. His son became a cabinet maker. *Ernst*ville commemorates these families.

EVITTS CREEK. A tributary of the North Branch of the Potomac River, near Cumberland, Allegany County. According to Footner the first white settler here was one Evart (d. ca. 1750), who lived in a secluded cabin on a nearby mountain. His name, changed a little by the folk, is today seen in *Evitts Creek*, *Evitts Creek*, a village, and *Evitts Mountain*.

EVNA. Village west of Hereford, Baltimore County. Perhaps it is from a female given name. As a placename it is most rare, with no U.S. post offices at all.

EWINGVILLE. North of Church Hill, near Foreman Branch, Queen Anne's County. The Kent and Queen Anne phone book for 1963 lists nine *Ewing*.

*EWING(S)VILLE. In Cecil County. Ewingsville was a post office as early as 1824. The 1834 Register gives James *Ewing* as postmaster.

F

FAIRBANK. Village. Near Avalon, Tilghman Island, Talbot County. Evalyn Fairbanks Lednam, postmistress at Tilghman, tells me that Edward Ned Fairbanks (1792–1863) was given the land that is now called *Fairbank* as "bounty land" for fighting in the War of 1812. It has been known as *Fairbank* since 1848.

FAIRFIELD. A Montgomery County community on Washington, D.C.'s New Hampshire Avenue extended. The name reflects "Fairfield," a rugged stone and clapboard house built in 1856 by Edward Peirce, a "birthright Quaker." (See: Martha Nesbitt, "To Fairfield with Love ... ," *MHM*, 79:1,1975).

FAIRHAVEN. A village near Nutwell, Anne Arundel County. So named because it is a *fair haven* on Herring Bay.

FAIR HILL. A village near Andora, Cecil County. Postal history indicates that in 1823 this place was *Fairhill Cross Roads*. Later it became the post office *Fayette*. The present name denotes a pleasant elevation, which in reality is 385 feet. Nearby are Cedar Hill, Cherry Hill, Egg Hill, and Pleasant Hill.

FAIRLEE. A village on Fairlee Creek, near Georgetown, Kent County. It *Farlo* on Herrman's map of 1670; Scisco mentions "... Farlo Cr, now called Farley on Fairlee Creek." A tract "Fairlee" was occupied in 1659; "Fairlee Manor" was created in 1674. The name may be from the family name Farlow (Varlow, Fairlaw, Fairley), or it may simply be "fair lea or meadow."

FAIRMOUNT. A Somerset County village near Fairmount Neck, Potato Neck, Upper Fairmount, and Upper Hill. *Jamestown* was the earlier name of Upper Fairmount; Potato Neck is sometimes called Fairmount Neck. Upper Hill and Upper Fairmount are on approximately the same tract. Evidently there is the idea of a mount or hill. However, the elevation here is only about 5 feet, and an explanation of the name is elusive. Fairmount may be a fair mount in contrast to adjacent Flatland Marsh; or indeed the name may be ironical in the sense that SOLDIERS DELIGHT and PINCUSHION ROAD are ironical.

Note: Some Eastern Shore folk wrongly attribute *Fairmount* to the phrase "a fair amount," said in regard to the sale of a local farm.

FAIRVIEW.   Village.   Two miles from Frederick, Frederick County. This is probably the village Oliver Wendell Holmes had in mind when, going to Frederick during the Civil War to find his wounded son, he wrote: "In approaching Frederick, the singular beauty of its cluster spires struck me very much, so that I was not surprised to find 'Fair—View' laid down about this point on a railroad map."

FAITH SCHOOL.   A village near Dry Run, Washington County. The name apparently relates to the family of Joseph Faith, who emigrated to Baltimore, and later to Ellicott City, from a "Rhineland Province." One of his fourteen children, William Faith, was a wheelwright and carriage builder in 1882.

FALLSTON.   A village near Bagley, less than two miles from Little Gunpowder Falls, Harford County. The post office "White House" was changed to "Fallston" in 1849. The nearness of Gunpowder Falls probably accounts for the name. This becomes more evident when one notices that at the "Western end" of Fallston is the Little Falls Meeting House. See UPPER FALLS.

FARMINGTON.   Southeast of Rising Sun, Cecil County. Farmington was a post office in 1831. Later postal names were "Principio" and "College Green." College Green is about a mile southeast; Principio Creek begins just south of Farmington. The name may mean merely "Farming town." Compare, however, Farmington River, Connecticut, which has been ascribed to Farmington, Gloucestershire, England.

FAULKNER.   Village near Bel Alton, Charles County. In 1906 this was *Lothair Sta.* or *Faulkner P.O.* on the Pa. Railroad's branch to Pope's Creek. *Lothair* may have a literary origin; compare Lothair, the hero of Disraeli's *Lothair*. *Faulkner*, variously spelled, is a frequent family name in Maryland. Kuethe found *"Forkner's Mill"* on the present Faulkner Branch, Caroline County.

FEDERAL HILL.   A village north of Jarrettsville, Harford County. It was a post office in 1843. The elevation here is 591 feet. Nearby are Chrome Hill, Cherry Hill, and Chestnut Hill. Compare Federal Hill, Baltimore, which was named from the first recorded celebration, in 1788, of Maryland's ratification of the U. S. Constitution. Cf. Federal Hill (el. 2106 ft.), Garrett County. (See: *Sun*, 29 April 1970).

FEDERALSBURG.   A town on Marshyhope Creek, Caroline County. An earlier name, *Northwest Fork Bridge*, suggests that Marshyhope

Creek was thought of as the northwest fork of the Nanticoke River. The town developed around a general store opened by Clonsberry Jones in 1789. The name was changed to *Federalsburg* in 1812 when a mass meeting of the Federalist Party was held here.

FENWICK. A village near Sligo, Montgomery County. The name probably commemorates the Southern Maryland Fenwick Family, founded by Cuthbert Fenwick (1614- ca 1654), who was active in the provincial legislature and became the first "Lord" of Fenwick Manor. Montgomery County produced a Father Fenwick, who in 1821 became Bishop of Cincinnati. Compare Fenwick Lane, Silver Spring.

FERRY NECK. A neck between the Choptank and Tred Avon Rivers, Talbot County. Here there was once a ferry between Talbot County and Cambridge. Compare Ferry Bay, Talbot, Ferry Creek, Dorchester, Ferry Farms and adjacent Ferry Point, Anne Arundel, Ferry Landing, Calvert, and several other Ferry Points. The names probably commemorate bygone ferries. However, *Ferry* can also be a family name.

FIDDLESBURG. Near Hagerstown, Washington County. The Guide attributes this name to "a group of itinerant fiddlers who in early days played at all social affairs in this section." The community referred to as "Fiddlersburg, old-fashioned village," appears to be the same place as *Fiddlesburg*.

FINKSBURG. A Carroll County village near Sandyville. The name may be from Charles E. *Fink*, one of the incorporators of the Western Maryland Telephone Co. of Carroll County. (See: *Warner et al.*, p. 52).

FINZEL. A village near Little Savage Mountain, "Cranberry Swamp," Garrett County. Ruth Finzel Buckley, of Cumberland, tells me that Finzel was named for her great-grandfather, John George Finzel, who was born in Germany in 1812. He came to America with his wife, Margaret Wittig Finzel, before the Civil War. Later he fought with the Union Forces.

FISHTOWN. In the hollow north of Pikesville, Baltimore County. It is not in the 1904 Gazetteer; in 1909 the Baltimore trolley cars on the Pikesville line stopped here. To explain the name there are these conjectures: (1) a load of fresh fish was upset here—the fish spoiled in the sun and gave rise to "Fishtown"; (2) the "fishmen" who came here by trolley gave away their unsold fish at the end of the line; (3) Fishtown was journey's end for a walking fish peddler named Al; (4) in the 1900's a walking "basket man" cam here once a week to sell crabs in the summer, oysters in the winter. (Credits: Hope Burroughs, Baltimore Co. Public Library, Pikesville; Beryl Frank, Northwest *Star*, May 4, 1978).

FLINTSTONE. Village on Flintstone Creek, near Gilpin, Allegany County. Christopher Gist mentions Flintstone Creek in his journal of 1750. Some say that it was named from "the abundance of Indian flint-stones found in that locality." Ralph Reppert favors the explanation that the name is from a large stone of dark, waxy flint, which was destroyed in 1958, when parts of U. S. Route 40 were relocated. (See: *Sun* (Mag), 23 April 1961).

FLORENCE. Village near Lisbon, Howard County. Warfield noting that Florence was named by Gassaway Watkins Warfield, remarks that he was present when the name was given but "cannot remember the favorite lady thus honored." John Dorsey states that the first store, made of logs, was built here in about 1855. Dorsey's authority declares: ". . . Florence was named after a girl who lived around here, but who she was and when she lived I don't know." (See: *Sun* (Mag), 8 September 1963).

*FORDS STORE. Village in Queen Anne's County. In 1878 H. B. Ford was the postmaster here, and William Lloyd Ford was a local farmer. See GRASONVILLE.

FOREST. Maryland has such villages as FOREST GLEN, Montgomery, FOREST SCHOOL, Frederick, FORESTON, Baltimore, and FORESTVILLE, Prince George's. In addition there are *23* other *forest* names. Most of the "forest" villages arose in the mid-nineteenth century. The names of later ones are often owing to the real estate developer. Maryland's forests are not extensive, and Marye calls it a "popular fallacy" to suppose that primeval Maryland and Virginia were covered with "vigorous and unbroken forests."

FOREST GLEN. A Washington suburb near Kensington, Montgomery County. The elevation is 300 feet, and in the area are small hills. Tradition relates that this was once a trading post on an Indian path. The land is part of a grant made in 1680 to an ancestor of Archbishop John Carroll. Here was the home of Daniel Carroll, a cousin of Charles Carroll of Carrollton.

FOREST HEIGHTS. Village. Near Washington, in Prince George's County. Forest Heights was part of an original land grant made in 1667 to John Addison. The town was named in 1941 by Southern Maryland Homes, Inc., a real estate concern. The situation is on a hill-side above the Potomac River and was once heavily wooded.

FORESTVILLE. A Washington suburb near Meadows, Prince George's County. Postal history uses the spelling *Forrestville*; and until 1854 it had the post office name, "Long Old Fields." The early spelling with two *r*'s suggests that the name may be from the family name *Forrest*.

Note: W. H. Babcock (JAF-L, 1:146–47, July–Sept. 1888) deplores the change of *Long Old Fields* to *Forestville*. The former, he says, was for generations the spot of long old fields, an item of local history. *Forestville*, on the other hand, is cheap, jerky, and conventional. "Now it is Forestville and Commemorates nothing." Babcock speaks, however, of "the fertile forest of Prince George."

FORT ARMISTEAD. A park on the Patapsco River near Solley, Anne Arundel County. The name is in honor of Major George Armistead (1780–1818), U. S. Artillery, who commanded Ft. McHenry during the

British attack on Baltimore in September 1814. (See: McWilliams, *Capital*, March 16, 1978).

FORT (George G.) MEADE. Village. Near Jessup, Anne Arundel County, mapped in 1907 as *Fort George G. Meade Military Reservation*. This place has been called *Camp Meade* and also *Camp Leonard Wood*. Camp Meade was first organized in 1917, for World War I, and it was rebuilt later for World War II. *Camp Leonard Wood* was named for the Major General (1860–1927) who held troop-training assignments in W. W. I; he had earlier helped to recruit "the Rough Riders." The present name is for Major General George Gordon Meade (1815–1872), whose troops defeated Lee at the Battle of Gettysburg.

Note: An item in the *Capital* (Jan. 18, 1982) mentions a 72-year-old person who was born "at Admiral, Md., the site of Fort George G. Meade..."

FORT WASHINGTON. Village. Ten miles below Washington on the Potomac River, Prince George's County. An earlier name was *Fort Warburton, for "Warburton Manor," 1667. George Washington chose the site for this fort in 1794 when construction of a fort on the Potomac was being discussed. It was the earliest fortification built for the defense of the national capital. Two forts were built. The first stood five years. The new fort was finished in 1824, it was abandoned in 1872. The village takes its name from the fort.

FOUNTAIN. In 1941 Maryland had FOUNTAIN, Frederick, FOUNTAIN GREEN, Harford, FOUNTAIN MILL(S), Frederick, FOUNTAIN ROCK, Frederick, FOUNTAIN ROCK SCHOOL, Washington, FOUNTAIN VALLEY, Carroll, and FOUNTAINDALE SCHOOL, Washington. *Fountain* in these names probably means *spring*. History relates that FOUNTAIN ROCK SCHOOL, Washington County, takes its name from Samuel Ringgold's mansion, "Fountain Rock." The mansion, in turn, was named from a spring that gushed from beneath a rock near the house. Compare "Fountain Inn," Baltimore County, whose name is from a pictorial signboard, showing a spouting fountain.

FOUR CORNERS. Village. At an important crossroads, below Burnt Mills, Montgomery County. It is on Martenet's maps, 1866. Manual 1962 also lists a "Four Corners" (2) in Anne Arundel and in Caroline Counties.

FOWBLESBURG. Village. South of Arcadia and Upperco P.O., Baltimore County. Davidson mentions tollgates here, a stone tavern kept by a "Mr. Fowble," and "great-grandfather Fowble," who donated the land in the community over which the Western Maryland Railroad was built. The railroad station and post office were named for him. Pronunciation: *FABBELS-burg*.

FOXVILLE. Near Lantz and Smithsburg, Catoctin Mt., Frederick County. It was a post office in 1834. *Fox* here is evidently from the family name. Living here in 1878 were George H. *Fox*, Justice of the Peace; George L. *Fox*, timber merchant; Thomas C. *Fox*, general merchandise; and six farmers named *Fox*.

FRANKLIN. Village. George's Creek, near Westernport, Allegany County. It was a post office in 1834. Franklin Mines flourished in 1866. At that time the "Franklin Coal Company" was active in the great coal beds here. The name of the village is probably from this company. It in turn may commemorate Benjamin Franklin.

FRANKLIN MANOR ON THE BAY. Anne Arundel County community near Annapolis. It is *Franklin Manor* in Manual 1947. I have heard the unlikely story that descendants of Benjamin Franklin lived here. Not a "true" manor.

FRANKLINVILLE. On the Little Gunpowder River, northeast of Upper Falls, Baltimore County. Postal history relates that "Jerusalem Mills," Harford County, became "Franklinville" in 1841 and was "changed back" to "Jerusalem Mills" in 1842. Cotton mills were built here in 1826; in 1857 there were the "Franklinville Iron Works."

*FRANKVILLE. In Garrett County, nine miles from Westernport. It was a post office in 1852, and in 1941 it was still a Baltimore and Ohio Railroad station. Governor Francis Thomas, of Maryland, retired here, but the dates of his administration (1823-1876) seem to make it unlikely that the *Frank* of *Frankville* is from the *Francis* of Governor Thomas's name. (See: Piedmont (W.Va.) *Herald*, 26 July 1972).

FREDERICK. A city near the Monocacy River, Frederick County. In 1792 it was *Fredericktown*. Daniel Dulany, land speculator, laid out Frederick in 1745; it was incorporated in 1817. Most historians attribute the name to the sixth Lord Baltimore, Frederick Calvert, son of Charles Calvert. Delaplaine, however, suggests that the name is for Lord Baltimore's friend, Frederick, Prince of Wales. Lord Baltimore VI was fourteen when Frederick was laid out.

FREDERICK COUNTY. The county was formed in 1748 from portions of Prince George's, Anne Arundel, and Baltimore Counties, and originally included the whole territory north and west of these counties. The name is usually attributed to Frederick, heir apparent. But Delaplaine thinks that the name could be from Frederick, Prince of Wales.

FREDERICKTOWN. On the Sassafras River, opposite Georgetown, Cecil County. Both towns are mentioned in a clergyman's journal, 1759. Early names were *Pennington's Point* or *Happy Harbor*. The present name is for Frederick, brother of King George III. See GEORGETOWN.

FREEDOM. Village. Near Eldersburg, Carroll County. It was a post office in 1818. This village is on the Liberty Road, which today—beginning in Frederick—passes through Libertytown and finally becomes Liberty Heights Avenue, Baltimore City. Freedom, Libertytown, and Liberty Heights Avenue reflect the name of the road. However, Warner et al. attributes *Freedom* to the manner in which lots here were originally sold. For each lot purchased, the buyer was given an adjoining lot free. See LIBERTYTOWN.

FREELAND. Near the Pennsylvania border, Baltimore County. The Baltimore telephone directory of 1969 lists fifty-three *Freelands*. The family probably originated in Southern Maryland, where Quaker Robert Freeland settled on the Upper Cliffs, Calvert County, in 1659.

FREETOWN. A rural black community near Pasadena, Anne Arundel County. It is hard to tell whether Freetown originated before or after the establishment of the federal post-Civil War Freedmen's Bureau—which began in 1865 and continued its educational activities until 1872. However, Mr. Sherman T. Bouyer, of Freetown Road, estimating the population to be about 153 families, assures me that the name arose because the people here were never slaves. See: *UPPER FREETOWN (Som. Co.).

*FRENCHTOWN. On the Elk River, opposite Scotland, Cecil County. This place was once *Transtown, established by Swedes in the late 1600's. Between 1827 and 1858 it was the terminus of the pioneer Frenchtown and Newcastle Railroad. An early traveller mentions the name La Ville Francaise." This and the present name are usually attributed to the French Acadian refugees of 1755.

Note: A boatload of Acadian refugees gave rise to "Frenchtown," a Baltimore City neighborhood that bore this name for a century.

FRENCHTOWN. A village on the Susquehanna River near Perryville, Cecil County. It is in the 1904 Gazetteer. Perhaps the name is from the family name, *French*. In 1790 there were two *French's* in Cecil County.

FRENCH WOMAN'S BRANCH. A branch of Tuckahoe Creek, Queen Anne's County. It is mentioned in the 1729 Vestry Records of St. Paul's Parish. The name suggests the French presence.

FRIENDSHIP. A village near Fair Haven, Anne Arundel County. It was founded in 1804 and has had the earlier name, *GREENHEAD. The name is explained by the experience of Eli Towne, who preached here in 1807. He became ill after the sermon and spent the night lying on the floor of the meeting house. He was treated kindly during the night and awoke next morning feeling much better. This hospitality pleased Rev. Towne, and he proposed a new name, *Friendship*. There were already communities of Friends in this region.

Note: A different version of the story is that Rev. Towne had been severely beaten by a local drunkard, and became ill in the middle of his sermon. (See: Constable, *Capital*, Oct. 27, 1974).

FRIENDSVILLE. Near *Selbysport, Youghiogheny River, Garrett County. In 1832 the post office "Friends" was changed to "Friendsville."

Tradition relates that there was a Shawnee Indian village on the Youghiogheny River here in 1764. At that time John Friend and his brother arrived from the Potomac. Within a year they bought the Indian claim to the land. John Friend (1732-1803) was Garrett County's first settler.

Note: See: "A gentle man fears for the future," *Capital*, Sept. 20, 1983, in which James Augustine Ross, presently of Friendsville, is described as "a sixth generation descendant of John Friend, the wandering Swede who was the first white man to settle among the Shawnee Indians in what became Garrett County ..." Ross fears the destruction of Western Maryland's wildlife. He sees fewer snakes, for instance, probably owing to pesticides. And he grieves about strip mining.

FRIZZELLBURG. Near Fountain Valley, Carroll County. Daniel Smith built a house here before 1800. In 1814 Nimrod Frizzell moved here and opened a blacksmith shop, an inn, and a general store. Frizzell was active in local affairs and the village became known as "Frizzells." (See: Reppert, *Sun* (Mag), 26 Nov. 1961).

FROGEYE. Village. Near Rehoboth, Somerset County. Pocomoke River and Marumsco Creek are nearby. Frogs abound in this region. Elmer Brittingham calls this a "nickname." Compare *Frogtown*, near Forest Hill, Harford County.

FROSTBURG. Town west of Cumberland, Allegany County. Early names were *Mt. Pleasant* (el. 1919 ft.) and *Frost's Town*. The name of Josiah Frost appears in a list of settlers of Military Lots surveyed for the state in 1788 by Francis Deakins. However, the name of the town is from Meshach and Catherine Frost, who opened a tavern here in 1812.

FRUITLAND. Village near Salisbury, Wicomico County. This was the post office of *Forktown* in 1840. The present name arose in 1867 when the railroad reached here. *Forktown* was perhaps owing to a *fork* in the road. The original fruit of the place was strawberries. With the presence of the railroad, the village became a canning and shipping center.

*FUNKSTOWN or *HAMBURG, once occupying the present site of Washington, D.C. Tradition states that Henry Funk established this place, known also as the "old town." It failed to develop because of the nearness and growth of Daniel Carroll's establishment, "Carrollsburg." Henry Funk is said to have removed to Washington County. See FUNKSTOWN.

FUNKSTOWN. On Antietam Creek, southeast of Hagerstown, Washington County. The first name of this place was *Jerusalem; but it was Funkstown post office in 1816. The Guide attributes the present name to Henry Funk, formerly of *Funkstown—*Hamburg. He was granted land

Note: See: "Funkstown abounds in antiques, history," *Capital* Nov. 24, 1982. In July 1863, preparations were made here for the bloody battle of Antietam. Today the town does "a vibrant antiques business."

by Frederick Calvert in 1754. Others assign the name to Jacob Funk, who built a mill here before 1768.

FURNACE. Village on Nassawango Creek, near the Wicomico River, Worcester County. An earlier name was *Furnace Mills. This is the site of an early furnace for smelting iron. BOXIRON, from "bog iron," is about twelve miles away.

Note: Compare FURNACE BRANCH, near Glen Burnie, Anne Arundel County. It is the site of an early furnace and ironworks.

G

GAITHERSBURG. Town, northwest of Rockville, Montgomery County. The name reflects the *Gaither* family, whose members here were abundant. Greenbury Gaither was among seventeen members of the first grand jury, 1777, and Henry Gather was a member of the court in 1778. The first will probated when Montgomery County's Orphans Court was set up was that of Edward Gaither, 1777. Benjamin Gather had "Gather's Choice" surveyed in 1781. B. Gaither and W. R. Gather were farmers here when the population was only 200.

GALENA. Town near Massey, Kent County. In 1789 this was *Georgetown Cross Roads. Another early name was *Down's Crossroads, from William Down's tavern. The present name is from a small deposit of galena, a sulphide of lead. The ore was being mined in about 1813; and a Baltimore writer states that it was brought to Philadelphia and made into knee buckles, spoons, and casters.

GALESTOWN. Near Eldorado, at the mouth of Gales Creek, Dorchester County. In 1790 George Gale was living in Dorchester County. Robert Marine, interviewed in this vicinity in 1966, mentioned "... a certain Dr. Gales." The correct spelling of the surname may be *Gale* not *Gales*.

GALESVILLE. On West River, Anne Arundel County. It is adjacent to Galloway, where John Galloway settled in about 1845. George Gale owned the land here and encouraged the coming of other settlers. In 1860 Mrs. S. Gale lived in this vicinity. See GALLOWAYS; see LERCH.

Note: Dunham (p. 15) states that in the early 1800's George Gale (1799–1856) became the proprietor of Belle Grove, and Brownton plantation (fr. John Brown) and for the first time the region became known as Galesville. Here lies the historic Quaker Burying Ground. Also nearby is Hartge's Yacht Yard (fr. Emile A. Hartge).

GALLOWAYS P.O. West River, Anne Arundel County. Riley states that John Galloway "... had a large tract of land in this neighborhood under a grant from Lord Baltimore...." See GALESVILLE.

GAMBER. Village, three miles s. w. of Finksburg, Carroll County. Perhaps an earlier name was *Pleasantville. A Mrs. Burns, of this place, tells me that *Gamber* was the name of a former postmaster. A minister, she says, tried unsuccessfully to revive a former name, *Mechanicsville. A more sophisticated name—Statewood—was proposed. The citizens also turned it down.

GAMBRILL STATE PARK. Frederick County. This park was named for "the late" James H. Gambrill, Jr., of Frederick. He was a vigorous advocate of the conservation of natural resources. (See: *Sun.* 28 Oct. 1962).

GAMBRILLS. Village. Near Odenton, Anne Arundel County. Earlier this was *Sappington Station*, Sappington Post Office, with Mary M. Sappington, for postmistress. The change to Gambrills was in 1885, and the latter name, according to Raymond Storms, is from Augustine Gambrill "... who had a plantation in the neighborhood of Annapolis from about 1723 to 1774 ..." (See: *Capital*, Dec. 1, 1965).

Note: Warfield states that the will of *Alexander* Gambrill, who died in 1774, is the oldest on record in Annapolis.

GANNONS. Village. Near Franklin and Westernport, Allegany County. The place was evidently named for "Gannon's Store," kept by "the late" M. P. Gannon. When it was torn down in 1964 it had been unoccupied for twenty-seven years.

GARRETT PARK. Village. Near Kensington, Montgomery County. Incorporated in 1891. Forty families from the District of Columbia settled here in 1890. The name is for John W. Garrett, then president of the Baltimore and Ohio Railroad.

GARRISON. Village. Near Owings Mills, Baltimore County. Ten miles below this place there was once a "garrison," maintained to keep the Indians away. John Oldton, Captain of the Baltimore County Rangers, built it at the close of the seventeenth century. Marye situates the fort at the head of a branch of Jones Falls now called Slaughterhouse Run. Compare Baltimore's Garrison Avenue, Garrison Boulevard, and Garrison Forest Road.

GEANQUAKIN CREEK. On the Manokin River, Somerset County. This Algonquian name appears to consist of *chinqua* "big, high," the inanimate copula *-at-*, and *-ki* "it is." The meaning would be "Where it is high." However, there is no high land here, unless in contrast to the nearby Dames Quarter Marsh. Pronunciation: jin - KAWK - n, jin - KAWK N.

GEMMILLS. Village. Near Whitehall, Baltimore County. The village lies between First Mine Run and Second Mine Run, which may account for its occasional appearance as "Gem Mills." *Gemmill* (Gemmell) is a common surname in the Baltimore area. The Baltimore phone book of 1969 has five Gemmell and 31 *Gemmill*. Pronunciation: JEM - ul.

GEORGES CREEK. Flowing south from beyond Lonaconing, it enters the Potomac River at Westernport, Allegany County. An earlier name was *Lonaconin Creek. Legend tells that Indian *George* had a hunting camp in the valley between Dan's Mountain and Savage Mountain, traversed by this stream. *Lonaconin* Creek became *George's Creek* at about the time when *Caicuctuc* became *Will's Creek*, Cumberland. *Will* was perhaps a Shawnee Indian. See LONACONING.

*GEORGETOWN. Once in Montgomery County, Maryland; today an important part of Washington, D.C. The traveller, Ebenezer Hazard, described it in 1777 as "... George Town on Potowmack, a small town in Maryland, built on a hill." Wilstach conjectures that Georgetown lies on the site of *Tohogae*, an Indian town visited in 1632 by Captain Fleet. There was a ship landing here as early as 1703. It was a post office in 1789. The present name is attributed to Ninian Beall's son, George, who owned the land the town is built on. See *TOHOGA.

Note: For Ninian Beall, see BEALLSVILLE; see DUMBARTON.

GEORGETOWN. On the Sassafras River, Kent County. It is opposite Fredericktown; both places were laid out in 1736. Georgetown takes its name from the British prince who became George III. Fredericktown was named for Frederick, George III's brother. See FREDERICKTOWN.

Note: Postal history records the post office of *Georgetown Cross Roads*, Kent County, 1789.

GERMANTOWN. Near Gaithersburg, Montgomery County. On the Seneca Quadrangle, 1908, it is *Germantown, Old Germantown*. It became the headquarters of the Atomic Energy Commission during the closing years of the Eisenhower Administration. The town was founded in 1849 by German immigrants. Jacob Snyder, in 1849, was the first buyer of land. In this he was followed by other Germans, some of whose family names were *Adler, Grisendorff, Metz, Richter*, and *Stang*. In 1873, when a branch of the Baltimore and Ohio Railroad was built here, farmer F. C. Clopper donated the land for a station. Hence the village name CLOPPER, CLOPPERS.

Note: Maryland has six *Germantowns*. Compare Germantown School, Annapolis. Compare Germantown, a black community near Berlin. It consists of an abandoned barber shop and a row of unpaired houses. Today there are no Germans there.

GIBSON ISLAND. An island and postal community at the mouth of Magothy River, Chesapeake Bay, Anne Arundel County. A monument here commemorates "Stuart Symington, Jr. 1874–1926. Founder of Gibson Island, 1921." However, the name is from Gibson, one of the original owners of the island. See MOUNTAIN POINT; see MOUNTAIN ROAD.

GILMORE. Village near Lonaconing, Allegany County. Mr. McAlpine, of Knapp's Meadows, tells me that Gilmore was once *TAN-NERY, from Tannery Run. And he adds that the run was named for a tannery which his father had helped to tear down. The family name *Gilmore* is infrequent in Allegany County. I find only three instances in the 1969 Allegany phone book.

Note: The present author recalls that one John Gilmore, probably of this place, was for many years chief desk clerk at the Kenny House (Piedmont, W. Va., opposite Westernport, Allegany County, Maryland).

GILPIN. Village near Flintstone, Allegany County. This was *Gilpin-town in 1866. The name is from the family name Gilpin. The Allegany phone book of 1968 lists seven Gilpins, one of them living in Flintstone. Compare Gilpins Point, Caroline County; also Gilpin's Rocks (from Samuel Gilpin), Cecil County.

Note: Miller remarks that the founder of the Gilpin family in this country was Joseph Gilpin, who settled in Delware County, Pennsylvania, in 1695.

GINGERVILLE CREEK. On the South River, near Annapolis, Anne Arundel County. It was mapped as Gingerville Creek in 1860. If one may rely on the early spelling, Ginger*well*, *-well* has become *-ville*, perhaps by folk etymology. I suppose there was an abundance of wild ginger here. Ginger was widely distributed in the Virginia area. Compare Pepper Creek, Indian River Bay, Delaware.

Note: Compare *Green Ginger Cr.*, which appears on a fictitious map ("Some Plantations in Anne Arundel and Baltimore Cos.... 1650–1667.") in James E. Moss's fantasy, *Providence Ye Lost Towne at Severn in Mary Land*, Washington, D.C., 1978.

GINGERVILLE. A real estate development and community on Gingerville Creek, near Annapolis, Anne Arundel County. Mrs. Ralph Decker, of Peppercorn Place, Gingerville, tells me that eleven years ago her husband, a builder and contractor, named the community from the name of the creek. It appears that he bought 100 wooded acres here in January 1964, and in that year built the first residence. By 1972 seventy houses had been completed. The streets were named for spices and herbs.

GINSENG "Hollers." Near Oakland, Garrett County. In the spring ginseng begins to sprout in the hollows or "hollers" of this mountainous county. See SANG RUN.

GIRDLETREE. Village near Snow Hill, Worcester County. There are several explanatory stories, the commonest being that a drunkard tried to saddle his horse one night near Bishop's Tavern and instead saddled a tree. A second story relates that one day in 1869 a local whittler completely girdled a big tree. In 1964 Nellie Scarborough, daughter of James Scarborough around whose store the village arose, denied the whittling story. She declares that the name is from "Girdletree," her grandfather Bishop's farm. The farmhouse, she says, was built on ". . . a knoll upon which grew a birch tree girdled with wild grape vines." I am skeptical of these contradictory stories. It appears most likely that the name is from a tree that was marked or girdled by surveyors. Compare the "girdle pine" which in 1722 partly divided Anne Arundel and Baltimore Counties.

Note: Lewis 1878 lists Girdle Tree Hill, and gives a population of 400. This suggests that Girdletree was first known as *Girdle Tree Hill.

*GISBOROUGH. Community, near Washington, in Prince George's County. Bowie attributes the name to an estate in England with which the Dent family was connected. A historic brick house at Gisborough Point was burned in 1931 to make way for Bolling Field.

GIST. Village, near Freedom, Carroll County. This was the post office of "Gists" in 1828. The name commemorates a pioneer family. Christofer Gist, the immigrant ancestor of General Mordecai Gist, settled on the south side of the Patapsco River in 1682. The 1963 Carroll County phone book lists sixteen *Gists*.

GITTINGS. Village, near Glenarm, Baltimore County. Gittings is near LONG GREEN. The first owner of "Long Green Farm" was Thomas Gittings, great grandfather of John S. Gittings. Thomas Gittings came to Maryland in about 1684, and in 1720 patented the tract, "Gitting's Choice."

Note: W. B. Marye tells me that Long Green is from the name of a place in the north of Ireland. Near it and Glen Arm was the estate of Marye's great grandfather, Richard Gittings (d. 1830).

*GLASCOW. A village in Cecil County. In 1776 *Glascow was called *Aikens or *Aikentown. Aikin near Perryville still exists. However, there is no current mention of *Glascow. "Aikens or Aikentown" has been attributed to a man named Aiken who kept a hotel there. *Glascow is probably from the family name. In the West Nottingham Presbyterian graveyard eight miles from *Glascow, one finds a tombstone inscribed to John Glascow, d. 1769 aet. 47.

Note: Manual 1947 spells CLASGOW (Wicomico) with a *g*.

GLENARM. Village, near Long Green Creek, Gunpowder Falls, Baltimore County. Davidson attributes the name to the old home in Scotland of Thomas Armstrong, former treasurer of the Md. & Pa. Railroad. I am not aware of a *Glenarm* in Scotland, and William B. Marye declares that he knows Glen Arm to be definitely a name from the northeastern corner of Ireland.

GLEN BURNIE. A town south of Linthicum, Baltimore County. The name is for John Glenn, who had an estate here in the 1880's. According to Riley, it was earlier known as *Tracey's Station* and *Myrtle Post Office*.

Burnie suggests a *burn*, which is a Scotch word for a small stream. Compare "Glen Burnie," the home of Colonel James Wood, founder of Winchester, Virginia.

GLEN ECHO. Washington suburban village, Potomac River, Montgomery County. In the 1890's this place was a Chautauqua Center and a summer resort; for many more years it was an amusement park. The *Echo* of the name is fanciful; *Glen* appropriately suggests the gullies of this scenic, hilly area. Imported Indian street names such as Walhonding Road, originated in the days of the Chautauqua movement.

GLENELG. Village, el. 633, near Dayton, Howard County. The name is from Glenelg Manor, variously known as "the Tyson Mansion" and "the Governor Lowndes Estate." Folger McKenzie attributes *Glenelg Manor* to General Joseph Tyson, assistant postmaster in 1845, "from an old estate in Scotland." Glenelg, Scotland, also names a village and river in Australia, and a bay in Canada.

Note: Warfield gives the owner of Glenelg Manor as General Joseph *Tyler*. Compare Glenelg, W. Inverness, Scotland.

GLENNDALE. Village, near Bowie, Prince George's County. The invariable spelling *Glenn* suggests that the placename is from a family name. The 1967-68 phone directory for this region has 28 *Glenn*. And under *Glenn* Passano has ten genealogical items. However, the area is slightly hilly (el. 150) and Glenn here could be merely descriptive (glen).

GLENWOOD. Village, near Cooksville, Howard County. In 1841 this place was *Matthews Store P.O.*, for James B. Matthews, who had long kept a store here. The surrounding countryside has knolls ranging in height from 500 to 600 feet, and it appears likely that the present name is simply descriptive. Compare Glendale, Skye, Scotland.

GLYNDON. A village near Reisterstown and Emory Grove, Baltimore County. Davidson states that a Western Maryland Railroad Station called *Reisters-Town Station* or *Emory Grove* post office was built here in 1860. But an all-inclusive name was needed, and in 1879, at a drawing to select such a name, *Glyndon* was chosen. Prominent at the drawing were Messrs. Townsend and Hook, and Dr. Charles A. Leas, who had laid out the streets of the town in 1871. *Townsendville* was considered and rejected. Some think Dr. Leas chose *Glyndon* for a town he loved in England. An old Temperance Camp here was later called Glyndon Park.

GOLD MINE ROAD. Montgomery County. George F. Nesbitt, Silver Spring, 1975, tells me that there is an out-cropping of gold-bearing quartz some distance off this road. It was mined for a time, possibly in 1845-50, but the work was more costly than the yield and the project was soon abandoned.

GOLDEN. Baltimore County (Register 1834) See COCKEYSVILLE.

GOLDEN HILL. Village, near Smithville, Dorchester County. Postal history records that "Griffins and Robinsons Store" was changed to "Golden Hill" in 1841. The village is alongside a marsh (el. 2 ft.). In a discussion of Boddy Run or Golden Branch. Baltimore County, Marye mentions the tract, "Miners Adventure." He explains: "The presence of iron pyrites in the soil might account for names like these." Compare Golden Quarters Neck, Worcester County, probably named from the yellow English daisies planted here by the same English immigrant woman who, with seedlings from abroad, planted the famous *Ayres elm*.

GOLDSBORO. A village northeast of Greensboro, Caroline County. *Oldtown, probably from Old Town Branch, was an earlier name. When the D. & C. Railroad came here in 1867 the people decided to give the village "a more modern name." Therefore in 1870, since the land surrounding the village was owned by Dr. G. W. Goldsborough, the name was changed from "Oldtown to Goldsborough." it is now *Goldsboro*.

GOLDSBOROUGH. Village near Easton, Talbot County. Goldsboro and Peachblossom Creeks are nearby. Nicholas Goldsborough, of Dorset County, England, and later of Kent Island (1670), was the ancestor of all the Goldsboroughs in Dorchester County and Maryland. Local history mentions Judge H. H. Goldsborough, of Talbot County, Colonel F. C. Goldsborough, of "Ellenborough," on Peachblossom Creek, and Hon. Robert Goldsborough, a member of the Assembly from Talbot County and in 1719-1740 Chief Justice of the Provincial Court.

GOLTS. Village near Massey, Kent County. In 1952 (*MHM*, 47:I) Robert C. Golt asked for "information about the naming of this village." Compare *Golts Tavern* (1795), twelve miles northeast of Snow Hill.

GOOD LUCK. Village near Glenndale, Prince George's County. Postal history indicates that "Magruders" was changed to "Good Luck" in 1830. Compare Goodhope (Frederick County), Goodintent School (Frederick County), and Goodhope Road (Washington County).

GOODWILL. Village, east of Pocomoke City, Worcester County. The Goodwill Baptist Church is situated here. Compare *Good Intents* Ldg., near Pocomoke City.

GOODY HILL. I had thought this was a village. Instead it is a stream, Goody Hill Branch, near Ironshire, Worcester County. Mr. Hastings, of Ironshire Sta., tells me that he was born at Good "Town" Hill, now Goody Hill. *Goody* and *Gudde* are rare Maryland surnames.

GORMAN. Village, near Kearney, Garrett County. For Senator Arthur Pue Gorman, who had to do with the opening of the Western Maryland Railroad, and whose name is also found in Gorman's counterpart, *Gormania*, on the West Virginia side of the Potomac River.

GORSUCH. Village, near Sykesville, Carroll County. See GORSUCHS MILLS.

GORSUCHS MILLS. Village, near Maryland Line, Baltimore County. It was a post office in 1853. Compare "Old Gorsuch Tavern" between Cockeysville and York, Pa. Captain Joshua Gorsuch built the north wing in about 1810. Here also was "Gorsuch Stone Barn," where Joshua's son, Edward Gorsuch, a slave trader, kept his Negroes. There are the following *Gorsuch* names in the vicinity of Baltimore City: *Gorsuch Pt.; Gorsuch Creek; and Gorsuch Street. "Cold Comfort" was surveyed for Lovelace Gorsuch in 1661; and "Rich Neck Level" was surveyed for Charles Gorsuch in 1667. In 1661 Charles Gorsuch had patented a tract on *Whetstone Neck.

GORTNER. A village near Oakland, Garrett County. Gortner is situated at "Swans Meadow," earlier the property of General John Swan. The name is attributed to Peter and Barbara Gortner, Prussians, who moved here by oxcart in 1849. The Gortners bought the Swan Meadow farm and gave their son, Peter, that part of it on which the village now stands. The post office was in the Gortner store.

Note: The o /aw/ in *Gortner*, instead of the more usual (*Gartner*) a /ah/, illustrates the Western Maryland dialectal peculiarity responsible for such pronunciations as *born* for *barn*.

GOSHEN. A village near Laytonsville, Montgomery County. To speak strictly there are Goshen Branch (or Creek), Goshen, and Goshen Mills, all within three miles of each other. PHC notes that "Goshen Mills," a post office in 1818, became successively "Cracklintown" in July 1848, and "Laytonsville" in August 1848. Boyd remarks that Goshen has land "in fine cultivation," which bears out the biblical origin, from the fruitful "Land of Goshen."

*GOT CREEK. It is parallel to Herring Creek, near Tracey's Landing, Anne Arundel County. This stream was the earlier name of Rockhold Creek. Here in 1659 Richard Gott surveyed 600 acres and named the tract "Rams Gott Swamp." (See: Bisbee, *Capital,* 24 Sept. 1979). See ROCKHOLD CREEK.

GOTTS. Village near Millersville, Anne Arundel County. Probably a station on the bygone Baltimore and Annapolis Railroad. The name is from the family name *Gott.* In 1790 there were one *Got* and one *Gott* in Anne Arundel County. See *GOT CREEK.

GOVANSTOWN. Today a part of north Baltimore City. Marye mentions "Friends Discovery," near Towson, and remarks that it probably lay within a resurvey made in 1755 for "Captain William Govane." The *s* (Govanstown) is probably possessive; compare the French surname *Gauvain(e).*

GRAHAMTOWN. Village, near Frostburg, Allegany County. TW mentions Dr. Thomas Jennings Johnson Graham (d. Frostburg, 1891), a descendant of Gov. Thomas Johnson and "a leading physician and surgeon at Frostburg, where he settled when a young man."

GRACEHAM. Village, near Thurmont, Frederick County. Graceham arose in about 1750. As a post office, it appears once or twice as "Grace-town." To explain the name, the story is told that a visiting Lutheran bishop liked the place so much that he exclaimed: "May this be a hamlet where the grace of God abounds!"

GRANITE. Two places bear this name, one near Frostburg, Allegany County, and another near Randallstown, Baltimore County. In Baltimore County there is also *Granite Branch*. The earlier name of the Baltimore GRANITE was *Waltersville. Here in 1830 Captain Alexander Walters opened two Waltersville Granite Quarries. The present name was given in 1873; the quarries closed in 1925.

Note: From the Waltersville Quarries stone was taken to build Baltimore and Ohio Railroad bridges and many public monuments of Baltimore and Washington.

GRANTSVILLE. East of Keyser's Ridge, Garrett County. Postal history records that "Tomlinsons" was changed to "Little Crossings" in 1834, and "Little Crossings" was changed to *Grantsville* in 1846. The present name is from Daniel Grant, a Baltimorean. Weeks describes him as "of the noted Fountain Inn of Baltimore," and adds "In 1785 he patented 'Cornucopia' and moved to his property on the Braddock Road. When the Cumberland Road was built the old village site was abandoned and 'New' Grantsville grew up on the new highway."

GRASONVILLE. Near Queenstown, Queen Anne's County. Warfield mentions William Grason (1786–1868). Maryland's twenty-eighth governor. He was born in Queen Anne's County and was called "the Queen Anne Farmer."

GRATITUDE. Village, near Rock Hall, Chesapeake Bay, Kent County. It lies on a deep waterfront; an earlier name was *Deep Landing. The present name (adopted "around the turn of the century") comes from the Philadelphia steamboat, "Gratitude," which in times past regularly docked here.

Note: Reppert (*Sun*, May 5, 1969) lists the following places "considered a part of Gratitude": Puppyville, Biscuit Hill, Skinners Neck, Piney Neck, and Dodge City (with a citizen whose nickname is Matt Dillon).

GRAY. Village, near Ellicott City, Howard County. Davidson mentions Gray's cotton manufactory—bought from Thomas Mendenhall, who earlier had a paper mill here. Edward Gray (1776–1856) was from Bowera, near Londonderry, Ireland. His daughter, Maria, closed the factory in 1888.

GREENBACKVILLE. Near Stockton, Worcester County. It is partly in Accomac County, Virginia. The story is told that years ago northerners who came here to buy clams and oysters paid their bills with "greenbacks." However, there are two additional explanation: (1) When

Civil War oystering made the salt marsh lots here twenty times more valuable, a man named the town for the "then current" greenback money; (2) a jubilant oysterman and land buyer declared that to him the oysters were real "greenbacks." (See: *Star*, 30 July, 1967).

GREENBELT. A model village near Beltsville, Prince George's County. Greenbelt was the second "new town" built (1935-38) in the United States with the intention of creating a planned community protected from irregular growth by a permanent green belt of parkland or open country. Credit for this development belongs to Professor Rexford Tugwell and the Franklin Roosevelt regime, whose Resettlement Administration, using workmen on relief, did the construction. (See: *Star*, 24 August, 1967).

GREENFIELD MILLS. Village, near Licksville, Monocacy River, Frederick County. This was a post office in 1836. The 1790 census lists eighteen occurrences of the surname *Greenfield*, and the Greenfield of this placename is also probably from a surname. Radoff remarks: "On the Western Shore the Greenfields, the Hammonds, the Brooks, and the Taskers grew in worldly goods and meaningful alliances."

*GREENHEAD. See FRIENDSHIP, Anne Arundel County.

GREENSBORO. Village, Choptank River, near Ridgely, Caroline County. In 1732 an act was passed to establish this town at the bridge near the head of "Great Choptank River." Its first names were *Choptank Bridge* and *Bridge Town*. The change to *Greensborough* came in 1791 after a resurvey. The *Green* of the present name is from a family name. In 1878 Nathan Green was a farmer here.

GREEN SPRING. Village, Green Spring Valley, Baltimore County. Green Spring was a post office in 1832. It was Green Spring Junction—Chattolanee in 1906. Evidently this place is alternately *Chattalonee* Springs. The common source of both names and of Green Spring Valley was a *green* or grassy *spring*. See CHATTOLANEE.

GREEN SPRING FURNACE. Village, near Big Spring, Washington County. An ironworks was built here in about 1768. In 1848 there was still standing here the stack of a later furnace.

GREEN SPRING RUN. Washington County. In about 1765 Thomas Johnson and Lancelot Jacques, a Huguenot, inquired about mineral lands containing iron ore lying on Green Spring Run near Fort Frederick. The lands they sought were to be suitable for setting up a Forge Mill and other conveniences for carrying on "an Iron Work." The Green Spring *Furnace* was built in 1768, and the pig iron manufactured here was pushed by Negro slaves down the Potomac River to Georgetown.

GREY ROCK. Near Pikesville, Baltimore County. In 1700 "Grey Rock" was the name of a grey, stone house near Pikesville; there was also Grey Rock Lane. Compare the early post office "Grey Rock," Harford County. Postal history records that "West Connewingo" was changed to

"Grey Rock" in 1839. I suggest that the latter name refers to a *gray rock* near the Susquehanna River.

GRIMES. Village, near Spielman, Washington County. In 1904 Grimes was a station on the Norfolk and Western Railroad. The name is from the Grimes family, whose homestead was in Bakersville. Here lived James Grimes (1787–1860). A "Doctor Grimes," doubtless of this family, was elected to the state legislature in 1874.

*GUETOWN. Harford County. In 1841 it lay between the Susquehanna River and Conewago. Perhaps it is from the surname *Gue(y)*, *McGue(y)*.

GUILFORD. Village, near Savage, Howard County. In 1750 Guilford was the locality of a mill jointly owned by Alexander Warfield and Elizabeth Ridgely; in 1866 it was mapped as *Guilford Factory*. The Granite Company of Baltimore began quarrying here in 1834. A little stream nearby was called "Guilford stream." Though the name *Guilford* could come from Guilford, Surrey, England, it seems to me more likely that it commemorates Lord Guilford, the guardian of Charles, the fifth Lord Baltimore.

Note: Warfield indicates that *Wincopin Neck* was the name of the site of *Guilford*. See *WINCOPIN.

GUNPOWDER. In 1941 there were four villages by this name in Maryland. Two were in Baltimore County, the third was in Carroll County, and the fourth was on the Gunpowder River near Magnolia, Harford County. Of one of these, PHC notices: " 'Gunpowder' Baltimore County, was changed to 'Joppa Cross Roads,' Harford County, in 1819. 'Joppa Cross Roads' . . . was changed to 'Little Gunpowder,' Baltimore County, in 1829." Apparently, all these places have a connection with the Gunpowder. See GUNPOWDER RIVER.

GUNPOWDER RIVER. A branch of Chesapeake Bay, flowing between Baltimore and Harford Counties. A tributary, Gunpowder Falls, illustrates the antiquated use of *falls* to mean "stream." "Powderby," a tract laid out in 1658 by Godfrey Harmer, an Indian trader, appears to be an allusion to this river. There is no truth in the tradition that the name arose because the Indians, when they first saw gunpowder, thought it was seeds and sowed it on Gunpowder Neck. Saltpeter is an ingredient of gunpowder, and it is Marye's opinion (and mine) that the name is from Salt Petre Neck, bounded on the south by Carroll's Island. As a matter of fact, Carroll's Island was once known as *Gunpowder Island. See SALT PETRE CREEK.

GWYNN(S) FALLS. Baltimore City suburb. Compare Gwynnbrook and the present post office, Gwynn Oak. Each of these places owes its name to the stream, Gwynn Falls, which begins at Glyndon and flows through Baltimore City. Marye attributes the name of the stream to

Richard Gwin (*Gwinn* or *Guin*) who, with Edward Halton, "took up" the tract "New Town," in the angle or neck made by the junction of Gwinn's Falls and Gwinn's Run. The smaller of the streams, today called Peck's Branch, still appears on maps as *Gwinn's Run.

GWYNN OAK.   Suburban Baltimore City. See GWYNN(S) FALLS.

H

HABNAB.   A village in Somerset County, which the Guide describes as a "rundown hamlet" still called by its old name, though it became *Venton* officially in 1921. *Venton* was considered more "dignified." Compare "Habnab at a Venture," surveyed in 1688, and now a part of Druid Hill Park, Baltimore. "Habnab," the early spelling of *hobnob*, was a tract of land. The name suggests a real estate venture taken "with free leave, at random." See VENTON.

HACKETT CORNER.   Village, near Sudlersville, Queen Anne's County. In 1970 Thomas and William Hackett were in Queen Anne's County. The Kent and Queen Anne's phone directory for 1963 lists six Hacketts. The founder of the Dorchester family of Hacketts was one Thomas Hackett, a blacksmith, who settled in Annapolis in 1674. His son owned "Hackett's Adventure," 1732. To this family may perhaps be attributed HACKETT POINT, Anne Arundel County. *Corners* refers to the corners of a crossroad, and abounds in such Queen Anne names as Anderson *Corner*, DuHamells *Corner*, and Murdocks *Corner*.

*HACKS TOWN.   Sassafras River, Cecil County. This forgotten place seems to have been the Hack's Town tract, first owned in 1658 by Sepheron Hack. When Sepheron Hack was killed at Iron Hill in 1662 it passed to Dr. George Hack, who patented it as Hack's Town.

Note: Johnston (Cecil, p. 71) attributes HACK POINT (on the Bohemia River, Cecil County) to Anna Hak (b. Amsterdam, Holland) and her sons, George and Peter (both b. in Virginia). They were all naturalized on May 1, 1666, and were among the first petitioners for naturalization in colonial Maryland. (See: Wyand, p. 5).

HAGERSTOWN.   City, Washington County. Jonathan Hager (1719-1775) patented "Hager's Choice" in Dec. 1739, and "Hager's Delight" in 1753. He was called "Captain" and had reached America from Germany in 1730. The town, when laid out in 1762, was *Elizabeth Town, in honor of Hager's wife. Elizabeth Kershner Hager. However, the name was not popular, and in January 1814 the Assembly passed "an act to change the name of Elizabeth Town . . . to Hager's Town, and incorporate the same."

HALETHORPE.   Village, near Lansdowne, Baltimore County. The mother of Carville D. Benson, (State senator 1912-1914) named Halethorpe; it means "healthy village." In 1937 the part of Halethorpe from the Washington Boulevard to the Pa. R.R. tracks was known as the "East Side." The land on the other side was called the "West Side."

HALF PONE POINT. On the Patuxent River, Cuckold Creek, St. Mary's County. The Virginia Algonquian word for "bread" was *apones*, *appoans*. I think, therefore, that (H)*alf Pone* is a folk etymology of the local Indian word for "bread."

HALFWAY. Village, near Williamsport, Washington County. Williams mentions ". . . the village of Halfway, on the Hagerstown turnpike . . ." In earlier days this place was midway between Williamsport and Hagerstown. Cf. *Halfway House, Anne Arundel, a post office in 1826.

HALL'S CROSS ROADS. Village? Queen Anne's County. This place is mentioned in the court records of 1803. The family name *Hall* (*Halle, Halls*) occurs 110 times in Heads 1790, and nine of these occurrences are in Qu. Anne's County. TDr Qu. Anne's (1963) has eleven listings for *Hall*.

*HALL TOWN. See MARYDEL.

HALLOWING POINT. East bank, Patuxent River, near Bowens, Calvert County. This was a place where people hallowed or shouted—probably across the river. See *HOLLAND'S POINT.

HAMBLETON. Village, near Trappe, Talbot County. Ingraham speaks of William Hambleton, an early settler near St. Michaels. He emigrated from Scotland in about 1659. William Hambleton was High Sheriff of Talbot County in 1663 and a "Worshipful Justice of the Peace." One of his descendants, Samuel Hambleton, became a member of the House of Delegates, a state senator, and a colonel of cavalry. He was elected to Congress in 1870. See *HOLE IN THE WALL.

HAMMOCK POINT. In the Little Annemessex River, Somerset County. *Hammock* is probably a form of English *hummock* (related to *hump*) and means "mound, hillock."

HAMMONDS. The Hammond family has given Anne Arundel and Howard Counties such names as HAMMOND BRANCH (Ho), HAMMOND BRIDGE (Ho), HAMMOND(S) FERRY ROAD (AA), and HAMMONDS (AA). The first Hammond to remain in Maryland was John Hammond (d. 1707), whose titles and positions were Judge of the Vice-Admiralty, Major-General of the Western Shore, and member of their Majesties' Council. In 1796 Col. Rezin Hammond patented "Hammond's Inheritance," Howard County. Between 1770 and 1774, Rezin Hammond's brother Matthew built the Hammond-Harwood House, Annapolis, It appears that Rezin Hammond also had a "dwelling plantation" called Hammond's Inclosure," near Millersville (AA).

HAMMOND(S) FERRY ROAD. Anne Arundel County. In 1975 restoration of "the old Benson-Hammond House at Hammonds Ferry Road" was discussed. It is near the Baltimore-Washington International Airport and was built in 1830 by Joseph Benson. John T. Hammond and Rezin

Howard Hammond bought the property from Benson's heir in December 1887.

HAMPDEN.   A Baltimore City neighborhood linked industrially with Woodbury. These sister neighborhoods were born as "Baltimore County industrial communities" in the nineteenth century. At that time English and Welsh workers operated cotton duck mills here and made sailcloth for the Baltimore Clippers. The names of the mills were Mount Vernon, Woodberry, Meadow, Clipper and Druid. They gave rise to lesser areas, such as Stone Hill, Brick Hill, Druidville, Clipper Village, Sweet Air, and West Woodberry. According to Jacques Kelly, Hampden derives its name from John Hampden, "an historical figure from the Charles I period." See: Jacques Kelly, *News American*, Nov. 4, 1976. Probable pronunciation: HAM-den.

HAMPSTEAD.   Village, near Manchester, Carroll County. The townsite is part of the "Spring Garden" tract, patented to Dutton Lane in 1748. Early names were *Spring Garden* and *Coxville*, the latter for a Mr. Cox, who bought half of the original town lots. The town's historical plaque states: "Spring Garden. Christopher Vaughn laid out the town of Hampstead in 1786 on land called Spring Garden, located along the Indian path from Patapsco (Baltimore) to Letort's Spring (Carlisle) . . ." Hampstead and Spring Garden were well-known London localities.

HANCE POINT.   Northeast River, near Northeast, Cecil County. Noticing that Shawnee Indians once lived in Elk Neck and that the part of Elk Neck bordering on the North East River was once called *Shawnah*. Miller declares: "The name of Chief Hance, according to tradition, is perpetuated at the point which bears his name. The former Shawnah School in Elk Neck and the Shawnah tribe of the Red Men in North East both recall this group of Indians."

HANCOCK.   Town, Potomac River, Washington County. This was *Hancock's T.* in 1794. Hancock municipal pamphlet of 1958 states that: "Joseph Hancock, who evidently was in possession of a Crown Grant, settled in the area in 1749 and, while the records are rather vague, it is generally assumed that our town was named after him." The first settlers in this area came in 1732; the town was incorporated in 1853.

Note: In early days this area was known as North Bend Country, from the large northerly bend in the Potomac River. The municipal pamphlet suggests that a lost place *William's Town* once existed here. John Donovan, in 1790, had bought a local tract from *William* Russell, of Baltimore County.

HANDYS HAMMOCK.   A small marsh or hammock in Newport Bay, Worcester County. In 1790 there were six members of the Handy family in Worcester County, including Colonel Samuel Handy. See HAMMOCK POINT.

HANESVILLE. Village, near Melitota, Kent County. In 1878 this place was the post office of Mary A. Hanes.

HANOVER. A Howard County post village near Elkridge (G Md 1904, 1941; Manual 1947). The name of this place was at first *Hanover-ville.* I learn from Postmaster M. D. Thompson (1983) that the first settlers, arriving here in about 1880, came from Germany. The name is for the German city.

HANSONVILLE. Near Walkersville, Frederick County. The Hansons came to New Sweden in 1642. Eleven years later Andrew, John, William and Randel Hanson moved from New Sweden to Kent Island. The present village is related to John Hanson (b. 1715) of Charles County, who in 1773 moved to Frederick County. He was a grandson of "the immigrant of the same name" and represented Charles County in the Md. Assembly between 1757 and 1768. (See: Richardson; Hill).

HARDESTY. Village, near Hall, Prince George's County. The name represents the Hardesty family, whose founder, George Hardesty, a Virginia Puritan, settled in Maryland before 1652. His son was described in 1694 as "George Hardesty, Gentleman." The latter had six children, some of whom settled in Prince George's County. (See: Stein).

*HARDSWAMP'S TOWN. Dorchester County. This name illustrates folk etymology and commemorates an early Algonquian Indian. Marye finds "Hardswamp's Town" in a Dorchester County deed of Jan. 1, 1689-90. He was probably *Hatsawapp,* mentioned in *Archives* (1669) as "Hatsawap and the rest of the Indians." *Archives* 34 (for 1720-1723) calls him "Ababco Hatsawap (Indian)."

HARFORD. County, village, and furnace (Harford Furnace). The village (Harford—head of Bush River) was a post office in 1789. At Harford Furnace there was an ironworks. Of these names Gannett states: "... names for Henry Harford, the natural son of Lord Baltimore, the sixth, and proprietor at the time of the Revolution." Frederick, the sixth Lord Baltimore, died in Italy in 1771 (aet. 41). He left no legitimate children, and by his will his natural son, Henry Harford, a minor, was made proprietary of Maryland. See *HARFORD TOWN.

*HARFORD TOWN. Now the village of Bush, near Abington, Harford County. Ebenezer Hazard mentions Harford Town "... formerly called Bush Town, a very small shabby Place, though a County Town." *Harford Town was the county seat of Harford County from 1774 to 1781. The name is for Henry Harford, mentioned in connection with HARFORD and HARFORD FURNACE. (See: Fred Shelley, *MHM,* 46:1). See BUSH.

HARMANS. Village, near Severn, Anne Arundel County. In 1878 the village was *Harman Sta.,* on the Baltimore and Potomac Railroad. F. Harman, J. Harman, and E. Harman were living nearby.

*HARMER'S TOWN. In 1658 it lay on part of the land that is now Havre de Grace. The name is from the Indian trader, Godfrey Harmer. He was a Swede who was naturalized in 1661. Marye finds that in 1727 *Harmer's Town was "commonly called the Ferry." *Ferry* comes from the fact that the place was situated "one mile above the mouth of Susquehanna River at the old ferry landing." See HAVRE DE GRACE.

*HARMONDS SWAN TOWN. Baltimore County. In April 1658 an area of 200 acres was surveyed for Godfrey Harmer and James Robertson "... neare Swan Creek ..." *Harmonds* is apparently a corruption of *Harmer's.*

HARMONY. Village, near Meyersville, Frederick County. This was the post office of *Beallville from 1834 until 1842. The change to HARMONY came about when the present post office was established. Grove mentions *Beallville, now "Harmony," and adds that the name suggests peace; Maryland *Bealls* are abundant.

Compare Harmony (Caroline), Harmony (Kent), Harmony Grove (Frederick), Harmony Hall (Baltimore), and Harmony Hill School (Washington). Notice "Harmony Hall," a home (see OXON HILL).

HARNEY. A village northwest of Taneytown, Carroll County. When the citizens here petitioned for a post office in 1856, they discovered that their town's present name, *Monocacyville*, was already the name of another Maryland post office. They then asked James Elder, postmaster at Eldersburg, to choose a name. Elder having just read an account of a conflict in Utah between the Mormons and the U.S. government, suggested *Harney*, in honor of General W. S. Harney (1800–1889), commander of the federal troops involved in the trouble. (See: Warner et al.).

HARRIS LOT. Village, near Tompkinsville, Charles County. Postal history relates that "'Harris Lot' was changed to 'Milton Hill' in 1839. 'Tompkinsville' was changed to 'Harris Lot' in 1850." Lewis in 1878 mentions H. H. *Harris* in a list of farmers living here.

HARRISONVILLE. Near Randallstown, Baltimore County. It was a post office in 1843. Richard Harrison settled in Anne Arundel County in about 1651; Richard Harrison, Jr. (1665–1716) was the first of his family to live in Calvert County. The name *William Harris* appears in the census of 1800. Stein comments that later generations of the Harrison family moved to Baltimore City.

*HARRYSTOWN. This was once the name of a section of Hagerstown. Williams mentions Jacob Harry, hatter, "who made the addition (in about 1790) to Hagerstown known as Harry'stown."

HARUNDALE. A community near Glen Burnie, Anne Arundel County. Compare Martindale, near by. Is this name a surname? The 1970 census lists one *Heron*, two *Herrin*, and one *Herron*. The Maryland phone book for 1974–75 has three *Herren*, 35 *Herron*.

HARWOOD. There are Harwood, Howard County, Harwood, St. Mary's County, and Harwood P.O., Anne Arundel County. Warfield identifies "Harwood" (Rhode River, near Butlers) as a 1651 survey in the name of Robert Harwood. Succeding generations of the Harwood family have descended from either Robert Harwood or "a certain Thomas Harwood, D. D." He was of "Streatley" (England) and Rector of Littleton, Middlesex.

Note: Richardson has the immigrant, Richard Harwood, settling in Anne Arundel County before 1698. He owned "Brazen Thorpe Hall," Prince George's County, afterwards called "Harwood Hall."

*HASHAWA. Formerly in the Manocacy watershed. It was described in 1732 as "... the land called HASHAWA '... or where the Indian Cabin or Old fields are ..." Marye declares: "The Indian names of Monocacy, Olacin, or Olacip and Hashawa ... seem to indicate that there were Indian settlements in this region in historical times." The name may come from Algonquian *ācow* "across," and the meaning would then be "The place over across." Or it may be from Algonquian *ācaway* "long ago," with the consequent meaning of *Old Town*.

Note: The stems for "across" and "long ago" are in Fox, respectively, *ācowī-* (Michelson) and *acawaye*.

HAVRE DE GRACE. Town. Susquehanna River, Harford County. The town was laid out for Godfrey Harmer in 1658. The survey was called *Harmer's Town. In 1659 Harmer assigned his property to Thomas Stockett, whence *Stockett's Town. The ferry here had meanwhile been known as "The Lower Ferry." After 1700 *Susquehanna Lower Ferry became the name.

Havre de Grace, which became the name in 1795 when the town was incorporated, means "Harbour of Grace," and comes from Le Havre ("The Harbour"), France, whose earlier name commemorated a chapel dedicated to Notre-Dame de Grace ("Our Lady of Grace").

The reason for such a name in Maryland appears to be that General Lafayette, when he crossed the Susquehanna at the *Lower Ferry in 1782, was astonished by the resemblance of this place to Le Havre, France. An earlier French traveller had exclaimed, "C'est Le Havre; Le Havre de Grace!" Lafayette agreed, and was equally enthused; soon the new name took hold. Pronunciation: Havver de GRASS, Havver de GRAYCE. (See: Kidwiler).

Note: Compare "Havre-de-Venture," Charles County, the home (1743) of Thomas Stone the Signer. Other spellings were "Habre-de-Venture" and "Haber-de-Venture."
Commentary: The date, 1782, troubles me. Lafayette, receiving a hero's welcome, revisited the U.S. in *1784*.

HAWLINGS RIVER. A presently obscure stream in Montgomery County. Mrs. George F. Nesbitt writes: "I think there was someone named Hawlings in this area very, very early."

Note: *Hawlings*, now rare in Maryland, appears to be a variant of the British surname *Hollings*, "Dweller by the holly or holm-oak." (See: Reaney).

*HEAD OF ELK. Early village at the head of the Elk River, Cecil County. It was established as early as 1652, and became successively, *Elk Town and Elkton. See ELKTON.

HEATERS ISLAND. South of Point of Rocks, in the Potomac River, Frederick County. In 1971 a Mrs. P. S. *Heater* lived at Point of Rocks. See *CONOY ISLAND.

HEBRON. Village, northwest of Salisbury, Wicomico County. Like more than a score of similarly named places in the United States, Hebron probably commemorates the biblical town of Hevron (Hebron), Israel. However, owing to certain similar surnames, one cannot be sure that all such names are biblical. See below.

HEPBRON. Village, near Stillpond, Kent County. This place is in the vicinity of Kennedyville, the locality of "Hebron," a house owned by the Hebron family. The land, in 1683, was patented for James Heborne. The family name was also spelled *Hepburn*.

*HEISTERBORO. An early section of Hagerstown. General Daniel Heister, a Pennsylvanian and an officer in the Revolutionary Army, married a Jonathan Hager's daughter in 1772. He built a colonial farmhouse "Heisterboro," and laid out a southern addition to Hagerstown in streets and lots. In deeds and records it appears as "Heisterboro." See *HARRYSTOWN.

HELEN. Village, near Morganza, St. Mary's County. Frank Henry finds that this place (with the sign "Helen, Md." in front of the post office and general store) was named for Helen Hancock, daughter of Oscar Hancock, the first postmaster. He quotes Mrs. Latham, the postmistress at that time: "I can't tell you the date when the post office was named. It was a long time ago, sort of early in the 1900's." (See: *Sun*, Nov. 5, 1961).

HELLEN. Village, near Mutual, Calvert County. Stein mentions Nathaniel Hellen, immigrant of 1671 and founder of one of Calvert County's historic families. He thinks that the Hellens were French Huguenots, and that perhaps Christian Hillan, Huguenot goldsmith of London, was of the same family. This suggests that the surname *Hillen* (*Hillan*) became *Hellen*.

HENDERSON. Village, near Goldsboro, Caroline County. Cochrane states that the first post office in this region was *Melville's Crossroads*, established in February 1855 and named for Thomas Melville, local builder. The change to Henderson was in July 1868. The 1790 Census lists 31 *Hendersons*, but none for Caroline County.

HENRYTON. A Carroll County village near Sykesville (GMd 1904, 1941; ~, Henryton Road, Manual 1947). In 1919 a B. & O. Railroad stop; today (1983) the site of an institution for the mentally retarded. From Postmaster Edward M. Budelis (assisted by Doug McQuade) I have learned that Henryton takes its name from Henry Devries (storekeeper), who once owned vast tracts of land in this area on both sides of the Patapsco River.

Note: Mr. McQuade has kindly sent me a four-page history of Henryton in which the compiler, an unnamed resident here from 1919 until 1928, gives a nostalgic account of Henryton in the days before its culture and economy were disturbed by the coming of, first, a tubercular hospital and, second, a mental hospital. McQuade states that Henry Devries fired a resounding cannon on the days when the railroad delivered new goods to stock his store. The anonymous author blames "motor travel and truck transport" for the deterioration of small communities in the Patapsco Valley. He concludes: "A striking example of this is the now extinct village of Daniels, once known as Alberton, and the village of Oella which is nearing extinction."

HERALD HARBOR. A village lying between Valentine Creek and Little Round Bay, on the west bank of the Severn River, Anne Arundel County. The name of this erstwhile beach resort is attributed to promotional efforts made by the Washington *Herald* in 1924. One of its articles was "Herald Harbor Plans Announced"; and it is said that on one day in 1924 1,000 lots were reserved. Permanent residents began to arrive in the late 1930's; but no colored residents were allowed.

HEREFORD. Village, near White Hall, Baltimore County. Postal history records that "Loveton" was changed to "Hereford" in 1821. John Merryman of "Clover Hill" (his estate in Baltimore) received the deed to 1,000 acres of land here in 1714. The Merryman family had come to Virginia from Herefordshire, England, two generations before; the village of Hereford, part of the original 1,000 acres, commemorates the English County.

*"Herod's Line." Mentioned in the Rent Rolls of Baltimore County as "Land Called Harrods Lyon formerly taken up for Capt Harrod" (July 1962). Another version was "*ye Land Called Herod's Line ...*" A folk etymology perhaps worth notice.

*HERRING TOWN. Anne Arundel County. *Herrington, Harrington* and *Herring Town* have been somewhat confused. Riley mentions both Herrington (Herring Town) and Herring Creek (1686). Compare Herringtown Creek, Kent County. Maryland has an abundance of families named *Herring*.

Note: Garrett County's Herrington Creek, Herrington Manor, and Herrington Manor State Park are all from the family name Ha(e)rrington.

"Hibernia Woods." Emory remarks that camp-meetings were frequent in Queen Anne's County "quite early in the present century." A "Methodist-Protestant" camp meeting was held in Hibernia woods, near Centreville, in July 1835.

HICKORY. Village, near Belair, Harford County. In 1831 this was the post office of Hickory Tavern. I am inclined to attribute this name to hickory wood or to a location amidst hickory trees. Compare Hickory Avenue (Baltimore). Hickory Thicket (Kent), etc.

Note: There is the possibility that *Hickory Tavern owes its name to the well-known sobriquet ("Old Hickory") of President Andrew Jackson. Jackson was re-elected in 1832.

HIGHLAND BEACH. Village and summer resort on Chesapeake Bay, seven miles below Annapolis, Anne Arundel County. It has been an incorporated municipality since 1922. Charles Douglass, son of Frederick Douglass, the abolitionist, bought land here in 1892, and built the first house in 1894. Though it is principally a summer resort, ten families live here the year round. The name is somewhat descriptive; there is an open shoreline, and the land is obviously high when compared with the waters of the Bay.

HILLSDALE. It is on Gwynn's Falls, five miles from the Baltimore City Hall. Having been founded in 1832, this place has had the earlier names, *Dickeyville* (William Dickey) and *Wetheredville* (John Wethered). It became *Hillsdale* in 1911. The name is fitting because of the somewhat hilly terrain.

HILLTOP. Village, near Ironside, Charles County. (*Hilltop*, Scott 1807). This place is directly at the top of a little hill beyond Ironside.

*HOCKLEY. A lost place near Parole, Anne Arundel County. Mapped by Griffith in 1794. This was "Hockley-in-the-Hole," and represented the ancestral home of the Dorseys. Evans, describing "Hockley-in-the-Hole" as the name of a land grant made in 1664 by Cecilius Calvert to Edward, Joshua, and John Dorsey, remarks: "'Hockley-in-the-Hole' evidently derived from a place with a similar name situated in ... Clerkenwell, London." The English place is mentioned by Boswell and Dickens, and was celebrated for bull-baiting and bear-baiting.

*HOFFMANVILLE. Erstwhile Baltimore County village, now lying beneath the waters of Prettyboy Reservoir. What was probably the first paper mill in Maryland appears to have flourished here from 1775/76 until 1893. The post office was *Paper Mills* until the 1880's. Then the name was changed to *Hoffmanville in honor of William H. Hoffman, grandson of William Hoffman, the founder.

*HOLE IN THE WALL. Talbot County. It is on Griffith's map of 1794. The post office name of *Hole in the Wall is today *Hambleton*. There are three stories to explain the former name: (1) smugglers on boats from England to Oxford, Maryland, secretly traded their goods through a hole in the foundation of an old house; (2) the daughter of a protective father made a hole in the wall for her suitors to peep through and reconnoiter; (3) having seen enough through the hole in the wall to feel a jealous rage, a suitor shot and killed his rival. Unaware of his crime the girl married her jealous lover who confessed the murder on his deathbed.

*HOLLACA SNOOZE. Also, *HOLLOW CUTS NOOSE. A large coastal bight at Kent Point, Queen Anne's County. *Noose* here refers to a *bight*, "... a bend in a coast, forming an open Bay." The explanation of *hollaca* (*hollow cuts*) is difficult. Perhaps *hollow* means a "tidal cove"; but I am more inclined to attribute it to the English family name *Halket(t)*. The origin then would be *Halket's Noose, with an intrusive *a* in Halket to give *Hallaket* ("Hollaca," "Hollow Cut"), and the *s* of Halket's becoming joined to Noose to give "Snooze."

HOLLADAY. In Anne Arundel County. From a family name, variously spelled. Henry Hollyday relates that John Holliday was brought to St. Mary's County by Richard Taylor in April 1677. This Richard Taylor was perhaps the brother of Col. Thomas Hollyday, I, who founded the family in Maryland. There were other important *Hollidays* in Calvert, Talbot, and Queen Anne's Counties. The 1790 census for Anne Arundel, lists John Holliday (six slaves). Cf. Holliday Street, Baltimore City. (See: "The Hollyday Family," *MHM*, 26:2, June 1931, pp. 159–71).

HOLLAND'S CLIFFS. Patuxent River, near Huntingtown, Calvert County. Mapped in 1904 as *Hollin Cliff*. Stein mentions *Abington's (now Holland's) Cliffs. See HOLLAND'S POINT.

HOLLAND'S POINT, a mistake for HALLOWING POINT, Patuxent River, opposite Benedict, Calvert County. Stein remarks that the name *Holland's Point* was used for *Hallowing Point*, and so appears on "certain old maps." He comments: "... the name, Hallowing Point, with its connotations of Indians and early white settlers shouting to call the ferryman from the other side of the wide Patuxent River, has been revived in recent years." See HALLOWING POINT.

HOLLAND'S POINT. Chesapeake Bay, Anne Arundel County. Stein states that Francis Holland, a Virginia Puritan, settled in lower Anne Arundel in the early Puritan days. His son, Col. William Holland, together with Richard Harrison and Samuel Chew, bought the landed estates of the Abington family, Calvert County, in about 1695. Col, William Holland, when he died in 1732, left his plantation, "bought of John Abington," to his son, William Holland.

HOLLY. As early as 1663-64 one finds in Maryland *Holly Hill and *Holly Neck. In later years have arisen the villages of HOLLYGROVE (Worcester), HOLLYWOOD (St. Mary's), and HOLLYWOOD PARK

(Montgomery). Most of these names are from the shrub, American holly, which is especially abundant on the Delmarvan Peninsula. Compare *Green Holly Point* (St. Mary's).

HOMEWOOD. This English family name is found in HOMEWOOD, an Anne Arundel village, in HOMEWOOD, an obscure place in Montgomery County, and in HOMEWOOD and HOMEWOOD HOUSE, Baltimore City. James, John, and Thomas Homewood were on the Magothy River in the mid-seventeenth century; Homewood, Baltimore, was surveyed in 1670 for John Homewood. The surname *Homewood* means "wood near the manor-house."

HONGA RIVER. A tributary of the Chesapeake Bay at Hooper Strait, Dorchester County. Early spellings besides *Honga* are *Hunger*, *Hungar*, and even *Hungary*. Bozman concludes that this is the stream called **Rappahanock* by Captain John Smith. **Rappahanock* probably means "the alternating stream." And *Honga* appears to be an abbreviation (*-hunge*) of Powhatan *kahunge* (kahangoc) "goose." *Hungar* (*Hunger*, *Hungary*) are folk etymologies.

HOODS MILLS. Village, near Sykesville, Carroll County. James Hood, who inherited a large estate surrounding this mill, was the postmaster here in 1834. At first it was a flour and grist mill. It burnt down and was replaced by a rolling mill.

*HOOKSTOWN. *Hookstown has become ARLINGTON, Baltimore City. The road to this site was first known as the "Hooksville Road"; later it became Pennsylvania Avenue, Baltimore. Davidson relates that in about 1785 John Hook, of Manchester, settled with all his family in "a log house on the Reistertown Road near the bridge." In 1800 there were fifty or more families here, and the name of the settlement became *Hookstown*. The change to ARLINGTON was made in about 1870 when it looked as though *Hookstown would be engulfed by Pimlico. See ARLINGTON.

HOOPERSVILLE. On Middle Hooper Island, Dorchester County. This village takes its name from the Hooper family of Hooper Island. The island is on Fry and Jefferson's map of 1775; Hoopersville seems to have arisen between 1852 and 1866. Henry Hooper, of England, first settled in Calvert County where, in 1658, he was a gentleman justice. In 1667 he moved to Dorchester County and obtained a survey of 100 acres on Hooper's Island, near Hungar (Honga) River. In the *Star* (4 June 1967) Benjamin Ruhe gives a photograph of Walter Hooper, Jr., 81, whom he calls "the dean of the clan which gave the Chesapeake Isle its name."

HORSEHEAD. Village, near Baden, Prince George's County. This was the post office of *Horse Head* in 1819. Although there was once the "Horsehead Store" here, with a wooden sign showing the head of a horse, the name of the village and the locality probably comes from the ancient "Horsehead Tavern," supposed to have been visited twice by Lincoln's assassin, Booth. It is likely that the tavern also had a sign showing a horse. "Horseshoe Road" is nearby. Compare RISING SUN.

HOUCKSVILLE. Near Hampstead, Carroll County. In 1849 this was the post office of *Houck's Store.* Today in this vicinity the family name *HOUCK (HOCK)* abounds. There are 18 *Houcks* in the 1963 Carroll County phone book. Pronunciation: *HOCKS-ville.* See MEXICO.

HOWARD. This celebrated family name has given HOWARD COUNTY, HOWARDSVILLE (near Pikesville, Baltimore County), and such urban names as Howard Heights, Howard Park, Howardale, and Howard Street. Howard County was formed in 1851. It and nearly all the other Howard names in Maryland are from Col. John Eager Howard "of Revolutionary fame," who was Governor of Maryland from 1788 until 1791. There is strong evidence that Col. Howard and his grandfather, Joshua Howard, were the descendants of Matthew Howard, who received a patent of land on July 3, 1650.

HOYES. Village, near Accident, Garrett County. Early names were **Hoyesburg* (p.o. 1841), *Hoyestown* and **Johnstown P.O.* In 1799, to credit Schlosnagle, William Waller Hoye (1768–1836), an Irishman from Frog Harbor Manor, on the Potomac River, near Williamsport, moved with his family and slaves to Ginseng Hill, Garrett County. The family name, in Ireland, is O'Hoye; Charles Hoye, a descendant, refers to the "little known part of norther Ireland" the original Hoye was from.

HUDSON. This family name is commemorated in Maryland by *Hudson*, Dorchester County; **Hudson Creek* (or **River*), Dorchester County; *Hudsons Corner*, Somerset County; and *Hudson's Corners*, Cecil County. **Hudson Creek* and **Hudson River* are identical. The names once designated Little Choptank River, but the U.S. Geographic Board has ruled "Not Hudson." The surname *Hudson (Hodson, Huttson)* abounds on the Eastern Shore. The family has graveyard sites in protestant cemeteries in Snow Hill, Rehobeth, and Berlin. The 1790 census has 26 entries, fifteen of them being for Worcester County. In Dorchester the name appears as *Hodson.*

HUGHLETT. An obscure place in Talbot County. The first William Hughlett came to Maryland from Virginia in 1759, and settled near Greensboro, Caroline County. Thomas Hughlett became a member of the Maryland legislature; William Hughlett, the second son, was an extensive landholder. The most likely originator of HUGHLETT seems to be Col. Thomas Hughlett, whose father owned "Warwick Manor," Dorchester County. This Colonel Thomas Hughlett (1826–1896), a planter, and Clerk of the County Court, lived in Easton.

HUNGARY NECK. Somerset County. See HONGA.

HUNGARYTOWN. Worcester County. See HONGA

HUNTING CREEK. Stream and village, Patuxent River, near Barstow, Calvert County. It is on Griffith's map of 1794. Stein remarks that "in the very early days" Hunting Creek had been known by "the Indian name of 'Chingaware' Creek." See HUNTINGTOWN.

HUNTINGTOWN. A crossroads village southeast of Lower Marlboro, Calvert County. It lies near the site of old Huntingtown on Hunting Creek. Old Huntingtown—at the head of navigation, Hunting Creek—was established in 1683, when the Assembly of Maryland passed an act for the laying out of towns. Old Huntingtown was attacked by the British in 1814 and completely destroyed by fire. Meanwhile the creek became too full of silt for further navigation.

Note: There are four Hunting Creeks in Maryland, Cf. *Hunting C, Hunting Cr. T.*, Caroline County. Cf. Fowling Creek, Caroline County.

HURLOCK. A town, northeast of East New Market, Dorchester County. This was the site of a railroad station in 1867. John M. Hurlock built the first store in 1869 and the first dwelling in 1872. In 1878 J. M. Hurlock, a miller and farmer, was the local postmaster. Pronunciation: HERLUCK.

HURRY. Village, near Chaptico, St. Mary's County. This odd name is from the English family name *Hurry* (*Hurrey, Hurrie, Horrey, Horry*, etc.). In 1970 there were three families of *Hurry* in Maryland. The St. Mary's County phone book (1963) lists five families.

HUTTON. Village, near Crellin, Garrett County. In 1866 this was *Huttons Switch Sta.*, on the B. & O. Railroad. A large tannery there later burned down. I cannot find the Hutton family in the annals of Garrett County. However, the 1790 census lists nine examples for Maryland in general.

HUYETT. Village, west of Hagerstown, Washingtown County. Also "Huyett Cross Roads." Williams relates that "at an early day" Louis or Ludwick Huyett (1739-1828) came to "The Willows," Washington County. Two of his sons were Jacob and Daniel. The 1971 Washington County phone book lists five Huyetts near here. Pronunciation: HEWITT.

HYATTSTOWN. Village, near Clarksburg, Montgomery County. It was founded in 1800 by Jesse Hyatt. According to Bowie he was "another member of the Hyatt family/of Prince Geoarge's County/..."

HYATTSVILLE. Town, near Bladensburg, Prince George's County. An item in the *Star* (29 March 1878) indicates that before the nearby branch of the Potomac River became filled with silt this was the "port town" of *Bealltown*. The present name is for Christopher Clark Hyatt, who bought land here in 1845, Green has him settling in 1860.

HYNSON. Village, near Preston, Caroline County. When Thomas Hinson (d. 1668) came to the province of Maryland in 1650-51, he became Clerk of the Isle of Kent, and "High Sheriff for ye Countie." Thomas's son

(d. 1679) later settled in Talbot County where, in April 1666, he became Sheriff. "Hynson's Town" was the name of Thomas, Jr.'s Talbot County estate.

*HYNSON TOWN. Queen Anne's County. Reed's Creek was known as *Hynson Town Cr. and *Hynson's Cr. The lands were known as *Hynson Town and *Hynson Town Addition. The owner was Richard Hynson.

I

*I. B. A village, north of Church Hill, Queen Anne's County. Emory remarks that in 1811 *I. B. had been in existence many years. See (and compare) *I. U. and T. B.

IDLEWILD(E). Villages. Maryland has two, one in Baltimore County, and the other in Anne Arundel County near Shadyside. Cf. *Idylwild* Wildlife Demonstration Area, Caroline County (1962). *Idlewild* usually denotes an idyllic, pastoral locality. However, the Anne Arundel *Idlewild* is unusual. For I learn from Ferdinand Wilde (WILL-dy), a resident (1971), who estimates the age of the village to be about eighty, that the name is probably owing (in part) to his grandfather, a German, who was among the region's earliest settlers. Mr. Wilde sees a strong likelihood that the family name *Wilde* (WILL-dy) gave rise to the placename *Idlewild*.

IGLEHART. Village. Near Crownsville, Anne Arundel County. In 1811 Juliana and Leonard Iglehart built a mansion, "Iglehart," near the Baltimore and Annapolis railway line. Today their graves are nearby. According to Warfield the original Igleharts were from Germany and settled near Marlborough, Prince George's County, in 1740. Stein remarks: "The Igleharts, distinguished in law and medicine, trace their Saxon lineage back to the second crusade." Pronunciation: EYE-gull-hart.

IJAMSVILLE. Bush Creek, near Bartonsville, Frederick County. An earlier name, *Ijams' Mill (1832), comes from a grist mill built here by John Ijams. And this was the name assigned to the new depot in return for Plummer Ijams' permission for the Baltimore and Ohio Railroad to run its

---

Note: Henry Wright Newman (*Anne Arundel Gentry*, Vol. I (Annapolis, Md., 1970, pp. 293 ff.) gives an extensive genealogy of the Ijams families and comments, as follows, on the family name: "It is not listed among the ancient names of Britain, although some believe that it is a corruption of James or the Scottish Ian. In the seventeenth century the letters i and j were interchangeable, and the family and Christian name of James was often written as Iames. In the early period of the family in Maryland, however, there is a persistent double "ii" which is certainly not characteristic of the English language. Double vowels are an unmistakable characteristic of the ancient Dutch and Flemish tongues, and there is more reason to believe that the origin is Dutch or Flemish rather than British. The clerk of the Probate Court wrote ... "Eyoms," which would indicate that it was pronounced at that time with two syllables."

first line through his land. Evidently the change from *Mill* to *-ville* was rapid. Postal history records *Ijamsville* post office for 1832; in 1834 Plummer Ijams was the postmaster. (Thanks to Ruth English, Frederick County librarian, who cites Charles Moylan, *Ijamsville, The Story of a Country Village*, 1951).

ILCHESTER. A village on the Patapsco River, near Ellicott City, Howard County (GMd 1941 [Balt. & How.], Manual 1947 [Ilchester, Balt. Co., Ilchester Road, Howard Co.]). Doris M. Chickering, of the Howard County Historical Society, kindly informs me (Sept. 1983) that: (1) the future Ilchester site was acquired by the Ellicott brothers in 1772; (2) a post office was established at *Ilchester Mills in 1842; and (3) that the dates of the Golden Jubilee of the Redemptorist Novitiate here are 1907–1957. There seems little doubt that Ilchester derives its name from the English market town of Ilchester, Somersetshire, in the valley of the River Yeo.

INDIAN BONE. Dorchester County. Indian bones are said to have been found here. In the old Indian fields near "Indian Bone Farm," stands the colonial mansion, "Algonquin Manor."

"Indian Bridge." St. Mary's County. Forman states that Wolseley Manor, patented in 1664, lay at the head of St. Mary's River, near the "Indian Bridge."

"Indian Cave." In Cross District, Howard County. Balt. & Howard 1878 mentions Mrs. M. O. Davis, "Indian Cave."

"Indian Caves." On "Snow Bird Valley" Farm, Montrose, near Reisterstown, Baltimore County. It is told that a schoolteacher, Miss Smith, who ventured into these caves, found them thirty or forty feet high and leading from one to another. The discovery of tomahawks, feathers, arrows, and flintstones indicates that Indians once lived here (See Davidson, pp. 88–89, p. 157).

INDIAN CREEK. Maryland has: (1) *Indian Creek, or *Eastern Branch*, Anacostia River; (2) Indian Creek, a tributary of the Patuxent River between Charles and St. Mary's Counties; (3) Indian Creek, a tributary of the Choptank River, Dorchester County; (4) Indian Creek, a tributary of Levering Creek, Somerset County; and (5) Indian Creek, St. Mary's County, mentioned in 1738–45. The Anacostia *Indian Creek begins about a mile east of College Park (Prince George's County) and is joined by Paint Branch, a stream with Indian connotations. The Patuxent Indian Creek probably commemorates the Indians called *Patuxents*; the Choptank Indian Creek, once known as *Sopetank* Creek, commemorates the *Choptanck* Indians.

INDIAN FIELDS. At Maddox, Wicomico River, St. Mary's County. According to Knight these fields take their name from having been tilled by Indians.

Generally, such names as "Indian Fields," "Old Indian fields," and even "old Indian fort" are mentioned as landmarks in early land transactions.

Actual places are: "Indian fields" (Mattawoman on St. Thomas Creek, Charles County); "an Indian Field" (opposite Chingoemuxon Creeke) in Piscataway River (1674); "Old Indian Fields," Wicomico River, Charles County (1673); and "... an olde Indian field," Charles County (*Archives*, LX, 1664–74). Most Maryland and Delaware *old field* names have arisen from the Indian custom of clearing patches of land on them and dwelling there for a time. See OLDFIELD. See OLDTOWN.

"Indian forte, The." Known as the Anacostin Fort, this structure was situated on the Anacostia River where "the village of Twining," D.C., now stands. See *Archives* (LX, for 1664–74).

INDIAN FORT BRANCH. In February 1687/8 Indians attacked three Baltimore County settlers (killing one Richard Enock), returned to the "Indian Cabbin," and then escaped. Marye conjectures that this "cabbin" was the place for which INDIAN FORT BRANCH, of Deep Creek, Back River, was named.

"Indian Graves." On Broad Run, Baltimore County, between the Great and Little Falls of the Gunpowder River. Weslager observes that a 1769 deposition by Moses Greer mentions "... three heaps or Piles of stones which stand nearly in a triangle ... by the name of the Indian Graves ..." (See: *MHM*, XLII:1).

"Indian Heap." About four miles from *Askiminikonson "Indian Town," on the way to the Shockley Farm Lane. It was an Indian custom to build wayside memorial brush heaps to which each passerby added a twig or branch. Compare "The Indian Heap," Sussex County, Delaware. The Maryland heap quit growing after 1915. Legend attributes its construction to an Indian's wish to memorialize a dead sweetheart.

INDIAN HEARTH. A locality near Shavox, Wicomico County. Wilber Jones (1966) tells me that the ground here is as hard as iron. Near Waste Gate (and environs) the earth (he says) is almost impervious and resists drilling.

"Indian Hill." In the southeastern part of Pikesville, Baltimore County. The many "fighting implements" that have been found in the vicinity indicate the former presence of Indians.

INDIAN ISLAND. This feature (now probably submerged) lies below "the Bald Friar Ferry House" and One Tree Island ("still so called when lately submerged"). It was "taken up" by John Kirk in 1820. (See: Marye, "Place-Names of Baltimore and Harford Counties," *MHM*, XXV:4, Dec. 1930, p. 329).

INDIAN LANDING. On the Severn River, near Severn Crossroads, Anne Arundel County. *Archives* (XLVI for 1750) mentions "Indian Landing Warehouse" on the Severn. There were four other *Indian Landings*: (1) Pocomoke River; (2) Great Monie Creek; (3) Barren Creek (Nanticoke River); and (4) Blackwater River, Dorchester County. Compare *Emperor's Landing (on Rewastico Creek, Wicomico County), which probably commemorates Unnacocassinon, Emperor of the Nanticoke Indians (about 1677).

INDIAN MOUNTING STONE. Indian Fields, St. Mary's County. Knight, indicating that its age is 300, describes this stone as two steps hewn out of rock not found in St. Mary's County. He adds, quite implausibly, that it was used by Indian chiefs to "mount and dismount." Captain William F. Maddox, owner of Indian Fields, says that his father brought the stone here from Knotley Hall, on the Wicomico River, a few miles below his estate. See INDIAN FIELDS.

*INDIANS' NECK. In the "Choptank Indian Lands." *Archives* (XXXIV, for 1722) mentions 600 acres of land called "Indians' Neck." The name refers to a neck of land.

INDIAN POINT. It lies in Harris Creek, Talbot County. Compare INDIANHEAD POINT.

INDIAN QUEEN BLUFF. A bank or cliff on Broad Creek, Potomac River, Prince George's County. In colonial times, when *Queen* designated the wife of an Algonquian chieftain or "emperor," the bluff here was perhaps thought to resemble an Indian. The wife of Chitomacon, the King of Piscataway, was called a *Queen*. Riley states that as late as 1840 the people of Annapolis could remember the visit of (Indian) King Abraham and his wife, Sarah. Compare "The Indian Queen Tavern," Baltimore, "The Indian Queen Hotel," Pennsylvania Ave., Washington, etc.

"Indian Range." The Rent Rolls of Anne Arundel County, Herring Creek Hundred, indicate that Robert Franklyn and Richard Beard surveyed the tract "Indian Range," near "Beards Habitation," in February 1664. Compare "Indian Range," Delaware.

*INDIAN RIVER. Somerset County. *Archives* XXVI, for 1704-06, mentions the petition of Robin, Indian and Chief of the Indians belonging to the Indian Towne at the head of the Indian River in Somersett County.

INDIAN ROCK. Formerly a visible island in the Susquehanna River, Cecil County; now submerged because of the Conowingo Dam. The name refers to Indian rock carvings. Raymond Thompson's title (*Sun*, March 20, 1960) describes them: "Signs of Civilization, Maryland's Most Ancient are Carvings on Susquehanna River Rocks." Compare "Indian Rock," on Rock Creek, north Chevy Chase, Montgomery County, and "Indian Rock," a granite stone twelve feet high, lately destroyed in the Kensington area of Montgomery County.

INDIAN RUN. Three are of interest: (1) a branch of Blackrock Run, Baltimore County; (2) a branch of Grave Run, Baltimore County; and (3) an arm of the East Branch of the Patapsco River, Carroll County. Baltimore County had no known Indian towns of importance in historical times, and the first stream may owe its name merely to the presence of a few Indian cabins belonging to a temporary settlement. The second stream is perhaps more properly "Indian *Grave* Run," and apparently has its name from an Indian grave. The land records of Baltimore and Harford Counties make three specific references to Indian graves.

"Indian Spring." The Matapeakes, the real Indians of Kent Island, once lived near Indian Spring. Emory states that here there have been found many Indian relics and arrowheads.

INDIAN SPRING PARK. A village in Montgomery County, near Takoma Park. The spring here has been described as one of the freest flowing in the Washington area. It feeds a branch called Indian Creek. There was also an "Indian Spring Farm." Compare *Indian Spring* near the Patuxent River, Prince George's County.

INDIAN SPRINGS. Near Frederick, Frederick County. Evelyn Korrell, of Indian Springs, writes me: "There is a large spring on the property on which we live. Years ago the Indians were said to have a camp by this spring and gave the spring the name Indian Spring and this little vicinity has been called Indian Springs."

Perhaps this is the spot described by Dulany: "At a spring on Little Monocacy, about five miles from ... where this ... stream discharges its waters into the Potomac, axes, chisels, augers, spearheads, arrowpoints, drills, and pieces of curious pottery have been found deeply imbedded in mud and sand. Some of these implements were of native copper, and some of stone, ... well wrought out ..." (See: Dulany's *History of Maryland from 1632 to 1891*. Baltimore, 1891 p. 130.)

INDIAN SPRINGS. A village in Washington County. It lies within four miles of Clearspring, Indian Spring (whence its name), and Green Spring Furnace Road.

INDIANHEAD. A town near the Potomac River, Charles County. Shannon (1916) explains: "A high ... wooded point of the Potomac end of .../Indianhead Neck/ has been called Indian Head ever since white men found Indians there ... the name "Indian Head" has now come to be applied to several square miles of territory." (See: *Rambler*, II, 49). See INDIAN QUEEN BLUFF.

INDIANTOWN. There are several. The 1941 Gazetteer gives one for Queen Anne's County, another for Dorchester County. Indiantown, on the Wicomico River, Southern Maryland, is the site of an Indian Cemetery. Indiantown, Worcester County, has been referred to as (1) the Askiminikonson Indian Town, (2) Askiminikanson ... known as Indiantown, and (3) Askimenkonsen ..." now lying in Coulbourns district, and still called Indiantown." See INDIAN CREEK (Dorchester County).

INGLESIDE. On Beaverdam Ditch (or Causeway), Queen Anne's County. Emory (pp. 330–31 states that Ingleside was first *Long Marsh* ("Tappahannah or Long Marsh") and later *Beaver Dam*. *Long Marsh*

Note: *Tappahannah* is the only occurrence I have seen of a Maryland counterpart of the Virginia *Rappahannock* (*Toppahanock*). It is Powhatan for "Stream of the lapping waves."

became a post office in 1837. The name was later changed to *Ingleside*, perhaps from a local farm. The word *ingleside* suggests a cozy rural locality.

*INLET CREEK. At the Head of Assawoman Bay above the Narrows, Worcester County (Surveys of 1686, 1688). This vanished name suggests the earlier presence of an inlet between Mattapony Inlet and a place two miles south of Bethany Beach, where the mainland and the seashore unite. See MATTAPONI.

IRELAND CREEK. Dorchester County. See ISLAND CREEK.

IRISH CREEK. Between Treadhaven Creek and Broad Creek, Talbot County. (Fisher 1852).

"Irish Grove, The." Rumbly Point, Pocomoke Sound, Somerset County. A 1400-acre tract of marshland and loblolly pine known since 1665 as "The Irish Grove."

IRONSHIRE. A community near Berlin, Worcester County. Earlier *Poplar Town*. But there were no poplars here in 1966. The present name is from a local family. The 1790 Census lists Esther *Ironshier*, Worcester County.

IRONSIDES. Village, near Hilltop, Charles County. Steve Risko (Ironsides, 1971) attributes the name to "Old Ironsides" (the frigate *Constitution*). However, Lee Millstead (Ironsides) tells me that his house (built in about 1886) was once renovated by having its sides covered with tin. I prefer to explain the name by this fact.

Note: For twenty years the tin has been covered by "siding."

*ISIDORAS CREEK. Prince George's County. Warrants of 1662 and 1787 mention a creek called *Isidoras*. Shannon remarks: "It is puzzling to know where was Isidoras Creek, unless that were the earlier name of Oxon Run." (See: *Star*, May 18, 1924). See OXON CREEK, OXON RUN.

ISLAND CREEK. Village and stream. The village is on the headwaters of the creek and was evidently named for it. The stream, however, begins in Solomons Island District and flows from there past Broomes Island into the Patuxent. Thus it appears uncertain which island the creek was named for.

ISLAND CREEK. It flows through a salt marsh, past Grays Island, into Fishing Bay, Dorchester County. The islands here are dry places in an extensive salt marsh.

*ISLAND POINT. This is the now vanished elongation of Rickett Pt., towards Spry Island, at the mouth of Gunpowder River, Harford County. The hurricane of 1893 is said to have damaged this former peninsula. The land was laid out in 1683 for Mary Stansby, the daughter of Oliver Spry. It was then called "Island Point." Seen from the Bay, the peninsula may have looked like an island. See RICKET POINT; see SPRY ISLAND.

*ISLINGTON. Early village, Little Choptank River, Dorchester County. Private records indicate that early sessions of court in Dorchester County were held in various family homes at *ISLINGTON, on Nicholas Mayner's Point, Little Choptank River. Cf. Islington, a town in both Middlesex and Norfolk Counties, England.

ISRAEL CREEK. (1) Monocacy River, Frederick County; (2) Potomac River, Washington County, listed in Fisher, 1852. These two names are from either the given name *ISRAEL* (*Izrel*) or the surname *Israel* (*Isral*). Heads 1790 lists Israel *French* /*Friend*?/ and John *Israel* and his son for Frederick County. No *Israel*s occur in Heads 1790 for Washington County. But it is known that from Washington County came Midshipman *Israel*, who died heroically in Tripoli Harbor, 4 Sept. 1804.

Note: A survey of 1734 that mentions "Israel Friend's Mill Road ... where the said road crosses a hill called Kittawkin." Perhaps this is the Israel *Friend* (Fred. Co.) listed in the 1790 Census as Israel *French*. *Kittawkin* is for *Catoctin*. Grove (p. 368) mentions a tract, "Four Friends," on Israel Creek on the Baltimore and Annapolis road from Frederick. I suggest that ISRAEL CREEK, Frederick County, takes its name from *Israel Friend*.

ISSUE. Village, near Tompkinsville, Charles County. John Dorsey, estimating the village to be about eight years old, finds that the name arose from the *issue* of whether the first post office should be at the north of the town or the south end. The debate was lengthy and the annoyed Post Office Department began calling the town "Issue" in its correspondence. "... when the post office was finally built in a compromise location the name became official." (See: *Sun*, Jan. 13, 1963).

*I. U. Village. Worton District, Kent County. Hill, speaking of a parish church (1765) "I. U.", Kent County, remarks: "... this name ... is believed to have been the name by which a small village at the crossroads was formerly known." Hill cites the following occurrences of the lost name: (1) tract ... called IU (1728); (2) tract vulgarly called IU (1728); and (3) "... Forrest Plantation, always known by name of I. U. ..." (1753). Usilton explains that the I. U. probably means J. U., with the *J* probably standing for "John, Jim, or Jonas" and the *U* for Ute, Usilton, Urie, etc. Ridgely goes so far as to ascribe I. U. to "... John *Usidon*, a considerable landowner, whose initials decorated a signpost at the crossroads where the chapel stood." (See: Hill, MCC, 187; Usilton, p. 92; Ridgely, Old Brick, pp. 16–17). See T. B.

IVORY. Village, near West Friendship, Howard County. Cf. Ivory Mill (Harford), Ivory Run (Charles). A 1904 spelling (*Ivery*) suggests an origin from the surname *Ivery*, noticed by Passano as having been mentioned by Torrence, MHS, and DAR. The Annapolis telephone book for 1970 lists two *Ivrey*. The Baltimore phone book (1969) has three Ivery, three Ivory, two Ivrey, and one Ivry. (British; Anglo-Norman).

IVY...In such names as IVY NECK, Anne Arundel County, *IVY RUN (Marye); and IVY TOWN (Talbot County), there are three plausible explanations: (1) ivy, the vine; (2) the surname *Ivy*; and (3) the (mountain) laurel. The 1790 Census lists Joseph *Ivy* for Harford County. And the Annapolis phone book (1970) lists two *Ivy's*.

Marye gives two indications that *ivy* in Maryland sometimes means "(mountain) laurel": (1) a statement by Heath Steele (St. Mary's County, 1951) that *ivy* was used for "laurel" in St. Mary's County; and (2) the following lines from a Md.–Del. surveyor's journal (1751) "... a small Ridge of Ivey or Laurel ..." See LAUREL; see LONG GREEN RUN.

J

JACKSON. Village, near Lonaconing, Allegany County. In the vicinity are JACKSON JUNCTION, JACKSON MINE, and JACKSON RUN. The mine on Jackson Run is a coal mine. The junction would be on the Cumberland and Pennsylvania Railroad. Since the run was probably named before the mine, one supposes that an early settler is commemorated. In 1968 there were three telephone listings for the family name *Jackson* in the Lonaconing area.

JACOBSVILLE. Near Armiger, Anne Arundel County. I conclude from Hopkins 1878 that the name is from the *Jacobs* family. Near the village Hopkins charts the residences of "Dorsey Jacobs Hrs" and "Thos. S. Jacobs," whose home apparently was "Temperance Hall."

JAMAICA POINT. Opposite Indian Creek and Oyster Shell Point, Talbot County. In view of Delaware *ktemaque* "beaver," there is some reason to believe that *Jamaica* here is Algonquian. The *Ja-* may be equivalent to the *kte-* of the Delaware word. Tooker attributes *Jamaica*, Long Island, to the Algonquian word for "beaver." He cites a 1656 certificate: "Ye bever pond, commonly called Jamaica." But an even stronger argument can perhaps be made for the origin of Jamaica Point from Jamaica, British West Indies. After 1658 Jamaica, B.W.I., was a British Colony; and the island was an important slave market (1672) and a producer of coffee and sugar. No doubt there was appreciable trade between Jamaica and Maryland. Marye found two early backwoods tracts in Baltimore County named "Jamaica" and "Poor Jamaica Man's Plague."

JAMES. Village, near Hudson, Dorchester County. Cf. *James Island* and *James Point*, Dorchester County. The 1790 census gives only two instances of the family name *James* for Dorchester County. However, the Dorchester phone book (1963) gives twenty such instances. The address of one of them (Mrs. Mittie James) is Hudson. (See Above.)

*JAMESTOWN. Somerset County. This was the earlier name of UPPER FAIRMOUNT. However, the Postal History Catalogue has

"Jamestown 1849–1850," and remarks: " 'Fairmount' was changed to 'Jamestown' in 1849." See MANOKIN.

*JAMESTOWN. Sassafras River, Cecil County. See OLDTOWN.

*JAMESTOWN. Rhode River, Anne Arundel County. Its earlier name was *SCRABBLETOWN. Riley (p. 110) notes that a Capt. Ball built the first house here in 1840. The earlier name arose owing to the remark William McCarter made to Capt. Ball when he paid Ball a visit in this wooded area: "I've been scrabbling about here all day trying to find you." Riley states that the present name, given "about five years since," has no historic or local significance. See *SCRABBLETOWN.

JAMISON. Village, near Hagerstown, Washington County. Williams described the men perhaps responsible for this name: John I. Jamison, farmer and merchant (b. Frederick Co.); and J. V. Jamison (b. Urbana, Frederick County, 1851), the son of John I. Jamison. In 1897 John V. Jamison went into the coal and grain business in Hagerstown. In 1901, he began manufacturing lumber at Big Pool, Marykand. He became president of the Hagerstown Cooperage Co. (Pronunciation: JEM-i-son).

JARBOES, village. Near Mechanicsville, St. Mary's County. See *JARBOESVILLE.

*JARBOESVILLE. Near Herman(s)ville, St. Mary's County. John Jarboe, in about 1648, built a house at Long Lane Farm, overlooking Chesapeake Bay. This could have been John Jarbo, of Dijon, France (1619–1676). The latter enlisted in the force to restore Gov. Calvert's authority, and took an oath of fealty to the Lord Proprietary on 2 Jan. 1646/47. In 1666 he was Lieutenant Colonel Jarbo of the Regiment of trained bands (St. Mary's County); in 1674 he was a delegate to the Lower House of Assembly. However, the present name may have come from a much later *Jarbo(e)*. (See McHenry Howard, *MHM*, XV: 4). See LEXINGTON PARK.

Note: Gregory A. Wood (*The French Presence in Maryland 1524–1800*. Baltimore, 1978, p. 18) gives other details, such as that he became a naturalized citizen in 1666 and that his term of office in the Lower House was from 1671 to 1674.

JARRETTSVILLE. near Coopstown, Harford County. The Postal History Catalogue states that " 'Carmens' was changed to 'Jarrettsville' in 1838." In 1878 there were living at Jarrettsville: Dr. Martin L. Jarrett; and J. W. Joshua, and a W. B. Jarrett (farmers). It appears that Jesse Jarrett became real estate assessor for Harford County in January 1798. Preston notes that in February 1858 A. Lingan Jarrett was one of the commissioners who contracted for the erection of the new courthouse at Bel Air. Using a different spelling, "Capt. A. Lingan Jarrett" was for many years Clerk of the Harford County Circuit Court. The father of Captain Jarrett was "Abraham Jarrett."

JAVA, "JAVA FARMS." Situated in the vicinity of Rhode River, near Muddy Creek Road, Anne Arundel County. "Java Farms" was the former name of what is today the Chesapeake Bay Center for Environmental Studies. The present owner is the Smithsonian Institution, to which Roger Lee Forrest, an interim owner, willed the land in 1962. The *Java* of the two places comes from the name of the British warship which Robert Contee, an earlier owner, helped to sink in 1812. (See: Frances Jacques, *Capital*, June 30, 1977).

JEFFERSON. Village, near Feagaville, Frederick County. Settlers were here in 1743. The Postal History Catalogue relates: " 'Newtown Trap' was changed to 'Jefferson' in 1832. 'Trap' is always used with this 'Newtown' . . . probably to distinguish it from the Newtown office in Worcester County." Because of highway robbers this spot was known as "The Trap." Grove remarks that it was therefore customary for six or eight wagons to travel together. The present name is for President Thomas Jefferson (d. 1826). Cf. Jeffersons Corners (Somerset County), which was changed to "Bell Mount" in 1850.

JENNINGS. Village, near Bevansville, Garrett County. It arose in the late 1800's and was named for the Pennsylvania timber and railroad capitalists, Cord H. and Worth B. Jennings, who had enterprises here. (See: Schlosnaggle, 76–77).

*JENNINGS RUN, Village and stream, Allegany County. The stream is a tributary of Wills Creek, at Corriganville. Postal History records that *Jennons Run* (1840) was changed to *Mt. Savage* in 1847. Here in 1842 were the "Mt. Savage Iron Works," later the village of Mt. Savage. *Jennings* is a British family name, a diminutive of *John*. See MT. SAVAGE.

JERICHO PARK. A village in Prince George's County. It is sometimes spelled with a *G*. I have the feeling that horses were raced here. Older instances of the name *Jericho* in Maryland are: " . . . Land Called Jerichoe" (1678, Prince George's County); "Jericho" (1747, Anne Arundel County); "Dan" and "Jericho" (1684, Anne Arundel County); and *Jericho (Gunpowder Falls, between Jerusalem and Franklinville). "Jericho Bridge" is near Jerusalem Mills. For the famed biblical city of the miraculous walls. See *JERUSALEM MILLS.

Note: Attention should be called to the historic Jericho Covered Bridge (near Kingsville and spanning the Little Gunpowder Falls), which, after being closed for two years, was reopened on July 7, 1983. This structure, 118 years old, is one of the few remaining covered bridges in Maryland. It is now reinforced with steel. See: "Covered bridge re-opened to traffic," *Capital*, July 6, 1983.

JERUSALEM. In 1941 there were two villages, one in Frederick County, near Myersville, the other near Bagley, in Harford County. Sallie Marker, of Meyersville, informs me that eleven migrants from Cecil County came here in 1710 to search for iron ore in the Catoctin Mountains.

They built two churches, the second in 1716. A biblical name was appropriate. The Harford County village was near *Jericho. See *JERUSALEM MILLS.

Note: Scott 1807 mentions "*Jerusalem or Funkstown ... on Anti-Etam creek /near/ Elizabeth-town." Here there was a German church.

*JERUSALEM MILLS. A village near Jericho and Clayton, Harford County. Postal history records that "Jerusalem Mills" was changed to "Franklinville" in 1841, and was changed back to "Jerusalem Mills" in 1844. Eventually it became the present JERUSALEM. Reppert (*Sun*, 24 Sept. 1961) finds that the village grew up around the mill that Quaker David Lee built on Little Gunpowder Falls in 1772. Another Quaker, Elisha Tyson, built on the Little Gunpowder at what became Jericho. Marye remembers that the river bottom at Gunpowder Falls, below Franklinville, was called "Egypt." See JERICHO; see JERUSALEM.

Note: Compare Somerset County's Jeric(h)o, Jeric(h)o Marsh(es), and *Jerusalem.

JESSUP. A village on the B. and O. Railroad near Savage, Howard County. In 1866 this was "Jessups Cut Sta or Hooversville P. O." And *Jessups Cut* was the former name of *Jessup*. The "cut" was a passageway or channel for the new B. & O. Railroad. According to Brown, it was built under the direction of contractor Jonathan Jessup. Hungerford mentions Messrs. Gardner and Jessup, contractors (ca. 1829). Cf. Paxton's Cut, on the B. and O. Railroad between Harper's Ferry and Opequon Bridge. (See: *Sun*, March 5, 1978).

JESTERVILLE. Near Nanticoke, Wicomico County. Heads 1790 lists *Jester* four times. In July 1966, Mrs. Eloise Darby called my attention to the mention of Jno. F. Jester (presumably of this place) in her copy of Atlas 1877.

*JEWSBURG. Near Taylorsville, Carroll County. Authorities in western Carroll County tell me it is no longer heard of. However, I have later learned that *JEWSBURG is now called MARSTON. See MARSTON.

JOHNNY CAKE ROAD. In Catonsville, Baltimore County. Remarking that in 1916 the residents of Johnny Cake Road made an unsuccessful petition to have this name changed, the *News American* (25 May 1973) explains: "The road was named for the cakes and candies ... sold in taverns and shops in the area. A Johnny cake is a bread made of Indian meal,

Note: A deeper look at the phrase *Johnny Cake* raises the question of whether it comes from *journey* cake or even from the American Indian *Shawnee* Cake. Kuethe (*Am. Sp.*, X, 202) favors an origin from *Shawnee*; Mencken (1937) puts *Johnnycake* in the Colonial period and calls it "originally *Shawneecake* or-bread." He and Lowdermilk think the term may have originated in Maryland. Compare other Indian breads, such as *pone*, *pone* bread, corn *pone*, *hoecake*, and *hominy*.

flour, water and eggs. At the time the area was surveyed, the mapmakers were told that the road was called the Johnny Cake Road supposedly out of derision ... "

*JOHNNY CAKE TOWN. On the Johnny Cake Road, west of Baltimore. Davidson states that about eighty years ago, when James Lee kept a tavern on Johnny Cake Road, "all the region from Baltimore to Frederick was so called." He explains that at this tavern " ... one of the ladies of long ago ... served the teamsters and other travellers ... delicious Johnny cake so often for breakfast that the fame of the inn spread through the countryside and they decided to name it Johnny Cake."

*JOHNNYCAKE. See CATONSVILLE.

JOHNSON. Village near Pearre, Potomac River, Washington County. Williams relates that Thomas Johnson, III, first Gov. of Maryland, died in Frederick County in 1818 at the age of 87. Governor Johnson was one of the organizers of Green Spring Furnace, a furnace for making iron. Williams describes the farm where the Johnsons are buried " ... as being in sight of the C. & O. Canal ... about 10 miles from Hancock." This is approximately the location of the present JOHNSON. Cf. JOHNSON MOUNTAIN, near Clearspring, Washington County.

JOHNSON'S CROSS ROADS. A village in Dorchester County. Shannahan (p. 65) speaks of the Patty Cannon Gang (abhorrent to the Negroes of Delaware and Maryland), and declares: "It was ... noteworthy as much for the villainy of Joe Johnson, Patty's son-in-law, as for Patty herself, and to this day the site of Joe Johnson's tavern is on the map as 'Johnson's Cross Roads.' "

JOHNSTOWN. Village, near Solomons, Calvert County. The Johns family (the *Johns* of Johns Hopkins) was founded by Richard Johns (1645–1718), born in Bristol, England, of Welsh parentage. When the Quakers were expelled from Virginia, he fled to Maryland, and in 1694 was elected to the Lower House of the Maryland Assembly. Descendants of Richard Johns, II, left Calvert County in the later eighteenth century. But, states Stein, "We still find a Benjamin Johns listed as a resident of the Upper Cliffs in the Census of 1800."

JOHNSVILLE. Near Libertytown, Frederick County. It was a post office in 1830. The name may commemorate a descendant of the Calvert County *Johns* family. The descendants of Richard Johns, II, (including his son, Benjamin), left Calvert County in the later eighteenth century and resettled in Prince George's, Anne Arundel, Montgomery, and *Frederick* Counties. (See: Stein, pp. 278–79).

*JONAS TOWN. In 1732 the Maryland Assembly authorized the laying out of a town on the east side of ... /Jones Falls/ to be called Jonas Town. The name was later changed to Jones Town. See *JONES TOWN.

JONES. Village, near Taylorville, Worcester County. In 1906 this was Friendship Sta. or Jones P.O. The Guide (p. 440) speaks of " ... the crossroads settlement ... called Jones on most maps but Friendship locally ... "

JONES. An Anne Arundel County black community described by Christine Neuberger (*Capital*, May 4, 1983) as "a pocket of modest bungalows and tiny farmhouses hugging Old Annapolis Boulevard in Severna Park." Commenting on the changes wrought by the coming of the Ritchie Highway, Ms. Neuberger adds: "Some local commuters who use the boulevard know of the existence of Jones, a cluster of black families whose community was named for a late sea captain who retired and sold fruit and nails long before Severna Park had a name." See: SEVERNA PARK.

JONES CHAPEL. Village, near Williamsport, Washington County, About Jonathan Jones (b. Williamsport, 1791) and his descendants, Williams remarks: (1) that Jonathan Jones was a preacher in the United Brethren Church; and (2) that the father of Jonathan Jones was Joseph Jones, of Wales, who came to Maryland from Virginia. His farm as near Mt. Tabor Church, six miles from Hagerstown. He died at Williamsport.

JONES' CROSSROADS. See LAPPANS.

JONES FALLS. A creek in Baltimore County and City. It arises in Green Spring Valley and flows through Baltimore City into the northwest harbour of the Patapsco River. Land on the west side of Jones Falls near the water was surveyed for a planter, David Jones, in 1661. He acquired Cole's Harbour in 1679 and was a resident on the land in 1682. Captain Jones died in 1686–87, and it was Marye's opinion that "oldfield by the ffalls" (deed, 1701) may have been his "dwelling plantation." (See *Guide*, p. 199; *MHM*, XXXV: 2).

*JONES TOWN. The earliest part of Baltimore City. Already established in 1730, and "erected" in 1732 by an Assembly bill into "a town on a Creek Divided from the Town lately laid out in Baltimore County called Baltimore Town ... " This area, the Guide points out, "older in point of settlement than Baltimore Town," is still called Old Town. In 1745 the Assembly made *JONES TOWN and *BALTIMORE TOWN "one entire Town, and for the future called and known by the Name Baltimore Town ... " *JONES TOWN takes its name presumably from the *Jones* of JONES FALLS. See JONES FALLS; see *OLD TOWN.

JOPPA, JOPPATOWNE. An aged hamlet near the boundary line of Baltimore and Harford Counties. Nearby is Gunpowder River at about the point where it becomes an estuary of Chesapeake Bay. Farther north is JERUSALEM. Postal history relates that *GUNPOWDER (Baltimore County) was changed to *JOPPA CROSS ROADS, Harford County, in 1819, and that *JOPPA CROSS ROADS was changed in 1829 to *LITTLE GUNPOWDER, Baltimore County. Joppa once gave promise of becoming the big city of Maryland. In 1712 the Baltimore County seat was moved here from *BALTIMORE TOWN; this lasted until 1768. Joppa was the center of the tobacco business. it was the site of "Joppa Iron

Works," and there is a tradition that there was once a shipyard here. Like nearby JERUSALEM and JERICHO, *Joppa* has a biblical origin. It comes from what is today Jaffa, the harbor city adjacent to Tel-Aviv, Israel.

Note: In 1962, "Joppatowne," a planned community, was built near Joppa. Cf. Columbia.

JOURNEYCAKE NECK. There are two, one on the Patuxent River, Calvert County, the other between Island Creek and the Chester River, Queen Anne's County. The latter is better known as Wilmer Neck. See JOHNNY CAKE ROAD.

*JOURNEYCAKE TOWN. East of Franklin and northwest of Catonsville, Baltimore County. It is *Journeycaketown* on Martenet's map of 1866. The spelling precursor of *JOHNNY CAKE TOWN. See JOHNNY CAKE ROAD.

K

KAESE MILL. Garrett County village near Accident. The name is for Henry Kaese, who built a mill here in 1868. (See: Schlosnagle, p. 89). Pronunciation: CASE-y.

KALMIA. Village, near Gibbon, Harford County. On Rand-McNally's map, 1884. There was probably an abundance here of the evergreen shrub, Kalmia, of the heath family, which takes its name from Peter Kalm, a Swedish botanist. Cf. Kalmia Road, Washington, D.C.; Kalmia Road, Montgomery County (Md.); and Kalmia, Alabama.

KEEDYSVILLE. Near Sharpsburg, Washington County. In 1852 this was *Keedysville P.O.* or *Centreville*. Evidently *Centerville was the first name. Because of postal confusion with Centerville, Queen Anne's County, the citizens later asked the post office department for a different name. So many Keedys signed the request that *Keedysville* was selected. Williams, however, attributes the name directly to John J. Keedy, who built the Baker Mills here. In 1878 C. M. Keedy, railroad agent, Samuel Keedy, carpenter, and Jacob H. Keedy, farmer, were all living here.

KEENE DITCH. A village at Keene Ditch Stream, near Bucktown, Dorchester County. Related names are Keene Broads (pond) and Keenes Point. Maryland has 26 *named* ditches, the majority of them being in Wicomico and Worcester Counties. Some were dug by farmers for drainage; others are natural watercourses. In the present case the name appears to represent the Dorchester Keene family, whose founder, Richard Keen, settled in Calvert County in about 1661.

KEEPTRYST. Village, near Sandy Hook, Washington County. (*Keep Trieste* 1853 PHC; *Sandy Hook Sta.* or *Keeptryst P.O.* Martenet 1866). The Postal History Catalogue remarks: "After . . . /1855/, this office also appears as 'Keep Triest' and 'Keep Tryst.' The last spelling is still used for the town." The name seems to have acquired a folk etymology based on the resemblance of *tryst* to the Italian city, *Trieste*. See SANDY HOOK.

KEMPS. Village, near Williamsport, Washington County. Williams speaks of David C. Kemp, a native (b. 1849) of Loudoun County, Virginia, who lived near Williamsport, on the Williamsport and Greencastle Turnpike. His grandfather, David C. Kemp, had a mill and a distillery, and built the first grain elevator in Frederick County. Williams remarks that David C. Kemp was several times a member of the state legislature.

KEMPTOWN. Village, near Bartholows, Frederick County. It was a post office in 1853. Perhaps the name is from David C. Kemp (son of Christian Kemp, and grandfather of David C. Kemp, II), who was a soldier in the American Revolution, and built the first grain elevator in Frederick County. See KEMPS.

KENDALL. A village, near Friendsville, Garrett County. Apparently an earlier name was *Manor Land*, from the Yough Manor Land Co. In about 1890 the Kendall Lumber Co. operated a sawmill here, and the name became *Kendall*. This was the terminus of the abandoned (1942) Confluence and Oakland Railroad, and the locality once had a post office, a clubhouse, a store, and residences. (See: Weeks, p. 35).

KEN GAR. Washington, D.C., suburb in Montgomery County. It was founded in 1887, and as late as Aug. 19, 1972, the *Star* describes "the Ken Gar Section" as " . . . a small, largely black community of Kensington, long contemplated for redevelopment . . . " The *Ken-* may be from *Kensington*; the *Gar* may be from nearby *Garrett* Park. The *gar-* of *gar*den is also possible.

KENT COUNTY. An upper Eastern Shore county bounded on the north by Cecil and on the south by Queen Anne's. It was founded in 1642 and takes its name from Kent County, England. In 1642 the area was designated the "Isle and County of Kent." However, by an Act passed in 1695, Kent Island, which, to cite Mathews, "had given the name to the County," was removed from county jurisdiction owing to a change in boundaries. Today, Kent Island is in Queen Anne's County.

KENT ISLAND. Between Chesapeake Bay, Eastern Bay, and Chester River, Queen Anne's County. Capt. William Claiborne settled the island, and gave it its present name in honor of his former homeland, the English County of Kent. Claiborne had come to Virginia as a surveyor in 1621. In 1624 he became a member of the Governor's Council. In 1626 he was given a license to explore Chesapeake Bay and trade with the Indians. On p. 80 Emory points out that in 1638 the island was officially mentioned as "Kentish Island." See *MONOPONSON.

KENTUCK SWAMP. The 1950 Map of Dorchester County depicts this feature as an extensive swamp lying east of Little Blackwater River in Church Creek District. The name is probably short for *Kentucky*. And since *Kentucky* is an Iroquoian name, it is not likely that *Kentuck*, as found here, has any linguistic or aboriginal position. It is pronounced *canetuck*.

KENWOOD. Washington suburb near Chevy Chase, Montgomery County. Farquhar (p. 64) gives a clue to the origin of this name when he remarks that the Kenwood Golf and Country Club, (near Bethesda) was "organized by Mr. E. S. Kennedy in 1927." Cf. Kenwood, a village near Catonsville, Baltimore County.

KEYMAR. Village, near Middleburg, Carroll County. *Key-* stands for the family of John Ross Key, father of Francis Scott Key: *-mar* probably signifies *Maryland*. In the fall of 1822 Francis Scott Key sold his father's large mansion and estate on Pipe Creek near here. "Keymar" was probably the name of the mansion, or the estate, or both. (See: Delaplaine, *MHM*, XXX: 2; Grove, p. 69).

KEYSER. Hamlet (el. 2880). Near Oakton, Garrett County. Early map spellings suggest that the hamlet takes its name from nearby Keyser's Ridge. See below.

KEYSER'S RIDGE. A Western Maryland community (el. 2880) near Oakton, Garrett County. In 1852 this was *Keyser's Ridge* (Mt. and post office). Schlosnagle, speaking of "squatters" near the mouth of Savage River in 1787, mentions, "John Kiser" (from whom Keyser's Ridge takes its name). (See: Schlosnagle, p. 51; TW, II, p. 1106).

*KEYSER. Potomac River, Allegany County. The Guide (p. 517) remarks: "(McCool . . . a suburb of the larger Keyser /W. Va./ across the river, was called *Keyser before West Virginia was formed." See McCOOLE.

KEYSVILLE. Near Bruceville, Carroll County. Commenting on "Terra Rubra," the Guide (p. 506) writes: " . . . through Keysville . . . to Terra Rubra, birthplace on August 1, 1779, of Francis Scott Key . . . The tract, patented to Francis' English grandfather, Philip Key, was named for the color of the soil." Grove (p. 68) remarks that "The Keys lived near the Monocacy, near where Mt. St. Mary's College was later built, at a village then called Keysville."

KILDURE. GMd 1941: " . . . in Prince George's County." Probably an error for Kildare. Bowie (pp. 365–367) mentions "Kildare," an Oxon Hill home, and cites a personal letter from Edith Heiskell recounting the tradition that Dr. Tolson, earlier owner of the place, had had a governess from County Kildare, Ireland. " . . . And she gave the name to the place when Dr. Tolson built the house here . . . "

KINDY HOOK. A village near Bryantown, Charles County. Martin VanBuren's Lindenwall estate was at Kinderhook, N.Y., overlooking the Hudson; and "Old Kinderhook" was a Democratic catchword when Van-Buren, "a Northern man with Southern principles," was nominated in

1835 at a Baltimore convention. Political enthusiasm could have brought the name (Kindy = Kinder?) to Charles County. But why does it not appear on earlier maps?

KINGSTON. Near Marion, Somerset County. It was a post office in 1834. Guy E. Windsor, of Westover, discussed "Kingston Hall" with me in 1966 and mentioned King's Creek, which is north of Kingston, well above Westover. "Kingston Hall," the home of the King family, was probably built by Robert King III, who died in 1750. Richardson (II, 156–57), noticing that Thomas King Carroll inherited "Kingston Hall" from his mother, Elizabeth Barnes King, explains that " . . . a small village of the artisan class grew up on one extremity of the great estate, which is still called Kingston."

*KINGSTON (KINGSTOWN). On the Chester River, opposite Chestertown, on the Queen Anne's County side. The General Assembly in 1732 provided for the erection of a town on the Chester River to be called Kingston, apparently in honor of "the reigning monarch." It was evidently in existence in 1835, since in that year the Queen Anne's County Court gave William Primrose a license to keep a tavern there.

KINGSTON, KINGSTON LANDING. The two names represent one and the same place on the Choptank River, near Mathews, Talbot County. Perhaps this is the spot referred to, in an Act to set up ports and towns for unloading ships with Negroes, etc., as "King's Town in great Choptank." (See: *Archives*, XXVI, pp. 336–37, 1706).

KINGSVILLE. Near Bradshaw, Baltimore County. George King was the postmaster here in 1834. However, Marye states that Kingsville takes its name from Abraham King, who was born in Pennsylvania and came to Maryland from Willistown, Chester Co., Pa. He was probably descended from Michael King (or Koenig; 1714–1790), of Chester Co., a native of Wittenburg, Germany.

Note: PHC notices that " 'King's Tavern' was changed to 'Kingsville' in 1829. 'Kingsville' was changed to 'Fork Meeting House' in 1839." Fisher 1852 lists both *Kingsville* and *Fork Meeting-House.* He calls the former a village, and the latter a post office.

*KITTAMAQUINDI. An extinct Conoy (Algonquian) village at the junction of Tinkers and Piscataway Creeks, Prince George's County. Brinton spelled this place *Kittamaque-ink*. The name appears to consist of *Ke?t (Kitta-)* 'great' and **amexkwa* 'beaver.' The meaning would be "place of the big beaver."

The King of Piscataway, the vanished Southern Maryland Indian nation, was named Chitomacon (= Kittamaquindi). It is plausible that the beaver was the totem of the Piscataway gens, and that King Chitomacon (= Kittamaquindi) himself was the "big beaver."

KITZMILLER. A village on the North Branch of the Potomac River, near Swanton, Garrett County. Sometimes *Kitzmillersville.* The site of

Kitzmiller was originally Military Lot 300, bought in 1796 by Thomas Wilson II. In later years, Ebenezer Kitzmiller married the daughter of Thomas Wilson III and operated the Wilson grist mill and saw mill. On page 522 the Guide remarks that in 1882, when the railroad reached this point, there was a lumber boom. Twenty years later coal mining began.

KLEJ GRANGE. Village, Stockton District, Worcester County. Gannett states that the name is a combination of *K*ate, *L*ouise, *E*mma, and *J*osephine, daughters of J. W. Drexel, New York. Elmer Brittingham, of Pocomoke City, mentions, instead of the Drexels, the Girard family of Philadelphia.

KLONDIKE. Allegany County. The Klondike Coal Mining Company named this George's Creek village. Cf. Alaska, West Virginia. The original Klondike (Yukon Territory, Canada) may mean "River" full of fish.

Note: Coal mine names are often exotic, even fantastic (e.g., Ocean, Moscow, Pekin). Cf. VINDEX.

KNAPPS MEADOWS. A village near Lonaconing, Allegany County. The name is from the local *Knapp* family. Postmaster McAlpine, of this place, besides explaining that there was once a tannery near here, gives me (1965) two pronunciations: NAP and ku-NAP. Cf. *Knapp Narrows* (Talbot County), whose pronunciation is NAPS.

KNOWLES. Village near Kensington, Montgomery County. The village evidently existed in 1878. Lewis, at that time, gives *Knowles* as the post office address of farmer George Knowles.

KNOXVILLE. Near Brunswick, Potomac River, Frederick County. Knoxville was laid out in 1772 on several lots of "the Merryland Tract." It was a post office in 1829. In 1790 Maryland had seven persons by the name of *Knox*. See WEVERTON.

KOLBES CORNER. Village, near Largo, Prince George's County. In 1976, for the Washington suburban area of Prince George's and Montgomery Counties, there were telephone listings for 24 Colbys, 7 Kolbes, and one Kolbye. The pronunciation of the present place is COAL-bees.

KOOGLES. A village near Middletown, Frederick County. Between 1765 and the beginning of the American Revolution, five brothers by this name came to Maryland from Darmstadt, Germany, and settled near Bolivar, about three miles west of Middletown. The correct spelling of this German family name is *Kugel*. (See: Williams, II, 825–27).

KREIGBAUM. A village near Cumberland, Allegany County. This is virtually the same place as Corriganville. The name is probably from Conrad Creighbaum, whose will is mentioned for March 1821 in a list of Allegany County wills. (See: *Index to the Wills of Allegany County*, ed. Joan Hume, Baltimore, 1970). See CORRIGANVILLE.

*KROH'S MILLS. Wingate's Maryland Register for 1857 indicates that the postmaster here was John Kroh. (See: Warner et al., p. 52).

*KUS: flu: (*KUSKARAWAOK, village; KUSKARAWAOKS, na-tion). Former designations of the Nanticoke River and its watershed, so spelled on Virginia 1608 Smith.

Because Captain Smith commented on the abundance of "Rawranoke" / roanoke/ or white beads" here, William Wallace Tooker divided this name into *cusca-rawran-oke* and translated "A place of making white beads." For technical reasons, such as the facts that Tooker's *-rawran-* has an *r* that does not appear in Smith's spelling and that Tooker's *-oke* is not supported by correct analysis, it appears prudent to question the accuracy of Tooker's translation.

A more enlightened knowledge of the Algonquian language bolsters the view that *Kuskarawaok* represents a combination of Primitive Algonquian *kacki-* "expert," *-lal-* "(to) smoothe," and *-ahw-* "alternate motion (polishing)." The ending (*-waok*) appears to reflect Primitive Algonquian *-awaki* "they-them." The revised translation would be "They are expert at smoothing them" (i.e., sea shells for wampum).

L

LADIESBURG. A village near LeGore, Frederick County. Ladiesburg, founded in about 1820, owes its name "to the disproportion of seven women to one man in its early population." (See: Guide, p. 506).

LAKE ROLAND. A lake and an adjoining village, near Towson, Baltimore County. The artificial lake, begun in 1858 and retired, so to speak, in 1915, availed itself of the waters of Jones Falls and was meant to serve as Baltimore's main waterworks reservoir. In the beginning the lake's name was both *Lake Roland* and *Jones Falls Lake*. Later it was renamed *Swann Lake* for Mayor Thomas Swann. McGrain states: "The name stems from Roland Run, a stream mentioned as long ago as 1694, when Roland or Rowland Thornberry had a tract surveyed called 'Selsed.'" The occasional mistake "Swan Lake" perhaps suggests the influence of the celebrated ballet.

In 1872 the post office, *Lake Roland*, was established. It was soon discontinued; but it arose again and flourished between 1876–1896. (See: John W. McGrain, "Historical Aspects of Lake Rowland," *MHM*, 74: 3, pp. 253–73).

LAKELAND. Leon Wynter ("Lakeland ...," *Post*, 11 Feb. 1982) describes this place as " ... an 80-year-old all-black neighborhood in College Park ..." [Prince George's County]. He relates that twenty years ago, to stop flooding, pave roads, and replace substandard housing, the citizens here arranged an urban renewal project. The renewal was disastrous. Though the flooding was eased, and though some roads were paved and some high-rise tenements were built, 104 of Lakeland's 150 households vanished. The rest of Leon Wynter's title reads: "Urban Renewal Erases College Park Community."

The *Post* article does not explain the origin of the name. However, Lakeland is in the Paint Branch flood plain; and it was the annoyance of flooding that led to the ill-fated urban renewal. The name may therefore have arisen because of occasional "lakes" or flooded areas.

NOTE: A surname origin cannot at present be ruled out. The surname *Lakeland* occurs once in TDr 1981 Md. Suburban; and in that directory there are about 53 listings for *Lake*.

LAKESVILLE. Near Crapo, Dorchester County. During the Revolution of 1776 this vicinity was called "Lakes," for the *Lake* family, represented in particular by Captain Henry Lake, of the Dorchester County Militia. In 1797 he became High Sheriff. The family name persisted through 1878, when the postmaster was lumber dealer, Charles Lake. (See: Jones, p. 110, pp. 379–80; Lewis 1878).

LAMBSON. A village near Galena, Kent County. This is from a rare surname. There are no *Lambsons* in the Kent and Queen Anne's phone book for 1963. The Baltimore phone book for 1969 has four *Lambson*, one *Lamson*. The Md. Suburban Directory for 1974–75 has one *Lambson*, three *Lamson*.

LANDOVER. Village near Bladensburg, Prince George's County. The Gazetteers list *Landover, Landover Depot, Landover Road*. The name is probably from Llandovery, a market town and ancient municipal borough in Carmarthenshire, Wales.

LANHAM. Village near Seabrook, Prince George's County. It is on Martenet's map, 1866. On p. 21 Farquhar mentions Aaron Lanham, one of the seventeen members of the first Montgomery County grand jury, August 12, 1777.

LANSDOWNE. Village near Arbutus, Baltimore County. The spelling varies as to *d* and a final *e*. In 1904 it was *Lansdown*. The Baltimore phone book for 1969 lists three *Lansdowne*. Compare *Lansdowne*, a suburb of Philadelphia, Pa.

Note: The name may be from *Lansdown*, Somersetshire, England. There it is the name of a ridge, at which is *Langridge* (See: Ekwall, p. 288).

LANTZ. Near Sabillasville, Frederick County. On Rand-McNally's map of 1906 this was *Deerfield Sta.* or *Lantz P.O.* Christian Lantz, "late of Lancaster County in the Province of Pa., mason," became a resident of Leitersburg District in 1755 and bought a tract of 476 acres. John Lantz was in Frederick County in 1790.

LAPIDUM. A Harford County village on the "fall line" of the Susquehanna River opposite Port Deposit. At this place the river becomes too rocky for safe navigation.

Marye gives 1700 as the date of the first white settlements here. At that time Lapidum was the site of the historic *Susquehanna Upper Ferry, sometimes called *Perkins's Ferry. The name *Lapidum* is a form of *lapis*, the Latin word for "stone." The designation is appropriate because Lapidum is at the mouth of Rock Run and is, in general, a stony place. In the vicinity are Slate Hill and Slate Ridge. (See: Marye, *MHM*, 15: 4, pp. 374–75).

LA PLATA. A village near Waldorf, Charles County. It is on Martenet's Map, 1866. La Plata became a scheduled stop, "La Plata Station," when the Pope's Creek railroad was built through here in 1873. The station stood on "La Plata," the Chapman farm; and in Nov. 1873 Robert F. Chapman became the first postmaster.

The land here is flat, and "Le Plateau" was the original name of Chapman's farm. Evidently "Le Plateau" became "La Plata." Compare "La Grange," on the outskirts of La Plata. Pronunciation: luh-PLAY-tuh. (See: BK, pp. 138–40).

Note: Earl Arnett (*Sun*, June 14, 1975) gives "another version," namely, that Chapman may have visited Argentina and named his farm after the Rio de la Plata.

LAP. Village near Mt. Savage, Allegany County. Probably from the surname Lap(p). William *Lap* was in Frederick County in 1790. In the Allegany County phone book in 1968 there are seventeen entries for *Lapp*.

LAPPANS. Near Balls, Washington County. In 1843 this was the post office of *Lappons Cross Roads*. The Guide refers to "Lappans (Jones Crossroads)." This is evidently the possessive form of a surname. *Lapin* appears nine times in the Baltimore phone book for 1969. Compare Lipins Corner, Anne Arundel County.

LARGO. Village near Rigley, Prince George's County. Probably from an early tract or mansion. Ultimately from Largo, or Largo Bay, County Fife, Scotland.

LAURAVILLE. Near Baltimore City. It was a post office in 1851. Eva Slezak, of the Enoch Pratt Free Library, Baltimore, informs me (1980) that this name commemorates Laura, the daughter of John Henry Keene. Mr. Keene, a landowner, established the post office.

LAUREL. Town near Savage, Prince George's County. In 1837 this was the post office of *Laurel Factory*. Laurel, like Savage, seems to have begun as a cloth "factory." The *laurel* tree no doubt abounded in the more wooded local areas. Laurel has been called the "half-way city of tomorrow." And in recent years it has become the site of such dormitory developments as Laurel Hills (1960) and Maryland City.

LA VALE. A suburban village near Cumberland, Allegany County. It occurs in the 1941 Gazetteer. The name appears to be a combination of

French *la* and English *vale*. It means "the valley," and apparently refers to the valley of Braddock Run, near the Cumberland "Narrows."

See, however, Harder, *Illustrated Dictionary of Place Names* . . . 1976, p. 292: "Named by a local citizen for his birthplace, a farm in Pennsylvania."

LAWNDALE. Village near Patapsco, Carroll County. In January 1894 James A. Clark and 59 others petitioned the Carroll County Board of Commissioners for a road to run through Clark's land and, among other places, to touch upon Clark's lawn. According to Marye the "lawn" mentioned in the petition was situated at *Lawndale*. (See: *MHM*, XV; 4, 1920).

LAWSONIA. Village near Crisfield, Somerset County. It occurs in the 1904 Gazetteer. The *-ia* has the effect of making a placename out of the family name, *Lawson*. Oriole states that Thomas Bloyce, Jr., who came to Somerset County from Virginia in 1649, was a direct ancestor of the Lawson family. He built on tracts of land along Little Monie Creek, across from what was later known as "the Lawson place." Cf. Nelsonia, Accomac Co., Va.; Wilsonia Neck, Northampton Co., Va.; etc.

LAYTONSVILLE. Near Claysville, Montgomery County. Earlier names were *Goshen Mills* and *Cracklintown*. Zekiah Layton made his will in 1850. However, Farquhar attributes the present name to John Layton.

*LEE'S MILLS. See JERUSALEM MILLS.

LECOMPTE BAY, CREEK. Near Lloyds, Dorchester County. The bay is an inlet of Choptank River. The creek is a branch of the bay (GMd 1941, Manual 1947). Wood (p. 22) mentions the notable Huguenot, Antoine Lecompte, from Picardy, who occupied 800 acres, called "Antonina," near the Choptank River. His family name was widespread in Maryland, especially Dorchester. From 1669 to 1671 he was a justice. It was rumored that he had a thirst for killing Indians who came too near his land. Tradition records that the Lecompte family bore for many years the Indian curse of blindness.

LEITERSBURG. Village near Smithburg, Washington County. It was a post office in 1826. This place was on the 1300-acre tract, "Well Taught," granted in 1754 to George Poe. In 1762 Poe sold 362 acres to Jacob Leiter (d. 1764). Andrew Leiter, the son of Jacob Leiter, Jr., and grandson of Jacob Leiter, the pioneer, inherited this land in 1811 and laid out Leitersburg in 1815. (See: Leitersburg, p. 102; Williams, pp. 683–85).

LEONARDTOWN. Near Breton Bay, St. Mary's County. It appears as *Benedict Leonard Town* in *Archives* XIX, for 1693-97; and in 1792 it was the post office of *Leonardtown*. Lantz states that "tradition" carries the town back to 1652, "when it was known as Seymourtown." *Seymourtown was named for Provincial Governor, John Seymour. The present name, given in 1733, commemorates Benedict Leonard Calvert, fourth Lord Baltimore. (See: Lantz, p. 247; McHenry Howard, *MHM*, XV: 4, 1920).

Note: In at least one reference book Leonardtown has been mistakenly attributed to Leonard Calvert (1608–1746), brother of Cecilius, 2nd Lord Baltimore.

LERCH CREEK. A branch of the West River, near Galesville, Anne Arundel County (GMd 41). Dunham (p. 19) states that Emile E. Lerch, Galesville's first postmaster (1889), left his name on a creek [Lerch Creek] and a street (Lerch Lane). According to Riley there were seven Lerch brothers in 1845.

LEXINGTON PARK. Town near Herman(s)ville, St. Mary's County. Its earlier name, *Jarboesville*, is in the 1904 Gazetteer. In 1942 the U.S. Government built a $90 million air flight test center here, and *Jarboesville became Lexington Park. The name is from the World War II aircraft carrier "Lexington."

Note: This ill-advised and unfortunate change obscures the fact that the earlier name *Jarboesville commemorates one of Maryland's earliest French pioneers, John Jarbo, of Dijon (naturalized in 1666). See *JARBOESVILLE.

LIBERTYTOWN. Near Oldfield, Frederick County. The town was laid out in 1782 on a 6000-acre tract called "Duke's Woods." Lewis in 1878 describes neighboring Unionville as being "... on the Liberty Road, 2 miles east of Liberty." The proximity of Unionville favors the notion that Libertytown was named for patriotic reasons. However, in colonial days, certain areas of the Baltimore vicinity were known as "The Liberties." Perhaps, indeed, "Duke's Woods" was a *Liberty*. The term denotes a district free from the jurisdiction of the British crown. Liberty Road, between Libertytown and Baltimore City, eventually becomes Liberty Heights Avenue.

LIBERTYTOWN. On Libertytown Branch, Worcester County. Norman Adkins, of Goody Hill, tells me that until 1850 the name of this place was *Reedsville*. And Jeff Webb, of Whiton, tells me that it is known locally as "Hungrytown." According to Adkins, "Hungrytown" arose when a travelling salesman tried in vain to get something to eat here. The present name was probably given for patriotic reasons. I assume that the run was named for the town.

LICKSVILLE. Near Pleasant View, Frederick County. In 1897 it was mapped as *Licksville P.O.* or *Tuscarora Sta.* Grove describes the village as being near the Potomac River on the road to the mouth of the Monocacy. He cites the local sentiment that the name comes from the fact that "a visitor here had to be a pretty good man if he didn't want to get licked; that is, provided he didn't behave himself." It appears to me more likely, however, that the name came from a salt lick.

LILYPONS. Village near Sugar Loaf, Frederick County. In 1917 G. L. Thomas began to hatch goldfish and raise water lilies here; in 1966 there were 800 ponds. Washington journalists David Braaten and John

McKelway have discussed this name. Braaten states that the name is for Lily Pons, the opera singer, "as well as for the lily ponds." McKelway states that when a post office was established here in 1930, a postal official hit upon the name of Lily Pons. (See: *Star*, 13 April 1965, 23 August 1966).

LIMEKILN.   Village near Buckeystown, Frederick County. The first name of Limekiln was *Slabtown*; and it appears as *Slabtown* on Martenet's map of 1866. Grove explains *Slabtown* by pointing out that when the B. and O. Railroad was built to this point the place became a center for railway construction men and a number of slab houses were built for them. Even in Revolutionary days lime was burnt here for building and plastering. When B. and O. Railroad officials appointed the first agent, lime burning activities were at their height. The name was therefore changed from *Slabtown* to *Limekiln*. (See: Grove, pp. 72–73).

LINCHESTER.   Village. Hunting Creek, near Preston, Caroline County. Linchester lies on the border between Caroline and Dorchester Counties. Evidently the name is a combination of *Lin-* (from Caro*line*) and *-chester* (from Dor*chester*). See MURRAYS MILL.

*LINCOLN BANKS.   Maryland local name near Washington. W. H. Babcock, writing in 1888, describes this bygone feature as a bluff near a landing and spring on the Anacostia River. And he relates that "an old resident of the neighborhood" told him that "Lincoln Banks" in his boyhood was called "Lickin Banks." Babcock mentions a Potomac River "Deer Lick" he slept near in 1874. Presumably deer and other animals once licked at "Lickin Banks." When Abraham Lincoln rose to fame, it is probable that the folk altered "Lickin ..." to *Lincoln*. (See: *JAF-L*, 1:146–47, July–Sept., 1888).

LINEBORO.   Near Alesia, Carroll County. Gazetteer 1904 lists it. The village lies directly on the Mason and Dixon line, and the name is a combination of *line* and *-boro*. Cf. MARYLAND LINE.

LINGANORE.   A village on Linganore Creek, near Unionville, Frederick County. In 1724 the creek was spelled *Linganoa*. The village takes its name from the creek, and was a post office in 1855. It is evidently folklore to suppose, as some have, that *Linganore* is a combination of German *linke(n)* "left" and *ohr* "ear," and denotes "Left Ear," an Indian chief who once lived on its banks. However, as an Algonquian name, *Linganore* is a difficult word. I have decided that it can best be explained as a development related to Delaware *linkteu* "it melts" plus *-anwi-*, a copula referring to natural phenomena. One would translate "It melts (copiously) in springtime." (See: Kenny, p. 79).

LINGANORE CREEK.   See LINGANORE.

LINTHICUM, LINTHICUM HEIGHTS.   El. 135. Both names represent one and the same town near Pumphrey, Anne Arundel County. The land on which Linthicum stands was acquired in 1801 by Abner Linthicum, a descendant of the Thomas Linthicum, of Wales, who came to Anne Arundel County as early as 1658. Henry J. Paul, postmaster in 1950, informs me that the present town arose on the 700-acre farm of Sweetser Linthicum, Sr., descendant of Abner, and was platted and recorded as LINTHICUM HEIGHTS in 1920. Meanwhile, a family concern, The Linthicum Heights Realty Co., had been organized. (See: "The Linthicum Family of Anne Arundel County," *MHM*, XXV: 3, pp. 275–84).

LISBON. Village near Poplar Springs, Howard County. Lisbon was a post office in 1815. Warfield states that Caleb Pancoast built the first house here. Judging from the regularity of the houses on both sides of the National Pike, Warfield assumes that the village was laid out after the pike was surveyed. The name Lisbon commemorates Lisbon, the Portuguese capital city famed for its earthquake. In 1905 there were 22 Lisbons in the United States.

LITTLE. ... The early settlers often used *little* to denote a smaller mountain or stream adjacent to, or even a part of, an evidently bigger feature. Thus, in Anne Arundel County, the Little Patuxent River is a tributary of the (big) Patuxent River, and in Garrett County, Little Savage Mountain is adjacent to Big Savage Mountain. Many of the features whose names begin with *Little* are Indian mountains and streams. See below.

LITTLE ALLEGANY MOUNTAIN. North of Jennings Run and west of Wills Creek, Allegany County. See ALLEGHENY.

LITTLE ANNEMESSEX. A tributary of Tangier Sound, Somerset County. Sixth USGB forbids the spelling "... Little Annemessic." See ANNEMESSEX.

LITTLE ANTIETAM CREEK. It enters Antietam Creek near Leitersburg, Washington County. See ANTIETAM.

LITTLE CATOCTIN CREEK. A branch of Catoctin Creek near Myersville, Frederick County. See CATOCTIN.

LITTLE CHOPTANK RIVER. It enters Chesapeake Bay between Ragged and Hooper Points, Dorchester County. Sixth USGB: "Not Hudson." See CHOPTANK.

LITTLE MAGOTHY RIVER. A tributary of Chesapeake Bay, Anne Arundel County. The 1904 Gazetteer describes it as a tributary of the Magothy. See MAGOTHY.

LITTLE MONIE CREEK. It flows into Monie Bay, Somerset County. See MONIE.

LITTLE MONOCACY RIVER. A tributary of the Potomac near the Monocacy River, Montgomery County. See MONOCACY.

LITTLE PATUXENT RIVER. This tributary begins in Howard County and flows into the big Patuxent River at Priest Bridge, Anne Arundel County. See PATUXENT.

LITTLE SENECA CREEK. A branch of Seneca Creek, Montgomery County. The 1904 Gazetteer describes it as a tributary of Great Seneca Creek. See SENECA.

LITTLE TONOLOWAY CREEK. It enters Tonoloway Creek, Washington County, near the Pennsylvania state Boundary. See TONOLOWAY.

LITTLE TUSCARORA CREEK. A tributary of the Tuscarora Creek that enters the Monocacy River three miles northeast of Frederick, Frederick County. A second Tuscarora Creek, Frederick County, flows south into the Potomac River near the village of Tuscarora. See TUSCARORA.

LITTLE YOUGHIOGHENY RIVER. A branch of the Youghiogheny River, Garrett County. See YOUGHIOGHENY.

LITTLE ORLEANS. A village on the Potomac River, east of Cumberland, Allegany County. It is on Martenet's map of 1866. TW mentions Orleans District, LITTLE ORLEANS, and Orleans Road. Gannett refers to three places by this name, and states: "... named from the city in France." Cf. Orleans Street, Baltimore. (See: TW, I, 483). Pronunciation: Little Or-LEANS.

*LLANGOLLEN. A former mining village at the junction of Savage and Potomac Rivers, Garrett County. It was *Llangollen Mines* in 1852. Postal history records that "Llangallen" was changed to "Bloomington" in 1855. The Maryland name is from the Langollen Coal Company. Remotely, however, Llangollen commemorates the market town and summer resort of Llangollen, Denbighshire, Wales. See BLOOMINGTON.

LLEWELLENBURGH. An obscure village in St. Mary's County. It was a post office in 1832. The 1790 census lists, for St. Mary's County, Charles *Llewellin* (27 slaves) and Richard *Llewellin* (18 slaves).

LLOYDS. Village near Cornersville, Dorchester County. It is in the 1904 Gazetteer. Probably from the family name *Lloyd*, and not from the given name. The 1963 Dorchester phone book has seven Lloyds. The 1790 census lists four—two in nearby Talbot County.

*LLOYDSVILLE. Wicomico County. Rand-McNally's map of 1877 has: "Lloydsville, see Quantico."

LOARTOWN. A village near Vale Summit, Allegany County. El. 2075. Schlosnagle indicates that George Loar occupied a Military Lot in 1815.

LOCK LYNN. Sometimes *Lock Lynn Heights*. El. 2420. A village near Mt. Lake Park (el. 2403), Garrett County. Spellings alternate between *Loch* and *Lock*. Hoye points out that in about 1827 David Lynn sold a Military Lot in the local glades; Weeks calls him Captain David Lynn, the owner of nearby "Lynn Pasture." Although there was a planing mill here in 1881, the name was probably given in 1894 when the Loch Lynn Hotel was planned. *Loch* ("lake") is the correct spelling, suggested perhaps by Mt. *Lake* Park, or by Loch Lein, near Killarney, Ireland.

LOCH RAVEN. A village, a lake, and a dam (Loch Raven Dam) near Towson, Baltimore County. The dam, created in 1922 by curbing Gunpowder Falls, forms a lake ten miles long. The name is evidently a folk corruption of the name of one Luke Raven, *Luke* having become *Loch* ("lake"). Luke Raven, the uncle of Tobias Stansbury and the possessor of land near Sterlings Branch, is mentioned twice in the 1721 land records of Baltimore County. Howard McHenry concludes: "The common impression is that Loch Raven was so called from ravens having nested or frequented there. But Luke Raven owned several tracts of land in that locality." (See: Howard McHenry, *MHM*, XX, 1925, p. 288).

*LONACONIN CREEK. This is the original Indian name of George's Creek, a tributary of the Potomac River at Westernport, Allegany County. It occurs as *Lonaconin Creek* on Fry and Jefferson's map of 1751. By 1795 it had become George's River; by 1818 it was *George Creek*. See GEORGE'S CREEK.

LONACONING. A town on George's Creek (earlier *Lonaconin Creek), Allegany County. It was a post office in 1837. Because Seldom Seen Run and four other streams meet at this place, the townspeople believe that *Lonaconing* means "Where many waters meet." Scharf, stating that Lonaconing was once the home of an Indian, George, even goes so far as to identify George's "tribal chieftain" as Lonacona, "Where many waters meet." This is absurd. The foregoing meaning is probably wrong, if only because *Lonaconing*, analyzed as a Delaware Algonquian word, gives no hint of either "meeting" or "waters." However, it is reasonable to believe that its ending, *-in(g)*, is the common Algonquian suffix "Where." For the rest of the name there are two technically correct explanations.

1. The opening syllables may be a development of Primitive Algonquian *lāwi-*, "to fail, fall short of." In Delaware, on the analogy of Cree *yāni-na-kwan*, the form would be *lāwi-na-kwan-ing*, which gives *Lonakoning*. Here, as in Cree, the meaning is "Where it disappears from view."

2. The opening *l* may be a contraction of Delaware *wul(i)-* "good, pretty." The next syllables may constitute *-anahkw-*, "a summit." Alto-

---

Note: In addition to its Indian origin, Lonaconing has an industrial history that deserves attention. For it appears that from 1839 until 1855 a pioneer iron furnace, using coal and coke instead of charcoal, flourished here on land bought in 1836 by the Georges Creek Coal and Iron Company. Declares Ms. Mary Meyers: "It was the largest furnace that was built up to that time." In 1981, through the efforts of Ms. Meyers, the venerable furnace was restored; and in the same year there arose Lonaconing Furnace Park. The park today is a tourist attraction and commemorates the English, Welsh, and Scotch pioneers "who came to work in the coal mines and at the furnace when it was turning out 60 tons of pig iron in a week." (See: "Furnace Town Lives Residents Preserve Memory of Workers," *Capital*, Dec. 18, 1982). Addendum: R. B. Levy's *A Wee Bit O' Scotland* ... Baltimore, 1983.

gether, with the addition of the copula -an-, one arrives at w'l-anahkw-an-ing, which gives Lonakoning. Here the meaning would be "Where there is a beautiful summit." In both cases the reference may be to nearby Dan's Mountain (whence Vale Summit).

*LONDON TOWN. On the South River, Anne Arundel County. Notable as the site of the ancient South River Club. Calling this bygone place "a busy port of entry" to whose wharves came the latest London fashions, Richardson states that William Burgess founded *London Town in 1680. He owned the land and wharves at which vessels were permitted to land and unload; and Eugenia Holland remarks that the town was once commonly referred to as Burgess' Wharf. The Act of the Assembly to establish a port of entry here was passed in 1683. Compare Londonville, Somerset County. (See: Holland, MHM, XLIV: 1 March 1949).

Note: For a more complete, up-to-date account of *LONDON TOWN, see: Donald Shomette, London Town A Brief History (Londontown, Maryland, 1978).

LONG. Near Cumberland, Allegany County. See ALLEGANY GROVE.

LONG GREEN. A village, a creek, and a station (Long Green Station) near Glen Arm, Baltimore County. William B. Marye informed me in 1965 that Long Green takes its name from a place in the north of Ireland. He also attributed to the north of Ireland "Berry Hill," a farm on the nearby Gittings estate. See GITTINGS.

LORD. A village near Midland, Allegany County. It is also mapped as Lorddolph, and the two names evidently denote one and the same place. Lord probably commemorates C. K. Lord, president of the Consolidation Coal Company, which was organized in 1864 and eventually came to own the Cumberland and Pennsylvania Coal Company and the greater part of the Allegany Coal Field. (See: TW, I, p. 459).

LORD DOLPH. This is the same place as Lord, and appears to be the family name Lord combined with the -dolph of another family name, or even a given name, such as Randolph, Rudolph, etc.

LORETTO. A village and erstwhile railroad station near Princess Anne, Somerset County. The same place as LORETTA. In 1877 it was mapped as Loretto Sta. Compare Loretto, a Pennsylvania borough, explained by Gannett as ". . . from the city in Italy."

LOTHAIR STATION. Erstwhile Charles County railroad station of Faulkner and Port Tobacco. In 1877 it was mapped as "Lothair, see Port Tobacco." The name is probably for Lothair, the leading character in Benjamin Disraeli's popular Victorian novel Lothair (1870).

LOTHIAN P.O. A village near Harwood P.O., Anne Arundel County. Listed by Lewis in 1878, Lothian is the post office name of Mt. Zion. In connection with Anne Arundel historic estates and mansions, Mrs. R. H.

Nelker has written: "There was Lothian built by Philip Thomas about 1804." The name Lothian is from Great Britain where, in the eleventh century, it designated the English part of Scotland. In Maryland it has a Scotch family background. Compare Midlothian, Allegany County. (See: *Capital*, March 6, 1969).

LOUGHBOROUGH. Montgomery County village near Washington, D.C. In 1800 Nathan Loughborough owned land on the present site of American University; and in 1808 he occupied "Milton," whose later owner, Hamilton Loughborough, gave plots of land to his emancipated slaves. This resulted in a large Negro settlement along River Road near Milton. (See: Farquhar, p. 213). See TOBY TOWN.

*LOVETON. North of Baltimore City, Baltimore County. It existed in 1812. PHC notes: "'Loveton' was changed to 'Hereford' in 1821." Cf. Loveville. See HEREFORD.

LOVEVILLE. On Pincushion Road, near Morganza, St. Mary's County. Journalist Paul Fleming states that this name, given in 1890 when a new post office was established, is for a lawyer, Albert K. Love, the first postmaster. But journalist John Sherwood, remarking that Kingsley Love and Bernard Love, brothers, were early postmasters, attributes the name to Kingsley Love, who opened a post office in 1895. In any event, *Love* here is from a family name. (See: *Sun*, Feb. 9 [Mag.] 1964; *Star*, Feb. 14, 1970).

LOWER MARLBORO. A village on the Patuxent River, Calvert County, about twelve miles below Upper Marlboro. It was a post office in 1796. Remarking that *Marlborough* was shortened to *Marlboro* late in the nineteenth century, Stein points out that an earlier name was *Coxtown* and that the present name commemorates John Churchill (1650–1722), victor at Blenheim. *Lower* was added to avoid postal confusion with *Upper* Marlboro. (See: Stein, pp. 91–92). See UPPER MARLBORO.

*LOWER TRAPPE. A village several miles south of *Upper Trappe, now Allen, Somerset County. It was mapped by LGS in 1877. The change of *Upper Tract to Allen may have been made to prevent confusion with Lower Traape. See ALLEN.

LOWNDES. A hamlet and railroad station near Cumberland, Allegany County. It is in the 1904 Gazetteer. The name is probably for Lloyd Lowndes, Cumberland lawyer, who became Governor of Maryland in 1895. (See: TW, I).

LUKE. A town near Westernport, Allegany County. It was first known as *West Piedmont* because Piedmont, West Virginia, lies opposite to it across the Potomac River. The present name is for the Luke family, whose members came to America from Scotland in 1850 and eventually established at this place the West Virginia Pulp and Paper Company. TW mentions William Luke, John G. Luke, and Allen L. Luke, and states that

William Luke, was the company's founder and first president. (See: *Town of Luke Maryland 50th Anniversary of Incorporation 1922 thru 1972*. Luke, Md. 1972).

LUTHERVILLE. Near Timonium, Baltimore County. In 1866 it was *Timonium Sta - Lutherville P.O.* The name is evidently for the German theologian, Martin Luther (1483–1546). In 1878 a Lutheran church and the "Lutherville Female Seminary" were situated here. And the Seminary, later the Maryland College for Young Ladies, had been chartered in 1853 through the efforts of D. B. Kurtz and J. G. Norris, Lutheran ministers. In 1952, after its last graduation, the college closed. (See: Vincent-Verplanck, "College Days at Lutherville," *Sun* [Mag.], Sept. 23, 1962).

M

MACKALL. Village. St. Leonard Creek, near Wallville, Calvert County. The name is from the family founded by James Mackall, who came to Maryland in 1666, perhaps as a Scotch prisoner of war. One of his descendants, Dr. Richard Mackall, of lower Calvert County, served several terms in the General Assembly. (See: Stein, pp. 292–93).

MADDOX. A village near Hurry, St. Mary's County. Named for the numerous Maddox family. Heads 1790 lists 25 *Maddox* and five *Maddux* for Maryland; but only two of these (*Maddox*) are in St. Mary's County. However, the Charles and St. Mary's County phone book for 1963 lists 20 *Maddox*.

MADISON. A village on the Little Choptank River, Tobacco Stick Bay, Dorchester County. This was **Tobacco Stick P.O.* in 1866. On Rand-McNally's map of 1906 it is *Madison*. Remarking that there was a village here in 1760, Elias explains the earlier name by repeating the story that an Indian, upon being pursued by the settlers in "early colonial days," jumped across the channel at the mouth of the cove here by means of a "tobacco stick." The present name may well be for James Madison (1751–1836), who became our fourth president in 1809. (See: Elias, p. 108).

"Madame Elsie's Branch." Queen Anne's County. Emory, describing St. Paul's Parish, mentions a stream commonly called "Madame Elsie's Branch." (See: Emory, p. 204).

MADONNA. Village, near Jarrettsville, Harfore County. It was mapped by Rand-McNally in 1906. Earlier names were **Briar Ridge*, **Kings Corner*, and **Cathcart*. Cherrill Anson attributes to "unofficial historians" the story that the name is for *Madonna* McCurdy, a daughter of Dr. McCurdy, former postmaster. See BETHEL, Upper Node Forest. (See: *Sun* [Mag], 11 March 1962).

MAGNOLIA. Village, near Edgewood, Harford County. It was a post office in 1866. Lewis in 1878 attributes this name to the magnolia trees that grow in the neighborhood. Compare MAGNOLIA, Howard County.

MAGOTHY RIVER. A tributary of the Chesapeake Bay, Anne Arundel County. The earliest spelling of this name was *Magoty*. In 1795 Griffith spells it Mago*th*y. Compare similar names elsewhere—such as Magothy Bay, Va., Maggoty Run, W. Va., and *Maggotty Cove, Newfoundland. Keenleyside thinks that the Newfoundland name means "Full of Maggots." The citizens found the name "repellant" and changed it to Hoylestown.

If Magothy is an Indian name, its most likely derivation is from the Delaware Algonquian word *magucke*, "a wide plain," "without timber." However, this meaning does not correctly describe the Maryland stream's locality. If *Magothy* is an English name, it means "maggoty" and indicates an abundance of maggots or grubs, in the sense perhaps of gnats and mosquitoes. Perhaps the colonists found this meaning repulsive and unconsciously changed the *t* to *th*. (See: "Place Names of Newfoundland," *Canadian Geographical Journal*, XXIX [1944], No. 6).

MAGO VISTA. A development in the vicinity of the Severn and Magothy Rivers. *Mago* is probably from *Magothy*. The meaning would be "Magothy view."

MAGRUDER. A village on the Patuxent River, Prince George's County. In 1904 it was the post office of *Magruder-Tuxedo*. The name is from the Magruder family, whose first member, Alexander McGregor, came here in 1692 from Perthshire, Scotland, changed his name to *Magruder* for political reasons, and obtained a patent for 5000 acres of land in Calvert County. Cobb states that he founded "the Bethesda community of Scotland"; Greene states that his son, Samuel, married the daughter of Ninian Bell and became "the ancestor of the Maryland Magruders." (See: *Star*, April 5, 1969; Richardson II, 178–81; Green, 24–25). See SCOTLAND.

MANADIER. A village near Stumptown and Hambleton, Talbot County. Ingraham recounts that in 1711 the Rev. Mr. Manadier, a Huguenot, was rector of White Marsh church, one-fourth of a mile from Hole-in-the-Wall (Hambleton). He and his wife are buried in the White Marsh churchyard. Cf. MAYNADIER, Garrett County.

MANAHOWIC CREEK. A tributary of the Wicomico River, St. Mary's County. In 1608 Captain Smith mentions the *Mannahokes*; later the anthropologist Mooney uses the spelling *Mannahoacks*. The Maryland word resembles Mooney's form, the *-ic* being an English adjectival ending.

Taken as Algonquian, *Manahow-* appears to consist of *man-* "dig," *-ahw-* "action by tool," and *-äwaki* "they-them." The meaning would be

"They dig them," a reference, perhaps, to shellfish or tubers. Mooney, however, regarded the Mannahoacks as Eastern Sioux and believed that the name contains the Siouan locative root *mo* (*ma*), "place, earth, country."

I recommend the Algonquian analysis. It is more complete than Mooney's. Besides, it is reasonable to believe that all of Smith's Indian names are Algonquian.

*MANASSAS. Talbot County. Ingraham states: "Not far from Trappe lies the village, also island, of Manassas, where there is a church, stores, and school house, and where a good highway leads to a landing on the Choptank." Cf. Manassas, Va. The name in both cases appears to refer to Manasseh, a King of Israel, or to the apocryphal Old Testament book, Prayer of Manasses.

MANCHESTER. A town near Greenmount, Carroll County. Warner et al. relates that Captain Richard Richards laid out Manchester in 1790 and named it for his native English city. Warner adds that the German custom of making noodles gave the village the nickname "Noodle Doosey."

Note: Cf. Noodle Doosey, Columbia County, Pennsylvania, mentioned in Walter M. Brasch's *Columbia County Place Names* (Col. Co. Historical Society, Orangeville, Pa.).

MANKLIN CREEK. A tributary of Isle of Wight Bay, Worcester County. The name is pronounced MACK-lin, which makes it likely that it comes from the *Macklin* family. However, *Manklin*, although rare, is also a family name. Benjamin Manklin lived in Frederick County in 1790.

MANNINGTON. An obscure village in Allegany County. Stein mentions Captain Thomas Manning, an early Puritan settler of Calvert County. In 1651 he was assigned 600 acres on the Lower Cliffs. Perhaps the Allegany place represents a branch of this family. Cf. Manning Range, Dorchester County; Mannington, W.Va.

MANOKIN RIVER. A Somerset County tributary of the Chesapeake Bay. The name is related to Captain Smith's *Monacans* of 1608. Some early Maryland spellings are *Monoakin*, *Manaoke*, and *Manaco-River*.

The name is probably Virginia Algonquian. Tooker, studying Smith's Virginia form, states that it contains Algonquian *man-* "dig, dig away, remove." He translates "People who dig the earth." However, Smith's *Monacan* lacks the grammatical ending it should have to justify Tooker's translation of it as a reference to people. I agree, though, that the opening part of the name contains Algonquian *man-*. In addition, it is likely, especially in view of the Maryland spelling *Monoakin*, that the mid part of the name is a contraction of *āwak-* "earth." This would account for the *-ac-* (*-ok-*) of the various forms. The final *-in* (*-an*) could be from the inanimate copula *-enwi*. This analysis with *āwak-* and *-enwi* seems best. The meaning would be "Earth is dug out." The reference is to a cutting stream. Pronunciation: Ma-NOKE-in.

MANTUA. MANTUA MILLS. Baltimore County. Probably from Mantua, Lombardy, Italy, the birthplace of Virgil.

MAPLEVILLE. Washington County. The Guide (p. 350) explains: "...originally... *Mt. Pleasant* a trading post for an area where strawberries, blackberries, raspberries, and cantaloupes are intensively cultivated." For the abundant maple trees.

MARBLE FRONT. George's Creek, near Barton, Allegany County. The cemetery here, with its marble tombstones, was once visible from the highway.

MARBLE HILL. Near Cockeysville, Baltimore County. Among the stones of Maryland, Scott (1807) lists marble and granite. B. B. Perlman, writing about the Baltimore city hall, mentions "Baltimore County marble," a white magnetic limestone referred to as "Beaver Dam Marble." It is found in quarries near Cockeysville. Cf. Marblevale Baltimore County. (See: *MHM*, XLVII: 1, p. 50). See GRANITE.

MARDELA SPRINGS. A village near Barren Creek, Wicomico County. In 1895 there was a resort hotel here, and visitors disported themselves at a bubbling sulphur spring. An earlier name was "Barren (...formerly Baron) Creek." The present name is composed of *Mar-* (Maryland) and *Dela-* (Delaware). The southwest corner of Delaware is two miles away. (See: *Sun* [Mag], 23 June 1963, p. 2).

MARBURY. Near Pisgah, Charles County. Francis Marbury was an emigrant from Chestershire, England, who settled near Piscataway. In 1693 he obtained a deed for "Carroll's Kindness," on Piscataway Creek. In 1698 he obtained a second grant on Piscataway Creek. This was "Marbury's Chance." (See: Bowie, p. 549).

*MARLBOROUGH. Prince George's County. Greene points out that in 1706 the Assembly ordered the survey and erection of *Marlborough, named for the Duke of Marlborough, of Blenheim. On a later page he calls it Upper Marlborough and remarks that, excepting the defunct *Charlestown, the original county seat, it was the first town set apart in the county. See LOWER MARLBORO; see UPPER MARLBORO.

MARRIOTTSVILLE. Near Woodstock, Howard County. It was a post office in 1834. The name is from the estate of General Richard Marriott, a descendant of John Marriott who, in 1681, lived on Peter Porter's plantation, Indian Landing, Severn River. Compare Marriott Hill, Anne Arundel County. (See: Warfield, p. 488).

MARSHALL HALL. A village on the Potomac River below Fort Washington, Charles County. Wilstach, calling Marshall Hall the "ancient seat" of the Marshalls of Maryland, believes that this was the location of "Marshall," a 500-acre tract surveyed for William Marshall in 1651. Thomas Hanson Marshall represented Charles County at the provincial convention in Annapolis in 1775; in 1776 John Marshall was First Major of the Lower Battalion. In bygone days Marshall Hall was well-known to Washingtonians for its amusement park, built in 1888. (See: BK, pp. 52–53, p. 56; *Star*, 21 June 1967).

MARSHYHOPE CREEK. Flowing from Delaware, it is a branch of the Nanticoke River, Caroline and Dorchester Counties. In 1732 it was spelled *Marshy hope*. *Hope* in this name, and in Eel Hope Point, Dorchester County, is a survival of the Middle English placename element *hope* (Old English *hop*) "Valley, enclosure." In Maryland *region* is apparently the best meaning. Marshyhope is a region of marshes; Eel Hope is a region (oceanic) of eels. Cf. Marshy Hope, Antigonish County, Nova Scotia.

MARSTON. Carroll County village, near New Windsor. Manual 1947 gives the same coordinates for both *Jewsburg and Marston; evidently they are one and the same place (*Marston* GMd 1941; also, "Jewsburg: in Carroll County").

I learn from the Wilt brothers, of Marston, 1981, that this place arose in the late 19th century, when several Jewish families lived here and had a country store. The present name (*Marston*, Manuals 1962, '67; *no* *Jewsburg) is from the British family name *Marston*, rare in Carroll County today and occurring only once (Jane *Marstin*, Charles Co.) in Heads 1790.

MARTIN MOUNTAIN. GMd 1941 describes this feature as *Martin Mountain Ridge*, lying 3¼ miles west of Flintstone, Allegany County (*Martin's Mt.* Bradford 1838, Colton 1852; *Martins Mountain, Martins Spring Run* Martenet 1866; *Martin Mountain* GMd 1904, Manual 1947, State Highway 1978). The progressive loss of the *'s* is interesting. And it appears likely that the Martin (or Martin family) of *Martins Spring Run* gave his name also to the mountain.

MARTINAK STATE PARK. Watts Creek, Choptank River, Dorchester County. The name is for George Martinak, retired government printer, who gave this 100-acre tract to the state of Maryland in 1961.

MARTINS CROSSROADS. Near Cearfoss, Washington County. David Martin came to what is now Cearfoss in 1828. His son, Nicholas Martin, born in 1828, was a tanner. Nicholas Martin lived here and there, near Cearfoss. Williams has him dwelling on a tract of 35 acres in 1901. (See: Williams, II, 1271–72).

MARUMSCO. The Algonquian name of a large creek, Marumsco, in Somerset County, and a smaller stream, Morumsco (Meramscott) Creek, in nearby Wicomico County. There is also the identically spelled Marumsco Creek, Prince William County, Virginia. Derived from the Maryland name are Marumsco, a village, and Marumsco Marsh.

The last two syllables of Marumsco probably consist of a cognate of Natick *-ompsk* (*-ompsq*) "stone" plus the pronominal ending *-wi*. The incomplete meaning would be "Where there is a stone of some kind."

The meaning of the opening syllable, *Mar-*, is complicated by the fact that Lucas in 1841 spelled this element with an *n* (Ma*n*umco), which suggests that the Indians who originated the name spoke both an r- form of it and an n- form. If this was the case Ma*r*um- (Ma*n*um-) may be related to Massachusetts *manum*, which Tooker found in *Merrim*ac and translated "noise, sound, mysterious noise." However, 1841 is perhaps too late a date for a new form (*Manumpco*) to crop up; the *n* is probably a mistake for *r*. Moreover, it is not clear that Massachusetts had such a word as *manum*. I dismiss as coincidence the fact that Rumbly Point (i.e., windy, noisy) is at the mouth of Marumsco Creek.

To pursue further the idea that Marumsco has two valid forms, one in *r* (Ma*r*umsco) and the other in *n* (Ma*n*umpco), one may seek a general Algonquian explanation. Here a likely source would be Primitive Algonquian *myāl-* "bad, dangerous." On this basis the meaning would be "Where there is a dangerous rock."

However, further reflection leads me to feel that it is unwise to found a confident conclusion on a spelling (Lucas, 1841: *Manumpco*) that occurs so late and may be merely a mistake (*n* for *r*). The safest course then, is to regard *Mar-* as unsolved. There remains the incomplete "Where there is a stone [of some kind]." See PATAPSCO.

Note: Rumbly Point (at the mouth of Marumsco) needn't mean "windy, noisy." Its origin from the family name *Rumbly* is a clear possibility. See RUMBLEY.

MARYDEL. A village on the Maryland-Delaware state line, Caroline County. The first name was *Halltown, after William Hall, who in 1850 bought a tract covering parts of Caroline County, Maryland, and Kent County, Delaware. After three years, *Halltown was changed to *Marydel*, whose syllables denote the two states. (See: Cochrane, p. 175). See *HALLTOWN.

MARYLAND CITY. On the Anne Arundel County line near Laurel. Aaron Ruvinsky, discussing in 1963 the growth of the Laurel area, mentions a projected MARYLAND CITY as one of "the larger communities" in the Laurel neighborhood. Five thousand houses were planned. (See: *Star*, Dec. 14, 1963). See COLUMBIA or HOWARD CITY; see ST. CHARLES.

MASON. Mentioned in 1941 for Washington County. The name is for the Washington County Mason family. Some of its more prominent members were Reverend Jeremiah Mason, who settled on Licking Creek soon after frontier days, and Jeremiah Mason, born at Pecktonville in 1849. The latter, the grandson of Rev. Jeremiah, owned Castle Howe Farm, on Licking Creek, and kept a store at Park Head. (See: Williams, II, passim).

MASON SPRINGS. Near Indian Head, Charles County. The Guide locates this place three miles from an estate, "Araby," and notes that

George Washington referred to it as the home of Widow Elbeck. Her daughter was the wife of George Mason, master of Gunston Hall, Virginia, and author of the Virginia Bill of Rights.

MASSEY. Pennsylvania Railroad Junction and post office, Kent County. In 1866 it was *Masseys X Roads P.O.* For the local Massey family. Daniel Massey owned 700 acres near here in 1754. In 1878, to rely on Lewis, C. H. B. Massey, a doctor and peach grower, lived here, and R. B. M. Massey was a local farmer.

*MATAPEAKE, MATTAPEX. *Matapeake, was the name of the discontinued Chesapeake Bay ferry from Sandy Point to Kent Island. Matta pex is presently a Kent Island village. Historically, Matapeake was the name of the Indians of Kent Island who lived on Matapax Neck and at Indian Springs. In early records one finds *Mattapex Creek* (1634–55) and *Matapeck Creek* (1652). There seems little doubt that *Matapex* has an English plural (Matapeakes) and that the word we have to deal with here is *Mat(t)apeake.*

The last syllables of *Mat(t)apeake* appear plainly to come from Primitive Algonquian *-āpyäki (*-epyäki) "water, current, expanse of water." *Mat-*, the opening syllable, can be derived from PA *mat "bad," PA *māt "moving," and general Algonquian *mat-* "junction, join." I prefer the third of these possibilities (*mat-*) which, added to *-āpyäki, would give *mat-āpyäki* "Junction of waters." It should be noticed that *massa-*, meaning "great" in some New England dialects, occasionally appears as *matta-* (cf. *Matta*chusetts, *Massa*chusetts). However, there is no clear evidence that *matta-* equalled *massa-* in Maryland and Virginia.

MATTAPONI. A tributary (Mataponi Creek) of the Patuxent River, Prince George's County; a creek and landing (Mattaponi), Worcester County. Of historical interest is *Mattapany Street* (*Mattapany Path*, 1639), St. Mary's County. Cf. Mattaponi River, Virginia, and Mattapan, Massachusetts.

In 1635 the name appears in the English adjectival form, *Mattapanian*; and in 1639-40 one finds the adjectival *Mattapanient*. These forms may refer to the Mattapony Indians.

The missionary, John Heckewelder, analyzed *Mattachpona* as a compound of two Delaware words meaning "No bread at all." But such a compound violates correct Algonquian composition.

Huden and other students of Massachusetts *Mattapan* derived this New England name from Natick *Mattappu* "He sits down." The meaning would be "Sitting down place, landing place, place of portage." In Maryland Mattaponi was indeed a "landing." However, Maryland is not a region of lakes and portages, and the Natick interpretation seems quite inappropriate here.

In both New England and Maryland the ending of the name may well be the inanimate copula *-anwi* "It is." And I prefer to regard the opening syllables of *Mattaponi*, Maryland, as *matta-* "joined" and *-apo* "water." The meaning would be "Meeting of waters [at a sand spit?]." Pronunciation: Matta-po-NYE.

MATTAWOMAN. A tributary (Mattawoman Creek) of the Potomac River, Charles County; a village near the headwaters of that creek; an obscure stream (*Mattowamon) on the Eastern Shore, mapped by Herrman in 1673. For 1659 and 1663 the Maryland *Archives* have "Matawomen Creeke." Compare Captain Smith's *Mataughquamend of 1608.

Ruttenber, relating *Mattawoman* to *Matteawan* (N.Y.), accepts Gerard's translation, "It debouches into." Dunlap and Weslager, studying Herrman's obscure Eastern Shore *Mattowamon, accept an analysis based on Tooker's translation of *Mattawommax* (N.Y.).

But it is a mistake, I think, to regard the Maryland Mattawoman as any other than Captain Smith's original Mataughquamend of 1608, whose ending *-quamend*, by folk etymology, has evidently become the modern ending *-woman*. In brief, so reason dictates, it is *Mattaughquamend*, not *Mattawoman*, that one must solve.

In keeping with this conviction one puts aside the opening *Mat(t)a-* of the Maryland form, and seeks an Algonquian word to account for the opening *Mattaughqua-* of Smith's Mataughquamend. As it turns out, Fox *matakwi* "delightful, pleasant" seems to be the answer. The rest of the word would be an impersonal form, appearing here as *-mind*. The consequent compound (*mātakwi -mind*) would mean "Where one goes pleasantly."

MAUGANSVILLE. Near Hagerstown, Washington County. It is on Rand-McNally's map, 1906. The name is from the *Maugans* family, two of whom had telephones in Maugansville in 1971. The name of Martin *Maugans* occurs in a roll of Civil War soldiers who enlisted in 1862-63 for Leitersburg District. (See: Bell, p. 66).

MAYNARD. Near Jacobsville, Anne Arundel County. Henry Maynard, an English merchant, settled in Anne Arundel County before 1702. He spelled his name *Maignard*. (See: Richardson, II, 181–82).

MAYO. Beach, village, and point near Annapolis, Anne Arundel County. Perhaps the earliest Mayo in Anne Arundel County was Joshua Mayo, who married Hannah Learson in 1707. Colonel Allen Jackson Lamb attributes the present placenames to Commodore Isaac Mayo, who served under Captain James Lawrence in the War of 1812. According to Jane McWilliams Commodore Mayo, born in about 1795, was awarded a silver medal by the U.S. Congress for distinguished military service; Maryland awarded him a gold-mounted sword. Commodore Mayo's naval career ended in 1861 when, in a letter, he protested Abraham Lincoln's denial "... to millions of free men the rights of the Constitution ..." He was summarily dismissed "with prejudice." But in later years "Dismissed" was changed to "Resigned." He died on May 18, 1861. His "forlorn" home, "Gresham," was still standing in 1977. (See: *MHM*, 25: 3, 1930; *Showcase," So. Co. *Sentinel*, 12 March 1970; *Capital*, 19 Aug. 1970).

MAYONE RESERVE. In Accokeek, Prince George's County. The area has a celebrated Indian burial plot. See ACCOKEEK INDIAN VILLAGE SITE: see *MOYAWANCE.

McCONCHIE. Near Port Tobacco, Charles County. Brown and Klapthor state that the Rev. William McConchie, of "Port Tobacco and Durham parishes," reported on education to the Bishop of London in 1724. He was a minister in the Port Tobacco parish from 1711 to 1742. In Nov. 1774 William McConchie is mentioned in a list of voters for representatives to the Continental Congress.

McCUBBINSVILLE. See STAR'S CORNER.

McDANIELTOWN. Compare Daniel, near Claiborne, Talbot County. Lewis in 1878 lists Charles W. and James McDaniel as farmers who used the post office at McDanieltown.

McHENRY. Buffalo Marsh Inlet, near Hoyes, Garrett County. Weeks, stating that McHenry was named for the McHenry family of Baltimore, mentions Dr. James McHenry (1753–1816), Secretary of War in the cabinets of George Washington and John Adams. He spent his summers in Wild Cherry Meadows with Colonel John Lynn. And in 1810 he bought land in Locust Tree Bottom . This purchase included the Buffalo Marsh, site of McHENRY. To Dr. McHenry Gannett ascribes the name FORT McHENRY.

McKINSTRYS MILL. A village near New Windsor, Carroll County. In 1814 Evan McKinstry came to Carroll County from Pennsylvania and bought Pusey's Mills, west of New Windsor. According to Wingate's Maryland Register, Samuel McKinstry was postmaster here in 1857. In 1878, so Lewis indicates, Samuel McKinstry was postmaster, and he and M. C. McKinstry were local millers. (See: Warner et al, p. 46, p. 52).

MECHANICSVILLE. There are at least two places by this name, one in St. Mary's County and one in Somerset. The St. Mary's village arose in connection with the crossroads tavern of the Adams brothers, who also had a forge and a blacksmith shop. In the Somerset village in 1878 there were two blacksmiths. Notice Mechanicstown and Mechanics Valley, Maryland. Compare Mechanicsburg, Pa., which Espenshade ascribes to ". . . a number of mechanics . . . who worked in the foundry and machine shops." (See: Guide, p. 477; Lewis 1878).

MELITOTA. A village near Hanesville, Kent County. It is in GMd 1904. In Attic Greek *melitoutta* means "sweetened with honey." But the reference as to whom or what was sweetened is, in this case, unknown. (See: Liddell & Scott, *Greek-English Lexicon*, 8th ed., N.Y., 1897).

*MELVILLE'S CROSSROADS. See HENDERSON.

MERCERSVILLE. Near Grimes, Washington County. It is on Martenet's map of 1866. The 1790 census lists seven families by this name. In the 1971 phone book for Washington County there are three entries for

Mercer. Compare the Mercer family of Cecil County, where Thomas Mercer and his sons occupied "Indian Range." (See: Richardson, II, 1837).

MERRICKTON. Queen's Anne County. Lewis lists C. H. R. Merrick and James Merrick as farmers whose post office address in 1878 was *Merricktown.* Compare Merrick Cemetery, Talbot County.

MESONGO. Though Johnson and Gannett list Mesongo as a Maryland stream, it appears, on more reliable evidence, to be a hamlet and creek six miles below Maryland, in Accomac County, Virginia. C. W. Sams spells it *Mes-son-go.*

Johnson sees Delaware *"Meshakan* a wound" in this name and remarks "probably referring to some accident, or where someone was badly wounded. Gannett, without citing an authority, goes so far as to translate "Where we killed deer." Compare Fox *mehcw* "wound by shooting," Cree *miswew* "Il le blesse."

However, since the connection between Algonquian "wound" and *mes-* is phonetically doubtful, and the rest of the name, *-ongo*, is unexplained, I am inclined to reject the explanations of Johnson and Gannett. It is more reasonable, to satisfy phonetic analogy and to explain all of the name, to view *Mesongo* as a local development of Primitive Algonquian **mes* "bare" and Primitive Algonquian **-ahki* "earth." The consequent prototype, which would appear with a nasal [n] in Maryland, is **mes-ahki* "Bare earth."

MEXICO. In Cranberry Valley, northeast of Westminster, Carroll County. It is on Martenet's Maryland map of 1873. M. R. Farrell states that from 1883 to 1889 to post office here was **Brummel, for Elisha Brummel, the first postmaster. Kathryn Geraghty indicates that the present name, Mexico, came about when a man named Santa Anna came here from Mexico and built a home, "Mexico," at the roadside. Farrell, however, contends that the name commemorates "Mexico House," a hotel built here in the early 1870's by one Myerly, who had lost a relative in the Mexican War. Compare *Mexico*, Cecil County, and Mexico Farms Airport, Allegany County. (See: Farrell, *Sun* [Mag.] March 12, 1961; Geraghty, *Sun* [Mag.] Dec. 4, 1960).

*MICHAELSVILLE. The 1944 Gazetteer situates Michaelsville within Aberdeen Proving Grounds, Harford County. In 1834 the postmasters here were Ethan Michael and Henry A. Greenfield. In 1878 the postmaster was J. J. Michael. (See: Register 1834; Lewis 1878).

*MIDDLEBROOK. Listed in Register 1834.

MIDDLEBURGH. Listed in Register 1834.

MIDDLETOWN. Eight miles west of Frederick, Frederick County. There was a post office here in 1834. Donald Smith writes that Lauder, an English gunsmith, "staked out a field near the west end of the present town around 1710." He adds "In the *center* of the valley [between the Catoctin and Blue Ridge Mountains] glittering through the morning haze, lay *Middletown.*" Other Maryland Middletowns are in Baltimore, Carroll, and Charles Counties. Compare Middletown Branch, Transquaking River, Dorchester County. (See: Lewis 1878; Smith's "Several Ages of Middletown," *Star*, 8 Dec. 1968).

MIDLAND.   Also sometimes listed as *Midland Junction* and *Midland Mines*. Thomas and Williams describe this village as being ". . . located 3 miles north of Lonaconing and 5 miles south of Frostburg, in the same deep valley." It was incorporated in 1902. (See: TW, I, 498–99).

Note: The town was probably thought of as being midway between Frostburg and Lonaconing.

MIDLOTHIAN, MIDLOTHIAN JUNCTION.   Coal field village near Frostburg, Allegany County. One finds the *Midlothian* Coal and Iron Company in a Table of Properties containing "the Great Coal bed of the Cumberland Basin." The name comes originally from Edinburghshire, or Midlothian, a Scottish county where coal at some points is extensively mined. The two other Midlothians (Pr. George's County, Calvert County) suggest Scotch immigration. (See: TW, I, 455 [1869]).

MILES RIVER.   It enters Eastern Bay, near Claiborne, Talbot County. It was spelled *Miles River* in 1782. The name was originally *St. Michaels*, to commemorate St. Michael, on whose "feast day" the colonists paid their semi-annual rents to the Calverts. In the process of becoming *Miles*, *St. Michaels* lost *Saint*, perhaps because of the Quakers, who disliked titles. The slurring or elision of the *-ch-* of *Michael* brought about the change to *Miles*. Compare the British family name *Miles* which, so Reaney states, can come from *Michael* through the form *Miel*. The Maryland pronunciation of *Miles* is MAHLS. (See: Archives, XLVII, 97; Guide, p. 391; Kenneth Carroll, *MHM*, 53: 4, 1958). See ST. MICHAELS.

*MILFORD TOWN.   Emory mentions the Supplementary Act of 19 Nov. 1686 establishing an additional town in Kent County on the land of William Stanley, Swan Creek, to be called Milford Town. (See: Emory, pp. 315-16).

MILLER CHAPEL.   Village near Leitersburg, Washington County. Michael Miller, probably a Mennonite, lived near the Little Antietam in 1765. Jacob Miller paid part of the cost of building Miller's (Mennonite) Church, on Jacob Miller's ground, in 1835. This was probably Miller's *Chapel*. (See: Williams, I, 512–13).

MILLERSVILLE.   Near Gambrills, Anne Arundel County. Stating that the village originated in "the 1940s," Riley attributes the name to George Miller who, soon after the railroad came, built a store and residence on land belonging to John Miller, his father. (See: Riley, p. 114).

MILLINGTON.   On the Chester River, Kent County. Emory states that *Head of Chester* became *Millington* in about 1819, and that its postal name became *Millington* in 1827. The Guide, mentioning the "six or more" water wheel mills around which the town grew, implies that the name arose because of the milling industry. And Emory, at first, attributes *Millington* to "the woolen mills of Messrs. Mallalien." Later, however, in a correction, citing Folger McKinsey, Emory declares that the name is today believed to be for Richard *Millington*. (See: Guide, p. 413; Emory, p. 327, p. 374; *Sun*, Oct. 13, 1940, p. 16).

*MILLTOWN. See BISHOPVILLE.

MINGO BRANCH. A tributary of Gunpowder Falls, Baltimore County. The *Archives* for 1660–1661 mention *Minqua* or Sinigo Indians, and also *Minquas Country Minquaas* appears on Md. 1676 Speed. The backwoods of Baltimore and Harford Counties, when they were first colonized, had many scattered. Indian cabins and tents, as such placenames as *Indian Cabin Branch, Indian Cabin Cove, Indian Cabin Neck* and *Indian Quarters* reveal. These dwellings were probably Algonquian. But *Mingo Branch*, and the two *Seneca* Creeks of Baltimore and Cecil Counties, indicate the earlier presence of the Iroquois. *Mingo* was the Delaware term of contempt for the Iroquois, and comes from Delaware *Mingwe* "stealthy, treacherous." (See: Marye, *MHM*, 25: 4, 1930; *Handbook* I, 867).

*MIOWAIKE. A forgotten stream near the Wicomico River, Charles County. In the *Archives* for 1663–66 it is spelled *Miowaike, Myowickes* Creekes mouth. Probably a Southern Maryland form of Primitive Algonquian **melwi-* "good" and Primitive Algonquian **-axki* "earth." There is a close resemblance here to Cree *miyo* "good," where the *l* of Primitive Algonquian *melwi* appears as *y*. *Milwaukee*, Wisconsin, has a similar origin. The meaning is "good earth." (See *Archives* XLIX).

MISKI RUN. A tributary of McIntosh Run, St. Mary's County. If it is Indian, *Miski* may mean "It is red." Fox *me'kwi* means "red"; in Ojibwa *Miskwagam* . . . , "Red Lake," *miskwa* means "red." Compare Miskimon, a village in Northumberland County, Virginia.

MITCHELLVILLE. Near Collington Branch, Pr. George's County. On Martenet's map of 1866, it is *Mullikin Sta-Mitchellville P.O.* Lewis, 1878, lists George A. Mitchell as a general merchandiser here, and George and James Mitchell as farmers using the Mitchellville post office. See MULLIKIN.

MOCCASIN POND. On Isle of Wight Bay, Worcester County. Stating that *moccasin* came into English through Powhatan as well as through "Massachuset," Chamberlain gives these variants: (Powhatan) *mockasin;* (Massachuset) *mohkisson;* (Narragansett) *mocussin;* (Micmac) *m'cusun;* and (Ojibwa) *makisin.* The region is too far north for the moccasin snake. The name is best explained by the possible presence of either the moccasin fish (Maryland *sunfish*) or the moccasin flower (lady's slipper or Indian shoe). (See: Handbook, I, 916).

MONIE. [muh-NYE]. A bay, two creeks, a neck and a post office, Somerset County. Some early spellings are *Mannij* in *Archives* III, for 1605, and *Manaye* on Md. 1780 Mt. & Page. Two Algonquian words suggest *Monie*: Natick *munnoh* "island"; and Natick *moonôi* "(It is) deep." However, the waters of Monie are not deep, and there is no island.

It seems to me more likely that *Monie* is an abbreviated form of Virginia *Nominy*, as in *Nominy Bay*, itself a contraction of Powhatan **Onawmanient*. *Nominy* could give *Monie* by losing its unstressed opening syllable, *No-*.

If it is true that Monie is from Nominy, both names have a common origin from *Onawmanient*. To solve *Onawmanient*, one must first remove the final *-ent*, which is evidently an English adjectival suffix. The basic Indian word is then *Onawmani-* and it may, indeed, consist of Primitive Algonquian **aeāmi-*, which in an *n-* dialect is *anāme* and means "beneath, within, deep down," plus *-anwi-* "It is" and *-wi*, a pronominal ending. Altogether, for the Indian part of *Onawmanient*, one would translate "It is beneath (within, deep down)."

MONKEY LODGE HILL (el. 2660). (Monkey Lodge, GMd 1904; ~ Hill, GMd 1941; ~ Manual 1947). Mary V. Jones, of Oakland, describes its location as being north of Swanton in Election District No. I. The name has not been solved. I find, though, that in some parts of Maryland (e.g., Anne Arundel Co.) trees children like to climb are called "monkey trees." Perhaps on Monkey Lodge Hill there were such trees, or even a tree house or lodge.

MONKTON. A village near Corbett, Baltimore County. It is *Monkton Mills P.O.* on Martenet 1866. The name is from Monckton, Nova Scotia, and commemorates a Canadian sojourn and love affair on the part of Robert Cummings, a Pennsylvanian. The lady was Rosanna Trites, of Monckton, N. S., and when Cummings returned from Canada in 1773 he settled twenty miles from Baltimore on a part of his uncle's estate and, remembering Ms. Trites, named it "Monckton Mills." (*See:* Esther Wright, *MHM*, 52: 3, Sept. 1957).

MONOCACY. [moe-NOCK-uh-see]. A tributary of the Potomac River, Frederick County. Compare *Monocasy Creek*, Lehigh River, Bethlehem, Pa., and **Menagachsink*, Delaware name of the site of Bethlehem. Early Maryland spellings are *Monocasey, Mononknissa, Monocassy*.

Heckewelder, Boyd, and Donehoo derive *Monocacy* from *Menagassi*, a "stream, with several large bends." Johnson derives it from *menen-achk-hasik-hanne* "At the garden creek." And Scharf really exfoliates when he sees *mashanne* "rapid stream" and *okehanne* "crooked or winding stream" in the name and translates "A rapid stream containing several great bends or windings."

There is no dictionary support for Heckewelder's translation. However, Johnson's translation is borne out by Delaware *menachk* "fence, fort."

Even better than Johnson's analysis is Delaware *menachk(h)asu* "forti-fied, fenced, a garden." The last syllable of *Monocacy* may be from Primi-tive Algonquian *-(e)nki* "where or at," but I see no element for "stream" or "creek" in the name.

*MONOPONSON. The Indian name of Kent Island, Queen Anne's County. The *Relation of Maryland* in 1635 has "Island of Monoponson"; the *Archives* mention "Indians of Monoponson."

Frank Speck describes *Monoponson* as a Nanticoke name. It closely re-sembles *Monoponsett*, Massachusetts, which Kinnicutt defines as "It is a deep pond."

It is plausible to regard the final *-on* of Maryland *Monoponson* as the grammatical equivalent of the final *-et(t)*, "It is," of Massachusetts *Mono-ponsett*. The two names then become identical, and Kinnicutt's translation applies to both of them. However, Kinnicutt's analysis rests on the ques-tionable assumption that the *-son* of these names comes from *paug* "pond."

Because of this flaw in the Kinnicutt explanation, I am inclined to give up the New England connection and divide *Monoponson* into *mon-* "dig," *opon(i)* "tuber," and a form of Algonquian *menesi* "island." The preferred translation, then, is "It is an island where tubers are dug." (See: L. N. Kinnicutt, *Indian Names of Places in Plymouth . . . County, Massachu-setts*, Worcester, 1909).

MONROVIA. Frederick County village near New Market. It was a post office in 1834. Probably from U.S. President James *Monroe* (1758–1831). Compare the Negro colony (now republic) of Liberia, Africa, founded in 1822 by American slave trade abolitionists. Freetown, Sierra Leone, and Monrovia, Liberia, resulted from this movement.

MONTEVIDEO. Village, near Dorsey, on the boundary line between Howard and Anne Arundel Counties. Probably from a similarly named house or estate. Compare "Montevideo," a ponderous manor house near Big Seneca Creek, Montgomery County. Farquhar states that the Mont-gomery County mansion was probably built in the 1820's.

MONTGOMERY COUNTY. It lies northwest of the District of Co-lumbia. The Wooton Bill to create this county was passed on September 6, 1776, and the county came into "legal and actual existence" on October of that year. The name is for General Richard Montgomery, who was killed in December, 1775, while leading an attack against Quebec. Farquhar states that Montgomery, born near Raphoe, Ireland, in 1736, never set foot in the county named for him. In Bethesda there is a monument to General Montgomery. (See: Farquhar, p. 20; Guide, p. 514).

MONTGOMERY VILLAGE. Near Gaithersburg, Montgomery County. Work on this place, described as "an entirely new town," began in March 1966; it was finished in 1967. The builders were Kettler Broth-ers, Inc. And it was hoped, at the time, that someday it would have a population of 30,000. (See: Poole, "Montgomery Village - Work Starts on New Town," *Star*, March 4, 1966; *Star*, Sept. 27, 1977).

MONTPELIER. There are villages by this name in both Washington and Prince George's Countries. The Prince George's village takes its name from "Montpelier," a mansion whose construction was begun in about 1740 by Thomas Snowden, the son of Richard Snowden, "The Iron-master." The mansion takes its name from "Montpelier," Anne Arundel County, the birthplace of Ann Ridgely, Thomas Snowden's wife. The first Snowden was Richard "The Immigrant," who came to Maryland in about 1669 after serving under Cromwell. The Snowdens mined and smelted iron ore and established the "Patuxent Iron Works" at Muirkirk and the "Snowden Iron Works." The Patuxent River, in the vicinity of the Snowden homes, was at one time known as "Snowden's River." (See: M. H. Edsall, "Montpelier Mansion . . . Laurel, Md.," *Capital*, 26 Sept. 1978).

MORANTOWN. Near Mt. Savage, Allegany County. It is on Martenet's map, 1866. The 1968 telephone book for Allegany County lists 14 *Morans*. One of them was in neighboring Mt. Savage. Compare *Morantown, on Tom's Creek, Frederick County. Helman, stating that it existed in about 1723, attributes the Frederick County place to a Methodist preacher.

MORGAN, MORGAN RUN. Both village and stream are near Woodbine, Carroll County. Morgan Run is on Martenet's map, 1866. Marye notices that in this vicinity there were two streams called *Little Morgan's Run. Probably for an early Morgan family. The Carroll County phone book of 1963 lists six *Morgans*. (See: *MHM*, 52: 2, June 1955).

MORGANTOWN. Potomac River, near Wayside, Charles County. Manual 1947 lists *Morgantown, Morgantown Bridge*. The 1963 telephone book for Charles and St. Mary's Counties has 34 entries for *Morgan*. One of these is John W. Morgan, of Banks-O-Dee, near Morgantown.

MORGANZA. A village near Leonardtown, St. Mary's County. Mary H. Tennison, postmistress here in 1950, tells me that the Morganza office was established between 1875 and 1880, and that the name is for the Morgan family, who owned a large tract of the land. Knight identifies the "Goodrick Farm" as "The farm once owned by George W. Morgan from which Morganza derives its name." Compare Morganza, Pennsylvania, whose name Espenshade attributes to "the famous Morganza farm" of Colonel George Morgan, local Indian agent from 1776 to 1779. (See: Knight, pp. 19–20).

Note: To me the final -*za* indicates *abundance*, cf. *extravaganza*.

MORGNEC. Near Kennedyville, Kent County. A document signed by William Stone, associate of Lord Baltimore's, mentions Henry Morgan, sheriff in 1648 of the Island of Kent. Morgan had come into the province in

1637, and in 1650 Stone assigned to him a parcel of land adjoining his own plantation. This land was probably *Morgan's Neck*, of which *Morgnec* is a contraction. (See: Hanson, p. 42).

MORNINGSIDE. A suburban community near Suitland, Prince's George's County. Development was in the decade of 1940–49. It appears that the builders gave this name for no other reason than that it sounded romantic. (See: George Flynn, "Prince George's County Past and Present," *Star*, April 10, 1955). Cf. MORNINGSIDE HEIGHTS, N.Y.C.

MORRISON, MORRISON'S MILLS. A community near Western-port, Allegany County. It is recorded in Manual 1947. The Piedmont, W.Va., *Herald*, of June 4, 1964, tells of the death of the married daughter of James Morrison, of Virginia, who began to live at Morrison in 1890. He is described as ". . . a member of one of the pioneer families of Alleghany County . . ."

MOSCOW, MOSCOW MILLS. A George's Creek coal village, near Pe-kin, in the heart of the Cumberland coal basin, Allegany County. *Moscow Mills* is on Rand-McNally's map of 1876. The pioneer landowner was William Burns Shaw, an Englishman. His son, Andrew Bruce Shaw, developed the region by building a stone grist mill and a lumber mill, and by laying out sites for communities. "Pekin mine" was situated here, and *Moscow* and *Pekin* belong in the category of unexplained, far away, and exotic colliery names, such as *Caledonia Mines, Klondike,* and *Midlo-thian Mine*—all of them in Allegany County. (See: Reppert, *Sun* [Mag.], Dec. 11, 1960). See BARTON; see PEKIN (NIKEP).

MOTTERS. A village near Emmitsburg, Frederick County. In Manual 1947 it is *Motters, Motters Station*. In 1878 William Motter was the post-master here. The family name was originally *Mottrie* or *Mottieur*, according to Williams, who mentions Henry Motter, of Frederick County, and relates that the Huguenot ancestors of the Motter family fled to America during the reign of Louis XV. (See: Lewis 1878; Williams, p. 648).

MOUNTAIN LAKE PARK. El. 2500. A mountain resort and village near Oakland, Garrett County. In 1881 The Mt. Lake Park Association established a vacation community here. The site was earlier "Hoyes Big Pasture," in the Little Youghiogheny glades. The park was a forest of oak trees; the lake is formed by Broad Ford Creek and Crystal Spring. (See: Weeks, p. 22, p. 32, pp. 92–93).

MOUNTAIN ROAD. The highway, via Pasadena, to Gibson Island, Anne Arundel County. Hoping that I will "Find a little mountain" in "Mountain Road," Valerie Parker, Glen Burnie, writes me that, in the Wishing Rock area of Mountain Road, there are "solid, huge boulders that seem to indicate only one thing—Mountains!" She states that a traveller, standing on the "Wishing Rock," can see "all the way over" to Route 301, where there seems to be another ridge. Evidently, in the days of unpaved roads and fewer houses, it was appropriate to describe this region as mountainous.

However, despite Ms. Parker's kindly wisdom, I continue to seek a more tangible explanation of this name. And I find such an explanation in the fact that Mountain Road leads to Mountain (Bar) Point at the southern tip of Gibson Island. The island itself has a quantity of small hills that are sometimes called the "Seven Mountains of the Magothy." (See: Joel McCord, "Mountain Road: Fabric of Life Changes with Times, *Sun*, Feb. 25, 1979).

MOUNT AIRY. A town near Ridgeville, Carroll County. When the Baltimore and Ohio Railroad was planned this was "Parrs Spring Ridge (the present Mount Airy) . . ." On March 9, 1854, The Mt. Airy Coal and Iron Company was incorporated. The townsite is on an *airy* ridge, 800 feet high. (See: Hungerford, *Story of the Baltimore and Ohio Railroad 1827–1927*, I, 52; Warner et al, pp. 48–59).

Compare the following Maryland mansions and estates: "Mount Air," on an elevation above the Potomac River, Port Tobacco Creek; "Mt. Airy," the home of Benedict Swingate, "Calvert of 'Mount Airy'"; "Mt. Airy," near Rosaryville, Prince George's County; and "Mt. Airy," a Montgomery County home mentioned by Farquhar.

MOUNT CALVERT. El. 50. Earlier **Charles-Towne*. This village is near Upper Marlboro, Prince George's County. It is also MT. CALVERT LANDING. The *Archives* for 1711 mention ". . . a Ferry over Patuxent River at Mount Calvert . . ." Lantz states that the first county seat of Prince George's County was **Charles-Towne* ". . . known as Mount Calvert . . ." The *Charles* suggests that the present name is for Charles Calvert. (See: *Archives*, 29, p. 70; Lantz, p. 196).

Note: W. H. Babcock doubts that Mount Calvert is the site of the earliest settlement in Prince George's County. But "at all events," he says, it is very old, with nothing now (1888) remaining but an estate bearing the historic name. Babcock in 1888 saw a National Museum map that charted Mount Calvert as Mount *Calvary*. And he feared that in the future the name would perhaps take on this change. I see, however, that the original name continues to hold its own—it is still Mt. *Calvert* (village) in Manual 1969. (See: *JAF-L*, I: 146–47, July-Sept., 1888).

"MOUNT MISERY." Fisher in 1852 mentions "the celebrated cold waters of Mount Misery," in the neighborhood of Port Tobacco. Carleton Jones mentions an 1805 homestead, "Mt. Misery," paradoxically situated in Talbot County near "Mt. Pleasant." The Anne Arundel County MOUNT MISERY, in the Round Bay Community, Severn River, was known in 1837, and had been a military outlook in the War of 1812. Mrs. Pearl Podlich thinks that the soldiers stationed at a campsite here were miserable owing to hot humid summers and icy winters. Compare SOLDIERS DELIGHT, Baltimore County. (See: C. Jones, "The Sounds of

History," *Sun* [Mag.], Oct. 8, 1978; F. Jacques, "Lucky to Find Misery," *Capital*, Aug. 11, 1979.

MOUNT NEBO. A mountain in Garrett County; communities in Montgomery and Washington Counties. Mary Mish terms *Mt. Nebo*, near Pecktonville, Washington County, a "symbolical" name. She explains: It was from Mt. Nebo in Micah that Moses first saw the Promised Land." (See: *MHM*, 51: 1, March 1956).

MOUNT PLEASANT. Montgomery County suburb of Washington, D.C. Farquhar remarks that this place gives "a sweeping view for many miles towards the north and west." Compare Mount Pleasant (el. 450), Frederick County, and Mounty Pleasant (el. 816), Carroll County.

MOUNT RAINIER. Prince George's County suburb of Washington, D.C. (el. 120). "Many years ago" several army officers from Seattle subdivided 100 acres here and named them *Mt. Rainier* for the 14,000-foot mountain in their home state. A syndicate of six men bought the tract in 1902; upon incorporation in 1910 the name became official. Anne Christmas remarks that the unpaved streets of early Mt. Rainier were so muddy that the village was called "Mud Rainier." Pronunciation: RAINY-er. (See: *Star*, April 15, 1960; Mount Rainier *News*, July issue, 1965).

MOUNT SAVAGE. Town. El. 1206. Near Frostburg, Allegany County. In 1866 it had a foundry and coal mine. In 1906 it was mapped as *Mt. Savage Jct.* or *Corriganville P.O.* Mount Savage, settled at the beginning of the nineteenth century, was first known as **Jennings P.O.* It especially flourished between 1839 and 1847, the life of The Mount Savage Iron Works. The name is evidently related to adjacent Great Savage Mountain. (See TW, I, 488–89, 495). See JENNINGS, JENNINGS RUN.

MOUNT VERNON. A village near Widgeon, Somerset County. There are also Mount Vernon, Carroll County, and Mount Vernon, Frederick County. These three Maryland names probably commemorate the original Mount Vernon, Virginia, George Washington's birthplace. The Virginia place, in turn, commemorates the British Admiral, Edward Vernon (1684–1757), who took Puerto Bello in 1739, but was repulsed before Cartagena in 1741. Lawrence Washington, an admirer of Admiral Vernon's, took part in the Cartagena expedition. See CARTAGENA; see *PORTO BELLO*.

MOUNT VICTORIA." Charles County. Footner describes "Mount Victoria" as a "huge structure" on a hill "with a superb view over rich fields to the distant Potomac." It was built in 1905; Queen Victoria had died in 1901. This was the home of the "late" Robert Crain (d. 1928), whose name is found in the "Crain Highway."

Note: The "Old Crain Highway" is near the (Upper) Marlboro Fairgrounds, Anne Arundel County. Today the principal span runs north and south between the Glen Burnie Bypass and the John Hanson Highway (Route 50).

THE PLACENAMES OF MARYLAND

MOUNT WASHINGTON. Baltimore City suburb in the Jones Falls Valley. Martenet 1866 notices a tavern here. B. L. Weston, describing the place as "sitting on its hills and looking back 140 years," indicates that its first name was *Washingtonville, "... said to have derived from a nearby tavern." On March 16, 1810, the Washington Cotton Manufacturing Company was opened here. (See: *MHM*, XLIII: I), March 1948).

MOUNT WILSON. Baltimore City suburb, near Randallstown. The Guide mentions Mt. Wilson Lane and Mt. Wilson tubercular sanatorium, opened for the poor children of Baltimore in 1884. Thomas Wilson, Baltimore's Quaker merchant, was the benefactor of the sanatorium.

MOUNT WINANS. Baltimore City suburb. C. C. Hartman describes this place as five square blocks "tucked away" in a corner of southwest Baltimore. The name is from Ross *Winans* who in 1833 invented a steam engine and built special baggage cars and eight-wheeled coaches. (See: *News-Am.*, Feb. 22, 1969, 4-B). See WINANS.

*MOYAWANCE. Piscataway (Conoy) town and tribe near Broad Creek, Prince George's County. Some of Captain Smith's spellings were *Mayaons, Mayaoones, Moyowances*. The opening syllables may be related to Primitive Algonquian *melwi- "good, fair, fine," as in *Mil*waukee. The rest of the word suggests a nasal form of Fox *-atesi* "exist, get along, have such a way of life." See James A. Geary's analysis of *werowance* (*The Roanoke Voyages*, Quinn, ed., II, 899).

As for archeology, Dr. Frank W. Porter, III, explains: "In 1935, Henry and Alice Ferguson began the excavation of an Indian village site along the edge of the Potomac River, which they tentatively identified as MAY-AONE, the principal village of the Piscataway Indians. Excavation of the Accokeek Creek site identified the principal cultural traits of the historic Algonkian site of the Lower Potomac, those traits being ossuary or group burial, grit-tempered pottery, stemmed projectile points, and stockade villages."

Note: See Stephen E. Fitzgerald's "Lost Indian Village Found," *Sun*, Aug. 13, 1939, Section 1, p. 3. Fitzgerald describes the site of *Moyaone as being on the Maryland side of the Potomac River diagonally across from the land now occupied by Mt. Vernon. More specifically, the place is at "Hard Bargain," the estate of Mrs. Alice L. L. Ferguson and her husband Henry Ferguson, a geologist. At "Hard Bargain," so Fitzgerald remarks, "... diggers have found some 1600 skeletons, pipes, mortars, clam-shell knives, stone gorgets, hundreds of potsherds." It is believed that there was a village here in pre-Columbian times. Some of the artifacts indicate that in colonial days there was extensive and amicable trade between the natives and the whites. In the early eighteenth century the Piscataways disappeared from Maryland. There had been massacres, and it is believed by some that *Moyaone was wiped out and burned by vengeful colonial Virginians in about 1623.

MUDDY CREEK FALLS. It is in Swallow Falls State Park, Garrett County, and consists of a fifty-foot waterfall at a point near the Youghiogheny River. The creek, which flows forth from the Cranesville Swamp, is clear and sparkling and completely belies its name.

MUIRKIRK. Village near Beltsville, Prince George's County. (*Muirkirk P.O./*I. Furn/, Martenet 1866). The Guide points out that Muirkirk was named for Muirkirk, Scotland, by the Scotchmen who in 1747 built an iron furnace here. In 1940 six of the "hive-like brick-charcoal" ovens were still standing.

*MULBERRY HILL. Region near Easton, Talbot County. Cf. Mulberry Hills, Anne Arundel County. Ingraham (p. 238) relates that in 1838, when there was a silkworm craze, many Talbot County farmers planted mulberry trees. To use the foliage of these trees, other persons built a "cocoonery" on Mulberry Hill. Within a year both ventures failed. Maryland has four Mulberry Points—named, perhaps, for more natural reasons.

MULLIKIN. Village near Collington Branch, Prince George's County. (*Mullikin Sta./*nr. Mitchellville/, Martenet 1866). Ingraham (p. 286), writing of the Mullikins of Talbot County, mentions Col. James Clayland Mullikin. He was the owner of a farm which his first American ancestor received from Lord Baltimore in 1662. See MITCHELLVILLE.

Note: Compare "Mullikin's Delight" (Prince George's County?), which the Guide (p. 474) describes as having been built in the seventeenth century for James Mullikin, former governor of a West Indian island.

MURRAY's HILL. Mentioned by Cochrane (for 1779). See LINCHESTER.

*MURRAY'S MILL. See LINCHESTER.

MYERSVILLE. In 1866 it was mapped as *Myersville P.O.* Postmistress Sallie Marker tells me that James Stottlemyer cut a clearing here in 1742 and built a log cabin. He was soon joined by other Stottlemeyers from the vicinity of Philadelphia. Says Miss Marker: "It is thought that Myersville obtained its name from the Stottle*meyer* families."

MY LADY BRANCH, MY LADY'S MANOR BRANCH. Near Phoenix, Baltimore County. Manual 1969 lists *My Lady Manor Branch, My Lady Manor Mill.* The name is explained by Laura Pearce: "My Lady's Manor is a tract of several thousand acres which Lord Baltimore gave . . . to his young wife, Lady Baltimore, in the early part of the 18th century." Ms. Pearce remarks that "in time the tract was broken up into farms which by 1900 were still occupied by the descendants of the original owners." In recent years, she adds, many of the old places have begun to be divided into housing developments. (See: Pearce, "[I Remember] a Magic Box of Youth and Beauty," *Sun*, [Mag.], Oct. 22, 1978).

N

NANJEMOY. A creek, and a village on that creek, near Grayton, Charles County. Mary Croft Ward, postmistress here in 1950, tells me that some maps give this place as *Cross Roads, and that before 1890 it was *Nanjemoy Cross Roads.

The Algonquian name *Nanjemoy* is probably a descendant of Captain Smith's *Nushemouck (Nussamek)*, of 1608. Noticing Delaware *nachenumook* "raccoons," Green defines *Nanjemoy* as "Haunt of raccoons." But his analysis fails to account for the present ending in *y*, with loss of the final *k*. And let me point out at this juncture that Blanchard's translation of *Nanjemoy* as "Poor fishing" is also wrong.

The truth appears to be that here there were two related Indian dialects—one of them (*Nussamek*) had no *n* before consonants, and the other (*Nanjemoy*) did have an *n* before consonants. The Algonquiam components of the name may be (for *Nanjemoy*) a cognate of Ojibwa *nânji-* "descend" and (for *Nussamek*) a primitive form, *nushi-mo-waki*. In each case the meaning would be "They go down to the river or landing place." *Nussame-k* seems to mean "One goes on downward."

Note: In about 1674 Nanjemoy Creek (spelled Nangemy) was known as *Avon River*.

NANTICOKE. This Algonquian name designates a river that flows into Tangier Sound, a village on that river, near Jesterville, Wicomico County, and an important group of early Maryland Indians. The village is mentioned in Fisher 1852; Speed in 1676 spells the river *Nanticok*. Captain Smith's name for this stream is *Kus: flu:* or *Kuskaraock (Cuscarawaock)*.

The *Handbook* attributes *Nanticoke* to *Nentego*, a variant of Delaware *Unalachtgo* "Tidewater people." This analysis correctly recognized the presence in the two words of Algonquian "tidal river, waves" (Ojibwa *tigow*). Evidently there was a local Nanticoke dialect in which internal *m* appears as *l*. On this assumption, *Nanticoke* and *Unalachtgo* are dialectal variants, with the *u* of *Unalachtgo* taken as an archaism indicating the third person. The *-nan-* is analogous to Delaware *nal* "go up." The primitive form would be *U-nal-eteg-wa-ki*, whose fourth syllable (*-wa-*) becomes ō. The meaning, verifying the earliest commentators, is "Tidewater people; they who ply the tidewater stream."

NARROWS. A village near Grasonville, on the eastern bank of Kent Island Narrows, Queen Anne's County. The name is evidently from the adjacent strait or *Narrows*.

As a maritime term one finds "Narrows" in Narrow Point, Kent County, and in Gunpowder Hundred (1695) on the north side of Gunpowder River ("The Narrows"). As a terrestrial term it occurs in "The Narrows," a spectacular gorge in the Alleghany Mountains near Cumberland. From the latter feature come *Narrows*, a post office in 1840, and *Narrows Park*. Local pronunciation: Narz.

NASSAWADOX. A neck of land on the lower Pocomoke River, Somerset County. Torrence spells it *Naswadux*; in the *Archives* it is *Nasswatex*. For 1667–88 there is an Archival reference to the "Kings of ... *Musswattax*. In keeping with its position as "neck of land," *Nassawadox* appears to contain Algonquian *nassaw-* (*nashaue*), "midway, between," and *-e?tuk* "stream." The meaning would be "Between the streams." The final *-x* (=*s*) is probably the English plural or possessive. Compare Nassawadox, Northampton County, Virginia.

NASSAWANGO. A creek flowing into the Pocomoke River, Worcester County; also a woodland area, the NASSAWANGO FOREST. An *Archives* entry for 1667–88 indicates that Nassawango once bore the alternate name, **Askimenokonson* Creek. Churchman's map of Delaware, 1787, has the spelling *Nassiungo*.

The most likely components of this Indian name are cognates of Natick *nashaui* "midway, between" and *-āwang-ā-wi* "ground, surface, soil." The *-āwang-ā-wi* would contract to *-ang-ā-wi*, whence *-ōngo*. The meaning altogether would be "Ground between the streams." See ASKIMINIKONSON.

NATIONAL P. O. A colliery village on George's Creek, Allegany County. An alternate name is *Carlos Junction*. NATIONAL takes its name from the National Coal Company, listed in an 1869 table of "properties" in the Great Coal Bed, Cumberland Basin. (See: TW, I, 455). See CARLOS JUNCTION.

NAYLOR. A Patuxent River village, near Nottingham, Prince George's County. This was **Naylors Landing* in 1866. The name is from the family name *Naylor*, which is mentioned six times for Prince George's County in the 1790 census. Compare Naylor Road, S.E. Washington, D.C.

NEAR EDEN SCHOOL. Village, near Maugansville, Washington County. Paradise Church is two miles east. The height of these places (Near Eden School, 700; Paradise Church, 636) may have had some bearing on the origin of these names. Maryland has three places with *Eden*, and eight with *Paradise*. Eden Street, Baltimore, and DENTON, Caroline Cunty, have been attributed to Provincial Governor Robert *Eden*. See DENTON.

NEAVITT. Town, near Bozman, Talbot County. Edward S. Neavitt (b. 1895), of Neavitt, informs me that Henry Neavitt, his great uncle, was running a general grocery and merchandise store when the post office was established here. My informant had not yet been born. "... the post office settled there at his store they called Neavitt post office and has always gone by that name."

NEGRO MOUNTAIN. E1. 3082. This range lies east of Meadow Mt., Garrett County. On Bradford's map, 1838, it is spelled *Negro Mt.* The name is for Goliah, the "gigantic" Negro "body servant" of Colonel Thomas Cresap. Local historians relate that it was here, near Grantsville, on June 30, 1756, that Goliah, along with Colonel Cresap and his sons Daniel and Michael, attacked a band of Indians in an attempt to avenge the death of Thomas Cresap, Jr. (See: TW, I, 12; FBC, p. 20), See DANS MOUNTAIN.

*NETHKEN. A "lost" Garrett County community. Compare *Nottken Run*, Garrett County. My notes suggest that *Nethken is near *Shallmar*, itself a lost village. Moreover, it appears likely that *Nethken, Maryland, and Nethken in adjacent West Virginia, are one and the same place. The name is from the Nethken family. Weeks finds Nethkens living on Bartlett Street, Oakland, in 1874; in 1972 there were five *Nethken* phone numbers in Oakland. (See: Weeks, p. 44; see my *West Virginia Place Names*, p. 440. See SHALLMAR.

NEWARK. A village near Queponco Creek, Worcester County. It was a post office in 1824. The railroad station here was named Queponco (Queponco Station) to prevent confusion with other Newarks. The name does not appear to relate to the biblical *Ark*, but comes ostensibly from Newark-upon-Trent, Nottinghamshire, England, a village whose name originally meant "New work, fort, building." (See: Ekwall, ODEP, 4th).

*NEW BREMEN. Northeast of Sugarload Mountain, on both sides of Bennett's Creek, Frederick County. The place declined rapidly in the years following 1804. Earlier it was the site chosen and occupied by Johann Frederich Amelung for his famous glass works. He reached Baltimore from Bremen, Germany, on Aug. 31, 1784. See Dorthy Guynn's "Johann Friedrich Amelung at New Bremen," *MHM*, XLIII: 3, Sept. 1948, pp. 155–179.

Note: The glass business here failed; the property was sold on June 18, 1804.

NEW GERMANY. Village, near Jennings, Garrett County. The name commemorates Germany, the native land of many of the first inhabitants. Family names in the vicinity are *Bittinger, Hummell, Otto, Warnick, Weimer,* etc. The tiny lake here, *Swauger's Mill Dam,* is the center of the "New Germany Recreation Area," and owes its name to John Swauger (1817–1878). (See: Schlosnagle, p. 64, p. 348).

*NEW IRELAND. The *Archives* (XVII, p. 230, for 1683) mention two manors "in New Ireland ... Cecil County ... lying between Elk River and North East ... River." Discussing why George Talbot's manor, "Susquehanna," was renamed "New Connaught," Johnston (pp. 114–15) remarks that "... for some time about this period Susquehanna Manor and the country east of it was called New Ireland, no doubt because other large grants of land were made to Irishmen there . . ." See * SHANNON.

NEW GLATZ. A village, near Silesia, Prince George's County. The name commemorates *Glatz*, a fortified German town in the Prussian province of Silesia. It was no doubt the origin of the first settlers. See SILESIA.

NEW MARKET. Maryland has five such places; and what appears to be the largest one is the town of NEW MARKET, near Ijamsville, Frederick County. It was a post office in 1800. Compare EAST NEW Market, Dorchester County, an 1803 post office which the Postal History Catalog describes as having been changed from "New Market" to "East New Market" in 1827. Today, however, it goes by both names. United States market names are usually self-explanatory, although the oldest of them, Newmarket, N.H. (1727), is supposed to be from Newmarket, County Suffolk, England. (See: Hunt's *New Hampshire Town Names*. Peterborough, 1970, pp. 180–81).

"NEW MUNSTER." George Talbot in 1683 patented this 6,000-acre tract on Big Elk Creek, Cecil County, for Edwin O'Dwire and fifteen other Irishmen. Talbot's intention was to set up a "border-protective" "County of New Ireland"; and his penchant for Irish placenames led him to rename the Northeast River *Shannon* and to call "Susquehanna Manor" *New Connaught*. H. J. Ford regarded the "group settlement of New Munster" as the earliest definitely recorded one. (See: Guide, p. 300; C. R. McKenrick, *MHM*, 35: 2, June 1940).

NEWPORT. Maryland has at least twelve places by this name, including a bay, a branch, a creek, a marsh, and a run. Their origins, for the most part, are either geographical, hence self-explanatory, or commemorative—commemorative, that is, of some similarly named place in America or Europe, or of the family name *Newport*.

Newport, a Charles County village, was a post office in 1806. Fisher in 1852, spelled it *New-Port*. Today it is a half mile from a tiny tributary of the Wicomico River. One supposes that there was a "new" port here before Maryland's streams began to silt up. Compare Newport Creek, Worcester County, once a deep stream.

*Newport-Town(e), on Assateague Creek, Worcester County, was earlier *Trappe (ca. 1744). And related to *Newport-Town* are *Newport River*, now Assateague River, and Newport Bay, Worcester County. These oceanic places, particularly this bay, were probably named for Captain Newport. (See: Marye, "Sea Coast of Maryland," *MHM*, XL: 2, June 1945).

Note: For the namer of Newport Bay, Worcester County, consider "Captain Christopher Newport," mentioned in *The Proceedings of the English Colony in Virginia* (ed. Tyler, p. 122) as ". . . a Marriner well practiced for the western parts of America." His name is found in *Newport* News.

*NEW PROVIDENCE. Stein describes *New Providence as a forti-
fied town at Greenbury Point, on the Severn River. It was built in 1649 by
the Puritans who came here in 1649 from Virginia after the passage of
Cecilius Calvert's Toleration Act. *PROVIDENCE (later *Annapolis*) was
the name of the region until the establishment in July 1650 of Anne Arundel County. See *PROVIDENCE; see ANNAPOLIS; see ANNE
ARUNDEL.

*NEW TOWN. The Guide remarks that the county seat of Kent
County was moved from *New Yarmouth to *NEW TOWN, the present
Chester Town, in 1696. See CHESTERTOWN.

*NEW TOWN. Anne Arundel. An addition of ten acres (near Powder
House Hill) to the city of Annapolis in 1718. See Ridgely, p. 113).

*NEWTOWN. In Newtown Hundred near Bretton's Bay, St. Mary's
County. Mentioned by the *Archives* for the 1750's. Compare Newtown
Neck, Bretton's Bay, the site of the old "Newtown Neck manor house."
The *Archives* for 1693-97 cite "Newtons Point upon Wicomico River in
Potomock ..."; but this is a different place. (See: "Some Early Colonial
Marylanders," *MHM*, XV: 4, 1920; Knight, pp. 6-7, p. 21).

Note: Edwin Beitzell locates at Newtown Hundred John Medley's plantation,
"Newtowne," and expresses bewilderment at the mention, in early records, of
*Newtowne River. (See: *MHM*, 51: 2, June 1956, pp. 125-28).

*NEWTOWN. Worcester County. *Newtown, the earlier name of Po-
comoke City, is given in the Postal History Catalog as "Newton Wo," for
1810, and as "Newtown" in a note. See POCOMOKE CITY.

NEW WINDSOR. A town at the junction of "the Monocacy and Buffalo roads," where in about 1788 Isaac Atlee, of Philadelphia, built a tavern. Lots were recorded here in 1797; and until 1816 the place was *Sulphur Springs*, on account of a nearby sulphur spring. The present name
came about when Mr. Atlee, modestly refusing to have the town named
for himself, suggested that it be named for a friend of his from Windsor,
England, who was then visiting him. (See: M. Hill, Baltimore Evening
Sun. Sept. 13, 1973, # C 2; Warner, et al., p. 52).

*NEW YARMOUTH. A "lost" Kent County town. Hanson states that
*New Yarmouth—situated on Gray's Inn Creek—became a "port of en-
try" in 1682, and the county seat in 1686. The Guide explains that *New
Yarmouth was perhaps named from "Great Yarmouth, England," and
comments that it rapidly deteriorated after the county seat was moved to
"New Town" (now Chestertown) in 1696.

NICHOLSON. An obscure place in Kent County. Richardson men-
tions Colonel Joseph Nicholson, High Sheriff of Kent County and Deputy
Commissary and Colonel of the Kent County Militia. Joseph Nicholson,
Jr., was a participant in the Convention in 1775 and a member of the Coun-

cil of Safety. Compare Nicholson Street, Annapolis, which the Evening *Capital* of May 14, 1968, attributes to Governor Sir Francis Nicholson (1694).

NIKEP. A village on George's Creek, at Pekin, Allegany County. It is the reversed post office name of PEKIN. Pronunciation: NICK-up. See PEKIN.

*NINE BRIDGES. Caroline County. According to Cochrane "Nine Bridges (Bridgetown)" was known in 1774. "Nine Bridges," a post office in 1811, was changed to "Bridgetown" in 1841. (See: PHC, n. 25). See BRIDGE TOWN.

*NINEPIN, NINEPIN ROAD and SWAMP, NINEPIN BRIDGE CREEK. The creek is a tributary of the Pocomoke River, Worcester County. In June 1966 I entered the Ninepin cypress swamp (near Walter Webb's grocery store, Whiton) and observed the multitude of small cypress knees or "ninepins" growing there. From one of these knees Mr. Webb's son had made a lamp.

*NOODLE DOOSEY. See MANCHESTER.

NORBECK. A village near Oakdale, Montgomery County. It was a post office in 1866. The name is from the family name *Norbeck*. The Baltimore phone book for 1969 lists one *Norback* and four *Norbecks*. And at Silver Spring, about 12 miles from Norbeck, H. K. Norbeck was living in 1967.

NORRISVILLE. Near Carea, Harford County. In about 1690 Benjamin Norris, "the elder," settled in Harford County (then Baltimore County) on a farm called "Everly Hills." Lewis, 1878, indicates that Norrisville then was the address of Benjamin, George, and Nicholas Norris, all farmers. (See: Preston, p. 210).

NORTHEAST. A town on the Northeast River, near Charlestown, Cecil County. It was a post office (*North East*) in 1809. The town owes its name to being at the head of Northeast River, a stream mentioned by Cyprian Thorowgood as early as 1634. The first settlement here was in 1716, when iron works and a flour mill were built. (See: Marye, "The Great Maryland Barrens," *MHM*, 50: 3; *The Upper Shoreman*, 88: 9, 1970).

NORTHEAST RIVER. It enters Chesapeake Bay from the northeast, below Perryville, Cecil County. Miller cites the evidently misconceived tradition that this stream was named by early settlers who were looking for "the Northeast Passage": "Arriving at the mouth of a river flowing from the northeast, they marked the change in direction and named the river 'North East.' " George Talbot, of County Roscommon, Ireland, and a cousin of Charles Calvert, the third Lord Baltimore, insisted on calling the Northeast, the *Shannon River* and even petitioned for this name in 1684. And so we find in *Archives* 17 for 1683 mention of "North East (als Shermor [=Shannon] River)." Captain John Smith's

*Gunter's Harbor was perhaps at this point. (See: Miller, p. 77; Johnston, p. 2, pp. 111–115). See *SHANNON RIVER.

NORTH MOUNTAIN. Leitersburg cites a Pennsylvania *Archives* survey of May 1793 that mentions ". . . the top of the most westerly hill of a range of hills called the Kittochtinny hills [North mountain] . . ." Scott, describing "the Appalachian or Allegany Mts.," names South Mountain as the most easterly mountain of the range. Thence westerly are NORTH MOUNTAIN, "Will's, Evit's, Warriors, Sidelinghill, and the great Allegany . . ."

NORWOOD. A village near Sandy Spring, Montgomery County. Farquhar mentions an ivy-covered colonial brick house called "Norwood." Robert R. Moore had come here for his health; his son, Joseph, bought "Norwood" in 1867. Gannett, observing that there are twenty-three places by this name in the United States, comments: ". . . generally named from the town in Middlesex, England." However, the *family* name *Norwood* should not be ruled out in this Maryland instance. The Maryland and D.C. suburban phone directory for 1976 lists forty-three Norwoods.

NOTKEN RUN. In Garrett County; see Hoyes Run. See *NETHKEN.

NOTCH CLIFF. Village, near Glenarm, Baltimore County. Marye declares that he is "morally certain" that Notch Cliff, "on or near the road from Cromwell's Bridge to Long Green," is also the name of a place in the northern part of Ireland. He explains: "Near it is Glen Arm, which I know to be definitely a name from the north eastern corner of Ireland." However, the M. & P. Railroad of long ago ran past a steep hillside at this point. (W. B. Marye, Letter, 28 Dec. 1965).

*NORTHWEST FORK BRIDGE. On the Northwest Fork (Marshyhope Creek) of the Nanticoke River, Caroline County. There was perhaps a post office here in 1804. The Md. Postal History Catalog states that the office "appears in a Delaware route," but adds the notation "or Federalsburg." Cochrane makes the entry: "Northwest Fork (now Pine Grove)." See FEDERALSBURG.

NOTTINGHAM. Cecil County. ". . . see WEST NOTTINGHAM."

NOTTINGHAM. A village near White Landing, Patuxent River, Prince George's County. There was a post office here in 1796. Calling Nottingham a "ghost town," Greene remarks that before the Revolution Nottingham had a population of 1500 and was expected to become "what Baltimore City is today." The 1790 census lists three Maryland persons by the name of *Nottingham.* However, it seems to me likely that the Maryland name is from the city of *Nottingham,* Nottinghamshire, England.

*NOX T. Griffith 1795 puts *Nox T.* in a sequential list with *Apoquinimy C., Comegys⁰, Choptank River,* & c. Is this not properly *KNOX TOWN, from the family name *KNOX*?

O

OAK. In Maryland's counties GMd 1941 lists: OAK CREEK, Talbot; OAK CREST, Prince George's; OAK FOREST, Baltimore; OAK GROVE, Caroline; OAK GROVE, Prince George's; OAK ISLAND, Worcester; OAK ORCHARD, Frederick; OAK SHOALS, Garrett; OAK SPRING, St. Mary's; and OAK SPRING LOCK, Montgomery. The Guide remarks that most of the trees "dominating the hardwood zone" are diffused throughout Maryland. It adds that "Black and white oak and beech are sometimes found in pure stands, but mixed forest is more common." There are no oak names listed for Calvert County. However, Stein states: "Calvert County . . . /is/ a natural forest region, and red and white oaks . . . abounded in the forests."

OAKDALE. Village, near Olney, Montgomery County. Probably from the name of a house. Cf. "Oakdale," a "forest home" built in 1838 by Albert G. Warfield, a school commissioner. (See: Warfield, p. 455).

*OAKENSHAW. An early neighborhood on "the fringe of Guilford near Calvert Street and University Parkway . . ." Baltimore. Audrey Bishop speaks of a region of quiet blocks that have an "architectural style . . . faintly British." She continues: "Today this is a neighborhood without a name. Yet on the eve of America's entry into World War I, when the Mueller Construction Co. built the first homes on Guilford Terrace, the development was called Oakenshaw, undoubtedly a variation of Okenshawe, as Henry K. Wilson's farm in the area was known." (See: *Extra*, 30 April 1972).

OAKHILL SCHOOL. Village, near Le Gore, Frederick County. Cf. "Oak Hill," Montgomery County, near Drayton. Farquhar describes the latter as an "attractive farm house" and remarks: "The name is derived from two very large white oak trees still standing on the highest hill in the manor."

OAKINGTON, OAKINGTON STATION. Near Havre de Grace, Harford County. MHGP (for 1964) mentions the Harford County house, "Oakington." It is on the original tract surveyed by Cecilius Calvert in 1659 for Colonel Nathaniel Utie. Cf. Oakington, Cambridgeshire, England.

OAKLAND. Town and county seat near Deerpark and Mt. Lake Park, Garrett County. This was the post office of *Yough Glades* in 1803. Reflecting the fact that Oakland is situated near the Youghiogheny River and its glades, its earlier names were as folows: *Yough Glades*; *Yox Glades*; *Armstrongs* [Wm. Armstrong p.m. Yough Glades]; *Armstrongs in the Green Glades*; and perhaps *Green Glades*. It appears, further, that some B. & O. Railroad records refer to Oakland as *Mc Carty's Mill*, from Isaac Mc Carthy, p.m., 1843.

The present name was given because of an abundance of oak trees. Felix Robinson has stated that the streets here were once "aisles of oak and maple." According to Weeks, *Water, Oak,* and *Alder* were early street names; in 1874 giant oaks shaded the grounds of the Glade Hotel. (See: PHC, n. 99; Weeks, p. 80).

OAKLAND. The 1941 Gazetteer lists this name for places in Baltimore County, Caroline County, Carroll County, and Prince George's County. It also lists two unidentified OAKLAND[S]—one in Harford County, and the other in Howard. The most likely explanation of all these names is an abundance of oak trees. But a surname origin is possible.

Note: TDr 1967 Baltimore has one instance of the surname *Oakland.* And Gannett states that Oakland, Nebraska, takes its name from the man who bought the town site from the original owner.

OAKLAND MILLS. A village near Columbia, Columbia Turnpike, Howard County. It was a post office in 1821. Warfield remarks that "Oakland Manor" and "Oakland Mills" arose around "Dorsey's Adventure," a tract north of "Athol" on the Ellicott City-Laurel highway. It was surveyed for the Hon. John Dorsey and willed by him to his grandson, Edward Dorsey.

OAKLEY. GMd 1941 fails to locate OAKLEY, Charles County. OAKLEY, St. Mary's County, is situated near Milestown. There were two families of *Oakley* in Charles County in 1790; and for 1688 one finds the will of Lyonel *Oakley,* St. Mary's County. (See: Index of Wills . . . St. Mary's County . . . 1633–1900 [M. R. Hodges, compiler].

OAKS. Village near Charlotte Hall, St. Mary's County. Probably from the trees signifying "the Oaks." However, the surname *Oaks* is abundant. TDr 1967 Baltimore has nine instances of *Oaks,* fourteen instances of *Oakes,* and twenty instances of *Ochs.* There are no examples of these surnames in Heads 1790. And there are none in TDr 1963 Charles & St. Mary's.

OAKVILLE. Near Laurel Grove, St. Mary's County. Knight (p. 101) declares that the history of Oakville antedates the Revolutionary War. It was named, he states, for the many oak trees along its borders.

OAKWELL. GMd 1941. Harford County. I can find no surname, *Oakwell.* The name is probably a combination of *oak* and *well,* with *-well* perhaps meaning "spring" or "fountain."

OAKWOOD. Listed in GMd 1941 for Cecil, Harford and Anne Arundel Counties. OAKWOOD, Cecil County, is a village. These and similar names are, for the most part, correctly explained by Gannett's remark: "oak; a prefix much used in combination with lodge, mont, park, point, ridge, summit, ton, town, vale, and valley, and generally so given on account of the preponderance of this species of trees."

OCEAN. A village near Midland, Allegany County. On Martenet's map of 1866 it is *Ocean P.O.* "Ocean Mine." According to Ralph Reppert, when a coal mine was dug here in 1837 it was called the Ocean Mine because parts of it filled up with water. Later mines dug here were named similarly, from Ocean No. 2 up to Ocean No. 16. TW relates that William Aspinwall, of New York, bought a tract comprising the basin near Squirrel Neck and Wright's Run and organized the Ocean Steam Coal Co. In 1864 the newly organized Consolidation Coal Co. included the lands of the Ocean Steam Co. (See: "Ocean in the Mountains," *Sun* (Mag.), 27 Nov. 1960; TW, I, 454).

OCEAN CITY. Sinepuxent Beach, east of Berlin, Worcester County. Cf. "Ocean House" [mainland, opposite Sinepuxent Beach], Martenet 1866. The Guide remarks that "Some of the streets of Ocean City were laid out in 1872 by a group of promoters, but not until 1875 was the first hotel, The Atlantic, opened." W. B. Marye (6) declares: "It is reliably reported that Ocean City was founded by a company of well meaning Eastern Shoremen and was formally open to visitors on July 4, 1875."

Note: Marye describes "Ocean House," mentioned on Martenet 1866, as a "spot" on the west side of Sinepuxent Bay, opposite the site of the future Ocean City.

OCTORARO. A creek that flows into the Susquehanna River near the Conowingo Dam, and a hamlet (Octoraro) at that junction. Perhaps the earliest spelling is *Octoraaro*, on Herrman's map of 1673.

The name is Iroquoian (Tuscarora) and, according to the Smithsonian (BAE) card index, it means "Where the water is shallow and swift." The Guide has: "Rushing waters."

Stewart suggests that *Octoraro* owes its somewhat classical form to a clerk who wrote "a sort of nonsense Latin." In any case it has the earmarks of a Tuscarora Iroquoian name, and I am inclined to accept the following analysis of it by Yale Iroquoian scholar, Professor Lloyd Lounsbury (Dec. 1952): (1) the *-ora* of Tuscar*ora*, for example, means "covered, covering" in Tuscarora Iroquoian; (2) Tuscarora *yohtawakarera* could mean "the sound of rushing waters," but it could not give *Octoraro*; and (3) a form *ohtawora* ("covered water, it is covered with water") is possible. But, asks Prof. Lounsbury, if *Octoraro* comes from this last word, how has it gotten an *r* for the *w*? A plausible answer is that in this case the settlers came to pronounce *r* for *w* either by assimilation or by folk etymology.

ODENTON. Village near Severn, Anne Arundel County. The Guide points out that Odenton, founded in 1867, was named for Governor Oden Bowie (1868–1872). It was a new Baltimore & Potomac railroad station, and Governor Bowie was president of the company. Mrs. Marshall Nelker comments: "The little town sprang up around the crossroads of the railroad and the Annapolis, Washington and Baltimore Road." (See: Riley, p. 112; Evening *Capital*, 21 Nov. 1968). See BOWIE. [Pron.: OADEN-tun].

O'DONNELL STREET. In southeastern Baltimore (Arrow 1948). Named for John O'Donnell, captain of the *Pallas*. See CANTON; see HAMPSTEAD HILL.

OELLA. A village on the Patapsco River, near Ellicott City, Baltimore County. Charles L. Wagandt, of Oella Avenue, Ellicott City, informs me (July 1969): "I have a report that the deed to the Union Manufacturing Co. of Maryland . . . March 31, 1809, stated: '. . . called Oella, in commemoration of . . . the first woman who applied herself to the spinning of cotton on the continent of America.'" Later, in a Baltimore *Sun* article, Wagandt explains more fully: "In 1808, the Union Manufacturing Company became the first textile mill in Maryland to be granted a corporate charter and . . . selected this site . . . for its works. Later known as Oella, the area commemorates the name of the first woman to spin cotton in America." (See: "Oella, a Heritage of Cotton, Fire, and Flood, *Sun* [Mag.], 2 Nov. 1975).

OFFUTTS CROSS ROADS. It lies on or near the present site of Potomac, Montgomery County. *Potomac* was a post office as early as 1830; *Offutts X Roads*, on Martenet and Bond, 1865, bears the annotation "T. M. Offutts P." Lewis, 1878, lists W. Offutts as postmaster and mentions, for the vicinity, Dr. B. Offutt, the general merchandise firm of Offutt and Perry, and farmers L. M. Joshua, and John Offutt.

OGLETOWN. Queen Anne's County. On Aug. 8, 1732, the General Assembly created a town to be called "Ogletown-upon-Chester." It was named, presumably, for Samuel Ogle, then Governor of Maryland. In 1734, according to Queen Anne's County records, James Hollyday bought "Macklinborough, lying on [the] . . . main road leading to Ogletown." Emory could find no further mention. (See: Emory, p. 321).

OHIO BRANCH. A tributary of Big Pipe Creek, Carroll County. It is not on Carroll 1877. Arthur G. Tracey, of Hampstead, however, tells me, February 1951, that the first mention of Ohio Branch he has seen was in a survey for a tract called *Ohio*, made for Samuel Owings in 1765. Tracey adds: "Samuel Owings was a very active man and an extensive land owner, and it is likely that he was responsible for the name." There are other Indian names in the vicinity and an Indian trail probably passed near by; but I am not aware that *Ohio Branch* has any aboriginal significance for Maryland.

OKAHANIKAN COVE. On Bloodsworth Island, Dorchester County. The U.S. Geographic Board has ruled: ". . . (Not Hanikan, Occohannock, nor Onkanikan.)" In 1657–60 there was a Maryland place, *Occahannock*; in 1866 one finds *Onkanikan Cove* (Bloodsworth Island).

Green translates the Virginia river, *Accohanoc*, as "as far as the river." Mentioning other forms (Accahanock, Accohanock), he makes two additional suggestions, "Narrow, winding stream," and "People of the bending (curving) stream."

The name evidently contains "stream." And there is some justification for "people," insofar as -*ock* could be an inanimate plural ending. At Scarborough's Neck there was a village of the Occahannock Indians.

I conclude that the correct elements of the name are: (1) *-wāki* "bend, curve"; (2) -*ahan*- "flow, stream"; and (3) -*ihkān* "numerous, where there are many." The meaning would be "Winding river," or "Place where there are many bends in the stream."

OKLAHOMA. A Carroll County village near Eldersburg and Sykesville. This modern, imported name has no aboriginal significance in Maryland. Compare OKLAHOMA, Harford County.

Note: Perhaps it is significant that, though this place is not in GMd 1904 and does not appear on R-McN 1906, it is given on USGS 1906 Ellicott. Oklahoma (Choctaw "red people") became a state on Nov. 16, 1907.

*OLACIN LAND (OLICCIN LAND). See OREGON.

*OLD BALTIMORE. *Old Baltimore was on the Bush River, about seven miles south of Perrymanville and two miles northeast of the Phila. & Washington R.R. bridge. For some years before 1683, it was probably a port of entry and the county seat. Scharf speaks of six maps which locate the town accurately. All traces of it had disappeared by the seventies of the last century. (See: Stockett, p. 38).

Note: L. M. Passano (*H. of Md.*, 5th ed., p. 58) states that there is still a boat landing on the Bush River called "Old Baltimore." This was about 1901.

"Old Burnt Store." Knight (p. 65) mentions the "Old Burnt Store," located today at what is known . . . as Clements, Maryland . . . "

*OLD BUSH TOWN. On Bush River, Harford County. Hill indicates that a locality near the Philadelphia Road, on the east side of Bynum's Run near Abington, is still known as *Old Bush Town*. A monument here states that this was the site of the first courts of Harford County, from March 1774 until March 1780. The present village of BUSH appears to be at this spot; the headwaters of Bush River are nearby. See BUSH; see *HARFORD TOWN.

*OLD CHARLES COUNTY. Hill (p. 191) relates that in 1650 Lord Baltimore directed that a Charles County, named for his son, Charles, be formed from lands bordering on the Patuxent River. However, its new Commander, Robert Brooke, sympathized too much with the Puritans. On July 3, 1654, Brooke was deposed and the new county was abolished. At the same time Governor Stone "created" both sides of the Patuxent River into Calvert County, named for the Proprietor's family. The abolished county was remembered as "Old Charles County."

Notes: Calvert County was called *PATUXENT COUNTY in 1654; it was changed back to CALVERT in 1658. A new Charles County was established in 1658. Its western limit was undefined until the formation of Prince George's County in 1695.

OLDFIELD. Near Libertytown, Frederick County. Compare Old Field Point, Kent County, and Old Field Point, Cecil County. The term "old field" was used in frontier days to describe timberless land, earlier cultivated by the Indians and left fallow. The "Indian Old Fields" of the Potomac River's North Branch had been deserted in this manner by the Shawnees. Perhaps at this Frederick County place there had been clearings and an Indian settlement. See my *Origin and Meaning of the Indian Place Names of Maryland*, p. 101.

*OLD HARFORD TOWN. On Bush River. See BELAIR, BUSH, *HARFORD TOWN, and *OLD BUSH TOWN.

"Old I. U. Church." Near Smithville, Worton D., Kent County. The Guide (p. 383), stating that the present church was built in 1868 to replace an older structure (1768), attributes the name to initials found on a large boundary stone near by. The parish was established in 1765. Cf. *I. B.* (Town), Queen Anne's; and *T. B.* (vil.), Prince George's.

*OLD FORGE MILL. Queen Anne's County. Emory (p. 326) thinks that this name is from an iron forge in the neighborhood. He explains that bog iron ore was found "in considerable quantities" near Church Hill many years ago.

OLD STATION ROAD. In the Round Bay Community, Severn River, Anne Arundel County. The name commemorates an old station of the now defunct Baltimore and Annapolis Railroad. At No 4, Station Road, there still stands the historic house that was once used as the railroad station. The home is a stop on the annual Round Bay tour; there is a historical marker.

OLDTOWN. Village, about twelve miles southeast of Cumberland, on the N. Branch of the Potomac River, Allegany County. This place, on the Maryland side of the Potomac River, is about a mile from the "Shawnee Indian Fields Deserted" of the early maps of Warner and Mayo. Scott 1807 has: "Oldtown, properly Skipton, a post town"; and Fisher 1852 lists "Old-Town ... the oldest village in the County, having been settled ... /in/ 1741 by Col. Thomas Cresap and several other families." One supposes that Cumberland and Oldtown occupy, respectively, the sites of *CAIUCTUCUC and *KING OPESSA'S TOWN, the Shawnee villages abandoned by the Indians before the middle of the eighteenth century. TW explains "Shawanese Oldtown, now simply Oldtown." See *SKIPTON.

*OLD TOWN. Baltimore City. Stockett states that *Old Town," situated across Harrison's Marsh, was laid out in 1732 on "the land where

Edward Fell kept a store," some distance north of Fells Point. See *JONES TOWN.

*OLDTOWN. Caroline County. See GOLDSBORO.

OLDTOWN. Cecil County. Johnston (p. 83) relates that the first courthouse of Cecil County was built on the north side of Sassafras River, near Ordinary Point ". . . at what was afterwards called Jamestown, and is designated now on the map of Cecil County as Oldtown."

*OLD WYE MILL. Emory (p. 277) states that WYE Mill was spoken of as "Old Wye Mill" in 1748. See WYE MILL.

OLNEY. Town, near Sandy Spring, Montgomery County. Farquhar points out that in 1832 the post office here was known as *MECHANICS-VILLE. The present name is from "Mt. Olney," built in about 1800. The Farquhar family lived in this dwelling for 100 years. They and the Elgars admired the poetry of William Cowper. And the name "Olney" comes from Olney, Buckinghamshire, England, where Cowper lived for nineteen years. The "Mt." in this name is explained by Farquhar's remark that Mount Olney (el. 544) is one of the highest points in lower Montgomery County.

Note: J. Sherwood ("Olney is Still 'the Village,'" *Star*, 7 March 1965) writes that ". . . Olney is no longer just plain Olney. It's Williamsburg Village, Sycamore Acres, Timberwood Estates, Olney Acres, or Olney Estates." A similar item (*Star*, 23 May 1969) tells of the beginning of Olney Village, a housing development on Georgia Avenue Extended.

ONE STOP. A vicinity on U.S. Route I, near Jessup, Howard County. The name is from a big sign, "Home of One-Spot Flea Killer," that marks a dog-shaped dwelling house alongside the highway near Jessup. A striking photograph of the house in "What's Happened to Route I?" (*Star* /Mag/, 7 Feb. 1965) bears the caption: "A Route I landmark, this dog-shaped house is now a private dwelling, near Jessup. It told motorists they were nearing Baltimore."

ORAVILLE. At or near Turner, St. Mary's County. *Oraville has lost its identity and merged into Turner. Lilly Harding (Oakville, 3 Dec. 1971) tells me that *Ora* was the daughter of "Mr. Hopkins," one-time milliner; she had died two years ago at the age of 80. Robert E. Wigginton (Leonardtown 1969) explains that TURNER (the abiding name) is from Mr. Jesse Turner, who kept a store at Oraville for many years.

ORDINARY POINT. It projects into the Sassafras River near Earlesville, Cecil County. Blanchard remarks: "There used to be a hotel there in colonial days, hence the name 'Ordinary.'" Usilton cites a reference (1679) to an ordinary house or inn that was used as a courthouse. Cochrane, speaking of licences (1774) for keeping ordinaries and houses of entertainment, indicates that such places were permitted at Tuckahoe Bridge (Hillsboro), Murray's (Linchester), Nine Bridges (Bridgetown), Potter's

Mill (Williston), Chapel Branch (Piney Grove), and Cross-Roads, near Kingston (Smithson). *Ordinary* . . . is a notable name, in that it commemorates an archaic word and usage long gone.

OREGON. This name occurs (1) in *Oregon Branch*, near Cockeysville, Baltimore County, (2) in *Oregon* (village), near Oregon Branch, Baltimore County, and (3) in Oregon (and Oregon School), near Taneytown, Carroll County. The earlier name of Oregon Branch was *Shawan Cabin Branch*.

Compare with the above names "the land called Olacin," mentioned in a 1724 Land Office reference. Marye locates "Olacin (Oliccin) Land" between Glades and Linganore Creeks. It should not be overlooked that the *l* of *Olacin* could give *r* (hence Oregon) in a neighboring Algonquian dialect.

Excepting "Olacin Land" (1724) all these names are modern. Oregon Branch appears to date from about 1885. The dates on the Oregon schoolhouse are 1867–1900. Oregon had become a state in 1859. My best thought, then, is that Maryland's Oregon—for reasons not clear—is from the state name *Oregon*. Cf. OKLAHOMA and TEXAS. (See: Kenny, *Origin & Meaning of the Indian Place Names of Maryland*; Marye, letter, June 5, 1949). See SHAWAN.

ORIOLE. A village near Monie, Somerset County. Writing in 1961, Ralph Reppert relates that "eighty years ago" a leading citizen, William Thomas Smith, petitioned the Post Office Department to name this place *St. Peters*. However, there was already a St. Peters and, because large flocks of orioles nested in the village trees, *Oriole* was chosen. Mrs. Ruth Muir, postmistress here in June 1966, when I met her, tells me that it was in about 1886 when Mr. Smith chose the name. The post office was in his store, and his son, Sidney Smith, was the first postmaster. Pronunciation: this village has the standard dictionary pronunciation; but in Baltimore the sound would perhaps be "ORYUL." (See: "Oriole in Maryland," *Sun*, 9 April, 1961).

Note: Marion Hall, *History of Oriole and its Satellites* (1964?), mentions *St. Peter's Creek* and St. Peter's Methodist Church.

ORLEANS. I take this village to be the same place as LITTLE ORLEANS, near the Potomac River, about six miles from Bellegrove, Allegany County. In 1838 it was the post office *Orleans*.

Mrs. J. E. McCusker, postmistress at Little Orleans, 1975, citing her ancestors, states that it was named by the Indians and called "Little Beautiful Valley." And a Frenchman, when the C. & O. Canal was being dug (1832), changed ". . . beautiful valley" to *Orleans*. Compare Orleans Cross Roads, directly across the Potomac River, in W.Va. (See: "A Welcome Oasis Along the Parched C. & O. Canal," *Star*, July 3, 1980). See LITTLE ORLEANS.

Note: This is a doubtful story, to say the least. The French had little to do with the building of the C. & O. Canal.

"OUT BACK." Dorchester County. John C. Schmidt describes the vicinity as "... an offshoot of ... Madison which lies on State Route 16 as it winds ... westward from Cambridge ..." Schmidt interviewed Charles Bromwell (91), of Madison, who explained that "out back" was simply a convenient way of referring to the community. The entire area was once known as *TOBACCO STICK. The landscape consists of farms and woodland. (See: "Out Back—Where and Why," *Sun* [Mag.], 21 May 1961). See MADISON; see *TOBACCO STICK.

OVERLEA. Suburban village. It lies on the eastern boundary of Baltimore City, near Fullerton. Audrey Bishop speaks of "Belair Road north and south of the hilltop at Overlea Avenue." The caption of a photograph in her article reads: "Once called Lange's Farm, the name was later changed to Overlea, the 'over the meadow' connotation apparently alluding to the elevation of the land along the 6800 and 6900 blocks of Belair Road." Bishop mentions that the Lassahn family had a mortuary business here as early as 1878. (See: "Overlea," *Extra*, 7 Nov. 1971).

OWENSVILLE. Anne Arundel County. The 1941 Gazetteer advises: "... see West River (village)." Mrs. Samuel Chew writes: "A new house is being built in Owensville. The old house, opposite the rectory, is being torn down. The original house was the home of the late Henry Owens, who was one of the founders of the village. He owned a large farm and the Wheelwright shop. ..." (See: "Olivers Visit Owensville," *Capital*, 6 June 1969).

OWINGS MILLS. Suburban village, near Garrison, Baltimore County. It was a post office in 1833. Marye mentions a Nov. 1733 court record appointing Samuel Owings overseer of "the roads from Henry Butlers up by the Garrison to the North Run and from said Butlers ... to Gwynn's Falls ..." MHGP ascribes the name to Samuel Owings, prominent in early Green Spring Valley history. On Gwynn's Falls he built the three grist mills known as "Upper," "Lower," and "Middle." According to a 1969 *Street Map of Reistertown, Glyndon, Owings Mills, Garrison,* Samuel Owings also built "Ulm," named from the initial letters of his three mills. (See: Marye [3], p. 214, n. 9; *MHGP*, 1964, p. 13).

OXFORD. A village on the Tred Avon River, Talbot County. Shannahan states that the site of Oxford was settled as early as 1635. It bore the two early names, *Thread Haven* and *Third Haven*. The first name (*Thread Haven) was a corruption of Tred Avon, and the second name was a corruption of the first.

In 1668 thirty acres were set aside here for a town; and in 1669 Charles Calvert proclaimed it a port of entry. Oxford was officially laid out in 1683. The name has persisted, except for a brief period (ca. 1695) when it was called *Williamstadt to honor William of Orange. In 1702, with the accession of Queen Anne, it became *Oxford* again. The name, of course, commemorates England's great university and university town (Oxford, Oxfordshire). (See: Guide, p. 398; Shannahan, p. 25; Ingraham, p. 28). See CAMBRIDGE; see TRED AVON.

Note: I consider it nonsense to suppose that *Thread Haven is from hemp rope and ship's cordage. All of these early names are folk etymologies of *Tred Avon.*

OXON, OXON CREEK, OXON HILL. Oxon (el. 260) is southwest of Silver Hill, Prince George's County; Oxon Hill (el. 260) is southwest of Oxon, Oxon Creek is nearby. The source of all these names appears to have been the estate of "Oxon Hill Manor," built in the seventeenth century by Colonel John Addison, a privy counsellor of Lord Baltimore and the "first in America" of a family that, for several generations, has been prominent in Southern Maryland life. W. B. Marye refers to a general belief that Colonel Addison was a member of the family of Joseph Addison, of *Spectator* fame, and that there was "some close connection with Oxford." Perhaps Maryland's *Oxons* are from *Oxon*iensis "of Oxford." In any case Oxford, England, was the origin. (See: Wilstach, pp. 109–10; Guide, pp. 486–87; Marye, letter, Aug. 1957).

Parran (p. 55) has Col. John Addison coming to Maryland in 1677; he built Oxon Hill Manor in 1685. Oxon Creek and its branch Oxon Run (earlier *St. John's Creek) take their names from Oxon and Oxon Hill. (See: Marye, *MHM*, 33: 2, June 1938).

OXON CREEK, RUN.   See *ISIDORAS CREEK.

P

PADDY PIDDLE COVE. It is given for Cecil County in Manuals 1947, 1962, and 1969. In my Introductory Essay I treat this name jocularly. But, as Ekwall points out, the *Piddle* or Puddle (Dorsetshire) is an English river name of Germanic origin. Paddy may be a reduplication of *Piddle.* Cf. Piddle Brook (Worcestershire river name). Streams so named are small or *piddling.*

PADONIA. A village and erstwhile railroad station near Texas, Baltimore County. The name is probably a variant of the family name *Padden (Paden, Patton, Peyton)* with the addition of -*ia.* There are many parallels, such as *Irvona,* Pa., from E. A. Irvin, *Gastonia,* N.C., from William Gaston, etc. In the Potomac River, Frederick County, there is a Paton Island. Cf. Paden City, W.Va., from "Friend Payton," and Paden's Valley, W.Va., from Obadiah Paden.

PAINT BRANCH. A tributary of Indian Creek, near College Park, Prince George's County. Its banks have mineral pigments suitable for paint. Compare *Wallamünk,* "Place of paint," a tract in New Castle County, Delaware, where Indians "procured supplies of colored earth, which they employed in painting." (See: Brinton, *Lenape,* p. 60).

PALMER. The family name Palmer is found in two villages (Carroll County and St. Mary's County), in *PALMER'S ISLAND (nr. Havre de Grace), in *PALMER'S TAVERN (a Prince George's post office in 1829) and in *Palmer Park*, whence Palmer Highway, a Washington D.C. suburb. *PALMER'S ISLAND bears the name of Edward Palmer (ca. 1625); John Palmer was the postmaster of *PALMER'S TAVERN; Palmer Park and Palmer Highway appear to commemorate George N. Palmer.

Note: To account for the villages of PALMER, one notes that in 1963 (see phone book) there were twelve *Palmers* in Carroll County and eight in St. Mary's. At that time Windsor Palmer was living in PALMER, St. Mary's. With *PALMER'S TAVERN compare today's PALMER CORNERS, Prince George's.

PAMUNKEY. See POMONKEY.

*PANGAYO. The alias of *ZEKIAH SWAMP, Charles County. It appears on Herrman's 1670 map as *Zachkia Swamp als Pangayo*. See ZEKIAH.

PANGBORN. A village near Security, Washington County. The name arose in about 1935 and comes from Thomas *Pangborn*, head of the Pangborn Corporation, makers of sandblast-cleaning and dust-control equipment. Mr. Pangborn donated Pangborn Park (Hagerstown), "a public recreational area."

PAPER MILLS. This Baltimore County place was a post office in 1851. On Martenet's map of 1866 it is "Paper Mills P.O.," situated near Dug Hill. Martenet has five notations of "Pap" in this area; and I conclude that this was a district of paper mills. Evidently, in early times, local papermaking was a thriving business. In Cecil County for instance, according to Johnston, the making of paper was the most important industry besides iron. See *HOFFMANVILLE.

PARADISE. There are places by this name in Allegany, Baltimore, and Harford Counties. Sometimes the name is compounded, as in *Paradise Beach*, Anne Arundel, and *Paradise Church* (Washington). Paradise, Allegany, which stretches towards Dans Mountain (el. 2796), was perhaps named for its height; Paradise Beach was perhaps named for its idyllic qualities; Paradise, Harford, takes its name from the 1721 tract, "Paradise." Near Paradise, Washington County, one finds Paradise School and Near Eden School. Bell, remarking that Paradise School was probably built in 1830, explains that Dr. Frederick Dorsey cried out, "Call it Paradise!" when he passed "Paradise School and Meeting House" at the time it was being built.

PARK HALL. A village near St. Mary's City, St. Mary's County. It was the post office of *Park Hall* in 1851. Forman finds that by 1640 Snow Hill Manor extended northward "as far as Porke Hall, now Park Hall," and that at the village of Park Hall lay "Gerrards Freehold" or "Porke Hall Freehold" surveyed in 1640 for Thomas Gerrard. I believe that the *porke* and *park* of these names are one and the same word (*park*) and that the variation in spelling is the result of the Maryland speech characteristic whereby *a* and *o* are strangely influenced by a following *r*. Thus *pork* becomes *park, barn* becomes *born*, etc. See: Introduction, #V, Matters Linguistic.

PARKHEAD, PARKHEAD Station. A village on the W. Md. R.R. near Millstone, Washington County. It was a post office in 1831. According to the Postal History Catalog "Park Head" was changed to "Indian Spring" in 1842, and back again to "Park Head" in 1843. In 1854 "Park Head" became "Millstone Point." The Indian Spring post office of 1842–43 was more than five miles from the Indian Spring office established in 1854. The village in early days was probably at the beginning or "head" of a park.

PARK MILLS. A village near Hopeland, Frederick County. Grove indicates that Park Mills lies at the foot of Sugar Loaf Mountain. Its original name was *NEW BREMEN, from a tract named by the historic John Frederick Amelung (ca. 1784) from Bremen, Germany, his native city. The present name may be descriptive; or, indeed, may have come from the surname, *Park*. TDr Frederick 1971 lists James *Park* and Margaret *Park*. See *NEW BREMEN.

PARKERS. A village on the Patuxent River, near Broome Island village, Calvert County. No doubt all mentions of *Parker* in Southern Maryland are traceable to William Parker, whom Stein describes as one of the Puritans who, in 1649, founded Anne Arundel County. In 1651 he was granted two tracts, one of them being Parker's Cliffs on Middle Cliffs at Parker's Creek. Later he returned to England, where he died in 1674. Stein remarks that descendants of William Parker's nephew, George (d. 1681) still live in Calvert County. He attributes the name *Parker Wharf* to Dr. John Clare Parker, who represented Calvert County in the state legislature, where he was President of the Senate. (See: Stein, p. 32, pp. 299–300).

PARKVILLE. Near Overlea, Baltimore County. This was Parkville, Parkville Heights in 1969. Stan O'Brien relates that in 1874 Simon J. Martenet promoted residential sites here and spoke of the area as "one of the healthiest and pleasantest locations near Baltimore." Stein adds: "Martenet called the property Parkville, presumably after a 360-foot-long park he envisioned along Towson Avenue between Chestnut and Oak Avenues." I gather from O'Brien that the area bore the postal designation, *LAVENDER HILL. (See: *Extra*, June 11, 1972).

Note: To illustrate how names proliferate, let me point out that in 1946 the Parkville Lions Club developed forty-two acres called *Double Rock Park*. It was so named owing to "... twin boulders which rise steeply out of a swift-moving stream that bisects the property."

PAROLE. This erstwhile suburban village was annexed to Annapolis in 1951. It is *Roll Camp Stan* on Hopkins 1878; in 1941 it was listed as *Parole, Camp Parole*. During the Civil War the place had become a camp for Union soldiers of "uncertain loyalty." Such soldiers were drafted men who had been paroled by the Confederates and picked up by the Unionists. To follow Norris, the Civil War soldiers brought here were first received behind St. John's College and later taken to Camp Parole. Manakee describes the place as "a large installation for training and for prisoners of war exchange." (See: Guide, p. 469; W. B. Norris, *Annapolis, Its Colonial and Naval Story*, N.Y., 1925, pp. 274–75; Ralph Reppert, *Sun* [Mag.], March 26, 1961).

Note: In a letter to *Capital*, 21 Sept. 1970, Marshall Andrews remarks that Camp Parole, intended for 50,000 men, was established by the War Department on June 6, 1862. Paroled prisoners from New England and the "middle states" were brought here, and official correspondence soon began referring to the place as "Camp Parole."

*PARRAHOCKON NECK. Somerset County. *Archives XV*, 1671–81, "... one other neck of land called Parrahockon ..."; XLII, 1742, "... the main Road called Parahawkin Road." The last two syllables of this name appear to be "earth, ground" (cf. Delaware *haki*, etc). The opening syllables may represent an *r*-dialect form of Primitive Algonquian **pelawa* "turkey" (cf. Del. *bloeu*, Shawnee *palawa*). The meaning would be "Turkey Land."

PARRAN. A village near the head of Plum Point Creek, Calvert County. The founder of the Parran family was Alexander Parran (d. 1729), a Huguenot who settled near the head of St. Leonard's Creek, Calvert County. In 1706 he was granted the landed estate, "Parrans Park." Thomas Parran, former state senator, was a lumberman known as the "Alfalfa King" of Maryland. He lived at Prince Frederick, five miles south of Parran. (See: Stein, pp. 300–302; Lantz, p. 36).

PARRSVILLE. Near Mt. Airy, Carroll County. It was a post office in 1830. The Postal History Catalog notes that "Ridgeville" was changed to "Parrsville" in 1830 and again to "Ridgeville" in 1837. Compare Parr's Ridge, Carroll County, described by Fisher, in 1852, as a "low ridge" of the Alleghanies dividing Frederick and Carroll Counties. The name is from the somewhat rare family name, *Parr*.

PARSONBURG. Village near Pittsville, Wicomico County. *Parsonburg*, Parsons District, Martenet 1866. Lewis in 1878 lists the following residents of Parsonburg: D. F. Parsons (carpenter); D. J. and John H. Parsons (millers); and D. J., E. H., and J. J. Parsons (farmers).

PASADENA. Village near Earleigh Heights (el. 70), Anne Arundel County. In 1874 fruit growers brought the Algonquian word, *Pasadena*, from Indiana to California. BAE Smithsonian lists it as Ojibwa, "a gap

188   THE PLACENAMES OF MARYLAND

between mountains." Baraga has *Passadina* "... There is a low place between two mountains; a valley." The imported Maryland Pasadena (el. 90
ft.) somewhat befits this description by being on or near the Gibson Island
highway called "Mountain Road." (See: *New Int. Enc.*, 1907, 18, p. 134).

Note: The "mountain" in Mountain Road is not easily explained. Evidently,
even a moderate elevation could, in earlier times, be called a mountain. On nearby
Gibson Island, for instance, there is *Mountain Point* (at sea level). Two nearby
knobs, each about 80 feet high, seem to explain the name.

PASQUAHANZA POND. Charles County. Not given in Gazetteers
1904, 1941, but appearing (*Pasquahanza Pond*) in Manuals 1947, 1962, and
1969. On a map I have seen, this pond appears as a small significantly in-
dented body of water. The indentation suggests that *Pasqua-* reflects Algonquian *pāskwi-* fork," a stem corroborated by Cree *pāskwi-*, Micmac
pēskū-, and Fox *pa'ck*. Taking *-hanza* as a mistake for *-hanna*, I assume
that the rest of the name means "stream" (fr. PA *-aha-, -ahahw* "waves,
flood, alternate motion"). One would translate "Divided or forked
stream."

PASSAPAE LANDING. Village near Denton, Choptank River, Caroline County. The present book gives me an opportunity to correct an error
in my *Origin and Meaning of the Indian Place Names of Maryland*
(1961). There I analyzed *Passapae* as though it were Anglo-Algonquian.
However, despite the close resemblance of *Passapae* to Capt. John
Smith's **Paspahegh* (James and Chickahominy tribe and villages), I now
feel that I was mistaken. The name is probably from a family name. Heads
1790 lists Moses Passipa for Dorchester County; *MHM* mentions Wm. M.
Passapae. TDr 1969 Baltimore has seven entries for *Passapae*. (See:
MHM, XX: 1, March 1925).

PASSERDYKE CREEK. A tributary of Wicomico Creek, Wicomico
and Somerset Counties. Torrence, 1867, spells it *Passedyke Creek*. It may
be that this name is simply *pass* and *dyke*. But such a compound seems
unlikely, and I prefer to relate *Passerdyke* to Capt. Smith's (Powhatan)
*Pasaughtacock, in both of which names the two opening syllables appear
to be Algonquian "split, gouge, gap" (Ojibwa *pasihkw* "grove"). The -
augh- of the Powhatan name may in *Passerdyke* be represented by *-er-*
(*Pasaugh* = Passer); *t* may have become *d*. By contraction one gets *Pasar-
dock*, which the folk could have changed to *Passerdyke*. As for meanings,
-tacock and *-dyke* may be Algonquian "stream" (Ojibwa *tigow*, Abnaki
tegw, etc.) and the locative *-ock*. One would translate, "Stream that scoops
banks."

PATAPSCO. A river flowing into Chesapeake Bay at Baltimore; vil-
lages in Carroll and Anne Arundel Counties; the former name of Elkridge
Landing; and "Patapsco Falls," earlier the **Western or Delaware Falls* of
Patapsco River.

The *Bolus flu* on Virginia 1608 was probably the Patapsco River, Captain Smith having given it this name because of the clumps of clay, resembling medicinal Armenian Bole, he found on its banks. Tyler thinks Smith meant the Gunpowder River; and I have somewhere seen *Bolus* for Bush River (*Bolus* = Bush?). But Bozman declares: "This (the Bolus) has been generally deemed to have been the *Patapsco*, which opinion seems to be warranted by Smith's map."

John Heckewelder derives Algonquian *Patapsco* from Delaware *petapsqui*, which he defines as "back-water, tide-water." It is probably from Heckewelder's "Back-water" that the prevailing mistake arose of translating *Patapsco* as "black-water."

Heckewelder's conjecture is ill-founded, and lacks geographical corroboration. However, thanks to C. W. Bump, aided by W. W. Tooker, an entirely acceptable analysis of *Patapsco* has been reached. Tooker had proposed that *patapsco* contains *pota-* "to jut out, bulge, *-psk* "ledge of rock," and *-ut* "at." The consequent meaning, "At the rocky point or corner," was defended by Bump, who realized from local knowledge that the "rocky point" could well be the White Rocks, ". . . that group of limestone rocks jutting out of the river opposite where Rock Creek joins the Patapsco." (See: Bozman, I, 116; Heckewelder, *Names Which*, p. 51; Bump, "Indian Place-Names in Maryland," *MHM*, II (1907).

Note: For a technical criticism of Tooker's analysis, see my *Origin and Meaning of the Indian Place Names of Maryland*, p. 106.

PATUXENT. A river flowing into Chesapeake Bay, near Solomons, St. Mary's County; and the following places named *Patuxent* because of being on or near that river—Patuxent, near Ft. Meade, Anne Arundel County, Patuxent (Patuxent City), near Hughesville, Charles County, Patuxent Mills, Anne Arundel County, and Patuxent Station (Woodwardville), Anne Arundel County. Compare *Patuxen M.* [manor], on Homann's map of 1759, and *Patuxent Forge, an 1831 post office.

Smith, 1608, maps *Pawtuxunt, Pawtuxunt flu.* In *Archives*, V, for 1667–1687/8, it appears as *Pettuxent, Patuscent, Puttuxan*. The BAE card index, Smithsonian Institution, identifies the Toag (Doag) or Taux Indians with the Patuxent Indians.

In all forms of the Algonquian name, *Patuxent*, one finds *pawi-* "to shake" (Ojibwa *bawitig*) "rapide," Cree *pawistik* "rapide," etc.). Gerard, Trumbull, and Nils M. Holmer all agree that the meaning is "At the falls or rapids." A similar name is Pawtucket, Rhode Island. (See: Nils M. Holmer, *Indian Place Names of North America* . . . (1948), p. 25).

Note: Trumbull thinks that the *Patux-* of *Patuxet* is from the diminutive *Pautuckese* PLUS *-it*, a locative suffix. In this event a more complete translation is "At the *little* falls or rapids." The fact that the Maryland form ends with an *n* (*-ent*) is explained by supposing that there was a mishearing of *-enk* (where *-en* is the inanimate copula "is").

PATUXENT CITY. See PATUXENT.

*PAWATINIKA, Camp. A former Y.W.C.A. camp near Annapolis, Anne Arundel County. It appears that the camp was sold in 1949 and that the name is no longer used.

It is important to correct the error that *Pawatinika* means "Camp of our dreams." The truth is that this Algonquian word is a compound of "at the falls" (cf. Ojibwa *pawi'ting*) and *-ika* (Fox *kä, hkä, gä*) "activity; there are many." The real meaning would be "There are many falls or rapids."

PAW PAW COVE. On the west side of Choptank (Tilghman's) Island, Talbot County. This name is probably from the Caribbean word, which in Maryland and Virginia designates a tree or shrub. Matthews describes the paw paw as "Any one of various North American trees or shrubs of the genus *Asmina*, esp. A. tril*o*ba. Compare Paw Paw, West Virginia. (See: *Dictionary of Americanisms*, II, p. 1195).

PEABODY HEIGHTS. Baltimore City. I include this name in memory of W. B. Marye who considered it important. Howard describes the area as an ". . . elevated plateau" of fity acres ". . . laid off into broad streets and avenues . . ." It was three fourths of a mile north of the Washington Monument, with Charles Street and Maryland Avenue on its west and "North Street" on its east. The name (coming directly from the Peabody Heights Company) commemorates George Peabody (1795–1869), the philanthropic banker who founded the Peabody Conservatory of Music. (See: Howard, *Monumental City*, 1873, p. 420).

PEALIQUOR LANDING. Village. On the Choptank River, near Denton, Caroline County. This name came into being "some years ago" when the Phillips Packing Company rented a tract of dairy land here and installed several stationery pea vinery machines to separate pea hulls from harvested pea vines, and then to separate the peas from the hulls. The discarded vines and hulls, by-products of this activity, were stacked, compressed, and sold as forage to nearby dairymen. The resulting "pea juice" was so abundant that a drainage ditch had to be built. Since *juice* and *liquor* are in some cases synonymous (cf. meat liquor, pot "likker," "pickle liquor" [an iron-rich waste]) I am content to believe that "*pealiquor*" in this name simply means "pea juice."

However, there are those who think that the *liquor* of "pealiquor" was intended to mean an intoxicating alcoholic liquid. To explain this, a story is told about a local dairy farmer's ailing herd of cows. Surprisingly, the cows one evening failed to return for milking. And the alarmed farmer eventually found them lying sick on the ground near the ditch. A veterinarian, observing that each of the prostrated animals had a greenish slobber on its lips, soon came to a startling conclusion. Turning to the bewildered farmer he announced: "Your cows are drunk! They got through the fence and have been drinking the pea juice in the ditch which apparently has fermented a bit in the time it has been there." According to my informants "The story relates that the cows ... [recovered] ... and ever since that time the names *Pealiquor Landing* and *Pealiquor Landing Road* have designated that area."

Note: For the foregoing data and story I gratefully acknowledge the help and kindness (Feb. 9, 1981) of Messrs. Tony Evans (Md. Dept. of Agriculture, Annapolis) and Max Chambers, Preston, Maryland.

PEARRE. A village, near Exline, Washington County. TW mentions several possible sources—Judge George A. Pearre (fl. Cumberland, 1839), for instance, or Col. George A. Pearre, Jr. (b. Cumberland, 1860), former member of Congress. It is likely that one of these prominent Pearres had an interest in the W. Md. R.R. and that a station (*Pearre*) was named for him. Local pronunciation: Puh-REE. (See: TW, I, p. 300, p. 320).

PECKTONVILLE. Near Parkhead, Licking Creek, Washington County. The Rev. Jeremiah Mason established this place, and its first name was *Licking Creek Mills* (fl. 1833). After the flood of 1889, Martin L. Peck, the Reverend Mason's grandson-by-marriage, moved the mill to higher ground and changed the name to *Rosedale Mills*. In 1893, in honor of Martin L. Peck, the official post office name became PECKTONVILLE. (See: Mary Mish, "Park Head Church ...," *MHM*, 51: 1, March 1956).

PEKIN. Village near Lonaconing, Allegany County. Martenet, 1866, maps *Pekin Mine*. The coal mine here was probably named by the Atlantic and George's Creek Coal Co. PEKIN, the village, grew up near the mine. Lately, to avoid postal confusion, the name has been spelled backwards. See NIKEP.

PEN MAR, PEN MAR PARK. A village and resort area (el. 1400) on the Pennsylvania-Maryland state boundary, Washington County. In 1980 architectural plans were afoot to revive enthusiasm for what Carleton Jones calls "Maryland's oldest surviving formal resort spot." It had been launched in 1877 by John Mifflin Hood, a Western Md. Railroad tycoon; its popularity ebbed in the 1930's. The combination of *Pen* and *Mar* suggests an unusually picturesque view of the two states. (See: "Pen Mar Lives Again," *Sun* [Mag.], June 22, 1980).

*PEPOMETAN (POPEMETAN). A Cecil County tract ("Steelman's Delight," patented in 1711) and a creek thereon. An 1822 survey identifies the creek as the present PRINCIPIO). The opening syllables of *PEPOMETAN require guesswork. But it may be said with some certainty that the end of the name (-*etan*) represents Primitive Algonquian *-*ehtan* "flow, current." Cf. CHOPTANK (*kehtci-āpi-ehtan-ki) and Powhatan (*pāwi-*ehtan*-wi). Cf. POPOMENTANG, Columbia Co., Pennsylvania.

Note: My thanks to Dr. Richard H. Hulan, of Arlington, Virginia. His sources are original Cecil County patents and the Cecil County Rent Roll in the Calvert Papers at the Maryland Historical Society. Professor C. A. Weslager, of Hockessin, Delaware, first called my attention to this name.

PERRY HALL. Village near Whitemarsh, Baltimore County. Land records show that in 1774 Henry Dorsey Gough bought a 1000-acre estate, "The Adventure," and changed its name to "Perry Hall." Apparently he made this change because "Perry Hall" was the name of the Staffordshire (England) family seat of Sir Henry Gough (d. 1724). Presumably Henry Dorsey Gough was a relative of the Goughs of Anne Arundel County. The American "Perry Hall" was slightly north of the present village. (See: Edith Bevan, *MHM*, XLV, I, March 1950).

PERRYMAN. A village near Aberdeen, Harford County. This was the post office of *Perrymanville in 1838. In 1878 the spelling was still *Perrymansville*. And living here at that time was Eugene Perryman, a farmer. (See: Lewis, 1878).

PERRYVILLE. A Cecil County village opposite Havre de Grace and adjoining Perry Point. It was the post office of *Perryville* in 1837. However, so Miller states, the first post office here was *Chesapeake* and the town was also called *Lower Ferry*. Another earlier name was *Susquehanna*.

To rely on Miller, "Perry Point" was surveyed as early as 1658. But the identity of the first *Perry* seems to be unknown. A much later Perry, Captain Richard Perry, of London, bought the tract in 1710; and in 1728 it passed into the hands of John Perry, George Perry, and others (See: Miller, Cecil, p. 92, pp. 95–96; Johnston, p. 132).

PERSIMMON. Maryland has Persimmon Creek (St. Mary's County), Persimmon Island (now inundated, near Conowingo), five Persimmon Points, and Persimmon Tree Road (Montgomery County). The name is from the *persimmon* tree, which Captain Smith spells *putchamin*, and which appears in *Archives* LI, for 1679, as *Pisamon* (Creek). It contains Algonquian *-min(i)* "berry," and is evidently Virginia Algonquian.

PETERSVILLE. Near Brunswick, Frederick County. It was a post office in 1813. Grove states that in 1826 /?/ St. Mary's Catholic Church, Petersville, was built on the "Merryland Tract." This tract and "Needwood Forest" were "social centers" that had been settled at an early time by Catholics. For the Peters family Passano cites Williams (2; II, 762–763).

PHILOPOLIS. A village near Phoenix, Baltimore County. It was a post office in 1847. Presumably "City of Love." Fisher 1852 explains: "The inhabitants, who are mostly 'Friends,' are entirely occupied in agricultural pursuits." The Guide mentions "Lamb's School at Philopolis among whose pupils were John Wilkes Booth and his brother Edwin.

PHLUGERS MILLS. GMd 1941: "... in Frederick County." Cf. Phluger's Mill, owned by John Phluger. Grove locates it on "Shoaf or Ballenger Creek" (Frederick County) and states that it delivered flour to Limekiln, "the shipping point."

PHOENIX. Maryland has Phoenix, near Westernport, Allegany County, and Phoenix, near Cockeysville, Baltimore County. The legendary bird, the *phoenix*, a symbol of rebirth and vitality, is an appropriate name for these places. The Allegany Phoenix, a coal mining village, is recorded by Fisher in 1852 as **Phoenix Mines*. There was also *Phoenix Hill*. The name is from the *Phoenix* Mining and Manufacturing Co. The Baltimore County Phoenix, mapped by Martenet in 1866, appears to have taken its name from the *Phoenix* [cotton] Manufacturing Co. Eliza Fisher relates that the cotton mill here, built in the 1820's, went out of business in about 1930 because of the backing up of water at the Loch Raven Dam. (See: *Documents Relating to the Phoenix Mining and Manufacturing Co. Cumberland*. (N.Y. 1852); "I remember Life in an Old Maryland Mill Town," *Sun* [Mag.], Feb. 11, 1962).

PICCOWAXEN CREEK. A Charles County tributary of the Potomac River. Its early forms are extremely variable. *Archives* for 1649–50 has *Pukewaxen*, and for 1663 *pickyawaxent*. One also finds the colloquial *Piciowaxon*. The form in the 1947 Manual is *Piccowaxton*.

Delaware authorities have analyzed *Piccowaxen* as a combination of *pixu* "ragged" and "shoe, sock." The meaning would be "Torn shoes." However, the phonetics of this explanation are faulty.

It would be more correct to derive *Piccowaxen* from cognates of Ojibwa *piqwi-* "break" and Ojibwa -*ahkisin* "shoe." The consequent meaning, "Rugged, pierced or broken shoe," bears witness to the crags and brambles of the wilderness. Cf. such colonial names as *Tearcoat* Creek (W.Va.) and *Tear Wallet Creek* (Va.).

*PIGTOWN. An erstwhile Baltimore neighborhood west of Washington Boulevard. Baltimore *Sun* features, in 1970 and in 1978, tell of the Baltimore bi-weekly *Pigtown Post*, of "Sid's Little Tavern," of "shuffle-bowl," and of bar teams that had their own World Series. According to Dilts, "Pigtown derives its name from the days when ... livestock was driven through the streets to the stockyards ..." Cf.: PIG QUARTER CREEK (1715: Kent Island); also *PIG POINT, the early name of Bristol. (See: James Dilts, *Sun*, 29 March 1970; Jack Dawson, *Sun*, 15 Oct. 1978). See BRISTOL.

PIKESVILLE. Northwestern suburb of Baltimore City. It became a post office in 1817 although, to cite the Guide, it was settled before the American Revolution. The name—given by his friend, Dr. James Smith, a landowner here—honors Brigadier General Zebulon M. Pike (1779–1813), who was killed in the War of 1812 while leading an assault on Fort York, at Toronto. (See: Davidson, p. 93).

PIMLICO. Baltimore City suburb and racecourse. On Hopkins's Atlas of Baltimore, 1877, there are the Baltimore, Pimlico, and Pikesville Railway, "Pimlico Farm," Pimlico Hotel, Pimlico Company, Pimlico Fair Ground, and Pimlico Road. In 1699 an 800-acre tract, "Pimlico," on the site of the present racetrack, was surveyed for Thomas Hedge and John Oldton (Oulton). Oldton (d. 1709), once a captain of the Rangers, had been in England in about 1698. And it is supposed that on his return he named his land "Pimlico" for the district of Pimlico, London, which in turn, so Marye remarks, "... is said to have originated with a certain Pimlico, an Italian who resided several centuries ago." Thackeray mentions Pimlico in *Vanity Fair*. (See: W. B. Marye, *MHM*, 16:3, Sept. 1921, p. 217).

PINEY POINT. A village on the Potomac River, near Drayden, St. Mary's County. It was a post office in 1855. Knight has: "A little over 100 years ago, Piney Point [was] only referred to as 'The Point.' " To account for the name Lantz explains: "Piney Point, densely green with pine, holly and tulip poplar trees ...". (See: Lantz, p. 232).

PINTO. Village near Cresaptown, Potomac River, Allegany County. *Potomac Station* is the name of the local railway depot (B. & O. R.R.). And R-McN 1949 indicates that *Pinto* is the post office name of *Potomac*. Postmistress Viola Johnson (August 1973) tells me that PINTO was once on a short route between U.S. 40 and U.S. 50 and had a stagecoach stop. "... and it is assumed that PINTO received its name from the pinto ponies stabled here." However, when I visited Pinto on an earlier occasion, I was told about an obscure episode involving this place with the pinto horses of the American Southwest.

PIPE CREEK, PIPE CREEK STATION. Village near New Windsor, Carroll County. Cf. Double Pipe Creek, a post office in 1825. In my *Origin and Meaning* (p. 10), citing Arthur Tracey, of Hampstead, I state: "... Pipe Creek (whence Little Pipe Creek, Double Pipe Creek, and Double Pipe Creek ... village) is thought to owe its name to the peace pipes of local red clay used by Indian tribes at occasional meetings near Union Bridge." However, a non-Indian origin is perhaps to be inferred from the mention by Frederick Klein of a brick kiln (ca. 1797) "... constructed near the creek, known in previous years as Pipeclay Creek." See DETOUR. (See: Klein, *MHM*, 52: 4, Dec. 1957, p. 292).

Note: Compare "Pipe Tomahawk," Washington County, surveyed in 1798.

PISCATAWAY. Village on Piscataway Creek, near Fort Washington, Prince George's County. It was a post office in 1792. If *Piscataway* were an Anglo-Algonquian name found only in Maryland, I should be quite satisfied to derive it from Delaware *peechg* (plus general Algonquian *atawau*). The meaning would be "High passable bank around a bend in a river." However, the same name seems to occur in New Jersey (*Pescat'taway*), New Hampshire (*Piscataqua*), and Maine (*Piscataqua*); and I am inclined to believe that Ruttenber's more general "The division or branch of a stream" is preferable. See my analyses in *Origin and Meaning* ...

Note: In March 1969 (v. *Capital*, 13 March 1969) an Ohio Congressman proposed that *Piscataway* be renamed to honor an Ohio Congresswoman who had served for twenty-eight years. I think that Indian placenames are precious relics. Such a change as the one proposed would be miserably improper. The Piscataways were a kingly Algonquian people!

PITTSVILLE. Near Parsonburg, Wicomico County. The Guide (pp. 378-79) ascribes the name to Dr. H. R. Pitts, ". . . a president of the little Wicomico and Pocomoke Railroad completed in 1868 from Salisbury to Berlin as a continuation of the line from Claiborne." The District (Pittsburg) was also probably named for Dr. Pitts.

PIVOT. Village on the C. & D. Canal, near Chesapeake City, Cecil County. (*Pivot Bridge*, Cecil 1850 Martenet). The name is from a "pivot bridge."

Note: R-McN 1877 (Indexed . . . Md., D.C., Del.); "Pivot Bridge, see Chesapeake City."

PLAINDEALING CREEK. A branch of the Tred Avon River, near Bellevue, Talbot County. Carleton Jones, writing about an estate that takes its name from this stream, remarks that the locality is supposed to have been an early trading ground for Quakers and Indians. (See: Jones, "The Sounds of History," *Sun* [Mag.], Oct. 8, 1978).

Note: Hays and Hazleton, in *Chesapeake Kaleidoscope* (Cambridge, Md. 1975, p. 29) explain the name of this stream: "Plaindealing Creek got its name from the Indians who went to that location to trade with the Quakers. Because the Indians considered the Quakers honest and fair traders, they referred to them as plaindealers." It is rather obvious, however, that the unlettered Algonquians could not have said this in English.

PLANE NO. 4. Village near Bartholows, Frederick County. (Lewis 1878;—[on B. & O. R.R.] USGS 1909 Mount Airy). Michael R. Farrell explains that PLANE NO. 4 was the fourth in a system of four inclined planes designed to solve the B. & O. Railroad's early difficulty of hauling cars over Parrs Ridge, near Mt. Airy—which at first the tiny pioneer locomotives could not do. Regular locomotives pulled the cars to the foot of the ridge; horses then pulled the cars, one at a time, to the top of the ridge. By gravity, the cars rolled down the other side. In 1900 PLANE NO. 4 was bypassed, and the station and other railroad buildings were torn down. (See: "A Place in Rail History," *Sun*, 13 May 1963, p. 16).

*PLEASANT HILL. Brown and Klapthor locate this village on the main road between Port Tobacco and Piscataway. It was a post office in 1825. Compare Pleasant Hill, Baltimore County, near Reisterstown, and Pleasant Hill, Cecil County. The two latter places also seem to bear the name of Delight and Chrome Hill, respectively. See DELIGHT, PLEASANTVILLE, and SOLDIERS DELIGHT.

PLEASANT VALLEY. The name is from "Pleasant Valley" which, according to Williams, lies between South and Elk Ridge Mountains, extending from Weverton to Trego, and includes the land between Crampton's Gap and the ridge west of Keedysville. The spirit of this name is expressed in the opening lines of Arthur Blessing's poem, *Pleasant Valley:*

"Beloved valley, where the soul oppress'd
Turns for comfort and finds rest;
Adorned with nature's lavish hand,
Fairest of vales in Maryland."

Other *Pleasant Valley's* are in the counties of Allegany, Baltimore, Carroll, Harford, and (Pleasant Valley *Run*) Garrett. (See: Williams, II, 931–33; Balt. Weekly *Sun*, 25 July 1903).

PLEASANTVILLE.   Village near Scarff, Harford County. (*Pleasantville* 1849 PHC). About this place Fisher (1852) remarks: "The location and climate have given origin to the name of the village—both are pleasant and are said to communicate their charms to the inhabitants."

POCAHONTAS.   Sometimes encountered as the name of suburban streets in Baltimore City and the District of Columbia. See "Pocahontas-Matoaka," where Charles Edgar Gilliam defends the usual derivation from Powhatan *pokachantesu* "She is playful."

However, the following different derivation is possible; *pok-* "break"; *-at-* "by some means"; *-awān* "fog"; *-ta-* "for to"; *-aswa* "action by (sun's) heat." The meaning is a reference to the personal radiance of Pocahontas: "It (the sun) breaks through the fog with its rays and heat." (See: Gilliam, *Names*, 2: 3, 1954).

POCOMOKE CITY.   On the Pocomoke River, twelve miles southwest of Snow Hill, Worcester County. The present name is from the river the town is on. But it has had a succession of earlier names. Hilda Stevenson tells me (20 Aug. 1950) that her uncle, Eben Hearne (d. 1944 at 89), in a leaflet "Old Newtown and New Pocomoke City ..." (1943), tabulated the earlier names as follows: (1) *STEVENS' FERRY (est. 1670); (2) *MEETING HOUSE LANDING (1683); (3) *WAREHOUSE LANDING (1700); (4) *NEWTON (1780); and (5) *POCOMOKE (1878). The Guide mentions "Pitts Creek (Pocomoke City)."

POCOMOKE RIVER.   In Somerset, Wicomico, and Worcester Counties. It rises in Delaware and debouches in Pocomoke Sound. Smith spells this stream *Pawcocomocac*; in *Archives*, IV, 1637, it is "river of Pocomoque."

There is no evidence for "black (dark) water." Heckewelder proposes "broken ... by knolls and hills"; the BAE (Smithsonian) has "general Algonquian for 'at the clearing.' "

Heckewelder's "broken ... by knolls and hills" and the BAE's "At the clearing" are substantiated by the Algonquian stem *pōhkwi-* (Fox, Ojibwa) "to pierce." Its Primitive Algonquian form would be **pōxkwi*; and, relying on Smith's *Pawcocomocac*, one may hypothecate a form consisting of *pōxkwi* pierced, broken," *ahkami* "ground," and *-aki* "it is." The meaning would be "It, is pierced or broken ground."

POCOSIN.   This Algonquian word appears in **Porcosen Run*, an alternate name for Brady's Run, Baltimore County. And in the Rent Rolls of

Baltimore County one finds such phrases as (1673) "nigh a *pocoson*" and (1678) "by a *pocoson*." *Pocosin* is usually derived from *pakwesen* "It (the land) is in a slightly watered condition." The settlers used the word to mean "swamp" or "marsh." (See: "Some Baltimore City Place-names," *MHM*, 54: I; J. Louis Kuethe, "Pocosin," *MLN*, LII, March 1937; *Handbook*, II, 287).

PODICKERY POINT. An item in *Capital* (27 Jan. 1983) describes this Anne Arundel point as a community cut off from Route 50 by a section of Sandy Point State Park. Log Inn Road and Tydings Road are mentioned. Perhaps the *d* is a mistake for *h*. Cf. Captain John Smith's *pawcohiccora* (*Handbook*, I, 547) whence English *hickory*; also *Pohick (Talbot Co.).

*POHICK. This Algonquian word appears as follows in *Archives* LIV, for 1666: ". . . in the County of Talbott one Thousand Acres of maine good Land Called Pohic." Cf. Pohick Church, Va. Occurrences of this name pertain to Captain Smith's *pawcohiccora*, whence English *hickory*. (See: *Handbook*, I, p. 547).

POINT LOOKOUT. Point, village, and creek. St. Mary's County near Scotland. The point projects into Chesapeake Bay at the mouth of the Potomac River (GMd 1941). *Pt. Lookout* (Herrman 1670); *P? Lookout* (Van Keulen 1682); *P. Lookout* (Moll 1717). Kuethe (*Strange Origins*), commenting on Catholic names, remarks: "Smith's Sparkes Poynt was changed to St. Mitchaell's Point, but this name, in turn, was soon changed to Point Lookout." However, note ". . . Point Lookeout. . ." (*Archives*, II, 1666–1676). As to the origin, Knight (p. 58) explains: "In colonial times the settlers believed that by standing on this point one could see out to the Virginia Capes on clear days."

POINT OF ROCKS. Village on the Potomac River, southeast of Brunswick, Frederick County. There was a post office here in 1832. Hill speaks of the "natural barrier" at this place formed by Catoctin Mountain and the "steep granite walls of the river bank. . . ." He adds that the construction gangs of the C. & O. Canal and the B. & O. R.R. both reached the Point in the same month (1828?). A battle for the right of way began in 1830. In 1867 the railroad won and proceeded to tunnel the mountain. (See: Hill, MCC, p. 47).

POKATA CREEK. A tributary of Island Creek, Dorchester County. Dunlap and Weslager, citing Ruttenber, Trumbull, and Brinton, analyze *Pokety*, Delaware, as *pok* "open, clear," combined with a variant of *etek* "where it is." However, for technical reasons, it is more likely that -*etek* is a changed conjunct form of *-atek* "where it is put." And D. and W.'s interpretation thus becomes inapplicable.

A more satisfactory analysis is to regard the name as containing *pōhkwi* "to pierce." The -*wi* of *pōhkwi* could then, by contraction, give the -*o*- of *Pocoty*. The rest of the word would be -*te-ki*, where the *te* is a passive inanimate element. The result, in all, would be *poko-ty* "Where it is opened or cleared." (See: A. R. Dunlap and C. A. Weslager, *Indian Place-Names in Delaware*, Wilmington, 1950).

*POLAND. Bygone village near Westernport, Allegany County. The name POLAND is on a road sign near a W. Md. R.R. watertank. Mrs. Harry L. Biggs, of Westernport, describes the site (letter, 29 March 1970): "There is no town as such. The area, marked by a railroad switch and water tower and survey stone, ... [is] merely an extension of Westernport's business and industrial enterprises, with no post office or school." Mrs. Biggs has shown me genealogical data that indicate that the family name *Poland* was originally *Poling*, and that the first *Poling* who came to Allegany County was perhaps John Poling, a landowner in Monmouth County, N.J. She continues: "Poland was changed from Poling by John Poland. Early recorders spelled according to sound and whim. *Polen* and *Polan-Poland* were different clerks' ideas but represented Poland or Poling." POLAND, then, has no apparent connection with the European country. Instead, it represents the English placename and surname, *Poling* (v. Ekwall).

Note: Smith (*Am. Surnames*, 1969) remarks that "English people with PO-LAND as a surname derive from a residence of the early ancestor who lived on the homestead on which there was a pool, or through which a stream flowed."

POLISH MOUNTAIN [POLE—ish]. GMd 1941 has Polish Mountain (el. 1800) bordering Town Creek, Allegany County, and stretching northeastward into Pennsylvania. To me there seems little doubt that this range, mapped by Colton in 1852, takes its name from some once resident Polish family or families.

Note: I am obliged to Dr. Gordon E. Kershaw (Frostburg State College, 1981) for the opinion (held by Donald Workman, local historian, LaVale) that POLISH MOUNTAIN owes its name to the fact that in earlier days the leaves of the trees on this mountain had a *polished* appearance. See Introductory Essay, #VI, where I reject this theory.

POMFRET. Village near La Plata, Charles County. Brown and Klapthor state that in 1763, when the Catholic Church acquired "Pomfret Chapple Land," a small frame chapel was built here. However, the name is appreciably older. *Archives* (XXXVI, for 1729), listing Chapticoe, Port-Tobacco Creek, etc., mentions "the Head of Pomphrett Rac[?]." Though *Pomfret* is sometimes a family name, it is likely that in the present case, it commemorates the Yorkshire market town, Pontefract, which is pronounced and sometimes written "Pomfret."

POMONKEY. Village on Pomonkey Creek near La Plata, Charles County. (*Pomonkey* 1833 PHC). BK notices that William Turner (d. 1793) had fifteen slaves at "Pomunkey Quarter." John Dorsey remarks that "residents of the surrounding countryside ... think of themselves as citizen of Pomonkey rather than of the neighboring communities of Bryans

Road, Pomfret or Indian Head." "Pomonkeyites," Dorsey continues, "don't know how long their tiny town has been there, but William P. Jameson, a longtime resident, knows that there has been an Episcopal church in the area for at least 125 years. A post office was established about 75 years ago but was closed in 1942." (See: "Pomonkey, Without Indians," *Sun* [Mag.], 11 Nov. 1962).

POMONKEY CREEK.   A tributary of the Potomac River, Charles County. Marye remarks: "It appears to me scarcely doubtful that *Pamacocock* was . . . the Pamunkey Indian town of history." It appears as *Pamunky Indian Land* on Herrman's map of 1673.

Heckewelder derives this Algonquian name from Delaware *pihmunga* "Where we sweat"; Tooker reaches the meaning, "Place of secrecy in the woods"; and Gerard sets up the prototype **pamunki* "sloping hill, rising upland."

The early spellings of this name, in Arber's edition of Captain Smith's writings, indicate that *Pamaunke* is the word to be solved. And the -*au*- of this form appears to be from an earlier long *a*. If this is the case, the last part of the word may be taken as -*awang(k)* "land" and -*ya* "it is." If *pām*- means "sloping," one arrives at Gerard's translation. If, instead, it is the counterpart of Fox *pyäm*- "(to) twist, twisted," the meaning may be "(River) twisting in the land."

*POMPEY SMASH.   Village. Now VALE SUMMIT, near Clarysville, Allegany County. (*Pompey Smash*, Martenet 1866; *Vale Summit*, USGS 1908 Frostburg). H. M. Parker (p.m., Sept. 1950) tells me that the change from **Pompey Smash* to *Vale Summit* occurred when the first post office opened. Mr. Parker mentions a Negro, Pompey, whose cart of vegetables had a smash. Pompey cried: "Pompey had a smash!" Other stories to account for the name are: (1) that Pompey was a Negro or Italian fruit vendor who had a runaway and smash ("Pompey smash! Pompey smash!"); (2) that Pompey was a bootlegger and spilled his *mash*; and even (3) that Pompey, a Negro, wrecked his automobile here. See VALE SUMMIT.

Note: Andrew Roy, stating that *POMPEY SMASH was laid out in 1851, relates that at that time coal from the local mines was hauled from here in wagons and sold to neighboring blacksmiths. The Negro Pompey (a slave) did such hauling, and one day smashed his wagon on the site of the town. "Pompey's Smash" came into being. Roy declares that the change to *Vale Summit* came about because the coal miners were ashamed of the name. (See: *History of the Coal Miners of the United States*. Columbus, 1907, 3rd ed., p. 48).

PONE.   An island near Bloodsworth Island, Dorchester County; also, a cove north of Pone Island. Cf. Pawn Run, Garrett County. *Pone* appears as *appoan* in Strachey's Dictionary and may be defined as Powhatan for a cake made of corn meal and hot water. Its Maryland occurrences may be authentic Indian survivals. The *Archives*, recording an examination of Indian prisoners in 1681, has: "Love Jones . . . Declares that she saw this

Man ... in the boate at Point Looke out and gave him a Pone and a fish ..."

Gerard derives *pone* from *apan* "(something) baked." Compare Fox *apwā (apwä)*- "cook, boil, roast." (See: *Archives*, XV, 364–373; *Handbook*, II, p. 279). See HALF PONE POINT.

POOLESVILLE. Near Dickerson, Montgomery County. PHC remarks that "Pooles Store" was changed to "Poolesville" between Sept. 30, 1823 and September 30, 1825. Farquhar (p. 256) mentions "Richard Poole's House," and states that, in a deed dated Nov. 23, 1769, the land on which this and much of the village stands is called "Poole's Ratification." The tract was "conveyed" by John Poole to Joseph Poole. Farquhar cites Scharf and a "strong local tradition" to the effect that the name was given in 1793 and comes from John Poole, builder of the first village house. Grove (p. 388), however, has: "Joseph Poole after whom Poolesville is named."

Note: In "Development Encircling Poolesville" (*Star*, 2 Feb. 1973) John Birchfield relates that in 1758 Capt. Joseph Chiswell was given title to "Joseph's Choice," near the present town, and that in 1760 John Poole was granted land paralleling "Joseph's Choice" on the east side of Route 109. The town began when John Poole II built a log house "just north" of the present Town Hall. John, Joseph, and Benjamin Poole all had stores in the town.

POPES CREEK. Village. Potomac River, near Faulkner, Charles County. Hill cites this entry in the records of 1662: "... ye ducking stool to be set up at Mr. Pope's Creeke ..." Though the date is somewhat at variance, Hill was perhaps referring to an *Archives* item which states that at the January 1663/4 Charles County Court the Sheriff was ordered to have erected a ducking stool "at Mr. Pope's Creek." "Mr. Pope" was evidently Francis Pope. BK (p. 43) remarks: "[The] First Negroes in Charles County are said to have been imported in the seventeenth century by Francis Pope whose land grant on the Potomac River included Pope's Creek..." (See: Hill, MCC, pp. 200–201; *Archives*, LIII, 1659–72, p. 30).

POPLARS. Village near Sunderland, Calvert County.

POPLAR SPRINGS. Village near Lisbon, Howard County. (*Poplar Springs* 1807 PHC) Noting that at this place the Frederick Turnpike crossed the National Pike, Warfield remarks that a large spring provided a halting place for the traveller. In later days, with the Poplar Spring Hotel, the village became a summer resort.

Note: That the poplar tree abounds in Maryland is shown by the presence in GMd 1941 of twenty-two *poplar* names. In three cases (*Popular, Popular Neck, Popular Springs*) one finds the folk etymology *popular*.

POPLARTOWN. Worcester County. (*Poplartown*/Poplartown Cross Rds. 1811 PHC). PHC has this note: "... 'Trap' in 1797. ... 1810 ...

'Trap or Poplartown Cross Roads. '. . . for about ten years [after 1811] . . .
'Poplartown or Trap.' In the 1822 list [and thereafter] . . . Trap is omitted." See IRONSHIRE.

POPULAR. Village. GMD 1941: ". . .; see Ironshire." Probably a folk
version of *poplar.*

*PORCOSEN RUN. See POCOSIN.

PORT DEPOSIT. Town. Susquehanna River, near Perryville, Cecil
County. (*Port Deposit* 1816 PHC). Johnston and Miller both point out that
in 1729 there was perhaps a ferry here, called *Smith's Ferry* for Captain
John Smith, who probably reached this point when he explored Chesapeake Bay. I cannot think that such a name was given for Smith, except
perhaps in retrospect. However, the early name *Creswell's Ferry* (fr.
Col. John Creswell, early landowner) is an actuality; and Johnston remarks that the town had also probably been called *Rock Run.* According
to Miller, Gov. Winder in 1812 signed the bill that changed the name to
Port Deposit. Miller relates: ". . . when a suitable name for the town was
discussed someone said, 'It is a port of deposit for lumber, Why not call it
Port Deposit?' " After 1880, however, the lumber became depleted.

Note: Besides Miller's explanation (v. above), there are other somewhat different accounts. The Guide, for instance, attributes the name to the idea "that the
town would be a port of deposit for products coming down the Susquehanna." And
Gannett (p. 251) delcares: ". . . so named because it is one of the principal depots
for the pine lumber rafted down the river." Tropical storm "Agnes" (1972)
brought about a revitalization of Port Deposit, leading to its consideration for
mention in the National Register of Historic Places, and involving the restoration
of the Paw Paw Building for use as a library and museum. An item, "Flood Led
Town to Rediscover Lost Heritage" (Capital, 3 Dec. 1975), explains: "The Paw
Paw Building, named after two flourishing trees that used to grace its front door,
was built in 1821 of Port Deposit granite . . ."

PORT HERMAN. Village. Elk River, near Town Point, Cecil County.
(*Port Herman* 1852 PHC). Johnston points out that this village was
founded "about thirty years ago" and is *not* the town Augustine Herrman
projected but never built. Using the spelling *Hermen,* Johnston notes that
Augustine Herrman's "name and nationality have been perpetuated by
being applied to Bohemia River, Bohemia Manor, St. Augustine Church,
St. Augustine Manor, and the pretty little town of Port Hermen."

PORT REPUBLIC. A village four miles southeast of Prince Frederick, Calvert County. (*Port Republic* 1836 PHC). Port Republic lies on a
low plateau (153 el.) between tiny headwater branches of Governor Run
and Parkers Creek; overland, it is less than two miles from Chesapeake
Bay. Vicki B. Horsmon, of Prince Frederick has explained to me: "No one
seems to know just how Port Republic got the name . . . It is thought to
have been a port of entry. There was an old dirt road that went by Christ's
Church to what is now Port Republic. There people stopped to water their

horses before travelling on to Governor's Run, where there was a wharf, or to Parker's Creek." Cf. Port Republic, Virginia, and Port Republic, New Jersey—both on or near streams.

Note: Port Republic, Virginia, takes its name from the fact that it was once a shipping and loading port for flatboats carrying flour, grain and other farm products, as well as pig iron from the Port Republic foundry, down the Shenandoah River to the B. & O. Railroad at Harpers Ferry. This river traffic occurred between 1790 and (ca.) 1860 . . . (See: "Names along the Line," *N. & W. Magazine,* 28: 12. p. 662).

PORTERS. Village near Freedom, Carroll County. (*Porters* 1834 PHC). *Porter* is an abundant surname in Maryland. Passano (Index) lists thirty-three genealogical items under this name. Heads (1790) has sixty *Porters.* However, there are only six *Porters* in TDr Carroll 1963.

PORTERS BRIDGE. Village. GMd 1941: ". . . in Cecil County; see Richardsmere." Johnston (p. 357, ff.) mentions Stephen Porter, "a lawyer of some distinction, who lived at Porter's Bridge, on Octoraro Creek in 1784." See RICHARDSMERE.

Note: Richardson (II, 207–08) states that "the Porters" were early settlers on Susquehanna Manor, alias New Connaught, granted by Lord Baltimore II to George Talbot in 1680 for the encouragement of British settlers. Robert Porter, "son of the emigrant," inherited his father's part of the manor, and later served in a troop of horse, Cecil County, 1739–40. His son, Captain Robert Porter, fought in the Revolutionary Army.

PORTOBELLO. Village. St. Mary's River, near Drayden, St. Mary's County. Pogue (p. 141) states that "Porto Bello" (whence the village name) was built by William Hebb in the mid-1740's after he returned from the British expedition against Spanish South America. Admiral Vernon was the leader, and the British had succeeded in taking Porto Bello.

Note: To resolve a conflict with Wilstach, who attributes the name to Edwin Coade, Mr. Pogue writes me (22 Sept. 1973): "According to the Chronicles of St. Mary's and the Annapolis Land Office Records (St. Mary's Co., 1742, Ctf. 352) Porto Bello was built by Wm. Hebb. He is buried in the family cemetery there. The second owner was his son Vernon Hebb. The family owned it until about 1815. The Coad family bought it in this century. It is my belief that the Coads lived at nearby Cherryfields."

PORT TOBACCO. A village on Port Tobacco Creek, near La Plata, Charles County. (*Port Tobacco* 1792 PHC). PORT TOBACCO takes its name from the creek it is on. And the creek (*Potopaco,* Va. 1608 Smith; *Portobacke,* Md. 1635 Lord Baltimore), in turn, represents a well-disguised folk etymology from the Algonquian. I favor, for the original Powhatan, *Potapaco,* meaning "A jutting of the water inland." See below.

Note: Philip Sheridan Proctor (Piscataway Indian, Mechanicsville, Md.) spoke to me (14 March 1962) about the "Port Tobacco Hills." Wilstach (p. 101) notes the phrase "Portobacco Cliffs" in Tom Dent's will, 1676. In 1728 PORT TOBACCO was officially named *CHARLESTOWN (with a courthouse to be built at *CHANDLER'S TOWN). Officially, in 1820, the name was changed to PORT TOBACCO. CHANDLER'S TOWN relates to Captain William Chandler who, in 1740, joined the expedition against Cartagena. (See: Brown and Klapthor, p. 46).

PORT TOBACCO CREEK. A tributary of the Potomac River, Charles County. Early map spellings are *Potopaco*, Virginia 1608, Smith, and *Portobacke*, Maryland 1635, Lord Baltimore. E. R. Hayden declares: "We often read that the name comes from the fact that the town was a port from which tobacco was shipped to England; but the spellings in earliest documents show that the name was certainly a corruption of the Indian 'Potopaco.' "

Trumbull translates *Potopaco* as "bulging out, a jutting of the water inland." Tooker, feeling that the *pota-* of *Port Tobacco* is the same as the *pata-* of *Patapsco*, also translates "A jutting of the water inland. They both cite Eliot's *pootuppog* (*pootuppag*) "bay" (cf. Abnaki *podebag*). I agree with the conclusions of Trumbull and Tooker. And, though Port Tobacco Creek has silted up, its meaning befits the local topography. (See: Hayden, "Port Tobacco, Lost Town of Maryland," *MHM*, XL: 4, 261–76)

PORTERS. Village near Rawlings, Allegany County. TW (1100–1101) mentions John M. ("Squire Jack") Porter, a pioneer settler of Allegany County, who opened the area's first coal mine for "domestic purposes" on "Rose Meadows" near Frostburg. There were other prominent *Porters*, e.g., Glissan Thomas Porter (b. 1849). He was the author of a history of Frostburg, and a leader in the fight to bring natural gas to Allegany County.

POTOMAC. Village on the River Road, several miles from Great Falls (Potomac River), Montgomery County. (*Potomac* 1830 PHC). The Postal History Catalog relates: "This office was originally established as 'Section Eight,' but after three months it was changed to 'Potomac.' " Cf. two similar villages, POTOMAC VALLEY JUNCTION (nr. Williamsport, Washington County), and POTOMAC VIEW.

POTOMAC RIVER. Together with its North and South Branches, this river constitutes Maryland's common inland border with both Virginia and West Virginia, and debouches into the Chesapeake Bay beyond Point Lookout, St. Mary's County.

On Virginia 1608 Smith, one finds *Patowmeck, Patowmeck Flu* [river]. On Mayo's map, 1737, one finds *Patomack Cr., Patomack River, Wappācomma Riv*, and *Cohongorooto river*. *Cohongorooto (with variants) appears to represent the North Branch. It evidently contains Delaware and Powhatan *kaak, kahunge* "goose." *Wappacomo*, naming the South

Branch, contains *wāpi* "white" and *ahkamiku* "ground" and apparently means "White ground."

The Powhatan word *Potomac* contains either *pyä-* "to come," or *pō(t)-* "into." Considering Smith's spelling, *Patawomeck*, the Primitive Algonquian prototype was probably **pyä-taw-ameki* "Where it is brought in," or "Where one comes in." Gerard was correct in his conception that the name contains a form of the verb "to bring." Tooker thought it was steatite that the Indians brought in. But C. E. Gilliam (letter, Sept. 1966) skeptically suggests antimony, corn, and the fur of local beasts. (See: *Names*, 15. 3, p. 87).

POTOMAC VIEW. Village. Smith Creek, near Wynne, St. Mary's County. Cf. "Potomac View" (nr. Harpers Ferry), about which the Guide has: "From Potomac View the river is visible, flowing through Harper's Ferry gap, between the steep and craggy slopes of Maryland Heights and Loudon Heights, Virginia." See BENVILLE (St. Mary's Co.).

Note: There are also Potomac Heights (Charles and Washington Counties), Potomac Hill (Allegany County), Potomac Park (Cumberland, Allegany County), Potomac State Forest (Garrett County), etc. All of these names are from proximity to Maryland's most important river, the Potomac. See my *Origin and Meaning* (pp. 115–16) where I conclude that the Algonquian name *Potomac* (Smith *Patawomeck*) probably means "Where goods are brought in," i.e., "Landing place for goods," or even "Emporium."
... Of all the views from the Potomac River, none can rival (so it seems to me) the silent grandeur and still primitive majesty of this great stream's massive banks near Gunston Hall, Virginia, opposite St. Mary's, Maryland.

*POTTER'S LANDING. Choptank River, five miles below Denton, Caroline County. Footner states that until 1847 this place was the stronghold of "Maryland Potters, whose first ancestor was Captain Zabdiel ("Zeb") Potter, of Rhode Island." Cochrane gives the mid-eighteenth century as the date of Zabdiel Potter's settlement; he adds that the landing was named "in his honor." Zabdiel Potter died at sea in 1761; General Potter, a descendant, died in 1847. At that time Colonel John Arthur Willis, of the First E. Sh. Regiment of Volunteers, bought Potters Landing. States Cochrane: "In later years the name of *Potter Town was changed to Williston in memory of the Colonel and his family." See WILLISTON.

Note: It is not clear when *POTTER TOWN enters the picture. Cochrane mentions "Potter's Mill (Willistown)" for 1774. Hulbert remarks: "a Mr. Willis" bought the estate and sought to change the name to Williston. "Nowadays it is either Potter's Landing or Williston."

POWELLS. Village. Pocomoke River, near Rehoboth, Somerset County. Its existence is doubtful. Richardson mentions Walter Powell, a Virginia Quaker who became a citizen of Somerset County before 1671.

His plantation was on the Pocomoke; one of his sons, Levin, died in 1764. (See: Richardson, II, 403–17).

POWELLVILLE. Near Truitt, Wicomico County. Lewis 1878 spells Powellsville and lists E., J., and J. L. Powell as farmers living there. Norman Adkins (a native) tells me (June 1966) that the *s* is sometimes used, sometimes omitted.

POWHATAN. A Baltimore City suburb, today better known as Woodlawn. In Maryland, *Powhatan* seems to have no aboriginal significance. However, the fact that the meaning of *Powhatan* ("A fall or rapid in a stream") somewhat befits this suburb's location (near Gwynn's Falls) suggests that the name may have been given by someone familiar with Virginia Algonquian.

The original *Powhatan*, designating the Indian town at the *falls* of the James River, contains Primitive Algonquian **paw(i)*- "(to) shake" and PA **-ehtan* "flow current." Its prototype, **pāw-ehtan-wi*, is a verb in the independent mode and means "It is a fall or rapid in a stream."

PRESTON. Village near Bethlehem, Caroline County. (*Preston P.O.*, Martenet 1866). The Guide remarks: "In its central section one or two old houses remain from the days when it was a tiny settlement called Snow Hill." J. L. Christopher, postmaster, informs me that the change to *Preston* was in 1856. He attributes the name to Alexander Preston, "a prominent Baltimore lawyer of that day."

*PRESTON MILLS ... R-McN's 1877 Index Map has "Preston Mills, see Chrome Hill." See CHROME HILL.

PRICE. Village near Church Hill, Queen Anne's County. (*Price's Station*, Martenet 1866) Lewis 1878 lists M. *Price* as a farmer living near here.

PRIEST BRIDGE. A bridge and village on the Patuxent River, near Conaways, Anne Arundel County. Cf. PRIEST FORD.

PRIEST FORD. GMd 1941: "... in Harford County." Marye, citing Baltimore County Court proceedings, finds mention of *Johnson Ford and remarks: "This is the first direct allusion I find to Johnson's Ford, which was on Deer Creek at the mouth of Thomas's Run, and is identical with the famous Priest's Ford." The "priest" in this name was Reverend Bennet Neale, S. J., who bought land here in 1750. "Priest Neale's Mass House (Pb. Doc., 1756) gave occasion (to quote Preston) to "the fording being called Priest's Ford." (See: *MHM*, XVI: 2, p. 137: Preston, pp. 160–61).

Note: In Cecil County there are BALD FRIAR, and BALD FRIAR KNOB. John W. McGraw, Jr., declares: "Neither does the Bald Friar Knob place name refer to Father Neale or any other known clergyman. Dedicated men as they seem to have been, neither Bennett Neale or John Digges ... left any trace of their quiet ministration, least of all a phrenological likeness in stone, not on this side of paradise." (See: "Priest Neale and His Successors, Pt. II," *MHM*, 63: 2, p. 157).

PRIESTLAND. A Branch, a School, and a Valley near New Windsor, Carroll County. With the intention that the region become a Catholic community, Thomas Diggs, in April 1743, acquired the 600-acre tract, "Mountain Prospect." However, Diggs's intention eventually came to naught, for the Catholics sold the land to Samual Godfrey and James Gillingham in 1793 and moved away to *Connewago (Hanover).

PRIESTS POINT. Village. St. Mary's County. The point separates Smith's Point from the St. Mary's River. Martin (p. 95) states that the land here was patented to Thomas Copley (d. 1653), the Superior of the Jesuit Mission in Maryland. His clerical name was Father Philip Fisher. The heir to this land (2000 a.) was Father Lawrence Starkey; and ever since the Jesuits have owned it.

PRINCE FREDERICK. A town south of Stoakley, Prince Frederick D., Calvert County. (Prince Fredericktown 1824 PHC). Stein (p. 57) states that this place was first known as *Old Fields. The Guide (p. 457), however has *Williams Old Fields, "until 1725." It appears (v. Stein) that the land was originally patented to William Williams under the name of "Little Fields." Later, Aaron Williams owned it. Today's name is for Frederick, eldest son of King George I. The Assembly established the town in 1725. Cf. FREDERICK.

PRINCESS ANNE. Town. Manokin River, Somerset County. (Princess Anne 1792 PHC). Torrence states that in 1733 this town was "laid out and established as Princess Anne Town ..." James Wilfong, Jr., after mentioning the portrait of Queen Anne in the Somerset courthouse, declares: "The ... town was named for Queen Anne while she was still a princess." The Guide, however, attributes the name to a lesser Anne (1709–1759), the daughter of King George II. The accuracy of the latter belief is somewhat supported by the fact that the town's Prince William Street seems to commemorate the lesser Anne's husband (m. 1734), William, Prince of Orange. (See: Star [Mag.], 6 Oct. 1963).

Note: Hulbert Footner favors the lesser Princess Anne. Richard D. Steuart comments: "Mr. Footner makes ... statements which are apt to shock some of the natives. In the courthouse at Princess Anne ... hangs a ... portrait of good Queen Anne ... and Queen Anne is pointed out as the patron saint of the town. But Mr. Footner says that Princess Anne was not named for Queen Anne ... but for another less distinguished Princess Anne, the daughter of George II." (See: MHM, 39: 4, pp. 351–52).

PRINCIPIO, PRINCIPIO FURNACE [prin-SIP-io]. Village and town, respectively; Furnace Bay and Principio Creek, Cecil County. (Principio 1840 PHC, Principio Furnace 1850 PHC). These names all relate to Principio Creek, whose name until the rise of Cecil County's iron works (ca. 1715) was *Back Creek. The following letter from Joshua Gee, English entrepreneur, to Joseph Farmer, English ironmaster (ca. 1715), accounts for the present name: "... I am sending Stephen Onion and Wil-

liam Russell and William's son Thomas to help thee start the ironworks
... I will charge thee to change the stream's name from Back to Principio.
That means 'first' or 'in the beginning' if thou knowest thy Latin." Hill,
Johnson, and Kidwiler mention "The Principio Co.," "Principio Iron
Works," etc. And there is a reference to "Principio Iron Works" by Eben-
ezer Hazard in his *Travels through Maryland in 1777* (v. *MHM*, XLVI: 1,
March 1951). (See: E. C. May, *Principio to Wheeling 1715–1945 A Pageant
of Iron and Steel.* New York, 1945).

Notes: (1) PHC states that "Farmington" was changed to "Principio" in 1840,
that "Principio" was changed to "College Green" in 1849, and that "College
Green" became "Principio" again in 1849. (2) Scott (1807, p. 113) speaks of mines of
iron ore in Cecil County, and continues: "... manufactured into pigs, hollow ware,
bar iron, and nails. Cecil furnace consists of a wind and air furnace. It is ... on
Principio Creek."

PRIZE HOUSE POINT. It juts out from Wilmer's Neck, between Island Creek and Chester River, Queen Anne's County. Emory explains:
"Prize-house derived its name from the fact that inspectors of tobacco
were required to prize or press the tobacco in a hogshead until the latter
weighed 950 pounds nett. The house in which the pressing was done came
to be known as the prize-house, i.e. press-house."

PROCTORS WHARF. Village. Mattawoman Creek, near Marbury,
Charles County. Brown and Klapthor point out that in Charles County in
1790 there were thirteen *Proctors*, all of them mulattoes. Philip Sheridan
Proctor (of Mechanicsville; 1962), a descendant of the Piscataways, speaks
of an old "Doctor Proctor" who knew some of the Piscataways. Cf. "Proctor's Chance, whence *Proctor's Landing, Severn River. Warfield (p. 11)
mentions Robert Proctor, a surveyor. He acquired "Proctor's Chance,"
on the westside of the Severn River, in 1679. (See: BK, pp. 179–95).

*PROVIDENCE. See ANNAPOLIS. Kelly points out that before
1650 the western shore between the Magothy River and Herring Bay was
a favorite region for the settlement of the Quakers, who called the land
"Providence." In 1650 the General Assembly changed the name to Anne
Arundel (County). See ANNAPOLIS, Anne Arundel, SEVERN, etc.

PUBLIC LANDING. Village. Chincoteague Bay, near Spence, Worcester County, The Guide speaks of the Public Landing Road, leading to
PUBLIC LANDING "... on the shore of Chincoteague Bay, here five
miles wide." Adds the Guide: "Until the railroad era, the place was a busy
shipping point for freight going the short distance overland between vessels here and at Snow Hill." Cf. PUBLIC LANDING, Queen Anne's
County.

*PUNCH HALL. Caroline County. Cochrane speaks of the "adjoining
villages of UNION CORNER and PUNCH HALL. According to Cochrane, runaway slaves, hiding under a hall there, were punched out by citizens using a long pole. Another explanation is that a man by the name of

Hall kept an inn here and sold punch. UNION CORNER was the hamlet (at a crossroads corner) and "Punch Hall" was the central group of buildings. See BURRSVILLE; see *UNION CORNER.

PUCKUM BRANCH. A tributary of Marshyhope Creek, Ennall's Wharf, Dorchester County. *Archives*, XV, 1671-81: ". . . neck of Land called . . . Puckamee . . ." This may be a local variant of Powhatan *poughcone*. Strachey defines it as "the red paint or dye." Cf. *poke, poke-berry, poke*weed.

Note: Torrence (Old Somerset, pp. 142-43) mentions the baptism, in 1682/3, of John Puckham, a member of the Monie Indian tribe of Somerset County. Torrence adds: ". . . we have evidence . . . that people by the name of Puckham were living at a later date near this Monie Indian town site."

PURNELL. GMd 1941 lists PURNELL BAY,—COVE,—POINT, and—POND (2), all in Worcester County; also PURNELLS CROSSING and PURNELLS SHOPS, both in Worcester. The Guide mentions two men who may have been responsible for these names: Major John Purnell, who built "Genezir" (Sinepuxent Neck) in 1732; and Thomas Purnell, who built "Scarborough House" in about 1780.

Note: The 2,000-acre tract, "Genezir," was patented (under that name) in 1684 by Edward Whaley and Charles Ratcliffe. BC 1879 mentions Thomas Purnell who, in 1664, came from Beckley, Northamptonshire, England, and settled in "Fairfield," Worcester County. His most illustrious descendant was perhaps William U. Purnell, a lawyer, who served twice in the Maryland House of Delegates and twice in the State Senate.

PUSEYS LANDING. Village. Corsica River, near Brownsville, Queen Anne's County. Miss Lillian Callaway (Courthouse Centerville, 30 Aug. 1967) pronounced the name PEW-zy. Heads (1790) gives 3 *Pusey* and 2 *Puzey*. None of them is in Queen Anne's County. Passano makes four genealogical references.

PYLESVILLE. Near Whiteford, Harford County. Lewis, describing this place as being three miles from Delta, Pa., gives N. Pyle as the postmaster, Nathan Pyle as a general merchandiser, Nathan and E. Everett Pyle as millers, and D. Pyle as a surveyor. I suppose that N. Pyle and Nathan Pyle are óne and the same person.

Q

QUAKER NECK, QUAKER NECK LANDING. Neck and village, Chester River, near Pomona, Kent County. These names relate to the settlement in Maryland of members of the important Society of Friends, popularly called Quakers. Kinney calls attention to "Providence Plantation," a dwelling built in 1781 by William and Mary Trew, a Quaker couple.

QUANTICO. Village and creek, Nanticoke River, Wicomico County. Cf. Quantico Creek, Prince William County, Virginia (Smith 1608-12: *Quantico*). The Maryland spellings are almost invariably *Quantico*. The divergent spelling *Quanticott*—which one finds in Cotton III (p. 63), for 1705—occurs rather late, but it certainly suggests that, like Connecticut the name originally ended in *t*.

Quantico is Virginia Algonquian; and the BAE (Smithsonian) card index—apparently basing its conclusion on the Delaware and Natick forms for "long" ([Del.] *guneu, quin*; [Natick] *qunni*)—translates "At the long inlet." Heckewelder, however, finds Delaware *gentgeen (gintkaan)*, "to dance," in the name, and translates "Place of dancing and frolic." In 1947 Elizabeth Myers, siding with Heckewelder, declared: "The Nanticoke Indians called it [Quantico] 'The Dancing Place.'"

I feel obliged to deny Heckewelder's explanation, because of the phonetic difficulty of deriving a word beginning with *Q* [kw] (Quantico) from a word beginning with a *G* or *K* (Delaware *gintkaan* "to dance," Powhatan *kantokan* "to Daunce"). The same objection does not hold as strongly for the BAE's derivation of *Quantico* from "long," since the Delaware, Natick, and Powhatan words for "long" to some extent favor *Q* (Del. *quin*, Natick *qunni*, Powhatan *cunnaivwh*).

These considerations greatly favor the correctness of the BAE (Smithsonian) "At the long inlet," where *inlet* could as well be "creek" or "stream." Indeed, it is quite unobjectionable to regard the *Quan-* as a version of Primitive Algonquian **kenw* "long," and the second element *-tic-* as a version of Primitive Algonquian **ehtekw* "creek, inlet, stream." A lost *-t* ending (**-atwi* "it is") may be assumed, and accounts for the *-o*. The word differs little from *Connecticut* ...

Notes: (1) See Myers, "Quantico, One of the Shore's Oldest Towns ...," *Salisbury Advertiser and the Wicomico Countian*, Oct. 23, 1947; (2) My decision to accept "long" (PA **kenw-*) as the first syllable of *Quantico* makes superfluous and inapplicable the conclusion I reach in my 1961 book on the subject (p. 118).

QUEEN ANNE. GMd 1941 describes this village as being in Queen Anne's and Talbot Counties, near Tuckahoe Creek. The Guide (p. 417) has it in Talbot County "practically constituting one settlement" with Hillsboro. Compare QUEEN ANNE (Pr. Geo. Co.), a post office in 1796 which, according to PHC (n. 144), appears in the early records as "Queen Anns." Both of these names commemorate Anne (1665-1714), Queen of England, Scotland and Ireland, and the last British sovereign of the House of Stuart.

Note: QUEEN ANNE (Pr. George) is adjacent to Hardesty.

QUEEN ANNE'S COUNTY. Emory (p. 32): Named in honor of "good Queen Anne" of England. It was established in 1706, four years after Queen Anne's accession.

QUEENSTOWN. On Queenstown Creek, near Grasonville, Queen Anne's County. Emory, citing an Act of 1707, notes that the new county seat was named "Queenstown or Queen Anne's Town." An act of 1710 mentions "Queens-Towne." According to Emory a post office was opened here on July 1, 1800.

QUEPONCO. This is Queponco Station, adjacent to Newark, Worcester County. Early spellings in the *Archives* are *Capomco* (V, for 1667–88) and Necke of Land called *Quapanquah* ... *Quapomquah* (XV, for 1671–81). Maryland 1841 Lucas spells *Quepongo*.

Boyd, evidently having in mind Delaware *cuwe* "pine tree" and *ponk* "dust," translates "Ashes of pine woods." Cf. Delaware *ponxu* "full of sand flies" with Strachey's (Powhatan) *poenguwh* "a gnatt."

The simplest Algonquian linguistic model of Boyd's analysis would be **cuweuponga*. However, this form lacks an initial element to make it more idiomatic. Such an initial element could be ***axkwi* "to limit, extend, as far as." On this basis, a more adequate model would be **axkwi- penkuwiwi*, **penkwi* being the Primitive Algonquian word for "dust." The full meaning, differing somewhat from Boyd's, would be "It is the limit of the sand or dust." See *PANGAYO.

*QUINDOXUA NECK. This is perhaps the neck of land between East and Marumsco Creeks, today known as *Richardson Marsh* (Somerset County). Manual 1947 lists Quindooque Church, Somerset. Early spellings appear to be **Quandonquan* (*Archives*, V, for 1667–88), **Candocway Point* (Cotton, III, p. 1701), and *Condocua Neck* (Cotton, III, p. 137, for 1708–09). Martenet 1866 has *Quindoxua*. If one stresses the first syllable of this name and gives the *k* sound to the *x*, *c*, or *q* of the early spellings, the phonetic result strikingly justifies the opinion that *Quindoxua* is a variant of *Quantico*. See QUANTICO.

QUIRAUK. A mountain (2145 ft.) near Pen Mar, on the Appalachian Trail, Washington County, and a village (Quirauk School) a little more than a mile from the mountain. The name is foreshadowed by **Cwareuuoc* (Va. 1585 White); **Quiyough flu* [river], **Quiyoughohanock* (Va. 1608 Smith); and **Quowaughkutt* (*Archives*, III, for 1657–60).

Though it is eighty-five miles from Captain Smith's Virginia, I am inclined to regard *Quirauk* as a phonetic variant of **Quiyough*, the stream name that appears on Va. 1608 Smith as **Quiyough flu* [river] and today, in Stafford County, Va., as *Aquia Creek*. One supposes that the *a*- of *Aquia* (*Quiyough*) was added by the settlers, perhaps on the analogy of Latin *aqua*. The -*y*- of *Quiyough*, appearing in *Quirauk* as *r*, suggests folk etymology.

The analysis and correct translation of *Quirauk* are difficult because *quiyough*—which I take to be the original Virginia Algonquian form—has two different meanings: (1) "god(s)," spelled *Quiyoukosuck*, and having cognates such as *Kewás* (Carolina Algonquian "... a god"), *Quiyouko-*

suck (Virginia Algonquian [Smith] "gods"), *gwaiak*, (Ojibwa "just, right, upright"), and *kwaiusku* (Cree); and (2) "Gull(s)," spelled *Quiyough*, and having cognates such as *coiahqwus* (Strachey "a gull"), *gaiashk (kiyask)* ("young gull"), *kiyask* (Cree), *kaakw* (Abnaki, "a gull, a small, grey gull"), *kiawk* ("Malecite Algonquian," [BAE Smithsonian] "sea gull") *quiyough* ("gulls" [Hewitt, Bull. 30]). Geary (See *Roanoke Voyages 1584–1590 . . .* ed. Quinn, II . . . p. 888) shows clearly how Smith arrives at the spelling *quiyough . . .*, as in *quiyoukosuck* ("gods") from Algonquian *Kewas* (Ojibwa *gwaiak*, Cree *kwasiusku*, etc). In stream names (e.g., Quiyough flu, Quiyoughohanock) Smith was evidently using the word for "gull," and Gerard (Bull. 30) correctly translates *quiyoughohanock* as "Gull river people." Hewitt, accordingly, translates *quiyough* as "gulls" (Bull. 30).

One can derive Quirauk phonetically from either "gull(s)" or "God(s)" (just, true, straight, upright). If "gull" is selected one must keep in mind that *Quirauk* is an inland mountain; if "god(s)" is selected, one is faced with such dubious interpretations as "God's Mountain," "Straight or upright mountain," etc.

R

RACCOON.   Maryland has *Raccoon Creek* and *Raccoon Creek Marsh* (Dorchester County), *Raccoon Creek* (Talbot County), Raccoon Point (Somerset County). The name is from a typically American beast whose designation—evidently from Virginia Algonquian—was spelled variously (*rahaugcum, raugroughcum* [Smith 1608]; *aracoune* [Strachey 1612]; etc.). Mencken states that the word didn't emerge as *racoon* until 1612.

The name, as Smith and Strachey spell it, seems to have no apparent linguistic ties to Delaware (*nachenum*), Natick (*ausup*), Abnaki (*asban*) Ojibwa (*essikan*), or Micmac (*amalchoogwech*). However, noticing that the racoon has the habit of scratching the bark of trees with the sharp nails of its paws, Gerard posits the linguistic model *ara'kunem (ara'ku)* and translates "He scratches with hands."

The name *Raccoon Point* (Somerset County) is explained by the folk tale that here an oyster once grabbed and drowned a raccoon! This is a curious inversion of the fact that raccoons (v. Bull. 30, II, 348) eat a mollusk called the raccoon *oyster*.

RALPH.   Village near Vienna, Dorchester County. In July 1966, while visiting Wicomico County, I was impressed by the abundance of the surname *Ralph*. TDr 1963 Dorchester lists Geo. L. Ralph and Walter T. Ralph, Vienna, and Helen D. Ralph, Cambridge. Cf. RALPHS LANDING (Queen Anne), ROLPHS (vil., Queen Anne), etc. Manual 1969 gives ROLPHS (Landing and village). See also ROLPHS WHARF.

Note: (v. Reaney): *Ralf(e)* and *Rolf(e)* have been confused.

"RANDALIA." A tract on the peninsula formed by Back Creek, Elk River, and Herring Creek (Cecil County). MGHP 1963 (p. 65) states that this part of "Bohemia Manor" (Herrman 1670) was once called "Sodom." In 1792 it was divided by an act of the Legislature. It was later deeded to John Randall, Jr.

RANDALL(S) WHARF. Landing, Cecil County. Perhaps for John Randel, Jr., civil engineer, of Albany, N.Y. Johnston (p. 389, p. 391), spelling his name in this way, calls him the proprietor of "Randalia," and states that in 1823 he estimated the supply of water obtainable from Big Elk Creek. He also resurveyed the route for the Chesapeake and Delaware Canal. See "Randalia."

RANDALLSTOWN. Village near Harrisonville, Baltimore County. (*Randallstown* 1824 PHC). According to the Guide (p. 344) Thomas Randall and Christopher Randall, Jr., founded this village in the early eighteenth century.

RANDLE. GMd 1941: "...In Prince George's County." Farquhar (p. 92) mentions "Aix La Chapelle," more recently known as the Randle's Farm, four miles northwest of Dawsonville (Montgomery County). Cf. RANDLE CLIFFS, Calvert County. Maryland Tel. Directories give *Randle* as a variant of *Randall, Randol.* Baltimore TDr 1969 has 15 *Randle*s. Md. Sub. Wash. TDr 1974–75 lists 7 *Randle*s, two of them in Montgomery County, the rest in Prince George's.

RAPAHANOCK. flu [River]. Charted on Virginia 1608 Smith for the Dorchester County region of Maryland. Bozman declares: "... this river on the Eastern Shore, which ... [Smith] called the Rapahanock, could be no other than the river in Dorchester County called on Griffith's map *Hungary* river, but more commonly by the neighboring inhabitants— Hunger River."

Beauchamp defines *Rappahannock* as "Current returning and flowing again," The *Handbook* gives the almost identical "The alternating stream."

I agree with the meaning given by Beauchamp and the *Handbook*. The late Professor James A. Geary explains: "The word seems to be composed of **thāpi* 'back again as before' ... plus **-ahan-* 'alternate movement, as of ... lapping of waves' (... frequently used in river names) ..." The ending (*-ock*), to follow Prof. Geary's analysis, consists of the inanimate copula **-at-* (or **-an-*) "it is" combined with the 3rd singular inanimate ending **-ki*. One would translate "It is an alternating stream." (See: Bozman, I, 114; Beauchamp, *Indian Names in New York*, 1893, p. 105; *Handbook*, II, 354–55; Geary, in *The Roanoke Voyages 1584–1590*. D. B. Quinn, ed., II, p. 879). See HONGA RIVER.

RASIN. Baltimore City suburb. *Rasin*, GMd 1941. The Guide (p. 45) mentions I. Freeman Rasin, Baltimore politician, who (along with Arthur Pue Gorman) controlled Maryland politics from 1869 to 1895.

RAWLINGS. Village near Fort Hill, Potomac River, Allegany County. The Guide (p. 517) states that this place was at first called "HICKORY FLATS." TW (I, 487) speaks of District No. 7 as ". . . generally known as Rawlings Station District . . ." The same authority, calling Colonel Moses Rawlings a "pioneer resident," remarks: "The Rawlings family was the first to settle in this district prior to the Revolution." The village evidently owes its name to the aforesaid Colonel Rawlings, who was commissioned, July 1, 1776, as lieutenant-colonel of a Maryland rifle regiment, and marched with Captain Cresap from Oldtown, Allegany County, to the Revolutionary defense of Boston. The present writer recalls several visits to the somewhat stately mansion at RAWLINGS. It is situated alongside the B. & O. Railroad tracks (and the Potomac River) at what was once (probably) *Rawlings Station.

*RED DOOR. see DARLINGTON.

REDHOUSE. Village near Sunnyside, Garrett County. (GMd 1941). The Guide (p. 523) describes this place as a "crossroads hamlet with several roadhouses," and states that "The Red House" was once a tavern for cattle drivers following the Northwest Pike (U.S. 50). A *Sun* article ("Red House Maryland," 5 March 1966, p. 24) states that an inn, painted dark red, was built here in the early 1830's; . . . "and from this the small turnpike community was named: Red House." It appears that the original inn was torn down a few years after 1877. A second, smaller house, also red, was constructed on the same spot; it stood until 1939–40. Today the site is occupied by a two-story colonial house.

Note: This inn of the 1830's does not seem to be the inn mentioned by Weeks (p. 15): "Joseph Tomlinson surveyed in 1760 and patented in 1761 "Good Will," the first land patented in Garrett County. This tract included the historic Little Meadows on the Braddock Road; here Tomlinson built of logs the Red House Inn."

REHOBETH. Village. Pocomoke River, near Hudson's Corner, Somerset County. Torrence (p. 169), indicating that there is evidence from 1708 that describes Rehobeth as *"Pocomoke Town Called Rehoboth,"* remarks that Rehobeth was laid out in 1683 on a portion of William Stevens' plantation called "Rehoboth." He writes: "William Stevens' home was 'Rehoboth on Pocomoke, a name apparently given by him to his home plantation with the full recognition of the biblical significance of the word—'roominess' or 'room for all.' " As the Guide expresses it (p. 433): "The name Rehobeth (there is room) was applied by Colonel Stevens

Note: The *Sun* article (see above) discusses the question of whether REHOBETH should be spelled with an *e* or an *o*. The U.S. Postal Guide, the maps, the local canning house, and the county tax records spell it Rehobeth. And there were many complaints (in the days of Postmaster General James Farley) when there appeared a postoffice sign written "Rehoboth." As for other instances of the biblical name, a Historical Marker (seen July 21, 1966) points out an old home, Rehoboth," near Eldorado, Dorchester County. Cf. REHOBOTH BEACH, Delaware.

(1630–1687) to the tract he patented in 1665 near here along the Pocomoke." The *Sun* (22 June 1940)—on the name's 275th anniversary (to take the date of 1665)—relates similarly: "Col. William Stevens, of the Colonial Governor's Council, named the town Rehoboth in 1665 . . .

REIFFS. Village near Hicksville, Washington County. Williams (II, 694–95) relates that David Reiff, born near Farmersville, Lancaster County, Pa., came to Washington County in 1839. He died in 1890. He and his wife belonged to the Reif Mennonite Church and are buried there.

Note: According to Williams, David Reiff lived for nineteen years on the farm "... where C. R. Strite now lives."

REISTERSTOWN. Near Glyndon, Baltimore County. (*Reistertown* 1802 PHC). Davidson (pp. 80–81) states that George Washington gave the name *Washington* to this village when he was asked to name the place after spending the night at Colonel Bower's. It appears that *Washington* was only the northwestern part of the town. The southeastern part was called *Reisterville*; later the whole village was called *Reistertown*. Davidson attributes the *Reister* names to the fact that at time three fourths of the inhabitants were members of the Reister family. The Guide (p. 500) states, more specifically, that John Reister, a German immigrant, gave the name "Reister's Desire" to a tract of land the Calverts granted him. A large population of *Reisters* arose; hence the present name.

Note: *Street Map of Reistertown Glyndon Owings Mills Garrison* (Pb. by Reistertown Chamber of Commerce /1969?/ declares that John Reister settled here in 1758 on a 20-acre grant.

RELAY. Patapsco River, near Halethorpe, Baltimore County. (*Relay House*, Martenet 1866). This name marks the fact that America's first railroad (Baltimore and Ohio, 1828) began by using horses for its motive power. Here the horses were changed. The change was called a *relay*, and the station a "Relay House." Davidson (p. 185) says: "This term, at first applied to the change of horses, was used in speaking of the terminal and also of the surrounding neighborhood, continuing to this day."

Note: Hungerford, noting that *Relay House was "then known as Elkridge Landing," states (I, 73) that here occurred "the first change of horses upon the cars ..." As a Baltimore writer in *West Virginia Hillbilly* (7 Nov. 1970) puts it: "Early company records state that these trains received a 'fresh' relay of horses."

RENONCO CREEK. A tributary of the Nanticoke River, Wicomico County. Compare *Reconow-Creek* (1673 Journal of George Fox). The Primitive Algonquian elements of this name appear to be *leni-* "real, genuine," and *-anakwi* (Fox *wanakwi*) "hollow." The consequent compound would be *len-wanakwi*, which by syncopation could become *lenōn'ku*. This, in a dialect where *l* becomes *r*, would give *renonco*. The meaning would be "Real or genuine hollow."

Note: In April 1672 George Fox, the famous and compelling Quaker fanatic, reached the Patuxent River, Maryland, on a voyage from Jamaica (see: *The Journal of George Fox*, rev. ed., John L. Nickalls ... Cambridge [England], 1952). Fox attended the celebrated General Meeting held at West River, and eventually crossed the Delaware, lying in the woods by a fire "and sometimes at Indians' houses or cabins." In 1673, again in Maryland, after a year of devious American travels, Fox found himself near the Tred Avon River, where he has occasion to mention *Reconow Creek*.

REVELL (REV-L). Village near Arnold, Anne Arundel County. Riley (p. 112) mentions James Revell, President of the Mutual Building Association of Annapolis, and states that in 1867 this association bought the tract that is now Eastport. It made a plat of the place and built a bridge from Annapolis to Horn Point, "as it was then called." On p. 122 Riley mentions "Revell's Station."

Note: *Revell* (on the Baltimore and Annapolis Shortline R.R., USGS 1907 Relay). I have learned (field trip, June 1966) that the surname *Revel* is sometimes pronounced ruh-VELL.

REWASTICO CREEK. A tributary of the Nanticoke River, Wicomico County. Compare Indians of *Rasoughteick* (*Archives*, III, for 1657-60). *Cotton*, III, for 1703-13, spells *Reiwasticoe River*. The first element of the name is probably Delaware *liwasquall* "weeds," where the opening *l* is in an *l*-dialect and would become *r* (as it does) in a Maryland *r*-dialect. With the combining form of *liwasquall* being *liwasqu-*, the rest of the name is quite plausibly "stream" (Primitive Algonquian *-etekw*). The consequent compound (*liwasq- *etekw*) would give *rewastico* in an *r*-dialect. The meaning would be "Weedy stream."

Note: The Primitive Algonquian consonant *l* appears in modern Algonquian sometimes as *l* (Delaware) and sometimes (Maryland) as *r*. Such changes characterize dialects.

REYNOLDS. George's Creek, Allegany County. GMd 1941: *Reynolds*: in Allegany County. The family name *Reynolds* is moderately frequent in the Mt. Savage-Cumberland area. Webb's *Cumberland Directory 1880-81* lists seven persons by that name. TDr Allegany 1968 lists twenty-five. The community is still known (See: Manual 1969).

RHODESDALE. Village near Ennalls, Dorchester County. There are five *Rhodes* in TDr 1963 Dorchester. Heads 1790 lists seven *Rhodes* in as many as six different counties. See Passano for genealogical items.

RICHARDSMERE. A village near Colora, Cecil County. It and Porters Bridge are one and the same place. *Richards Oak* is nearby, and gives a clue to the name. The second element *-mere* means "lake," and one supposes that *Richardsmere* means "Richards Lake."

RICHARDSON. Village near Medford, Carroll County. Perhaps this name has given way to MEDFORD. There are eight *Richardson*[s] in TDr Carroll 1963. The family name is well documented in Passano.

RIDER (RIDERWOOD, RIDERWOOD HILLS). Suburban. Near Ruxton, Baltimore County. Rider existed in 1904; in 1941 it and Riderwood were identical places; in 1969 *Rider disappears and Riderwood and Riderwood Hills are adjacent. The name is from the family name *Rider*, which abounds in Baltimore County. TDr Baltimore 1969 lists 57 members. (See: GMd 1904, Manual 1969).

Note: Sher*wood* is adjacent to Riderwood; the area on the east is sharply hilly (el. 285–495). Doubtless the name consists of *Rider* plus *-wood*(s). I have a note reading: "Col. Rider's Mill. See James Billings's Mill."

RIDGELY. Village southwest of Greensboro, Caroline County. The Guide (pp. 416–17) tells of the failure in 1867 of an attempt to lay out the town of Ridgeley, when there was a land promotion scheme. Later, with the coming of a railroad, the project succeeded. Both the Guide and Hill ascribe the name to Rev. Greenbury W. Ridgeley. The Guide mentions that he had been a law partner of Henry Clay; Hill states that his home was "Oaklawn." (See: Hill, MCC, pp. 238–39).

RIDGEVILLE. Village near Mount Airy, Carroll and Frederick Counties. (*Ridgeville* 1827 PHC). Note 130, PHC, explains: "'Ridgeville' was changed to 'Parrsville' in 1830 and was changed back to 'Ridgeville' in 1837. 'Ridgeville' was moved into Carroll County in 1844 or 1845 and was changed to 'Mount Airy' in 1845." The village (el. 850) is on an early "Ridge Road" and probably takes its name from PARRS RIDGE.

RIDOUT CREEK [RIDE-out]. A branch of Whitehall Creek, near St. Margarets, Anne Arundel County. In 1878 (see Hopkins) there lived in this area Weelus and Horatio Ridout, and Rev. Samuel & Jno. Ridout, M.D.

In neighboring Annapolis, the Anne Arundel County Committee of the Maryland Historical Trust is the custodian of an annual Orlando V. Ridout IV award. In 1977 The London Town Publik House and Gardens was the Recipient. (See: *Capital*, 17 May 1977, "Historic Trust Presents Orlando Ridout Award").

RIGGS MILLS. The family name *Riggs* abounds in the nomenclature of this area. Warfield (p. 354) mentions John Riggs, of "Riggs Hills," probably near Annapolis Junction north of the present Laurel. Farquhar (p. 164) notices Remus Riggs and Reuben Riggs (fl. 1833). F. B. Culver remarks that John Riggs, the family's founder, is first mentioned in Maryland records in 1716, when John Marriott devised him fifty acres of "Sheppard's Forest," in Anne Arundel County. The Md. Manual of Coordinates, 1969, lists *Riggs Mill Village*, *Riggs Mill Manor*, and *Riggs Road* all in Prince George's County, near College Park. An examination of coordinates makes it evident that Riggs Mill Village and Adelphi are today one and the same place. I conclude that *Riggs Mill Village has been renamed Adelphi.

Note: Important members of the Riggs family lived in Montgomery County. The Evening *Capital* (Jan. 3, 1980) calls attention to an effort to save from a landfill "The Oaks," the former home, near Laytonsville, of ". . . the Riggs family, which founded the District's largest bank and was prominent in Montgomery County affairs of the last century." See ADELPHI.

RINGGOLD. Village near Leitersburg, Washington County. (*Ringgold* 1850 PHC). Both the Guide (p. 515) and Williams (p. 510) state the first name of this village was *Ridgeville. When the post office was established (1850) the name became *Ringgold*, for Major Samuel Ringgold, of the Mexican War. According to Williams he was born at his father's house ("Fountain Rock," Conococheague Manor; *General* Samuel Ringgold) in 1800. He died at the Battle of Palo Alto in 1846.

Note: I conclude from Williams (I, 197) that *General* Samuel Ringgold, son of Thomas Ringgold, was born in Kent County in 1762.

"RINGGOLD'S GREEN." Caroline County. Cochrane (p. 245) describes this community as a crossroads near the Delaware state line. It was known in Revolutionary times. Cochrane thinks that the name was given owing to the constant "greenness" of the surrounding swampy region.

Note: *Not* in GMd 1941; *not* in Manual 1947; but *Ringgolds Green*, Manual 1969. Heads 1790 lists no Ringgold[s] for Caroline Co. However, TDr . . . Caroline 1963 lists five.

RISING SUN. Town, seven miles from Port Deposit, Cecil County. (*Rising Sun* 1802 PHC). The Guide, Miller, and Johnston all agree that the first name of this place was *Summer Hill. The Guide attributes the present name to "a tavern whose shingle depicted the sun peeping over the horizon." Miller, however, though he acknowledges the existence here of a tavern called "Sunrise Tavern," declares that the origin of the name is "shrouded in uncertainty." He repeats the story that the name arose because the people who used to rise before daylight to take produce to Port Deposit passed through Rising Sun at about daybreak. In support of the tavern theory, one keeps in mind Vallandigham's remark: "Old inns furnish such names to villages and hamlets as . . . Rising Sun . . ." (See: *Delaware and the Eastern Shore*, 1922, pp. 57–58).

Note: Maryland has three additional "rising sun" names: "Rising Sun," a Baltimore Inn (Stockett, p. 122); "Rising Sun Tavern," Hagerstown (Williams, I, 157): and "Rising Sun Tavern of 1753" (Mrs. M. H. Nelker, "From the Colorful Past," *Capital*, March 6, 1969). Mrs. Nelker describes the third place as being on the road to Crownsville from Route 3 (Anne Arundel County). Cf. "Rising Sun Tavern," Windmill Street and Tottenham Court Road, London, England (fl. 1954?).

RISON [RISE-n]. Village near Marbury, Charles County. Mrs. J. R. Scott (of Welcome, Charles County; 1971) gave me the pronunciation. She remarked that some say it is from "rising sun." That, however, is untrue. The name comes indubitably from the surname. Md. Sub. TDr 1974-75 lists twelve *Risons*, five of them in the vicinity of the village (RISON) and one (Robert *Rison*) from Rison itself.

RIVA [REE-vuh]. South River, near Annapolis, Anne Arundel County. (*Riverview*, GMd 1904; *Riverview*, USGS 1905 Owensville; *Riva*, GMd 1941; *Riva*, Manual 1969). Thelma W. Billings (p.m., Riva, Aug. 1950) informs me that the earlier name was *Waterview*, and that the change to *Riva* occurred "sometimes in /the/ 1920's." Ms. Billings was probably wrong about *Waterview*. For it appears from the map spellings that the earlier name was *River*view. The location on or near South River accounts for the names.

Note: Etymologically, *Riva* is from Latin *rivus* "small stream of water, a brook." The name is of great rarity in the United States. Cf. Riva, a steamship station at the northern end of Lake Garda, Tirol, Austria, near the Italian frontier.

RIVERDALE. Town near Hyattsville, Prince George's County. In 1800 the region of present-day RIVERDALE—"low, meadow-land" lying between the "upper reaches" of Paint Branch and the N.W. Branch of the Anacostia River—became "the plantation of Riversdale." And in 1803 George Calvert (1768-1838) and Rosalie Eugenia Stier (1778-1821) moved from Mont Alban to "Riversdale" mansion. It appears that by 1927 the mansion was no longer known as "Riversdale," but as the "Calvert Mansion," And the name "Riversdale," modified to *Riverdale*, had been given to the suburban community which developed around the local B. & O. R.R. station. Notice the characteristic loss of *s*. (See: *MHM*, XLV: 4, Dec. 1950, pp. 271-93).

Note: Today the grounds of the Calvert Mansion, Riverdale, are known as "Calvert Gateway Memorial Park." (See: *Md. Clubwoman*, 42: 3, March 1969, p. 30).

RIVERSIDE. Village near Nanjemoy Creek, Potomac River, Charles County. The Guide (p. 490) mentions this place as ". . . one of several river resorts of the peninsula frequented by Washingtonians in summer . . ." Cf. *Riverside*, a Baltimore suburb; *Riverside*, a Kent County village, Chester River; *Riverside*, a Talbot County village; etc.

RIVERSIDE. Community? Near the junction of the Hawlings River and the Patuxent, Montgomery County. ("*Riverside*: in Montgomery County." GMd 1941). Farquhar (p. 262) speaks of "Riverside" (built in 1855), a "delightful old house," on a promontory four hundred feet high, ". . . the land sloping steeply to the Patuxent through thick woods."

RIVERTON. Hamlet near the Ashton-Brighton Road (in early deeds, the Bladensburg-New Market Pike), Hawlings River, Montgomery

County. Farquhar (p. 264) states that before the Civil War the land here was known as BROOKE BLACK MEADOW. James Brooke, the elder, had died in 1784. Mrs. George F. Nesbitt relates that Elisha Hall, moving here in about 1860, renamed the house at BLACK MEADOW "Riverton." Mrs. Nesbitt writes me (19 April 1975) that it is situated "beside the Hawlings River." (See: "To Fairfield with Love," *MHM*, 70: 1, Spring 1975; p. 79).

*RIVERVIEW. See Riva.

RIVIERA BEACH. A village on the Patapsco River, near Solley, Anne Arundel County. Across the river at this place one can see Bethlehem's Sparrows Point steel plant. *Rivera Beach* (GMd 1941, Manual 1947); *Riviera Beach* (Manuals 1962, 1969). Evidently, between 1947 and 1962, the spelling was changed from *Rivera* to *Riviera*. The present pronunciation is indicated by the following title of a *Sun* article by Robert Fugetta: "Call it 'Rivera'; Rive-ee-era Sounds too Ritzy."

Fugetta describes Riviera Beach as "... a crowded, middle-class community of duplex and single homes, on a peninsula along the county's north shore." The region did not become a summer resort until the 1920's, when T. W. Pumphrey and his brothers bought the peninsula and formed the Riviera Beach Development Co. There was an influx of defense workers during World War II. (See: *Sun* [Mag.] 11 Feb. 1979).

ROBERTS. Village near Cumberland, Allegany County. The proximity to Cumberland suggests that this place takes it name from one of the Roberts[8] mentioned by TW (II, 856–58): William Milnor Roberts I, civil engineer and railroad builder; William Milnor Roberts II (d. Cumberland, 1920), railroad builder; and William Milnor Roberts III (b. Brazil, 1865), a General Manager of the Edison Electric Illumination Co. of Cumberland, Cf. Roberts (Queen Anne's County), Roberts Island (Harford County), Roberts Mills (Carroll County).

Note: Roberts was probably a station on the B. & O. R.R. Stein (p. 306) points out that Robert Roberts (d. 1728) was the first of the line in Calvert County, and that the Roberts family is one of the most widely dispersed Puritan families that settled in the Colonies.

*ROBEYSTOWN. Prince George's County. In a letter asking *Why*, Congressman Frank Small indicates that the Clinton Community, Prince George's County, was once called *Robeystown*. He adds that in the "mid-19th century" the community was called *Surrattsville*. (See: N. & Q., *MHM*, XLIX: 2, June 1954). See CLINTON.

Note: A. L. Keith mentions marriages of Esther Smallwood and Ann Smallwood with *Rob(e)ys*. Keith mentions Harriet, Grace, Walter, Garrett, and Leonard S. Robey; he lists several marriages with Prince George's County families. (See: "Smallwood Family of Charles County," *MHM*, XXII: 2, June 1937).

ROCKAWALKING CREEK. A tributary of the Wicomico River, Wicomico County; also a village (Rockawalking) on that Creek. Footner remarks: "The Wicomico River was originally called Rockiawackin." *Archives* (38, for 1697) mentions the "Nations of Rockawakinmany ... Summersett County." Cf. *Righkahauk* (Va. 1608 Smith).

The Sixth USGB decision, ". . . Not Rock a-walking," brings to mind that the folk explanation of this name rests on the totally false story that one day, when Mr. Rock came to town without his horse, someone cried" "Here comes Rock a-walking!" The truth is that *Rockawalking* is Maryland Algonquian and has recognizable Delaware language *r-* dialect counterparts on Long Island (*Rockaway*) and in Pennsylvania (*Lackawaxen Creek*).

There are two solutions, the simplest one being that *Rockawalking* contains an *r-* dialect form of Delaware *lehauwak* "fork." One has only to add the locative suffix *-ink* to obtain **lechauwak-ink*, which in an *r-*dialect gives **rechauwakink* or *rockawalking*. It means "Place of the fork (in a road or stream)." The second solution, which I prefer and which has the support of Tooker, Gerard, and Ruttenber, also explains several comparable names, for instance Rahway, N.J. It consists simply of deriving *Rockawalking* from Delaware *lekau* "sand" (Prim. Algonquian **lākaw*). Compounded with *-āwank-* "land" and the locative *-ink*, it becomes the primitive **lākaw-āwank-ingki*. This in an *r-* dialect, contracts to *Rockawalking* and would mean "At the sandy ground." (For a full discussion of Algonquian dialects and related placenames, see the present author's "Place-Names and Dialects: Algonquian," *Names*, 24: 2, June 1976).

ROCK HALL.   Town at Rock Hall Harbor, 5 miles south of Tolchester Beach, Kent County. (*Rock Hall*, Griffith 1794; *Rock Hall* 1806 PHC). Note 70, PHC reads: "'Rock Hall' was changed to 'Eastern Neck' in 1840 and was changed back to 'Rock Hall' in 1841." The historic marker here attributes the name to "Rock Hall Mansion," which stood at the landing one mile west of the town. Cf. "Rock Hall," a 300-a. tract near Rohrer's Mill, Washington County. Cf., also, "Rock Hall" a colonial mansion of local white sandstone, built at the foot of Sugar Loaf Mountain, 1812.

Note: The Guide mentions the theory that Rock *Hall* is from "rock *haul*," so given because of the large *hauls* of rock fish made there. Usilton, while conceding the existence of "Rock Hall Farm," owned in 1774 by Richard Spencer, believes that the town takes its name *not* from the rocks, ". . . of which there are none to be seen," but from "a large haul of rock fish" taken before Baltimore was incorporated, Lantz (p. 172) also accepts the rock fish origin. Cf. ROCKHOLD (ROCK-HOLE) CREEK, Anne Arundel County, and ROCK HOLE, an inlet of Tangier Sound, Somerset County.

On second thought, I am persuaded that *Hall* in Rock Hall may well mean "hole." *Hall*, *haul*, and *hole* are similarly pronounced; and the meaning, **Rock Hole*, is analogous to Rockhold (Rockhole) Creek, Anne Arundel, and to Rock Hole, Tangier.

ROCKHOLD CREEK.   GMd 1941 describes this stream as a branch of Herring Bay near Deale, Anne Arundel County. It also lists a variant,

Rockhole Creek. The variant spelling suggests that this was once a *hole* abounding in rock fish.

Note: Gene Bisbee remarks that "At the time of the Revolutionary War, Rockhold Creek was named Gotts Creek." (See: "Deale Ways ...," *Capital*, 24 Sept. 1979; Hopkins 1878 [Got Cr]). See *GOTTS CREEK; See ROCK HALL.

ROCKLAND. GMd 1941: "Rockland: in Montgomery County." Perhaps this name comes from "Rockland," which Farquhar (p. 267) gives as the old frame house where Benjamin Hallowell came to live in 1842. Cf. the village of ROCKLAND, near Ellicott City, Howard Co. See ROCKLAND, Baltimore County.

ROCKLAND. A village south of Brooklandville, Baltimore County. The Brooklandville post office is here; Rockland cannot be a post office because of Rockland, Howard County. This place came to light in 1978 when the Azola Building Co. bought & restored the Rockland Grist Mill (1813) and proceeded to built 73 expensive new homes. They are described as being of "rough-hewn wood and stone to harmonize with the landscape."

Rockland is in an area of wooded hills; stone appears to be an abundant building material. The name is evidently descriptive.

Note: The village has an industrial history. The grist mill once housed the Rockland Calico Print Works. And in a nearby building in 1831 Robert Wright, an Englishman, opened the Rockland Bleach and Dye Works. (See: Charles Flowers, "Rockland is home to very new houses, very old mill," *Sun*, Feb. 17, 1980).

ROCK SPRINGS. Village near Richardsmere, Cecil County. (*Rock Springs* 1830 PHC). The elevation is about 500 feet and there are hilly slopes Cf. Rock Springs Church, one mile north, in Pennsylvania.

ROCKVILLE. Five miles southeast of Gaithersburg, Montgomery County. (Rockville 1817? PHC). PHC has the following note (129): "'Montgomery Court House' was changed to 'Rockville,' probably in 1817.... It seems most likely that the change of names took place in May, 1817. In one appointment book a notation reads: 'Blackshears—see Montgomery Court House.'" The Guide states that ROCKVILLE was first called *Montgomery Court House* and later *Williamsburg*. Farquhar (pp. 193–94) notes that after 1774 it was known as *Hungerford's*, and that in 1784, when it was surveyed for William Prather, it was laid out in streets and became *Williamsburg*. *Hungerford's* was from Charles Hungerford's tavern (1774); the name *Montgomery Court House* persisted even after the change to *Rockville*. In a slightly different version Farquhar declares:

Note: Peter L. Smith (letter, *Star*, Dec. 22, 1962), commenting that ROCKVILLE was once known as *Hungerford's Tavern* and *Williamsburg*, objects to the present name. He proposes that it be changed to *Hungerford, King William*, etc. And he comments that the mayor and city council have twice rejected proposals to change the name.

"At that time the name of Williamsburg was changed to Rockville apparently to honor Rock Creek, one of the most beautiful streams in the state
of Maryland.

RODGERS FORGE.   Baltimore suburb. (GMd 1941: a town two miles
s.w. of Towson). The following excerpt indicates what happened to more
than one Baltimore suburb following World War II: "Rodgers Forge,
farmland when Scott Fitzgerald lived there, became a maze of brick, each
block with its garbage-truck mews." (See: "Joke Was on Us," *News-
American*, 23 Feb. 1969),

ROE.   A village near Price, Queen Anne's County. This name is probably an abbreviation of *ROESVILLE*, a post office in 1866. Emory states
that in 1841 James Roe and his son kept a store at *Roe's Cross Roads,
afterwards *Roesville.

ROHRERSVILLE.   Near   Locust   Grove,   Washington   County.
(Rohrersville 1836 PHC). Williams names Frederick Rohrer (b. France,
1742), who came to Washington County in 1766, as the progenitor of the
Rohrer family and the father of David Rohrer "founder" of the town. Bell
mentions the pre-Revolutionary "Rohrer's Mill," situated on Antietam
Creek, four miles from Hagerstown. I notice that in 1878 (v. Lewis) J. V.
Rohrer was the postmaster here, D. A. Rohrer, the railroad agent, D. A.
Rohrer and J. V. Rohrer, general merchants, and M. T. Rohrer, a miller.
(See: Williams, II, 963; Bell, Leitersburg, p. 114).

Note: PHC (n. 61) states that "Cramptons Gap" was changed to "Rohrersville in
1836. Today the village of Crampton Gap is two miles southeast of Rohrersville.
And Trego, the site of Rohrersville Station (B & O. R.R., Hagerstown Branch), is
three-fourths of a mile from ROHRERSVILLE.

ROLAND PARK.   Northern suburban region of Baltimore City, comprising Lake Roland and Roland Avenue. One of the nation's oldest
planned garden suburbs, it was named for Roland Thornberry, a Baltimore County landowner. The Roland Park Company was incorporated on
July 30, 1891. For a description of the historical marker recently erected
here by the Roland Park Civic League, see *News and Notes* [MHS], 6, n.s.,
5 January 1978.

*ROLL CAMP Sta.[n]   Anne Arundel County. This is *Roll Camp Sta.[n]* in
Hopkins 1878. Cf. CAMP PAROLE, which this form may stand for. See
PAROLE.

ROLPHS.   [*o* as in rose].   Village. Chester River, near Church Hill,
Queen Anne's County. (*Rolphs* Landing and Vil, Manual 1969). Here (30
Aug. 1967) I found the marina of the Rolph Point Yacht Club, Inc. It was
for sale for $45,000; and the descriptive brochure states that it was once a
"busy little port" with a post office and store. Members of the *Rolph* family are abundantly listed by Emory. It appears, for instance, that in 1808
(v. Emory, p. 380) Ensign James Rolph was a member of Captain

Fogwell's military company. Richard S. Rolph was postmaster at *Sudler's Cross Roads in 1834, and again at Millington in 1845. In 1860 James O. Rolph had a store at Church Hill. See RALPH.

ROMANCOKE [ROMAN-coke]. A hamlet in the southeastern part of Kent Island, Queen Anne's County; also the name of the Romancoke-Claiborne Ferry, which was discontinued on Dec. 31, 1952. The name was brought here from Virginia by Colonel William Claiborne to denote his plantation on Kent Island. *Romancoke in Virginia—where Claiborne was known as "Claiborne of Romancoke"—was spelled *Romangkok* (Patent, 1653) and designated a region near Cohoke Creek and the junction of the Pamunkey and Mattapony Rivers.

Sams (*Conquest of Va.*, p. 319) includes *Ro-man-coke* in a list of Indian names retained in eastern Virginia. Green (*Word book* ..., p. 524) defines it as "Circling Waters."

There appears to be no linguistic basis for Green's translation. However, there are two Powhatan words that may, to some degree, explain *Romancoke*. I refer to *rom-* "low," which one finds in Strachey's *romutton* "hill of small mount" (where *-utton* means "hill"), and *cohoke*, which contracts nicely to *-coke*. I have no meaning for *cohoke*. But it is plausible to combine Strachey's *rom-* with general Algonquian "ground" (Fox *-āwak*, Ojibwa *-awank*) and obtain the indicative prototype *rom-awank-at-wi*. To arrive at the present form one would replace *-at-wi* by the conjunctive ending *-ak*. The result would be *rom-awank-ak* (*Romancoke*) "Where there is low-lying ground." Cf. *Chericoke*, Pamunkey River, King William County, Va., and Cohoke, a Virginia post office. (See: Nathan C. Hale, *Virginia Venturer a Historical Biography of William Claiborne 1600–1677* [Richmond, 1951], pp. 296–97).

Note: I think of *Cohoke* as a suffixal fragment standing alone as a name. Perhaps it is a denasalized form of Delaware and Powhatan *kaak, kahunge* "goose."

ROSARYVILLE. Near Cheltenham, Prince George's County. Here, in Rosaryville State Park, a little woods where there are blacksnakes and raccoons, one finds the somewhat restored ruins of an old manor house, "Mt. Airy."

Mr. John M. Walton, Jr. (Park Historian, The Md.-National Capital Park and Planning Commission) informs me that Rosaryville takes its name from "Holy Rosary Church or the Church of the Holy Rosary," the first Catholic church to be built here (ca. late 1850's). He adds: "The original church was destroyed by a storm in the 1920's and was replaced by the current Holy Rosary Church ..."

Note: Site visited on Oct. 19, 1978.

ROSE HILL. Villages: Dorchester County (GMd 1941); Antietam Creek, near Funkstown, Washington County (GMd 1941); Charles County

(Manual 1969). The name appears to come from homes and estates. The Guide mentions Rose Hill (Dorchester County) as one of the "... seven Rose Hills in Maryland." It had been inhabited by the Webster family. Kinney (p. 440) notices Rose Hill, Charles County: "Travelling north from St. Mary's into Charles County, I came to Rose Hill, home of George Washington's personal 'chirurgeon.' ... Since the State has at least six other Rose Hills, this one must be called Dr. Brown's Rose Hill."

ROSLYN. Village near Pikesville, Baltimore County. "Roslyn," whence this Baltimore County name, was the estate of Benjamin C. Howard, son of one Colonel Howard, and, for several years, a member of Congress from Maryland. "Roslyn," whence the apparently extinct Montgomery County name, was the home of Henry Stabler, horticulturalist, who came here between 1842–44. Both Roslyn⁵ are probably Scottish. *Roslin* ("moor of hollies") is in Edinburghshire, Scotland. A battle was fought there in 1803. The Scotch placename is probably seen in the title, Earl(s) of *Rosslyn*. (See: Davidson, p. 111; Farquhar, p. 281).

ROSSVILLE. Village near the town of Stemmer Run, Baltimore County, (*Rossville* 1839 PHC). Cf. Rossville, Prince George's County, and Rossville, Prince George's (where there is the Rossville Area Resettlement Administration). *Ross* is an abundant family name in Maryland. There are thirty-two *Ross* in Heads 1790, six of them in "Baltimore Town." The families have grown; TDr Baltimore 1969 has 462 entries.

ROTH ROCK MOUNTAIN. Near Redhouse, Garrett County. [El. 2860]. (*Roth Rock Mountain*, GMd 1941). The name may be from the surname *Roth*. On the other hand, especially if the name applies to an entire mountain, the abundant family name *Rothrock* (*Rotruck*) appears likely.

ROTTERDAM. Archives, LI (p. 12, p. 33, for 1669), mentions: "... Fifty Acres called Rotterdam lying near Nangemoy Indian Town ..."

ROUNDTOP. Hill and village. Tonoloway Ridge, near Hancock, Washington County. Williams (I, 212–13) describes a cement mill near a precipitous cliff on the "ber*m* side" of the C. & O. Canal: "This mill is situated at the commencement of the very heavy work at Round Hill, which reaches about a mile. This mill is the same long owned and operated by Bridges and Henderson, and the Round Top Cement enjoys a reputation which is greatly increased since ... /April 1839, the day the C. & O. Canal was opened at these points/ ..." The el. of the hill is 1,388; the village is 450.

Cf. Roundtop Mountain (in Catoctin Mountain), Frederick County. (GMd 1941; el. 1,640).

ROWLANDSVILLE. Near Colora, Cecil County. (*Rowlandsville* 1826 PHC). Miller (p. 134) states that Rowlandsville is "prominently linked" with the Rowlands. He finds the name of *Rowland* on the records of Cecil County in 1749, when James Rowland and his sons, William and Robert, bought part of a tract called "Glass House." William Rowland owned land and mills on Basin Run. For ROWLANDSVILLE in 1878, Lewis lists Dr. Samuel Rowland, and Postmaster W. B. Rowland.

ROXBURY MILLS. Village near Glenwood, Howard County. (*Roxbury* Mills 1832 PHC). Warfield (p. 440) mentions ". . . a new store and postoffice, a mill, a blacksmith shop, with its residence, all upon the Cattail River, upon the site of 'Roxbury Hall' . . ." He adds that the survey was made by Colonel Richard Dorsey; the settlement was "rocky and Romantic." Cf. Roxbury (today part of Boston), Massachusetts, which *Origin of Mass. Place Names* (Mass. WPA, 1947) explains as "So named because of the large number of rocks found on the surface of the land." However, both names appear to be secondarily derived from *Roxburgh*, Scotland ("Castle of /the/ rook/s").

Note: Col. Dorsey's survey was of "the Cat-tail . . ." (today Cattail Creek).

ROYAL OAK. Village near St. Michaels, Talbot County. (*Royal Oak* 1837 PHC). The Guide attributes the name to "a giant tree" that was hit by two British cannonballs during the bombardment of St. Michaels in 1813. Muriel Dobbin relates that a cannonball lodged in the tree. Shannahan (pp. 43–45), repeating the bombardment story, calls the tree "a gigantic white oak." But he indicates that perhaps the town was known as Royal Oak before the War of 1812, its name having come from this self-same tree. Ingraham (pp. 114–15) speaks of ". . . the famous oak that from this engagement /bombardment; War of 1812/ was called Royal, a veritable monster of the forest . . ." According to Ingraham it fell in 1864. (See Dobbin: "A Shot that Named a Town," *Sun* [Mag.], July 30, 1961).

Note: Cf. Royal Oak, near Wetipquin, Wicomico County. Frederick A. Crockett, of this place (July 21, 1966), speaks of the royal oak as an oak tree from the royal forest. He states that there used to be several big oaks here.

RUMBLEY. Village. Manokin River (at Goose Creek), three miles west of Fairmount, Somerset County. Cf. *Rumbley point*, Tangier Sound, Somerset County and *Rumbley Point* [pron: rumbling], Pocomoke Sound, Somerset County. The name of the village is related to the name of a point. Carroll Bozman (crab packer) and Cecil Ford (Fairmount) both agreed (June 28, 1966) that there are no rumbling noises at Rumbley Point, Tangier Sound. Bozman suggested thunder; Ford seemed to recall another "Rumbling Point." As for Rumbley Point, Pocomoke Sound, those whom I talked to at D. H. White's store, Shelltown (June 28, 1966), all agreed that the water at this point does not make a rumbling noise. They suggested that perhaps the wind was accountable.

Note: William McLane, postmaster at Manokin (June 12, 1953), explained to me that "/The/ water here makes a rumbling noise." See TULL'S POINT. It should not be overlooked that Rumbley in these names could be from the family name *Rumbly*. Heads 1790, for Caroline County, lists Mary *Rumble*, Henry and Lydia *Rumbly*.

RUSHVILLE. Potomac River, Seneca Creek, near Seneca, Montgomery County. (*Rushville* 1832 PHC). PHC notes: " 'Seneca Mills' was changed to 'Rushville' in 1832. 'Seneca Mills' was changed to 'Dawsonville' in 1854." There are only three *Rush* in Heads 1790. TDR 1974-75 Md. Sub. D.C., however, lists forty-eight families.

RUTHSBURG. Village near Hope, Queen Anne's County. (*Ruthsburg* 1842 PHC). Emory (p. 330) state that in 1812 Ruthsburg was known as the "Cross Roads by Henry Pratt's." He adds that the village had the name *Ruthsburg* or *Ruthsborough* in 1861, and perhaps even earlier. Emory (p. 129) mentions Christopher Cross Ruth, a county justice in 1765. As for the Ruth family in general, he declares that no names in the pages of Maryland history are more honorable than those of *Ruth*, ". . . who have served their state and country in various posts of trust and honor."

Note: MHGP (1963, p. 38) describes the *Pratt* mansion near Ruthsburg and remarks that the early wing of the house, built in 1710, belonged to "the Ruth family."

RUXTON. Town near Towson, Baltimore County. MHGP (1964, p. 32) relates that in 1885 the Northern Central R.R. built a station here. It explains that the name is from the Ruxton family, whose immediate progenitor, Nicholas Ruxton Moore, was a Revolutionary War officer and a Maryland congressman. Towards the end of the 18th century he owned "the farm just west of Ruxton railroad bridge."

S

SABILLASVILLE. Near Lantz, Frederick County. (*Sabillasville* 1830 PHC). Lewis lists Wm. M. Sibley (blacksmith and wheelwright) under Urbana, near Ijamsville. Perhaps Sabillasville is from the family name *Sibley*. On the other hand, it could be from a girl's given name. Williams (I, 113) mentions the marriage, in 1792, of one Captain Carberry to the "amiable Miss Sybila Schnertzell of Frederick County."

Note: PHC (p. 87) notices that " 'Sibylsville,' which also appears as 'Sybilisville,' was changed in 1830 to 'Sabillasville,' which also appears as 'Sabillisville.' "

SAINT. ... Kuethe (". . . Strange Origins") remarks that (in 1634) "Lord Baltimore's colonists . . . Devout Catholics that they were . . . named places in honor of the saints . . . St. Mary's town, county and river, St. Catherine Island, St. Clement Bay, St. Inigoe Creek, St. George Island, to name a few . . ."

St. AUGUSTINE. Village near Chesapeake City, Cecil County. (*St. Augustine*, Mitchell 1865). Augustine Herrman founded "Bohemia Manor" near here.

St. CHARLES. Community near Waldorf, Charles County. The *Star* (8 Jan. 1965) describes this place as "St. Charles City," a "planned community located at Waldorf . . ." Construction was to begin "soon." The same source (three years later; 1 March 1968) states that ". . . it is planned for an ultimate population of 100,000." The name is probably from *Charles* County. Cf. St. Charles College (near Doughoregan Manor, Howard County, founded by *Charles* Carroll of Carrollton.

*St. CLEMENTS ISLAND. St. Mary's County. Named in 1634 by the first colonists; later renamed *Blackistone* (for Nehemiah Blackstone). See BLACKISTON (BLAKISTONE) ISLAND. See CLEMENTS.

St. DENIS. Town near Relay, Baltimore County. (*Saint Denis* 1851 PHC). Lewis 1878 remarks: "The Washington Branch /B. & O. R.R./ joins the main line here and it is known as Relay Station." Davidson (pp. 186–87) explains that *St. Denis* is from a certain *Denis* A. Smith, former state treasurer, who owned much of the land. "He was instrumental in having a post office established in the village." According to Davidson, the nickname "Saint" was given to Denis by his associates because of "high doings" in the "stone house where he entertained." See RELAY.

Note: Davidson goes on to say that Denis Smith "failed," and his property was bought by Samuel Sutton. It was low and swampy and was called "Chile Valley" before being named "St. Denis."

St. GEORGE. Village near Reisterstown, Baltimore County. Directly or indirectly, the name comes from St. George (d. 303), patron saint of England. The first use of St. George as a placename in Maryland was probably in *St. George's River*, St. Mary's County. Today it is *St. MARY'S RIVER*. See *St. MARY'S CITY;* see *YOWACCOMOCO.

Note: St. George can be a given name (e.g., *St. George* Tucker, Virginia jurist).

St. HELENA. Village near Sparrows Point, Baltimore County. Its first name was perhaps *Longwood* (v. Davidson, pp. 217–18), so given because the southern boundary ran "right to the woods." When Col. Arthur Bryan lived here, he called it "Bonaparte." His daughters objected to "Bonaparte," and he changed the name to *St. Helena*, for Napoleon's place of exile. *Bonaparte perhaps arose from the fact that *Longwood was also the name of the estate where Napoleon was imprisoned. (See: Davidson, pp. 217–18).

Note: Cf. St. HELENA ISLAND, Anne Arundel County. In "St. Helena" (*Extra*, Dec. 10, 1972, pp. 9–10), Clark Smith cites a local member of the Colegate family who has documents tracing this settlement to William Colegate (1675–1722), of Colgate Creek. It appears that Davidson's Arthur Bryan was an Englishman who had fought in the Napoleonic campaigns.

St. INIGOES. Village near St. Mary's City, St. Mary's County. (*St. Inigoes* 1801 PHC). *Inigo* was the baptismal name (*Inigo* Lopez de Recalde) of St. Ignatius of Loyola (1491–1556), founder of the Society of Jesus. Lantz states that St. Inigoes Manor was patented to the Jesuit priest, Thomas Copley (d. 1653). According to Andrews, the manor church, built later, was called St. Ignatius.

Note: Riley (p. 4) cites Father Andrew White as calling St. Ignatius the patron saint of Maryland. It appears that the saint signed his name both *Ignatius* and *Inigo*. Andrews designates him as Eneco of Inigo (a Moorish name handed down in his family). The more correct form is said to be *Inigoes*.

St. LEONARD. Creek and village, near Port Republic, Calvert County. The name of the creek precedes that of the village. Stein finds that "the town of St. Leonard's, at the head of navigation of St. Leonard's Creek," was reestablished by the Commissioners in 1683. The creek had by then lost some of its depth, and the new town was located slightly farther downstream. Stein mentions that "An Act of Assembly of 1735 authorized a new and enlarged St. Leonard's Town . . ." The new town was to have better facilities for handling increased shipments of tobacco.

Note: St. Leonard was the patron saint of captives. One supposes that St. Leonard Creek (whence the town name) was named by (or for) *Leonard* Calvert.

St. MARGARETS. Village near Skidmore, Anne Arundel County. (*Saint Margarets* 1855 PHC). The place is in ". . . the St. Margarets area," formerly known as Broad Neck Hundred. Here was made the first Annapolis settlement (1649). MHGP (1964) states that the parish was founded in 1692. Riley explains: "The village of St. Margaret's takes its name from St. Margaret's Parish, whose church is in the village. The parish is supposed to have taken its name from St. Margaret's Chapel, Westminster, England. St. Margarets, though venerable in name, is an origin of the present century, probably three fourths of a century old."

Note: Rosamond Beirne (*MHM*, XLV, 1950, p. 305) states that there have been three churches here. The first, which burned down, was in 1692. The second, built in 1731, burned down in 1823. The present church, the third, is the one that gives the community its name.

St. MARY'S CITY. Town. St. Mary's River, St. Mary's County. The first settlers, having reached Maryland in two boats, the *Ark* and the *Dove*, on Ladie's Day, Feast of the Annunciation, March 25, 1634, landed on St. Clement's Island. Their next move was to ascend what became St. MARY'S RIVER. Here, along with thirty miles of land, they bought *Yaocomico*, an Indian village whose occupants were on the point of moving away to escape the ravages of the Susquehannock Indians. The colonists renamed the village St. MARIES. Radoff refers to Leonard Calvert's purchase of the Indian village which he named after the Virgin Mary. Forman explains: "Because the founders of Maryland were devout Roman Catholics, the first capital was named for the Virgin. St. Mary's was *her* city, dedicated to *her,* in almost the same way that Notre Dame de Chartres Cathedral was built as *her* palace. Every time the name of the little Maryland settlement was spoken she was indirectly complimented." See *YAOCOMICO; see St. GEORGE RIVER.

St. MARY'S COUNTY. Riley indicates that the area bought by Leonard Calvert from "King Yocomico" was first named "Augusta Carolina." In time it became *St. Mary's County.* Wilstach explains that Lord Baltimore named St. MARY'S COUNTY "... for the patron saint selected by the Pilgrims in the *Ark* and the *Dove."* Gannett however, attributes the name to Queen Henrietta *Maria,* the source also of *Maryland.* Certainly the name of the City is from the Saint (B. V. M.); and I have little doubt that this is true of the County. However, see St. MARY'S RIVER (where I cite Stevens). (See also: Mathews, p. 421).

Note: Hill (MCC, p. 70) points out that in 1654, after the Puritan Commissioners seized the Provincial government, *St. Mary's County* was changed to *Potomac County,* "... reverting to the original name after the return of the Proprietary Government."

St. MARY'S RIVER. Stevens (*Annapolis,* p. 30) relates: "After preliminary explorations and peaceful dealing with the Indians, Leonard Calvert entered the river or 'inlet' of the bay (still known by the name he gave it as a devout Catholic, '*St. Mary's*') and laid the foundation of a settlement on the east bank, which he called St. Mary's City. Perhaps too, these names did graceful homage to the patron saint of the queen for whom the new colony was officially named *Terra Mariae.*"

St. MICHAELS. Town about eight miles from Easton, Talbot County, (*Saint Michaels* 1801 PHC). St. Michaels is on the *Miles* River, itself supposed to have taken its name from *St. Michaels River.* Parran (p. 78 ff.) notes that Edward Elliott, an immigrant to Maryland in 1667, donated the land for St. Michaels Church "Around which the town of St. Michael grew ..." Lantz (pp. 292–93) states that this church, the first building here, was built in 1690. According to Ingraham, St. Michael's Parish was Episcopalian.

*St. MICHAELS RIVER. (*St. Michalis R.* Senex 1719; *Miles River,* USGS 1904, St. Michaels, Md.). See MILES RIVER.

St. PETERS CREEK. Village near Oriole, Somerset County. The village is at the head of St. Peter's Creek, a tributary of the Manokin River. "St. Peters" (St. Peters District) is today the name of the Methodist church near Oriole. Marion Hall (*Oriole*) states that Peter Elzey was granted 400 acres between St. Peter's Creek and Genngaukin [sic] Creek. Many families settled here; the place grew and needed a post office. William Thomas Smith, who requested the office, was given the privilege of finding a name. Because of St. Peter's Creek, St. Peter's Methodist Church, and St. Peter's District, *St. Peter's* was the logical choice. However, there was already a St. Peter's in Maryland. *Oriole* was therefore preferred. See ORIOLE.

St. STEPHEN. Village near Bethel, Somerset County. The name is from St. Stephen's Church. Hall (*Oriole*) explains: "Not caring to travel over the long, rough road to Oriole to Church, the people of Genngaukin and surrounding territory built a church [St. Stephen's] nearby . . ." Soon there were homes, a schoolhouse, and later a store.

SALISBURY. [SAULS-bury]. City on the Wicomico River, Wicomico County. (*Salisbury* 1792 PHC). According to the Guide (p. 293) the exact spot was "Handy's Landing, in the forks of the Wicomico. Here in 1732, by authorization of the Provincial Assembly, twenty lots to be called *Salisbury-Town were surveyed and laid out. Gannett speaks of "towns in Wicomico County, Maryland, and Essex County, Massachusetts, named for the city in England." Truitt (.21) declares: "That the town was named for Salisbury, Wiltshire, England, there can be no doubt. Many of the large landowners emigrated from the vicinity of the ancient English city. John Rhodeson, who acquired 200 acres on the river April 3, 1667 gave it the name 'Salisbury.' John Glass received a grant of 500 acres on June 13, 1675 and called it 'Wiltshire.' "

Note: Until 1867 Salisbury was partly in Somerset County and partly in Worcester County. After a bitter contest, the petition to set up Wicomico County was granted and SALISBURY became the county seat.

SAMS CREEK. Village near Marston, on the border between Carroll and Frederick Counties. (*Sams Creek* 1826 PHC). *Sams Creek Church, Sams Creek* /stream/, USGS 1911 Taneytown; GMd 1941). The village probably takes its name from the creek. And the name of the creek probably represents the family name *Sams* (*Sames, Sammis, Samms*). TDr Frederick 1971 has one instance each of *Sames* and *Sammis*.

*SAN DOMINGO. Baltimore neighborhood near an old tollhouse (razed in 1907) on the west side of Belair Road. J. P. Foote comments: "I don't know why they called the neighborhood San Domingo." It is to be remembered, however, that in July 1793 Baltimore became the refuge of "more than 500 whites and Negroes," who had fled the slave rebellion and massacre of Cap Francois, French Colony of San Domingo. By July 22, fifty-three ships had brought 1000 whites and 500 mulattoes and blacks. In Baltimore, French ". . . methods of husbandry . . ." were introduced; and for one of the newcomers, Edme Ducatel (ca 1757–1853), who became a druggist on Baltimore Street, *Ducatel Street* was named. Cf. SAN DOMINGO CREEK, St. Michaels, Talbot County. (See: "I Remember Colorful, Bustling San Domingo," *Sun* [Mag.], April 30, 1961; *MHM*, 38: 2, June 1943, pp. 109–32)."

*SANDTOWN. Emory (p. 327) states that an Act of 1798 gave *Sandtown* the privilege of voting for commissioners. Heretofore, Bridgetown in Kent and *Sandtown* in Queen Anne's were practically one and the same place. There was a bridge over the Chester River at *Sandtown* ("which retains its name to the present day").

"SANDTOWN." Baltimore Negro neighborhood. (TV broadcast, 9 April 1968). Mention was also made of *Gum [town? ville?]). See: New American Road Show, Balto. TV Ethnic, May 14, 1981.

SANDY HILL. Village? Worcester County. (*Sandy Hill* 1830 PHC). Cf. Sandy Hill, Dorchester County; and Sandy Hill Landing, Wicomico County.

SANDY HOOK. Village. Potomac River, west of Weverton, Washington County. (*Keeptryst, Sandy Hook*; GMd 1941). The Guide states that Sandy Hook came into being in about 1832, when the C. & O. Canal was completed. "First known as *Keep Tryst*, the present name is said to refer to a nearby quicksand pool in which a teamster lost his horses." Cf. SANDY HOOK (village), near Allibone, Harford County.

Note: PHC 1847 lists *Sandy Hook*, Harford. And there is the note that " 'Deer Creek Works' was changed to 'Sandy Hook' in 1847." See KEEP TRYST.

SANDY SPRING. Village between Olney and Ashton, Montgomery County. (*Sandy Spring* 1817 PHC). According to Forman (p. 205), Sandy Spring was founded in 1728 by James Brook of the "De la Brooke Manor" family. Farquhar, describing a pilgrimage to the Springs, states that now the water flows out of the earth and no longer bubbles up through "the white sand that gave the spring its name . . ." "We now see only the plain, ordinary spring of our common fields." He complains that wagon loads of stone, together with "alluvial deposits of other soil" have almost covered the large original basin. "The white sand of the original Sandy Spring exists only in history." (See: Farquhar, Annals, I [1884], XIV–XV).

Note: *Sandy Spring* Md Edward Stabler /p. m./, *Register 1834.*

SANG RUN. Village at the mouth of Sang Run, s.w. of Hoyes, Garrett County. (*Sangrun* Ag 1837 PHC; *Sang Run*. GMd 1941; *Sang Run Village*, Manual 1969). Weeks (p. 20) states that John Friend, Jr. (1764–1849) settled in 1795 on part of "Friend's Delight" at the mouth of *Ginseng Run (> Sang Run)*. Ginseng, an "article of trade" among "our pioneer settlers," was so abundant here that the area was generally known as the "Sanging Ground." The post office—opened in 1837 with Elijah Friend, postmaster—was called Sang Run.

Note: Ginseng [jin SANG]. The Glade Star (19 [30 Sept. 1955]) describes a power line, completed here in 1945, as the "Sanging Electric Line."

*SANTO DOMINGO. Community near Sharpstown, Dorchester County. Ms. Severn Cooper (p.m., Sharpstown, 22 July 1966) tells me that this is a colored locality. However, she adds, the Negroes of Santo Domingo prefer to say they are from Sharpstown.

SAPPINGTON.   Near Odenton, Anne Arundel County. Warfield (p. 129) states that John Sappington of All Hallows settled his son, John Sappington, Jr., upon an estate known as "Sappington." Here (in Warfield's time) a cottage stood at "Sappington Station, of the Annapolis and Elkridge Railroad." He mentions that farther south and leading to Laurel were two Warfield estates which Thomas Sappington bought and resurveyed into "Sappington's Sweep." "Sappington Ford," on the Little Patuxent River, was named ". . . for a kindred family."

Note: On Hopkins Atlas 1878, M. Sappington is given as the postmaster of *Sappington Sta. & P.O.*

SASSAFRAS.   Village near the Sassafras River, Kent County. (*Sassafras T.*, Griffith 1794). Map spellings indicate that this village was once known as **Head of Sassafras* (because of its situation at the head of the Sassafras River). Muriel Dobbin, citing Mrs. Harry Robinson, finds that the sassafras tree is the source of the name; there are still some here. However, the villagers no longer brew sassafras tea. Mrs. Robinson remarks: "Years back I used to do it . . . You get some sassafras root, dry it, then put it on the back of the stove with water, and just let it brew. Tastes a bit like root beer." (See: "Sassafras in Kent County," *Sun* [Mag.], 17 Dec. 1961).

Note: Cf. the early P.O., *Sassafras and Oak* (SM 1837–1848 PHC).

SASSAFRAS RIVER.   A tributary of the Chesapeake Bay, Kent and Cecil Counties. The stone tablet on Sassafras River Bridge, Georgetown, Md., states: "Sassafras River Discovered and Explored by Capt. John Smith 1607–1609 Who named it Tockwough after the tribe of Indians who inhabited its banks Tockwough was the original Indian name for sassafras root from which they made a form of bread."

DAE (II, 1460) regards the ultimate origin of *sassafras* as obscure; it may be from American Indian. "The derivation . . . from Latin words . . . is doubtful." See **TOCKWOUGH FLU* and TUCKAHOE.

SAVAGE.   Village northeast of Laurel, Howard County. (**White's Mill*, Griffith 1794; *Savage* AH 1846 PHC). Vera Ruth Filby states that Joseph White owned a tract, "Mill Land," here in 1753. In 1823, his son (Gideon) sold "Mill Land" and 500 acres of "White's Contrivance" to John Savage, a Philadelphia merchant. Mr. Savage and the Williams brothers had been developing a cotton mill at the falls of the Little Patuxent River. It was the Savage Manufacturing Co., incorporated in 1821–22 for the manufacture and sale of cotton goods. In 1835, when the Washington branch of the Baltimore and Ohio Railroad was completed, Savage Station was established, at about one mile southeast of the mill. (See: Y. R. Filby, *Savage, Maryland* . . . Savage, 1965).

Note: Ms. Filby relates that (pioneered by the Williams Brothers, et al.) the cotton industry began in 1808, with cotton being shipped to Baltimore from the South and hauled overland to mills located at the falls of streams. By 1832 there were thirteen cotton mills in the vicinity of Baltimore. Cotton duck was first made here (1822).

SAVAGE RIVER. A tributary of the North Branch of the Potomac River, near Bloomington, Garrett County. Its headwaters are in Johnson District. *Savage River als. No. Fork* (Warner 1738); *Savage R.* (Trader's 1752, F & J 1751, Map Country 1787, USGS Frostburg 1908). The earlier name, *North Fork*, was probably given because the stream enters the Potomac River from the north at Bloomington. The present name was probably given for Thomas Savage, a surveyor with the historic Mayo Expedition of 1736. The West Virginia State Markers booklet (p. 59) gives as follows the words of a commemorative highway plaque at the top of Kenny Hill, Piedmont (Potomac River), West Virginia: "Near here, William Mayo, Thomas Savage, and party spent the winter of 1736 on their expedition for the British King to determine the headwaters of the Potomac River and fix the boundary between Maryland and the lands of Lord Fairfax...."

Note: A doubtful tradition has it that Savage was blind, felt himself expendable, and offered his body to be eaten by his starving companions.

SAVAGE MOUNTAIN. Little and Big Savage Mountains, Garrett County, owe their names to the Savage River. It, in turn, was named for Thomas *Savage*, a member of the Mayo Expedition of 1736.

Mt. Savage, the Allegany County village, is in sight of Big Savage Mountain.

SAVAGE'S NECK. A highway marker indicates that this Delmarva Peninsula name is not a reference to the Indians, but to Thomas Savage (1608), first settler of the Eastern Shore. The land (according to the marker) was given to him by the "Laughing King of the Indians," Debedeavon.

SAVANNAH LAKE. It lies in a swampy area near the Nanticoke River, Dorchester County. The U.S. Geographic Board prefers *Savanna*, forbids *Savannah* and *Savannah Lake*. The *h* of this word results from confusion between **Savanna* and *Savannah*, Georgia. DAE (II, 1461) cites: "The army has been moving through magnificent pine woods—the savannahs, of the South, as they are termed." Was the Maryland name given because of the presence of plains, or because of the presence (once upon a time) of the Shawnee Indians? The region is a low, fresh marsh; it has no Shawnee Indian history. All in all, I favor the topographical explanation. (See: *Handbook*, II, p. 532).

SCARBORO (SCARBOROUGH'S) SCAR-burr-uh. Village between Snow Hill and Girdletree, Worcester County. The pronunciation is that of Elmer Brittingham, Pocomoke City (June 1966).

Note: Cf. Scarboro (village), near Dublin, Harford County. Heads (1790) lists eight persons by this name—five are in Harford County and three are in Worcester. Today (1963, 1966) TDr Harford lists two *Scarboro*, 25 *Scarborough*, and one *Scarbrough*; TDr Som & Wor 1966 has six *Scarborough*.

*SCHAEFFERSVILLE. Garrett County. Schlosnagle attributes this name (1840) to Jacob Schaeffer. See GORMAN.

SCHLEYS. GMd 1941: "Schleys: in Frederick County." Grove (pp. 371–72) mentions "Franklin Street, at *Schleysville* ... known [i. e., Franklin St.] as Adlum Lane, then a part of Locust Level." He says that John Thomas Schley (?1767–1835) built the first house in Frederick, and that Mary Schley (nursed by an Indian squaw) was the first white baby born here.

SCIENTISTS CLIFFS. Village in or near Calvert Cliffs State Park, Chesapeake Bay, Calvert County. Muriel Dobbin calls this place "the unusual cliffside town in Calvert County." It began in 1935 when Flippo Gravat, a forest pathologist in the U.S. Dept. of Agriculture, bought a tract on the side of the cliffs and built a house of chestnut logs. His plan was to found a community of scientists, insofar as the Calvert Cliffs are a treasury of age-old Miocene fossils. It appears that the roads in the community are named for plants, and that the original name was not SCIENTISTS CLIFFS but ("successively and temporarily") "Pathologist's Quagmire," "Flippo's Folly," and "Anne's Aggravation." (See: "Scientific Cliffdwellers," *Sun* [Mag.]. 26 Aug. 1962, p. 14).

SCOTLAND, SCOTLAND BEACH. There are two SCOTLAND'S (one near Rockville, Montgomery County; another near Ridge, St. Mary's). SCOTLAND BEACH (Chesapeake Bay) is adjacent to SCOTLAND, St. Mary's. Apparently the Montgomery County *Scotland* is a black community. The *Star* (4 Dec. 1969) speaks of the place as "... a community of about 50 Negro families that has been rebuilt near Rockville ..." It mentions further "the Scotland Community Development Corporation, which organized the rebuilding of delapidated houses into a community of 100 townhouses, about 75 of them low-rental units." In any event, it is likely that the name of both Scotlands arose owing to an early preponderance of Scotch residents.

Note: In 1965 (v. Anne Christmas, "Neighbors Aid Negro Town," 7 March) the *Star* had described Scotland as "The century-old Negro community of Scotland, now bounded by plush Montgomery County subdivisions ..." See also June Saylor's "Scotland's Renewal: How to Rebuild a Small Town" (*Star*, 29 Nov. 1968).

*SCRABBLETOWN ... See JAMESTOWN; see WESTERNPORT. Cf. *Scrabble Alley* (Baltimore City 1896 Bromley).

SEAT PLEASANT. Suburb of Washington, D.C. Near Fairmont Heights, Prince George's County. J. Kiker (Andrews AFB 1964) finds that the earlier name of this place was *Chesapeake Junction,* so called because at this point there was the junction of a railway line to the Chesapeake beaches. The line was discontinued during the Depression of 1929. Citing "Historic and General Information of some Communities of Prince George's County," *Star,* May 20, 1906, p. 10, Kiker remarks that while the junction was active hoodlums gave the place a bad reputation. Desirous of changing the name, the leading citizens met on May 20, 1906, and proposed "Gregoryville," "Distmar," "Seat Pleasant," "Advance," "Pine Pond," "District Line," etc. For no clear reason, *Seat Pleasant* was chosen. The name suggests a pleasant place to live.

SECRETARY. Town. It is on Secretary Creek, Warwick River, Dorchester County. Frank Henry says that the town "became a reality in the latter 1800's"; incorporation was in 1900. The town takes its name from the stream it is on. Marye describes the stream as "Secretary's Creek (now Warwick River) named for Henry Sewall, then Secretary of the Province of Maryland." Lord Sewall (d. 1665) was the Secretary in 1661 of Charles Calvert, the third Lord Baltimore. Jones (p. 356) terms him "Henry Sewall of London"; Ingraham (pp. 294–95) calls him "Hon. Henry Sewall" and remarks that he was a "Privy Councillor." During Charles Baltimore's rule his home was "the government house of the Province." (See: "The Town of Secretary," *Sun* [Mag.] 25 June 1961; *MHM.* 2: 5, Oct. 1937, p. 3)

Note: Emory indicates that an Act of Assembly, May 8, 1660, mentions "Secretary Sewell's Creek."

SELBYSPORT. I learn from Beverly Otto, of Oakland, that *Selbysport, near Friendsville, Garrett County, was submerged in 1943 by the Youghiogheny River Flood Control Authority. Scott 1807 has "Selby Port, a small town 38 miles west of Cumberland ... on ... Big Crossing Creek." It was a post office in 1834.

The Guide attributes the name to Evan Shelby, who had a tract surveyed here in 1772 and laid out lots in 1798. The Glades *Star* describes Shelby's tract (patented 1773) as *Buffalow Run "in Garrett County at the south of the present Buffalo Run. The run was so called because early settlers had killed a buffalo on the north bank near its mouth. The -*port* in the name is explained by the Glades *Star* as indicating that the pioneers

Note: The identity of Evan Shelby is not clear. The Guide has him becoming the Governor of Kentucky, in 1792. The Glades *Star* calls him Captain Evan Shelby, a fighting Welshman of the Frederick County Rangers, who moved to Tennessee. TW (I, 309) spells the name *Selby* and relates that "Samuel Selby, the third, came to the Allegany bar in 1791." TW adds: "Selbysport is said to have been named after his brother."

hoped to use the Youghigoheny, or a canal on one of its shores, for transportation. (See: "Selbysport, Maryland," The Glades *Star*, No. 11, Sept. 30, 1943).

SENECA.   Village. It is southwest of Darnestown and within a mile of Seneca Creek, Montgomery County. PHC (n. 125) remarks: "Apparently 'Seneca' was an early alternative name for 'Middlebrook Mills.' Entries of 'Seneca' (also spelled 'Senica') say 'Seneca—see Middlebrook Mills.' The name of the village is from *Seneca* Creek. And *seneca* (ultimately from the Algonquian) means "stony, and activity in regard to stones (i. e., quarrying)." For this region Martenet 1866 charts "Fine Red Sandstone" and *Quarry Pt.*

SENECA CREEK (2), SENECA POINT.   One of the creeks is a tributary of the Potomac River, Montgomery Count. The other Seneca Creek is a tributary of Chesapeake Bay, Middle River Neck, Baltimore County. Seneca Point is on the Northeast River, Cecil County. Early spelling of the Montgomery County stream are *Sinegar Cr., Sinegar Falls* (1751), *Senegar Cr., Senegar Falls* (1751), etc.

The Montgomery County Seneca names are attributed by Scharf to "the Seneca tribe of Indians at one time so numerous ... in Western New York, as well as in Western Maryland."

The Middle River Seneca Creek, however, has a local history. Scharf points out that in July, 1663, the Senecas murdered several settlers " at the head of the bay" and "near Patapsco River." Marye cites records of attacks in the Gunpowder region, 1680, attributed to the "Sinniquos." He remarks: "... a highway of the Seneca Indians passed through the western part ... of what is now Baltimore City, and crossed Gwynn's Falls near the mouth of that stream."

Seneca—though it is the name of an Iroquoian tribe—is Algonquian for "There are plenty of stones," or "Where activity is carried on in regard to stones." Its components are "stone" (Delaware *achsin,* Ojibwa *assin,* etc.) and "activity, abundance" (Fox *e'ka*). One wonders whether the Montgomery County *Seneca* names—where there are *Seneca Quarries*— do not simply mean "stony," with no reference to the Iroquoian at all. (See: Scharf, *Western Maryland,* p. 646, p. 51; "The Old Indian Road." *MHM,* XV (1920), pp. 110–114).

*SENECA MILLS.   Fisher 1852 mentions Seneca Mills as a Montgomery millseat and post office with ten or eleven inhabitants. And PHC has *Seneca Mills* Mg 1819. PHC's note is " 'Seneca Mills' was changed to

Note: George Kennedy ("The Rambler," *Star,* April 20, 1960) describes a visit to Block House Point (Potomac River near Seneca) and the ruins of the stone-cutting mill at Seneca. He mentions the quarries at Seneca Creek, and continues: "The stone walls of the cutting mill are still standing—red standstone, the same as was produced here before the Civil War for the construction of the Smithsonian Institution ..."

'Rushville' in 1832. 'Seneca Mills' was changed to 'Dawsonville' in 1854."
RUSHVILLE (q. v.) is at the mouth of Seneca Creek.

SEPUS'S TOWN. Mentioned by William B. Marye along with Shawan, Oregon Run, *Shawan Hunting Ground, *Shawney's Run, *Shenese
Glade, and *Olacin (Olacip, Olicin Land)—all of them in the erstwhile
Shawnee region of central Maryland. Compare the Algonquian (Munsee)
word and place *Esopus* (today Kingston, N.Y.), which appears on Schuy-
ler (1693) as *Sepus*, and has been analyzed by Mooney as *sip* "river" and
-us "small."

Arthur G. Tracey, of Hampstead (letter, Feb. 8, 1951) mentions the local
story that *Sepus's Town was named for Sepus, an Indian chief. I believe
however, that "Chief Sepus" is a folk creation, and that, as Mooney
thought, *Sepus* is the diminutive of Algonquian "river" (Cree *sepe*, Fox
sibō, Delaware *sipo*, etc.). The meaning is "Little river." (See: Marye,
"The Old Indian Road," *MHM*, 15, 1920, pp. 365–69; Handbook, I, 437).

*SETH'S MILL. Near Queenstown, Queen Anne's County. Emory (p.
27) notices that "Miss Sally Harris' Mill" ... was originally known as
Seth's Mill and derived its name from the Seth family. It is mentioned in a
deed (28 Jan. 1717) from Charles Seth, carpenter, to Norton Knatchbull.

SEVERN. Village and erstwhile railway station, south of *Harmans*,
Anne Arundel County. It is about two miles north of Severn Run, a tribu-
tary of the Severn River, On Atlas Hopkins 1878 it is *Severn Sta.* See
SEVERN RIVER.

SEVERN RIVER. With its mouth at the Naval Academy, Annapolis,
it reaches into Anne Arundel County almost as far as Benfield. Early
spellings are *Seavorn R*, (Herrman 1670), *Anne Arundel al Seavorn R*,
(Van Keulen 1682), and *Seavorn R*, (Moll 1717). Kelly describes Colonel
Edward Lloyd as commander (1650) of the armed forces of the Severn section and a member of the Governor's Council. He adds: "To him is probably due the very name of the river, which like his name is obviously Welsh.
When he moved to the Eastern Shore, he bestowed other Welsh names,
Wye and Tred Avon, on rivers there. "It appears that Lord Baltimore
favored the name *Anne Arundell* for this stream. For many years it was
referred to as the "Anne Arundell River, alias the Severn."

Note: The Maryland Severn is from the SEVERN RIVER of England and
Wales. The Welsh river begins in the vicinity of Plinlimmon, Montgomeryshire,
and flows about 210 miles to the Bristol Channel. Like the Maryland stream, it is
in part an estuary. The etymology of *Severn* is not clear.

SEVERN CROSSROADS (village), SEVERN HEIGHTS (village), and
SEVERNSIDE (village)—all in Anne Arundel County—owe their names
to proximity to, or location on, the Severn River.

SEVERNA PARK. Community. A half mile from the Severn River,
near Robinson, Anne Arundel County. (*Boones*, GMd 1941; *Boone*, USGS

1907 Relay; *Severna Park*, (GMd 1941). Nelson J. Molter, State Librarian, Annapolis, tells me (May 1970) that this name is the result of a contest to select a name. The winner, a black woman, proposed "Severna Park." See his *An Illustrated History of Severna Park* (Annapolis, 1969).

Note: In a Letter to the Editor (*Capital*, 4 March 1975), Mr. Molter insists that "The community, as such, was never known as Boone...." He refers to plats made in 1906 and in 1908, and declares: "These plats clearly show that the name of the community was Severna Park. However, the post office, which was established on April 7, 1914, was designated as Boone." The railroad station was called Boone until about 1919. The post office name was changed to *Severna Park* on June 16, 1925.

Further note: In her story about JONES ("Jones A Community that Gets in the Blood," *Capital*, 4 May 1983), Christine Neuberger remarks: "What many probably don't know is that Severna Park was called that only after a black woman dreamed up the name to win a contest held in the late 19th century. She received cash instead of the prize of acreage because land at the time couldn't legally be sold to blacks or Indians."

SEWELL. Village, near Abingdon, Harford County. The *Sewall* family was represented among the Puritan settlers of Virginia, Maryland, and New England. Cf. Sewall Branch, Kent and Queen Anne's Counties near Millington. Of the twenty-one *Sewell* (*Sewel*) entries in Heads 1790, only two are in Harford County. TDr Harford 1963 lists one *Seawell*, one *Sewall*, and eight *Sewell*. Two of the entries are for Abingdon. (See: Stein, pp. 309–310).

SHADYSIDE, WEST SHADYSIDE. Village. West River, near Idlewilde, Anne Arundel County. Marie Bailey comments: "... the place called Shadyside appears to be aptly named." And Jane Adams remarks: "The name is appropriate for a land shaded by trees and sided by the waters of the Chesapeake Bay, the West River and its small tributaries ..." She adds: "... the area officially became Shady Side in 1886 when postal officials in Washington, D.C., gave it a post office with the name. In earlier times it had been known as Parrishe's Choice and Rural Felicity." *Shady Rest Road* is the name of a street here. (See: "Artists Enjoy Shadyside Living," *Capital*, 26 Sept. 1970; "Shady Side Clings to its Ways," *Capital*, Oct. 8, 1979). See IDLEWILDE.

ATTENTION: In this vicinity, so my notes indicate, lies COLUMBIA BEACH, a 98% black community of 150 houses. It has been referred to as "Gem of the Bay," a community within a community.

Note: George Dunn ("Shady Side's Beloved Lady," Nautical *Times* [Annapolis, Md.], 2: 2, Feb. 25, 1982, p. 4) states that the earlier name of this place, before the coming of the post office, was *Sedgefield*, so given because of "the sedge grass, common in marshy areas, and naturally flourishing in Shady Side."

SHAFT. Village. George's Creek, Allegany County. (*Shaft*, GMd 1904, 1941). See BORDEN SHAFT.

SHALLMAR. [SHELL-mar]. Village near Kitzmiller, Garrett County. Felix Robinson ("New Forests Now Beautify Old Region," *Sun*, 27 June, 1965) remarks that "Shallmar is the name in the reverse for Marshall, a New Yorker who founded the community."

Note: Among towns along the North Branch of the Potomac River, Robinson mentions "Wallman, *Schell*, Hubbard, Gleason, Dotson, Harrison...." An appended map charts *Schall* near Laurel Run. Weeks (p. 34), speaking of a Pennsylvania railroad organized in 1881 and taken over by the Western Maryland Railroad in 1905, lists Augustus *Schell* as one of the directors. One wonders whether there is a connection between *Schell* (W.Va.), from Augustus Schell, and SHALLMAR.

*SHANNON RIVER ... McGrath (Pillars, p. 119) states that Colonel George Talbot (ca. 1680), a cousin of the Lord Baltimore, "called his tract New Ireland and named a nearby stream the Shannon River, but the mingling of Irish blood and Irish whiskey caused his undoing." See *NEW IRELAND; see NORTH EAST RIVER.

*SHARKTOWN. Kent Island, Queen Anne's County. Emory (p. 326) states that in 1835 a license was given to R. H. Gardner to retail merchandise at Sharktown, Kent Island. See Fauna and Flora, III, 7, Introduction.

SHARPSBURG. Antietam Battlefield Site, adjacent to Antietam Creek, Washington County. (−1792 PHC). Near Sharpsburg, on July 9, 1763, Joseph Chapline, a real estate investor, laid out on "Joe's Lot" the town of SHARPSBURG. He named it for Gov. Horatio Sharpe, "... the Proprietor's active representative at Annapolis." (See: Williams, I, 23–24).

Note: The town is notable because of the tragic Battle of Antietam. Here the battle was fought; here lies "Bloody Lane" (*Sunken Road). The village of Antietam is nearby. See ANTIETAM.

SHARPTOWN. Village. Nanticoke River, Wicomico County, near Delaware. (−1845 PHC). On July 22, 1966, I talked to Robert and James G. Marine about this and neighboring places. They attributed the name to Governor Horatio Sharpe, remarking that earlier it had been *Slabtown*. Cf. Sharptown, Kent County, for which I have no data.

SHAVOX. [SHAV- rhymes with *have*]. Community on the Shavox Road one mile north of Waste Gate Road, Wicomico County. The Waste Gate Road (observed on June 18, 1966) appears to go from east to west at Shavox, and to pass under a small bridge. *Shavox* is from "shaft ox," a beast which, with shaft and cart, was much used here in earlier days.

*SHAW. Community? George's Creek, Allegany County. It is now spoken of as "at Moscow." The place is noteworthy for a restored old-fashioned brick and stone mansion about which the Piedmont [W.Va.] *Herald* remarks: "Shaw Mills turned out the lumber and Millwork and

Andrew Bruce *Shaw* supervised construction . . ." TW (I, 649) mentions "Andrew Bruce Shaw, of Moscow," and points out that his father was Major William Shaw (b. nr. Cresaptown 1794). (See: "Shaw Manion at Moscow," Piedmont [W.Va.] *Herald*, Apr. 3, 1968). See BARTON, MOSCOW, PEKIN.

SHAWAN. [shu-WAHN]. Village near Cockeysville, Baltimore County. (*Shawan, Shiwan* 1837 PHC). MHGP (1963) mentions the land grant, in 1714, of "Shawan Hunting Ground." And it describes Shawan House as one of "the early Worthington houses," built in 1740. Of SHAWAN Gannett states: ". . . an Indian word meaning 'south.' " Locally, however, the name (and *Shawan Cabin Branch, *Shawney's Run) probably arose from "small settlements of the Shawnee Indians, which the first settlers discovered at the head of Rowland's Run and on Oregon Run in Baltimore County." Marye suggests that these particular Shawnees were members of Martin Chartier's band, which appeared in Cecil County in 1692.

Shawnee had such variants as *Shawana* and *Shawanoe*; and it is from one of these, with loss of the final syllable, that *Shawan* has come. *Shawnee* is usually defined as "south," "southerners" (from *shawun, shawunōgi*). However, considering Fox *cawa* "warmth," it is possible (from *cawä* PLUS the copula -*anwi*) to define a form like **Shawenwi* as a reference to the *blowing of wind*, or to the *weather* resulting *therefrom*.

Note: Johnston relates the tradition that the Shawnee on their migration north stopped in Elk Neck, ". . . and for a long time after it was settled by the Europeans that part of it along the North East River was called 'Shawnah.' "

SHELLTOWN. Village. Pocomoke River, near Marumsco, Somerset County. (*Shell Town*, Fisher 1852). There are old oyster beds here.

SHERWOOD (SHERWOODVILLE). Near Wittman, Talbot County. Talbot County also has a Sherwood Forest. The names of both village and forest appear to commemorate Major Hugh Sherwood (1632–1710). According to Parran (p. 78) he emigrated to Maryland in 1661 and died at Sherwood Forest in 1710. He was a member of the Maryland Assembly, a justice, and an officer in the militia. Cf. SHAREWOOD ACRES, Howard County.

Note: Jones (p. 293) mentions Hugh Sherwood, early Talbot County settler, and also Colonel John Sherwood, of "Pitts Range," Talbot. He served in the Revolutionary War. Cf. *Sherwood (Riderwood).

SHERWOOD FOREST. Village near Iglehart, Anne Arundel County. (*Sherwood Forest*, GMd 1941; *Sherwood Forest Village*, Manual 1969). Christine Neuberger (*Capital*, 6 July 1983) describes this place as follows: "Called 'The Forest' by local residents, Sherwood is a community of 330 summer and year-round cottages nestled within a dense natural forest of tall poplars, locusts and oaks hugging the Servern River."

Note: Manual 1969 lists Sherwood Forest, Montgomery County, and Sherwood Forest, Prince George's. Cf. Sherwood Forest, England, which the eleventh Britannica (24, p. 853) calls "One of the ancient English forests, in Nottinghamshire."

SHILOH. Village on the East Branch of the Patapsco River, above Hoffmans Mill, Carroll County. (*Shiloh, Shiloh Park Church*, Manual 1969). The name is probably biblical (Joshua 18:1; Hebrew "Place of rest"). However, it could be commemorative of the Civil War battle of Shiloh (April 1862), an important Union victory.

SHIPLEY'S CHOICE is an Anne Arundel residential vicinity near INDIAN LANDING and the headwaters of the Severn River. The highway marker here (on Benfield Road?) states that: ADAM SHIPLEY CAME TO ANNE ARUNDEL COUNTY IN 1668, ON MARCH 30, 1681 200 ACRES WERE SURVEYED AND PATENTED IN HIS NAME. THIS TRACT WAS THE EARLIEST PATENTED IN THE SHIPLEY NAME. MARKER WAS DEDICATED DURING THE DEVELOPMENT OF THE SUBDIVISION NAMED IN HIS HONOR. SHIPLEY'S CHOICE COUNTY ASS. IN. ... MD.H. SOC....

SHIPLEY CORNER. Village near Harman's, Anne Arundel County. (*Shipley Corner*, Manual 1969). Atlas Anne Ar. Hopkins 1878 names an abundance of Shipleys in the vicinity of Harman's (e.g., R. A. Shipley, J. W. Shipley, L. R. Shipley, Geo. E. Shipley, etc.).

Note: Cf. "Shipley's Choice," mentioned by Warfield (p. 485). Robert Shipley settled at an early time near Sykesville. "This tract [lying] upon the river side of the Severn is the earliest in the Shipley name ..." It was surveyed March 30, 1681, for Adam Shipley ... held later by Peter Porter and James Barnes. Howard's Range and Porter's were granted by Richard Shipley to his brothers, Adam, Robert, and Peter.

SHOWELL. Village near St. Martin, Worcester County. Of this place, the Guide remarks: "... named for one of the largest slaveholding families of the region." In Heads (1790), however, Eli and Samuel Showell, of Worcester County, appear to have had no slaves.

*SHREWSBURY TOWN. Emory (p. 320): "... at Sassafras River where Shrewsbury Town was ..." This place (v. Act of ... 1707) was later to be "deserted," and a new town laid out on land bought by the Commissioners. The name is not necessarily from Shrewsbury, Shropshire, England.

*SHREWSBURY, SHREWSBURY TOWN (Kent County). Hanson (p. 27), citing the Act of 1706 "... for ... erecting Ports and Towns in the Province of Maryland," mentions a town "At Sassafras River, where Shrewsbury Town was." As Usilton (p. 152) suggests, *Shrewsbury Towne was probably by this time deserted. Usilton (pp. 50–51) states that Shrewsbury Parish probably takes its name from the deserted town on the Sassafras. When the latter was ordered to be laid out /at Meeting House Point, 18 April 1684/, the Rt. Hon. Charles Talbot, Earl of Shrewsbury, was Great Britain's principal Secretary of State. The town may have been named in his honor, or it may have taken its name from Shrewsbury, Shropshire, England.

SIDELING HILL, SIDELING HILL CREEK [SIDE-ling]. The hill runs north easterly in Washington County; the creek is in Allegany and Washington Counties. TW (I, p. 11) notes that *Side Long Hill* appears on FJ 1755, and in Col. Thomas Cresap's contract with the Indians (for widening the original path). *Archives* (LVI, p. 105, 1758) mentions ". . . the Mouth of Sidling - Hill Creek . . ."; Hill (p. 100) gives *Sidelong Hill Creek*. The name means "sloping, askew, slanting . . ."

SILESIA. Village near Friendly, Prince George's County. Some of the early settlers were probably from the former Prussian province of Silesia.

SILLERY BAY. An inlet of the Magothy River, Near Mt. Carmel, Anne Arundel County (Not in Hopkins 1878); *Sillery Bay*, USGS 1904 North Point; GMd 1941). It is near Sylvan View; folk etymology describes it as "Silvery Bay."

Note: Sillery is a standard French family name. Armstrong explains *Sillery*, near Quebec City, Canada, as a village and parish name in honor of M. Noel de Sillery, who (amongst civic activities in both France and Canada) founded an institution for the education of Indian children.

Evidently the name in Maryland is comparatively recent. Dr. William Sillery, of Naples, Florida, tells me (1983) that he is a member of a branch of Sillerys who emigrated first to Northern Ireland and later to New York and New Jersey. Dr. Sillery never lived in Maryland; has never seen or heard of SILLERY BAY. He characterizes the family as "adventurous."

SILVER HILL. Suburban village near Suitland and the S.E. section of Washington D.C. Daniel Corder (Andrews AFB, Jan. 1964) relates Effie L. Swan's story that a customer of the erstwhile country store at Branch Avenue and the present Silver Hill Road one day lost a silver shoe buckle on a nearby path. The inhabitants searched the entire hill for it. The hill thereafter was called *Silver Hill*, and the path, *Silver Hill Road*.

SILVER SPRING. Montgomery County suburb of Washington, D.C. The Guide ascribes the name to the "mica flakes visible on the bottom of "a near-by spring." Farquhar (pp. 285–286), depicting the spring as once bubbling up with particles "which looked like silver," states (ca. 1952) that it has "gone completely dry." In 1961 Bodine (Face, p. 101) spoke of a park at the site of the spring. He gives a photograph of its restoration, and remarks: "The glitter of mica sand in its water, on a sunshiny day in 1840, led its discoverers to call it . . . /*Silver Spring*/, and in time the name was conferred also on the community that grew up about the Montgomery spot . . ."

Note: Farquhar (p. 285) mentions the story that Francis Blair, when his horse Selim ran away and was captured at this point, observed a "strong, freely flowing spring stream of very cold water bubbling up with white sand in it which looked like particles of silver." Pleased with "the beauty of the spot, and with its fine timber," Blair bought the land and built here his mansion. (This was Francis Preston Blair [1791-1876], father of Montgomery Blair).

SIMPSONVILLE. Near Laurel, Howard County. (*Simpsonville* AH 1850 PHC). Warfield mentions "an old tiny mill later destroyed (on Middle Patuxent River)" that (1) was *Dr. Warfield's Mill* (in some of the Howard Co. wills), (2) *Richard Owings Mill*, and (3) today SIMPSONVILLE. Warfield (p. 417) mentions a William Simpson (ca. 1798).

SINEPUXENT. A bay adjoining Chincoteague Bay, Worcester County. Also Sinepuxent Neck and village. Several early spellings are *Sene Puxone, Cinnepuxon Inlet* (*MHM*, X, for 1698) and *Senepuchen* (Md. 1757 Kitchin).

The two opening syllables may be from Algonquian (Delaware) *esseni* "stony." One supposes that the opening *es-* of *esseni* has been lost, thus giving *sen(e)*. The rest of the word (*puxen* PLUS superfluous adjectival English *-t*) could come from Algonquian **päkwi-* "shallow" joined by Algonquian *-sen* "lie, be placed." The meaning would be "stones lie shallow." If, however, one supposes that *-puxen-* comes from Algonquian **pōxkwi* "break crosswise . . .," the meaning would be "Stones are lying broken up" or "Stones lie shallow."

The bay may owe this name to a nearby stone, to the stony appearance of its rippling waves, or to the stony terrain adjacent to Sinepuxent Neck. See *POCOSIN.

SINES. A village southeast of Sang Run, Garrett County. According to Schlosnagle (p. 57), families related to Henry Sines moved to Sang Run during the first three decades of the 19th century.

SKIPNISH. Village near Crellin, Garrett County. (—GMd 1904; *Skipnish, Skipnish Junction*, GMd 1941; —Manual 1947; not in Manuals 1962, '69). The Sixth USGB (1890-1932, p. 698) has decided: "Skipnish: railroad station, Garrett County . . . (Not Skipnish Junction.)" Cf. Skipness (Tarbert), Scotland; spelled *Skipnish* in 1260 (v. James B. Johnston, Place-Names of Scotland /rpr. 1970, p. 296/).

*SKIPTON. The alternate early name of OLDTOWN, Allegany County. Scharf (II, 1458-59) remarks: "Old Town was called by Col. /Thomas/ Cresap 'Skipton,' after a little town in Yorkshire, England, from which he emigrated. In my *Origin and Meaning* . . . (p. 102, n. 3) I state: "As early as 1741 . . . Col. Thomas Cresap established a frontier post at . . . Old Town, or Skipton, . . . then called Shawnee Old Town, presumably from the fact that a village of the Shawanese, or Shawnees, had once been located there."

SKIPTON. Village southeast of Wye Mills, Talbot County. (*Skipton*, GMd 1904, 1941: *Skipton, Skipton Creek*, Manual 1969). Ingraham (p. 140), citing the first court record, states that court was held in Talbot County at the house of William Courcey, of Skipton, on a creek of the same name and a branch of the Wye, Oct. 25th, 1662. Cf. Skipton, Yorkshire, England.

Note: Emory (p. 316) mentions "... the court house on Wye River, near the locality now known as Skipton."

SLIGO [SLY-go]. Suburban village. Near Silver Spring, Montgomery County, Sligo Branch is near by. (*Sligo* 1835 PHC; *Eagle Inn* see *Sligo*, R-McN ... 1877; *Sligo, Sligo Branch*, GMd 1904, 1941; *Sligo, —Branch, —Creek—Creek Park, Sligo Park Hills* /vil./, *—Park Knolls*, Manual 1969). Cf. County Sligo, Province of Connaught, Ireland.

Note: According to PHC the extinct post office of *Simpsonville* (Montgomery County) was changed to *Sligo* in April 1835. In May of that year the name was changed to *Gettings*. Shortly afterwards it became *Sligo* again.

*SLAUGHTERTOWN. On the south side of Chester River near Rousby's Branch (adjacent to land laid out for Christopher Rousby). Emory (p. 43) cites a 1714 county land record to the effect that 500 acres were "taken up" here on Dec. 7, 1675, for John Slaughter.

*SLOAN, SLOAN MINE. Village near Church, Allegany County. One wonders which of the two progenitors named *Sloan*, mentioned by TW, is responsible for these names. Alexander Sloan (b. Scotland) came to the U.S. at the age of eighteen and became a coal mine superintendent and owner. In 1850 he lived at *Boston Mines, near Eckhart, Matthew S. Sloan (b. Birniesknowe, Ayrshire, Scotland, 1817) came to the U.S. from Cape Breton, N.S., in 1837 and settled at *Jennings Run (now Mt. Savage). TW (II, 809) states that he worked for the Union Mining & Iron Co. and (at Lonaconing) the American Coal Company. Matthew Sloan (d. 1863) was a pioneer worker in the coal development of George's Creek.

*SLOAN'S VILLE. Garrett County. Schlosnagle (p. 63) states that in 1801 John Sloan bought most of the "Grassy Cabin" tract east of the Little Crossings below the Grant Settlement. He laid off four lots adjacent to the Braddock Road. This was *Sloan's Ville. The road soon bypassed it, and in 1815 the village was abandoned. Hoye cites a deed of 1812 whereby John and Mary Sloan convey to George Newman, "tanner," two lots "in the town of Sloan's Ville." (See: C. E. Hoye, *Garrett County History of Pioneer Families*, p. 11).

SMALLWOOD. Village near Westminster, Carroll County. Arthur Keith states that James Smallwood (Md. 1664) and his descendants were *with very few exceptions* the sole bearers of the name in Maryland until comparatively recent imes. Two exceptions are Thomas Smallwood, south side of the Patapsco (Balto. Co. records, 1692–1695), and Samuel

Smallwood (Balt. Co. records, 1713). (See: "Smallwood Family of Charles County," *MHM*, XII: 2, June 1927, pp. 139–86).

SMITHSBURG. Village near Cavetown, Washington County. (*Smithsburg* 1829 PHC). Lantz (p. 302) locates it at the foot of South Mountain and remarks that it was founded by Christopher Smith before 1815. Bell (p. 17) gives the same explanation as Lantz, and points out that the village is situated on the W. Md. R.R. Williams (I, 1302) mentions the Smiths who settled near the Antietam between Keedysville and Sharpsburg, but he does not say which family was responsible for SMITHSBURG. Lewis 1878 lists J. M. Smith, general merchandise, for Smithsburg—but I am not sure that this was the Washington County village.

*SMITHFIELD. Apparently the early name of Middletown. Grove (p. 446) states that the first settler was Frederick (Fritz) Lauber, German gunsmith, who built his cabin here in 1736 ("near the present residence of Charles Butts ... on the old Indian Trail ..."). "A settlement was then started which was at first called Smithfield, named for Lauber Smith, his shop and clearing which is now Middletown." See MIDDLETOWN.

*SMITHVILLE. Evidently a bygone quarter of Annapolis. Smithville St., Annapolis, commemorates it.

*SMITHVILLE or Dunkirk. Stein (p. 49) mentions Thomas Smith (d. 1684) a Quaker from the West River Community, Anne Arundel County. In 1670 he was granted the tract at Highland that is presently marked by a brick house often called "the old Smith house near Dunkirk." Stein states that Thomas Smith was the progenitor of the Smiths of "Smithville" or Dunkirk.

*SNOWDEN'S RIVER. Mrs. George S. Nesbitt, of Sandy Spring, informs me (19 April 1975): "This is the Patuxent River and I can only assume it was called 'Snowden's River' because of Richard Snowden, the younger's, extensive land-holdings alongside it. They extended from Prince George's County at least as far as the Mink Hollow bridge near Ashton."

*SNOW HILL ... Talbot County? See PRESTON.

SNOW HILL. Town on Pocomoke River, Worcester County. (*Snow Hill* 1792 PHC). Torrence (pp. 413–17) indicates that "the town of Snow Hill, then in Old Somerset County, now in Worcester ... (by subdivision in 1742) had its origin and founding in 1684–86." He adds that the town was established by direction of the Maryland Assembly of 1686. C. T. Merriam cites what he calls "the engorged derivation" given by G. A. Townsend in *The Entailed Hat*. This explanation is that the streets, gardens, and fields here once abounded in mounds of white sand, swept in "by the wind from a receded sea ..." The owner, calling the mounds a hill, "put his own name thereto, perhaps with memories of old Snow Hill in London." The Guide says that the site was part of the tract Colonel William Stevens patented in 1676 and called Snow Hill after a London suburb of the time. Still another authority attributes the name to a group of English settlers from Snow Hill, London, England. I am satisfied with the London theory. (See: Hill. pp. 312–15).

Note: (Md. Cal. Wills, II, p. 18) Jno Snow /Somerset County?/ witness ... 1687; (*Archives*, VII, 1678–83. p. 442) Chr: Snowhill ...

SOLLERS. Village. St. Leonard's Creek, near Appeal, Calvert County. The Calvert County name seems to have come from John Sollers, who settled in Anne Arundel County in 1670 and later moved to Calvert County and the Upper Cliffs. (See: Stein, pp. 315–16).

SOLLERS. Village. It is northwest of Sparrows Point, Baltimore County. Sollers Point is nearby. Stein remarks that John Soller's son, Sabrett Sollers (1680–1760), owned land at Sollers Point which he left to his son, Thomas Sollers.

Note: Stein finds that Sollers, a surname of Huguenot origin, has been traced to a French nobleman, Guilbert de *Solario*.

SOLOMONS, SOLOMONS ISLAND. Village and island. Patuxent River, near Appeal, Calvert County. Stein (p. 183) indicates that at first the island was a plantation owned by Alexander Somervell, and known as *Somervell's Island*. He adds: "The island originally has been part of Eltonhead Manor and had been known as 'Bournes Island.' ...'' The present name is accounted for by the fact that Captain Isaac Solomon, of Philadelphia, chose the island in 1869 to establish the "first large-scale fishery" in southern Calvert County. See *SOMERVELL'S ISLAND.

Note: Under *Solomons Island* Lewis (1878) lists Charles S. *Solomon* as an agent for both General Merchandise and Marine Railways.

*SOMERS COVE ... The Guide notices that the name of Benjamin *Summer* (*Somers*) is preserved in *Somers Cove*, "formerly the name of the wharf-hamlet here /presentday Crisfield/." The Guide adds that Upper Crisfield is on tracts surveyed in 1663 by John Roach and Benjamin *Summer* (*Somers*). See CRISFIELD.

SOMERSET COUNTY. Adjacent to Wicomico and Worcester Counties. Torrence (p. 5) apparently concludes the matter when he cites a proclamation by Cecil Lord Baltimore in Aug. 22, 1666. It announced the erection of Somerset County, named "in hon^r to our dead Sister, Lady Mary Somersett." Torrence identifies Lady Somerset as the wife of Sir John Somerset and the sister of Anne Arundel, the wife of Cecil, the second Lord Baltimore. The two sisters were the daughters of Thomas Lord Arundel (1560–1639) and Anne Philopson (v. *MHM*, XXII, p. 315). (See: Mathews, p. 421).

Note: When Ethan Allen (p. 41) describes Lady Mary Somerset as Lord Baltimore's *sister*, he probably means *sister-in-law*. One wonders about Gannett's curious statement (p. 287) that the name is from "Edward Somerset, husband of the daughter of Lord Baltimore."

*SOMERSET TOWN (*SOMERTON). The Guide, situating this place "Directly across the /Manokin/ river, where the house of Clifton now stands on the point of Revell's Neck," remarks that (as "Sommerton or Somerset Town") it was ordered laid out in 1688 (v. Herrman 1670). Torrence, however, gives the date of the order (by Gov. Charles Calvert and council) as June 5, 1668. And he cites a deed that describes the locality as "att Deepe Point att Randall Revell's." Various names (v. Torrence, p. 181) were *Somerset Town, *Sommerton, and *Monocan Town.

Note: The Guide calls attention to "Double Purchase Tract," later Revell's Neck, Somerset County. Hill (MCC, p. 134), specifying 1668 like Torrence, states that Gov. Calvert's order concerned a plot of twenty acres called "Somerton," to be obtained from Randall Revell (v. REVELL'S NECK) and laid out in streets for a town. The Somerset County court met here in 1669, but the town never materialized.

*SOMERVELL'S ISLAND. The earlier name of SOLOMONS ISLAND (SOLOMONS). The Somervell family was founded by Dr. James Somervell, a Scotch supporter of "Bonnie Prince Charlie." The English captured Somervell in 1715 and sent him to the Colonies to be sold as an indentured servant. He settled on the Lower Cliffs in about 1719; in 1744–1747 he became High Sheriff. He died in 1754. (See: Stein, pp. 316–17).

Note: The surname *Somervell* (in Virginia, *Somerville*) is said to be a version of (French) *St. Omerville*, the first settler by this name in Britain, probably a Huguenot, having come from St. Omer, France. (v. Stein, *loc. cit.*)

*SOPETANK. See CHOPTANK.

SOTTERLEY. Village. Patuxent River, near Hollywood, St. Mary's County. The name of the village appears to have come from "Sotterley," "a delightful mansion house ... built near St. Leonard's Creek on part of old Resurrection Manor (v. McGrath, p. 122)." Marian McKenna relates that George Plater II (d. 1755) completed his house and renamed it "Sotterley" from Sotterley, Suffolk Co., England, the home of his ancestors, the English Playters. (See: "Sotterley ...," *MHM*, XLVI: 1, Sept. 1951).

Note: MHGP (1964) remarks that the manor was built in about 1727 and named from "the English ancestral home of the Plater and Satterlee families. Its present owner (1964) appears to be Mrs. Mabel Satterlee. *Satterlee* is a phonetic variant of *Sotterley.*

SPARKS. Village near Phoenix, Baltimore County. Probably from the British surname Spark (Sparke, Sparkes, Sparks). Heads 1790 lists 23 *Sparks*, 18 of them living in Queen Anne's County, and only two (*Josias* and *Francis Sparks*) living in Baltimore County (in Mine Hundred District). TDr 1981 (for Greater Baltimore) lists 133 *Sparks*. Two variants of the surname are *Sparck* and *Sparkes*.

SPARROWS POINT. Town on Patapsco River Neck, near North Point, Baltimore County. Davidson (p. 203) states that the Lord Proprietary granted Patapsco River Neck to Thomas Sparrow in Nov. 1652. Ever since then it has been known as SPARROWS POINT. Cf. "Sparrow's Nest," a house Solomon Sparrow, son of Thomas Sparrow, built here. Note also Sparrow Beach, near Annapolis. Thomas Sparrow (between 1750 and 1775) was an Annapolis silversmith (Guide, pp. 160–61). See Audrey Bishop and Fred G. Kroft, "Sparrows Point, Ghost Town in the Making," (*Extra*, 14 Nov. 1971).

Note: Did the town begin in 1840? It appears that it has also been called *Steelton, from the Maryland Steel Co. Cf. Steelton, Pa., associated with the plant at Sparrows Point.

SPENCE, SPENCE COVE.   The village is near Public Landing, Chincoteague Bay, Worcester County. The cove is in Sinepuxent Neck. The Guide mentions *Spence* among the old families of Sinepuxent Neck, and points out that Judge Ara Spence (1793–1866) lived many years at Public Landing near Spence, in the Mansion House, a building once owned by the Spence family.

Note: (Md. Cal. Wills, I, 216) David Spence, Wicomico, Somerset Co., 1678/79).

SPENCERVILLE.   On the Sandy Spring Road, near Burtonsville, Montgomery County. Boyd (p. 142) mentions W. H. Spencer, postmaster here at the time of Boyd's book (1879).

SPESUTIE ISLAND.   In Chesapeake Bay, off Aberdeen Proving Ground, Harford County (*Spes Utia* 1658 grant to Col. Nathaniel Utie; *Spesuty Creek*, Md. Rent Rolls, 1663; *Spes Utie I*ˢ, Ches. Bay 1735 Hoxton; *Spesutia Island, Archives* XLIII [1779–1780], p. 40; *Spesutie I.*, Md 1795 Griffith; *Spesutia* (p.o. Harford), 1828–1831 (PHC), etc. L. D. Scisco (*MHM*, XXXIII: 4, Dec. 1938) in his notes on Augustine Herrman's map, speaks of the single word *Spes* and comments that Utie's 1658 grant was previously known as BEAR ISLAND. The name *Spesutie* (*spes* [Latin] "hope" combined with *Utie*) means "Utie's hope," and was probably coined by him when the bold adventurer took possession of his 1658 grant. Colonel Utie was one of the earliest settlers above the Patapsco, probably soon after the treaty with the Susquehannocks in 1652. According to Johnston (Cecil, 28–30) he was a Councilor in 1658, Captain of all the forces between the coves of the Patuxent River and the Severn Mts, and (in 1665) represented Baltimore County in the House of Burgesses. Utie was also licensed to trade with the Indians for beavers, etc. Preston surmises that Colonel Utie was a relative of John Utie of Virginia.

Note: Johnston (Cecil, 28–30) sees evidence that the Dutch of Altona called Utie's grant *Bearson's Island.

SPIELMAN.   Village north of Grimes, Washington County. (—R-McN 1906; USGS 1930 Williamsport). William H. Spielman (1822–1889) owned a farm near Keedysville, and was a member of the Keedysville Reformed

Church. He had nine children, some of them sons. (See: Williams, II, 886, 1104).

*SPOCOTT. At the head of Little Choptank River, Dorchester County. ("Specott, sometimes called Spocott," Tidewater *Times*, 13.5, Oct. 1968); "Spocot, old house . . ." (Guide, p. 261). The Tidewater *Times* states that it was patented from Lord Baltimore in 1663 for Stephen Gary, of Loo, Cornwall, England. Marye (*BASD*, 2: 5, Oct. 1937) states that the survey was in 1662.

Note: The late Hon. George L. Radcliffe, whose home was "Spocott," assured me (letter, 1 Oct. 1970) that the name is Cornish. Stephen Gary was Mr. Radcliffe's grandfather in the eighth generation, and probably came from East Loo, Cornwall.

SPRINGDALE. Apparently there are two, one in Montgomery County, and one in Washington County (*Spring Dale /2/*, GMd 1941). Farquhar (p. 289) mentions "Springdale," a brick house on the road from Ashton to Brighton (on Walnut Hill). It was built in 1837–38. He also states that water was carried from the spring at Springdale more than a century ago. Cf. Springdale Ave., Baltimore City; Springdale Gardens /real estate/, Prince George's County.

SPRINGFIELD. Principally, there are two, one in Prince George's County, near Bowie, and the other in Washington County. The Prince George's Springfield, lying between Newstep Branch and Horsepen Branch, appears to be in a watery region—which may explain the name. If the Washington County Springfield is in the Conococheague area, it perhaps owes its name to "Springfield Farm" (ca. 1755) near the celebrated "Fountain Rock," the "apex of an aqueous triangle." (See: Mary Vernon Mish, "Springfield Farm of Conococheague," *MHM*, XLII: 1, Dec. 1952).

Note: Harold Gray, in ". . . There's a Springfield Near You," *Star*, Nov. 10, 1963, makes fun of the abundance and duplication of *Springfield's* in thirty states and remarks that SPRINGFIELD is a new development in Montgomery County.

*SPRING GARDEN. Suburb. Baltimore City (*Spring Gardens*, GMd 1941). Cf. *Spring Garden Avenue*, Arrow Street Guide. Stockett (p. 40) states that the early settlers established a town on the Middle Branch of the Patapsco called *Spring Garden*, "as it is called to this day." Probably from New Spring Garden, later Spring Gardens, Lambeth, London. The London area was laid out as public gardens in about 1661. The U.S. Postal Directory (July 1961) lists Spring Garden, Alabama, and Spring Garden, Sta., in both Philadelphia (Pa.) and Quincy, California.

STABLER, STABLER HILL. Montgomery County. Annals (I, xxxii) mentions that in 1847–48 Edward Stabler "interested himself" in a Montgomery County Mutual Fire Insurance Company. Furthermore, in 1859, Sarah P. Stabler wrote a poem for the opening of the Sandy Spring Lyceum. In the census of Sandy Spring (April 1, 1879) there appear: James,

James P., William H., Philip F., Henry, George L., Frederick, Asa, Charles, and Hetty Stabler. It appears that earlier in 1797 there were the schoolboys, Thomas P. and Edward Stabler. See ALLOWAY.

Note: Passano (p. 301) has numerous items on this family, such as the ancestry of Caleb and Anne (Moore) Stabler, Sandy Springs, Md. Passano mentions the Golden Wedding of Edward and Ann R. Stabler, Sandy Springs, 1878.

STABLERSVILLE. Near Parkton, Baltimore County. (*Stablersville* 1853 PHC). Lewis 1878 indicates that at that time C. M. R. Stabler was the local postmaster and that A. J. Stabler and H. S. Stabler were resident carpenters and millwrights. TDr Baltimore 1969 lists five Stabler[s]. See Passano (p. 301).

STAFFORD. Village. Deer Creek, near Darlington, Harford County. (*Stafford Bridge* [of Deer Creek] USGS 1942 Havre de Grace). Note also *Stafford Mills* (GMd 1941: "... see Stafford"). Preston (p. 264) believes that the name was given by pioneer ironmaster, Stephen Onion. He came from Staffordshire, England, and bought the iron forge that had been built in 1749 by George Rock. The name dates from this period. See PRINCIPIO CREEK.

*STAR'S CORNER ... Harford County. Together with remarks on UPPER FALLS, Marye ("Place Names of Baltimore and Harford Counties," *MHM*, 53: 1, March 1958) explains: "When the post office /at Upper Falls/ was transferred to Star's Corner, at the junction of the old Joppa Road and the Franklinville Road, the name went with it. We generally called the place 'the Corner.' Star's Corner was originally known as *McCubbinsville. The McCubbins, who gave the place its name about 1800, were said to have been a race of very small men. One of them was seen climbing up a pokeberry bush, a typical example of country humor." See *McCUBBINSVILLE; see UPPER FALLS.

STARTZMAN. Near Hagerstown, Washington County. According to Williams, Frederick, Lord Baltimore, gave the deeds to the original Startzman property to Henry Startzman in 1752 and 1773. He notes that some of the land owned today by Jacob M. Startzman (b. 1832) has never been out of the possession of the Startzman family. The son of Jacob M. Startzman, Harry K. Startzman (b. 1868), was at one time postmaster of Hagerstown. (See: Williams, II, 717–18).

STEEL PONE ... See STILL POND.

STEPNEY. Village near Aberdeen, Harford County. (*Archives*, XXIII, 1696–98, p. 23) "*Stepney Parish* Consisting of Wiccomoco and Nentecoke Hundreds." Lantz (p. 320) indicates that Stepney Parish, created in 1692 by Sir Lionel Copley, Maryland's first royal governor, centered its religious activity in Green Hill Church (built in 1733), twelve miles from Salisbury. *Stepney* is both a surname (23 entries, Balt TDr 1969) and an eastern metropolitan borough of London, England.

STEVENS CORNERS. Village near Sudlersville, Queen Anne's County. BE mentions B. Gootee Stevens (b. Caroline Co., 1837), merchant. He was the son of Gootee Stevens, whose father had a steam sawmill. His mercantile business was at Potter's Landing. The Qu. Anne's Co. TDr (1963) lists 22 *Stevens*. As for *Corners*, USGS 1905 Barclay maps, within a four-mile radius of Sudlersville: Benton Corners, and Stevens Corners. Each was at a highway corner.

STEVENSON. Village near Pikesville, Baltimore County. Cf. (v. BE) Henry Stevenson, "extensive" Baltimore grain merchant. He was the uncle of John M. Stevenson, M.D., b. Baltimore, 1840. Dr. Stevenson's grandfather was John Stevenson (b. Ireland), who came to America in 1815. Notice Stevenson, a small Baltimore street. There are more than 180 *Stevenson*[s] in TDr Balto 1969.

STEVENSVILLE. Kent Island, near Chester, Queen Anne's County. Emory (pp. 313–14) calls Stevensville the oldest town within the present limits of Queen Anne's County, and locates it in the vicinity of Broad Creek. He states that it took its name originally from Broad Creek but in recent years has been known as STEVENSVILLE. Cf. (Warfield, p. 262) Governor Samuel Stevens, Maryland's twentieth governor (1823–25), who was born in Talbot County (1776) and died (1860) at "Compton," near Trappe (Talbot Co.).

Note: Emerson Roberts (*MHM*, 39: 4, Dec. 1944, p. 342) mentions William Stevens, "the immigrant," who settled in ca. 1650 in the Quaker colony of Calvert County. Here his first land grant was near the mouth of the Patuxent River. Later he moved to Dorchester County, where he became a Justice of the Peace.

STEYER. Village near Gorman, Garrett County. (*Steyer*, Stoyer . . . see Steyer, GMd 1941; *Steyer, Steyer Run*, Manual 1962). Passano (p. 306) indicates that Scharf mentions the family that gave rise to this name. TDr Garrett 1963 has sixteen *Steyer*[s], most of them in Gorman, two of them in STEYER. (See: Scharf, II, 1477).

STILLPOND. Creek and village two miles below Sassafras River (Chesapeake Bay), Kent County. (*Steelpond Creeke, Archives* XLI, 1661; *Steel Bone C*[r] Herrman 1670; *Steelpone Bay*, Deed 1672; *Steel Pond* Mitchell 1865). Scisco points out that Herrman's *Steel Bone C*[r] flows into a small bay. He finds that land records of 1659 have *Steelpone Bay* and *Steelpone Creek*, and he supposes that the modern *Stillpond* is "of later origin." Usilton attributes the name of the village (inc. 1908) to Still Pond Creek. He, Blanchard, and Lantz all seem to attribute the name to the stillness of local waters. Blanchard remarks that the waters are "so often still" perhaps because of "oil springs in the creek." Lantz speaks of a large pond near Galena whose "calm surface" no wind can ruffle. Perhaps Herrman mistook *pone* for *bone*. Cf. *Half Pone Point* (St. Mary's Co.) and (*The*) *pone Island* (and Cove), Dorchester County. (See: "Notes on Augustine Herrman's Map," *MHM*, XXXIII, 1938, p. 347).

Note: A surname (*Steel*) origin is plausible. Donnell MacClure Owings locates Worton Manor, Kent Co., 1658, on "a point by Steele Creek," and he explains that this was Still Pond Creek, then commonly called *Steel Pone Creek*. Scisco mentions a deed (Sept. 7, 1669) in which Axell Still, planter, conveyed 100 acres at Axell's Creek on the north side of Sassafras River, it being a plantation where *Still* lately dwelt. Scisco also notes that, in 1670 at Geo. Utie's house, one Axwell Steel acknowledged (a) conveyance of land. Cf. STEEL POND, Worcester County (Manual 1962). (See: "Private Manors: An Edited List," *MHM*, XXXIII, Dec. 4, 1938, p. 123; "Baltimore County Land Records of 1670, Continued," *MHM*, XXVI: 3, Sept. 1931, p. 229).

*STOCKETT'S, *STOCKETT'S TOWN. An early name of Havre de Grace. Kidwiler (p. 13) notes that in 1659 Godfrey Harmer assigned to Thomas Stockett land (now Havre de Grace) that had been assigned to Harmer in 1658. Stockett's ownership lasted until 1688. See HAVRE DE GRACE; see *HARMER'S TOWN.

STOCKTON. Village. Stockton District, below Girdletree, Worcester County. (*Stockton*, Harford 1878). I learn (Visit, 15 June 1966) that eighty or a hundred years ago the name of this place was *Sandy Hill*. Today there are many Black people here. Heads 1790 has only one *Stockton* (Cecil Co.). TDr 1964 Worcester has none. Cf. STOCKTON, near Jerusalem, Harford County. TDr 1963 Harford lists no *Stockton*[s]. TDr 1969 Baltimore, however, has eight. The name may well have come from Stockton, England, which is found in Cheshire, Durham, &c.

Note: Passano has two genealogical items for *Stockton*. One of them concerns Richard Stockton, of New Jersey. Gannett attributes Stockton, California, to the family name.

STOKLEY. Village near Prince Frederick, Calvert County. (*Stoakley*, USGS 1938 Prince Frederick; *Stoakley* ... see *Stokley*, GMd 1941). This name comes from "Stoakley," the plantation of Woodman Stoakley (d. 1662), a Puritan who settled on Hunting Creek in 1652. He was a Puritan Commissioner of Calvert County and served in the militia. After the Restoration of 1658 he removed to Somerset County. (See: Stein, pp. 37–38).

STONEBRAKER. Village near Weverton, Washington County. Historians mention John W. Stonebraker, whose grandfather was John Stonebraker, and whose great-grandfather, "an immigrant from Denmark," settled in Western Maryland in 1730. Williams comments that the Stonebraker house in Funkstown District remains the property of lineal descendants. He adds that they still have the letters patent (1730) for their land. (See: Williams, p. 898).

Note: Stonebraker is in the Sandy Hook region, where (Williams, pp. 947–48) "Glen Rose" farm was situated, an estate that has been in the Stonebraker family for three generations. It was first occupied by Christian Stonebraker (d. 1865), a Catholic. At "Glen Rose" in 1857 was born William F. Stonebraker, a son of George E. Stonebraker and grandson of Christian Stonebraker.

STREET. Village near Highland, Harford County. (*Street, Highland,* USGS 1901 Belair). The *Sun* /Mag/, 22 April 1962, calls this place "A Village with Two Names," and states that it began as a one-name town in 1774 when a group of Scotch-Irish Presbyterians settled here and called the community *Highland.* Later, when a post office was opened, it was called *Street.* The *Sun* quotes a 78-year-old citizen, Jerome Heaps: "We talk about living in Highland but we give our address as Street." Preston (p. 226) explains the post office name by noting that Thomas Streett, before the Revolution, patented a tract called Streett's Hunting Ground" above the Rocks of Deer Creek. He was living there in 1774. A member of this family, Col. John Street (1762–1837), of Marshall's District, served twelve times in the Maryland Legislature. (See: *Sun* [Mag.], April 22, 1962).

Note: I am indebted to Mrs. Gladys Carr, of Edgewater, Md., for helpful correspondence on this subject.

STRITES MILL. Village near Leitersburg, Washington County. (*Strites School, Strites Mill,* GMd 1941). The Guide relates that this flour and feed mill was built in 1792 "on Leiter land." Bell (p. 345) states that Christian Strite (1798–1826), son of John Strite, owned and operated the mill near Leitersburg and the farm connected with it ..." Williams calls John C. Strite (b. 1871), son of Samuel Strite (b. 1837), "a miller near Leitersburg, Md." According to Williams, the Strite family of Washington County stems from Christian *Streit,* a Palatine Mennonite who came to Pennsylvania (d. 1823). Samuel Strite, great-great-grandson of Christian Streit, settled in Leitersburg District in 1842. The genealogy given by Bell differs appreciably from that given by Williams. (See: Williams, II, 1032).

STUMPTOWN. GMd 1941 lists three, one in Carroll County, one in Kent County, and one in Talbot County. The Carroll County village is not on Carroll 1862. However, TDr 1963 lists three *Stump*[s]. The Kent County village is not on Kent 1860; nor does TDr 1963 Kent and Queen Anne's list this family name. The third Stumptown (Talbot County, near Manadier) is not on Martenet 1866. There is one *Stump* in TDr 1963 Talbot and Caroline.

Note: Cf. with these Maryland villages the two *Stump Town*[s] I discuss in *West Virginia Place Names.* One, in Gilmer County, was named for Michael Stump, the first settler; the other, in Monongalia County, takes its name from a large tree stump that stands near the first house.

SUDLERSVILLE. Near Barclay, Queen Anne's County. (*Sudlers Cross Roads* 1811 PHC). Emory (p. 331) points out that *Sudler's Cross Roads became a post office in 1811, and that the name was changed to *Sudlersville* in 1839. The Guide remarks that the original spelling was

"Sadler's Cross Roads," a "misspelling of Sudler . . ."; Clark has ". . . Sadler (now spelled Sudler)." It is hard to know which member (if indeed any *one*) of the Sudler family was responsible for the name. Hanson notes that Joseph Sudler was a Grand Jury member in 1694. And Biog. Enc. (1879) declares that the village is on the estate of the family's first American ancestor. It mentions Richard Sudler (d. 1797). As late as 1878 (Lewis) there were at Sudlersville Dr. William J. Sudler, Dr. A. E. Sudler, J. M. Sudler, of the American Grange, and the merchandise firm of Sudler, Pierce and Co.

Note: In Feb. 1964 the Md. Hist. Soc. was given a quantity of manuscripts having to do with the Sudler family.

SUDLEY. Village near Churchton, Anne Arundel County. Kelly (p. 102) mentions Sudley "or Cumberstone as it was known until 1798," and locates it three miles south of the Quaker Burying Ground just off Route 468 on Sudley Road. He adds that the name "Cumberstone" was taken from a grant of land; and he indicates that John Johns (s. of Kensey Johns II) gave the name "Sudley" to the estate. Cf. Sudeley, Gloucestershire, England. (See: Kelly, "Old Quaker Burying Ground . . . West River . . . Anne Arundel County . . .," *MHM*, 55: 4, Dec. 1960). See CUMBERSTONE.

SUGAR HILL. A colored community half a mile from Upper Marlboro, Prince George's County. In 1968 it had thirty houses (see *Star*, Oct. 9, 1968). In October 1970 the residents I talked to at Sugar Hill were all skeptical of the notion that the name is from the sugar maple tree despite the fact that the hamlet is on a small hilly bluff where maple trees are acknowledged. Wentworth (*Am. Dial. Dict.*, 1944) defines "sugar tree" as the "sugar maple." *Maple Shade Lane* is half a mile east of Upper Marlboro. (See: Donald Hirzel, "Sugar Hill Getting Help," *Star*, 29 May 1972).

Note: Cf. "Sugar Hill," a Baltimore City colored neighborhood; also Sugar Hill, Harford County. Sugarland, Montgomery County, is a rural settlement (probably Black) near Dawsonville.

SUITLAND. Village near District Heights, Prince George's County. My pupil at Andrews Air Force Base, D. Cordek, citing *Star*, Sept. 1937, attributes *Suitland* to Colonel Samuel Taylor *Suit*, who lived in the area from 1834 until his death (1888). He was active in local politics and became a state senator.

Note: Prince George's Co 1861 Martenet charts *J. S. Suit Tavern* (Bladensburg).

SULPHER SPRING. Community (thus spelled) in Baltimore County. GMd 1941 has ". . . see Arbutus," which suggests that this was the earlier name of Arbutus. (*Sulphur Springs*, Martenet 1866). In Manual 1962 Arbutus and Sulphur Spring Terrace (Baltimore) have almost the same coordinates. See ARBUTUS.

*SULPHUR SPRINGS. See NEW WINDSOR.

SUMMERFIELD. Village. Gunpowder Falls, five miles from Towson, Baltimore County. (GMd 1941). Query: Is this the Summerfield Farms [Balt. Co.] given in Manual 1969? A surname origin seems likely. TDr 1969 Baltimore lists five *Summerfeld*, one *Summerfeldt*, four *Summerfield*.

*SUMMER HILL. See RISING SUN.

*SUMMERSEAT ... St. Mary's County. (*Summerseat* 1831 PHC). Not in Fisher 1852. PHC notes: " 'Dorsey,' which also appears as 'Dorsey's,' almost certainly did not operate during the thirty-eight days of its existence on paper before it was changed to 'Summerseat.' "

SUMMERVILLE. Calvert County. Cf. SOMERVILLE, Charles Co. (GMd 1941). A surname origin seems likely for both of these names. Heads 1790 lists Philip *Somerville* for Charles County. TDr 1963 Calvert lists Alex *Somervell*, Jack *Somerville*. TDr 1963 Charles and St. Mary's has nine *Somerville*, one *Sommerville* ... See *SOMERVELL'S ISLAND.

SUNDERLAND, SUNDERLANDVILLE. The former is near Chaneyville, Calvert County. The latter is adjacent to Sunderland, Calvert County. (*Sunderland* 1840 PHC; *Sunderlandville P.O.*, Martenet 1866). PHC notes: " 'Sunderland' was changed to 'Chestnut Hill' in 1848." According to Stein, John Sunderland—the founder of the Sunderland family in Calvert County, probably a Puritan—came to Calvert County from Anne Arundel County before 1669 and settled on "Hopewell," a tract not far from "the crossroads center of Sunderland ..." The name *Josias Sunderland* is found on a 1733 tax list. In 1753 he owned 250 acres of "Lordship's Favor." Josias Sunderland Jr., owned part of "Upper Bennett." A tax list of 1782 lists John and Thomas Sunderland; the 1800 census lists John and Benjamin Sunderland. (See: Stein, pp. 320–21).

SUNNYBROOK. Near Jacksonville, Baltimore County. Davidson (p. 159) relates that when a post office was established at Kings Hotel in 1870 it was named SUNNYBROOK "on account of the little stream that runs nearby." The nearest mapped stream appears to be Overshot Run. Cf. SWEETAIR (*Sweet Air*, Martenet 1866), two miles away.

SUNSHINE. Village near Unity, Montgomery County. Lucy Harvey "About Sunshine, Md.," Sun /Mag/, 9 April 1961, says that her father and her uncle bought "the store property at Sunshine" in about 1890. The name SUNSHINE had been given years earlier, when the post office came (with mail from Hoods Mill). Later the post office was moved to UNITY.

*SUNSHINE. Garrett County. It was known in the first decade of the 18th Century (Schlosnagle). See CRELLIN.

*SURRATSVILLE. Near Camp Springs, Prince George's County. (*Surratts* 1854 PHC). Maynard W. Binge (Andrews AFB 1964) attributes the name to "an early settler named Surratt." He explains that the name was quickly changed to CLINTON in 1864 or 1865, when Mrs. Mary E. Surratt was cruelly hanged in connection with Abraham Lincoln's assassination. It was alleged that the conspiracy was plotted at her tavern, Surrattsville. Mr. Binge asserts that many residents still refer to the town as SURRATTSVILLE, and that all three of the public schools here—elementary, junior high, and senior high—have *Surrattsville* in their names. Pronunciation: SooRATSvil. See CLINTON.

SUSQUEHANNA. Grand tributary of the Chesapeake Bay at Havre de Grace, Hartord County. Three early spellings are *Sasquesahanough flu* (Va. Smith 1608), *Susquehanok River* (Md. 1666 Alsop), and *Sasqusahana R.* (N. Am. 1680 Thornton). The repetition of the initial *sa-* persisted for a century. Compare Powhatan "water" (Strachey *Secqwahan, Suckquohana*; Smith *Suckahanna*).

"Muddy stream," based on Heckewelder, is the most frquent translation of *Susquehanna*; and the latest, most elaborate translation is Tooker's "People of booty or spoil obtained in war." To reach this interpretation, Tooker persisted too literally in his pre-judgment (based on Smith) that the **Sasquesahanoughs* were men of booty and spoil, and he therefore sees Massachusetts *sequ-* "booty, spoil" in the beginning of the name, and *-anock* (*-anough*) "men" at the end. The truth is, however, that such an analysis contradicts Algonquian grammar, which requires that an element meaning "booty or spoil" be followed by something verbal (such as "seizers").

All told, the simplest explanations of *Susquehanna* are the best, and I feel confident that *-hanna*, at the end of the name is the widely used Algonquian element (meaning "stream, river") one finds in Allegh*any*, Toby*hanna*, Loyal*hanna*, Rappa*hann*ock, etc. The opening part is probably from Algonquian "smooth," whose variants occur in Massachusetts as *sooskwa*, in Ojibwa as *cōcw*, and in Fox as *cockwi*. This is also the analysis of N. W. Jones (*Jones* 1868), who translates "Smooth flowing stream." (See: Tooker, *The Names Susquehanna and Chesapeake* (No. III, *The Algonquian Series*).

SWANSCUT CREEK. Also spelled SWANSECUTE (etc.). A tributary of Chincoteague Bay, Worcester County. Several colonial spellings are *Swanscutt* (Md. 1670 Herrman), *Swansicot* (Md. 1684 Thornton), and *Swanscutt* (Ches. Bay 1735 Hoxton).

Sw is not an initial cluster in Algonquian. Moreover, though the early forms of *Swan Gut* look very Algonquian, the only real difference between *Swan Gut* and *Swansecut* is the additional vowel (*e* or *i*) before *s* and *c*—a circumstance easily explained as a colloquial intrusion on the order of the *a* in "athaletic" or the *i* in "Patapsico."

It is therefore surprising to find Marye commenting, in regard to *Swansicut* in a Virginia will of 1679, that "The Indian name has been corrupted into Swan's gut." The following remark by Harry Covingtom suggests that the name was the English *swan*: "The Dutch named ... [a] region in 1651 Zwaanendael or Valley of the swans, while the Maryland - Virginia divisional line of 1668 ran east from Watkins Point to a creek called Swans Cut ..." Despite Marye, then, I reject an Indian origin and find it most likely that *Swanscut* is from *swan* and *gut*. Swan point and Goose Point are in the vicinity. (See: Marye, *BASD*, III, Feb. 1940, p. 22; Covington, "The Discovery of Maryland or Verrazano's Visit to the Eastern Shore," *MHM*, 10, 1915, p. 217).

Note: In such forms as Swanscut, *gut* has become *cut* by assimilation. *Gut*, meaning "run, sluggish stream," occurs in two other Maryland *swan* names. McJimsey gives thirty-five instances of the use of *gut* in Virginia, the first being in 1636. (See: "Topographic Terms in Virginia (III)," *Am. Sp.*, XV (1940), No. 3).

SWANTON. Village near Wilson, Garrett County. Weeks notices that in 1823 SWANTON was mapped as *Swan's Mill*. And, remarks the Guide, "It was named for Swan's Mill." It was once a B & O. shipping point for yellow and white pine timber. Early settlers were Patrick Hamill and Abraham Wilson, of Wilson's Station. Cf. Swanton Hill (summit), Allegany County. See GORTNER. (See: Weeks, pp. 21–22).

Note: Rand-McN 1877 has *Swanton*, Kent County, near the Sassafras River. The name (Cf. Swanton Creek) comes probably from one of the Swan Creeks of Sassafras River.

SWEETAIR. Village near Jacksonville, Baltimore County. (*Sweet Air* 1850 PHC). See Ralph Reppert, "Sweetair: A Town Aptly Named" (*Sun* /Mag/, 10 June 1962). It appears that SWEETAIR arose in connection with "Sweet Air" estate (Georgian style brick home, 1750) and took its name in 1812. The name was more than usually apt owing to the abundant locust trees which "scented the spring breezes."

Note: Reppert states that the Sweet Air estate was part of a 1704 grant to Charles Carroll, founder of the family in this country. He was attorney general, agent, and receiver of lands for his kinsman, Lord Baltimore III. The 1704 grant (5,000 acres) was divided into "Ely O'Carroll," "Litter Luna" /sic/, "Clynmalira," and "Sweet Air," all named for the landholdings of the Carrolls in their native Ireland.

SYKESVILLE. Town. Below Eldersburg, Carroll County. (*Sykesville* 1832 PHC). For 1831, Hungerford mentions "... Sykes Mills—now Sykesville." Warfield (p. 485) explains: "It takes its present name from

Note: Hungerford (I, 125–126), for March 1832, indicates that the B. & O. Railroad, some 31 miles from Baltimore, regaled its passengers by stopping for dinner at "the Halfway House." "Both the plantation and the tavern belong to a Mr. Sykes, and already the little town springing up around the railroad depot is being called Sykesville." I notice that Lantz (p. 69) describes James Sykes as "... son of John Sykes, of Baltimore ..."

Mr. James Sykes, the Englishman who converted a flour mill into a cotton mill and lived to regret it."

SYLMAR. A village northeast of Rising Sun, Cecil County. It is at the Pennsylvania border. The name is a combination of syllables from *Pennsylvania* and *Maryland*. Cf. DELMARVA, MARDELA SPRINGS, MARYDEL, etc.

T

TAKOMA PARK. Montgomery County suburb of Washington D.C. (*Tacoma or Tacoma Park*, R-McN 1892; *North Takoma, Takoma Park*, Matthews 1902). The name has no aboriginal significance in Maryland. The Haskin Information Service (20 Sept. 1949) has suggested that *Takoma* was selected "because the area (el. 200) lies higher than the National Capital ..." Compare the Pr. George's County, Washington suburb, Mt. Rainier. Mt. Rainier (el. 120), named in 1902, was (in Washington State) earlier called **Mt. Tacoma*.

Proctor describes Takoma Park "as unnamed" in 1884. However, W. A. Hooker, of the Takoma Park Historical Society, writes me (1950) that Benjamin Gilbert, on the suggestion of his friend, Ida Summy, named Takoma Park in 1883–84. Adele Chidakel is definitive: "It was invented, named, promoted and, to a large extent, built by Benjamin Franklin Gilbert, a Washington real estate man who drove through the area one day in 1883 ..." (See: *Washington Past and Present* [N.Y., 1930, I, 155]; Chidakel, "Takoma Park's First Seventy-five Years," *Star* [Mag.], Nov. 16, 1958).

Note: Maryland's Takoma Park and Mt. Rainier are both, of course, primarily from **Mt. Takoma, later Mt. Rainier, a peak in Washington State. See MT. RAINIER.

TALBERT. Village near Cheltenham, Prince George's County. (GMd 1904). Heads 1790 lists six *Talbert*, two in Anne Arundel County and four in Montgomery. Reaney calls *Talbert* "A rare name, identical with the French Talbert. v. TALBOT." See TALBOT.

TALBOT. Village near Cheltenham, Prince George's County. (*Talbots*, Martenet 1866). The family name Talbot abounds in the area. Heads 1790 lists ten *Talbot* for Prince George's. Stein states that John Talbot (d. 1709), son of Richard Talbot, early Puritan settler of Anne Arundel County, was the founder of the Calvert County branch of Talbots. Their plantation was "Expectation," near the Upper Cliffs above Parker Creek.

TALBOT. ... see EASTON.

TALBOT COUNTY. It lies on the Eastern Shore of Chesapeake Bay, and borders Tuckahoe Creek and the Choptank River. According to

Mathews, it was named in 1662 for Grace Talbot, daughter of George, first Lord Baltimore. Parran and Clark call her Lady Grace Calvert Talbot, "sister of the Second Lord Baltimore and wife of Sir Robert Talbot, second Baronet of Cartown ... County of Kildare." Clark expresses the opinion that the name, Talbot County, may have been chosen as a "sweeping gesture" to all of the Talbots. And he and Mrs. Russell Hastings suggest the possibility that Lady Frances Arundell Talbot, sister of Anne Arundell, was the wife of Lord Baltimore II. (See: Hastings, "Calvert and Darnall Gleanings from the English Wills," *MHM*, 22: 4, Dec. 1927, pp. 315–16).

Note: Gannett (p. 295), quite unreliably and, I think, mistakenly, attributes the county's name to "a son of Sir Robert Talbot, of Ireland ...; though some authorities state that it was named for the uncle of Lady Talbot."

TALBOT or SUSQUEHANNAH MANOR. (*Archives*, XXXI, p. 524).

TALL TIMBERS. Village near Drayden, St. Mary's County. Also *Tall Timbers Cove*. Knight (p. 46), recollecting social activities between 1825 and 1853 at the "old Piney Point Hotel," mentions "... 'Tall Timbers,' as it is called now, taking its name from the tall pines that grow along the shore ..." Cf, "Tall Timbers," an 1845 Montgomery County home, so named because of "very tall oak trees still standing on the lawn" (Farquhar, pp. 9–10).

TANEYTOWN [TAHN-y]. Near Stumptown, Carroll County. (*Taneytown* 1795 PHC). Lantz and Stein give 1750 as the founding date; the Guide gives 1740. There is disagreement as to *which* Taney the name comes from. The Guide and Lantz cite *Frederick* Taney "of Calvert County" (Lantz). Stein, however, cites *Augustine* Taney. The latter, Stein remarks, was the best known of the Calvert County family founded by Michael Taney (Fr. *de Tani*). He was a Huguenot whom the Puritan leader, Thomas Letchworth, transported to Calvert County (with his brother) before 1655. (See: Stein, 322–23).

Note: "Tawney-town" (for 1783–84). See Edith Rossiter Bevan, *MHM*, XLI: 2, June 1946).

*TANNERY. Allegany County. See GILMORE.

TANNERY. Village near McGinnis, Carroll County. Cf. other similar names, such as TANHOUSE CREEK, Worcester, and TANYARD BRANCH, Caroline (at Federalsburg). Cochrane (p. 166) remarks that tanning had been introduced in America as early as 1830. Indeed, tanneries in Maryland were "quite numerous in rural sections before 1830." As for the Federalsburg tanyard, Clark comments that there was a "sizeable trade in tanbark" at Federalsburg. "Because the source of supply

---

Note: Warner et al., p. 46, enumerates 26 tanneries in Carroll County.

was nearby and plentiful it is not surprising to find that there was a tan-yard in the vicinity at an early date." Cf. also TANYARD COVE, Anne Arundel County. (See: Clark, II, 1111).

TASKER CORNERS. Village near Kearney, Garrett County. GMd indicates that the name is sometimes *Tasky* Corners. Weeks (p. 22) mentions Richard *Tasker* among "other early settlers" in the Kitzmiller area. TDr Garrett 1963 lists twenty-one *Tasker*, one of which (Mike Tasker) lives at Tasker Corners. Passano gives twenty-five genealogical items on *Tasker*. Stein notes that Thomas Tasker (d. 1700) settled in Calvert County in about 1668. His son, Col. Benjamin Tasker, helped to develop the iron mines of Anne Arundel County. Howard McHenry mistakenly concludes that there are ". . . none now living of the Tasker name in Maryland, though there are many descendants through Elizabeth Tasker Addison and the daughters of Benjamin Tasker."

Note: See Johnson's article on the Tasker family (*MHM*, IV, 191); also McHenry's "Some Early Colonial Marylanders," *MHM*, XVI: 2, June 1921. Speaking of early 19th century settlers in the Kitzmiller area, Schlosnagle (p. 67) lists the ". . . sturdy Scotch-Irish folk—Davises, Hamills, Harveys, Junkens, Paughs, Pews, Rafters, and Taskers."

TAYLOR. Village near Furnace, Harford County. (*Taylor* 1849 PHC). Marye, mentioning a fight with Indians at the head of Gunpowder River in 1661, speaks of the Foster brothers and John Taylor, a county magistrate who lived on "Taylor's Choice," the site of Joppa. Marye remarks that the names of Taylor and of the Fosters survive "to this day" in the names of small creeks. Doubtless the TAYLOR of today commemorates a descendant of the *Taylor* of "Taylor's Choice"—however, TAYLOR is about thirteen miles from (present) Joppa. Marye also notices "Taylor's Mount," for more than 200 years the estate of the Taylor-Day family. See TAYLOR ROAD. (See: Marye, *MHM*, XV: 2, June 1920; *Archives*, III, p. 419).

Note: Scisco ("Notes on Augustine Herman's Map," *MHM*, XXXIII: 4, Dec. 1938) speaks of Taylor's Cr., below Sim's Point/Gunpowder River?/, on the lands of John Taylor ("Taylor's Mount" tract, 1661), a "fellow justice of Herman" and the father-in-law of Sims and Windley. Herrman 1670 maps *Deep C*[r], *Fosters C*[r], *Taylor*[s] *Cr.*, *Sims Pt.* (for Baltimore County). Cf. *Foster Branch* (head of Gunpowder River, near Magnolia).

TAYLOR ROAD. Baltimore County. *Md. Hist. Notes* (22: 3, Nov. 1964, p. 11) speaks as follows about a genealogical study of the Taylor family by Carroll T. Sinclair, of Pittsburg: "The family is discussed from its original settlement in Anne Arundel County through intermediate generations to its status as a large land-owning family in Baltimore County, where its name is preserved in such places as Taylor Road and Taylor Chapel."

TAYLORVILLE. Near Gray's Corner, Worcester County. Cf. TAYLORSVILLE, near Winfield, Carroll County; and *TAYLORSVILLE,

Anne Arundel (1850–1852 PHC). Heads 1790 lists twenty *Taylor* for Worcester County. As for the Carroll County *Taylor*[s], Heads 1790 lists for Frederick County and Baltimore County are pertinent. For Frederick County, Heads 1790 lists three *Taylor*. For Baltimore County (excluding Baltimore Town) there are twelve. Heads 1790 lists for Anne Arundel County only four *Taylor*.

T. B. [TEE-BEE]. Village near Brandywine, Prince George's County. (*Tee Bee, P.O.*, Martenet 1866). The date it was founded is in doubt. Muriel Dobbin states that the first postmaster was appointed in 1862. Francis T. Monroe reports: "The name was derived from a boundary stone, with T on its west side and B on its east . . ., marking the boundary between the . . . acreage of my great-grandfather William Townsend (1768–1849) and that of Thomas Brooke." Stein (p. 27) describes Thomas Brooke as Major Thomas Brooke, second son of Robert Brooke (b. London, 1602). Muriel Dobbin calls him a former major in the British army, a member (1662–76) of the Maryland Assembly, and (in 1667) a presiding justice of the county court (d. 1676). She notes that on the site of the original marker of TB there is a notice stating that the boundary stone marked a corner of "Brookefield," a tract patented in 1664. (See: Dobbin, ". . . TB," *Sun* [Mag.], 19 Nov. 1961, p. 38; Monroe, *Names*, 1: 3, Sept. 1953, p. 209).

TEMPLEVILLE. Northwest of Marydel, on the Queen Anne's and Caroline County border. PHC (*Templeville* 1847) indicates that before 1847 the name of this place was **Bullockville*. And Emory (p. 533) has "Bullock-Town (now Templeville)." Emory adds that Templeville was incorporated at about the time of the decline of Crumpton (ca. 1870?). And he explains: "Templeville (formerly Bullock Town) . . . derives its name from the Temple family of which Ex-Governor Temple of Delaware was a member . . ." Heads 1790, for Queen Anne's County, lists George Temple. Lewis 1878 lists, among farmers living near the Templeville post office, J. H. Temple, John T. Temple, and John W. Temple. With **BULLOCK-VILLE* cf. SHAVOX. See SHAVOX.

Note: BE 1878 mentions James Temple, of Templeville, a member of the state legislature in 1850, and his son, William E. Temple, of Templeville (b. Templeville, 1836), who became sheriff of Queen Anne's County in 1869.

*TENLEYTOWN. Erstwhile northwest Washington suburb, Montgomery County (*Tenallyton*, Peale 1902). Proctor (p. 187) states that in 1899 TENLEYTOWN was described in the city directory as a "post village on the Rockville turnpike." He derives the name from John Tenley, "who had a tavern in Georgetown." Gannett, however, attributes the name (*Tenley*, as he gives it) to "two sisters, weavers, who lived near the old toll-gate." Cf. *Tenley* Circle, a derivative.

TERAM CREEK. Scott 1807 mentions this stream: "The land[s] in the s. parts of . . . [Dorchester] County are low and marshy; particularly along

Transquaking, Blackwater, and Teram creeks. . ." Perhaps this name is related to variants of the first syllable (*Trans-*) of Transquaking Creek, q. v.

TERRAPIN BRANCH. A tributary of the Middle Patuxent River, Howard County. The turtle designated by this name is well-known in Maryland. It has given rise to the contraction "Terps," which denotes the University of Maryland football players.

Despite its Latinate spelling, *terrapin* is the folk etymology of a common Algonquian word for "turtle, water turtle" (Delaware [Campanius] *tulpa*, *turpa*; Abnaki *turebe*, Lawson *terebins*, etc). (See: *Handbook*, II, 734; Alexander Chamberlain, "Algonquian Words in American English," *JAFL*, XV: 59, p. 261).

TERRAPIN SAND COVE POINT. The cove is on the northeast end of Smith Island, Somerset County. The point is a tiny island on the outer edge of the cove. Evidently terrapins abound. See TERRAPIN BRANCH.

TERRA RUBRA KEY FARM. Carroll County. Warner (et al.) notices (p. 21) that the Key and Bruce families came here from Frederick County. "Terra Rubra," a tract of 1865 acres, was patented to Philip Key, the grandfather of Francis Scott Key, in 1752. The name is an allusion to the area's "red earth" (*terra rubra*).

TEXAS. Village on Goodwin Run, Baltimore County. (*Texas*, /*Ellengowan P.O.*/ Martenet 1873). PHC (n. 83) states that "Taylor Hall" /1850/ was in that year changed to "Ellengowan." S. E. Kearns and S. F. Gavin identify *ELLENGOWAN as the *original* of TEXAS. Mrs. Gavin believes that *Ellengowan* became *Texas* soon after the Spanish American War. And she repeats the story that the change was made because Marylanders in that war had been stationed in Texas. Map entries show, however, that TEXAS was named at least twenty five years before the Spanish American War. (See: Kearns and Gavin, "Marylanders Identify Twelve of State's 600 'Lost Places,' " *Sun*, Oct. 1, 1946, p. 20, p. 26).

Note: The Md. Historical Society informed me (January 13, 1959) that TEXAS was named for "a group of Marylanders who fought in the war of Texas independence."

THACKERY POINT. On the north bank of the Elk River, Cecil County. The U.S. Geographic Board's decision, "Not Tackaras," indicates that this name has had a strange spelling. However, the presence of Thomas Thackery in Cecil County in 1790 makes it likely that the designation is from the family name, probably his.

THAYERVILLE. Near Oakland, Garrett County. Weeks (pp. 39–40) attributes the name to Murray Thayer, who bought land on Deep Creek in about 1830 and built "a large house of white pine." It appears that he and his brothers, Stephen and Job (descendants of Captain Abel Thayer, Braintree, Mass.), came to Yough Glades from New England in February

1819. Murray and Job went on to Lewis County, Virginia; Murray returned to Maryland to be near Stephen.

THOMAS ... This surname appears to be the source of eleven Maryland placenames (GMd 1941), two of them villages—THOMAS (near James, Dorchester County and THOMAS RUN (near Thomas Run, Gibson, Harford County). PHC has: "Thomas Run ... 1854-End." Heads 1790 lists 147 *Thomas*[s]; and to *Thomas* Passano makes thirty-six direct genealogical references. According to the Guide Thomas Viaduct (earlier *Carrollton Viaduct), completed in Dec. 1829, takes its name from the *given* name (*Thomas* Latrobe, its designer). Cf. Thomas Viaduct (Patapsco River, near Relay; completed in 1835). It was named for the first president of the B. & O. Railroad, Philip E. Thomas (Hill, MCC, p. 98).

THURMONT. Town near Graceham, Frederick County. (**Mechanicstown* 1815 PHC). The Guide relates that the first settler was here in 1751. Woody West notes that in 1894 the Maryland Legislature approved a change from *MECHANICSTOWN to THURMONT. But he gives no clue as to the origin of the present name. There is no doubt, however, that *Thurmont* is a variant of the surname variously spelled *Thurman, Thurmand, Thurmon, Thurmond*. TDr Md-D.C. suburbs 1974–75 lists 20 *Thurman*, one *Thurmon*. TDr Baltimore 1969 has 13 *Thurman*, one *Thurmond*. (See: West, "Thurmont Clings to a Slower Life," *Star-News*, Oct. 28, 1974).

THURSTON. Village. South of Urbana, Frederick County. GMd 1941; Manual 1947; Maryland, GMW, 1961/73. In the 1790 Census, there were no *Thurstons*[s] in Maryland; in 1941 the population was 50. TDr Frederick 1971 has John R. Thurston living on Carrollton Drive. Gannett 1905 lists three places (two counties and a town) by this name. The family name is Old Danish and means "Thor's Stone."

TILGHMAN [TILL-man]. Village, near Avalon, Talbot County. Adjacent, on Harris Creek, Chesapeake Bay, is TILGHMAN ISLAND (*Lows I.*, Martenet 1866). Earlier **Lows Island*; and "... once Great Choptank Island ... earlier Foster's Island ..." I learn from Shannahan (p. 28) that Matthew Tilghman once owned TILGHMAN ISLAND. George T. Harrison informs me (20 Nov. 1967) that his father and uncle founded the Tilghman Packing Co. here in 1897. (See: Roberts, *MHM*, XLI: 3, Sept. 1946).

Note: Roberts, writing later (*MHM*, XLII: 2, June 1947) states that Col. Vincent Lowe (whence *Lows Island) acquired *Foster's Island or *Great Choptank Island (now Tilghman Island) by marrying the daughter of Seth Foster. Lowe came to Maryland in 1672. As for Matthew Tilghman, Ingraham (p. 100) states that he was a member of the Md. Legislature from 1751 until the Revolution. He was called the "Patriarch of Maryland," and in 1783 resorted to his estate at Tilghman's Point. I assume that Matthew Tilghman was the descendant of Dr. Richard Tilghman (b. London, 1626). According to Skirven, Dr. Tilghman came to Maryland in 1657. In 1670 he was sheriff of Talbot County. (See: "Seven Pioneers of the Colonial Eastern Shore," *MHM*, XV: 4, Dec. 1920).

TILGHMANTON. Village near Fairplay, Washington County. Williams tells of the patriotism in 1807, of Dr. Frisby Tilghman, Hagerstown. Later he was Captain Frisby Tilghman, of the Washington Hussars. He lived at "Rockland" (Tilghmanton District) and drilled his hussars at the crossroads today called LAPPANS. In 1808 he was a delegate to the state legislature. See the Guide, p. 395. (See: Williams, I, 144).

TIMONIUM. Village near Lutherville, Baltimore County. (*Timonium* 1833 PHC). Genevieve H. Johnston (letter, Timonium, Sept. 1950) tells me that the present name comes from "Timonium Mansion," the home of Mrs. Archibald Buchanan, locally known as "the lady of sorrows." My informant notes that Mrs. Buchanan lost a close friend at sea, and later became blind. Consequent melancholia led her to call her home "Timonium" after the tower near Alexandria, Egypt, to which Mark Antony retired following Actium and the desertion of his friends. Mrs. Buchanan also fancied that her later life resembled that of Shakespeare's misanthropic *Timon* of Athens.

TIPPITY WICHITY ISLAND. It is at the head of St. Mary's river, near Great Mills, St. Mary's County. Manual 1947: *Tippity Wichity Island.* Ernest G. Dickey, the owner of this island (1971), tells me that it was also known as **Lynch's Island*, from a Southern Maryland family who may have once owned it. Mr. Dickey thinks the name is Indian, but he cannot explain it.

In truth, this name apparently refers to the Tipitiwitchet, once the popular name for Venus's fly trap (Dionaea muscipula), a remarkable insect-eating plant from North Carolina. The word is Virginia Algonquian and is analyzed as *tĭtĭpĭwĭtshik* by W. R. Gerard, who translates "[leaves] which wind around (or involve)." See *Handbook*, II, 759.

*TIPQUIN, TIXQUIN. *Archives*, XIII, for 1684, records "Tixquin on the south side of the said River, Tixquin, a town at Tipquin, Tipquinn on the south side of Nanticoke River." *Tipquin* is probably a contraction of *Wetipquin* Creek. It illustrates the Maryland and Virginia speech tendency to omit an intial syllable when there is stress upon the second syllable. And here we have *we-* omitted from *Wetipquin* to give *Tipquin*. Other examples from aboriginal names are *Coan* (from *Chicacoan*), *Quinton* (from *Acquinton*), *Wango* (from *Nassawango*). See WETIPQUIN.

TOBACCO RUN. A tributary of Deer Creek, Harford County. Cf. Tobacco River, Michigan. As the Guide remarks, tobacco early became the staple crop of the Maryland province. *Tobacco* (borrowed by the Spaniards) is perhaps from Taino, the language of the extinct natives of the greater Antilles and the Bahamas.

*TOBACCO STICK. Little Choptank River, Dorchester County, (*Tobacco Stick* 1837 PHC). Elwood Cheeseman, postmaster at Madison, tells me (June 1953) that **Tobacco Stick* (from TOBACCO STICK CREEK) post office has been changed to *Madison*. Cheeseman relates that an Indian is said to have jumped across the mouth of a stream near here by using a tobacco stick. This gave rise to *Tobacco Stick Creek*. He hints (cf. *Tobacco Stalk C*, Churchman 1787) that a tobacco *stick* was the *stalk*.

Note: The *Archives* (XL, for 1665; LI, for 1670; LIV, for 1666) record that a man in colonial times once used "a tobacco stick in his hand" to defend himself from an Indian arrow; that John Richardson assaulted his wife "with a certain Tobacco Stick to the value of one penny Sterling"; and that with "A Tobacco stick" a farmer broke three of a hog's legs. See MADISON.

TOBYTOWN. Montgomery County. (*Toby Town*, *Star*, July 3, 1968). On Dec. 30, 1965, the *Star* called it: "... a small Negro settlement at River and Pennyfield Lock Roads in Potomac ..." The name is probably from the family name *Tob(e)y*. Heads 1790 lists one *Tobey*, four *Toby*. Md. Sub. D.C. TDr 1967–68 lists six *Tobey*, two *Toby*.

*TOCKWOGH FLU. Probably the early name of what is now the Sassafras River, Cecil County. The same word designates the Indian tribe and their erstwhile nearby village. Smith spells *Tockwogh flu.*, *Tockwoghs*. On Herrman 1673 it is *Sassafrasx*, on Moll 1736 it is *Sassafras*. Earle concludes: "The Indian name gave way to ... 'Sassafras' ... shortly after the coming (1634) of the Calverts." (See: Earle, *Chesapeake Bay Country*, p. 311). See: TUCKAHOE.

TODDSTOWN, TODDVILLE. Both places are in Dorchester County. The former is barely identifiable (GMd 1941); the latter is near Wingate. The family name *Todd* applies to TODD(S) POINT (Baltimore & Dorchester Counties), to TODD(S) WHARF (Caroline), to TODDSTOWN and TODDVILLE (Dorchester), and to *TODDS CREEK, today Spa Creek, Annapolis. The Annapolis creek was named for Thomas Todd, a shipwright who came to the Severn area in 1649. L. D. Scisco has Thomas Todd in the lower Patapsco in 1660, and at the river's entrance in 1669. He lived at "Darinton," on what is today Sparrow's Point. As for the Todd in Toddstown and Toddville, there are 62 *Todd* in TDr 1963 Dorchester, one of them living in Toddville. TDr 1970 Annapolis lists fifteen *Todd*, presumably the descendants of Thomas Todd (*Todds Creek). Heads 1790 lists twenty-three *Todd*; Passano makes forty-seven genealogical references. (See: Kelly, p. 10, p. 20; Scisco, "Notes on Augustin Herrman's Map," *MHM* 33: 4, Dec. 1938).

*TOHOGA. According to *Washington City and Capital*,[1] the Indians of long ago established a village named *Tohoga* at the fall line of the Potomac River. It is suggested that the site is today Georgetown, and reference is made to "grants" to "individuals at Tohoga ..." This suggests that the name is recorded in early Maryland and Virginia land records. I have not seen such records, nor have I found *Tohoga* in the Maryland *Archives* or on a map. See, however, Wilstach, *Tidewater Maryland*,

---

[1] *American Guide Series* ... 1937, p. 715.

p. 332. As for a translation, *Tohoga* may be a badly spelled version of *tuckahoe*. See TUCKAHOE.

TOLCHESTER BEACH. Village. Chesapeake Bay, near George-town, Kent County. The Guide states that this "bay side resort" started in 1877; and Lantz (p. 169), for 1877, mentions the Tolchester Steamboat Co. The name itself is probably a compound of *Tol-* (fr. the surname *Tolson*) and *Chester* (probably fr. the river). W. B. Marye tells me (4 April 1970) that "Tolchester," 400 acres, was surveyed for William Tolson, 1 Aug. 1659. The same folio speaks of land resurveyed for Tolson ". . . by the name of Tolchester." (See: Rent Rolls of Kent County . . . Calvert Papers No. 883).

*TOMACKTICO RIVER. Somerset County. In *Archives*, LIV, for 1667–68, one finds: *Cuttomacktico, Tomacktico river*. Evidently a short-ened form of *Cutmaptico* Creek. The missing initial syllable was probably Algonquian "large" (Delaware *kit(t)-*.) See CUTMAPTICO CREEK.

TOMAKOKIN CREEK. A tributary of St. Clement Bay, St. Mary's County. Two early spellings suggest folk etymology: *Tomacookin* (Cotton, III, for 1703–13); and *Tomachokin* (*Archives*, XLVI, for 1750). I learn from Dorothy Shannon (1959) that the children of Leonardtown pronounce this name: Tuh-Moke-uh, Tuh-MOKE-n. Although a reduplicated version of Strachey's *tamokin*, "to swim," is a possibility, I prefer to explain *To-makokin* as a reduplicated form of Algonquian *tamaqua* (Delaware *kte-maque*) "beaver" PLUS the Algonquian locative suffix *-in(g,k)* [Prim. Alg. *-(e)nki*]. The meaning would be "Beaver place."

*TOMLINSON(S) . . . One of the early names of Grantsville, Garrett County. (*Tomlinsons* 1822 PHC; Tomlinson . . . Jesse Tomlinson /p.m./, Register 1834). Weeks (p. 15) points out that in 1761 Joseph Tomlinson patented the first land in Garrett County. On it he built the Red House Inn. In 1816 his son, Jesse (1754–1840), built the Stone House Inn. *TOMLINSON'S became *Little Crossings* in 1834. The latter, in 1846, became Grantsville. See GRANTSVILLE.

TONOLOWAY. It arises in Pennsylvania and flows through Maryland to the Potomac River at Hancock, Washington County. Also a hill in Han-cock District and a hamlet. In Hancock there is *Tonoloway* Street.

See Donehoo for Pennsylvania spellings. He declares: "There is no au-thority . . . for the form Tonoloway, which is used on all recent maps of . . . [Pennsylvania]." Some early Maryland spellings are *Toonaloway* (1737 Mayo), *Town Alloway, Cunnolleaway's Hill* (*MHM*, XV, for 1739), and *Conoloway Cr.* (1794 Griffith).

Donehoo, convinced that *C* is the correct opening consonant, regards this name as a corruption of *Conoy* or *Canhaways*. However, to judge from the folk spellings (*Town Alloway, Canallowais* [1775]), *c* and *t* were not always clearly distinguished by the early settlers—some may have pronounced *c* (*Canal*lowais), others may have said *t* (*Town* Alloway).

As it turns out, the spelling with *c* favors a Delaware derivation from *guneu* "long" and *Alloway* "tail," *Wulalowe* "beautiful tail." The meaning would be "Long tail," signifying "Wildcat, Panther." See ALLOWAY.

Note: The phonetic fumbling with *c* and *t* suggests a common indeterminate Algonquian sound.

TONYTANK CREEK. A tributary of the Wicomico River, Wicomico County. Compare Capt. Smith's *Tanxsnitania*. Maryland spellings are *Tundotenake, Tundotanck* (*Archives*, XV, for 1671–81); *Taney Tank Br.* (1841 Lucas); and *Toney Tank, Toney Tank Mills* (1884 Rand-McNally).

Folk etymology may have transformed Smith's *Tanxsnitania* into Maryland *Tonytank*. Therefore one should not ignore Tooker's interpretation of *Tanxsnitania*—which he modifies to *Tauxuntania*—as a compound of *tank* "little," *-itan* (PA*-*e?tan*), and *-anough* "people." The meaning (see Tooker) would be "People of the little rivers."

However, the Archival spellings strongly suggest that the forerunner of the Wicomico County *Tony Tank* is *Tundotenake* (*Tundotanck*). And this form I analyze as a compound of *tänk* (with a changed vowel) "little," *-aten* "hill," and *-e?tan* "stream." The resultant form (*tänk-aten-e?tan-ki*) is a "changed conjunct" and would mean "Where there is a stream at the little hill."

See: William Wallace Tooker, "The Algonquian Appellatives of the Siouan Tribes of Virginia," *Am. Anthropologist*, VIII (1895), pp. 376–92. For a description of the "changed conjunct" in Algonquian grammar, see James A. Geary, *Int. Journal Am. Linguistics*, XI (July 1945), 160–181, XII (April 1946), 66–78.

TOPHILL... Near Welcome, Charles County. PHC has "Top Hill (See Hill Top)." And in a note on Hilltop (1800–) PHC states: "The office appears once as 'Top Hill.' " On one's way to TOPHILL near Ironsides, the road of a sudden winds to the top of a little hill. See HILLTOP.

TOWN CREEK. Potomac River, Allegany County. (*Town Creek* 1839 PHC; *Town Creek, Town Hill*, Fisher 1852). TW (I,12) notes that the early records call it "Oldtown Creek." The same authority states that *Old Town Creek* is from the Shawnee Old Town, near its mouth on the Potomac River. Cf. Town Creek, St. Mary's County near California, mentioned in *Archives* XLVI, 498, for 1750, and *Archives* L, 317, for 1753. PHC (n. 26) thinks that despite some indication that there was a post office at Town Creek, St. Mary's, in 1850, "It is almost certain that this post office never operated." See OLDTOWN.

TOWSON. Northern suburb of Baltimore City, Baltimore County. Nearby, and from the same family name, are TOWSON HEIGHTS and TOWSON RUN (2). (*Towsontown* 1827 PHC). Both Davidson (p. 123) and the Guide, the latter giving the date of 1750, attribute the name to Ezekiel *Towson*. John Goodspeed, however, mentions "William Towson, innkeeper and founder." (See: Goodspeed, "Maryland Diary—of Towson He Sings," *Capital*, Dec. 5, 1969).

Note: Goodspeed's mention of William Towson brings to mind (see Marye) William Towson, the owner (ca. 1754) of "Gunner's Range," on the site of Towson, and "Vulcania," at the head of Towson Run. The English family name, *Towson*, sometimes alternates with *Townsend* and *Tolson*. (See: Marye, "The Old Indian Road, Pt. II," *MHM*, XV: 3, Sept. 1920, p. 211).

*TOWSONTOWN. See TOWSON.

*TRACEY'S STA (MYRTLE P.O.). See GLEN BURNIE.

TRACYS LANDING. Village near Nutwell, Anne Arundel County. (*Traceys Landing* 1803 PHC). In Heads 1790 I can find no *Tracy* for Anne Arundel County. However, TDr Annapolis 1970 has thirteen *Traceys*, nine *Tracy*.

TRANSQUAKING RIVER. A tributary of Fishing Bay, Dorchester County. An authentic forerunner of the Maryland name is Virginia Algonquian **Tramasquecook* (1621). Three early Maryland spellings are *Tresquaquin* (1673 Herrman), *Transquaquin* (Cotton, I. for 1675), and *Tresquegue* (Emperor Ababco). On Herrman and Mt. and Page, 1673, 1780, Transquaking is the alias of **St. Catharin(e) River*.

Gerard, citing a variant (**Tramasqueac*) of *Tramasquecook (1621)— which he designates as "Renape" *Teramaskekok*—makes a derivation from "Renape" *tēarar* (Delaware *talala*) "white cedar." This PLUS Delaware *maskek* "swamp" and the locative suffix *-ing* would give "Place of the white cedar swamp." Unfortunately, from the Algonquian standpoint, this analysis is unacceptable because Delaware *maskek* (full form *mackäkwi*) in composition would have to drop its *m*.

Yet all is not lost if the *m*—which must be accounted for if the name is to be derived from **Tramasquecooc*—be looked upon as a misreading (*r* misread as *m*) of the second *r* of *tēarar* (Del. *talala*), or if the *m* be looked upon as a substitute for *r* made by someone who knew that Delaware *maskek* means "swamp" but did not know that the combining form of *maskek* is *-ackwäki* (without *m*). (See: Gerard, *Handbook*, II. p. 801).

Note: By "Renape," a coined name, Gerard chose to designate an Algonquian linguistic group related in particular to Ojibwa. Prehistorically, the word for "true or native man" in this group was, as Gerard conceived it, *renape*. He assumed a dialectal change from *r* to *l* in historic times. "Renape" today is Lenape. And by modern *renape* Gerard embraces, as it were, the *l*-dialect Delaware word, of identical meaning, *lenape*. And his "Renape" *tēarar* is the Delaware *l*-dialect word *talala* "white cedar." (See: *Handbook*, II, 371; also my "Place-names and Dialects: Algonquian," *Names*, 24: 2, June 1976).

As for folk etymology, it is evident that **Tramas-* and *-queac* have been falsely fancied to mean *Trans* and *quake*.

*TRAP. Near Feagaville, Frederick County. This was later **Newtown Trap* and is now Jefferson, Frederick County. The name is attributed to gambling houses that "trapped" farmers and teamsters. (See: Grove, p. 374, p. 493). See JEFFERSON.

TRAPPE. A village near Hambleton, Talbot County. (*Trappe* 1813 PHC). *Talbot County Maryland A Tourist Guide* (Ch. Commerce 1968) gives two theories of the name's origin: (1) that a Trappist monastery, with ruins still existing in the first farm house off Main Street going south, once flourished here; and (2) that it is from a colonial tavern, "The Partidge Trap," whose patrons were described as "visiting the Trap." However, I feel that the following remarks by Emory (p. 10) are sufficiently explanatory: ". . . the location of wolf traps at certain points gives their names to certain bridges, roads, etc. A 'Wolf trap bridge' mentioned in a deed of July 14, 1724 would seem to explain the origin of the word trap or Trappe as used to designate a certain portion of Talbot County."

TRAPPE. A village near Fruitland, Wicomico County. Compare *Upper Trappe P.O.*, on the site of present day Allen, and *Lower Trappe*, farther south, in Somerset County, near Kings Creek. Three names are involved. Bradford 1838 maps **Trap*, near Princess Anne, and this I take to be the **Lower Trappe* of Martenet 1866; the 1941 Gazetteer has *Lower Trappe Point*, Somerset County. *Upper Trappe is today *Allen*, and only the TRAPPE near Fruitland survives. In the absence of contrary evidence, I attribute these names to animal traps. See ALLEN: see *LOWER TRAP.

*TRAPPE. Near Trappe Creek, Worcester County. The Guide relates: "Trappe declined as Berlin developed in the early 19th century on the new stage route." There is still Trappe Road.

TRAP RUN. Youghiogheny River, near Kendall, Garrett County. The following are several other Maryland *trap* names that—like TRAP RUN— were probably given owing to the early presence of animal traps: the "Trapp" (Preston, p. 153, Deer Creek): "a place commonly called *the Trapp*" (*Archives*, XLII, p. 424, for 1744); *Trap* [near Poplar T.] 1797; *Trap* or *Poplartown Cross Roads* 1816; *Trap*, Bradford 1838; *Trap*, Bradford 1838 (Manokin River, near Princess Anne); and *Trap*, Bradford 1838 (Pocomoke River, below Snow Hill). In the absence of explicit data, a surname origin is of course possible. Wm. *Trap* was in Baltimore County in 1790 (cf. Trappe Road, Baltimore City). TDr 1969 Baltimore lists twenty-one *Trapp*.

Note: "Trappe Shell Service Station," Trappe Road, Baltimore, suggests a locality. Alexander Levin (*The Szolds of Lombard Street*/1960/p. 86) mentions "the Trappe Road," Baltimore. Davidson (p. 200; after 1868) mentions "Trappe Road," in connection with Fifth Avenue, Canton, Baltimore City.

TRAVILAH. Village near Darnestown, Montgomery County. (*Travilah*, POD 1883). I notice *Travilah Road*, Rockville. Cf. TRAVILLAH WHARF, near Morgnec, Chester River, Kent County. Hanson (p. 141) mentions the marriage (ca. 1829) of Margaret *Travilla*. The name is Cornish; and the surname may be from Travillick, Cornwall. However, there are other comparable placenames, such as Treville, Herefordshire, England. The *Tre* may be Welsh "hamlet." In Cornish, *tra* means "beyond, over,"; and *tre* means "dwelling place, home, town." See TREVANION.

Note: I have seen *Travilla* as the name of a cinema costume designer.

TRENTON. Near Arcadia, Baltimore County. (Martenet 1866). The origin could be a surname. Richard *Trenton* was in Frederick County in 1790; Charles *Trenton* is listed for Anne Arundel County in TDr Balt 1969. Cf. Trenton, N.J., named for Col. William Trent (*Trent Town > Trenton). Ekwall mentions *Treanton* as an old Breton personal name. No doubt it originated from the river name *Trent*.

TREVANION. A village near Copperville, Carroll County. Also (GMd 1941) *Trevannon Farm* and *Trevanion Mills*. Warner (et al.) mentions Trevanion among the flour and grist mills of the 19th century. Its earlier name was Kepharts "Brick Mills." On March 19, 1855, "Brick Mills" was bought by William Wallace Dallas, who forthwith improved the flour mill and built a mansion, "Trevanion." Trevanion is a Cornish personal name, containing Cornish *tre* "dwelling place, home, town." Compare Trevanion, an English officer in Charles Lever's *Confessions of Harry Lorrequer* (1839).

*TRIADELPHIA. Inundated village, Patuxent River, near Unity, Montgomery County. (*Triadelphia* 1811 PHC). Manual 1962 mentions Triadelphia Turnpike, Triadelphia Road, and Triadelphia Reservoir, all in Howard County. Farquhar explains that this place—established in 1809 or 1810 on the Montgomery County side of the Patuxent River—was completely submerged in 1940 when the Brighton Dam was developed. Esther Stabler recounts that the founders (1809) were Isaac Briggs, Thomas Moore, and Caleb Bentley, brothers-in-law, who had married daughters of Roger Brooke IV. However, Warfield attributes the name to a tract called "Three Brothers," bought from Richard Dorsey by Caleb Bentley, Richard Thomas, and Thomas Moore (Quakers). (See: Stabler, "Triadelphia Forgotten Maryland Town," *MHM*, XLIIII: 2, June 1948).

Note: (1) The Brighton Dam now covers a six-mile tract north of Brookeville and inundates the Patuxent Valley from Brinklow to Triadelphia; (2) the name of the business here was the Triadelphia Cotton Factory; (3) William J. Boswell, Brookeville postal historian, remarks that *TRIADELPHIA was sometimes called *Sowbed* because on one occasion a sow had raised her family under the post office steps. A few old timers called the road in front of the office "Pig Tail Alley."

TRUXTON. Village near Cropley and Great Falls, Montgomery County. Compare Truxton Farm, Truxton Heights, Truxton Park (Anne Arundel). Also *Truxton Circle, a former Washington, D.C., street intersection. Truxton is both a given name and a surname. Truxton Park, Annapolis, for instance, was donated in 1931 by *Truxton* Beale. There are seven *Truxton* in TDr Balt in 1977; and in TDr D.C. 1975, one finds *Truxtun*-Decatur Naval Museum.

Note: The former *TRUXTON CIRCLE, Washington, D.C., was evidently named to commemorate Thomas *Truxtun* (1755-1822), American naval officer.

TUCKAHOE. A tributary of the Choptank River, Caroline County; a village near Denton, Caroline County. Captain Smith's spelling of the forerunner of this name was *Tochwogh flu*. Early Maryland spellings are *Tukkoho Branch* (Herrman 1670) and *Tockwoghs, Tukkoho Br* (Speed 1676).

According to Bozman **Tockwogh flu* was the early name of Sassafras River. *Tuckahoe Creek* has arisen independently as the name of a different stream. However, *Tockw(h)ogh* and *Tuckahoe* are evidently variants of one and the same word.

The stone tablet on the Sassafras River Bridge, Georgetown, Kent County, announces that *Tockwough* is Indian for "... Sassafras, a root from which they made a form of bread." Quite elucidating is a remark by the U.S. Coast Pilot Atlantic Coast Section (1947): "The flats [of Tuckahoe Creek] are covered with tuckahoes or marsh grass in the summer ..."

Gerard, Chamberlain, and Trumbull conclude that *Tucka* means a round root used as food. Gerard considers its source to be "Renape" *p'tukweu* "It is rounded"; Trumbull cites Massachusetts and Delaware *ptukqui* and Cree *p'ttikayoo* "It is rounded."

I am in general agreement with Trumbull and Gerard. However, the word can be derived from more than one related stem. If *Tuckahoe* is cognate with Fox *tagwi* "together" it can mean a fungus pressed together around the base and roots. With the meaning "corm, edible root," it could be ascribed to Fox *tagw-a'ā-* "compact by pounding, pound into meal." And if it concerns round roots or corms, it may well have come from what in Cree (Lacombe) appears as *pitikw-ā-w* "Il est fait en boule."

See: Bozman, I, 127; Gerard, "Virginia's Indian Contributions to English," *Am. Anthropologist*, n. s. 9 (1907); OED, X, Pt i.

TULL'S CORNER. Village near Ward, Somerset County. (*Tulls Corner*, GMd 1904). My visits to this area in June 1953, and again in June 1966, revealed that Rumbley Point in Pocomoke Sound was formerly *Tull's Point. Torrence, discussing *Tull's Creek, remarks that in February 1671 John Rhodes sold to Thomas and Richard Tull the tract "Salisbury," apparently in the vicinity of present Holland Pt. TULLS CORNER and Tulls Branch are about five miles south of Torrence's locality. Torrence thinks that Thomas and Richard Tull were brothers, and he has them coming from Virginia to the Annamessex vicinity in 1666. Cf. SCOTTS CORNER and CARROLLS CORNER, Somerset County. (See: Torrence, p. 121, pp. 512-513).

TUNIS, TUNIS MILLS. Villages. Tunis is near Claiborne, Talbot County. Tunis Mills is on Leeds Creek. The villages are six miles apart. Hill (MCC, p. 155) uses the spelling *Teunis* Mills. From Mr. and Mrs. Richard L. Tunis (of Pasadena, Md.), I learn (1) that Abraham Tunes, founder of the family in Pennsylvania, came to Germantown (Philadelphia) from Crefeld-on-the-Rhine, sixteen miles from Holland, in July 1683; (2) that his name appears in deeds as *Tunes*, though properly it was Abraham *Tennisen*; (3) that his grandfather's Christian name was probably *Tennis*—since it was then the custom of the Hollanders to add *-sen* to the father's Christian name to form the surname of the son; and (4) that *Abraham Tunnis* appears in a list of naturalizations for Sept. 28, 1709. The children of Abraham Tunes (I) and his wife, Bathsheba, bore the name *Tunis*. John Hansel Tunis (b. 1815) was perhaps the first Md. Tunis. He married Georgiana Lowe, of Talbot County.

Note: The mills at Tunis were planing mills. Blanchard (Rev. 2nd Ed., p. 93) states that a large saw mill was built here "nearly 100 years ago."

*TURKEYTOWN ... GMd 1941: "... in Cecil County." See COWEN-TOWN.

TURNER. Village near Sollers, Baltimore County. The surname is abundant, and I am not sure which *Turner* was involved. BE 1878 mentions William Turner and his brother, who came to Baltimore from England in 1795. Lewis Turner, of this family, was born in Baltimore in 1810. He was a prominent butcher.

Note: Turner, situated on two railroads, is also Turner's Station.

TURNER. Village near Mechanicsville, St. Mary's County. The Patuxent River and Calvert County are near by. Stein (p. 328) states that William Turner (d. 1663), probably a Puritan, founded the Calvert County family. He lived in Anne Arundel County before coming to Calvert County and was one of the original Puritan settlers on the Severn River. Stein notes that there were two families of Turners—one in upper Calvert County and one in lower.

Note: According to Stein, William Turner, of Calvert County, left his Calvert lands to his son William, and his Eastern Shore lands to his sons Edward and Richard. Cf. *TURNER'S POINT (Talbot County, near Easton), where the land was granted in 1659 to William Turner, a Quaker.

TURPIN COVE. An inlet of Chincoteague Bay, Worcester County. The surname *Turpin* could be the origin; but I think it quite likely that *Turpin* here represents a local pronunciation of *terrapin*. Cabell Greet has described the Delmarvan speech habit that makes *terrapin* "turpin" and *where* "whir": "... from Accomac County, Virginia, north to Pennsylvania, the vowel of *there, where* is that of *but* [ʌ] or [ə] followed by *r*. Educated as well as uneducated people say [delewer] Delaware. Both are apt to say [am∧rika] America."

I have observed the following analogous E. Shore pronunciations: Barren Island [barn, burn], Herring Creek [hurr-ing], Horse Island [harse], and York River (Va.) [yark].

See: W. C. Greet *in* Couch, W.T., ed., *Culture in the South* (Chapel Hill, 1935), pp. 606–07.

TUSCARORA. Village near Tuscarora Creek, Potomac River, Frederick County. (*Licksville P.O.*/on *South* Tuscarora Cr., Fred. Co./Martenet 1866). Grove (p. 92) describes Tuscarora as a station on "the Metropolitan Branch" of the Baltimore and Ohio Railroad, and notes that it derives its name from Tuscarora Creek, which empties into the Potomac River at this point. Citing Mrs. C. H. Lamar, of Tuscarora, Sophia K. Stunkle (postmistress, 1950) explains: "The town has always been called Licksville. Around 1925 the post office was moved from Tuscarora station to Licksville. So the town now goes by two names. The county uses *Licksville* and the post office uses *Tuscarora.*" See LICKSVILLE.

TUSCARORA CREEK. A tributary of the Monocacy River, Frederick County; also a Frederick County village. An early spelling is *Tuskarorah, Tuskrorah C* (1794 Griffith).

Tooker satisfactorily demonstrates that *Tuscarora* in Maryland is from the Iroquoian tribal name and has no connection whatever with **Kus:flu* (*Kuskarawaok*), former Virginia Algonquian designation of the Nanticoke River and its watershed (Virginia 1608 Smith).

Tuscarora, fashioned with some alteration from Iroquoian *Skarūrën* "hemp gatherers," designates an Iroquoian linguistic group that was first encountered in eastern North Carolina.

Maryland's Tuscarora names point to the temporary presence of these unhappy travellers in Frederick County towards the end of the eighteenth century. Hostility and injustice on the part of the colonists led the Indians to seek a reunion with the Iroquois of the north. They were on the council board of the Oneidas in 1712–15; in 1722, they had entered the League of the Iroquois. The trek from N.C. to N.Y. and Canada lasted ninety years.

TUXEDO. The former name of Magruder, Prince George's County; also real estate developments, such as one north of Roland Park, Baltimore City. Manual 1969 lists Tuxedo, and Tuxedo Colony, both in Pr. George's County.

Tuxedo in Maryland is a secondhand Algonquian name. Chamberlain in 1910 ascribed the original Tuxedo to "a summer resort in Passaic Co., N.J., on "the lake of the same name." However, I can find no such place in New Jersey, and Donald Becker omits *Tuxedo* in his *Indian Place Names in New Jersey* (1964). I am therefore obliged to accept Webster's locality, Tuxedo Park, near Tuxedo Lake, N.Y.

Beauchamp finds Tuxedo in Orange County, N.Y., and remarks: "Tuxedo is a doubtful name, appearing on early maps as Tuxseto. While he thought it of uncertain origin, Freeland called Tucseto, *lake of clear flowing water*, but there seems no reason for this."

Chamberlain gives reasons, however, and derives *tuxedo* from Delaware p'tuk-*sīteu* (*eu*=o) "He has a round foot" (i.e., "wolf"). *Tuxedo* and *Tuckahoe* both have the same stem (*p'tuk* "round") in the first syllable. Since the combining form of -*sīt* (Delaware *usīt*) "foot" is -*sitä*-, a better analysis of *Tuxedo* than Chamberlain's would be *p'tuk-sitä-wa*. The meaning would be the same.

See: *Handbook*, II, 858; Beauchamp, *Aboriginal Place Names of New York* ... Albany, 1907, p. 166.

TWIGGTOWN.   Village near Rush, Allegany County. (Martenet 1866). There was once a Big Pond here, with "flowing springs" and a "great Sink Hole Bottom." TW states that the place was so named because "... only Twiggs lived around the Big Pond, and its countrysides at that time and for long after ..." TW continues: "John M. Twigg was born in 1845 at Twiggtown ... The name is a misnomer, for there was never a town there, not even a village ... It is but a neighborhood, where once upon a time, long ago, there lived so many Twiggs that it came to be called 'Twiggtown' by some countryside wit, and the name hangs to it still ..." (See: TW, II, 1161–66).

Note: TW speaks of the three Twigg brothers who came to Murley's Branch along with its first permanent settlers. They arrived as early as 1787. The land records and the records of wills of Allegany County ... "establish the fact that their father was named John Twigg." TW (II, 1154–56) further notes that Austin Davis Twigg (b. 1863) was postmaster here in 1895.

TWO JOHNS.   Village. Choptank River, near Williston, Caroline County. According to "Maryland's Two Johns," *Sun*, 1 Jan. 1961 (probably by Ralph Reppert), this almost deserted community takes its name from John Hart and John Stewart Crossey, two ridiculously identical comedians who called themselves John Stewart Crossey and John Crossey Stewart and gave a vaudeville act known as "The Two Johns." In the 1880's at the peak of their popularity, they bought a farm on the Choptank River, and added a wharf and a dancing pavilion. The project failed after several years; the two Johns disappeared. The last building here burned down in 1947. The *Binnacle* Yachtsman's Guide (2: 1, June 1966) speaks of the Two Johns Landing, and adds that Baltimore-to-Denton steamships regularly brought people here for dancing and theatrical performances "in the round house on the shore."

Note: Reppert relates that one John had a wife and two children. Were the "two Johns" father and son?

TYASKIN CREEK. A tributary of Wetipquin Creek, Wicomico County; also, a village at the mouth of Wetipquin Creek. Compare *Achquank (Md. 1780 Mt. & Page). See also *Tayachquans (Heckewelder's Account; Handbook, II, 26).

The BAE (Smithsonian) card index defines Taiaskon (Taiaskwon) as General Algonquian "bridge." For the Tawachquan Indians the Handbook gives "Bridge people" (cf. Delaware taiachquoan "a bridge"). Scharf and Bozman make the variation "Bridge builders." The bridges, Bozman suggests, were for trapping. Jones (Rev. H. of Dorchester, 182) states that the bridges were of floating logs "made into rafts."

The Handbook's opinion seems best. Tyaskin is from taiachquoan (B & A, ZID) "bridge." And the Tawachquan Indians are "the Indians at (or of) the bridge." (See: Handbook, II, 26).

U

UNCLE. "Uncle: in St. Mary's County" (GMd 1941). Today this place is little known; though I find (TDr 1963) families with the surname Uncle living in St. Inigoes (1), near Park Hall (1), and at Great Mills (3). The text of a deed I have seen in the courthouse at Leonardtown, for 1872, uses the spelling Uncle, but the signers, Frederick and Parmelia, spell their name Unkle. Uncle (Uncles, Ungles, Ungless) is a British family name (v. Reaney).

UNDERWOOD. Near Oakland, Garrett County. Mrs. Hardesty (b. 1893), of nearby Aurora, describes this place as a farming community near the Underwood Cemetery. The 1790 census lists seven families by this name.

UNION BRIDGE. Village. On Little Pipe Creek, near Linwood, Carroll County. (Union Bridge 1816 PHC). Ralph Reppert states that the original name of this place was *Little Pipe Creek Settlement." Lewis (1878) and Reppert mention that a later name was *Buttersburg, given on account of the good butter made and sold here. Lewis states that the present name was given in 1810 when the village became a post office. Noting that the four Maryland "union" towns (excepting UNIONTOWN) were founded in colonial times, Reppert thinks that "enthusiasm for the new nation" probably accounts for their choice. Yet he and the Guide specifically attribute Union Bridge to a bridge built across Little Pipe Creek to unite the Scott area Pipe Creek settlements. (See: "Four 'Union' Towns," Sun [Mag], 25 Feb. 1962).

Note: PHC (p. 87) remarks: "In one early list this office appears as 'Farquharsville' (The postmaster's name was Farquhar), but there is no evidence the office ever operated under the name."

*UNION CORNER. Cf. AMERICAN CORNERS. See BURRS-VILLE; see PUNCH HALL.

*UNION MEETING HOUSE. Baltimore County. (*Union Meeting House* 1828 PHC). It was still a post office in 1834.

UNION MILLS. Village near Big Pipe Creek and Silver Run, Carroll County. (*Union Mills* 1803 PHC). Reppert, stating his belief that Maryland's four "Union" towns—with the exception of UNIONTOWN—seem to express by their names "enthusiasm for the new nation after the Revolution," cites Mrs. E. Roy Kindig, Union Mills storekeeper, as saying that in its earliest days "the settlement" was called *Meyersville*, after the Peter Meyers family. According to Reppert, the two Shriver brothers, Adam and Daniel, built a sawmill here at the time of the American Revolution. As late as 1878 (Lewis) the place had a "Fullen" mill, a sawmill, and four millers. Cf. UNION MILLS, Allegany County. (See "Four 'Union' Towns," *Sun* [Mag], 25 Feb. 1962).

Note: See Cherrill Anson, "Museum of Maryland at Union Mills . . .," *Sun* /Mag/ 20 Aug. 1961. F. S. Klein ("Union Mills, the Shriver Homestead," *MHM* 52: 4, Dec. 1957) relates that two brothers, Andrew and David Shriver (sons of David Shriver, of the Revolutionary Company of Safety) built a house and mills here in 1797, the original mill contract having called for "a set of mills," a grist mill and a sawmill. The fact that the mill "operated through the union of the brothers" seems to have suggested the name.

*UNIONTOWN. Near Baltimore City? Hill remarks that (so old maps indicate) the Philadelphia Road in 1802 left Baltimore at *UNIONTOWN, thence crossing Bird River near "the old Iron Works . . ." (See: MCC, p. 118).

*UNIONTOWN. District of Columbia. (*Uniontown/Anacostia*, Martenet 1866). Jacqueline Trescott, pointing out that this Washington neighborhood was incorporated in 1854, terms it ". . . the enclave called Old Anacostia or Uniontown." She gives the following explanation by a local historian Louise Hutchinson: "The community was the idea of . . . John Van Hook, who bought [land] in 1854 from Enoch Tucker . . . who farmed here. With his partners, John Fox and John Dobler, Van Hook operated the Union Land Association, hence the name Uniontown . . ." Mrs. Hutchinson adds: "The name remained until 1869, then people began saying Anacostia, which Congress legalized in 1886." My pupil, Charles Kiker (Andrews AFB, 1964) cites Dr. George Havenner's "Early History of Anacostia or Old Uniontown" (*Star*, 11 Sept. 1948) to the effect that the name caused a lot of confusion because of Uniontown, Pa. It was changed from *Anacostia* to *Uniontown* in 1854; in 1856 it was again Anacostia.

Note: Espenshade, finding that Uniontown, Pa., dates from perhaps 1780, remarks: "The name of Union was first applied to this place when the idea of union was becoming a part of the national consciousness. This would seem to be a sufficient reason for its use."

(See: "Uniontown A Neighborhood ... May be Restored," *Star-News*, 27 January 1974). See ANACOSTIA.

UNIONTOWN. Village. Uniontown Road, near Hahns Mill, Carroll County. (*Uniontown* 1815 PHC). Ralph Reppert ("Four 'Union' Towns," *Sun*, 25 Feb. 1962) states that the first record of this town (as *Uniontown*) occurs in 1813. Before that it was called THE FORKS. He adds: "All but Uniontown were founded in Colonial times, and it seems likely that enthusiasm for the new nation after the Revolution led to the eventual choice of names." See Espenshade (above).

UNIONVILLE. Near Oldfield, Frederick County. (*Unionville* 1826 PHC). Ralph Reppert ("Four 'Union' Towns," *Sun*, 25 Feb. 1962) reports that ("according to legend") this village was once called **Idletown*. He states that, with a stone tavern and several homes, the place began in the late 1700's. And he includes UNIONVILLE among the three "Union" towns that, since they were founded in Colonial times, probably got their names owing to "enthusiasm for the new nation after the Revolution."

Note: Lewis (1878) probably means this place when he mentions Unionville "... on the Liberty Road, 2 mi. e. of Liberty ..." Cf. Unionville, Baltimore Co. near Glenarm. This is probably the place designated by Martenet 1866 as *Unionville* or *Long Green Academy P.O.*

UNIONVILLE. Near Tunis Mills, Talbot County. See foregoing explanations.

UNIONVILLE. Near Pocomoke City, Worcester County. Today there is a Methodist church among the few houses here. Allen L. Hardester (Pocomoke City, June 1966) thinks that this name comes from Trinity Church (Worcester 1950).

Note: Elmer Brittingham (Poc. City, June 1966) describes Unionville's locality as Henderson's Neck.

UPPER FAIRMOUNT. Village near Freetown, Somerset County. There are no hills here; *upper* and *lower* are used from the standpoint of going up or going down (Cecil Ford, Fairmount, June 1966). See UPPER HILL.

Note: In PHC the post office of *Fairmount* is given for 1849; and note 79 (p. 83) states that *Fair Mount* was changed to *Jamestown* in 1849. Martenet 1866 gives Jamestown near Fairmount. However, I see that on my copy of Som. Co. 1950 I have written near *Upper Fairmount* the annotation "P.O. formerly **Jamestown*."

UPPER FALLS. Village one mile west of Little Gunpowder Falls, near Bradshaw, Baltimore County. (*Upper Falls* 1851 PHC). In his "Place Names of Baltimore and Harford Counties," William B. Marye cites *Upper Falls* as an example of placenames hard to explain: "This name is appropriate to neither of two places to which it has been applied. In 1877 it was the name of a post office situated between Franklinville and the present Upper Falls ... When this post office was transferred to Star's Corner, at the junction of the old Joppa Road and the Franklinville Road, the name went with it. We generally called the place 'the Corner. . . .' Cf. Fallston, one mile northeast of Little Gunpowder Falls. (See: *MHM*, 53: 1 March 1958, pp. 34–35).

UPPER HILL. Village. Due north of Upper Fairmount, Somerset County. (*Upper Hill* ... see *Freetown*, GMd 1941). There is no mention of Freetown (a half mile north of Upper Fairmount) on Somerset 1950. Cecil Ford (Fairmount, June 1966) remarks that *Upper Hill* became *Upper Freetown* after the Civil War. There are no hills here. *Upper* denotes going up; and *lower* denotes going down. See UPPER FAIRMOUNT; see FREETOWN.

UPPER MARLBORO. On the W. Branch of the Patuxent River, near Washington; Prince George's County. (*Upper Marlboro* 1792 PHC). *Upper* Marlboro is about twelve miles north of *Lower* Marlboro, Calvert County (1796 PHC). Both names are for John Churchill *Marlborough* (1650–1722), hero of Blenheim (1704) and Ramillies (1706). Stein states that Marlborough was very popular in the American colonies, and that *Coxtown, Calvert County, changed its name to *Marlborough* in his honor. To avoid confusion the two towns were thought of as *Upper* and *Lower*. Hill gives the date of the settlement of UPPER MARLBORO as about 1704, "by some Scottish merchants," and states that they gave the name, this being the time of the great victory at Blenheim. At that time the Western Branch of the Patuxent was navigable "into the town." According to Stein, the spelling *Marlborough* was shortened to *Marlboro* in the late nineteenth century. In this connection, Anne Christmas reports that a town ordinance to change Marl*boro* back to Marl*borough* was to go into effect in the summer of 1967. She adds that 1721 is the date of the name, and that the original plat shows that the village was *Marlborough Town. Ms. Christmas cites old postal guides as having *Upper Marlborough* from 1886 to 1892. Without explanation, the 1940 Guide has UPPER MARLBORO. She supposes that the longer spelling was too large to put on a rubber stamp. (See "'Ugh Bill' Corrects Name," *Star* [Sun.], 26 March 1967; Hill, pp. 91–92). See LOWER MARLBORO.

UPPER OCEAN. See OCEAN.

*UPPER TRAPPE. Now ALLEN, Wicomico County. (*Upper Trappe* 1849 PHC). Smith's letter (see below) explains the situation, but I am not clear about the exact location of *Lower Trappe*, or the part played in this matter by *Trappe* (about one mile northeast of Fruitland, Wicomico County). To support a surname origin, I find Wm. *Trap* (Balt. Co., Heads 1790), 22 *Trapp* (TDr Balt. 1967), and such names as *Trappe* Road, Baltimore (TDr 1967). See ALLEN; see TRAPPE.

Note: About UPPER TRAPPE, PHC (p. 80, n. 23) has: "This office was established as 'Brereton,' and 3 1/2 months later it was changed to 'Upper Trappe.' It may not have operated under the name 'Brereton.'" Joseph W. T. Smith, Circuit Court Clerk, Salisbury, confirms the change from *Upper Trappe to Allen* (letter, Sept. 1967): "I was born in Allen, and I have heard my mother and father say that Allen was once known as Upper Trappe.... Lower Trappe is a small settlement in Somerset County a few miles north of Allen."

UPPERCO. Village near Arcadia, Baltimore County. (*Upperco* 1841 PHC). About the surname *Upperco*, H. L. Mencken remarks: "What is now Upperco /the surname/ in Maryland was once *Oberkugen, Opferkuchen, Oberkuchen.*" One finds Jacob *Upercue* (Jr. and Sr.) in Baltimore County in 1790 (Heads). TDr 1967 Balt lists six *Uppercue*, four *Upperco*. (See: Am. Lang., 4th ed., 1937, p. 484).

URBANA [er-BANNA]. Village near Thurston, Frederick County. (*Urbana* 1833 PHC). *Urbanna*, Colton 1856. The Guide states that URBANA was settled in about 1830. Cf. Urbana, Ohio (laid out in 1805). Gannett states that Urbana, Illinois, takes its name from the Ohio town. He attributes the Ohio name to "... urban, 'pertaining to a city.'" Harder's *Illustrated Dictionary*, speaking generally, has: "URBANA From Latin Urbanus, 'citified.' The addition of -*a* is common in the United States to designate a place ..."

URIEVILLE. Kennedyville District, Kent County. (*Urieville* 1846 PHC). TDr Kent 1963 lists eight *Urie*, five of them in Rock Hall (Kent County). According to Usilton (p. 124), John D. Urie was a director of the Kent County Savings Bank in 1901, and served as "Counsellor" of the Kent Building and Loan Company. Urieville Community Lake is here.

Note: *Archives* XXXVIII, 377 (1725) mentions as *naturalized* "Michael Ury of Prince George's County a Greek ..." Heads lists for Montgomery County John and Thomas *Ury*.

"UTOPIA". ... Land records mentioned in *MHM*, XXI: 4 (Dec. 1926, p. 345) list 320 acres called "Utopia," surveyed on Dec. 28, 1670, for Robert Wilson, on the north side of the Patapsco River. Cf. "Paradise 300 acres surveyed on May 1673 for Giles Stevens in Back River, by a little Cove on the north side of the river" (*MHM* XXI: 4, Dec. 1926, p. 356). See PARADISE.

V

VALE. Village. Winters Run, near Belair, Harford County. VALE and adjacent WATERVALE are in the valley-like fissure of Winters Run. The sides of the run are more than 270 feet high.

VALE RUN. Allegany County. The stream begins a mile or so from VALE SUMMIT, and flows north into George's Creek, in the greater George's Creek Valley. It lies between two heights of about 2,000 feet each. The surname *Vale* is rare. It seems to me likely that *vale* here means "valley." See VALE SUMMIT.

VALE SUMMIT. Village (el. 1987), near Loartown, Allegany County. H. M. Parker (once postmaster here) tells me (letter, Vale Summit, Sept. 1950) that *Vale* is from nearby Vale Farm and that *Summit* is from the surrounding heights of Dan's Mountain (el. 2898). The village is within a mile of Vale Run. I therefore think that the name is from either the run or the tiny valley named for the run. It does not seem to me likely that the name of the farm (Vale) would be transferred to the *summit*; or, indeed, that *Vale*, in *Vale Farm*, is a family name.

Note: Since there is a surname, *Vale* (Smith, 1964: *Vail, Vale*), a surname origin is possible. However, the name as it appears in Md. tel. directories, is always *Vail*. Indeed, the only occurrence of *Vale* I have seen is this reference from Passano (p. 328): "Vale Family, Pa. Col. and Revolutionary families of Phila. . . ." See LA VALE: see POMPEY SMASH.

VANSVILLE. Near Beltsville, Prince George's County. (*Vansville* 1804 PHC). Kuethe mentions "Van Ville Tavern (Pr. Geo.).—at present Vansville." The following entry in *Post Offices 1811* well enough accounts for the name: "Vansville Prince George G-G. Van Horn /postmaster/." PHC remarks: "In 1835 the Vansville office was moved three quarters of a mile south, and the name was changed to 'Beltsville.' "

VAN BIBBER. Village near Abingdon, Harford County. I have no data about the Van Bibbers of Harford County; though (Heads 1790) I find three *Van Bibber* in "Baltimore Town," and one (Abraham *Van Bibber*) in Baltimore "county not separated." The latter person may have been living in or near Harford. For neighboring Cecil County, Johnston (p. 186) includes Isaac and Matthias Van Bibber among the early settlers of Bohemia Manor. Their father was Jacob Isaacs Van Bibber, of Holland, a settler of Germantown. The sons were naturalized in Maryland in 1702. In that year, and in 1704, Mat/t?/ias bought parts of the Labadie Tract. in 1708 Isaac Van Bibber bought 138 acres more. Today (TDr Harford 1963) one George L. Van Bibber lives in Bel Air.

VAUGHAN. Village near Indian Springs, Washington County. Gazetteer 1941 indicates that VAUGHAN is on USGS 1901 Hancock. But I do not see it there or on any other map. In Heads 1790 I find: six *Vaughen* for Baltimore Co.; Isaac *Vaughan* and John Vaughen for "Baltimore Town"; George *Vaughan* for Pr. George's County; and Thomas Vaughan for St. Mary's County. Under the family name *Vaughan*, Passano (p. 330) refers to the Ellicott Chart, the Lloyd family history of Wales, Pa., and Md., the M. Van V. Tyson pedigree chart, etc. In "Seven Pioneers of the Colonial Eastern Shore" (*MHM*, XV: 3, Sept. 1920, pp. 230–251), Percy Skirven notices Robert Vaughan (d. 1668), High Constable for St. George's Hundred, St. Mary's County, Feb. 1637/38. In 1648 he was Commander of the Isle of Kent.

VEIRS MILL, VEIRS MILL ROAD [VEERZ]. Washington, D.C. suburb, Montgomery County. (*Viers Mill Road, Viers Mill Village*, Manual 1962). Stating that on Veirs Mill Road, two miles south of Rockville, stands Veirs Mill, built after 1838 by Samuel C. Veirs, Farquhar comments: "It seems inexcusable that county officials ... made the mistake of spelling the name of this family who have been well known in Montgomery for over a century 'Viers' instead of *Veirs* as it should be." Boyd lists E. Veirs & Brothers as Rockville millers. Nearby farmers were E. M. and W. A. Veirs.

VENTON. Village near Monie, Somerset County. Oriole notes that this place was earlier *Habnab. Cf. the surname *Vinton* (2 in Heads 1790; Passano "Vinton. Hazelhurst charts. MHS."). Note also places by the name of VINTON in California, Iowa, Louisiana, Ohio; also Vintondale, Pa.

Note: Compare (Ekwall) Fenton in Cumberland and Devon, England; Reaney mentions the "derivative" surname *Venton*. See *HABNAB.

VERONA. Village near Glencoe, Baltimore County. Discussing a survey of a tract northwest of Glencoe, on the York Road, Marye remarks: "This milestone stands ... below a crossroads called Verona." Gannett refers to *Verona*, Maine, New York, and "seventeen other towns and villages, named from Verona, Italy." (See: "The Great Maryland Barrens, III, *MHM*, 50: 3, Sept. 1955).

VICTOR. Village near Mount Vernon, Somerset County. On a visit here (summer 1966) I learned that Victor Neck was earlier *HUNGRY NECK, q. v. The origin in probably the surname *Victor*. Heads (1790) lists four *Victor* for Worcester County (Somerset County lists destroyed). TDr 1964 for Somerset and Worcester lists two. Cf. Victor Haven (Annapolis, Back Creek). TDr Annapolis 1970 lists two *Victor*.

VIENNA. A town on the Nanticoke River below the mouth of Chicone Creek, Dorchester County. Vienna was laid out in 1706 at Emperor's Landing. Jones declares: "It was a town for some years prior to 1709." The emperor of *Emperor's Landing was the Nanticoke chieftan, Unnacocassinon. A State Road Commission sign just off U.S. Route 50 on the outskirts of Vienna announces: "Unnakokossimmon Emperor to the Nanticoke Indians Lived (about 1677) at Chicacone, an ancient Indian town north of this point...."

Vienna is not from the Austrian city of that name. Jones, citing "unofficial sources of tradition," derives it from *Unnacocassinon*. The name is, he states, "a derivative Indian language word abbreviated and amended by substituting a diphthong for a vowel by common usage."

Jone's explanation is hardly to be doubted. Since the *Unna-* of *Unnaco-cassinon* was sometimes printed as *Vnna-*, it appears likely that the founders gave *Vnna-* the alphabetical pronunciation "Vee-enn-na" and adopted it as a placename in honor of the erstwhile emperor. "Vee-enn-na" could not have come from the *pronunciation* of *Unnacocassinon*, since there the opening sound must have been the vowel *u*. (See: Elias Jones, *Revised History of Dorchester*, p. 82. p. 89; Hamill Kenny, *Origin and Meaning of the Indian Place Names of Maryland*, p. 25).

Note: According to William R. Marye (Letter, Aug. 1, 1957) *Emperor's Landing* was not at Vienna but on Rewastico Creek. He cites a 1681 survey: "... on Nanticoke River on the south side of a creek called Rowasticot, beginning at a marked white oak standing on a point of high land near the Emperor's Landing."
I have heard the pronunciations Vye-ANNA and Vee-ANNA.

VINDEX. Village. Three Fork Run, near Kitzmiller, Garrett County. Vindex was still a post office in 1962 (See "Portrait of a Dying Maryland Community," *Star*, May 18, 1962). The latter item states that coal mining here, dating back to 1907, began to slow down in 1950. An additional story (*Star*, 20 February 1967: "Company Town Goes May 1") states that the Johnstown Coal and Coke Co., which built Vindex in 1906 but had quit operating in 1950, was now selling the town and the adjacent land to the Douglas Coal Co. Felix Robinson, of Oakland (letter, 6 Dec. 1966), gives 1907 as the date when the Johnstown company founded Vindex. In an earlier article he had stated, somewhat contradictorily, (1) that the town began in about 1900; (2) that it had had the two earlier names, **Three Forks* and **Maysville*; and (3) that an unknown person chose *Vindex* when the name had to be changed because there were two *Maysvilles* in Maryland. I suggest that the namer(s) of Vindex had in mind *this* meaning of Latin *vindex*: "One who lays legal claim...." (See: Robinson, "Vindex—a Ghost Town in Maryland's West," *Sun* [Mag.], 19 Nov. 1961).

Note: In his 1966 letter, Robinson attributes the name to "A Roman General of the Army of Emperor Augustus." It could also mean "Vindicator," but with what local significance? *Vindex* is a typical coal mining name.

VINEGAR HILL. GMd 1941: "Vinegar Hill in Cecil County." Marye describes this place as "The hill which descends to the Falls down to ... Egypt." And he describes Egypt as the river bottom below Franklinville "... where ... /the/ road crossed over the Falls from Baltimore to Harford County." Marye notes that other persons have accounted for the name by the steepness of the hill -- his grandfather Gittings used to say: "Always trust in the Lord, until the breeching breaks going down Vinegar Hill." Marye himself, however, believes that the name came from

Note: Vinegar Hill, overlooking Enniscorthy, Co. Wexford, Ireland, is the place where the rebels were encamped when they stormed and burned that town in 1798.

abroad: "It is a Monmouthshire place name, also the name of a hill in County Wexford, Ireland. Possibly cotton factory employees at Franklinville named our Vinegar Hill for the place from which they came."

W

*WAKEFIELD. Village. In the midst of "Wakefield Valley," near Wakefield Mill, Carroll County. (*Wakefield* 1836 PHC). The family name, *Wakefield*, is the origin. Frederick County is adjacent to Carroll County; and Passano (p. 332) has: "/Genealogy/ Wakefield. Frederick Co. families. Markell. Ms. Personal list." TDr Baltimore lists twenty-one *Wakefield*[s].

WALDORF. Village near Beantown, Charles County. (Compare *Beantown Sta., Beantown P. O., no* Waldorf, Martenet 1866). BK (p. 140 describes WALDORF as "another" station on the Baltimore & Potomac railway line (1872), and states that it appears as a town and post office on a map put out by the P. O. D. before 1880. My pupil, H. S. Hamilton, of Waldorf, tells me (May 1966) that *Waldorf* means "Town in the woods," and came into being with the opening of "the Pope's Creek Branch of the Pennsylvania Railroad in 1868." However, this place is not in the woods and I do not think that the *meaning* of the name had anything to do with the reason why it was chosen. Walldorf, near Heidelberg, Germany, was the birthplace of the American financier, John Jacob Astor (1763–1848), whose great-grandson was William *Waldorf* Astor. I suggest that the Maryland name was given—perhaps by railroad officials—to honor this family. See BEANTOWN.

Note: Hamilton (see above) cites Bulletin 1, Charles Co. Board of Education, 1948, p. 37. The first syllable of *Waldorf* is properly *Wall-* (*Walldorf*, Germany, Nat'l Geog. Soc., map). The correct meaning of the name is, therefore, not "Town in the woods" but (Ger. *Wall* - "mound, rampart") "Village with a mound or rampart."

WALKERSVILLE. Near Woodsboro, Frederick County. Williams mentions W. H. Walker (b. Pa., 1832–d. Hagerstown, 1889), son of Dr. T. J. Walker, of Waynesboro, Pa. William remarks that the Walkers were early Scotch settlers in Pennsylvania. Note (Passano, p. 332) "Walker ... /Genealogy/ Frederick Co. families ..." (See: Williams, II, 1183–84).

WALTERS. Village near Essex, Baltimore County. Baltimore's most famous *Walters* was William T. Walters (b. 1820), of Scotch-Irish ancestry. He was educated in Philadelphia in civil and mining engineering; and in 1847 he established in Baltimore a "wine and spirits" business. He sponsored the Maryland scuptor, Rinehart, and founded the Walters art collec-

Note: William Walters' son, Henry, bequeathed the Walters Art Gallery to Baltimore in 1931 (Bodine, p. 13).

tion; but I have no evidence to connect him with the East Baltimore village. Baltimore TDr 1969 lists about 245 *Walters*—two of these are in Essex, three in Dundalk.

*WALTERSVILLE. See GRANITE.

WANGO BRANCH. A tributary of Nassawango Creek, Wicomico County. Wango village is near the junction of Wango Branch and Nassawango Creek. The village was named from the branch, which in turn appears to be a contraction of Nassa*wango*. See NASSAWANGO.

*WAPPLEMANDER. Carroll Merriam describes this Dorchester County Village and creek as a "lost" Maryland placename. For 1739-40 (see Cotton VIII) it is *Wappermando Cr.* On 1873 Martenet it is *Whappramander*. *Whapplemander*, a town, appears on Md. 1892 R-McN.

Perhaps this name contains the Algonquian stem "white" (Ojibwa *wāb*, Cree *wap*, Fox *wapi-*). Compare Fox *wapi-maneto'a* "white snake." I recall *White Snake Creek* on an atlas map of the lower Eastern Shore. (See: Merriam, *Chesapeake Cruise*, N. A. Hill, ed., p. 315).

WARFIELD. Village near Sykesville (—USGS 1906 Ellicott; GMd 1941). The scarcity of map entries for this place suggests that it no longer exists. See WARFIELDSBURG.

WARFIELDSBURG. Village near Lees Mill, Carroll County. (*Warfieldsburg* 1837 PHC). PHC (n. 159) throws light on this name: " 'Warfields Store' was changed to 'Warfieldsburg' in 1837."

Note: Lewis 1878 lists under Winfield (Carroll County) one R O D Warfield, physician. Richardson states that Richard Warfield (d. 1703/4) came to Maryland in 1662 and settled in Anne Arundel County. He was a vestryman of St. Anne's Church. (See: Richardson, II, 247-53).

WARING. Village near Germantown, Montgomery County. Bowie (p. 597) states that in England the family name *Warren* changed to *Waring*. He adds that Captain Sampson Waring, of Onslow, Shropshire, came to America in about 1646 and settled at "The Clifts," Patuxent River. Before 1650 he had been granted such tracts as "Sampson's Division" and "Warington," lying in Charles and Calvert Counties (now Prince George's).

*WARRINGTON. Calvert County. Stein remarks that *Warrington—on the road to Dare's Wharf—appears on early maps of Calvert County, "but has long since disappeared." The town was established in 1683 by an Act of Assembly. Captain Sampson War/r?/ing (1617-1670), of the Calvert County Puritan Militia, owned the townsite. See WARING.

Note: Bowie has Captain Sampson Waring coming to America in about 1646. Stein spells the Captain's name *Warring* and has him in Virginia in about 1643.

WARWICK [WAR-WICK]. Village east of Cecilton, near the Delaware border, Cecil County. (*Warwick* 1789 PHC). There are no *Warwick*s in Heads 1790; TDr Cecilton 1964 has *no Warwick*s. However, Balt TDr

1969 has 16 Warwick[s]. Cf. Warwick, Rhode Island (named for the Earl of Warwick), and Warwick, Warwickshire, England.

Note: WARWICK RIVER (bra. Choptank River, Dorchester County), earlier *Secretary Creek, for Henry Sewall, Secretary of the Province of Maryland in 1661/?/. "Warwick Fort Manor," overlooking *Secretary Creek, was built in 1720. The river name, WARWICK, is probably from Sir Robert Rich, second Earl of Warwick (1587-1658) and head (1643) of a commission for the government of the colonies. (See: Ingraham, pp. 294-95; Jones, p. 90).

*WASHINGTONVILLE ... See MOUNT WASHINGTON.

WATERLOO. Village near Dorsey, Anne Arundel and Howard Counties. (*Waterloo* 1819 PHC). Manual 1962 lists *Waterloo Point*, St. Mary's, *Waterloo Road*, Howard, and *Waterloo Run*, Prince George's. "Spurriers Tavern" was on the site of Waterloo (v. Kuethe's List). And if I follow Warfield correctly, "Waterloo Inn" succeeded "Spurriers Tavern." The inn was the area's "central headquarters" and a "popular resort for many years ..." Doubtless the name commemorates the famous battle (1815). Cf. Waterloo Row, Calvert St., Baltimore. Stockett states that Calvert Street was opened in about 1810, and that Robert Mills planned Waterloo Row in 1819.

Note: Warfield points out that near Waterloo two brothers, Col. Edward Dorsey and Hon. John Dorsey, had settled before 1700. Historic tracts situated here were "Troy Hill," "The Grecian Siege," "The Isle of Ely" (cf. Elioak), "Major's Choice" and "Long Reach."

WATERVIEW. Village near Nanticoke, Wicomico County. The village of Nanticoke is within a mile of the Nanticoke River. A *Wall Street Journal* article Aug. 18, 1967, describes WATERVIEW as a "... faded resort town near the Chesapeake Bay." The village had received attention because the D.C. Russian Embassy chose an old hotel here to spend summer with their children. An example of how circumstances can give sudden prominence to an obscure village and name. (See: "Will the Russians Return to Waterview ...?" *Wall St. Journal*, Aug. 18, 1967).

WAVERLY. Baltimore suburb. Also mentioned (GMd 1941) as being a place in Harford County, and in Queen Anne's County. Stockett (p. 294) speaks of the "village" of Waverly, "once called Huntingdon ..." And *The Kalends* of the Waverly Press denotes it as being in 1904 "... a sparsely populated, unpaved suburb ..." There is only *one* Waverly (Irene) in Balt TDr 1969. I am inclined to attribute the name to Sir Water Scott's Waverly novels—which is the source (so Gannett states) of Waverly in Illinois, New York, and Ohio. (See: *Kalends*, XLI: 5, Sept.–Oct., 1962).

WAYSON'S CORNER. Village. "South County," Anne Arundel. In an Evening *Capital* item, April 8, 1975, one reads of "Ed Wayson, whose family owns the Wayson's Corner restaurant ..."

WELCOME. Village near Hilltop, Charles County. Mrs. J. R. Scott (Welcome, March 27, 1971) cannot account for the name. She has "Welcome Inn" on the doormat of her grocery store; and she comments that the neighboring estates welcome visitors during the annual spring House and Garden Pilgrimage. Despite Mrs. Scott's suggestion of a literal explanation, it appears to me likely that the correct origin is the family name, *Welcome*. Passano (p. 341) lists "Welcome. Burbank family. Sedgley, MHS ..." and "Wellcome Family. Ms. MHS." Smith (*Am. Surnames*, 1969) mentions the surname *Welcome*, derived from Welcombe, Devonshire, England.

Note: TDr Charles & St. Mary's 1962 has no *Welcome*; and there are only two such entries in TDr Baltimore 1969. Mrs. Scott and a store customer (a native of southern Pennsylvania) have the astoundingly false notion that the names in this region (*Welcome, Newton, McConchie, &c.*) are Indian.

WELLS CORNER. Village near Marlboro, Prince George's County. Bowie (p. 471) states that the first known ancestor of the *Wells* family (in Md.) was Daniel Wells, of Anne Arundel County. "Bachelor's Delight" was surveyed for him in 1679. Daniel Wells III lived in Annapolis. He was a large landowner and had a pew in St. Anne's Church. University Park, Prince George's County, has *Wells* Avenue and *Wells Parkway*.

WENONA. A village and post office on Deal Island, Somerset County. (Md. POD 1883). The local postmistress (1950) informs me that "The Government gave this name to the Post Office at the time the first P.O. was erected here."

The name is a Siouan importation. Riggs defines it as "First-born child, if a daughter"; and Dunn remarks that "Wi-no-nah is a Sioux, female, proper name, signifying a first-born child." (See: Riggs, *A Dakota-English Dictionary*; Dunn, *True Indian Stories, with Glossary of Indiana Indian Names*, pp. 317–18).

WESLEY. Village near Snow Hill, Worcester County. Cf. Wesley Grove (V.) near Harwood, Howard County. I notice Henry *Wessley* in Heads (1790) for Frederick Co., and Harold *Wesley* (of Salisbury) in TDr Som & Wor 1966. On account of *Grove*, which suggests "camp meetings," I am inclined to attribute WESLEY GROVE (Howard Co.) to John Wesley, worthy preacher and founder of Methodism. Cf. Emory *Grove*, Washington *Grove*, etc.

*WEST BEACH. Mentioned by GMd 1941 as being "In Calvert County." J. Mayo Rector, President of the East Washington Railway Co. (Seat Pleasant, Md.), writes me (Aug. 8, 1950) that WEST BEACH—with "its own post office of that name"—is entirely within the corporate limits of Chesapeake itself, having materialized in about 1900, though it was named by a legislative act in 1894. See CHESAPEAKE BEACH.

WEST FRIENDSHIP. Village near Clarkson, Howard County. (*West Friendship* 1820 PHC). There appear to have been two *Friendship*s east of WEST FRIENDSHIP, namely, *Friendship* (community or church), near Friendship Airport (W.—B. Airport), and *Friendship*, Anne Ar. Co., near Nutwell. WEST FRIENDSHIP could have been so named to differentiate it from the other *Friendship*[s]. The name suggests Quakerism. See FRIENDSHIP.

WEST RIVER. The village is near Galesville, Anne Arundel County; the estuary (*West River*) is a branch of Chesapeake Bay, near Mayo. In 1834 Samuel Owens was the postmaster here, and for seventy or more years thereafter the place was mapped as *Owensville/West River P.O.* Reaney Kelley declares that it was not known where the West River post office was in 1814; but he adds that "in later years it has been in or near Owensville about three miles from 'Tulip Hill.'" According to PHC the post office "Lebanon" was changed to "West River" in 1824.

The village was named from the nearby "river" or estuary. And Fisher explains the name of the latter when he describes it as being "... immediately south and *west* of South River ..." See OWENSVILLE.

Notice the following *Archives* reference (XLIV for 1745-47): "... where the ships lie in West River."

WESTERNPORT. A town at the junction of George's Creek and the North Branch of the Potomac River, Allegany County. In 1803 the name was *Western Port* or *George's Creek*. In 1825 it was *Western Port*; and on Martenet 1866 it is *Western Port P.O.* The early spellings bear out the fact that *Westernport* was a western port on the Potomac River's northern branch. And at this point it may once have been somewhat navigable. TW states that James Morrison laid out the town at the beginning of the [19th] century, and that it was originally called "Hardscrabble." (See: Postal Lists for 1803, 1811, 1819, 1825; also TW, II, 487-88). See GEORGE'S CREEK; see LONACONING.

WESTMINSTER. Town near Cranberry Station, Carroll County. (*Westminster* 1800 PHC; *West Minster*, Register 1834; *Westminster*, Fisher 1852). The Guide points out that in 1764 *Winchester, was the earlier name of the village, given for its founder, William Winchester (b. 1710 London). Lantz states that he came to Maryland in 1729. Soon after the beginning of the Revolutionary War, the town was renamed owing to confusion with Winchester, Virginia. It was incorporated in 1837 (v. Footner, p. 119, Lantz, pp. 66-67). The reason for choosing *Westminster* is not explained. Gannett (p. 170) derives Westminster, Massachusetts, "from the borough of London."

Note: Daisy Malone, a descendant of the original William Winchester, describes him as the colonial proprietor of *Winchester. She adds, moreover, that he was a surveyor, a soldier in the French and Indian War, and a member of the Committee of Observation during the American Revolution. (See: Letter, *MHM*, XXXIII: 1, March, 1938, p. 56). On pp. 66-67, Lantz gives 1830 as the date of incorporation.

WEST NOTTINGHAM. A village near Rising Sun, Cecil County. (*Nottingham*, Register 1834; *W. Nottingham P.O.*, Martenet 1866). The original *Nottingham* arose when two Delaware settlers, James and William Brown, came to this region on the Octoraro River, in about 1702. Later, twenty more families arrived; and after the Revolution there were thirty-seven "Nottingham Lots." In about 1739, so Johnston conjectures, ". . . the names of East and West Nottingham were first applied to the respective parts of the original Nottingham Township." It is probable that some of the newcomers here were from Nottingham, Nottinghamshire, England. (See: Johnston, pp. 145–147, p. 154).

WESTOVER. Village near Cottage Grove, Somerset County. Manual 1969 lists Westover as a *station* on the Penn Central Railroad. Hill states that "In the early days of the Province" "Westover Farm" was situated at the head of Back Creek and near the site of the first courthouse in Somerset County. Guy E. Windsor, Westover postmaster, spoke of "Westover Manor" when I visited him in June 1966. *Westover* is not a local surname. The likelihood is that it comes from Westover, Somersetshire, England. (See: Hill, MCC, pp. 133–34).

WETHEREDVILLE. Near Franklinville, Baltimore County. (*Wetheredsville* 1848 PHC). The PHC notes (86) that "Franklin" was changed to "Wetheredsville" in 1848. Fisher (1852) states: "The mills of Wethered Brothers, celebrated for their fine cassimeres, are located here . . ." Annals (pp. 195–96) mentions James *Wetherald*; Heads 1790 lists Richard *Wethered* (Kent County). In TDr Balt 1969 there is only one *Wethered*.

WETIPQUIN. This creek flows into the Nanticoke River at Tyaskin, Wicomico County. Named from it is the village, Wetipquin, on Wetipquin Neck.

Early Maryland spellings vary from *t* to *l* (*Tipquin*, 1684; *Wellipqueen*, 1700; *Witipquin*, 1787; *Wilipquin Cr.*, 1795). And such an alternation—if it is not the result of a misreading of *l* for *t*—indicates that the name belonged to two dialects, an *l*- dialect (Delaware) and a *t*- dialect (Nanticoke), with both *t* and *l* harking back to an original Primitive Algonquian **l*.

The spelling *Wellipqueen* evidently denotes phonetic *l*. Heckewelder and Johnson use the form *Wilipquin*, with Johnson making it clear that he has in mind the Maryland place. As for meanings, Heckewelder translates "The place of interring skulls." Johnson confirms this, saying, "The word for head was *wihl, wil* . . . which bears out Heckewelder's definition of head or skull . . ."

I agree with Heckewelder and Johnson. Primitive Algonquian **wī̄lipkwin* would become *wītipkwin* in Nanticoke and *Wīlipkwin* in Delaware. And each of the forms contains Primitive Algonquian **wil* "head." Taking the endings of the variants as locatives, the meaning becomes

---

Note: Heckewelder states that the Nanticoke carried with them the skulls of their dead and buried the skulls in holes.

"Skull place." Compare *Wheeling* (W. Va.) "Place of the skull." (See: Heckewelder, *Names which*, pp. 53–54; Johnson, *Lindeström*, p. 402).

WEVERTON. Village near Sandy Hook, Potomac River, Washington County. (*Weverton* 1842 PHC). PHC (n. 119) indicates that "Wevers Mills" became "Knoxville" in 1828, and that "Knoxville" was changed to "Weverton" in 1842. The Guide explains that here in 1835 Caspar W. Wever, civil engineer, established a manufacturing town called WEVERTON. A file factory and a marble works came into being; but all was lost when Wever died. From Hungerford and Grove one learns that Wever was Superintendent of Construction for the B. & O. Railroad and had built many miles of the road through Ohio. (See: Hungerford, I, p. 31, p. 65, p. 120; Grove, pp. 39–39).

Note: A local geographical feature is WEVERTON CLIFFS.

WHALEYSVILLE. Near Willards, Worcester County. (*Whaleysville* 1836 PHC). H. S. Walker, Isle of Wight Bay, pronounces this name without the *s*. The Guide states that the village was named for Captain Seth Whaley, 18th century settler. He was perhaps a descendant of Edward Whaley (Whalley), whose grave is here. Torrence, giving such variants as *Wale*, *Whale*, *Walley*, and *Whaley*, finds Edward Wale in the Pocomoke area in 1666. He moved to the Sinepuxent region in 1676. Was Edward Whaley (Whalley) the English regicide?

Note: The Guide points out that Whaleysville, now a ghost town, was once the center of the shingle industry.

WHEATLAND SCHOOL. Village near Galestown, Dorchester County. I regard Wheatland as a folk etymology from the surname Wheat*ley*. Nelson Wheatley (of Brookview, near Eldorado) suggested this origin. Notice the many occurrences of *Wheatley* in the vicinity, such as *Wheatley* Camp Ground, *Wheatley* Point, and *Wheatleys* Wharf.

WHEATON. A Washington suburban city near Kensington, Montgomery County. (*Wheaton* [nr. Mitchell's X Roads], Martenet 1866; GMd 1904, 1941). From Mrs. George C. Rechen, of the Montgomery Co. Dept. of Public Libraries, I learn that this region originally bore the name, **Mitchell's X Roads*, from Richard T. Mitchell who, during the Civil War, ran a hotel-tavern with an "overflowing bar" on the spot where the Wheaton Pharmacy later stood. Wheaton itself takes its name from Union General Frank Wheaton who, encouraged by a visit from President Lincoln, commanded nearby Fort Stevens and successfully defended the city of Washington in a battle fought on July 12, 1864. Some of the soldiers killed in the battle were buried in a patch of land on Georgia Avenue. (See: The Maryland *Monitor*, July 30, 1964, p. 3).

Note: It is not certain who gave the name. Perhaps it was George Plyer, the first postmaster and a soldier under General Wheaton. Perhaps it was Wheaton's friend, George A. Eccleston, local farmer.

WHITTAKER. GMd 1941: "Whitaker: in Cecil County." Cf. Whitaker's Mill, Winter's Run, Harford County. Louise Ingalls relates that in 1689 the Harford County grist mill was known as Dunkeele Mill. She adds: "The mill owes its present name to Franklin Whitaker, a member of the Maryland legislature who operated it with slave labor in the 1850's." In 1900 the mill closed, and the building became a barn. It has since been restored. (See: Ingalls, "New Grist for Old Mill," *Extra*, Oct. 7, 1973).

WHITE HALL. Village near Hereford, Baltimore County. (*White Hall* 1833 PHC). Cf. White Hall Manor, Anne Arundel, and White Hall Manor, Montgomery. As for other places similarly named, my notes indicate that "White's Hall" (South Run, South River) was surveyed in 1663 for Jerome White; and Stockett (p. 175) points out that "White Hall" was the name of a famous Baltimore tavern. Charles Scarlett indicates that in 1695 the tract "Fuller" (near Annapolis) was renamed "Whitehall," "of London fame," by the Greenburys. This estate became the property of Governor Horatio Sharpe in 1763. And from it have come the names, WHITE HALL BAY and WHITE HALL CREEK. (See: Scarlett, "Governor Horatio Sharpe's Whitehall," *MHM*, XLIV: 1, pp. 9-10).

Note: Kelly (p. 96) points out that WHITE HALL, South River—for Jerome *White*—appears on Herrman 1670.

WHITEHAVEN. Village near Capitola, Wicomico River, Wicomico County. (*White Haven* 1809 PHC). In early times this place was in Somerset County; Wicomico County was formed in 1867. Torrence notices that Whitehaven was established "near the beginning of the 18th century, doubtless through the influence of Colonel George Gale (Anglican, and distinguished official; d. 1712), who came to Somerset County from Whitehaven, Cumberlandshire, England." (See: Torrence, p. 415).

WHITELEYSBURG. Village southeast of Greensboro, Caroline County. (*Whiteleysburg* 1800 PHC). PHC (n. 163) states that "Whiteleysburg" was moved into Kent County, Delaware, apparently in 1803 ..." Cochrane relates that in April 1775, when the American Revolution began, William Whiteley (1753-1816), a citizen of Caroline County (originally from Delaware), became a lieutenant in the Eastern Shore Militia. Later he commanded the Militia of Caroline County; and in 1811 he became a state senator. William Whiteley died in Delaware. (See: Cochrane, pp. 80-81).

WHITE PLAINS. Village near Middletown, Charles County. (*White Plain*, Martenet 1866). The Manuals give White Plain, a discontinued Pa. R.R. station, on approximately the same site as WHITE PLAINS. BK (p. 140) remarks that in 1873 the name of the post office at *Duffield* was changed to *White Plain*, and the location was moved two miles east to the railroad station (Balt. & Potomac, 1872). Compare La Plata. Both places were probably named for their flatness.

Note: In view of the Prince George's commemorative name, Brandywine, one supposes that WHITE PLAINS could celebrate the Battle of the White Plains (N.Y., 1776). And it should not go unnoticed that the surname *White* is rather abundant here. TDr Charles & St. Mary's lists twenty-four *White*[s].

WHITES FERRY. Village and ferry on the Potomac River near Martinsburg, Montgomery County. (*Conrads Ferry*, Martenet 1866). Farquhar (p. 95) states that WHITES FERRY was known as *Conrad's Ferry* before the Civil War. However, Montgomery 1865 lists *Conrads Ferry*— and at that time C. Conrad was living near *Tennallytown. Heads 1790 lists four *Conrad*[s] for Washington County, and five *Conrod*[s]. For Montgomery County, Heads 1790 lists eleven *White*[s]. This historic rural ferry was still operating in 1980.

WHITON. [WHITE-n]. Village near Powellville, Wicomico County. (*Locustville*, Martenet 1866). Esther Evans (Worcester County Public Library, Snow Hill) confirms the pronunciation (June 1966); and Jeff Webb states that it was earlier *Locustville*. The surname *Whiton*, at least in the form one finds it here, is most rare. It is not in Heads 1790, TDr Som & Wic 1966, or Passano. However, in TDr Balt 1969 there are Fred *Whiton* and Linda *Whiton*.

*WHITTEN'S CORNER. William B. Marye (II, p. 244) relates: "In my younger days the tavern at this place was kept by Isaac Tyson, and the place called *Tyson's Corner. His heirs sold it to William Whitten, station agent at Bradshaw, who thereafter kept the tavern. Compare WHITON.

WICOMICO. The opening syllable is pronounced WYE in Maryland and WE in Virginia. A river in Wicomico County, Eastern Shore; a smaller river in Charles County, Southern Maryland; a creek flowing into the Wicomico River, Eastern Shore; and a village in Charles County. Early spellings are: *Wighco flu*, *Wighcocomoco* (Smith 1608 Virginia); *Wighkawamecq*, *Wighco alias Pocomoke R* (Speed 1676 Virginia).

Heckewelder translates "Where houses are building." Kelton, considering Zeisberger's (Delaware) *wikeu* "He is building a house," states that *wag*, *wak*, and *wik* mean "something round." He cites Ottawa *waginogan* "a round lodge" and Ojibwa *wigiwam* "lodge," and defines *wicomico* as "There are houses there." Trumbull defines *-comoco* as "house, enclosure"; Mooney for the same element gives "stockaded village."

The most authentic choice for the opening syllable of *Wicomico* is general Algonquian "(to) dwell" (Fox *wi*-, Cree *wiki*, Abnaki *ik*, *ig*). The latter part of the name almost certainly means "house, village." However, an acceptable translation from *wik* "(to) dwell" eludes me. And I have chosen

See: Heckewelder, *Names Which*, p. 54; Kelton, *Indian Names of Places Near the Great Lakes* (1888); Trumbull, "Indian Names in Virginia," *Hist. Mag.*, n. d., VII: I (Wherein Trumbull translates Narragansett *sachimma-comock* as "a prince's house"); Mooney, *Handbook*, II, 950; Delaware *wingan* (Ojibwa *wīng-*) "It is sweet (-*an* is the copula "it is.")."

to regard the *Wic-* of *Wicomico* as Delaware *wik (wing)* "pleasant." One would translate "Pleasant dwelling or village."

"WITCHOTTS." Vexler (1978), in a section entitled Selected Documents (pp. 89–99), included *Lord Baltimore's Plantation in Maryland* (London, 1634), attributing it to letters to their friends in England by Cecil Calvert's brothers, Leonard and George. Here we find that the word *Witchotts* was used by the Indians of Yoacomoco (St. Mary's) to name the Indian houses that they later gave to the newcomers. From the same source comes Sioussat's reference to "... the town of the Yeocomicoes, with its witchetts, one of which was speedily taken for a chapel...." I have no doubt that *witchott* contains the Algonquian stem *wik-* "something round," in this case meaning "house." Cf. Zeisberger's *wikeu* "He is building a house." See WICOMICO.

WIDGEON. Village near Mount Vernon, about a mile from the Wicomico river, Somerset County. Cf. Widgeon Landing, Anne Arundel County, a name which MHGP attributes to "... the many ducks of that breed that frequent the quiet cove in Meredith Creek ..." The Widgeon is a fresh-water duck, a game bird ... that breeds in the American northwest and winters from Canada to South America.

WILLARDS. A village near Pittsville, Wicomico County. The Guide states that WILLARDS began as a "railroad station named for Willard Thompson of Baltimore, an officer of the line."

WILLIAMSBURG. Village near Hurlock, Dorchester County. (*Williamsburg*, Williamsburg District, Martenet 1866). Cf. *Williamsburg, Talbot County (1840 PHC). Lewis 1878 lists for Williams Wharf (on the Nanticoke) Postmaster J. H. Williams. Today (TDr Dorchester 1963) there are twenty *Williams* in Dorchester County—one of whom (Charles A. Williams) lives in Williamsburg.

Note: Jones (p. 96) recounts that Williamsburg District was laid out in 1859. He adds that its original name was *Bunker's Hill, a name given not for patriotic reasons but satirically—because of frequent "battles" at a local rum and whiskey store. Later the place was often called "Slabtown," owing to the use of slabs for building material. The change to *Williamsburg* was in 1840.

WILLIAMSPORT. Town. At Conococheague Creek, Potomac River, Washington County. (*Williamsport* 1796 PHC). The Guide remarks that the town was laid out in 1786 by General Otho Holland Williams (1749–1794), "for whom it was named." According to Williams, Otho Holland Williams was a deputy adjutant-general in the American (Revolutionary) Army under General Horatio Gates. Later, when he became a collector of the Port of Baltimore, he bought "Springfield Farm" and laid out Williamsport. Leitersburg (p. 17) explains the *-port* of the name: "The Potomac was then extensively used for the shipment of grain and merchandise, for which Williamsport possessed every advantage as a point of consignment." (See: Williams, I, 78–79).

Note: Leitersburg gives 1787 as the date when Williamsport was laid out, "... under authority of the Md. Legislature." Williams states that Otho Williams was born in Pr. George's County and died in Woodstock, Virginia. Mary V. Mish declares that the father of Otho Williams, Joseph Williams, was an early resident of "his Lordship's Manor of Conocheague Indian Reserve." Here he lived on Limestone Hill. Later, General Williams became the owner of "Leeds" and "Ezekiel's Inheritance" ... all of which in time comprised Springfield Farm and the town of Williamsport." (See: Mish, "Springfield Farm of Conococheague," *MHM*, XLII: 4).

*WILLIAM STADT (OXFORD). Mentioned in an Act of Oct. 1, 1704, providing for notched roads (v. Emory, p. 60). See OXFORD.

WILLISTON. Near Denton, Caroline County. (*Potters Landing* 1854 PHC). The Guide mentions the "Potter Mansion," built in about 1730 by Captain Zabdiel Potter, who had earlier taken over "Coquerious Fields" (surveyed in 1673). The place became a tobacco shipping center, with boats sailing forth to England and France. In about 1847, John Arthur Willis bought Potter's Mansion; and the name of the port was changed from *Potter Town to WILLISTON.

Note: I do not find mention of *Potter Town; but a comparison of *Potters Ldg.* (Martenet 1866) with Williston (USGS 1905 Denton) shows that they are one and the same place.

WILLS CREEK, MOUNTAIN. A tributary of the North Branch of the Potomac River, near Cumberland, Allegany County; a mountain alongside the creek; and *Will's Town, "A former settlement of the Shawnee at the site of Cumberland, Md." The earlier name of the creek was *Caicuctuck.

Several early spellings are *Cacutuck (Winslow's Plan 1736), *Caicuctuck or *Wills Creek* (Md. 1755 Fry & Jefferson), and *Wills Cr. Wills Mountain* (Md. 1794 Griffith).

Finding mention of the "town field" in a Survey of June, 1745, Marye thinks *Caicuctuck was the name, first of all, of a town or point of land near the creek. The *Handbook* identifies *Will*, of *Will's Town, as an Indian found living near the erstwhile Shawnee town at the mouth of *Caiuctucuc Creek. Thomas calls him an Indian sachem, and remarks that he died at the end of the American Revolution and is buried on "the uppermost peak of Will's Knob, a spot still pointed to ..." (See: "Notes on the primitive History of Western Maryland," *MHM*, 38, 1943, P. 162; *Handbook*, II, 956; *History of Allegany County* ..., I, 10. See *CAIUCTUCUC; see GEORGES CREEK.

WILMERS. Village near Booker, Chester River, Queen Anne's County. (*Wilmers Neck* /adjacent to Journey Cake Neck/, Martenet 1866). BE 1878 mentions Doctor John Lambert Wilmer, of "Wilmer Point

Farm." J. Hall Pleasants' edition of the "Memoirs of the Rev. James Jones Wilmer" indicates that the first established ancestor of the Wilmer family in Maryland was Simon Wilmer (d. 1699), who settled in Chestertown before 1680. He had come from an English family that lived in Chigwell, Essex. Simon Wilmer II (1686–1737) married Dorcas Hynson ... Simon Wilmer (from Lambert Wilmer) became Sheriff of Kent County, a justice of the county court, and a member of the Provincial Assembly (d. 1768/69). Percy Skirven states that the first Simon Wilmer was a Commissioner of Justice for Kent County (1687) and a Burgess from Kent County to the Provincial Assembly (1689). (See: Pleasants, *MHM*, XIX: 3, pp. 221–22; Skirven, *MHM*, XV: 4, 414 ff.).

WILSON. Village. Garrett County. There are two places so named: (1) near Altamont /W. Va./ on the B. & O. R.R.; (2) s. w. of Gorman, on the W. Md. R.R. GMd 1941 locates both places in Garrett County—yet each is on (or near) a West Virginia boundary. In Omni 1972 WILSON was not a Maryland post office. However, Manual 1969 lists WILSON, Garrett County. The present author's West Virginia placename study attributes Wilson (W. Md. R.R., s. w. of Gorman) to George W. Wilson, school teacher, lumberman, and first postmaster. Earlier names had been *Camden (fr. Johnson Newlon Camden) and *Wilson's Mills. More recently (1967), Dr. Paul Wilson (son of my first informant, Burt Wilson) has told me the different story that the name was from one Abraham Wilson, who at a family reunion in the 1920's was 100 years old and lived only ten days thereafter. He was the first cousin of George Washington Wilson, Dr. Paul Wilson's grandfather.

WILSON P.O. Village near Plum Point, Calvert County. (*Wilson P.O.* GMd 1941). The Wilson family of Calvert and Prince George's County, was founded by James Wilson (d. 1672) before 1652. His son, Major Josiah Wilson (d. 1717), was a major in the Militia of 1698. He became High Sheriff of Calvert County (1690) and a Justice (1700). Later, in Anne Arundel County, he was again High Sheriff. (See: Stein, p. 33).

Note: Biographical Encyclopedia (1876) mentions Hon. Joseph Alexander Wilson (b. Calvert Co., 1831), son of Joseph W. Wilson. He was a lawyer and state senator (1878). His ancestors on both sides came early to Maryland. "Both families own large estates on Chesapeake Bay in that County."

WILSON. Village. GMd 1941: "Wilson: (village) in Worcester County." BE mentions Col. Ephraim King Wilson (b. nr. Princess Anne, Somerset Co., 1771). His father, David Wilson—of early Maryland ancestry—later moved to Worcester County. Col. King Wilson (I) graduated from Princeton in 1790. He was twice elected to the national House of Representatives.

WINANS [WYE-nans]. There is no village. GMd 1941 has: "... see Mount Winans /a suburb of Baltimore City/." The Guide (p. 88) mentions

Ross Winans (1796–1877), Baltimore engineer, who invented the "camel-back /steam/ engine" in 1833.

WINCHESTER. Village on the abandoned Baltimore & Annapolis Short Line R.R., near Annapolis, Anne Arundel County. The place was earlier known as *Winchester Station. Atlas Hopkins 1878 shows Horace R. Winchester, John Winchester, and Jacob Winchester living in this region. The concept of a village probably arose with the coming of the railroad. (See: *MHM*, XLV: 4, Dec. 1950, p. 306).

WINCHESTER. GMd 1941: "Winchester: (town) in Queen Anne's; see Grasonville." Emory speaks of WINCHESTER in the southwestern part (Piney Neck) of Queen Anne's County. He also (pp. 37–38), citing a deed of 20 August 1709, mentions Winchester Creek—presumably the same as Matthew Reed's Creek—near the lands of William Hynson. The name, presumably, is from Winchester, Hampshire County, England.

*WINCHESTER. ... See WESTMINISTER.

WINGATE. Village near Crapo, Dorchester County. WINGATE Pt. is about a mile and a-half to the south. Compare WINGATE'S Pt. at the mouth of Wicomico River, Monie Bay, Somerset County. Jones indicates that in 1902 Urim G. Wingate was the postmaster at Wingate. The same authority mentions Lavinia Wingate, Pritchett Wingate, Thomas and Levin Wingate. Gilbert B. Wingate was an enlisted private for Dorchester County in September 1861. (See: Jones, p. 537).

WINKLEDOODLE CREEK. The Washington, D.C. *Star* (August, 1953) describes this stream as "meandering in and out of Southeast Washington." It is a tributary of Oxon Creek, and can be seen from a bridge at Southern Avenue and Barnaby Street, S.E.

If the name is Algonquian, folk etymology has played havoc with it. *-doodle* effectually disguises the ending. The initial syllables suggest Algonquian "good, fair, pleasant" (Strachey *wingan*; B & A *wingan, wingi*; Fox *wĩgi*).

To propose an English origin, *winkle-* could be from dialectal *wingle* "wind in and out." *Doodle* suggests the *doodle* of Yankee *Doodle*, monkey-*doodle*, etc. These, Mencken thinks (*Am. Lang.*, 1937, 176), "hint at German influences."

WIONA CLIFFS. Five miles up the Severn River from Annapolis, Anne Arundel County. *Wiona Cliffs* (Anne Arundel Co. 1940).

A variant of *Winona*, q. v. Cf. *Weona*, Arkansas (PG, 1936), and *Weona* Yacht Club, Dyckman Street, New York City. See WENONA.

*WITMERS STORE. See BEAVER CREEK.

WOLFSVILLE. Near Middlepoint, Frederick County. (*Wolfsville* 1828 PHC). Jacob Wolf was the postmaster in 1834. Grove speaks of a settlement made here by the Hoover, *Wolf*, and Blickenstaff ... families. *Jacob* Wolf appears to be the most likely source of the name. TW remarks that William G. Wolfe (b. here 1859), son of Cornelius Alexander Wolfe, closed Wolfe's Mills after milling for about twelve years. Lewis 1878 lists J. N. Wolfe, a local butcher, and J. Wolfe, a Wolfsville farmer. (See: Grove, p. 444; TW, II, 1194).

WOODBINE, WOODBINE MILLS. Doris A. Martin, postmistress here, tells me (letter, Sept. 15, 1983): "Woodbine is a small town located in the southern part of Carroll and Howard Counties, between Winfield and Lisbon in the early 1800." (PHC 1840; GMd 1941; *Woodbine, Woodbine Mills* Manual 1947). Ms. Martin adds that the village takes its name from "a running plant called Woodbine that grew in abundance on the banks and fields." She accounts for the *Mills* by remarking: "There was a large worm seed oil distillery that gave employment to many local people." Cf. Woodbine, Harford Co. (GMd 1941).

WOODENSBURG. Village on the W. Md. R.R., near Emory Grove, Baltimore County. (*Woodensburg P.O.*, Martenet 1866). Marye mentions John Wooden, Jr. and Sr., for 1757. At that time, near the main road to the Baltimore Iron Works, there were "John Wooden senior's plantation and John Wooden junior's lane ..." Lewis 1878 lists Frank Wooden among the blacksmiths and wheelwrights here, and B. Wooden and Frank Wooden as neighborhood farmers. (See: *MHM*, XVI: 3, Sept. 1921, pp. 246–47).

WOODLANDTOWN. GMd 1941: "... in Dorchester County." In Lewis 1878 one finds that WOODLANDTOWN is twenty-five miles from Cambridge, near the Honga River and Hooper's Straits. Lewis lists, as general merchandisers, JAM Woodland & Son. Heads 1790 has eight *Woodlands*. And it seems to me likely that this surname also accounts for Woodland, Allegany, Woodland, Talbot, Woodland, Cecil, and both Woodland Beach (Anne Arundel) and Woodland Creek (Talbot). See: LONDON TOWN.

Note: Woodland Beach, A. Ar., was renamed London Town in 1967.

WOODLAWN. Village and Baltimore suburb. Near Franklintown, Baltimore County. Cf. Woodlawn (Anne Arundel), Woodlawn Heights (Anne Arundel), and Woodlawn, Cecil County. The latter was a post office in 1821. Each of these names represents a combination of *wood* and *lawn*. Cf. Woodlawn, Beaver Co., Pa., about which Espenshade remarks: "A suitable tribute to the sylvan beauty of the new village site in the valley of Logstown Run."

Note: PHC (n. 10) states that "'Darlington' Harford County, was changed to 'Woodlawn,' Cecil County, in 1821. 'Woodlawn' was changed to 'Battle Swamp' in 1853."

THEIR ORIGIN AND MEANING 297

WOODMOOR. Village near Kolbes Corner, Prince George's County. There is also a Woodmoor in Montgomery County. For the Prince George's place Lewis 1878 lists L. R. Wood, postmaster, Louis R. Wood, merchandise, and James M. Wood, blacksmith. It appears likely, then, that *Woodmoor* is a combination of *-moor* (*more*) and the family name *Wood*.

WOODSBORO. Village near La Gore, Frederick County. (*Woodsboro* 1798 PHC). Among farmers near Woodsboro, Lewis 1878 lists Charles *Woods*.

WOODSTOCK. Village near Davis, Howard County. (*Woodstock* 1836 PHC). Cf. Woodstock, Anne Ar., Woodstock, Carroll, Woodstock, Harford, and Woodstock, Pr. George's. One supposes that the name is from Woodstock, Oxfordshire, England. This is the origin of Woodstock in both Connecticut and Vermont. I notice that Gov. George Howard's estate, "Waverly," was near Woodstock, Howard County. And Kelley (p. 366), for 1777, mentions "Dr. William Murray of 'Woodstock,'" the estate lying between "Lebanon" and "Tulip Hill" (Anne Arundel County). (See: Warfield, p. 489).

Note: Woodstock is about one and a-half miles from Granite. Warfield remarks that "Woodstock's granite quarries are represented in the handsomest public buildings in Baltimore." There is a *Woodstock Granite*.

WOODWARDVILLE. Village near Odenton, Anne Arundel County. (*Woodwardville P.O.*, Hopkins 1878). Lewis 1878 has WOODWARDS-VILLE, and lists A. G. Woodward as postmaster. No doubt this is the *Abram* G. Woodward who lived in the vicinity in 1878 (v. Hopkins 1878). Warfield (p. 127) refers to a Mr. Woodward who was born at Woodwardville but resided in Annapolis.

WOODYARD. Village near Meadows, Prince George's County. Cf. the early place called (descriptively?) "... the Woodyard." In Fred Shelley's edition of Ebenezer Hazard's travels through Maryland in 1777, one learns that the "Post Master" had a "Country Seat at the Woodyard," the place where Stephen West (d. 1790) manufactured linens, cottons, and woolens ... Shelley relates (p. 50): "... The estate, Woodyard, was built ca. 1692 at the home of Henry Darnall." Shelley's citation suggests a *wood yard*. However, *Woodyard* could be from a surname. Neptune Woodyard (Heads 1790) was a "free negro." And Md. Sub. TDr (1974–75) lists some ten *Woodyards* and one Woodyard Road (in the vicinity of Clinton and Camp Springs, Pr. George's Co.). (See: *MHM*, XLVI: 1, March 1951).

WOOLFORD. Village near Church Creek (t.), Dorchester County. (**Loomtown* [near Woodford Creek], Martenet 1866). Jones remarks that WOOLFORD twenty-five years ago was called *Milton (a P. O. D. name), and that 150 years earlier it was *Loomtown. He accounts for *Loomtown by explaining that (perhaps owing to a premium on the weaving of linen by a 1682 Act of Assembly) "... the industrious maidens there in every household had a weaver's loom." Jones adds that, "two hundred years ago," the Woolfords were residents of "the old place now known as Woolford ..." The same source states that Roger Woolford, of Manokin, Somerset County, came to Maryland (fr. England and Virginia) in 1662. Woolford was a Justice for Somerset County in 1676, 1680, and 1689. He died in 1701. To explain the present name, however, it is enough to mention that Samuel W. Woolford was the postmaster of WOOLFORD, Dorchester County, in 1902. (See: Jones, p. 107, pp. 486–87, p. 537).

WOOTENAUX CREEK. [Pronounced "Wooden Hawk"]. A tributary of Kings Creek, Talbot County. Marye spells it *Woodenhawks Branch*. He cites a 1704 Dorchester County deed signed by Woodenhoocke, an Indian. Dunlap and Weslager cite the comparable *Woodenhawk Bridge*, Sussex County, Delaware. The forms with *wooden* and *hawk* are evidently folk corruptions of an Indian personal name.

Wootenaux, as an Algonquian personal name, may designate an animal, a totemic being. On that assumption, supposing that the word had an *l*-form (Woo*l*enaux), I cite New England *Woollaneag (wullaneag)*, defined by Trumbull as "fisher [bird]" and by Gerard as "fine squirrel." An *l*- form of *Wootenaux* could also be derived from Delaware *wulit (wulik)* "good, pretty,' plus Delaware *haki* "earth, ground." But no *l*- form of *Wootenaux* exists, and the foregoing possibilities have no foundation.

As a stream name, given secondarily to the chieftain, *Wootenaux* could be a denasalized form of *Wyantenock*, general Algonquian for "Place of the bent channel" (BAE). However, a more acceptable solution arises if one regards *Wootenaux* as comprising *oot* (Fox *utci*) "thence," *-en* (PA **eth*) "thus, thither," and *-awank* "earth." This combination plus the diminutive *-su*, gives an acceptable prototype (**ut -eth- āwank -isä -wi*) meaning "It rushes forth from the ground."

See: Marye, "Indian Paths of the Delmarva Peninsula," *BASD*, II (Oct. 1937), Appendix, p. 16; *Indian Place-Names in Delaware*, p. 53; Gerard, *Handbook*, II, p. 974; *B & A wundschen* "wind comes from thence." *Enaw*, in an *n*- dialect, would be the instrumental "shoot forth."

WORTON. Village and creek, near Butlertown, Kent County. *Archives* LIX (1765, p. 299) notices (for Kent Co.): "... from the Head of Worton by Chester Town ..." Of *Worton Heights* (Kent 1849) PHC remarks (n. 166): "... in existence on paper for only twenty-five days and almost certainly never actually operated." It seems to me likely that these names are from the surname (Heads 1790: William *Worton*, Balt. Co.; Ben-

Note: Manual 1969 lists Worton as a discontinued station on the Pennsylvania Central R.R. (earlier the Balt. & Del. Bay R.R.).

jamin *Worton*, Dorchester Co.). However, there is the possibility that an English village may be commemorated. There are Worton (Oxfordshire, near Cassington) and Nether Worton and Over Worton (Oxfordshire).

WOYTYCH [WUR-tick]. Village near Iglehart, Anne Arundel County. Once a well-known station on the abandoned Washington, Baltimore, and Annapolis Railroad. *Capital* (Jan. 12, 1977) tells of the death (in Petersburg, Va.) of Louis B. Woytych, of Atlanta. He was born in Annapolis, and was a member of St. Mary's Catholic church. The surname is spelled variously: e. g., *Woytek* (Balt. TDr 1969).

WYE MILLS. Village northwest of Willoughby, Queen Anne's and Talbot Counties, (*Wye Mills* 1814 PHC). E. M. Barry ("The Old Wye Mills, 1690–1956," *MHM*, 52: 1, March 1957) states that on 16 Sept. 1664 James Scott patented "Old Mill," the land on which WYE MILLS now stands. Additional land records reveal that in about 1686 Henrietta Lloyd (1647–1697), widow of Philemon Lloyd, received timberlands from James Scott, Lloyd's overseer. Bodine (p. 62) remarks that in 1680 "Old Wye Mill" replaced the earlier one that gave the town of WYE MILLS its name. It is a grist mill, and MHGP describes it as ". . . still grinding corn today between huge water-turned stones." All these names (including Wye Neck Wye Narrows, etc.) have arisen, one supposes, from Wye River (a branch of Eastern Bay in Queen Anne's and Talbot Counties). (See: "The Old Wye Mills, 1690–1956," *MHM*, 52: 1, March 1957; MHGP, 1964, p. 53).

WYE RIVER. Arising near Queenstown, it is situated in Queen Anne's and Talbot Counties, and constitutes a branch of Eastern Bay. (*Wye River*: Herrman 1670; FJ 1775; Churchman 1787). To explain WYE RIVER there are three theories: (1) that it is so named because its course forms a "Y" (so believed by Mr. Fowler, post office, Wye Mills, 2 Oct. 1965); (2) that the name is from the family of the Rev. William Wye (d. 1744), who lived near it; and (3) that the name was brought here from Wales (along with *Severn* and *Tred Avon*) where, so Welsh records show, the old king, Evan Lloyd, ruled the lands lying between the Severn and the WYE. The last theory is assuredly the most likely. And Philemon Lloyd (of Lloyds Cr) was perhaps the namer. The British River Wye (rising in Montgomeryshire, on the eastern Slope of the Plinlimmon) is 130 miles long and eventually joins the Severn. (See: Johnston, pp. 220–21; Richardson, II, 196–97).

WYNNE. Village near Ridge, St. Mary's County. Oliver Martin ("The Chesapeake and Potomac Country," C. & P. Tel. Co., 1928, p. 95) describes WYNNE as "a little settlement centering around a fish packing house and a cannery." More fully, Martin speaks of WYNNE as ". . . formerly Miller's, on Smith's Creek, called Trinity Creek by Calvert in 1634 but later renamed by others in honor of Captain John Smith . . ." *Wynne* is probably from the surname. Heads (1790 [Pr. Geo. Co.]) has two *Wynn*[s].

Passano (p. 359) lists a *Wynne* genealogy and cites several sources. See BENVILLE. (See: Martin, "The Chesapeake and Potomac Country," C. & P. Telephone Company, 1928, p. 95).

*WYOMING. GMd 1941: "Wyoming: in Prince George's County." Cf. "Wyoming," Howard County, which Reuben Dorsey bought from Benjamin Howard in October 1845. "Wyoming" lay behind "Arcadia," whose farmhouse lay beyond St. John's Lane ("new U. S. . . . 40"). (See: *MHM*, XL: 1, March 1945, p. 61).

Note: *Wyoming* is not an indigenous Maryland word, but it is typically Algonquian, and may be related linguistically to Smith's *Massawomecke*. The name, usually translated as "great flats," occurs in Pennsylvania and was no doubt borrowed for use as an estate name.

Y

YEOHOE. Village near Cedar Grove, Baltimore County. The name is probably from a surname. There are ten *Yoho*[s] in Md. Sub. D.C. TDr 1967-68, and one in Annapolis TDr 1970. Other apparent versions of the surname are *Yoe* (Heads 1790), *Yeo* (Passano, p. 360, p. 156), and *Yee, Yohe* (Balt. TDr 1962). Compare John *Yeo*, mentioned in relation to Yorks hope, Gunpowder River, surveyed in 1664, and Mount Yeo (nr. Deer Creek), surveyed in June 1683 for John *Yeo*. The Guide notices that "the Reverend John Yeo" was an influential Anglican in Maryland, ca. 1694. (See: *MHM*, XIX: 4, Dec. 1924, p. 351, p. 356).

Note: OE *ēa* "river" (> Yeo) underlies these surnames, which signify "Dweller by a stream."

*YONKERS. An obscure place between Flintstone and Cumberland in Allegany County (*not* in Manual 1947; *Yonkers*, Manual 1969; *Yonkers*, Maryland (Dept. G. M. W. 1961-73). The German form of this name (v. Heintze, p. 153) is *Junker* (*juncherre*) "Junger Herr." In Dutch it is *yonkheer* "young man." Cf. Yonkers, Westchester, N.Y.C., from Adrian Van der Donck, who bought the land from Indians. See: Harder, who calls the Dutch form "possessive."

Note: The name, in Maryland, occurs in a part of the state very much settled by Germans. And Heads 1790, for Frederick County, lists Jacob *Yonker*. Is this one of Maryland's few *Dutch* names?

YORK. GMd 1941 lists "York Road . . . Carroll County; see Keymar." GMd 1941 also lists "Yorktown in Somerset County." The fact that Highway 194 passes through Keymar from Frederick to Hanover, Pa., and thence to York, Pa., no doubt explains the Carroll County name. Compare York Road, Baltimore, a direct route (I83) to York, Pa. The Somerset County name perhaps commemorates the Siege of Yorktown.

Note: In "A Visitation of Western Talbot," E. B. Roberts comments on "the many names common to western Yorkshire and to the western part of Talbot." He cites *Yorke ("in honor of the ancient city in Yorkshire"), a village "that grew up around the first Court House, on the headwaters of the Wye . . ." It was named by Act of Assembly in 1686. (See: *MHM,*. XLI: 3, p. 235).

*YOUGH GLADES [YOK]. Community and Glades of the *Youghio-gheny* River, Garrett County. (Register 1834; Burr 1839). See OAKLAND.

Note: *YOUGH GLADES, the early name of OAKLAND, was alternately "Yox" and "Yox Glades." Register 1834 gives John N. Armstrong as the first postmaster; PHC calls him *William*, and cites a letter (1815) from the Post Master General to *William* Armstrong. These references account for the alternate names *Armstrongs, Md., and *Armstrongs in the Green Glades. Another alternate name, *McCarty's Mill, arose from the *McCarty* family. Isaac *McCarty* was postmaster until 1842.

YOUGHIOGHENY RIVER. Largely originating in Garrett County, this stream flows thence into Pennsylvania and enters the Monongahela River at McKeesport. Green indicates that *Youghiogheny* was the former name of the Pamunkey River, Virginia; and it appears that Castleman's River, Garrett County, was once called *Little Youghiogheny.* Early spellings are *Ohio gani* (Trader's 1752), *Yoxhio geni* (Evans 1755), and *Yoghioghenny* (Bew 1780).

Heckewelder translates "Stream flowing in an opposite direction or in a circuitous course"; and he is joined in this opinion by Beauchamp, Ker, Espenshade, and Green. But Claude Maxwell, a West Virginia writer, divides *Youghiogheny* into *yiough* "four" and *-hanne* "river," and translates "Three main prongs and the main river."

The snakelike windings of the Youghiogheny, especially near McKeesport, somewhat support Heckewelder's definition. But, though *-gheny* could well mean "stream," there appears to be no suitable Delaware word to support Heckewelder's "opposite direction or circuitous course." On the other hand, Powhatan *yeough* (*yowgh*) "four" gives some truth to Maxwell's interpretation. (See: Green, p. 350; *Names Which,* p. 49; Maxwell, "Indian Names in West Virginia," *W. Va. Review,* II; 8, May 1925).

Note: The Delaware word for "round about" is *wiwuneiwi* (*wiwuniwi, wagawe*) and could hardly give *youghio-*. For another possibility, however, one could take the *-gheny* of *youghiogheny* as meaning not "stream" but "lands" (cf. Fox *ahky-ani*), which with *yeough* would mean "Four lands (stream)," Or, as a final conjecture, one may take *youghio-* from Cree *wiyak* "dirty" and make a combination with (*yo*) and *-agan* (*yo-wiyak-agan*) which could give *Youghiogheny* "It flows with a muddy stream." I am strongly inclined, considering the analogy of *Allegheny*, to regard the *-gheny* of *Youghiogheny* as meaning "stream, river."

YOUNGS SWITCH. Switch near La Plata, Charles County. *Switch* is explained by the village's location on the erstwhile Charles County branch of the Pennsylvania Railroad. Stein (pp. 336-37) mentions Captain Richard Young, the first of the Puritan *Youngs* in Maryland and an original settler of Anne Arundel County in 1650. Stein comments that the Youngs of Calvert County are probably descended from George Young and William Young, whose older brother was "Richard Young of the Cliffs." However, the Catholic Youngs appear to have been nearer the locality of YOUNGS SWITCH. Bowie (Across, p. 617) mentions the Catholic, Benjamin Young, a member of the Council of Maryland. Heads 1790 lists four *Young*[s] in Charles County; TDr Charles & St. Mary's lists 41.

*YOWACCOMOCO [yo-KAHM-ee-ko]. This name, variously spelled, was the Indian designation of St. Mary's. The word appears to contain Powhatan *yowgh* "four," Powhatan "land, dwelling site" (cf. Fox *-ahkamigi-*), and the copula *-ä-*. The meaning would be "There are four dwelling sites."

Z

ZACAYA MANOR. et al. Forman (p. 236): ". . . Another home of Charles Calvert lay in Charles County, and was what he called his summer manor of Zacaya, named for the Saccaia Swamp. In 1672 he wrote his father Cecilius. . . : 'I am now building upon your Lordship's Manor of Sachay. . . !' "

Note: The spelling in a later letter was *Zachya*.

ZEKIAH SWAMP, RUN. A marshy stream flowing into the Wicomico River, Charles County; the run crosses the swamp. Early spellings are: *Sacayo* [Indian Nation], *Archives*, V, for 1668; *Zachkia Swamp als* [alias] *Pangayo*, Md. 1670 Herrman; and *Saccaia Path*, *Archives*, II, for 1674.

The name could be from a Maryland Algonquian equivalent of Fox *si-käyaw(e)* "Where there is a bend." Or it could contain a Maryland Algonquian equivalent of Fox *sagwi-* "thick, dense," the *w* of which in *Saccayo* would be lost. (See: Michelson's *Stems*, p. 640: *sïgä-* "there is a corner.") See *PANGAYO.

ZIHLMAN. Village near Frostburg, Allegany County. GMd 1941 gives ZIHLMAN as the postal name for ALLEGANY. Probably for Frederick N. Zihlman (b. Carnegie, Pa., 1879). He was a member of Congress from the sixth Maryland district (64th Congress; 1916). Congressman Zihlman's father was Nicholas Zihlman, who came to Cumberland, Md., at the age of three. In 1909, and again in 1913, he was an active member of the Maryland state Senate. (See: TW,II, 738–39).

ZION. Village near Calvert, Cecil County. (*Zion* 1849 PHC). Compare ZION CHURCH (2), Manual 1962. Gannett mentions Zion, Illinois, and states that the name is from Mt. Zion, Palestine. P.O. Directory (1961) lists 3 Zion, 1 Zion Grove, 1 Zionhill, 1 Zionville, and 2 Zionsville.

Note: In 1966, from one Wilkins, of Waste Gate Road, Worcester County, I have heard the pronunciation ZAHN.

ZITTLESTOWN. Near Boonsboro, Washington County. The Guide (p. 335) has: "So named for the large Zittle family here." Williams (II, 825) remarks that Daniel and Michael Zittle and their wives lived and died here. See BOLIVAR.

Note: *Zittles Town*, Martenet 1866.

COMPREHENSIVE BIBLIOGRAPHY

I. ARTICLES AND BOOKS (*GENERAL*)

Allen (St. Ann's)	E. Allen, *Historical Notices of St. Anne's Parishes...* 1857.
Alsop	G. Alsop, *A Character of the Province of Maryland, 1666.*
Andrews	M. P. Andrews, *History of Maryland, Province and State*, Hatboro, Pa., 1965 (repr. orig. ed., 1929).
Annals	*Annals of Sandy Spring*, Baltimore, 1884–1929, 4 vols.
Archives	*Archives of Maryland* ... vol. 1 -. Baltimore, 1883-19-.
Babcock	W. H. Babcock, "Notes on Local Names Near Washington," *Journal of American Folk-Lore*, I: 146-47, July–Sept., 1888.
Bell	Annie (Walker) Burns Bell, *Maryland Land Records, Baltimore County Deeds*, Annapolis, (1938).
Bell Som.	_____, Index, Rent Roll, Somerset Co.
Bell Kent	_____, Index to Rent Roll ... Kent County.
	_____, Maryland Colonial Statistics and Indices ... Annapolis, 1936.
	_____, Maryland. "Early Settlers (Land Records)" ... Annapolis, 1936–40. 14 vols.
	_____, Maryland Genealogies and Historical Records, Washington, 1941.
BC	*Biographical Cyclopedia of Representative Men of Maryland and District of Columbia*, Baltimore, 1879.
Blair	G. Blair, *Annals of Silver Spring*, Washington, 1918.
Blanchard	Fessenden Blanchard, *A Cruising Guide to the Chesapeake* ... New York, 1950.
_____	F. Blanchard and W. T. Stone, *A Cruising Guide to the Chesapeake* ... [Revised and Updated 1983]. New York, 1983.
Bodine	A. A. Bodine, *The Face of Maryland*, N.Y., 1961.

Bonnett	L. Bonnett, T. S. Offutt, and E. B. Haile, *Baltimore County* ... Towson, ca. 1916.
Bowie	E. G. Bowie, *Across the Years in Prince George's County*, Richmond, 1947.
Boyd	T. H. S. Boyd, *The History of Montgomery County*, Clarksburg, Md., 1879.
Bozman	J. L. Bozman, *The History of Maryland*, ... Baltimore, 1837.
Brewer	J. M. Brewer, *List of Early Maryland Settlers* (1634–1682), Baltimore,
Brinkman	W. H. Brinkman, Never-to-be-Forgotten Tales of Catonsville, Baltimore, 1942.
Bromwell	H. E. Bromwell, *Old Maryland Families*, Denver, 1916– .
BK	P. D. Brown and M. B. Klapthor, *The History of Charles County*, La Plata, 1958.
Brown	B. B. Brown, "The Battle of the Severn," Baltimore, V Md. Hist. Soc. Qt. XIV, p. 154, 1919. 18 pp.
Browne	W. H. Browne, *George Calvert and Cecilius Calvert*, N.Y., 1890.
Brumbaugh	G. M. Brumbaugh, *Maryland Records*, vol. 1, Baltimore, 1915; vol. 2, Lancaster, 1928.
Bryan	W. B. Bryan, *A History of the National Capital*, N.Y., 1914.
Callcott	G. H. Callcott, *A History of the University of Maryland*, Baltimore, 1966.
Carey	G. Carey, *A Faraway Time and Place* ... Wash.-N.Y., 1971.
Carr	L. W. Carr, ed., *Our Streetts*, Edgewater, Md., 1973.
City	*City of the Highlands, Prince George County*, Washington, 1870.
Clark	C. B. Clark, ed., *The Eastern Shore*. 3 vols. N.Y., 1950.
Cochrane	L. C. Cochrane (et al.), *History of Caroline County*, Federalsburg, 1920.
Cotton	J. (B) Cotton, ed., *The Maryland Calendar of Wills*, vol. 1, Baltimore, 1904; vol. 2, 1906; vol. 3, 1907; vol. 4, 1914....
Covington	H. F. Covington, "Verrazano's Visit to the Eastern Shore," MHM, 10 (1915).
Croker	M. B. Croker, *Tales and Traditions of Old Saint Mary's*, Reisterstown, 1934.

Cunz	D. Cunz, *The Maryland Germans*, Princeton, 1948.
Dalrymple	E. A. Dalrymple, ed., *Relatio Itineris in Marylandium*, Baltimore, 1874.
Davidson	I. Davidson, *Real Stories from Baltimore County History*, Baltimore, 1917.
Davies	W. F. Davies, *The Caves of Maryland*, repr. 1952, Baltimore, 1950.
Dunham	D. L. Dunham, *Galesville Maryland, Its History & Its People*. The Paper Mill, Severna Park, Md. 1980.
Earle	S. Earle, *The Chesapeake Bay Country*, 3rd ed., Baltimore, 1929.
Eason	R. Eason, *History of . . . Glen Burnie*, Baltimore, 1972.
Eckhardt	M. S. Eckhardt, *The Story of Glyndon 1871–1971*, Glyndon, 1971.
Ekwall	E. Ekwall, *The Concise Oxford Dictionary of English Place Names*, 4th ed., Oxford, 1960.
Emery	F. Emery, *Queen Anne's County . . . History*, Baltimore, 1950.
Evans	H. R. Evans, *Founders of the Colonial Families of Ridgeley, Dorsey, and Greenbury*, Washington, 1935.
Farquhar	R. B. Farquhar, *Historic Montgomery County Maryland*, Silver Spring, 1952.
Filby	V. R. Filby, *Savage, Maryland*, Savage, 1965.
Fooks	N. H. Fooks, *Historical Compton . . . Dividing (or La Trappe) Creek*, Talbot County . . . 1930.
Footner	H. Footner, *Maryland Main and the Eastern Shore*, N.Y., 1942.
_____(2)	_____, *Rivers of the Eastern Shore*, N.Y., 1944.
Forman	H. C. Forman, *Jamestown and St. Mary's*, Baltimore, 1938.
Foster	J. W. Foster, *George Calvert: His Yorkshire Boyhood*, repr. fr. *MHM*, 55 (1960).
Gambrill	J. M. Gambrill, *Leading Events of Maryland History*, Baltimore, 1903.
Gannett	H. Gannett, *The Origin of Certain Place Names in the United States*, 2nd ed., Washington, 1905.
Geraghty	K. Geraghty, "Mexico in Maryland," *Sun*, Dec. 4, 1960.

Gordon   D. H. Gordon, "Hero Worship as Expressed in Baltimore Street Names," MHM, 43 (1948).

Green   B. W. Green, *Word-book of Virginia Folk-speech*. Richmond, 1912.

Greene   D. M. Greene, *A Brief History of Prince George's County*, Avondale, 1946.

Greet   W. C. Greet, "Delmarvan Speech," *AM. Sp.*, 8 (1933).

_____(2)   _____. "Southern Speech," *in* W. T. Couch, ed., *Culture in the South*, Chapel Hill, 1934.

Grove   W. J. Grove, *History of Carrollton Manor Frederick County*, Frederick, 1928.

Gutheim   F. A. Gutheim, *The Potomac* [Rivers of America], N.Y., 1949.

Hall   C. C. Hall, ed., *The Lords Baltimore and the Maryland Palatinate*, Baltimore, 1902.

_____(2)   _____, ed., *Narratives of Early Maryland 1633–1684* /Orig. Narratives of Early Am. History/, N.Y., 1910.

Handbook   *Handbook of American Indians North of Mexico*, 2 parts, 1907, 1910 (BAE Bull. 30).

Hanson   G. A. Hanson, *Old Kent*, Chestertown, 1936.

Hayes   H. A. Hayes, *The Antietam and its Bridges*, N.Y., 1910.

Heck   L. W. Heck (et al.), *Delaware Place Names*, /Geol. Survey Bull., 1245/, Washington, 1966.

Helman   J. A. Helman, *History of Emmitsburg*, Frederick, 1906.

Hill   A. Hill, ed., *Chesapeake Cruise*, Baltimore, 1944.

Hill (MCC)   H. W. Hill, *Maryland's Colonial Charm Portrayed in Silver*, Baltimore, 1938.

Hodges   M. R. Hodges, comp., *General Index of Wills of St. Mary's County* ... 1633–1900, /Carter-Braxton Chapter D. A. R./.

Howard   G. W. Howard, *The Monumental City, its Past History and Present Resources*, Baltimore, 1873.

Hoye   C. H. Hoye, comp., *Garrett County History of Pioneer Families* /Clippings; LC: F187.G287/.

Hume   Joan Hume, ed. *Maryland Index to the Wills of Allegany County*, 1784–1960. Am. Index Library. Baltimore, 1970.

Hungerford E. Hungerford, *The Story of the Baltimore and Ohio Railroad, 1827–1927*, N.Y., 1928, 2 vols.

Ingraham P. Ingraham, *Land of Legendary Lore*, Easton, 1898.

Jackson E. M. Jackson, *Annapolis*, Annapolis, /ca. 1936/.

Jacobsen P. R. Jacobsen, *Quaker Records in Maryland* ... /Annapolis: Hall of Records/, 1965.

Johnston G. Johnston, *History of Cecil County*, Elkton, 1881.

Jones E. Jones, *Revised History of Dorchester*, Baltimore, 1925.

Kelly J. Kelly, *Quakers in the Founding of Anne Arundel County*, Baltimore, 1963.

_____(2) _____, " 'Tulip Hill' ...," MHM, 60 (1965).

Kenny H. Kenny, *West Virginia Place Names, their Origin and Meaning*, Piedmont, 1945.

_____(2) _____, *Origin and Meaning of the Indian Place Names of Maryland*, Baltimore, 1961.

_____. _____, "Baltimore: New Light on an Old Name," MHM, XLIX: 2 (June, 1954).

_____. _____, "Place-Names from Surnames: Maryland," *Names*, 18: 3 (Sept., 1970).

_____. _____, "Place-Names and Dialects: Algonquian," *Names*, 24: 2 (June 1976).

Kidwiler E. Kidwiler, *History of Havre de Grace*, Havre de Grace, 1947.

Killough E. M. Killough, *History of the Western Maryland Railroad Company*, Baltimore, 1940 [rev. ed].

Kinney W. A. Kinney, "Roving Maryland's Cavalier Country," *Nat. Geog. Mag.*, 105 (1954).

Knight F. M. Knight, *Intimate Glimpses of Old Saint Mary's*, Washington, 1942.

Kuethe J. L. Kuethe, "Water Terms in Maryland," *Am. Sp.*, 10 (April, 1935), 153–154.

_____. _____, "Johnnycake," *Am. Sp.*, 10 (Oct. 1935), 201.

_____. _____, "Runs, Creeks, and Branches in Maryland," *Am. Sp.*, 10 (Dec. 1935), 256–259.

_____. _____, "Maryland Place Names Have Strange Origins," *Sun*, Sept. 8, 1940.

_____. _____, "Words from Maryland," *Am. Sp.*, 15 (Dec. 1940), 451–452.

Lantz	E. E. Lantz, *The Spirit of Maryland*, Baltimore, 1929.
Leitersburg	H. C. Bell, *History of Leitersburg District*, Leitersburg, 1898.
Linthicum	M. L. Linthicum, *A Brief History of Linthicum Heights and Vicinity* ... 1908 to 1959, Linthicum Heights, 1969.
Lowdermilk	W. H. Lowdermilk, *History of Cumberland (Maryland)*, Washington, 1878.
Lowther	M. K. Lowther, *Marshall Hall* ... 1925 /LC: F187. P8L8/.
MacReynolds	G. MacReynolds, *Place Names in Bucks County Pennsylvania*, Doylestown, 1942.
McGrath	F. S. McGrath, *Pillars of Maryland*, Richmond, 1950.
Magruder	J. M. Magruder, *Index of Maryland Wills, 1634–1777* ... Baltimore, 1967 /repr./.
McJimsey	G. D. McJimsey, "Topographic Terms in Virginia," *Am. Sp.*, XV (1940): 1, pp. 1–38; XV: 2, pp. 149–179; XV: 3, pp. 262–300.
Marriott	J. H. W. Marriott, *Picturesque Cabin John*, 1903 /LC: F189.C13M3/.
Marye (1)	Wm. B. Marye, "Early Settlers of the Site of Havre de Grace," *MHM*, 13 (1918).
_____(2)	_____, "The Baltimore County 'Garrison' and the Old Garrison Roads," *MHM*, 16 (June 1921).
_____(3)	_____, "The Baltimore County 'Garrison' and the Old Garrison Roads," Pt. 2, *MHM*, 16 (Sept. 1921).
_____(4)	Wm. B. Marye, "The Place-Names of Baltimore and Harford Counties," *MHM*, 25 (1930).
_____(5)	_____, "Notes on the Primitive History of Western Maryland," *MHM*, 38 (1943).
_____(6)	_____, "The Sea Coast of Maryland," *MHM*, 40 (1943).
_____(7)	_____, "Commentary on Certain Words and Expressions Used in Maryland," *MHM*, 46 (1951).
_____(8)	_____, "... Supplemental Commentary ...," *MHM*, 46 (1951).
_____(9)	_____, "The Great Maryland Barrens," *MHM*, 50 (March 1955).

____(10)   ____, "The Great Maryland Barrens," Pt. II, *MHM*, 50 (June 1955).

____(11)   ____, "The Place-Names of Baltimore and Harford Counties," *MHM*, 53 (1958), pp. 34–57.

____(12)   ____, "The Place-Names of Baltimore and Harford Counties," *MHM*, (1958), pp. 238–252.

____(13)   ____, "Some Baltimore City Place-Names," *MHM*, 54 (1959).

MHGP   *Maryland House and Garden Pilgrimage House Tours...*, 1963, 1964, etc. /Booklets/.

Maryland   "Maryland Place Names Depict Much of State's Early History," *Sun*, Aug. 9, 1942.

____(2)   *The Calvert Mansion 'Riverdale'...*, Pr. George's Co. Regional Office ... Pr. George's Co. Memorial Library, 1946.

Mathews   E. B. Mathews, *The Counties of Maryland ...* (Pt. 5 of /Md./ Geological Survey, vol. 6, 1906), 1907.

McSherry   J. McSherry, *History of Maryland*, Baltimore, 1904.

Miegel   C. H. Miegel, "What's in a Street Name?" *in* Report of the Society for the History of the Germans in Maryland, 25 (1942).

Miller   A. E. Miller, *Cecil County Maryland*, Elkton, 1949.

Molter   N. J. Molter, *An Illustrated History of Severna Park*, Annapolis, 1969.

Moss   J. E. Moss, *Providence Ye Lost Towne At Severn In Mary Land A Documented Relation ...* Washington, 1976 [sole distributor, Md. Hist. Society, Baltimore]. Note: The reader should be apprised that this elaborate and interesting book (XXIII, 560 pp.) is not really history but a sort of "documented" novel.

Mullikin   J. C. Mullikin, *Ghost Towns of Talbot County*, Easton, 1961.

Murray   J. Murray, *History of Pocomoke City, formerly New Town*, Baltimore, 1883.

Neill   E. D. Neill, *The Founders of Maryland*, Albany, 1876.

Newman   H. W. Newman, *Anne Arundel Gentry*, Baltimore, 1933.

_____(2)   _____, *Charles County Gentry...*, Washington, 1940.

_____(3)   _____, *Seignory in Early Maryland ... Manors and Manor Lords*. Published by Descendants ... Lords ... Maryland Manors, 1949.

_____(4)   _____, *Maryland Revolutionary Records*, orig. ed. 1938. Repr. Baltimore, 1967.

_____(5)   _____, *Anne Arundel Gentry A Genealogical History of Some Early Families* ... Annapolis, 1970.

Nickalls   J. L. Nickalls, ed., *The Journal of George Fox* ... A Revised Edition. Univ. Press, Cambridge, 1952.

Norris   W. B. Norris, *Annapolis its Colonial and Naval History*, N.Y., 1925.

Offutt   T. S. Offutt, *Baltimore County, its History* ... 1916. /LC: F187.B2.032/.

Oriole   M. Hall, ... *Oriole and its Satellites*, Oriole, 1964.

Palatinate   W. H. Browne, *Maryland, the History of a Palatinate*, N.Y., 1904.

Pangborn   J. G. Pangborn, *The Glades of the Alleghenies...*, 1882.

Papenfuse   E. C. Papenfuse and Joseph M. Coale, *The Hammond-Harwood House Atlas* of Historical Maps of Maryland, 1608–1908. Baltimore and London, 1982.

Parran   A. N. Parran, *Register of Maryland's Heraldic Families*, 1634–1935, vol. 1, Baltimore, 1935; vol. 2, 1938.

Passano   E. B. Passano, *An Index to the Source Records of Maryland*, Baltimore, 1940.

Percy   A. Percy, *Tobacco Rollings Roads to Waterways*, 1963 [See *Names*, 14: 4 (1966)].

Pogue   R. F. T. Pogue, *Old Maryland Landmarks ... A Pictorial Story*, Bushwood, 1972.

Preston   W. W. Preston, *History of Harford County ... 1608 ... 1812*, Bel Air, 1901.

Proctor   J. C. Proctor, *Proctor's Washington and Environs* /Written for *Star*, 1928–1948/, ... 1949.

Radoff   M. L. Radoff, *The Old Line State*, 3 vols., Baltimore, 1956.

Reaney · · · · · · · · R. H. Reaney, *A Dictionary of British Surnames*, London, 1968.

Richardson · · · · · · H. D. Richardson, *Side-Lights on Maryland History*, Baltimore, 1913.

Ridgely · · · · · · · · D. Ridgely, *Annals of Annapolis*, Baltimore, 1941 /LC: F189.A6R5/.

Riley · · · · · · · · · · E. S. Riley, *A History of Anne Arundel County*, Annapolis, 1905.

_____(2) · · · · · · · · _____, "The Ancient City," *A History of Annapolis*, ... 1887.

Robinson · · · · · · · · F. G. Robinson, /Vindex/ *Sun*, 11 May 1961.

Roy · · · · · · · · · · A. Roy, *A History of the Coal Miners of the United States*, 3rd ed., Columbus, 1907.

Scharf · · · · · · · · · J. T. Scharf, *History of Maryland*, 3 vols., Baltimore, 1879.

_____(2) · · · · · · · · _____, *History of Baltimore City and County*, Philadelphia, 1881.

_____(3) · · · · · · · · _____, *History of Western Maryland*, 2 vols., Philadelphia, 1882.

_____(4) · · · · · · · · _____, *Deer Park and Oakland...*, 1887 /LC: F189. D3 83/.

Schaun · · · · · · · · · G. and V. Schaun, *Everyday Life in Colonial Maryland*, Annapolis, 1959.

_____(2) · · · · · · · · _____, *The Greenberry Series on Maryland* (Issue 3), Greenberry Publications, Annapolis, /1965?/.

Schlosnagle · · · · · · S. Schlosnagle, *Garrett County, A History of Maryland's Tableland*, Garrett County Centennial Committee ... 1978.

Shannahan · · · · · · · J. H. H. Shannahan, *Tales of Old Maryland History ... Eastern Shore*, Baltimore, 1907.

Shomette · · · · · · · · D. G. Shomette, *Shipwrecks on the Chesapeake ...* Centreville, Md., 1982.

Shriver · · · · · · · · · J. A. Shriver, /Olney/, 1928. /LC: F182. S56. 1928/.

Simon · · · · · · · · · · L. Simon, et al., *Historic and General Information ... Prince George's County ...* 1957–58 /Stapled pamphlet/.

Sioussat · · · · · · · · A. L. Sioussat, *Old Manors in the Colony of Maryland ...* /First Ser. On the Potomac/. Baltimore, 1911. /Mentions: "... the town of the Yeocomicoes, with its witchetts, one of which was speedily taken for a chapel ..."/.

_____(2)   _____, [Second Ser. On the Patuxent]. Baltimore, 1913.

Skordas   G. Skordas, ed., *The Early Settlers of Maryland* ... 1633–1680, Baltimore, 1968.

Smith   E. C. Smith, *American Surnames*, N.Y., 1969.

Stegmaier   H. J. Stegmaier, Jr., et al., *Allegany County, A History*, Parsons, W. Va., 1976.

Stein   C. F. Stein, *A History of Calvert County*, Baltimore, 1960.

_____(2)   _____, *Origin and History of Howard County*, Baltimore, 1973.

Stevens   W. O. Stevens, *Annapolis, Anne Arundel's Town*, N.Y., 1937.

Stewart   E. N. Stewart, *History of Mt. Rainier*, /Leaflet/, 1954.

Stockett   L. Stockett, *Baltimore, A Not Too Serious History*, Baltimore, 1936.

Stonesifer   O. J. Stonesifer, *History of Union Bridge*, 1937. /LC: F189. U6S8/.

Streeter   S. F. Streeter, ... *Papers Relating to the Early History of Maryland*, ... 1876. /LC: F176.M37 no 9/.

_____(2)   _____, *The First Commander of Kent Island*, ... 1868.

TW   J. W. Thomas, and Judge T. J. C. Williams, *History of Allegany County Maryland...*, 2 vols., Cumberland /?/, 1923.

Tilghman   O. Tilghman, *History of Talbot County*, 2 vols., Baltimore, 1915.

Torrence   C. Torrence, *Old Somerset on the Eastern Shore*, Richmond, 1935.

Truitt   C. J. Truitt, *Historic Salisbury Maryland*, N.Y., 1932.

Tyson   M (Ellicott) Tyson, *A Brief Account of the Settlement of Ellicott's Mills*, 1865 /Also: MHS Fund-Pub., 4, 1871/.

Usilton   F. G. Usilton, *History of Kent County*, /Chestertown, 1916?/.

_____(2)   _____, *"City on the Chester" History of Chestertown*, ... 1899.

Vexler   R. I. Vexler and W. F. Swindler (Editors). *Chronology and Documentary Handbook of ... Maryland.* Dobbs Ferry, 1978.

Warfield   J. D. Warfield, *The Founders of Anne Arundel and Howard Counties*, Baltimore, 1905.

Warner et al.   N. M. Warner (et al.), *Carroll County, Mary-land, A History, 1837–1976*, Carroll County Centennial Committee, 1976.

Warner   W. W. Warner, *Beautiful Swimmers....* N.Y.: Penguin Books, 1977.

Weeks   T. F. Weeks, *Oakland Centennial History 1849–1949*, Oakland, 1949.

Williams   T. J. C. Williams, *A History of Washington County*, 2 vols., Hagerstown, 1906.

____(2)   ____, *History of Frederick County* /Continued fr. 1861 by Folger McKinsey/, 2 vols. /LC: F187, F8W7/.

Wilson   "Wye Island," *Lippincott's*, 19: 466 /Poole, Pt. II, 1802–1881/.

Wilstach   P. Wilstach, *Potomac Landings*, N.Y., 1921.

____(2)   ____, *Tidewater Maryland*, Indianapolis, 1931.

Wyand   J. A. and F. L. Wyand, *Colonial Maryland Naturalizations*, Baltimore, 1975.

Wysong   T. T. Wysong, *The Rocks of Deer Creek*, Baltimore, 1879, /Also: 1800; LC: F187. Ha. W92/.

II. INDIAN PLACENAMES, ARTICLES AND BOOKS

[Note: This is a list of the symbols, abbreviations, articles and books used in my detailed 1961 volume on Maryland's Indian placenames. Since those names have been included in the present work, the reader will find the following titles often referred to.]

A. *Phonetic and Etymological Symbols* (see: *Phonetic Transcription of Indian Languages*, Smithsonian Miscellaneous Collections, 66:6 [1916]).

PA	Proto—or Primitive Algonquian
? (also')	glottal stop
'	Aspirate, rough breathing, *h*
*	Hypothetical, extinct, or PA
ä	Original PA ä (as in *cat*)
c	Sound of *sh*
θ	Sound of *th*.

B. *Particular Abbreviations*

Arber	Travels and Works of Captain John Smith, two parts, 1910.
BAE	Bureau of American Ethnology.
Baraga 1853	A Dictionary of the Otchipwe Language, 1853.

Baraga 1879	A Grammar and Dictionary of the Otchipwe Language, 1879.
Baraga 1880	A Dictionary of the Otchipwe Language, Part II, 1880.
Beauchamp	Aboriginal Place Names of New York, 1907.
Boas	Handbook of American Indian Language, Pt. I, 1911.
Boyd	Indian Local Names with their Interpretations, 1885.
Brinton's Lenape	The Lenape and their Legends ... 1885.
B & A	Brinton and Anthony, A Lenape-English Dictionary, 1888.
Cotton	Maryland Calendar of Wills, 3 volumes, 1904–1907.
Cuoq	Lexique de la Langue Algonquine, 1886.
DA	Dictionary of Americanisms on Historical Principles, ed. by M. M. Mathews.
Donehoo	History of the Indian Villages and Place Names in Pennsylvania, 1928.
Douglas-Lithgow	Dictionary of American-Indian Place and Proper Names in New England, 1909.
Gannett 1905	Origin of Certain Place Names in the United States, second ed.
Gazetteer Md. 1852	Fisher's Gazetteer of Maryland.
Gazetteer Md. 1904	Gannett's Gazetteer of Maryland.
Gazetteer Md. 1941	State Planning Commission's Gazetteer of Maryland.
Gerard's Tapehanek	W. R. Gerard's Tapehanek Dialect of Virginia, 1904.
Gerard 1905	W. R. Gerard's Some Virginia Indian Words, 1905.
Gerard 1907	W. R. Gerard's Virginia's Indian Contributions to English, 1907.
Handbook	Handbook of American Indians North of Mexico, two parts, 1907, 1910.
Heckewelder's Account	... of the History, Manners, and Customs of the Indian Natives ... 1819.
Heckewelder's Names Which	... the Lenni Lenape or Delaware Indians gave..., with their Significations, ed. by W. C. Reichel, 1872.
Johnson's Lindeström	Amandus Johnson's tr. of Lindeström's Geographia Americae, 1925.
Jones 1867	The Rev. N. W. Jones's No. I Indian Bulletin, 1867.

Jones 1868	His No. II Indian Bulletin, 1868.
Ker	River and Lake Names in the United States, 1911.
LaCombe	Dictionnaire et Grammaire de la Langue des Cris, 1874.
Lemoine 1901	Dictionnaire Francais-Montagnais avec un Vocabulaire Montagnais-Anglais, etc., 1901.
Lemoine 1909	Dictionnaire Francais-Algonquin (Chicoutimi, 1909).
LSNA	Linguistic Structures of Native America.
Michelson's Stems	Fox Stems, pp. 616–658, 40th Annual Report, BAE (1918–19), 1925.
ONEAH	Original Narratives of Early Am. History (C. C. Hall, ed., Narratives of Early Maryland, 1633–1634 ... N.Y., 1910).
Rand	Dictionary of the Micmac Indians ... 1888.
Rasles	Dictionary of the Abnaki Language, in North America, 1833.
Ruttenber	Footprints of the Red Men, 1906.
Sixth USGB	Sixth Report of the U. S. Geographic Board (1933).
Strachey's Dictionarie	In History of Travaile into Virginia Britannia.
Tooker's Long Island	Indian Place Names on Long Island and Islands Adjacent, 1911.
Trumbull	Indian Names of Places ... in ... Connecticut, 1881.
Trumbull's Natick	Natick Dictionary, 1903.
Tyler	J. G. Tyler, ed., Narratives of Early Virginia, 1606–1625, 1907.
ZID	Zeisberger's Indian Dictionary, 1887.

C. General Indian References

Baraga, Rev. F.	*A Dictionary of the Otchipwe Language* ... Cincinnati, 1853.
———.	*A Grammar and Dictionary of the Otchipwe Language*, Montreal, 1879.
———.	*A Dictionary of the Otchipwe Language, Explained in English*, Part II. *Otchipwe-English* ... Montreal, 1880.
Beauchamp, W. M.	*Indian Names in New York, with a Selection from Other States* ... Fayetteville, 1893.

———. *Aboriginal Place Names of New York.* N.Y. State Museum, Bulletin 108, Archeology 12, Albany, 1907.

Becker, D. W. *Indian Place-Names in New Jersey,* Cedar Grove, N.J., 1964.

Bloomfield, L. "On the Sound-System of Central Algonquian," *Language,* I, (Dec. 1925), 130–156.

———. "Algonquian," *in Linguistic Structures of Native America.* (Viking Fund Publications in Anthropology, No. 6). New York, 1946.

Bolton, R. P. *Aboriginal Place-Names of the County of Westchester* ... N.Y. Public Library, 1942.

Boyd, S. G. *Indian Local Names with their Interpretations.* York, Pa., 1885.

Bozman, John Leeds *The History of Maryland, from its Earliest Settlement, in 1633, to the Restoration in 1660* ... Vol. 1. Baltimore, 1837.

Brinton, D. G., and Reverend A. S. Anthony, eds. *A Lenape-English Dictionary.* From an Anon. MS in the Archives of the Moravian Church at Bethlehem, Pa. Philadelphia, 1888.

———. "A Vocabulary of the Nanticoke Dialect," Proc. of the Am. Philosophical Soc., 31 (Nov. 1893), 325–333.

Bump, C. W. "Indian Place Names in Maryland," *Md. Hist. Mag.,* 2 (Dec. 1907). 287–293.

C.C. [E. A. Dulmymple's list of seventeen Pamunkey Indian words], *Historical Mag.,* 2 (June 1858), 182.

Campanius, J. *Luther's Catechism Translated into the American-Virginian Language.* Stockholm ... 1696; New York: 1938.

Chamberlain, A. F. "Algonkin Words in American English, ...," *Jour. Am. Folk-Lore,* 15 (Oct.–Dec. 1902), 240–267.

Cook, J. H. "Twilight of Maryland's Indians, ...," Sun [Mag.], Jan. 6, 1929.

Cooper, J. M. "Tete-De-Boule-Cree," *Int. Jour. of American Linguistics,* 2 (January 1945), 36–44.

Cuoq, J. A. *Lexique de la Langue Algonquine,* Montreal, 1886.

Curran, F. X., S.J. "The Mystery of Andrew White," *Woodstock* [Md.] *Letters,* 85 (Nov. 1956), 375–80.

Donehoo, Dr. G. P.   *A History of the Indian Villages and Place Names in Pennsylvania*, Harrisburg [ca 1928].

Douglas-Lithgow, R. A.   *A Dictionary of American-Indian Place and Proper Names in New England* ..., Salem, 1909.

Dunlap, A. R. and   *Indian Place-Names in Delaware* ... Wilmington, 1950.
C. A. Weslager

Dunn, J. P.   *True Indian Stories, with Glossary of Indiana Indian Names*. Indianapolis, 1908.

Espenshade, A. H.   *Pennsylvania Place Names* ... State College [1925].

Ferguson, A. L.   *Moyaone and the Piscataway Indians*. Washington, 1937.

Fitzgerald, S. E.   "Lost Indian Village Found, *Sun*, Aug. 13, 1939, section 1, p. 3.

Fleet, Captain Henry   *A Brief Journal of a Voyage Made in the Bark 'Warwick,' to Virginia and Other Parts of the Continent of America.* 1631 (*In* E. D. Neill, *The English Colonization of America During the Seventeenth Century.* London, 1871, pp. 221-237.

Fowke, G.   *Archeologic Investigations in James and Potomac Valleys* ... Washington, 1894.

Gatschet, A. S.   "The Massawomekes," *American Antiquarian*, III (1880-81), 321-324.

Geary, J. A.   "The Changed Conjunct Verb (without -Ni) in Fox," *International Journal of American Linguistics*, XI (July 1945), 169-181.

_____.   "The Changed Conjunct (with -Ni) and the Interrogative in Fox," *International Journal of American Linguistics*, XII (April 1946), 66-78.

_____.   "Strachey's Vocabulary of Indian Words Used in Virginia, 1612, *in* Appendix B of *The Historie of Travell into Virginia Britania* (1612) *By William Strachey, gent.* Ed. by L. B. Wright and V. Freund. London: The Hakluyt Society, 1953.

_____.   "The Language of the Carolina Algonkian Tribes," *in* Appendix II, Vol. II of *The Roanoke Voyages 1584-1590, Documents to Illustrate the English Voyages to North*

America under the Patent Granted to Walter Raleigh in 1584, ed. D. B. Quinn ... London: The Hakluyt Society (2nd Series, No. CIV, for 1952), 1955. 2 v.

Gerard, W. R.   "The Tapehanek Dialect of Virginia," *American Anthropologist* (n. s.), 6 (April–June 1904), 313–330.

——.   "Some Virginia Words," *American Anthropologist* (n. s.), 7 (April–June 1905), 222–249.

——.   "Virginia's Indian Contributions to English," *American Anthropologist* (n. s.), 9 (January–March 1907), 87–112.

Grubb, M. L.   "Indian War Relics are Still Cropping Up," The Baltimore (Sunday) *Sun*, September 28, 1941, no. 2, p. 12.

Hakluyt's Collection of the Early Voyages, Travels and Discoveries of the English Nation.   A New Edition with Additions. 5 v. London, 1809–12. [Vol. III, 1810 (pp. 357–64) has *The Relation of John de Verrazano, a Florentine, of the Land by him Discovered in the Name of his Majestie. Written in Diepe, July, 1524*].

Hale, H.   *Indian Migrations as Evidenced by Language* ... Reprinted from the *American Antiquarian* for January and April, 1883, Chicago, 1883.

Hall, C. C.   ed. *Narratives of Early America 1633–1684.* [*Original Narratives of Early American History*]. New York, 1910.

Harrington, J. P.   "The Original Strachey Vocabulary of the Virginia Indian Language," No. 46 *in Anthropological Papers Nos. 43–48.* (Bureau of American Ethnology, Bull. 157), Washington, 1955.

Harriot, T.   *A Briefe & True Report of the New Found Land of Virginia, of the Commodities and of the Nature and Manners of the Naturall Inhabitants.* ... A Reproduction of the Edition Printed at Frankfurt, in 1590, at the Expense of Theodore de Bry. Ed. by W. H. Rylands, F. S. A. ... Manchester, 1888.

Hayden, E. R.   "Port Tobacco, Lost Town of Maryland," *Maryland Historical Magazine*, XL: 4, pp. 261–276.

Heckewelder, Reverend J. *In Transactions of the Historical and Literary Committee of the American Philosophical Society,* Vol. I (Philadelphia, 1819): (No. I) ... *Account of the History, Manners, and Customs of the Indian Nations Who Once Inhabited Pennsylvania and the Neighboring States;* (No. II) *Correspondence between Mr. Heckewelder and Mr. Duponceau on the Language of the American Indians;* (No. III) *Words, Phrases, and Short Dialogues ... of the Lenni Lenape.*

——. *Memorandum of the Names and Significations which the Lenni Lenape, otherwise called the Delaware, had given to Rivers, etc. in ... Maryland and Virginia.* Pennsylvania Historical Society *Bulletin,* I: 121, 139, 1848.

——. *Names Which the Lenni Lenape or Delaware Indians Gave to Rivers, Streams and Localities, within the States of Pennsylvania, New Jersey, Maryland and Virginia, with their Significations.* Prepared ... from a ms. by J. Heckewelder, by W. C. Reichel. Bethlehem, 1872.

Hodge, F. W. ed.   *Handbook of American Indians North of Mexico.* Bulletin 30 ... Part I, Washington, 1907; Part II, Washington, 1910.

Holm, T. Campanius.   *Description of the Province of New Sweden, Now Called by the English, Pennsylvania, in America. Compiled from the Relations and Writings of Persons Worthy of Credit, and Adorned with Maps and Plates.* Translated from the Swedish, for the Historical Society of Pennsylvania. With Notes. By S. DuPonceau, Philadelphia, 1834.

Holmer, Nils G.   *John Campanius' Lutheran Catechism in the Delaware Language.* (The American Institute in the University of Upsala. *Essays and Studies on American Language and Literature,* ed. S. B. Liljegren ... III). Upsala, 1946.

Holmer, Nils Magnus.   *Indian Place Names in North America.* (The American Institute in the University of Upsala, *Essays and Studies on American Language and Literature*, 7). ... Cambridge (Mass.) [1948].

Horsford, E. N.   *The Indian Names of Boston, and their Meaning*. Cambridge, 1886.

———.   ed. *Comparative Vocabulary of the Algonquian Dialects*. From Heckewelder's Manuscripts in the Collections of the American Philosophical Society, Philadelphia. ... Cambridge, 1887.

Howse, J.   *A Grammar of the Cree Language: with which is Combined an Analysis of the Chippeway Dialect*. London, 1844.

Hunt, J. W.   "Across the Desk," Cumberland, Md. (Sunday) *Times*, April 17, 1949; July 10, 1949.

Jones, Rev. N. W.   *No. I. Indian Bulletin for 1867. Containing a Brief Account of the North American Indians, and the Interpretation of Many Indian Names*. New York, 1867.

———.   *No. II. Indian Bulletin for 1868. Containing a Brief Account of Chinese Voyages to the North West Coast of America and the Interpretation of 200 Indian Names*. N.Y., 1869.

Jones, William.   "Some Principles of Algonquian Word-formation," *American Anthropologist*, 6 (September 1904).

———.   *Algonquian (Fox)* ... Revised by Truman Michelson, in *Handbook of American Indian Languages*, ed. Franz Boas, Bureau of American Ethnology, Bulletin 40. Washington, 1911), Part I, pp. 739–878.

Kelton, D. H.   *Indian Names of Places Near the Great Lakes*, Vol. I. Detroit, 1888.

Kenny, H.   *Origin and Meaning of the Indian Place Names of Maryland*, Baltimore, 1961.

Ker, E. T.   *River and Lake Names in the United States* ... New York, 1911.

Kinnicutt, L. N.   *Indian Names of Places in Worcester County, Massachusetts, with Interpretations of Some of Them* ... Worcester, 1905.

———.   *Indian Names of Places in Plymouth, Middleborough, Lakeville and Carver, Plymouth County, Massachusetts, with In-*

terpretations of Some of Them ... Worcester, 1909.

Kuethe, J. L.   "Pocosin," *Modern Language Notes*, LII (March 1937), 210–11.

LaCombe, Alb.   *Dictionnaire et Grammaire de la Langue de Cris*, Montreal, 1874.

Lane, Ralph.   *Narrative of the Proceedings of Sir Walter Raleigh's Colonists in 1585*, in *Old South Leaflets* (General Series), 5: 119. Boston, 1900.

Laurent, J. ed.   *New Familiar Abenakis and English Dialogues. The First Vocabulary ever Published in the Abenakis Language, Comprising: the Abenakis Alphabet, the Key to the Pronunciation, and Many Grammatical Explanations* ... *to which is Added the Etymology of Indian Names of Certain Localities, Rivers, Lakes, &c.* St. Francis, P.Q., 1884.

Lemoine, Geo.   *Dictionnaire Francais-Montagnais avec un Vocabulaire Montagnais-Anglais, une Courte Liste de Noms Geographiques et une Grammaire Montagnai* ... Boston, 1901.

Lewis, C. M., S. J. and A. J. Loomie, S.J.   *The Spanish Jesuit Mission in Virginia 1570–1572* ... Published for the Virginia Historical Society by the University of North Carolina Press, Chapel Hill, 1953.

Lindeström, P. Martenson.   *Geographia Americae with an Account of the Delaware Indians Based on Surveys and Notes Made in 1654–1656* by Peter Lindeström. Introduction and an Appendix of Indian Geographical Names with their Meanings, by Amandus Johnson. Philadelphia, 1925.

Long, C. M.   *Virginia County Names* ... N.Y. and Washington, 1908.

Lorant, Stefan, ed.   *The New World. The First Pictures of America. Made by John White and Jacques LeMoyne and Engraved by Theodore de Bry.* N.Y., [1946].

McBee, A.   "Mysterious Village on Potomac's Shore. Indian Skeletons Lately Uncovered Arouse Archeologists' Interest," *Sun*, Baltimore Section, October 3, 1937, p. 5, p. 7.

McJimsey, G. D.   *Topographic Terms in Virginia.* (*American Speech Reprints and Monographs*, No. 3). N.Y., 1940.

MacReynolds, G.   *Place Names in Bucks County Pennsylvania Alphabetically Arranged in an Historical Narrative.* ... Doylestown, 1942.

Martin, J., ed.   *A New and Comprehensive Gazetteer of Virginia and the District of Columbia ... to which is Added a History of Virginia from its First Settlement.* ... Charlottesville, 1835.

Marye, W. B.   "The Old Indian Road ..." [Parts I, II, III], *MHM.*, 15 (June, September, Dec. 1920).

————.   "'Patowmeck Above ye Inhabitants.' ... Part One: ... Lloyd's Map of Western Maryland ...—circa 1721," *MHM.*, 30 (March 1935).

————.   "'Patowmeck Above ye Inhabitants.' ... Part Two: King Opessa's Town on the 'Warrior's Path.' ... Shawnee Settlements in Baltimore County," *MHM*, 30 (June 1935).

————.   "'Piscattaway.' ... Part One: The Piscattaway People. Part Two: Piscattaway, the Place," *MHM*, 30 (Sept. 1935).

————.   "Indian Paths of the Delmarva Peninsula (Part One: The Old Choptank or Delaware Path)," *BASD*, 2 (March 1936).

————.   "Indian Paths of the Delmarva Peninsula (Part One: The Old Choptank or Delaware Path Continued," *BASD*, 2 (Oct. 1936).

————.   "Indian Paths of the Delmarva Peninsula (Part II: The Choptank Indians) *BASD*, 2 (Oct. 1937).

————.   "'Patowmeck Above ye Inhabitants.' ... Part Three ...," *MHM*, 32 (Dec. 1937).

————.   "Indian Paths of the Delmarva Peninsula ... Part Three: Indian Paths Near the Seaboard," *BASD*, 2 (June 1938).

————.   "The Annacostin Indian Fort. (With Appendix: Potomac River Called Annacostin River)," *MHM*, 33 (June 1938).

————.   "'Patowmeck Above Ye Inhabitants.' ... Part Four: The Several Indian 'Old Towns' on the Upper Potomac River," *MHM*, 34 (Dec. 1939).

Mencken, H. L.   *The American Language: an Inquiry into the Development of English in the United States.* 4th ed., N.Y., 1936.

———.   *Supplement II The American Language ...* N.Y. 1948. [Note: Section X of this supplement deals with "Proper Names in America," pp. 396–575.]

Michelson, T.   "Preliminary Report on the Linguistic Classification of Algonquian Tribes ...," *in* 28th Annual Report of the *BAE* ... 1906–07. Washington, 1912.

———.   "List of [Fox] Stems," *in Fortieth Annual Report* of the *BAE* ... 1918–1919. Washington, 1925. Pages 616–658.

———.   "The Linguistic Classification of Powhatan," *American Anthropologist*, n. s., 35 (July–September 1933), 549.

Mooney, J.   "Indian Tribes of the District of Columbia," *American Anthropologist* II (July 1889), 259–266.

———.   "Geographic Nomenclature of the District of Columbia," *American Anthropologist*, VI (January 1893), 29–53.

———.   *The Siouan Tribes of the East.* (Bureau of American Ethnology, Bulletin 22, bound with Bulletins 14–24). Washington, 1894.

Myers, A. C. ed.   *Narratives of Early Pennsylvania West New Jersey and Delaware 1630–1707.* [ONEAH]. N.Y., 1912.

Nelson, W.   *The Indians of New Jersey ... With Notices of Some Indian Place-Names. ...* Paterson, 1894.

New Jersey,   Workers of the Writer's Program of the Work Projects Administration in ... *The Origin of New Jersey Place-Names.* Sponsored by N. J. Library Commission [1939?].

———.   *The Origin of New Jersey Place Names.* Reissued by N. J. Public Library Commission ... Trenton.

Norona, Delf.   *Wheeling: A West Virginia Place-name of Indian Origin.* Moundsville, W. Va.: West Virginia Archeological Society, 1958. 38 pp.

Phillips, P. L.   *The Rare Map of Virginia and Maryland, by Augustine Herrman, First Lord of Bohemia*

Manor, Maryland ... with Facsimile Reproduction from a Copy in the British Museum. Washington, 1911. 23 pp.

Pilling, J. C.   Bibliography of the Algonquian Languages ... Washington, 1891. [p. 525: "White (Rev. Andrew). Grammar, Dictionary and Catechism in the Language of the Maryland Indians. (*)"The asterisk within parentheses indicates that the compiler has seen no copy of the work referred to]."

Pollard, Jno. G.   The Pamunkey Indians of Virginia ... (BAE, Bulletin 17). Washington, 1894. [Contains Lawson's vocabulary (i. e., Dalrymple's 17 Pamunkey words?) of the Pamticough (Pamlico) Indians].

Prince, J. D. and   "Glossary of the Mohegan-Pequot Language,"
F. Speck   American Anthropologist, n. s., 6 (Jan.-March 1904), 18–45.

Quinn, D. B., ed.   The Roanoke Voyages 1584–1590 Documents to Illustrate the English Voyages to North America under the Patent Granted to Walter Raleigh in 1584 ... London, 1955. 2 v. [Note: Vol. 2 contains James A. Geary's "An Introductory Study of the Position of the Indian Language of Virginia and North Carolina in the Algonquian Family," and "List of Indian Words Found in the Documents, with Notes on their meaning."].

Rand, S. T.   A First Reading Book in the Micmac Language ... Also, Some of the Indian Names of Places and many Familiar Words and Phrases, Translated Literally into English. Halifax, 1875.

——.   Dictionary of the Micmac Indians, Who Reside in Nova Scotia, New Brunswick, Prince Edward Island, Cape Breton and Newfoundland ... Halifax, 1888.

——.   Rand's Micmac Dictionary from Phonographic Word Lists ... with a Grammar and List of Place-Names by Jeremiah S. Clark ... Charlottetown, P. E. I., 1902.

——.   Micmac Place-Names in the Maritime Province and Gaspé Peninsula Recorded between 1852 and 1890 ... Ottawa, 1919.

Rasles, Father S.   *A Dictionary of the Abnaki Language* ... in *Memoirs of the* [American] *Academy of Arts and Sciences*, n. s., I (1833).

Read, A. W.   "Boucher's Linguistic Pastoral of Colonial Maryland," *Dialect Notes*, 6 (Pt. 7) (1933), 353–360.

Rogers, P. B.   "Indian Names in Tidewater Virginia," *Names*, IV (September 1956), 155–159.

————.   "Tidewater Virginians Name Their Homes," *Am. Sp.*, 34 (Dec. 1959). [Note: Rogers remarks, p. 254, that "Although a place in Wiltshire, England, is named Purton, the Gloucester County home of the same name is certainly a telescoped form of Powhatan." [He also mentions the Virginia home names, "Chericoke," "Romancoke," and "Tuckahoe."].

Semmes, R.   "Aboriginal Maryland, 1608–1689. ... Part One: The Eastern Shore," *MHM*, XXIV (June 1929), 157–172.

————.   Aboriginal Maryland, 1609–1689. ... Part Two: The Western Shore," *MHM*, XXIV (September 1929), 195–209.

Shannahan, J. H. K.   *Tales of Old Maryland: History and Romance on the Eastern Shore of Maryland* ... Baltimore [1907].

Shannon, J. H.   "The Rambler": A Series of Articles on Washington and Vicinity Contributed to the Evening *Star*, 1912–1922 ... In four [scrapbook] volumes, Vol. I, 1912–1915. Washington. 1923.

Shea, J. G.   "The Identity of the Andastes, Minquas, Susquehannas & Conestogues," *Historical Magazine*, 1st ser., II (September 1858), 294–297.

Smith, Captain John.   *Travels and Works of Captain John Smith, President of Virginia, and Admiral of New England 1580–1631*, ed. E. Arber. ... A New Edition ... Part I, Edinburgh, 1910. cxxxvi, 382 pp. Part II (Vol. II), 383–984 pp.

Snowden, W. H.   *Some Old Historic Landmarks of Virginia and Maryland* ... 3rd ed. ... Alexandria, 1902.

Snow Hill   [Maryland] *Democratic Messenger*. [A *Sun* (May 14, 1941) item states: "Jack Culver, of the 'Jack Pots' column of the Snow Hill *Democratic Messenger*, has discovered that there are 90 names of Indian origin in Worcester County [Maryland]-including place names, river names and what have you."]

Speck, F. G.   *The Rappahannock Indians of Virginia*, in Indian Notes and Monographs, V: 3. N.Y., 1925.

———.   *The Nanticoke and Conoy Indians with a Review of Linguistic Material from Manuscript and Living Sources*. Wilmington: Papers of the Historical Society of Delaware, n. s. . . . 1927.

Stevens, Cj.   "The Rediscovery of the Indian Languages: A Survey," *American Speech*, XXXII (February 1957). See the present author's commentary on the above article. It appears in *American Speech*, XXXII (October 1957), under the heading "The Founders of Amerindian Linguistics."

Strachey, W.   *The Historie of Travaile into Virginia Britannia*, ed. R. H. Major . . . from the Original Manuscript in the British Museum . . . [On Cover: Hakluyt Society Strachey's Virginia] London, M. DCCC. XLIX.

———.   *The Historie of Travell into Virginia Britania* (1612), ed. L. B. Wright and V. Freund. London: The Hakluyt Society, 1953. [It contains: "Strachey's Vocabulary of Indian Words Used in Virginia, 1612," by Father J. A. Geary, Catholic University of America, pp. 208–214.]

Tooker, W. W.   "The Kuskarawoakes of Captain John Smith," *The American Anthropologist*, VI (October 1893).

———.   "On the Meaning of the Name Anacostia," *The American Anthropologist*, VII (October 1894).

———.   "The Origin of the Name 'Chesapeake,'" *Virginia Magazine of History and Biography*, 3 (1895).

———.   "The Problem of the Recahecrian Indians of Virginia," *The American Anthropologist*, XI (1898), 261–270.

———. *The Names of Susquehanna and Chesapeake, with Historical and Ethnological Notes ... (The Algonquian Series*, No. 3). N.Y., 1901.

———. *The Algonquian Names of the Siouan Tribes of Virginia, with Historical and Ethnological Notes ... (The Algonquian Series*, No. 5). N.Y., 1901.

———. *The Bocootawanaukes; or, the Fire Nation; with Historical and Ethnological Notes ... (The Algonquian Series*,No. 6). N.Y., 1901.

———. *The Algonquian Terms Patawomeke (Potomac) and Massawomeke, with Historical and Ethnological Notes ... (The Algonquian Series*, No. 8). N.Y., 1901.

———. *The Names Chickahominy, Pamunkey, and the Kuskarawaokes of Captain John Smith ... Notes ... (The Algonquian Series*, No. 9). N.Y., 1901.

———. "Meaning of Some Indians Names in Virginia," *William and Mary College Quarterly*, XIV (July 1905).

———. "Some More about Virginia Names," *The American Anthropologist*, n. s., VII (July–September 1905).

———. "The Powhatan Name for Virginia," *The American Anthropologist*, n. s., VIII (January–March 1906).

———. *The Indian Place-Names on Long Island and Islands Adjacent, with their Probable Significations ...* ed. Alexander F. Chamberlain ... N.Y., and London 1911.

Truitt, A. "Eastern Sho' Indians: their Nomenclature ... *Sun*, Magazine Section, February 10, 1929, p. 16.

Trumbull, J. H. "Indian Names in Virginia," *The Historical Magazine, and Notes and Queries Concerning the Antiquities, History and Biography of America*, VII (2nd ser.), 1870.

———. *The Composition of Indian Geographical Names, Illustrated from the Algonkin Languages. ...* the Connecticut Historical Society's Collection, Vol. II. Hartford, 1870.

———. *On Some Words Derived from Languages of North American Indians ...* the Transactions of the American Philological Association. (Boston), 1872.

———. *Indian Names of Places ... in and on the Borders of Connecticut: with Interpretations of Some of Them ...* Hartford, 1881.

———. *Natick Dictionary.* BAE, Bulletin 25. Washington, 1903.

Tyler, L. G. ed. *Narratives of Early Virginia, 1606–1625.* (*ONEAH*). N.Y., 1907. *United States Coast Pilot:* Atlantic Coast, Section C, Sandy Hook to Cape Henry. 5th ed. Washington, 1947.

Voegelin, C. F. "The Lenape and Munsee Dialects of Delaware, an Algonquian Language," *Proceedings of the Indiana Academy of Science*, 49 (1939).

———. "Delaware, an Eastern Algonquian Language," *in LSNA*. (Viking Fund Publications in Anthropology, No. 6). N.Y., 1946.

———. *Walam Olum ... Translation, in Walam Olum or Red Score ... A New Translation ...* Indianapolis, 1954.

Walam Olum or Red Score The Migration Legend of the Lenni Lenape or Delaware Indians A New Translation, Interpreted by Linguistic, Historical, Archaeological, Ethnological and Physical Anthropological Studies. Indianapolis: 1954.

Weslager, C. A. *Delaware's Forgotten Folk, The Story of the Moors and Nanticokes. ...* Philadelphia, 1943.

———. "The Nanticoke Indians in Early Pennsylvania History," *Pennsylvania Magazine of History and Biography*, LXVII (October 1943), 345–355.

———. "Indian Stone Piles in Maryland," *MHM*, XLII (March 1947), 46–49.

———. *Indians of the Eastern Shore of Maryland and Virginia, in the Eastern Shore of Maryland and Virginia,* ed. C. B. Clark. N.Y., 1950.

———. "Place Names on Ocracoke Island," *North Carolina Historical Review*, XXXI (January 1954).

———. "Robert Evelyn's Indian Tribes and Place-Names of New Albion," The Archeological

	Society of New Jersey, Bulletin 9 (November 1954).
White, J.	"Names of Birds and Fishes in the Indian Language of Virginia," *Proceedings* of the American Antiquarian Society, 32 (April 1860).
Whitmore, C. W.	"Early Maryland's Indian Neighbors. The Colony Lived in Amity with Them, Barring Occasional 'Accidents,'" *Sun* [Mag.] June 9, 1929.
Williams, R.	*A Key into the Language of America, or an Help to the Language of the Natives in that Part of America Called New-England* ... (London ... 1643). Providence, 1827.
Yonge, S. H.	*The Site of 'Old James Towne,' 1607–1698. A Brief Historical and Topographical Sketch of the First American Metropolis* ... Richmond, 1904.
Zeisberger, D.	*Grammar of the Language of the Lenni Lenape or Delaware Indians* ... Translated from the German MS of the Author by Peter Stephen Du Ponceau ... (Transactions of the American Philosophical Society, n. s., III). Philadelphia, 1827.
⸻.	*Zeisberger's Indian Dictionary. English German, Iroquois-the Onondaga and Algonquin-the Delaware* ... from the Original MS in Harvard College Library. ... Cambridge, 1887.

III. MAPS OF VIRGINIA AND MARYLAND

(The Earlier ones were all seen in the Division of Maps, Library of Congress. Cf. Coale and Papenfuse's *House Atlas* of Maryland's "Historical Maps").

Virginia 1585 With	By John White. Engraved by De Bry.
Virginia 1597 Wytfliet	Norumbega et Virginia.
Virginia 1608 Smith	From LC original.
Maryland 1635 Lord Baltimore	From *A Relation* ...
Hondius 1635	Virginia. From Mercator's Atlas.
Maryland 1662 Alsop	From George Alsop's *Land-skip*.
Herrman 1670	Virginia and Maryland. Stevens facsimile.
Maryland 1676 Speed	In Speed's *Theatre of Gt. Brit.* ...

N. America 1680 Thornton	From Stokes' *Iconography*.
Van Keulen 1682	From *Sea Atlas*, 1682.
Maryland 1682 Bowden	From Bowden's *History of the Society of Friends* ...
Maryland 1684 Thornton	In *Maps of America*, London.
Maryland 1690	Thornton & Fisher, London.
Moll 1717	Va. & Md. by H. Moll.
Senex 1719	Va., Md., Pa.
Lloyd 1721	Philcmon Lloyd's W. Maryland.
Hoxton 1735	Chesapeake Bay.
Moll 1736	H. Moll's Va. & Maryland.
Virginia 1737 Mayo	Virginia (Northern Neck).
FJ 1751	Va. & Md. Fry & Jefferson.
Maryland 1752 Bowen	Eman. Bowen's Va. & Md.
Maryland 1753 Evans	Lewis Evans' Pa. Boundary.
Potomac 1753 Cresap	Sources of the Potomac.
Maryland 1755 Vaugondy	Va. ... from Fry & Jefferson.
N. Am. 1755 Evans	Facsimile of Map in Pa. Archives.
Maryland 1757 Kitchin	By T. Kitchin, Geographer.
Homann 1759	*Atlas Geographicus Maior.*
FJ 1775	Va. & Md. Fry & Jefferson.
Maryland 1778 Hutchins	US., Va., Pa., Md., & N.C.
Maryland 1780 Erskine	Pa.-Md. Boundary.
MP 1780	... Maryland ... Mount & Page.
Churchman 1787	Peninsula between Del. & Ches. Bays.
Baltimore 1792 Folie	Baltimore and its Environs.
Griffith 1794	Maryland ... facsimile by U.S.G.S.
Maryland 1795 Lewis	Maryland from the best authorities.
Baltimore 1799	Improved Plan ... Warner & Hanna.
Baltimore 1801	... Warner & Hanna Reproduction.
Maryland 1804 Lewis	Including Western Part....
Baltimore 1818 Carey	From Carey's *General Atlas*.
Baltimore 1822 Lucas	...
Balt. 1823 Poppleton	...
AK 1824	Abert & Kearney, Patuxent and St. Mary's Rivers.
Maryland 1833 Tanner	From Me. to Ala.: "The great chain," properly "Allegheny."
Maryland 1834 Sumner	Sumner & Co., Hartford, Ct.
D. C. 1835 Bradford	In Bradford's *Comprehensive Atlas*.
Baltimore 1836 Lucas	F. Lucas, Jr.
Maryland 1836 Tanner	*Universal Atlas* Inserts Baltimore.
Bradford 1838	Maryland ... T. G. Bradford.

Maryland 1839 Burr	Va., Maryland, & Delaware.
Maryland 1841 Lucas	State of Maryland.
Baltimore 1845 Lucas	Improved to 1845.
Cumberland 1851 Bevan	Map of Cumberland, Alleghany Co.
Colton 1852	Maryland, J. H. Colton.
Cecil 1858	Martenet. Cecil County.
Anne Ar. 1860	Martenet. Anne Arundel County.
Kent 1860	Martenet. Kent County.
Pr. Geo. 1861	Martenet. Pr. George's County.
Carroll 1862	Martenet. Carroll County.
Mitchell 1865	...
Montgomery 1865	Martenet & Bond.
Martenet 1866	Maryland. Atlas Edition.
Delaware 1869	Boughman, Thomas & Co.
Frederick 1873	Atlas of Frederick County. Lake.
Maryland 1873 Martenet	*New Topographical Atlas.*
Maryland 1876 Gray	Maryland, Delaware, District of Columbia.
Baltimore 1876 Hopkins	C. M. Hopkins. City Atlas of Baltimore.
Baltimore 1877 Hopkins	Atlas of Baltimore. Vol. 2.
Atlas 1877	Talbot & Dorchester Counties. Lake, Griffing and Stevenson.
Carroll 1877	Carroll County, Lake, Griffing, and Stevenson.
Maryland 1877 Rand-McNally	Maryland, D.C., and Delaware.
Wicomico, &c. 1877	Wicomico, Somerset, Worcester. Lake, Griffing & Stevenson.
Balt. & Anne Ar. 1878	Fifteen Miles Around ... Hopkins.
D.C. 1878 Hopkins	Fifteen Miles Around.
Balt. & Howard 1878	Atlas of Fifteen Miles Around.
Harford 1878	Martenet. Harford County.
Hopkins 1878	Atlas of Anne Arundel County. (Repr. 1969).
Maryland 1883 Colton	Va., W. Va., Md., and Del.
Maryland 1884 Postal	Post Route Map.
R.-McN. 1884	Md., D.C., Delaware.
Md. 1888 Rand-McN.	Pocket Map of Md. & D.C.
Md. 1892	Rand-McN. Universal Atlas Map ... Md. & Delaware.
Maryland 1893 M.-N.	Matthews-Northrup.
Baltimore 1894 Lange	*Maryland* ... Road Map ... Lange.
Balt. 1896 Bromley	Atlas of the City of Baltimore.
Baltimore 1897 Sams	Conway W. Sams. Also: The City of Washington.
Maryland 1897	Also Delaware. Century Atlas.

Balt. 1898 Bromley	Atlas of Baltimore County.
Hagerstown 19-	Maryland Hagerstown Wards ... Md. Geol. Survey.
Maryland 1902 Century	Maryland Delaware. Century Co.
Maryland 1902 Matthews	J. N. Matthews Co.
Maryland 1902 Peale	Maryland & D.C. 1902 ... Peale.
Cumberland 1906 Fowler	Birds Eye View of Cumberland, Maryland.
R.-McN. 1906	Rand-McNally Large Scale.
Virginia (1907) Sams	Territory Rules by Powhatan C. Whittle Sams. 1907.
Cumberland 1912 Rizer	Cumberland (City of) ... 1912 Rizer.
Hagerstown 192? Dagmar	Hagerstown 192?. Dagmar Hotel.
Md. 1937 Transportation	U. S. Bureau of Pub. Roads.
Anne Ar. 1940	Anne Arundel Co. Md. Geological Survey.
Tunis 1947	Historical ... Eastern Shore.
Wicomico 1949	Wicomico County. Department of Geology, Mines and Water Resources.
Dorchester 1950	Dorchester County. Department of Geology, Mines and Water Resources.
Qu. Anne's 1950.	Queen Anne's County. Department of Geology, Mines and Water Resources.
Somerset 1950	Somerset County. Department of Geology, Mines and Water Resources.
Worcester 1950	Worcester County. Department of Geology, Mines and Water Resources.
Prince George's 1958 (Sheets A, B, C, D)	Street Map ... Pr. George's County. National Capital Park and Planning Commission.
Annapolis 1960	Annapolis Maryland and Vicinity. W. E. Jones 1960.
St. Mary's 1963	St. Mary's County ... St. Mary's Historical Society.
USC & GS (Seven Charts)	Coastal Charts of the U.S. Coast and Geodetic Survey. Chesapeake Bay; Potomac River.
USGS (Quad. and date)	Quadrangluar Maps of the U. S. Geol. Survey (Maryland Quadrangles and edition).
USGS (2)	Larger size Quadrangular Maps of the U. S. Geol. Survey (Maryland Quadrangles and edition).

ADDENDA

MARYLAND. A combination of *Mary* and *land*, probably first used in 1632, when King Charles I, writing it "Terra Mariae" (Latin for "Land of Mary"), coined the phrase to honor his young wife, Queen Henrietta Maria (1609–1666). She was the daughter of French King Henry IV, and was 23 when Lord Baltimore's provincial charter was being drafted. See Andrews, p. 11, ff.

ADMARIOTHRIA. The 1662 Prince George's manor of George Thompson, gent. It probably means "Devotion to Mary."

BOLIVAR. Frederick County village near Middletown. Probably for Simon Bolivar (1783–1830), South American liberator.

CARLOS JUNCTION. The alternate name of National P.O. The family name, *Carlos*, is not in Heads 1790 or in TDr Allegany. I am inclined to attribute the name of this George's Creek colliery junction to the British surname, *Carless, Careless, Carloss, Carlos* (from O.E. *Carlēas* "unconcerned, careless"). See Reaney, p. 61.

COCKEYSVILLE. Near Timonium, Baltimore County. Earlier name **Golden*. From the Cockey family. Baltimore County court records (1720) mention Col. Cockey's rolling road. In 1878 (Lewis) one finds living here G. Cockey, and Judge Joshua F. Cockey.

*GREEKTOWN. This Baltimore Highlandtown ethnic name represents the Greek immigrant tide that arose in that city after about 1900 (*Sun* [Mag.], 25 March 1984, p. 53).

*HAMMETTSVILLE. The lost St. Mary's County village where Dashiell Hammett (1894–1961), Maryland's celebrated detective-story writer was born. A bill of sale (St. Mary's County courthouse, 1782), mentioning a "storehouse known as Hammettsville," was signed by Samuel B. Hammett on April 2, 1889. Hammett's father was Richard Thomas Hammett. (Thanks to Mrs. Regina Hammett, Ridge, Md., and Mrs. Hope Grace, Leonardtown).

*HOSPITAL HILL. Near Williamsport, Washington County. In about 1833 a multitude of C. & O. Canal laborers were buried here. They were victims of a cholera epidemic that had swept down from Canada. Memorial stones were set up here. They no longer remain. See E. Kytle, *Home on the Canal*, Cabin John, 1983, p. 55.

MISCELLANEA

ARDMORE-ARDWICK. Industrial complex near New Carrollton, Prince George's Co. With Ardmore compare Ardmore, Co. Waterford, Ireland. Irish *ard* means "a height"; *mora* means "big, great." The *wick* of Ardwick is O.E. *wic* "dwelling-place." The names are inappropriate.

INDEX OF PLACENAMES

N.B.: An asterisk (*) denotes extinct, previous, or questionable names and forms.

Shawan, 20, 182, 240
*Shawan Cabin Branch, 20
Shelltown, 240
Sherwood (Sherwoodville), 240
Sherwood Forest, 240
Shiloh, 241
Ship Creek, 8
Shipley's Choice, S. Corner, 241
Shipyard Creek, 7
Showell, 241
*Shrewsbury, S. Town, 241
Sideling Hill, S. Hill Creek, 12, 14, 242
Sideling Mountain, 14
Silesia, 23, 171, 242
Sillery Bay, 22, 242
Silver Hill, 242
Silver Spring, 17, 242
Simpsonville, 243
Sinepuxent, 243
Sines, 23, 243
Sir Johns Run, 5
Skipnish, 243
Skipton, 244
*Skipton (now Oldtown), 70, 180, 243
Skunk Hollow, 9
Skywater Road, 19
*Slabtown, 239, 292
Slaughterhouse Run, 7
*Slaughtertown, 244
Sligo, 244
*Sloan, Sloan Mine, 244
Sloane, 21
*Sloan's Ville, 244
Sloop Creek, 8
Slough, The, 72
Smallwood, 244
*Smithfield, 245
Smithsburg, 245
Smithville, 2, 245
Snake Den Branch, 9
Smokehouse Cove, 7
*Snowden's River, 245
Snow Hill, *Snow Hill, 245
Soldiers Delight, 88, 164, 195
Sollers, Sollars, 22, 246
Solomons, Solomons Island, 4, 246, 247
*Somers Cove, 71, 246
Somerset County, 246
*Somerset Town (*Somerton), 247
*Somervell's Island, 246, 247, 255
*Sopetank, 247
Sotterley, 247
South Mountain, 174
Spa Creek, 8
Spaniard Neck, 36
Sparks, 8, 247
*Sparks Switch Sta., 9
Sparrows Point, 247
Spence, Spence Cove, 248

Spencerville, 248
Spesutie Island, 248
Spielman, 248
*Spocott, 249
Springdale, 249
Springfield, 249
*Spring Garden, 249
Squirrel Hill, 9
Stabler, Stabler Hill, 249
Stablersville, 250
Stafford, 250
Star's Corner, 156, 250
Startzman, 250
Steel Pone, 250
Steelyard Creek, 15
Stepney, 250
Stevens Corners, 251
Stevenson, 251
Stevensville, 251
Steyer, 23, 251
Stillpond, 250, 251
Stingaree Island (Bend, Creek), 11
*Stingeray Ile, 11
Stirrup Run, 15
*Stockett's, *Stockett's Town, 252
Stockton, 252
Stokley, 252
Stonebraker, 252
Strecker, 23
Street, 253
Striking Marsh, 15
Strites Mill, 253
Stumptown, 253
Sudlersville, 253
Sudley, 254
Sugar Hill, 23, 254
Suitland, 254
Sulpher Spring, 254
*Sulphur Springs, 255
Summerfield, 255
*Summer Hill, 255
*Summerseat, 255
Summerville, 255
Sunderland, Sunderlandville, 255
Sunnybrook, 255
Sunshine, * Sunshine, 255
*Surrattsville, 5, 255
Susquehanna, 256, 259
Swanscut Creek, 256
Swan Creek, 10
Swanton, 257
Sweetair, 257
Sweathouse Branch, 14
Sykesville, 257
Sylmar, 18, 258

Takoma Park, 258
Talbert, 258
Talbot County, 4, 258, 259